D1306398

Anabaptists Meeting Muslims

A Calling for Presence in the Way of Christ

Edited by
James R. Krabill, David W. Shenk,
and Linford Stutzman

Herald Press

Scottdale, Pennsylvania
Waterloo, Ontario

Library of Congress Cataloging-in-Publication Data
Anabaptists meeting Muslims : a calling for presence in the way of Christ /
edited by James R. Krabill, David W. Shenk, and Linford Stutzman.
  p. cm.
Includes bibliographical references and index.
ISBN 0-8361-9290-7 (pbk. : alk. paper)
1. Missions to Muslims—Congresses.
2. Mennonites—Missions—Congresses.
3. Anabaptists—Congresses. I. Krabill, James R. II. Shenk, David W., 1937-
III. Stutzman, Linford, 1950-
BV2625.A66 2005
266'.43'088297—dc22

                          2004024042

Scripture quotations are by the author or *New International Version* (NIV),
Copyright © 1973, 1978, 1984 by the International Bible Society. Used by permission of Zondervan Publishing House. All rights reserved.

Chapter 6 by Roy Hange, "Revelation and Reconciliation: The Vision of Concord in Abrahamic Traditions," was developed for a dialogue between Muslims and Mennonites in Qom, Iran, February 2004, and is published here by permission of the Toronto Mennonite Theological Centre. It is anticipated that this essay will be published in a forthcoming issue of *The Conrad Grebel Review*.
Chapter 22 by Chantal and Mark Logan, "Somalia: What's in a Name?" was first published in *Fifty Years, Fifty Stories: The Mennonite Mission in Somalia, 1953-2003* by Omar Eby (Cascadia, 2003). It is reprinted here by permission.
Appendix F by A. James Reimer, "Revelation, Reason, and Authority," is published by permission of the Toronto Mennonite Theological Centre.

ANABAPTISTS MEETING MUSLIMS
Copyright © 2005 by Herald Press, Scottdale, Pa. 15683
    Published simultaneously in Canada by Herald Press,
    Waterloo, Ont. N2L 6H7. All rights reserved
Library of Congress Control Number: 2004024042
International Standard Book Number: 0-8361-9290-7
Printed in the United States of America
Cover design by Gwen Stamm

10 09 08 07 06 05 10 9 8 7 6 5 4 3 2

To order or request information, please call
1-800-759-4447 (individuals); 1-800-245-7894 (trade).
Web site: www.heraldpress.com

Anabaptists
Meeting Muslims

Dedicated to Michael Sattler

*A pioneer of the Anabaptist movement half a millennium ago,
who was committed to living the suffering love of the cross
in all relationships, including the Muslim Turks.
That commitment contributed to condemnation
by the state-church authorities.
He was tortured and burned at the stake.
His witness joins that of a multitude of others
who with joy have invested their lives
as faithful witnesses of the gospel,
and as participants in the sufferings of Christ.*

Contents

SECTION TWO: Learnings and Vision

Foreword

The most powerful nation in the world has perhaps never been more frightened. Since September 11, the national psyche has been leavened with a foreboding sense that the security of the United States can no longer be assured, and with the disturbing awareness that global antipathy to America has its roots in the decades of self-serving and shortsighted policies and actions pursued by the American government and corporations on their behalf. As the United States struggles to salvage some honor and stability out of the complicated and bloody muddle precipitated in Iraq, its citizens are rediscovering that history is like a lobster trap: there can be no escaping the consequences of personal or collective behavior. The present always begins in the past, and stretches into the unknown future. Like Israel of Hosea's day, so today, having sown the wind, we must reap the whirlwind. For the law of the harvest is such that we not only reap what we sow, but more than we sow.

Christianity and Islam share much in common. Both agree that we live in a moral universe in which ordinary human behavior is of cosmic consequence; each insists that there is only one God, and each makes a similar claim to universality. Each claims, furthermore—with impressive, albeit selective, proofs—to be the religion of peace, par excellence; yet the history of each attests to the sorry ease with which their holy books can be invoked to legitimize or even demand violent means to achieve God-approved ends. Each has recourse, likewise, to a rich repository of highly selective, self-flattering memories, so that the excesses perpetrated in the name of its deity can be excused, overlooked, or reinterpreted. And each follows a holy book that, if read and understood in a certain way, can inculcate hatred and require genocide. On the positive side, each fosters strong traditions of piety, reverence, social action, hospitality, charity, and justice.

It is not their similarities, however, but the profound dissimilarities marking the two religions that made necessary the conference to which this book gives testimony. Christian-Muslim religious differences are not merely cosmetic, but epistemological, woven into the fabrics of intrinsically antithetical cosmologies. From these roots grow the limbs and branches of two systems of life that are seemingly fated to mortal combat. This is the "clash of civilizations" which Samuel Huntington elucidated in his groundbreaking study; and from these issues the bloody specter of medieval and contemporary religious violence—"Terror in the mind of God," as Mark Juergensmeyer aptly describes in his book by that title.[1]

What does all of this have to do with Anabaptists being present to Muslims in the way of Christ? Almost everything! In her splendid article, "Arabic Anti-missionary Treatises: Muslim Responses to Christian Evangelism in the Modern Middle East," appearing in the July 2004 issue of the *International Bulletin of Missionary Research*, Heather Sharkey shows how Christian missionary activity has been consistently portrayed in Arabic literature as "a grave threat to Islam and Muslims," and hence vehemently attacked. More than simply a religious threat, Christian missionaries represent the very life force of the west's three Gorgons: Wall Street, Hollywood, and the Pentagon.

Because they have for many centuries benefited directly from western intervention in the affairs of Muslim states, missionaries are seen as accomplices to the self-serving, imperial schemes of the west—the religious expression of a western military, economic, and cultural hegemony marked by imperviousness to local concerns. More than that, they are viewed as a religious wedge wielded to crack the cultural integrity of Muslim societies, making them susceptible to the west's insatiable appetite for money, pleasure, and control. Missionaries and missionary activities thus constitute both a grave danger to Islam and a humiliating sign of Muslim impotence.

In their recently published *Occidentalism: The West in the Eyes of Its Enemies*, Ian Buruma and Avishai Margalit show that western "orientalism" has its non-western counterpart, Occidentalism.[2] In its more extreme contemporary Muslim manifestation—at times uncomfortably reminiscent of God's white hot wrath as depicted in our Old Testament—the west is utterly diseased and irretrievably corrupt. Having embraced greed, sensuality, and self-interest as primary virtues, the west itself is a pestilence that has been unleashed on our world. According to this view, to speak of "saving the west" is to conflate the patient with the disease. The world is the patient; the west is its highly contagious and potentially lethal plague. The west should not, indeed cannot, be saved. It must be eradicated.

As Anabaptists, we like to think that what we embody in community and offer in mission is something unique. Citizens of the upside-down kingdom, we hold the Sermon on the Mount to be normative for our Lord's followers. We acknowledge that God's missionary purposes are not accomplished through strident aggression, but through quiet, self-giving participation in local human community wherever Christ's followers find themselves. Ours is a theology of the neighbor, a missiology of servanthood. Although we frequently fall far short of this ideal in our personal and institutional lives, our steady goal is to love our enemies, pray for our persecutors, do good to those who harm us, and reject violence as a solution to anything.

We believe that followers of the Way do not equate American hegemony with divine sovereignty, or blind nationalism with godliness. Nor do we see anything inevitable or universal about the plutocracy that we on the North American continent call "democracy." We try not to confuse legality with justice, or the nation's policies with virtue. Acknowledging the ease with which noble ends are subverted by selfish means, we place ourselves and our contexts within the larger vista of faith. By faith, we accept that God's strength is perfected in weakness, that in the deep operation of this moral universe, it is the weak who will be strong, the meek who will inherit, the sorrowing who will be comforted, the merciful who will be shown mercy, the peacemakers who will be called the children of God, and the persecuted who will be blessed. It was, after all, through his stripes that we are healed, and through his death that we have life.

St. Francis of Assisi was no Mennonite, but he manifested in his own life the Spirit who animates the Anabaptist imagination and directs our Christian realism. In our meeting with Muslims in the way of Christ, there can be no more appropriate prayer than the one attributed to him:

> LORD, make me an instrument of your peace.
> Where there is hatred, let me sow love.
> Where there is injury, pardon,
> Where there is doubt, faith.
> Where there is despair, hope.
> Where there is darkness, light.
> Where there is sadness, joy.

> O DIVINE MASTER, grant that I may not so much seek to
>   be consoled as to console:
> To be understood as to understand;
> To be loved as to love.
> For it is in giving that we receive—
> It is in pardoning that we are pardoned.
> And it is in dying that we are born to eternal life.[3]

This book, then, is an expression of hope, not triumphalism; of repentance of our sinfulness as we acknowledge our deep need for Christ's grace and forgiveness, of humble acknowledgment that we as a people do not aspire to brilliance, prominence, or domination. But one thing we can do: as sinners recreated and empowered by the Holy Spirit, we can meet Muslims; and meeting them as servants of the Servant, we can be a presence in the way of Christ.

—*Jonathan Bonk*
Executive Director
Overseas Ministries Study Center
New Haven, Connecticut

Preface

This book is about Muslims and Anabaptists.

The name Muslim means a believer in God. Muslim believers seek to submit to the will of God. Although Muslims believe that Adam was the first Muslim prophet, and that all people are born naturally Muslim, the early formation of the Muslim community as we know it today commenced in Arabia six centuries after Christ. Muslims believe that God's will is Islam, a belief system and way of life that is most fully revealed in the Qur'an and modeled most perfectly in the life of Muhammad. Muslims are a community (ummah) of faith who believe their mission in the world is to be faithful witnesses of the confession of faith that there is no God but Allah and that Muhammad is the prophet of Allah. In that witness and mission the faithful ummah seeks to extend the rule of God throughout the earth.

The mainstream of the Anabaptist movement of the early sixteenth century in Europe was a commitment to the authority of Jesus Christ and the total biblical witness concerning Christ. Anabaptist literally means a person who has been rebaptized. This is the nickname that European Protestant and Catholic leaders gave these followers of Jesus because they practiced adult baptism upon confession of faith in Christ. They were baptized upon confession of faith, even though they had been baptized as infants, and, therefore, the nickname: Anabaptists—rebaptizers.

The early beginnings of the movement were a Bible study fellowship in Zurich, Switzerland. Through the study of the Bible, this fellowship discerned that Jesus Christ is both Lord and Savior and that the faithful church are those who follow Christ in all of life, including Christ's teaching and example of peace, nonviolence, and love for one's enemy. They believed that the faithful church is the body of Christ serving one another and the world in the Spirit of Christ. Many Anabaptists were passionate evangelists for they believed that "the earth is the Lord's and everything in it, the world and all who live in it" (Ps 24:1). Therefore they sought to invite all people to repentance and new life in Christ.

Although severe persecution by state church authorities eventually dampened the evangelistic fervor of the Anabaptists, in time this movement gave birth to several denominations including the Mennonites, the Brethren in Christ, the Amish; even the early beginnings of the Baptist churches were considerably influenced by the Anabaptists.

It may seem presumptuous to use Mennonite and Anabaptist synonymously. Not all Mennonites are Anabaptist in their faith commitments; some denominations with Anabaptist roots are called by other names; there are many Christians in all denominations who embrace the foundational faith commitments of the Anabaptists. Nevertheless, recognizing that in its confessional commitments the Mennonite Church is committed to carrying forward the central Anabaptist commitment to follow Jesus Christ in all of life and that the largest global family of Anabaptist churches are the Mennonites, we have at times used Mennonite and Anabaptist synonymously.

Mennonites and Muslims

At the dawn of the twenty-first century the various Mennonite and Brethren in Christ expressions of global Anabaptists who are members of Mennonite World Conference (MWC) comprised 1.2 million members in sixty-three countries. The worldwide Muslim community comprises 1.2 billion people in every country on earth. For every member of the MWC there are a thousand Muslims!

This book is mostly a North American Mennonite reflection on Anabaptist engagement with Muslims as we "meet and greet," to use a phrase from Anglican bishop and Islamist, Kenneth Cragg. Although this book explores an Anabaptist-Mennonite journey with Muslims, we trust that this narrative and theological reflection will be helpful to other Christians who are committed to being present in the way of Christ among Muslims. We also hope that Muslims will discover in this book helpful insights into the nature of Anabaptist understandings of Christian faith, mission, and presence.

Although Anabaptists are quite miniscule when compared to the global reach of the Muslims, nevertheless, the engagement with

Muslims has influenced many Anabaptists significantly, and Muslims have also been influenced and transformed in their journey with Anabaptists. In rather amazing ways, Muslims and Anabaptists find themselves meeting in deepening and respectful relationships. Perhaps the reason is that both communities are at the deepest levels of faith committed to faithful obedience to the rule of God. We recognize that our understanding of the nature of the rule of God differs fundamentally (the revelation of God in Jesus Christ for Anabaptists and the revelation of God's will in the Qur'an for Muslims). Nevertheless, the commitment to faithfulness to the rule of God is at the center of both the Anabaptist church and the Muslim ummah.

Both Muslims and Mennonites resist dividing life into sacred and secular spheres—all aspects of life need to be brought under the authority of God. Furthermore, both are missionary communities committed to extending God's rule throughout the earth. However, the question that persists as Muslims and Mennonites meet is the nature of God's rule. J. Dudley Woodberry, in the chapter "The Kingdom of God in Islam and the Gospel," observes that there are both convergences and divergences between an Islamic- and gospel-centered vision of the kingdom. For Anabaptist-Mennonites and Muslims, their respective understandings of the kingdom of God help to inform their relationships with one another. That is true of all sincere Christians and faithful Muslims.

These understandings of the kingdom of God might provide a basis for respectful relations. However, that is not always true, for sincerity and faithfulness to one's vision of the nature of God's kingdom does not necessarily mean peaceful relations—Bosnian Muslim jihadists on the one hand and Serbian Christian militants on the other, have views of the kingdom of God that have provided a theological basis for destructive pyrolysis in the closing decade of the twentieth century.[1]

We recognize that it is not just Mennonites and Muslims who seek the kingdom of God. In fact, this is true of all the faiths that claim Abraham as the father of faith: Israel, the church, and the Muslim community. Each of these movements calls the believing community to submit to the rule of God and to be a witness for the kingdom of God to the nations. Yet the question persists: what is the nature of the kingdom of God?

Nearly five hundred years ago the early Anabaptists demonstrated a commitment to the kingdom of God that was centered in

Jesus crucified. That was profoundly counter to the theology of Christendom, as well as that of the Islamic Dar al Islam (the Muslim political order). These Anabaptist pioneers embraced a vision of the kingdom of God that in later centuries has helped to form Mennonite responses to the journey with Muslims wherever Mennonites and Muslims have met: Central Asia, India, Indonesia, the Middle East, Somalia, Algeria, modern Europe, North America, and over a dozen other regions as well.

During the nearly half millennium of the Anabaptist movement, what have Mennonites been learning about Muslims, ourselves, the church, the Qur'an or Muhammad, the nature of the kingdom of God, mission, or faithfulness to Christ? The sixteenth-century Muslim advance into Central Europe was significant for the Anabaptist movement. Just as was true of the Lutheran, Reformed, and Catholic communities, the early Anabaptists, as well as modern Mennonites and Brethren in Christ Christians, need to develop a theological and practical response to the Muslim challenge. Hence the title of this book: *Anabaptists Meeting Muslims: A Calling for Presence in the Way of Christ.*

The Mennonite response to Muslims has not always been as intensely significant as it was in the formative decades of the Anabaptist movement. In John Lapp's review of the history of Mennonite engagement with Muslims he observes that it is in the nineteenth century that the Mennonite awareness of Muslims has remerged as a significant dimension of the Mennonite journey. A century and a half ago (1851) the first Mennonite mission commitment outside of Euro-North America was among the Muslims of Indonesia through Dutch-Russian Mennonite endeavors. Lapp's essay traces the subsequent deepening involvement of Mennonites with Muslims.

The Mennonite commitment to meet and greet Muslims has expanded quite significantly in the last half of the twentieth century. At about mid-century North American Mennonite service-mission agencies initiated presence and service ministries within Muslim societies in Algeria, the Middle East, and Somalia. In the last half century North American Mennonites have significantly expanded such commitments. By the year 2000, Mennonite churches or service ministries were engaged with Muslims in scores of countries and communities. Modern mobility means that most Mennonites today, wherever they might live, have Muslim neighbors or acquaintances.

An Anabaptist Consultation on Islam

What are Mennonites learning as they meet Muslims? That was the theme of a gathering called, "An Anabaptist Consultation on Islam: the Church Meets the Muslim Community." The consultation convened at Eastern Mennonite University, Harrisonburg, Virginia, October 23-26, 2003. There were about 200 registrants with more than 300 attending some plenary sessions. Sponsored by the Mennonite Mission Network, Eastern Mennonite Missions, and the John S. Coffman Center of Eastern Mennonite Seminary, representatives from some fifteen agencies or church communities made presentations. Reports of "learnings" were shared from eighteen countries. In addition to overarching keynote addresses on pertinent themes, fifteen seminars focused on core concerns that engage Mennonites as they meet Muslims. The event brought together persons from a variety of perspectives and experiences.

The intent of the consultation and this book has not been an attempt to homogenize Mennonite commitments. Rather, the intent has been to listen and learn, to give and receive counsel. A listening committee has presented a word of counsel that came from what they had heard throughout our days together in the consultation (see appendix A). This book consists of most of the presentations that provided the grist for the counsel shared by the listening committee.

As planning commenced for the consultation, a decision was made that this would be a retreat for Anabaptists to caucus and listen to one another. So although no one was prevented from attending, we were open in communicating with our Muslim friends that this was intended as a time for Mennonites to retreat, listen, and share. We understand that several Muslim students from Eastern Mennonite University did drop in from time to time, and we have heard that they felt quite positive about the tone of the meeting.

We recognize that there is also value in convening forums where Muslims and Mennonites speak with one another. Some have felt that this consultation should be a precursor to that kind of meeting in the future. Of course, wherever Mennonites and Muslims meet and greet, there are conversations that often take us into the core commitments of faith and living. Public forums are important, but probably less significant than neighbor to neighbor conversations.

This was primarily a North American event. For example, European Mennonites were not involved, although a European voice would have been a significant contribution. There was only minimal, albeit very astute, representation from Asian and African churches that are very engaged in the meeting with Muslims. It seemed presumptuous by the North American planners to convene a global consultation. This would be the responsibility of the Global Missions Fellowship of Mennonite World Conference. So this was a North American consultation with a few invitees from Mennonite churches in Asia and Africa.

This Book

Some participants requested that their presentations not be published. We have respected those requests, including the request of a plenary presenter, Lamin Sanneh. He has elected to develop his paper, "War and Peace in Interfaith Perspective," into a larger more comprehensive tome which we trust will become available in due course when published. However, we are grateful for an alternative essay by Lamin Sanneh, "Islam—the West—Anabaptists." This is Sanneh's response to the overall thrust of the consultation. A few presenters or agencies also requested that we not publish their regional reports and a couple writers used pseudonyms. Although this book does not include all that was presented, we hope that this volume will be a helpful resource for all who are committed to the journey of understanding, meeting, and greeting Muslims.

The foreword by Jonathan Bonk and introduction by David W. Shenk explore global historical developments with particular focus on the context in which Mennonites and Muslims meet. These introductory essays are followed by presentations made at the consultation, except for one essay that is included because of its pertinence to this volume. There are four sections.

Section One: The Big Picture

This section explores several major themes that provide foundational understandings: "The Kingdom of God in Islam and the Gospel" and "A Global Perspective on the Current Status of Christian-Muslim Relations" by J. Dudley Woodberry; "Islam—the West—Anabaptists" by Lamin Sanneh; "The Mennonite Engagement with Muslims: A Historical Overview" by John A. Lapp; "Revelation and Reconciliation: The Vision of Concord in Abrahamic Traditions" by Roy Hange; "Women in Islam and the Gospel" by Chantal Logan. We also include one specific focus report that pulls together some of the key themes in The Big Picture, that of Indonesia presented by Mesach Krisetya.

Section Two: Learnings and Vision

These are brief regional reports that generally focus on three themes: (1) The story, (2) The learnings, and (3) The onward vision. The regional reports that are included provide insights into the sometimes exhilarating and other times sobering experiences of Mennonites meeting and greeting Muslims.

Section Three: Issues and Themes

Fifteen foci are explored in this section, with issues as varied as "Reconciliation and Justice" or "Apologetics." These essays are derived from the seminars and include twenty-nine contributions and twelve responses. Not all presenters in the seminars chose to have their contributions included in the book, but these themes provide the reader with pertinent insight into the nature of the Mennonite journey with Muslims.

Section Four: Wrap Up

Here we attempt to hear questions that Muslims ask Mennonites and all Christians, and we ponder our responses as Anabaptists to those questions. We tune in to Bedru Hussein reflecting on "Open Doors Through Walls." Then we read the counsel and witness of several participants.

The book concludes with a variety of appendixes. Noteworthy is a bibliography by James Krabill with a special focus on Mennonite writings in regard to Anabaptists meeting Muslims.

The Purpose

This book reveals a rich diversity of Anabaptist engagement with Muslims. Within your spirit you will find yourself in dialogue, questioning, agreeing, gaining new insights, amazement, and sometimes in dissent with the presentations; the same is true of the editors and the sponsoring and contributing agencies. We have not sought to homogenize the essays so that all that is written flows through a predetermined Anabaptist ideological grid. Rather, we commend this book as a forum for giving and receiving counsel as we open our hearts to one another, question one another, and challenge each other to continuing the journey of learning what it means to be faithfully present among Muslims in the way of Christ.

This book is not an occasion for self-congratulation; rather, it is a calling to repentant confession of our need for grace, forgiveness, humility, and wisdom in the journey with Muslims. It is an invitation to gratitude and thanksgiving for the many and surprising ways Muslims have opened their doors and hearts for Anabaptists to become servants and friends among Muslims. Our hope and prayer is that the stories and reflections of this book will encourage and help to equip Christians for the calling to presence in the way of Christ.

A Word of Thanks

We, as coordinators of the consultation and editors of this book, thank all those who contributed with excellence, energy, and focus to the consultation and the book. Seventy made presentations or led in seminars and public sessions; over 300 were present for some of the plenary presentations. All those who contributed and participated through their presence, prayer, and conversation have helped to form this book. We are grateful.

We also thank Eastern Mennonite University for providing facilities and significant staff time for the event and subsequent book. We thank Eastern Mennonite Missions and the Mennonite Mission Network for cosponsoring this event with the John S. Coffman Center of Eastern Mennonite Seminary. This has included significant staff time and finance. We are grateful to United Services Foundation for a very generous financial grant that paid for all consultation expenses that registration fees did not cover, including the subsidy cost for publishing this book. In all of this we have seen the hand of God, and we give thanks to the one who is the author and finisher of our salvation.

—*The Editors:*
  James R. Krabill, Mennonite Mission Network
  David W. Shenk, Eastern Mennonite Missions
  Linford Stutzman, John S. Coffman Center, Eastern Mennonite
    Seminary

Introduction

Three Journeys:
Jesus—Constantine—Muhammad

David W. Shenk

Here are three excerpts that provide context for this introduction to *Anabaptists Meeting Muslims.*

I, Linford Stutzman, am writing from Bethlehem, the birthplace of Jesus. Almost four months have passed since "An Anabaptist Consultation on Islam" in Harrisonburg, Virginia. I am reading parts of this manuscript coming out of that conference and reflecting on the conclusions in Bethlehem. This town in which Jesus was born is located in a part of the world that has seen more than its share of bloodshed in the name of God from earliest written history until last night when fifteen more Palestinians died in the ongoing violence.

When Jesus was born, one of Herod's palaces dominated the landscape to the southeast of Bethlehem. At the time of Jesus's birth, this town was a place of oppression and fear. Today a new Jewish settlement dominates the landscape to the north, with a brand new high-tech, lethal fence snaking through these communities to keep Jewish and Muslim neighbors apart. The city of Jesus's birth is still a place of oppression and fear for the people of Bethlehem, including the Christians.

In many ways, this small part of the world provides a preview of the future of the entire planet if believers in the God of Abraham do not live in ways that bless "all peoples" (Gen 12:3).

Yet within this cauldron of strife there are those Muslims, Jews, and Christians who are committed to a different way, the way of reconciliation and blessing. Many in the tiny Palestinian Christian community are an encouragement to all those who seek to walk in the way of peacemaking. Anabaptists and all Christians have much to learn from the bold suffering of Palestinian Christians in Bethlehem, who understand their Christian witness to all of their neighbors as one that demonstrates forgiveness and reconciliation between Muslim, Christian, and Jewish enemies.

Linford Stutzman[1]

The leaders of four major religions were challenged at the Davos World Economic Forum (January 2003) to commend to their faith community that violence no longer be considered acceptable to settle the affairs of men and nations. The representatives of Orthodox Christianity, Judaism, and Islam each lauded the principle, but reserved for themselves the right to use violence. The final speaker, a Catholic theologian, responded sadly and thoughtfully. He said . . . the audience must be discouraged by the answers from previous speakers. He would like to take the opposite view but would decline, since he doubted if his own leadership would support him.

Art DeFehr[2]

Some of our Muslim neighbors in Central Asia are very disturbed about the recent wars in our regions. These wars seem to them to be Christian wars again Muslims. Furthermore, some American Christian leaders have said some unkind and critical things about Islam. These statements are broadly publicized in our countries. Sometimes the anger of our Muslim neighbors about these matters turns into hate against our churches; we get blamed for the wars and the attitudes of American Christians.

Central Asian Pastors[3]

Shortly after the September 11 attacks, I asked Mark Oxbrow, a missions director with the Church Missions Society of the Church of England, "What do you say in churches in the United Kingdom when you are asked to speak on the Christian faith and Islam?"

Mark responded, "I speak about three different journeys for peace: Jesus, Constantine, and Muhammad. Those different journeys are options for each of us, and each of us needs to choose which one we will take."

Just as is true of British Christians, Anabaptists in North America and around the world are faced with the option of these three different journeys for peace. Bishop Kenneth Cragg, who has invested many years in the Middle East and is a reputable scholar of Islam, occasionally reminds both Muslims and Christians of the theological significance of two journeys: Jesus from Galilee to Jerusalem and Muhammad from Mecca to Medina. Mark Oxbrow reminds his audiences of a third journey as well, that of Constantine to Rome that laid the foundations for Christendom.[4]

J. Dudley Woodberry in his essay in this volume, "The Kingdom of God in Islam and in the Gospel," explores in some depth convergences and divergences between the way of Jesus and that of Muhammad. In this brief introduction I will not duplicate his observations, nevertheless, I believe it is essential to look at the Anabaptist journey with Muslims in the light of these three journeys for peace: Jesus, Constantine, and Muhammad. Those three journeys have shaped civilizational systems and faith communities, which provide the background and context of the present-day Anabaptist journey with Muslims.

The Journey of Jesus to Jerusalem

Jesus was at the height of his popularity in Galilee after feeding the five thousand men plus women and children by blessing and breaking five loaves of bread and two fish. The Galileans were impressed, and attempted to make him their king "by force" (John 6:15). Surely an army of Zealot independence fighters would have joined forces with Jesus to gain independence from the Romans, and then from the Galilee beachhead they could expand the kingdom of God throughout Israel and eventually throughout the earth. Jesus resisted that invitation and from that time onward he "resolutely set out for Jerusalem" (Luke 9:51). In the following weeks, Jesus tried to make his disciples aware that in Jerusalem the authorities would arrest the Son of Man and "mock him, insult him, spit on him, flog him and kill him," but on the third day he would rise again (Luke 18:32-33).

By this time the disciples were convinced that Jesus was the promised Messiah. They could not fathom that an arrest and death were possibilities for the Messiah. Peter, representing the convictions of all the disciples, rebuked Jesus for such notions, and Jesus responded very sharply, "Out of my sight! You are a stumbling block to me; you do not have in mind the things of God, but the things of men" (Matt 16:23).

Finally as Jesus approached Jerusalem, he mounted a colt. Jubilant children singing hosannas accompanied him. Yet as he came over the crest of the Mount of Olives and saw the city before him, he stopped his colt and wept, because Jerusalem would not receive "what would bring you peace" (Luke 19:41). Then with the children still singing, he and the children entered the temple and cleansed it of the merchants who were corrupting the whole system with their exploitative practices.

All of this is tremendously significant as it relates to the mission of Jesus and the nature of the kingdom of God. In that colt ride he was proclaiming the fulfillment of two biblical prophesies in regard to the messianic kingdom.

First, he was fulfilling Zechariah's prophecy of five centuries earlier. Most frequently we read only the introduction to the prophecy and miss the universal, peacemaking, nonviolent, and voluntary messianic rule that Jesus was announcing in riding that colt into Jerusalem.

> Rejoice greatly, O Daughter of Zion! Shout, daughter of Jerusalem! See, your king comes to you, righteous and having salvation, gentle and riding on a donkey, on a colt, the foal of a donkey. I will take away the chariots from Ephraim and the war-horses from Jerusalem, and the battle bow will be broken. He will proclaim peace to the nations. His rule will extend from sea to sea and from the River to the ends of the earth (Zech 9:9-10).

A second observation is that Jesus was announcing that he was fulfilling Ezekiel's prophecy that the radiant glory of God would enter Jerusalem from the east, fill the temple with the glory of God, and cleanse the temple of all corruption forever (Ezek 43:1-9). The contemporary British theologian, N. T. Wright, develops this theme. In regards to Jesus's entrance into Jerusalem and his encounter in the temple, Wright comments:

> Jesus of Nazareth was conscious of a vocation, given him by the one he knew as, "father," to enact in himself what in Israel's scriptures, God had promised to accomplish all by himself. He would be the pillar of cloud and fire for the people of the new exodus. He would embody in himself the returning and redeeming action of the covenant God.[5]

How, then, did Jesus establish the kingdom that he was inaugurating?

First, he went into the temple and drove those who exploited the poor from the temple precincts. In the confrontation he also made it known that the temple of stone was needed no more. He was the new temple; later the apostles proclaimed that the church as the body of Christ was the temple. "Place" was not necessary in the kingdom Jesus was establishing. The place of the kingdom was wherever Christ was welcomed.

Second, during his last meal with his disciples, Christ washed the feet of his betrayer. Consider for a moment the significance of this act. The One who is the radiant glory of God, who created the fifty billion galaxies in space, washed the feet of his betrayer!

Third, as Jesus the Christ was dying on the cross he cried out in forgiveness of those who crucified him. This is God in Christ seeking to embrace the world in his reconciling invitation. In that suffering embrace, we are reconciled to God and to one another and with all of creation. In that embrace, the kingdom of God breaks into human experience.

Fourth, after his resurrection he appeared to the disciples several times. John described an appearance where Jesus showed the disciples the nail prints in his hands and the wound from the spear thrust into his side. Then he said to them, "Peace be with you! As the Father has sent me, I am sending you. . . . . Receive the Holy Spirit" (John 20:21-22). In that same commissioning he proclaimed the forgiveness of sins.

Within several weeks the Holy Spirit came upon the gathering of disciples, and from that time onward the apostolic church believed that the journey of Jesus from Galilee to the cross in Jerusalem is the way of the kingdom of God. These first Christians believed that in Jesus crucified the God of all creation suffers for us and because of us. He identifies fully with the suffering of all humanity, and especially with the outcast and powerless. He was crucified between two thieves. He suffered a cursed death "hung on a tree" (Gal 3:13) outside the centers of power. He died in disgrace at Golgotha "outside the camp" (Heb 13:13). This one, who was crucified with the outcastes and stripped of all earthly power, is, in fact, the full in history presence and revelation of the power of God. Christ crucified and risen is the power center of the universe; he is the Lamb slain who stands in the center of the throne of God (Rev 5:6). In his redemptive sacrifice Christ forgives and redeems people from "every tribe and language and people and nation" (Rev 5:9). Christ crucified—the power of God (1 Cor 1:23-24)!

For the apostolic church, all kingdom ethics were grounded in the reality that in Christ crucified God revealed himself to be our suffering servant. Jesus proclaimed, "A new commandment I give you: Love one another. As I have loved you, so you must love one another" (John 13:34). The apostle Paul wrote, "Your attitude should be the same as that of Christ Jesus . . . who . . . made himself nothing, taking the very nature of a servant . . . he humbled himself and became obedient to death—even death on a cross" (Phil 2:5-8).

With remarkable consistency, for the next three centuries the church insisted that a cross-centered ethic meant that the Christian as a disciple of Jesus could not take arms. This was a costly commitment, for the church was a minority movement often persecuted for refusing to venerate the emperor. Yet the church confessed that Jesus is Lord—therefore disciples of Jesus could not venerate the emperor or participate in practices that were in variance with the way of the Lord Jesus Christ. This meant that Christians would not participate in sacrifices to the spirit of the emperor and they would not participate in the imperial military. Origen, who was one of the early pioneers in developing the Alexandrian Catechetical School, was a forceful yet typical voice insisting that Christians desist from any participation in warfare.

Informing the governing authorities on the commitments of the church Origen wrote, "No longer do we take the sword against any nation, nor do we learn war any more, since we have become sons of peace through Jesus who is our author."[6]

Celsus was a scathing critic of the church and accused the church of abandoning the responsibilities of patriotic citizenship. To this charge Origen responded, "Even more do we fight on behalf of the emperor. And though we do not become fellow-soldiers with him, even if he presses for this, yet we are fighting of him and composing a special army of piety through our intercessions to God."[7]

Cyprian was Origen's colleague in the Alexandrian Catechetical School. He denounced "wars scattered all over the earth with the bloody horror of camps. The whole world is wet with mutual blood; and murder, which in the case of the individual is admitted to be a crime, is called a virtue when it is committed wholesale. Impunity is claimed for wicked deeds, not on the plea that they are guiltless, but because the cruelty is perpetrated on a grand scale."[8]

Origen and Cyprian were only two voices. Equally clear in their renunciation of Christian participation in war were other church fathers such as Tertullian, Athanasius, or Lactantius. The main thrust of their writings is that even though the state may consider warfare lawful, a follower of Christ could not kill a fellow human being. For these leaders of the church, warfare was murder on a large scale. They would love their enemies, pray for the state, be loyal citizens, but as followers of Jesus they would not participate in the violence of warfare. They believed that the nature of the kingdom of God was revealed in the life, teachings, crucifixion, and resurrection of Jesus Christ. It was to Christ and his kingdom that they were committed. Many died as martyrs rather than deviate from the call of Christ— "take up [your] cross daily and follow me" (Luke 9:23).

The Journey of Constantine to Rome

However, the church's commitment to a cross-centered kingdom commitment began to undergo a dramatic transformation when Constantine gained the Roman imperial throne. For months Constantine had been engaged in a long march from Britain south to Rome, where he knew he would meet in battle his rival to imperial power and his enemy, Maxentius. Constantine commanded only 40,000 troops. Maxentius had the full force of the garrison in Rome at his command. Where could Constantine acquire adequate power for the military engagement ahead? Perhaps the divine sun? So Constantine turned to the sun in worship, a commitment that he never fully abandoned.

Then on the eve of battle on the outskirts of Rome, Constantine allegedly saw the sign of the cross in the sky with the words beneath that cross: *In hoc signo vinces* (under this sign, conquer). He took that as an omen and painted the *chi rho* sign of Christ crucified on his weapons of war.[9] The next day Constantine won a decisive victory in the battle with Maxentius. He went on to become emperor of the western empire, and Licinius emperor of the eastern empire. Licinius, in his wars in the east, also reported on a message from God. Every night an angel appeared instructing him to pray to the *Summus Deus*.[10] He encouraged his troops to do so likewise.

Within a year of Constantine's victory, he and Licinius issued the Edict of Milan (AD 313), which assured religious freedom throughout the Roman Empire, not only for Christians, but for all religions. Letters were sent throughout the empire proclaiming, "Everyone who has a common desire to observe the Christian worship may now freely and unconditionally endeavor to do so without let or hindrance. . . . To others also freedom of their own worship is likewise left open and freely granted."[11]

The churches rejoiced in the new freedom. Yet the vision quickly developed into far more than that of a pluralist society with benevolent government assuring the freedom of worship to all. Constantine tilted the western empire toward favoring the church. The church historian, Eusebius, was ecstatic when Constantine ordered Bibles to be made available for leaders in his seat of government in Constantinople. Eusebius believed that a Christian civilization was now a possibility. This civilization would unite political and ecclesial authority and power.

Eusebius wrote, "There was a multitude of rulers before the coming of Christ. All nations were governed by different tyrannies and democracies and men had no intercourse with each other . . . nation rose against nations and city against city."[12] However, in the mind of Eusebius, Christ and Augustus were corulers whose mission was to bring order, as well as peace. W. H. C. Frend observed, "Mankind was moving forward toward a universal monarch under one Church, and Constantine was God's chosen instrument, the reflection of his divine power."[13]

As long as the followers of Jesus Christ were a people committed to a kingdom that is not of this world (John 18:36), then his servants would not use force to protect the truth of Christ or the integrity of the kingdom. Ethics were grounded in the way of cross.

However, any notions of a cross-centered ethic seemed to be nonsense in a kingdom where authority resided in Caesaropapism (the union of emperial Caesar and papal authority), unless the cross was a radical denial of the cross of Christ. That is, of course, exactly what Constantine did. For him the cross became a talisman, a potent magic. This Constantinian cross used as a weapon for violence against the enemy is not the cross of the one who proclaimed forgiveness for his enemies as he died absorbing their taunting violence. The cross within a theology of Caesaropapism was a symbol of sacramentally effectuated grace, not a revelation of normative Christian ethics or the cross of the God who is our suffering servant, of the God who reaches out to us in forgiveness and redemptive love even as our sins crash upon his broken body, the cross of the one who has taken our place and in whom we are forgiven.

The implications were astounding and transformational for the church that had experienced three centuries of intermittent persecution, and which was always on the periphery of social and political norms. With astounding rapidity the church was seated with the empire at the centers of power. Nowhere was that more evident than in the Council of Nicea (AD 325), where the unbaptized Constantine presided over a council of bishops to determine christological and trinitarian doctrine. Not only did Constantine preside at the opening sessions, but he also implemented instruments of force to impose the decisions made at Nicea on recalcitrant churches, as for example with the Donatists of North Africa.

The marriage of empire and state required that normative ethics be severed from a cross-centered commitment. The Roman Empire had become the fulfillment of the kingdom of our Lord Jesus Christ on earth, but political power and the way of the cross were incompatible. It was only in the religious life of monasteries that the ethics of the way of the cross could be truly practiced. In the course of time, for western Christian society as a whole the confessional became a convenient alternative to discipleship. For the ecclesial authorities, the preservation of the truth of the gospel required temporal power. It is not surprising that before long the church joined hands with the political order to use "fire and steel"[14] to confront evil, such as the pagans who were outside the reach of the church. The imperial sword and the mission of Christ were merged.

This is not to say that there was no concern for ethics. A new foundation for ethics did develop, based on the pragmatics of political power and justice that served the centers of imperial power. The way of the cross might have been feasible when the church was a peripheral minority, but now it needed a more practical ethic that fit the norms of political power. Within less than a century of Constantine's victory at Rome, the North African, Augustine, set about developing a theology and ethic of power that could serve both church and empire. Augustine determined there are two kingdoms, the city of God and the city of man. The ethical foundations of the two are quite different. The Christian is equally loyal to both kingdoms, being aware, however, that at the end of the day it is the city of God that is eternal. That is, the kingdom of grace. The ethical alternatives to the way of Christ that we must embrace in the real world reveal that we are indeed saved by grace alone.

To help the individual Christian, as well as the Christian political authorities, discern how to live in a world of conflict and war,

Augustine developed a just war ethic. If a Christian nation had to fight, the bottom line was that the war had to be just and that there were no other alternatives. These principles of just war have been further refined, but Augustine, borrowing from the wisdom of some of the Greek political philosophers, has had significant influence on western Christian understandings of just war. However, inevitably justice was defined by those in power. Instead of hope for the powerless, Christianity had become a bulwark for the powerful. The realities of living within the city of man required recognition that we could not just be city of God citizens.

The implications of this kind of politico-ethical transformation were devastating for the churches in the east. For the first three centuries of the Christian era, it was mostly the churches in the west that were persecuted. However, with the emergence of Caesaropapacy in the west, it was the churches in the east that began to experience the wrath of the persecutors. Under Constantine, Christianity in the west had become transformed into the religion of western empire. Peace had come to the western church, as Bishop Mar Jacob of Edessa wrote, "Constantine, the chief of victors, reigns and now the Cross the emperor's diadem surmounts."[15] This legacy provided the paradigm for what became known as the Holy Roman Empire, and later as Western Christendom.

For the church in Persia, developments in the western church became the sentence of death. The Roman Empire and Persia had engaged in several centuries of conflict. Another war was pending when Constantine wrote to the Shah of Persia, Shapur II, "I rejoice to hear that the fairest provinces of Persia are adorned with . . . Christians. . . . Since you are so powerful and pious, I commend them to your care, and leave them in your protection."[16]

For the Shah, this letter meant only one thing: the Christians were a fifth column representing Rome by sabotaging Zoroastrian Persia from within. Twenty years later, Constantine massed his troops for war against Persia with bishops accompanying his armies. According to Eusebius, they accompanied Constantine "to battle with him and for him by the prayers to God from whom all victory proceeds."[17]

The rage of the Persians against the Christians knew no boundaries. For more than twenty years the Christians were systematically hunted from one end of the empire to the other, tortured and killed. The Persian church was nearly eradicated by this, "The Great Persecution." It has never recovered from that blow. Ever since

Constantine, the church in the east has sought to make it clear that it is not beholden to the church in the west. Constantine and the development of the Holy Roman Empire and later Christendom have made it necessary for churches of the east to become alternatives to the western church. Sometimes this need to preserve some distance from the western church has pushed the eastern church into directions that the western church considered to be heretical (for example, Nestorianism).[18]

These alternative definitions were also expressed in a thousand years of eastern missionary outreach across Central Asia into China; it is a remarkable story how these minority churches that had no imperial support reached out in mission across Asia.[19] This was quite different than the church in the west where the mission of the church was expressed in concert with empire and military conquest.

Nevertheless, the Constantinian transformation in the western church contributed to the opening for Islam in the east. This is because the persecutions in Persia decimated the church. It also meant that the churches of the east had to distance themselves from the churches of the west. One way they did this was by defining their theology as an alternative to that of the west. The Dutch historian of religion, Arend Theodoor van Leeuwen, insists that this redefinition has been most persuasively expressed by Islam for "islamic power . . . offered to anti-Byzantine sentiment a far more effective ideology than anything that heretical Christianity was able to provide."[20]

We should take note. Themes are emerging within the western church today that are similar to the Constantinian era: warnings from Washington instructing regimes to respect the rights of Christian minorities; a war on terrorism to defend the values of western Judeo-Christian civilization; support by many churches for any means necessary to bring that goal to pass; refurbishing just war ethical foundations that are grounded in commitments quite other than the way of the cross; a conviction that an ethic based on the way of the cross does not apply to the real world in which we live; a deepening global perception that the western Christian movement is the faith for the powerful that pushes the poor into despair. In the midst of all of this, an anti-Christian (western) backlash that is seriously affecting the well-being and even survival of some eastern churches.

A Palestinian Catholic priest, Father Labib Kobti, revealed this concern in comments about the occupation of the West Bank and the 2002 siege of Bethlehem's Church of the Nativity. He wrote,

Palestinian Christians of the Holy Land who have been living in harmony with Muslims for centuries feel abandoned and alone. They feel angry against the Christians in the west and especially the American Christians. Arab-Christians at the end are the losers; they lost their prestige, their future, and their hopes. I am very concerned for them, perhaps I am so concerned because I am also an Arab Christian.[21]

This Palestinian priest is caught within the ramifications of a legacy of a Western Christendom that conceptualized the world as divided into territory that is Christian compared with non-Christian regions. His suffering church is not within the parameters of Christian territoriality. Although Israel is not Christian, it nevertheless has forged strong alliances with the Christian west, a development that the largely Muslim Palestinians have not been able to emulate.

Christendom was intolerant of pluralism. Minority communities were ghettoized, as was the case with Jews in Europe for many centuries. As a modern example, recently Muslim girls in France have been forbidden from wearing the veiling in public places or in school, in fact all obvious religious symbols are banned. French civilization is now secularized, but a spirit of intolerance for pluralist culture prevails that has its roots in the Christendom ethos.

We now explore another journey that birthed an alternative vision of religion and territoriality, that of the Muslims.

The Journey of Muhammad to Medina

Six centuries after Christ and three centuries after Constantine, the unlettered Muhammad began preaching in Mecca in Arabia, among a people who were on the periphery of civilization and power. For twelve years he proclaimed portions of the Qur'an as they came to him. He warned the Meccans to leave their polytheistic worship and evil practices. He preached a message of hope for the poor and compassion for the dispossessed.

Very few Meccans accepted Muhammad's message, for he challenged the entrenched networks of polytheism that supported the political and economic structures of Arabian society. However, hope for the Muslim movement came from Medina; emissaries invited him to come to their city and become their prophet and statesman. This was the same invitation that Jesus had received from the Galileans six centuries earlier. Muhammad accepted the invitation, believing that this summons was a sign of favor and approval from God.

This migration to Medina is the *hijrah*, which took place in AD 622. It is significant that this event is the beginning of the Muslim era—not the birth of Muhammad in 570 or the advent of revelations in 610. The hijrah is most significant theologically, for this event enabled Muhammad to gain political and military control of a region. With those instruments of power he and his followers established Islam; in time Muslims referred to regions that they governed as Dar al Islam. This accomplishment was evidence indeed that Muhammad was a prophet of God and the thriving Muslim community had God's favor.

In Medina, a constitution was developed that in later centuries formed the nucleus for full-fledged Muslim systems of law known as the Shari'a. The goal of the Medina constitution was to include all minorities within a covenant of cooperation with the Muslims. The Muslims were tremendously disappointed when some minority communities resisted inclusion in the Muslim-led covenant. Subsequently these dissidents, who were perceived to be a threat to the Muslim community, were dealt with as traitors. Judgment included banishment or death.

Battles ensued between the Meccans and the Muslim armies; the Muslims were victorious, and within ten years a triumphant army of ten thousand Muslim soldiers were peacefully received by the Meccans who had been defeated on the battlefield. The Muslims then cleansed the Ka'bah of its idolatries, and Mecca became a Muslim city.

As Muhammad led the Muslim forces into Mecca he exclaimed, "Truth had come, and falsehood hath vanished away" (Qur'an 17:81).

Wherever Muslim government was established, Christian, Jewish, or Zoroastrian communities were circumscribed as *dhimmi*, protected communities. They were assured peace providing they functioned within the parameters established by the Muslim nation. This included paying a special tax. Regions outside the Dar al Islam were the Dar al Harb, or regions of war not yet brought under the control of Muslim authorities.

Kenneth Cragg observes, "Dar al Islam and Dar al Harb is a fundamental distinction running through all humanity; the household of submission to God and the household of non-Islam still to be brought into such submission."[22]

Muhammad left the suffering of Mecca for Medina, and later returned to Mecca as victor. This pattern is normative. Defeat for the faithful Muslim ummah is a theological anomaly, for God is all powerful and sovereign. Tactical retreat might be necessary, but in time the Dar al Islam of the Muslims must prevail.

Although Muslims are not to initiate aggression, if the ummah is under threat, then the defense of the ummah is mandated by any means necessary. This is jihad, a three dimensional striving in the defense of Islam (1) within one's soul, (2) with the pen, and (3) with the sword when necessary.

The Qur'an commands, "Fight in the way of Allah against those who fight against you. . . . And fight them until persecution is no more, and religion is for Allah. But if they desist, then let there be no hostility except against wrongdoers" (2:190-193).

The ummah will persuade and even seek to induce non-Muslims to convert, but are prohibited from using coercion to convert anyone. The Qur'an declares, "There is no compulsion in religion. The right direction is henceforth distinct from error" (2:256).

Within a century of the hijrah, the Dar al Islam had extended its political authority from the Indus River, throughout the Middle East, across North Africa, and into Spain. On the Western European front the advance was stopped in the Battle of Tours (AD 732), just over a century after the hijrah. Half of the Christian population on earth had come under the authority of the Muslim Dar al Islam. These churches across North Africa and the Middle East were circumscribed as dhimmi. Within all these regions within the Dar al Islam the primary function of the political system was protection of the integrity of the Muslim ummah.[23] Ideally, the churches and Jewish communities were protected as long as they did not threaten the integrity of the ummah. Eventually, this meant that Muslim political, community, and family systems cooperated to assure that conversions could go only one direction— toward the ummah and never away from Islam.

In modern times, the Dar al Islam vision of Muslim territoriality vis-à-vis the Dar al Harb persists with considerable resiliency. This is the reason that American military bases in Saudi Arabia in the wake of the Gulf War of 1991 became so tendentious, apparently contributing to the decisions by militant jihadists to initiate the tragedy of September 11. For the jihadists it is self evident that for regions of the Dar al Harb to place military forces within the soul of the territoriality of the Dar al Islam is theologically untenable and must be rectified by any means necessary.

However, there are also significant countervailing forces. It is exceedingly significant that at the beginning of the twenty-first century, one fourth of all Muslims live in regions that are not within the suzerainty of Muslim authority. This is a tremendous transformation—even a century ago it was exceptional for Muslims to reside outside the parameters of Muslim authority. Even the western colonial powers generally respected the authority of the Muslim jurists in regions under western colonial administration. However, there are now 300 million Muslims living outside the parameters of Muslim authority and whose neighbors are Hindus, Christians, atheists, or Buddhists. Notions of a monolithic idealized Dar al Islam is diluted by the realities of modern mobility and globalization. The vision for a Dar al Islam and Muslim diaspora are often in tension.

Christendom and the Dar al Islam

There are parallels between the theologies of territoriality within a Christendom worldview than that of the Dar al Islam. The community of faith and the political order converge, and the systems represent the kingdom of God. In Christendom the church is "established." In the Dar al Islam the primary function of the political order is to protect the ummah. In Christendom non-Christian communities were ghettoized. In the Dar al Islam non-Muslim communities became dhimmi. Prior to the Enlightenment, Christendom would countenance no dissent from the doctrines of the church; the Dar al Islam, when it heeds the counsel of the theologians, restricts personal freedom and dissent is forbidden.

In Christendom the world is divided into two regions—the civilized regions that are ruled by Christianized governments and the uncivilized regions that are ruled by other kinds of governments. In the Dar al Islam the world is divided into regions of peace under Muslim rule and those regions of war not yet brought under Muslim rule.

Christendom fights just wars; the Dar al Islam fights jihads. Christendom seeks to extend territory—in modern times the United States has frequently taken up a secularized version of this agenda through it vision of manifest destiny—extending the gift of democracy and free enterprise into regions not yet democratized. Likewise, the Dar al Islam from time to time has fought wars to extend the blessings of Islam into non-Islamized societies. Both movements have occasionally merged their missionary impulse with imperialist nationalist goals.

These themes suggest convergences between the political theology of the Muslim Dar al Islam and the Constantinian western church.

Both systems viewed their faith communities and the kingdom of God as identical to political control of territory. These convergences have provided ample grist for territorial conflict right from the beginning of the Muslim movement. In fact, when the Anabaptist movement was birthed, Christendom and Dar al Islam were engaged in another conflict. Vienna was under siege by the Muslims! We now explore that formative time for the Anabaptists.

The Anabaptists

The sixteenth-century Anabaptist movement, that birthed Mennonite and related denominations, emerged within the throes of sometimes violent conflict between divergent visions of the rule of God. The Muslim Dar al Islam and Western Christendom had experienced 900 years of intermittent conflict. On January 21, 1525, when a small Bible study fellowship in Zurich baptized one another on confession of faith in Jesus Christ, thereby inaugurating the Anabaptist movement, Christendom was engaged in a severe struggle with the forces of the Dar al Islam. However, the Anabaptists refused to participate in the war efforts against the Muslim Turks.

The Anabaptists were committed to joining Jesus on his journey from Galilee to Jerusalem. Had not Jesus commanded his disciples to take the cross and follow him? That was a terrifically difficult commitment. For many, the consequence was arrest, torture, and death. The Ottomans were attacking the west, and the ecclesial and political authorities would not tolerate detractors from the conflict.

Under Suleyman the Magnificent the Ottoman Turks were pressing forward into Hungary and toward Vienna. Surely the Muslim forces viewed their triumphs in the Balkans and Central Europe as rectifying the defeat of the Moors in Spain in 1492 and the defeat of Muslim armies in Russia with the concurrent pressure of Russian forces south toward the Caspian Sea. Although Muslim armies were forced into retreat in Russia and Spain, the Ottoman Muslims had occupied Constantinople and the Balkans, and were now advancing on Vienna.[24] Europe was terrified.

Western Christendom was mobilizing for war. In chapter 4 of this volume, "The Mennonite Engagement with Muslims," John A. Lapp comments that the Anabaptist refusal to participate in the war effort was considered treason. One of the Anabaptist prophets, Michael Sattler, stated at his trial which culminated in his execution, "If the Turk comes, he should not be resisted, for it stands written: thou shalt not kill (Matt 5:21). We should not defend ourselves against the Turks or our other persecutors, but with reverent prayer should implore God that he might be our defense and our resistance."[25]

Michael Sattler's commitment to nonparticipation in warfare against the Turks is in harmony with the commitments of the pre-Constantinian church that we have referred to above. Of course, he and the Anabaptists based their commitments on their understanding of Jesus and their study of the New Testament. They could not imagine Jesus killing his enemies. Jesus lays down his life for the enemy, he seeks to embrace the enemy and redeem the enemy.

The Anabaptist commitment to participating with Jesus in his journey to Jerusalem, and the cross was not only a veto on participating in the European military confrontation with the Muslim Turks, but it was also a veto on notions of territorial Christendom. Sattler said it plainly—the Turks in heart who do not know Christ are the ecclesial leaders who would kill a person for following Christ.[26] Territorial Christendom is not the kingdom of God.

In the Zurich Bible study group where the Anabaptist movement was born, another event happened that was a radical break with Christendom. The group baptized one another on the confession of faith. They believed that baptism was a sign of conversion and new birth; it was a public testimony of a person's decision to believe in and follow Christ.

A commitment to adult baptism meant that the state could not determine a person's faith. In that act the Anabaptists were planting the seeds that would transform Europe and eventually much of the world—a person is free to decide her faith. The implications were astounding. Church and state needed to be separate. That commitment birthed the free churches within the European context. It was only over a century later that the political philosophers of the Enlightenment began to carry forward these convictions with a call for separation of church and state; the United States political system is one of the consequences of that development. But the seeds of this transformation were planted in a small baptismal service in Zurich in 1525.

This is not to say that the Anabaptists had a direct influence upon the political philosophy of the Enlightenment. But they were pioneers in confronting the Christendom paradigm and they suffered profoundly for their insistence that the person is free to decide her faith.

Adult baptism meant that the church was a voluntary community within society. The church, therefore, was never the same as any political territory. It was a community within territory, but not convergent with any politically defined territory (nation state). This meant that the nation state would be a pluralist society. Because people are endowed by their creator with the right to choose, the nation state would be pluralist, for not everyone will choose Christ and the church; some might choose Islam and the ummah or a secularist option. Therefore no nation is Christian. It might be Christianized, but not Christian.

There was, of course, theological diversity within the Anabaptist movement. However, if Menno Simons[27] and the Schleitheim Confession[28] of 1527 are considered normative for the first century of the Anabaptist movement, then for the Anabaptists the church was the first fruit of the presence of the kingdom of God on earth. Christ and his kingdom commanded total allegiance. Therefore if the governing authorities or society invited commitments that were contrary to the kingdom of God, then the church needed to dissent even if that meant suffering or martyrdom.

The church was the visible community of disciples of Jesus Christ who gathered in his name; it was a community committed to repentance and who knew the grace of the forgiveness of sins through the atoning sacrifice of Jesus Christ, the Lamb of God. The church was a fellowship of born again believers who were committed to following Jesus Christ. Although the church eschewed political power, disciples of Jesus Christ did indeed influence the political systems as salt seasons and preserves food, or as light on a hill shows the way, or as leaven permeates bread.

In the Anabaptist rejection of participation in warfare and infant baptism, the Anabaptists were revealing a commitment to another way than the paradigms of either Christendom or Dar al Islam. They were committed to an alternative understanding of both the Muslim and Christendom understandings of the kingdom of God as regions defined by territory and political systems. This meant that for them, the whole world was the mission field, Christendom included. Being baptized as an infant or living within a Christian ecclesial and political order was no assurance that the person was a Christian. So every neighbor needed to hear and respond to the gospel. This commitment is revealed in their favorite preaching texts:

"The earth is the Lord's, and everything in it, the world, and all who live in it" (Ps 24:1). The Great Commission—"Go into all the world and preach the good news to all creation" (Mark 16:15-16; Matt 28:18-20).

In time, the severe persecution that befell the Anabaptists muted that calling and commitment. Yet the flame was not extinguished. When opportunity came their way, the Anabaptists were again pioneers to their neighbors, to Indonesia, to Central Asia, India, to their cities, and on and on. If the earth is the Lord's, then it is impossible to circumscribe the earth into territorial domains. Every person everywhere is loved of God and the calling of the church is to express God's love as revealed in Christ throughout the earth. All peoples in all territories deserve to be touched by ministries in the name of Christ; freedom to decide one's faith is God's gift to all humankind.

The essays and reports in this volume suggest that at the 2003 Anabaptist consultation on Islam at Eastern Mennonite University, we discovered that a gentle Anabaptist commitment to presence among Muslims, to identification with the aspirations of people, and respectful, loving, sensitive listening and learning is our best witness. This Anabaptist presence includes confession of our personal sins, the sins of the church, and the sins of our nations. It includes repentance and a commitment to cultivating relations that transcend political-territorial divisions, to peacemaking and identifying with local peacemakers, especially where there is conflict. It includes patient ministry and bearing witness in the name of Christ, to commending Christ in deed and word, to relating to Muslims as persons created in God's image, to respect Muslims as persons endowed with dignity, to believe that God's gift to every person is the freedom to choose, and to the conviction that all peoples should have the blessing of ministries that are expressions of the love of God. Anabaptist presence means a persistent and patient commitment to serving in the way of Christ, a commitment to local church, small and sometimes vulnerable as it might be, in all its variegated expressions, to accept suffering when it comes our way, to identify with those who suffer, and to pray. These commitments have opened doors for ministry and bearing witness that are quite frequently received with appreciation by Muslims and within varied expressions of the Dar al Islam.

Anabaptist commitments are an alternative to all territorial or politically defined expressions of the kingdom of God, whether Muslim or Christian. We observe that many Muslims welcome that alternative. We are grateful when Muslims receive us and serve us and permit us to serve them. Our consultation revealed remarkable accounts of trust-building and bridge-building across territorial divides.

One such bridge-building is Iranian Shi'a-Mennonite dialogues. A significant dimension of these conversations took place in Toronto in the fall of 2002 with a follow-up in Qom, Iran, February 2004. Anabaptists have miniscule political power. Yet the Islamic theological establishment in Qom, Iran, invites conversation.[29] However, the journey in dialogue and witness is fraught with challenges.

"Do not humiliate us," a mullah advised me when I asked what his counsel is to North American Christians.

Another observed that Jesus would also have taken the same path that Muhammad took in Medina, if he had an opportunity. His public ministry lasted only three years. Given more time, Jesus would also have commanded an army. Indeed, such dialogue often reveals that an Anabaptist understanding of the New Testament vision of the kingdom of God is radically other than the understandings of the kingdom of God among our Muslim friends.

Others commented that never before have they spoken with Christians about faith in serious open dialogue. This is significant. Yet even more significant are the hundreds and thousands of friendships that Anabaptists meeting Muslims are developing in neighbor to neighbor relationships, whether in North America or regions around the world.

Surely Anabaptists are called of God to transcend territorial divisions and in the spirit of Christ serve in ways that enable wider and wider circles of Mennonites and Muslims to meet one another. Every Mennonite needs a Muslim friend. I also wish that every Muslim had a Mennonite friend.

All Christian communities living in faithfulness to Christ have gifts of grace that they offer in the journey with Muslims. Muslims also offer gifts; who among us who has Muslim friends has not been challenged by their earnest quest for truth and commitment to submission to God? This introduction has not adequately explored those gifts, for this is a book about the Anabaptist vocation.

In this introduction I have explored the legacy of the Anabaptist journey within the context of three other journeys: Jesus to Jerusalem,

Constantine to Rome, and Muhammad to Medina. The essays and reports in this book are written with that Anabaptist legacy in mind, and with the awareness that as the twenty-first century commences territorial visions of the kingdom of God are clashing anew. A war on terrorism and jihadism are ominously colliding.

In times like these, what is the call of Christ to the Anabaptist community in the journey with Muslims? Hopefully this volume will provide indications of what the response to that question should be.

SECTION ONE

The Big Picture

CHAPTER ONE

The Kingdom of God in Islam and the Gospel

J. Dudley Woodberry

As I began to write this paper in Afghanistan, prior to leaving for Los Angeles, two governmental committees were working on constitutions for Muslim-majority countries, one in Afghanistan and the other in Iraq. Both have been under military occupation by non-Muslim troops! My new visa was issued in the name of the "Islamic Government of Afghanistan," and the Constitutional Committee has been wrestling with what it means to be "Islamic." Meanwhile, the Community Christian Church of Kabul, having just celebrated fifty years since its founding, is wrestling with what it means to be a Christian presence in a Muslim country. Both groups are asking how we should understand the kingdom of God.

Just prior to the first tour of our family in Afghanistan, an Afghan had a dream that he was walking and came to a fork in the road. A man, whom he later understood to be John the Baptist, was directing him to go on the path that followed Jesus. This is the picture we shall use to visualize our topic—the one route walked by Jesus and the other by Muhammad, each of whom followed his own understanding of the way of the kingdom of God.

Although Christians in history have frequently wandered onto the path walked by the Arabian Prophet, we shall seek to discern the original path walked by each pioneer of our respective faiths to see what implications it has for us. Both communities have been known as followers of "the Way"—Christians in Acts 9:2 and Muslims who follow the *Sunna* (or the way) of the Prophet.

The Qur'an repeatedly states that "to God belongs the kingdom (*mulk*) of the heavens and earth" (e.g. 2:107) and calls God "Master (*malik*) of the kingdom" (3:26). The term *mamlaka* (kingdom) then came to be used of God's power over creation, but also was used of power over a spatial entity. In geography, Qudāma b. Ja'far (ca. 928-32) spoke of the *mamlakat al-Islam* (or just *al-mamlaka*) to describe the areas of Islamic rule. The political divisions that arose within the Muslim empire after AD 1000, however, led to the disappearance of its use.[1] However, modern Islamists, like the widely read Sayyid Qutb (d. 1966) of the Muslim Brethren of Egypt, have used the term *hakimiyyat Allah* (kingdom of God), calling it the only legitimate framework within which humans may be governed.[2]

The kingdom of God in biblical understanding is God's sovereign reign, but it expresses itself in different stages throughout redemptive history.[3] Through Aramaic parallelism in the prayer he taught his disciples, Jesus defined the kingdom as God's will being done on earth as it is in heaven (Matt 6:10). Since it is the business of the Messiah to establish the kingdom,[4] we may with H. N. Ridderbos also say that it is "the lordship of Christ exercised in earth as it is in heaven."[5]

The church then is made up of the people of the kingdom and is the continuation of the people of God, the remnant, of the Old Testament.[6] Its counterpart in Islam would be the ummah, the community of Muslims, or the true ummah, those truly expressing God's rule. The New Testament understanding of the church, however, did *not* have the same political connotations that the ummah developed very early.

Since the gospel according to Matthew traces the theme of the kingdom of God (or heaven) in the life of Jesus, we shall follow the road Jesus traveled in this gospel and make comparisons with Muhammad's path as he pursued the similar goal of God's rule.

The Beginning of the Road: The Coming of the Kingdom

The roads that Jesus and Muhammad walked started in very similar circumstances. Both were born into humble homes (Matt 13:15; Qur'an 43:31), but had prominent ancestors. Jesus was of the house of David and Muhammad from the Quraish, the leading tribe of

Mecca, and was a great grandson of Hisham who had been a leader of the tribe in its expansion of trade with Byzantium, Abyssinia (present-day Ethiopia), and Persia.

There are accounts of both being recognized by other holy men before their ministries started. John the Baptist (Yahya in the Qur'an) said of Jesus, "But after me will come one who is more powerful than I, whose sandals I am not fit to carry" (Matt 3:11). A story with obvious apocryphal elements tells of Bahira, a Nestorian Syrian monk, who recognized Muhammad's spiritual potential while he was still a boy.[7]

Both preached a message of repentance (Matt 4:17; Qur'an 19:60) and were rejected in their hometowns (Luke 4:28-29). But ultimately their paths would diverge.

The Narrowing and Widening of Focus

The Bible and Qur'an start with God's creation of the universe and his governance of it through humans who are to be stewards of his in the earth (Gen 1:1, 26-27; Qur'an 6:101; 23:30). Matthew picks up the narrowing of the focus with the choice of Abraham and God's rule through the children of Israel until the birth of the Messiah, the King of the kingdom (1:1-17).

The Qur'an, too, describes creation and then traces the right religion to Abraham (6:161-63), but notes that the Israelites disobeyed God's commandments (e.g. 7:163) and now an Arabic Qur'an has been given for the Arabs (42:7; 43:44). When, however, it calls Jesus the Messiah (3:45), although it ascribes honor to him, this term has not traditionally been understood in its Hebrew meaning as the one "anointed" to establish the kingdom. Rather, its meaning has commonly been explained with only Arabic etymologies.[8] Instead, the primary focus in the Qur'an is on Muhammad and the Arabs.

At the end of Jesus's earthly journey, Matthew describes him as again broadening the focus to the world since his disciples are to make disciples of all peoples and teach them all that he has commanded them (28:19-20). And the Bible closes with the renewal of all creation (Rev 21:5). Likewise, the Qur'an broadens its focus from one people, the Arabs, to the world (34:28). It does not speak of a new heaven and a new earth, though it does have a return to the garden.

The Kingdom Starts from the Margins of Society

John the Baptist in Matthew's gospel announces that the kingdom of heaven had drawn near but did not mention establishing the throne of David or the overthrow of the occupying government, which the Jews expected of the Messiah (3:1-12). In fact, before the story is over even John the Baptist asked if Jesus was the expected Messiah (11:2). Instead, Jesus's followers were mostly from the edges of society, from Galilee far from the center of power (4:12-22).

Muhammad, like Jesus from a modest family, did not get his early followers from the powerful, the Quraish. In fact, some of his followers fled first to Abyssinia, then all escaped to Medina, a city of less note. The paths of the two spokespersons of their faiths thus started in similar contexts.

Identification with Sinners

Although Jesus was sinless (Heb 4:15; "faultless" in the Qur'an 19:19), he was to bear the sins of the world in bringing in the kingdom. Thus he identified with sinners by being baptized by John. Then the voice from heaven says, "This is my Son, whom I love; with him I am well pleased" (Matt 3:13-17). In this event, we see two surprises of his kingship revealed, the servanthood and the glory.

Muhammad in turn did not claim to be sinless. In fact, in the Qur'an he is even told to ask forgiveness for his sins (40:55; 47:19; 48:2), though most Muslims consider him to have been sinless. And, despite the veneration that has grown up around him, especially in Sufi circles, he never claimed supernatural power or glory.

Encounters with Satan and the Kingdom of this Age

In Christ's temptations we have the encounter between the kingdom of God and the kingdom of Satan. The temptation is to take the short cut, avoid the route of the cross, to win the kingdoms of the world. It would have involved a compromise of associating the devil with God in worship (Matt 4:1-11).

Muhammad faced a similar temptation in the "Satanic Verses" which recognized some local deities along with Allah and which, we are told, he temporarily included in the Qur'an. He ultimately rejected the compromise. The temptation to win a following by doing the spectacular was not Muhammad's because he never claimed that power. He later avoided Jesus's choice of choosing the route of the suffering servant by fleeing from Mecca to Medina.

Teaching Along the Way:
The Gospel of the Kingdom

Matthew clusters much of the teaching about the kingdom in two sections, one starting with the Sermon on the Mount (chapters 5–7) and the other with the parables (13:1–14:12). The qur'anic material is more dispersed.

Authority of the Teacher

Jesus begins the Sermon on the Mount with the authority of the King, promising the salvation of the kingdom to the poor in spirit, but denying it to those whose righteousness does not exceed that of the scribes and Pharisees (Matt 5:3, 20). He goes further to contrast the Law of Moses as interpreted by those scribes and Pharisees with his teaching: "You have heard that it was said to the people long ago . . . but I tell you . . ." (Matt 5:21-22).

In the Qur'an, what starts as a message to obey God becomes "obey God and his Apostle" (4:59). Noah and Jesus in the Qur'an also tell people to fear God and obey them (71:3; 43:63), but in Medina, according to both the Blachère and Cairo ordering of the suras, Muhammad goes further in asserting his authority by saying that "he who obeys the Apostle obeys God" (4:80).

Characteristics of the Citizens

The characteristics that Jesus uses to describe the blessed (Matt 5:3-12) have interesting parallels and contrasts with those given in the Qur'an. He talks of the poor in spirit (or poor in Luke 6:20) and those who mourn. The Qur'an speaks of giving alms to the poor (9:60), and the poor rather than the rich Quraish were those who originally followed Muhammad. Yusuf Ali, however, in his notes on the Qur'an, contrasts Islam with what he considers the "monastic" tendencies of the Sermon on the Mount with its emphasis on the poor in spirit, those who mourn, and the meek, noting that "Allah's kingdom requires also courage, resistance to evil . . . firmness, law and discipline which will enhance justice." God, he continues, does not mean that believers should have "gloomy lives."[9] Yusuf Ali misses Jesus's point. These people are blessed because their abject state makes them far more receptive to that which is vastly more valuable than earthly riches and happiness (Matt 6:19-34; 13:44-46).

The Qur'an speaks of the most righteous as most honored in the sight of God (49:13) rather than "those who hunger and thirst for righteousness," but Sufism added this element, as did the concept of *niyyah* or the importance of intention in all acts of Muslim worship. Jesus's blessing of the "merciful" certainly is a qur'anic value since God is repeatedly called the Merciful. Jesus's reference to "the pure in heart" is a theme developed in Sufism. Jesus says "blessed are the peacemakers." The Qur'an endorses those who make peace (e.g. 4:35; 6:34), but, unlike Jesus, advocates fighting and killing those who will not make peace (4:91).

Jesus goes on to say "blessed are those who are persecuted because of righteousness." The prophets in the Qur'an were certainly persecuted for righteousness' sake—Abraham, Moses, Jesus, and Muhammad—although in sura four of the Qur'an, Jesus, unlike the gospel account, seems to be rescued from the cross. The Qur'an describes Muslims as "the best of peoples evolved for humankind, enjoining what is right and forbidding what is wrong and believing in God" (3:110); so the emphasis is on faith plus the law. As we shall see, how the law is fulfilled is a major difference in what characterizes the members of the kingdom.

In the Bible, the members of the kingdom are called salt and light (Matt 5:13-16). In the Qur'an, God is called the light of the heavens and earth (24:35). These are images which express change without external force but after the hijrah, Muhammad and the Muslim community chose the use of force to create an ambiance that would change individuals rather than rely on internal means like salt, seed, or yeast (Matt 13) to transform quietly from within. It is interesting that in recent years the strategy for Islamic expansion in the west has been to reverse the process, starting with converted individuals, moving to an Islamic ambiance, and then to control of the government.[10]

The Law and the Religious Establishment

To see the similarities and differences in the attitude toward the law and the religious establishment in Islam and the gospel, it is helpful to note the similarity between Judaic law and its religious establishment and the two in Islam. The law in both Judaism and Islam applies to all areas of life.

The Qur'an includes the Ten Commandments though not together, and Sabbath observance was specified for the Jews only.[11] The social laws of the Qur'an are almost identical to rabbinic laws at the time.[12] Likewise, the scribes and the Pharisees and others in the religious establishment of Judaism have their counterparts in the *ulama*, *mujtahids*, and *qadis* of Islam. As the Talmud developed to interpret the details of the law so Shari'a developed to interpret the details of Islamic law.

In Matthew, the Sermon on the Mount becomes the counterpart to Mt. Sinai where Jesus explains the fulfillment of the law in the kingdom of God. He did not come to destroy the Law of Moses, but rejected the interpretation of it by the scribes and Pharisees. He called for a radical obedience that went deeper than the act to the thought and intent, what has been called niyyah in Islamic ritual, although Islam has never called for perfection as Jesus did (Matt 5:48). The new law is fulfilled by the law of love (even to the extent of loving your enemies, Matt 5:44). By way of contrast, God in the Qur'an loves those who love him, but not the disobedient (3:29-31). And enemies may be forgiven, but retaliation is permissible (42:40-41). Jesus also saw that in the very performing of the details of the law, people can be led to pride and hypocrisy.

Ultimately, for their followers, both Jesus and Muhammad have become models for their understandings of the kingdom of God. Both showed intolerance for violations of the rights of God, Jesus with the moneychangers in the temple, Muhammad with the idols in the Ka'bah. Although Muhammad forgave most of those from Mecca who opposed him, he ordered the killing of two women who chanted satires about him.[13] Jesus in turn bore suffering and death, and forgave and taught his followers to turn the other check.

The Parting of the Ways: The Power of the Kingdom

We see the parting of the ways as we look at the types of signs or miracles attributed to Jesus and Muhammad. One chose the approach of a suffering servant, the other chose the military-political option. One exhibits supernatural power and glory, the other that of an exclusively human messenger.

The Signs of the Kingdom

Both Jesus and Muhammad were asked to produce signs as proofs of their message, and both refused (Matt 12:38-40; Qur'an 21:5-6). Muhammad pointed to the signs of God in nature (Qur'an 2:164) and the reception of the Qur'an when he was an unlettered prophet

(2:23-24; 62:2). Subsequent accounts of his miracles are not in keeping with the earliest records and are of the character of spectacles, not evidences of the character of God's rule.

Conversely, Jesus's miracles in the gospels are signs that reveal the powers of the kingdom, though death and suffering will continue until the kingdom is consummated. His various miracles show the power to heal physical sickness (a leper), to control nature (the tempest on the lake), to overcome principalities and powers (casting out demons), to raise the dead (a child) and to forgive sins (the paralytic). In the Qur'an, Jesus heals the lepers, gives sight to the blind, and raises the dead, but always by the permission of God. Muhammad in the Qur'an does none of these and in addition needs his sins forgiven (Qur'an 48:2).

The Suffering Servant versus the Military-Political Route

The preaching of Jesus and Muhammad in their hometowns had similar results. In both cases there was rejection and even the attempt to kill them. However, their contrasting responses represented a major parting of their ways to the kingdom. Muhammad chose to rule in God's name rather than suffer and so made a flight (hijrah) from Mecca to Medina with his followers. He used an invitation to be an umpire between the tribes there to build a power base.

Jesus took the other route of suffering in God's name rather than ruling in an earthly sense. He rejected those who wanted to make him a king after the feeding of the 5,000 and instead "set his face to go to Jerusalem" knowing it would mean his suffering and death.

Muhammad chose the military-political route while Jesus rejected it by telling Pilate that his kingdom was not of this world and that, if it were, his disciples would fight. The Arabian Prophet did not force conversions: "Let there be no compulsion in religion" the Qur'an says (2:256). But, as he built his base, it meant that those who opposed him, like the Jewish tribes, were driven out or killed.

The contrast is symbolized by the way Muhammad conquered Mecca. He rode in with about 10,000 armed men, 400 of them on horses.[14] Jesus rode into Jerusalem on a donkey, a sign of a king coming in peace. He wept over Jerusalem with the words, "O Jerusalem, Jerusalem . . . how often I have longed to gather your children together, as a hen gathers her chicks under her wings, but you were not willing" (Matt 23:37). His approach was by invitation alone, not external force.

In the Topkapi Palace in Istanbul, what is purported to be the sword of Muhammad is proudly displayed. It would be impossible to do the same for Jesus. Medieval Christian pilgrims instead focused their attention on what were purported to be parts of the original cross. For the Arabian Prophet "striving in the way of God," or jihad, could take a military form. For Jesus it could not.

Muhammad and his followers believed that because human nature is good or at least neutral (Qur'an 30:30), the kingdom of God can be realized by introducing the law—which applies to all areas of life including the political. Then, as people got in the habit of following it, the kingdom would be actualized. Jesus, however, not only distinguished between the realm of Caesar and God, but told the law-abiding Pharisee, Nicodemus, that a person must be born again, transformed from within, to see the kingdom of God (John 3:3).

Muhammad fled from death, and most Muslims believe that God rescued Jesus from crucifixion and thwarted the forces of evil—though some significant Muslim qur'anic commentators allow for a real crucifixion.[15] On the other hand, the gospel witness is clear that Christ redeemed evil people by accepting death (Mark 10:45), thereby stopping the cycle of evil by accepting the consequences in himself and forgiving.

The success of Sunni Muslims was so rapid that they did not have to develop much of a theology of suffering, and within 300 years had developed a comprehensive political-military system and theory in Shari'a law. The Shi'ites, from their failure militarily and the deaths of Ali, Hasan, and Husein, did develop a theory of redemptive suffering.[16] But these three leaders were trying to set up the same type of military-political system that the Sunnis developed.

Although Jesus turned from the political-military route, and his followers remained a suffering minority for their first 300 years, Constantine and his successors soon developed a system with many parallels to Islam.

Supernatural Power and Glory versus a Human Messenger

Another surprise of the kingdom is that the Messiah's suffering and death is sandwiched between the supernatural glory of his transfiguration (Matt 17:1-13) and the supernatural power of his resurrection (Matt 28:1-20). In the Qur'an, Jesus and Muhammad, although honored above other humans, remain on the human level. Even Jesus's miracles are by the permission of God. According to the gospels, Jesus in his transfiguration expresses in himself God's glory. He does not just bring a message about it. A sign of the kingdom in the gospels is the demonstration of the conquest of death, not just the bringing of a message about it. In the gospels, God shows his power by raising Jesus after he has accomplished his work of redemption on the cross. This demonstrates the new life which characterizes the kingdom.

The End of the Road: Toward the Consummation of the Kingdom

As the end of the road is nearer, we see more clearly the task of the heralds of the kingdom, the judgment day, and the completion of the kingdom.

Heralds of the Kingdom

The calling of twelve disciples is parallel to the twelve tribes of Israel, but now they indicate a new people of the kingdom. By images of fishing ("fishers of men" Matt 4:19) and agriculture ("Ask the Lord of the harvest, therefore, to send out workers" Matt 9:38), they saw their task. As we have noted, in the beginning the disciples of Jesus and Muhammad saw their task as limited to the Israelites and Arabs respectively, but ultimately they learned that their message was for the world.

Both prophets started with followers drawn largely from the margins of society. Muhammad by conquering Mecca sought to bring in the leaders. Jesus, however, gives to his disciples from the margins the unlimited task of making disciples of all nations, teaching them all that he has commanded, and promising his presence until the end (Matt 28:18-20).

In their task we see our own: "As the Father has sent me, I am sending you" (John 20:21). Thus by our words and our deeds we are to proclaim the kingdom and demonstrate it by feeding the hungry, clothing the naked, and welcoming the strangers (Matt 25:31-36). As he avoided the military-political route to build the kingdom, so should we. In the tasks of proclamation and ministry the heralds of the gospel kingdom and the qur'anic kingdom share much. In the military and political route they part company.

Coming of Jesus and Judgment

Both Jesus and Muhammad taught concerning the final judgment and God's sovereign grace. Jesus taught that God is free to give the same salvation to those who enter the kingdom ("the vineyard") early or late (Matt 19:30–20:16). In the Qur'an, God forgives whom he wills and punishes whom he wills (48:14); thus for the Muslim there may be the expectation, but not the certainty of salvation.

In the gospel, the judgment is associated with the coming of the Son of Man as a judge (Matt 24:29-31; 25:31-46). While people's works will show whether they are kingdom people, there is not a teaching, as in Islam, of the scales in which good and bad works are weighed to see which is heavier. Since adjacent verses are about Jesus, most Muslims interpret Sura 43:61 ["he (or it) is a sign of the Hour"] as indicating that Jesus will return in the last day. Although there is not a hint in the Qur'an that God will share judgment with Jesus, a *hadith* says that Jesus will return as a wise judge (*hakam*).[17]

The Consummation of the Kingdom

For the Bible and the Qur'an, the world starts with creation and a garden. The Qur'an, however, does not see the problem of sin as being as serious as the Bible teaches, so Muslims believe that by the habit of following the law, humans actualize the kingdom and can return to the garden.

The Bible has a more pessimistic view of human nature without the work of God within. Humans cannot bring in the kingdom. The holy city will come down from heaven and God (Rev 21:2). There will be a new creation ("a new heaven and a new earth" Rev 21:1, 5). Our work then is by word and deed to proclaim and demonstrate the new power and life of the kingdom that is here now and will be fully realized when the King returns.

As our plane settled into the Los Angeles airport, we only knew that the draft of the new Afghan constitution stated that it is a Muslim nation. It was for the Loya Jurga (the Consultive Council) and the people to decide what that meant. In like manner, the members of the Community Christian Church of Kabul and the rest of us who bear the name of Christ must discern where his footprints lead.

The Afghan who followed the path indicated by John the Baptist in his dream faced the persecution similar to that of Jesus and the disciples who walked that path before him, but at the end of the road he will reach "the city whose architect and builder is God" (Heb 11:10).

∾

Response: Communities in Mission—the Church and the Ummah

–Bedru Hussein Muktar

J. Dudley Woodberry has clearly demonstrated the two different journeys toward the kingdom of God in the gospels and the kingdom of Allah in the Qur'an. This paper is well done and I deeply appreciate his work.

In the gospels, Jesus spoke about the power of God's kingdom and established its arrival by performing miracles through supernatural power. His death and resurrection demonstrated the kingdom's power in a way that completely contrasts to the way of Muhammad. There is no story in the Qur'an concerning the resurrection of Muhammad. Indeed, the story of Jesus and the cross in the Qur'an diverges substantially from the crucifixion and resurrection story in the New Testament.

Muslims believe that when a person submits to Islam (which they regard as a religion for all of humankind) and submit to the Shari'a of Islam, that person becomes part of the people of the Muslim region of peace.[18]

According to Badru Kateregga, co-author with David Shenk of the book *Islam and Christianity: A Muslim and a Christian in Dialogue*, the ummah, the community of Muslims, will continue to expand in the world until Muslims are the majority and the reign of Allah (the kingdom of Allah) will be experienced. The ummah transcends all tribal, national, linguistic, and racial loyalties.[19]

Kateregga argues that, following the example of the prophet Muhammad, it is the responsibility of the ummah to strive to fulfill its mission of establishing God's rule and law on earth. The Muslim concept of ummah includes a total program of social, economic, cultural, political, and religious organizations. All aspects of life are brought under the rule of the Shari'a within the ummah.

Islam relates to government structure with the goal of establishing what they call Dar al-Islam (house of Islam), a situation where God rules or the kingdom of Allah reigns. Abdo Shemsudin describes three ways in which Islam relates to government:[20]

1. Dar al-Islam

In this government structure Shari'a (Islamic) law regulates all of life.

The Muslims have privileges which include property and business rights.

Non-Muslims live by the courtesy of Muslims, and their freedoms are sometimes limited.

The territory under Muslim rule belongs to the Muslims.

Non-Muslims are guests to the Muslim community.

2. Dar al-Muahanda

In Dar al-Muahanda Islam and other religions coexist under the condition of religious freedom for all.

Some Muslims are not satisfied with this style of government because they have the goal to move toward total Islamic law and Muslim governance.

3. Dar al-Harb

In Dar al-Harb Islam does not have the freedom to expand or the Muslims feel oppressed and, therefore, a state of war exists in order to establish religious freedom for Islam in that land.

The mission of Islam is that everyone becomes a Muslim and for the world to come under the rule of Islam. The world is divided into two regions, the region of peace under Muslim rule and where Muslims live in peace, and the region of war where Muslims have no authority. Muslims seek to expand the region of peace.

In the Bible, the church also calls on people to bring all of life under the rule of God, a rule which Jesus the Messiah proclaimed as the kingdom of God. However, the New Testament Christians did not believe that the mechanisms of political power were appropriate to use in establishing the kingdom of God. Jesus the Messiah showed clearly that the kingdom of God could never be politically established. Although Jesus was pushed by his followers to become a political leader, he refused their request. Through Jesus, God revealed that it is in redemptive, suffering love that the kingdom of God becomes present in human history.

As Woodberry points out in his essay, God's kingdom in the gospel of Matthew (5:13-16; 13:33) is likened to the invisible yeast in bread, to a light in darkness, or to salt in food. The kingdom of God breaks in when people open their hearts and lives for the saving grace of God, not by the use of force, or jihad in Islam. The kingdom of God has no geographical or cultural orientation. It is present wherever people live in a right and joyous relationship with God and with others.

We can see from the above discussions that Jesus and Muhammad worked in contrasting ways and instructed their followers' to work as missionaries in these contrasting ways in order to bring about their respective kingdoms. Abd al-Masih explains these different journeys in establishing the kingdom of God and Allah. He observes that Jesus and Muhammad both commanded their followers to engage in world mission.[21]

Muslims around the world embrace the mandate to be a witness over the nations. In their mission, the majority of Muslims are committed to the qur'anic injunction, "There is no compulsion in religion" (Qur'an 2:256). However, there are a minority of jihadist Muslims who point out that Allah gave the order to the Muslims through their prophet, "Fight against them until there will no longer be a temptation and the religion (of Islam) will be reigning worldwide for Allah."[22]

Muslims believe that Islam brings the person to perfection, and in order for that perfection to happen, it is helpful (many believe necessary) to establish a Muslim political order. This means that the Islamic kingdom is to be built on this earth now with all means necessary. In Medina, Muhammad used military violence to defend and extend Muslim rule and authority. Although modern Muslim theologians debate to what extent the Medina experience is applicable in modern times, there are Muslim renewal movements that seek to emulate Muhammad's use of political and military power to establish Islam in Medina and throughout Arabia.

In contrast, mission as Jesus commanded is based on his redemptive death and the outpouring of the renewing power of the Holy Spirit (Acts 1:2, 8). Jesus did not train his followers for bloody combat. He chose to die for his enemies on the cross instead of killing them. Jesus strictly forbade his followers to fight with the sword (Matt 26:52; John 18:11). He commanded them to follow him in self-denial and love even their enemies in word and deed, and pray for them just as he did. Our Lord was meek and humble (Matt 11:29) and promised that the meek will inherit the earth (Matt 5:5). Thus, there are two very different and starkly contrasting approaches toward the establishment of the kingdom of God or the rule of Allah.

I am very happy to belong to this kingdom of God, that calls people from east, west, south, and north and makes them citizens of the kingdom of God that has broken into history in Jesus Christ. Woodberry's essay has clearly shown the contrasts between the kingdom of Allah in Islam and kingdom of our Lord Jesus Christ revealed in the gospel.

CHAPTER TWO

A Global Perspective on the Current Status of Christian-Muslim Relations

J. Dudley Woodberry

As we sang "I Heard the Bells on Christmas Day" at a Christmas program in the school where my wife teaches in Afghanistan, we came to the words:

> And in despair, I bowed my head:
> "There is no peace on earth," I said,
> "For hate is strong, and mocks the song
> Of peace on earth, good will to men."

In a land where Osama bin Laden had described Muslim-Christian relations as a global conflict, and, with guards outside because of weekly terrorist incidents, I was tempted to echo this verse of the carol in my analysis.

A few minutes later, however, we were guests of our Muslim neighbors in one of their two tiny rooms. As we sat cross-legged around the carpet and experienced their lavish hospitality, it was evident that the description of Muslim-Christian relations would need to be expanded. It could be better summarized by Charles

Dickens' first line of *A Tale of Two Cities*: "It was the best of times, it was the worst of times. . . ."

"The worst of times" has been evidenced by the anger of many Muslims against the west and, by association, against Christianity, which came onto the world stage with the Iranian Revolution of 1978-79 and into everyone's living room on September 11, 2001. And it has intensified with hostilities in Afghanistan, Iraq, and Israel/Palestine. This anger on the street has been reciprocated with negative views toward Islam expressed by Christian leaders and the general public. The same week as the Christmas program at my wife's school the Iranian President Muhammad Khatami spoke of this growing religious hatred.

"The best of times" is evidenced by the fact that President Khatami addressed these words in Geneva as the guest of the World Council of Churches and in a speech where he said that religious dialogue should help to remedy the mutual incomprehension.[1] Thus he mirrored what has been happening all over the world as Muslims and Christians have seen the necessity of opening mosques and churches to each other so that they might get to know each other and cooperate in conflict transformation.

Those expressing the worst of times have pointed to qur'anic references like Sura 2:190-193: "Fight in the cause of God those who fight you . . . and slay them . . . for tumult and oppression are worse than slaughter. . . . Fight them until . . . there prevails justice and faith in God." Those expressing the best of times, however, point to references like Sura 5:82: "The nearest in affection to the believers are those who say, 'We are Christians.'"

Prior to September 11, the Vatican, the World Council of Churches, and others like the Arab Working Group on Muslim-Christian Dialogue had sponsored many dialogues. Likewise, there were many Christian study centers for Islam sprinkled around the globe, and journals such as *Islamochristiana*, *The Muslim World*, and *Focus on Christian-Muslim Relations*. Though quite evidently their message did not filter down to the grassroots, they have provided the structures and contacts for working on present issues. The period before September 11 has been documented.[2] This survey will focus on the subsequent period, looking at specific regions that represent the major characteristics of the relations between the two faith communities and then making some general observations.

North America

American attitudes toward Islam and Muslims became more negative between March 2002 and July 2003 according to the Pew Research Center. In response to the question, "Does Islam encourage violence?" those who said yes increased from 25 percent to 44 percent, and those who said no decreased from 51 percent to 41 percent. In response to the question "Are Muslims anti-American?" those who said "all or most are" increased from 18 percent to 24 percent.[3] In like manner, foreign approval of the United States has plummeted since the last war in Iraq, especially in the Muslim world, according to a recent Pew Global Attitudes poll published in June 2003.[4] This trend has been confirmed by the Bush-appointed United States Advisory Group on Public Diplomacy for the Arab and Muslim World.[5] Needless to say, many Muslims and Arabs equate "American" and "Christian."

At the same time, anti-Muslim incidents increased by 15 percent over the previous year (from 525 confirmed incidents to 602) according to the Council on American-Islamic Relations.[6] The post-September 11 Patriot Act is also seen as having negative affect on Muslim civil liberties. There has been a special registration program for Muslim visa holders. Even some modernist Muslims like Canadian television journalist Irshad Mauji have joined the attack on Muslims and Islam with her book, *The Trouble with Islam*, which argues that it has deep problems with Jews, women, slavery, and authoritarianism.[7]

On the positive side, although the Task Force on Christian-Muslim Relations of the National Council of Churches had been closed shortly before September 11, they and the Roman Catholic Church, through leaders such as John Borelli of the U.S. Conference of Catholic Bishops, had established cordial relations with American Muslim leaders. The American Society of Muslims and the Catholic Focolare movement organized joint seminars to provide common spiritual values in modern, secular society.

After September 11, both churches and mosques opened their doors to those of the other community. Christians offered to accompany Muslims on errands or stay at mosques in case trouble started. Christians, Jews, and Muslims worked together in the Habitat for Humanity projects building homes for Muslim immigrants. Institutions like Hartford Seminary and the Center for Muslim-Christian Understanding at Georgetown University were already involved in considerable bridging between the two communities. Of particular note has been a student exchange program between the Toronto Mennonite Theological Center and the Imam Khomeini Education and Research Institute in Qom, Iran, since 1998, sponsored by the Mennonite Central Committee.[8]

Eastern Mennonite University and Fuller Theological Seminary have conflict transformation programs. Muslims have been anxious to dialogue with evangelicals at Fuller because evangelicals are a group they do not understand and with whom they think they have had little contact. According to an April 2003 survey of evangelicals cosponsored by the Ethics and Public Policy Center and Beliefnet, 76 percent believed that Islam opposed religious freedom, 72 percent that Shari 'a violates human rights, 66 percent that Islam is dedicated to world domination, and 70 percent that Islam is a religion of violence (a considerably higher figure than the Pew Research Center poll of the general public above).[9]

Despite the fact that President Bush described Islam as a religion of peace that has been hijacked by extremists, high-profile evangelicals have said the contrary. Franklin Graham called it "a very evil and wicked religion"—a remark he and his father are sorry that he made. Jerry Vine, former president of the Southern Baptist Convention, called Muhammad a "demon-possessed pedophile." And Jerry Falwell and Pat Robertson have made similar remarks.

Richard Cizik, vice president for Governmental Affairs of the National Association of Evangelicals, which represents 43,000 congregations, said, "Evangelicals have substituted Islam for the Soviet Union. . . . The Muslims have become the modern-day equivalent of the Evil Empire."[10] Such an onslaught led to a book by Akbar S. Ahmed, chairman of the Islamic Studies Department of the American University in Washington, D.C., entitled *Islam Under Siege: Living Dangerously in a Post-Honor World.*[11] Fortunately, in May 2003, the National Association of Evangelicals and the Institute of Religion and Democracy in Washington, D.C., offered *Guidelines for Christian-Muslim Dialogue*, which set a more positive tone. In article six it indicated the necessity to "affirm some points of theology and morality that Islam and Christianity have in common," and in article eight, to "work together with some Muslims on certain public issues in which we and they have similar concerns."[12] A further complicating factor has been considerable Evangelical support for Israel.[13] But for years Evangelicals for Middle East Understanding has given strong support for issues of justice for Palestinians.

Europe

During the month after September 11 there was an unprecedented backlash against the almost one million Muslims in Holland with over seventy attacks against mosques.[14] Muslim-Christian relations in Europe are affected by the large Muslim communities which have been formed by migrant workers who have brought their families at the same time as the population of traditional Europeans is dwindling. Muslims are seen as a threat to European cultural identity and Christian values even though Europeans have become secularized. This includes some opposition to mosque minarets in France even though there are five million Muslims and 1,500 mosques and prayer rooms in the country, and there are Muslim chaplains in hospitals, prisons, and the military.[15] These fears have been exploited by political movements like the National Front. The banning of Muslim head-scarves and other conspicuous religious symbols from public schools by France's National Assembly may be an attempt to uphold the principle of secularism (*laïcité*) by which equality before the law regardless of private beliefs is meant to be guaranteed by excluding religion from public life. But many Muslims have seen it as discrimination against them.[16] Yet the French government's appointment of an Algerian-born Muslim, Aissa Dermouche, as the education prefect of Jura region has been interpreted as taboo "positive discrimination" by some non-Muslims and opposed. So the government is caught between its desire to meet the needs of its Muslims (7 to 8 percent of its population) and its ideal of equality.[17]

In parts of Britain, Islamist groups are active, such as al-Muhajiroun, which claims to have offices in thirty British cities. They sell militant videos and stickers which even feature "The Magnificent 19," with pictures of those involved in the September 11 atrocities with a backdrop of the burning Trade Center towers. The press also sensationalizes the honor killings in London by Muslims of their daughters who have brought moral shame on their families.[18]

At the same time, there have been many meetings between Muslim and Christian leaders to build bridges, such as one hosted in 2002 by the Archbishop of Canterbury, George Carey, in Lambeth Palace, London, that included Prince Hassan of Jordan, and other Muslims from Africa and the Middle East along with Prime Minister Tony Blair and other Roman Catholics and Protestants. The Archbishop suggested that Christians should read the Qur'an and

Muslims the New Testament to understand each other's faith better. And he announced that he would sign an agreement with Mohamed Sayed Tantawy, Grand Imam of al-Azhar in Cairo, to have meetings at least annually between Sunnis and Anglicans.[19]

Germany represents an important religio-economic issue in Muslim-Christian relations. Statistics can create fear. For example, in 2001, 7.3 million foreigners lived in Germany and represented 8.9 percent of the population. Of these, 27.4 percent were Turks, who traditionally would be Muslim. At the same time, the German population is shrinking and aging and people have been leaving the churches. And many Turks would assert that some of the resistance to Turkey joining the European Union is really resistance to the further flooding of Turkish Muslims into countries like Germany.

But Germany has not had protests like those in England against Salman Rushdie's *The Satanic Verses* nor the conflict in France over schoolgirls wearing headscarves, though there was a dispute about a teacher wearing one. Germany does have a yearly "Foreign-born Citizens/Intercultural Week" in which the evangelical, Roman Catholic, and Orthodox leaders encourage all Christians to participate.[20]

Eastern Europe has, of course, had centuries of hostilities between Muslims and Christians. Though held in check for a time by the Soviet Union and Tito's regime, they were unleashed when these governments fell as the fighting in Bosnia, Kosovo, and Chechnya have shown so tragically. In the war crimes trials in The Hague during the fall of 2003, Serbian Christian officers say that eight years ago the massacre of more than 7,000 Muslims was intentional.[21] And Serbia has offered to send troops and police to Muslim Afghanistan.[22] Only a work of God can heal these wounds.

The Middle East

The Middle East has had centuries of Muslims and Christians living together with Christians usually protected by the dhimmi system as long as they have been loyal citizens. When a team of us writing a feature article for *Christianity Today* talked with Muslim leaders in Egypt, they told of the great toleration and protection of Christians. On the other hand, Christians wanted equality, not toleration, and spoke of the difficulties of getting permission to do such things as build or add to churches. At times there have been riots with Christians killed,[23] but this has been the exception. Yet between October 21 and 23, 2003, twenty-two converts to Christ from Islam were arrested in Alexandria, Egypt, for falsifying their identity papers. This was a result of the fact that converts to Islam can get their papers changed within twenty-four hours, but it is almost impossible for Christians converts from Islam to change their papers.[24]

Although there was considerable empathy for Americans immediately after September 11, 2001, once the war on terrorism started Muslims saw non-Muslims killing and imprisoning Muslims and they became angry. This was especially true with the invasion of Iraq. Now most Islamist Web sites list Iraq as the place most Muslim militants want to enter in order to wage jihad against the infidel.[25]

Attitudes are influenced by the family, the school, the place of worship, and the media. In a clannish social structure as found in the Middle East, families often criticize others. In the Muslim-majority schools, textbooks are sometimes biased against non-Muslims. An eighth-grade textbook in Saudi Arabia states that God curses Jews and Christians, and a tenth-grade textbook states that Muslims should consider infidels their enemies. The Saudi government, however, is in the process of trying to make the texts more tolerant.[26]

Attitudes are also influenced in the mosques. When there are demonstrations and riots, they are often after the Friday prayers in the mosque. Jews and Christians have been vilified in some Saudi mosques. Many of the imams have been removed or arrested by the government since the May 12 attacks against western civilians in Riyadh this year, and the government-appointed Council of Senior Islamic Scholars have said that terrorism has nothing to do with jihad.[27]

Finally, the media influences attitudes, and television stations like al-Jazeera and al-Arabiya, and the Arab press have been very inflammatory. Muslims on the street equate "westerner" and "Christian" just as the average westerner equates "Arab" and "Muslim." This poisons attitudes toward Middle Eastern Christians. However, they in turn can be a bridge between western Christians and Muslims even though they suffer in the process. In fact, many Iraqi Christians say that they felt safer under Saddam Hussein.[28]

Although there are many Palestinian Christians, the Palestinian cause has taken an increasingly Muslim flavor with slogans such as "Islam is the answer" and "Jerusalem and Palestine are Islamic endowments (*waqf*)." Even though attitudes on the street are bad, Yasser Arafat has for years tried to attend Christmas Eve mass in

Bethlehem, and chose his wife from the Christian community.

Gestures by prominent Christians have also helped intercommunal relations. During the war in Bosnia, some Muslims tried unsuccessfully to blow up a busload of Christians in Lebanon. When the culprits were captured, the Antiochian Patriarch Hazim asked the government to forgive them.[29] Also, Pope John Paul's visit with Sheikh Ahmad Kuftârô at the Umayyad mosque (formerly the Church of St. John the Baptist) in 2001 was seen by Muslims as a major step forward in Muslim-Christian dialogue.[30]

Back in May 1995, the Middle East Council of Churches (MECC) facilitated the formation of the "Arab Working Group on Muslim-Christian Dialogue" with members from Lebanon, Syria, Egypt, Jordan, Palestine, Sudan, and the United Arab Republic. Although none of the members officially represented any group, they have worked for the common good of the Arab nation. This group helped to calm people during conflicts in Kosovo, Bosnia, and Chechnya, and after September 11 by convening seminars, including ones with Lebanese and Egyptian youth.[31]

In November of 2001, the Saudi Islamic Organization called together a meeting in Cairo that included al-Azhar University, the World Council of Churches, the Vatican, the MECC, and representatives of the Muslim communities in France, Britain and churches of Jordan, Palestine, and Syria. They all publicly condemned the terrorist attacks on the United States and agreed to work together to enhance Muslim-Christian understanding.[32]

With the poor security in Baghdad, a gang of criminals threatened to kill members of St. George Chaldean Church if they did not pay $10,000. A local mosque offered to help. Until the fall of the Baath Party government in Iraq, the Presbyterians were the officially recognized Protestant denomination, but since the war other churches have started to spring up. However, some leaders of the established churches have expressed concern that these new churches might aggravate relations with the Muslims.[33]

In some of the most unlikely places we are seeing a thaw in Muslim-Christian relations. One of these has been the student exchange program between the Imam Khomeini Education and Research Institute in Qom, Iran, and Regis College of the Toronto School of Theology since 1998, which developed from the Mennonite Central Committee's long-term reconstruction and disaster relief after 1991.[34]

Africa

Since Muslims predominate in the North of Africa, and Christians and traditional religionists predominate in the south, it is the middle belt just south of the Sahara Desert where the population of the countries are more evenly divided that presents the greatest challenges to Muslim-Christian relations. Nigeria and Sudan are major examples.

Nigeria, Africa's most populous country, had a background of the dialogue of life where Muslims and Christians often shared in each other's celebrations, but increasingly religion became politicized. After independence in 1960 the northern Muslim political elite dominated, and after 1966 the northern Muslim military elite took over. There was a concerted effort of the Northern Peoples Congress and the Jama`tu Nasril Islam (society for the support of Islam) to foster Islamization. This was followed by efforts to add Shari'a to the constitution in 1978, 1989, and 1991. The government of General Ibrahim Babangida enrolled Nigeria in the Organization of Islamic Countries in 1986. Protestants, Roman Catholics, and African Independent Churches countered by forming the Christian Association of Nigeria in the same year.

With the gradual shift of the population to a Christian plurality over Muslims, a Christian Olesegun Obasanjo was elected president in 1999 and re-elected in 2003. Zamfara State reacted by adopting Shari'a in 1999 with financial backing from the Arab world and was followed by twelve other northern states including Kaduna, which led to interreligious riots involving hundreds of deaths.

Sudan, with its Arab Muslims in the north and its indigenous Christians and traditional religionists in the south, has experienced civil war since President Numeiri declared the introduction of Shari'a in 1983. The religious and ethnic differences were further complicated by the exporting of oil since 1999 and the government attempt to depopulate southern areas for further oil exploration and production. During the twenty years of fighting, two million people have been killed or starved. The Machakos Protocol of 2002 included the right of the south to seek self-determination in six years and the application of Shari'a in the north. At the present time, a comprehensive peace between north and south seems likely even as the government has apparently stepped up a campaign by proxy against the residents of Darfur in West Sudan.

Of particular value in Muslim-Christian understanding and Christian witness has been what started in 1959 as the Islam in Africa Project, and became in 1987 the Project for Christian-Muslim Relations in Africa (PROCMURA) with the stated purpose:

> To keep before the churches of Africa their responsibility for understanding Islam and the Muslims of their region in view of the churches' task of interpreting faithfully in the Muslim world the gospel of Jesus Christ.[35]

They continue this ministry by training sessions and publications.

As we commemorate fifty years of Mennonite life and witness among Muslims in East Africa, we draw special attention to Somalia where despite death of children, stabbing of workers, confiscation of property, and restrictions on evangelism, the Mennonite missionaries built and served in schools, clinics and hospitals, did agriculture, economic, and community development, led Bible classes, and administered relief. Although expelled in the 1970s, the Somali government asked them to return in 1981. They always asked, "How can we serve in Christ's name?"[36]

Asia

The Muslim Action Network, which serves in twelve Asian countries, has joined with the Catholic Federation of Asian Bishops and the Christian Conference of Asia. Besides holding peace seminars and workshops, they are developing a peace curriculum to be offered to imams, pastors, and those training for such ministries.

Afghanistan has had Christian workers in the country for over thirty-five years, but with restrictions on their religious activities. Many Afghans became refugees during the Soviet occupation, the fighting between the *mujahideen*, and the Taliban rule. Outside the country some became Christians, but at the present time there is no indication that they will be officially allowed to worship back in Afghanistan. It is not yet clear how the new constitution will affect the church. The constitution supports religious freedom, but nothing contrary to Muslim law is permissible. We do know that over thirty-five years of Christian health ministries have led to much good will. In my frequent visits to Afghanistan, people have sometimes stopped us on the road and asked, "Are you Christians?" If we ask why they are asking, they have responded, "Because Christians love us."

Pakistan is volatile. The Christians are about 2 percent of the population and come largely from a mass movement of outcaste Hindus 150 years ago. At the same time there are Muslim militants with calls to jihad everywhere—in the teashops and Urdu newspapers —despite the government attempts to crush or contain them. Poverty drives students to *madrasas* where they are taught militancy. There have been armed attacks on western Christians in Islamabad and Muree and on Pakistani Christians in Taxila and elsewhere. This has led Christians to meet in smaller groups and to vary their places and times of worship.

The Philippines have known years of fighting by the separatist Muslim Moros of Mindanao against the Catholic-dominated government. But Muslims and Christians are working together on development in 120 villages in the Muslim-Christian Agency for Rural Development (MUCARD), on justice issues in Zamboanga's Islamic-Christian Urban Poor Association, on peace issues in Peace Associates of Zamboanga (PAZ), on reconciliation in the Muslim-Christian Conference and the Moro-Christian People's Alliance, and on dialogue and education in the Silsilah group.[37]

Indonesia, the largest Muslim country, has been looked at as a model for interreligious harmony with its Pancasila form of government, which recognizes one God rather than Islam as the religious bond. Then in January of 2000 the Moluccas Christian troops killed 240-250 Muslims. And in turn, militant Muslims, called Laskar Jihad, massacred Christians. Since then, the major Istikal mosque and the cathedral of Jakarta were damaged by bombs and over 300 churches were burned.

Several factors were involved in the change. In 1997 there was an economic crash, which led to unemployment. When the Suharto government fell and the corruption in the leaders became evident, there was a breakdown in respect for authority and people looked for scapegoats which were found in other religious and ethnic groups. Muslims had political power. Christian Chinese had economic power. And a more militant form of Islam started to develop.

The troubles have drawn Christians together so there is a prayer movement in some 300 cities around the country, which is well accepted by Muslims. And Muslims and Christians of goodwill are working together for peace. A delegation that included the Cardinal Archbishop of Jakarta and the heads of Indonesia's major Islamic organizations went to Rome and Brussels before the Iraq war to talk with the Pope and the leaders of the European Union seeking peace.

General Observations

I highlight several current realities that are pertinent to the commitment to cultivating constructive relations between Muslims.

1. Unfortunately, it took the collapse of the World Trade Center to get everyone's attention. Before September 11 westerners knew little about Muslims and Arabs. Suddenly people were buying anything that they could find on Islam. My class at Fuller Seminary on current trends in Islam grew from an anticipated 35 to 135 students, including a Muslim.

2. A further impetus for understanding came from Samuel Huntington's thesis that the world was moving into a period of the clash of civilizations,[38] both Muslims and Christians began to work to keep his blueprint from becoming inevitable.

3. Many Muslims view the war on terrorism as a war on Islam. This view has been reinforced by remarks by Lt. Gen. William Boykin, a deputy undersecretary of defense who transfers intelligence to field commanders looking for Osama bin Laden. He likened the battle against Islamic militants to a battle against Satan.[39] Newspapers on September 29, 2003, reported a taped broadcast on al-Jazeera and al-Arabiya channels, purportedly by al-Qaeda leader al-Zawahri, which called on all Muslims to fight "the Christian-Zionist crusade . . . aimed at eradicating Islam and Muslims."[40]

4. This highlights another dimension of the challenge to building relations, the interrelatedness of events throughout the world facilitated by the communication explosion of television and the Internet and the use of petrodollars and educational materials from Saudi Arabia, although the Saudi leadership has been more active recently in trying to close down these as sources of terrorism.

5. On the other hand, there can be tremendous variety within a country like Indonesia where Muslim militants detonated bombs at the Marriott Hotel in Jakarta and a nightclub in Bali, but a church choir may be half Muslim with a Muslim director.[41] Other conflicts are motivated by mutual fear as, for example, in Indonesia and Malaysia where Muslims have political power and Christians have economic power.

6. There is a need to distinguish between the interrelated ethnic, economic, and religious roots of conflicts in places like Azerbaijan and Sudan.

We introduced this analysis of the current status of Muslim-Christian relations with the opening lines of Dickens' *A Tale of Two*

Cities: "It was the best of times, it was the worst of times." At the end of the story Sydney Carton finds meaning in life by sacrificing himself so that others could experience the best of times. May we follow the One who did that for us until the day when, with the writer of the Christmas carol we sang in the Afghan school, we, too, see:

> God is not dead, nor doth He sleep;
> The wrong shall fail, the right prevail,
> With peace on earth, good will to men.

☙

Response: Transforming Relationships
Jonathan Bonk

First, let me express my deep appreciation to J. Dudley Woodberry for his masterful overview of the current state of Christian-Muslim relations. I confess that his paper has elicited from me more of a *reaction* than a *response*. I apologize for this evident limitation. His essay is a global overview; my response is particularly focused on the North American role in Christian-Muslim relations, and especially the role of the United States. What is the calling of the North American church in times like these?

Woodberry has focused on the period following September 11, 2001, arguing that Christian-Muslim relations prior to September 11 are well documented. While this may be true, I'm sure he would agree that this does not mean that western Christians were or are well informed of pre-September 11 dynamics of Christian-Muslim relations. By drawing attention to the numerous Muslim-Christian dialogues that took place leading up to September 11, he has high-lighted the great gulf between the *good intentions* of official Muslim and Christian representatives, and their *actual ability* to deliver excellent Muslim-Christian relations on behalf of those of us for whom they ostensibly speak.

In the first paragraph of his paper, Woodberry alludes to "the reaction of many people [to September 11 and its aftermath] in churches and mosques who have seen the necessity of people of goodwill getting to know each other and who have cooperated on the grassroots level in conflict transformation." I appreciated this note of optimism—"the best of times"—at the very beginning of his paper, because it is at this level of interpersonal relationships, after all, that the Christian dynamic is most potent. There is no way to overestimate the power of loving neighbor as oneself. This mustard seed phenomenon is embedded in the very DNA of our moral universe. Not military might, not organizational power, not influence in high places, not conspicuously well-publicized public relations campaigns, not carefully orchestrated news releases. Our Christian faith began, not among the powerful or the influential or the noteworthy or the pedigreed of the day. It began with the stigma of a birth out of wedlock, in the rustic setting of a stable, witnessed by an assortment of common barnyard animals. Today, we remember and celebrate this birth, not Caesar's, whose apparent power obliged Mary and Joseph to be away from home when common sense would have had Mary at home, attended by midwives and family.

Is there any reason to believe that the American Caesar today is any more than a bit-player in the big scheme of things, as was the Roman Caesar then? The real power is behind the scenes, and we appropriate that power only when we pay close attention to the poor, the weak, the oppressed, the marginalized, the nobodies of this world. Christians who wield human political, economic, or military power face immense pressure to become corrupted by it, and by its troubling predisposition to keep the peace through brute force, rather than achieving genuine peace through justice and righteousness. Does the fact that our Christian scriptures are not strong on democracy, but adamant and uncompromising on justice, have anything to say to believers who function in a system ideologically committed to democracy, but supportive of whatever regime—however onerous— that serves our economic or military interests?

Woodberry's general observations constitute an apt reminder that: (1) we should be aware of the religious dimensions of the September 11 attack's motivation,[42] (2) we should as followers of Jesus resist our nation's temptation to retaliate in kind, (3) we should be aware that most of the world's peoples subscribe to a reading of North American history somewhat less flattering than our own self-congratulating myths, (4) viewers of CNN and ABC off this continent are acutely aware of our self-serving hypocrisies and biases when it comes to both government policy and media reporting and interpretation, and (5) we should be skeptical of the media's ability to provide information that is adequate—in either its volume or nuance—to really understand the "other," especially the *enemy* other. The parodies and caricatures of our enemies that emerge from their portrayal in our public media serve no one, since they are fundamentally false. These can be counteracted, not simply by an act of the will, but through personal relationships with actual Muslim men and women, complete with their complex personal identities, histories, families, communities, and dreams that move them out of the realm of subhuman caricature and into the family of humanity.

In his book *Humanity: A Moral History of the Twentieth Century,*[43] Jonathan Glover examines the roots and the rationalizations of state-or ideology-sanctioned murder of other humans, and shows that whether it be the indiscriminate violence visited upon ordinary people in My Lai, or Hiroshima, or Rwanda, or Europe, or Russia, or Cambodia, a key element in the universal template of conditions present when one group of human beings massacres another group is subhumanization or dehumanization of the other. Conditions are thereby created in which murdering the other becomes a necessary and even noble action. We must be convinced that their lives are not as worthy as our lives, and that if there is a choice between them and us, then they have to go.[44] But can any believer ever really think that his or her life is worth more than their enemy's life?

Woodberry's section on North America invites us to recall from the United States' history that what we enjoy today is simply one installment of a serial epic that reads very differently from the vantage point of the men and women and societies on whom our forebears visited both holocaust and genocide. Complicating the picture is the widespread understanding, both in this nation and abroad, that the United States is a Christian nation, pursuing de facto Christian ends that serve to justify any and all means. I believe that it is helpful for Christians to remember, with deep humility, that what we today enjoy in the United States is not the peaceable fruit of righteousness, but the spoils of an extraordinarily ruthless victor.[45]

My point is that there is more than one way to remember the United States' nation's history, and more than one legitimate interpretation of its present policies. Anabaptist Christians, of all people, are obliged to understand the United States' story from the vantage point of the conquered, the weak, and the oppressed, rather than merely the highly selective self-flattering and self-justifying elements of official national myths.

This is critically important, it seems to me, when it comes to Christian-Muslim relations. The rest of the world, perhaps in these times, especially the Muslim world, cannot be expected to judge the United States by its loudly proclaimed good intentions, but by the actual or perceived impact of these good intentions on their personal, family, and national well-being. This is the burden of the recent book by Clyde Prestowitz, *Rogue Nation: American Unilateralism and the Failure of Good Intentions.* "America," he says, "can be like a 'rogue wave,' a large swell that, running contrary to the general direction of the waves, takes sailors by surprise and causes unexpected destruction."[46]

It is for this reason that the note sounded by Woodberry's observation that "both churches and mosques opened their doors to those of the other community" is so hopeful. A nation state, especially a democratic one, cannot be expected to behave in a Christ-like way. But communities of faith and believing families can and must extend hospitality to the officially or popularly suspected ones among us—to enemies. Such an approach is quintessentially, uniquely Christian. One hopes that the grand gestures of Muslim and Christian leaders might migrate to the behavior of the rank and file. What would happen if every Christian family in North America made it a priority to cultivate friendships with Muslims? Only in such intimate, person-to-person relationships can we begin to counteract the relentlessly negative stereotypes being generated and employed as justification for American military violence.

It is tragic and idolatrous when high profile evangelicals, such as those identified in Woodberry's paper, publicly equate America's self-interest with God's will, and vilify the actions and motives of Muslims who, if read against the backdrop of the Old Testament prophets, may well be calling this nation to repentance. Whatever one's perspective on this, at the very least, such evangelical leaders are far from loving their enemies, or from inspiring their followers to love their enemies. And yet they purport to believe and proclaim the good news. Where is the good news in that?

European dismay and alarm with the steadily increasingly demographically significant Muslim presence among them is another argument for making personal and family friendship with real Muslims a Christian priority. This sense of alarm is, I imagine, reminiscent of Augustine's own disquiet as he and fellow beneficiaries of the Roman status quo quaked in dread at the looming prospect of a barbarian takeover. It was these concerns that elicited from Augustine, breaking with long Christian practice, an outline of the conditions under which a Christian might, or even must, wage war.

As a matter of historical record, of course, the barbarian threat *was* real enough; but also as a matter of historical record, despite Augustine's cleverly contrived way to permit or even require Christians to kill barbarians, it was to no avail in the end. Rome was overwhelmed. Happily, Augustine was wrong about the long-term impact of Rome's defeat at the hands of the barbarians. Christianity, far from being obliterated, survived and thrived. The greatest peril to Christian integrity has always been *inside*, not *outside*, the church. Augustine's doctrine of just war has done inestimable harm to the church's capacity to proclaim the kingdom that is not of this world, since every war ever waged has at some level been just (i.e. "justified") by those whose interests are served and preserved in waging it. And Christians have found themselves caught up in all of them.

Woodberry's section on the Middle East reminds us of the utter impotence of the "eye for an eye, tooth for a tooth" policy that lies at the root of almost all officially sanctioned or initiated violence. It also reminds us that nations cannot possibly adopt Christ-like approaches to enemies. By default, a nation's leaders, especially in democracies, serve as the extension of their population's collective ego and self-interest. It is unimaginable that any leader, like Jesus, would allow himself or herself to be crucified and his or her followers to be scattered to the winds.

Christians understand that we live in a moral universe, and that the key that cracked the code of the evil one's lock on the cosmos and everything in it was not revenge, but forgiveness; not strength, but weakness; not brute force, but acquiescent submission. The ultimately victorious kingdom of God will not arrive with a "shock and awe" bombardment of precision guided bombs and missiles, but with the gentleness and forgiveness against which Satan has absolutely no recourse. We Christians need to be faithful to this vision of reality in our relationships with our own fellow believers and with Muslims. Not redemptive violence, but redemptive suffering, marks the Christian way of dealing with fallen humanity.

Woodberry relates how a local mosque offered to help the members of St. George Chaldean Church when they were blackmailed by thugs is the sort of story that needs to be told. Such stories not only counteract the relentless flow of bad news about Muslims, but they serve as models of behavior for others who seek a better way. Christians should actively seek out good news stories like this, and disseminate them as widely as possible, so that they can have their mustard seed effect.

I cannot respond adequately to the section on Africa, but do we not need to ponder why in Africa there is such a disconnection between burgeoning, apparently vital Christianity, on the one hand, and the appalling tyranny, corruption, and general dysfunction of their leaders, governments, and political and judicial institutions, on the other? Just what role has, does or can Christianity play in all of this? Islam is rightly seen by many Africans as an attractive alternative to the chaos, corruption, inequities, and relative anarchy prevailing in many "Christian" African societies. What is wrong?

Woodberry's remarks on Asia also deserve more attention that I can possibly give in this limited compass. Asian perspectives on U.S. motivation in that region are somewhat different from our self-perceptions. Even U.S. satellites such as South Korea and Japan and Taiwan are beginning to show signs of restiveness, in light of the U.S.'s insistence of putting itself above the law, whilst at the same time advocating living by the law.

American Christians should be deeply self-conscious about what Prestowitz refers to as their country's "habit of expediency. With full knowledge that such actions undermined its credibility as an advocate for freedom, the United States frequently backed dictators and authoritarian rulers [such as] . . . the Shah of Iran, Ferdinand Marcos in the Philippines, and a succession of military dictators in Latin America, South Korea, Pakistan, and Taiwan." And Christians must avoid "Americanism," the peculiar religion founded on the "implicit belief that every human being is a potential American, and that his or her present national or cultural affiliations are an unfortunate but reversible accident."[47]

Conclusions and Observations

I am struck by how little Jesus seemed to have to say about the large, geopolitical questions of his day. I am equally struck by how attentive he was to the petty, personal agendas of ordinary people. I think that we Christians need to take a good, hard look at who we really are as North Americans. Change must begin with *us*, not *them*, for some very sensible reasons: (1) we have a very limited ability to influence our own leaders, (2) we have no capacity at all to influence non-American leaders, and (3) we have modest ability to try to adjust our own ways of understanding and behaving, vis-à-vis Muslims. It is on personal transformation that we need to concentrate our efforts. Woodberry's paper assists us along the way to personal and communal conversion into Christlikeness, and for this I thank him.

CHAPTER THREE

Islam—the West —Anabaptists

Lamin Sanneh

I had the strong impression from the presentations at "An Anabaptist Consultation on Islam" that the conversations moved full steam ahead by the force of two rather different momentums. One momentum was the stirring stories we heard from various Mennonite groups from various parts of the world reporting back to their supporting communities what is happening in their journeys of presence and witness among Muslims. The other momentum that may be not as bold or not as anecdotal is a trend of incipient self-criticism, of looking at the Anabaptist heritage and trying to find out how to reposition the heritage in the light of September 11.

Let me comment on the second part, because the reports are fortunately and thankfully self-explanatory. The assigned groups did their work and you've heard their stories and the sense of where things are going to proceed in the next few years. But the reassessment of the heritage in light of September 11, and in terms of your own experience of involvement in the Muslim world does seem to me to raise questions of a rather fundamental kind that, not only you, but all of us are confronted with. What is the relationship between the Muslim world and the west?

Let me say by way of personal anecdote that the World Economic

Forum which meets every January in Davos, Switzerland, and, at intervals, in Jordan, decided last year to create what they call, "Council of 100 Leaders." This council of 100 leaders has been charged with the responsibility for dialogue between the west and the Muslim world. For my sins, I have been elected to that council. We had our inaugural meeting in Amman, Jordan, at the end of June 2003. I was there when the Council of 100 Leaders was launched with the formal ratification of the council happening at the Davos meeting in late January 2004.

There is quite a long description of the issues between the Muslim world and the west that the Council is commissioned to address. In the description, a lot of attention is given to the importance of secularism in the west. The west is a post-Christian west, and secularism now forms part of the core values of the west. Putting it like that you can see the issue. How then do you North Americans from the west relate to the Muslim world which is not so much dominated by secularism as an ideology? The material artifacts of secular culture are not the issue. Rather, the issue is secularism as an ideology, as a core value, a value that is really very marginal in the Muslim world, at least in Muslim thinking when they articulate who they are and their identity. How then do we relate within this chasm between the Muslim world and the west?

It seems to me that this imbalance between the west and the Muslim world creates tremendous challenge, and I frankly don't know myself how the west will come out of this challenge. I am worried, however, by a west that has lost its moral core having to confront on its doorstep a resurgent Islam. When the centerpiece of the west's moral heritage has been torn out, that makes it hard to conceive a symmetrical relationship with resurgent Islam.

I recognize that secularism is a negative value deriving from the separation of church and state. Separation itself has to rest on a pillar, has to be supported by a premise of human equality. John Locke in his *Essay on Toleration* (1689) argues that toleration is a religious value, that it is derived from the notion that human beings, that you and I, are made in the image and resemblance of God. Without that fundamental principle it is hard to claim or sustain toleration against the demands of self-interest and personal or group advantage. I am concerned that the west's secular ideology leaves it helpless before the fundamentalists' radical ideology. Their religious excesses can be remedied only by the example and teaching of religious moderation, whereas secular dismissal of religion only inflames the radicals' passion.

In spite of its formal proximity to the west, the Muslim world seems disinclined to lend credence to the value of the kind of dialogue John of Segovia called for. There has been no important territorial retreat by Islam and no reconquest by Christianity, at least since the *reconquista* in Spain, and so there is no overt reason to revamp old certainties. On the contrary, as Muslims have continued to settle and to grow in the west, they have maintained adherence to Islam, sometimes taking over abandoned empty churches to convert them into mosques. The opportunity of Muslims resettling former Christian lands in the west seems to preempt any need or incentive for dialogue, though tactical alliances with local Christian institutions might be sought and welcomed.

The New Secular Mission

In place of the old theological mandate to undertake mission to Islam and to convert Muslims, there is now a secular mandate to modernize Islam and to fold Muslim societies into the unifying western secular net. The new secular mission as the successor to Christian mission is designed not so much to question Islam's truth claims as to bypass them in a bid to promote peaceful coexistence with other truth claims. Eventually, it is hoped, Islam's jihad reputation will be modified in favor of the secular accommodation. With Islam in the mix, secularism can resume its ascendant role and arbitrate among religions, throwing out religious differences where such differences threaten the secular truth dogma of a unified humanity.

That secular position notwithstanding, the fact that with its doctrine of jihad Islam has a recognized rubric for war and warfare has alike attracted and puzzled the west. It has attracted the attention of the west because a post-Enlightenment world, confident of its secular achievements, has only fading memories of religion as a pillar of the public order. The puzzle comes from the feeling that with Islam the forces of secularization seem inexplicably to have bypassed a whole swathe of the world inhabited by Muslims, and so the west clings to the wistful hope that in time Islam will remain an exception no longer to the impact of secularization. A resurgent radical Islamist ferment that appears to be stirring through much of the Muslim world has, however, shaken the west's complacency. It led, for example, *The Economist* to shake off its customary discretion and to devote a detailed investigative story to what it called "The fundamental fear:

Islam and the West" (August 6, 1994), saying there seems the distinct possibility of "a general war between Islam and the west." It softened that grim prognosis by acknowledging that Islam and the west as cousin-cultures have a lot in common beyond mere economic interests. Nevertheless, *The Economist* was not dewy-eyed about future prospects, with the uncertain prospects of embattled Algeria, north Africa's largest country, deepening the sense of alarm.

The Economist came close to putting its finger on what inflames Muslim opposition passion toward the west when it wrote, "The idea of Islam ignores the frontier that most [western] people draw between man's inner life and his public actions, between religion and politics." Jolted by what it sensed as steadily worsening relations with Islam, the paper called on its nerves to state the uncomfortable thought. "It may be the last such idea the world will see. Or it may, on the contrary, prove to be the force that persuades other [western] people to rediscover a connection between day-to-day life and a moral order," saying whatever the outcome, the issue is likely to simmer well into the twenty-first century. The paper could have added that what has ignited fundamentalist passion is the seeming unstoppable nature of the west's intellectual confidence of prescriptive secularism, in effect, of privatizing religion, a confidence that collides with the certainty of Muslims that they possess the infallible truth revealed syllable by syllable, verse by verse, to Muhammad. For such Muslims, religion is a matter of the public order, and, accordingly, they regard the west culpable for standing in the way of Pan-Islamic ascendancy. A collision seems inevitable, even if unnecessary.

The Islamic Impulse

The foundation of Islam is not that the word became flesh, which is grave anathema (*kufr*), but that the word became book, and dwelt among us as law. Fundamentalists have fed on the idea of revelation as a datum: the Qur'an may not be amended, translated, or superseded. Set in time and space, the event of revelation elicits an eventless relation between God and human beings. Sufi Muslims, by contrast, have adopted a radical mystical path to God, presuming to apprehend the shaft of divine truth directly rather than, as their more sober brethren affirm with trembling hope, only comprehending the world by that truth. No flesh may see God and live, as Moses testified (Exod 3:2-6), and that is reason enough for the fundamentalists to charge the Sufis with heresy, but perhaps also because the Sufis, in their absorption with God, have little scruple for worldly strategem.

The sense of divine efficacy in history, that God reveals but also commands, what the first Muslims called *jihad fi-sabil li-llah,* "holy war in the way of God," (Qur'an 4:76, 91f., 94f.; 9:5, 29, 36, 41, 122; 47:4) is demonstrated by the successful establishment of the early Muslim community in Medina, and that vision has inspired the fundamentalists to attempt, as an act of historical faithfulness, a replication of that triumph for their age and time. The vision of God under such a dispensation calls for public enforcement of the Shari'a code and of the solidarity of the ummah, the faith community. The modern national secular state has opposed Shari'a and splintered God's ummah into petty secular jurisdictions, and so must be subdued in order to institute the divine mandate for social order. The fundamentalists have appealed to fellow Muslims to assume a state of hijrah toward the modern secular state, to become what the Qur'an itself calls hijrah-bound in God's cause, *al-muhajirun fi-sabil li-llah* (24:22). One such movement declared: "All the Muslim people of Turkestan have lost their patience and have chosen the holy road to emigration for preparing for jihad-in-the-way-of-God."[1]

Sacred Truth and Secular Agency

Ironically, the American perspective on separation of church and state, and, by implication, on the distinction between the sacred and secular, may offer a way out of this impasse by ceding the religious ground without stripping it of public merit entirely. In that perspective it is inappropriate to employ the political instrument, with its skewed "secular" view of truth, to enforce religious compliance, with its springs in individual conscience, and that should resonate with the case the fundamentalists have made about making religion count in public life in terms of its fruits without neglecting its roots in religious truth claims.

Such qualified separation is congruent, too, with broader developments in Muslim thought. An instructive divergence of view exists among many Muslims about eliding religion with politics, the sacred with the secular, however much worldly interests may serve the ethical purposes of religion. There are sound religious reasons for not interchanging politics with religion, or religion with politics, lest between them sacred truth and secular agency become indistinguishable.

That issue lies at the heart of east-west tension and suspicion and belongs to the core of the radical forces driving Islam today. It happens that in the west, religion no longer provides a public framework of life and of the conduct of affairs, and so the church does not have it in its power to corral an unwilling secular west to accept a religious vision of peace for the world. In their pastoral letter on war and peace called "The Challenge of Peace: God's Promise and Our Response,"[2] the U.S. Catholic Bishops observed that the fundamental premise of world order in Catholic teaching is a theological truth, namely, the unity of the human family grounded in common creation and united by moral ties of rights and duties. While Catholic moral theology allows a real value to sovereign nation states in the structure of the international order, still that is only a relative value because the boundaries of the sovereign state do not dissolve the deeper relationships of responsibility in the human community.[3] Relations among states mirror those among individuals, but with this striking and defining difference: religion is restricted to personal life and conduct, and excluded from the jurisdiction of the sovereign nation state.

The international system of nation states has widened the gap between personal life and conduct, and the secular mandate of public order. International declarations on peace, justice and human rights, for example, assume the sovereign nation state to be the civil engine of implementation, with personal agency and its religious under pinning discounted. Yet the nuclear threat revealed the limitations of the sovereign nation state with respect to the wider human family. Nuclear weapons also proved that the nation state was not only the relative value of Catholic teaching; its sovereignty was relative, if not illusory. In an increasingly interdependent world where resources and burdens are unjustly shared, the seeds of conflict and instability abound while the unity of the human family is threatened. The fundamental belief of the new world order that technology and the free market can attain the unity of humanity without need of religion seems reasonable in light of secular globalization, unless, that is, technology and market advantage create new sources of violence and conflict, which does not at all seem an unreasonable possibility.

Conclusion

As I see it, pacifist arguments, in common with just war arguments, derive their cogency from the ethic of reconciliation, reconciliation in turn with God, within the religious community, with our fellow human beings, and with the world. War, on that count, is an attack on God's purpose for us and for the unity of the human family. The problem, then, is not whether peace is better than war, and reconciliation than enmity, and, therefore, whether renunciation of war is good for us, but, rather, whether we can devise effective and credible arrangements for a world order committed to reconciliation. William Barclay spoke with passion for his fellow Christian pacifists when he wrote: *"To put it bluntly, it is a sheer impertinence for the church as it stands today, to preach reconciliation to the world. It cannot set the world in order before it sets its own house in order.* And here precisely is the key problem of the pacifist position. We can be absolutely sure in our minds that Christianity demands the renunciation of war, but any such renunciation is doomed to failure unless it goes hand in hand with a revival of personal religion and a rebirth of the church as a body able to reconcile because it is reconciled."[4]

It seems increasingly clear that fruitful dialogue with Islam presupposes a refashioned international order inspired by a sense of the holy and the transcendent. Real engagement in dialogue might help advance such a prospect. Yet I am wary of the possibility that the wraith of Wycliffe may still haunt us in the sense of seeing ourselves as the obstacles standing in the way of God's will for the world. To require that we first set our house in order before doing God's bidding in dialogue, witness, and service places God under an embargo, and our lives on hold. The sins of the west would become an alibi for inaction.

In any case, do our efforts at repentance mean that Muslims must undertake a commensurate act of house cleaning to qualify as dialogue partners, or is their house to be left as irredeemable? Is an innocent Christianity the prerequisite for encounter with Islam as a nonpacifist religion? It is instructive to recall that the stocktaking of Christianity's assets and liabilities that Wycliffe undertook led him to a sunset view of the church without that in any way diminishing the strength of Islam. From all the labor and toil Wycliffe endured, and the learning and sophistication at his command, it is a meager harvest in an age noted for its scarcity of intellectual resources. Now I do not for a moment blame all this western cultural pessimism on Wycliffe, but I do see the danger of inaction in his fainthearted view of intercultural encounter. We should do better today.

CHAPTER FOUR

The Mennonite Engagement with Muslims: A Historical Overview

John A. Lapp

The role of the church is to offer the redemptive values of Christ to the community with the ultimate hope that the narrative of the community will eventually be transformed into the narrative of God's redemptive relationship with creation. . . .

There is no time when the world has been in greater need of the gospel of Jesus Christ, yet, there has also been no time in the history of Christianity when the gospel has been more trivialized. The Kosmos is hungering for redemption, not through propositional truth, but by means of a narrative into which we live. —Bruce Bradshaw, Change Across Cultures[1]

Islam, too, in the first instance, was fully admitted by Christian theologians to be an Arian heresy. Only when it evolved into a complete Corpus Islamicum, a counter-image to the Corpus Christianum, was it transformed into a self-supporting and comprehensive religion. Right down to the present time, however, Islam has invariably held a mirror up to Christianity. Although the Crusades are of course a thing of the past, Christianity has never yet been able to answer the vital question, which Islam sets before it: whether it is not itself a Hellenistic "heresy" of the primitive Church, which has unfolded in the form of Western Civilization.—Arend Theodoor Van Leeuwen, Christianity in World History[2]

Religiously it has been an eye-opener to meet Islam face to face, and to be in the minority. In North America, the dominant official religion is Christianity. Other religions get little serious thought. Suddenly the tables are turned. All propaganda, and religious radio and TV shows are Islamic, including in public schools. Islam is "in" not Christianity. . . .
Christian witness has a "more excellent way." The way of love. Christian witness does not rely on media or psychological pressure to convert people. True Christian witness wins trust through a life of integrity, openness, and compassion which gives authenticity and credibility to the Good News.—John Duerksen, "Monthly Report from Egypt to MCC"[3]

We cannot proceed upon convictions of universality without incurring relationships with religions. Intercultural expression means interreligious responsibility. For it is by their faiths that cultures have been historically determined and spiritually inspired. Christianity cannot address men and ignore their gods. It may act in the present and disown the past or wisely hold forth salvation and withhold salutation. In seeking men for Christ's sake, it is committed to the significance of all they are in their birth and their tradition, both for good or ill.—Kenneth Cragg, Christianity in World Perspective[4]

Introduction

It is always important to explore and reflect on what we do and how we do it, particularly at this juncture of history when the Muslim world not only expresses a vigorous alternative understanding of faith and life, but also focuses even more widely-held dissatisfactions with western culture and religion. Those of us concerned with Christian witness need to help one another to deeper understandings of our task.

At the same time, the Christian world is also in considerable disarray. Particularly the church in the United States is in an extraordinarily precarious situation as it is being wooed and perhaps coerced to provide a spiritual rationale for the American empire. The exposure of the propagandistic ideology of Lt. Gen. William Boykin merely caricatures a deeply held, widespread Americanized theology justifying military voyeurism and imperial domination.

The apostle Peter says judgment begins in the household of faith.

The current situation, I believe, calls every Christian community, including Mennonites of all persuasions, to wrestle again with the central issues of Christian purpose and mission in this particular context.

This book will not fulfill its high goals unless we recognize the timeliness and critical nature of this exploration. In writing this chapter, I again ran across some questions Edward Said posed in *Orientalism* twenty-five years ago. (Said, who died recently, expressed a profound, far-reaching critique of the distortions of much intercultural understanding. His densely argued books are essential reading for anyone interested in international mission.)

Here are Said's questions:

> How does one represent other cultures (religions)? What is another culture (religion)? Is the notion of a distinct culture (race or religion or civilization) a useful one or does it always get involved either in self-congratulation (when one discusses one's own) or hostility and aggression (when one discusses the "other")? Do cultural, religious, and racial differences matter more than socio-economic categories, or political historical ones? How do ideas acquire authority, normality, and even the status of natural truth? What is the role of the intellectual? Is he there to validate the culture and state of which he is part? What importance must be given to an independent critical consciousness, an oppositional critical consciousness?[5]

I make these prefatory remarks to let you know a certain discomfort I have speaking for all Mennonites and all Muslim communities. I know I'm too self-congratulatory. I hope I am appropriately critical of distorted gospels. You will have to decide whether I have avoided hostility and aggression.

Constructing Our Narrative

Bruce Bradshaw in his instructive book, *Change Across Cultures*, says, "We renew our minds when we transform the narratives that govern our lives; only then can they empower us to live into a different story."[6] Bradshaw adds that Christian mission has to do with changing narratives both within and across cultures. Each of us could tell the story how we became interested in Islam and what helped to determine the outlook or approach which dominates our insight.

I am not an Islamicist, neither have I had extended experience with Islamic peoples, and since you'll soon discover I have some decided opinions, you might appreciate how I came to these. I see myself as a generalist historian who has had the unusually rich opportunities of both the academic community and as a Mennonite Central Committee (MCC) administrator. I am one who believes that unless the gospel is practiced it will not be authentic, and that unless the word "Mennonite" carries particular meanings we should go out of business and return to the mother church—Catholic, Lutheran, Reformed, Orthodox.

As I reflect on my journey there were four incidents and one book that were especially influential in extending my interests. The first of these occurred fifty-two years ago here at Eastern Mennonite University (EMU)—then called Eastern Mennonite College (EMC)—when as a college sophomore I had the honor of being the roommate of Issa Khalil, as I recall, the first Middle Eastern student at this institution. Issa was devoutly Greek Orthodox whose prayer life easily shamed my own. Now I regret not using that opportunity to delve more deeply into the Orthodox tradition. Issa impressed on me how Christian churches lived side by side with Muslims for more than 1,300 years. Issa found his way to EMC after having worked with MCC relief workers in Bethlehem, his home town. Later he became a professor of comparative religion at San Diego State.

A second clarifying moment also occurred at this same institution fifteen years later when I was a history faculty member. By the mid to late 1960s we had a number of Muslim students from Palestine and Somalia.

In 1966-67 there were three vocal, articulate young men—Elias George, also Orthodox from Jerusalem; and Muhammad Shadid and Walid Sharif, both Muslims from Dura outside of Hebron. All had Mennonite connections through Ada and Ida Stoltzfus, EMC alumni, who directed an orphanage near Hebron. On campus that year was a visiting professor, J. P. Jacobszoon from the Netherlands. Jaap, as we knew him, lived through World War II and was deeply impacted by the Nazi treatment of the Jews. He believed the new state of Israel had a special place in God's order. Alice and I rather naïvely decided it would be an interesting evening to have the three Palestinians and Jaap face off in our family room one Friday night. It was a memorable moment. There was anger and shouting. There was no consensus. I learned that one need not be a premillennial dispensationalist to have a

Christian bias toward Israel. I learned the depth of the conflict without any Israelis present.

A third critical moment was when I accepted the invitation to serve as executive secretary of the MCC peace section. Only after the decision in 1969 was made did I learn that the MCC chief executive, William Snyder, had determined that the Middle East required deeper understanding on the part of MCC and its constituents. Part of the rationale was the vigorous appeal of Palestinians, with whom MCC worked, that unless MCC and other agencies became advocates for their cause, MCC and other agencies should pack up and leave. Like most administrators, Snyder had a strong political sense. He was being squeezed between powerful voices that MCC should be a stronger advocate for peace in Vietnam and many who thought that this would be too political for a Mennonite agency. By stoking up the Middle East, Snyder thought he might divert some Mennonite and Brethren in Christ energies away from controversies surrounding Vietnam.

Frank H. Epp, a *Canadian Mennonite* journalist and historian, was given a half-time assignment to work on Middle East topics. I was expected to supervise him. I joined the first Middle East study tour in June 1969, which was the first of eight journeys to the region, including living in Jerusalem during a 1978-79 sabbatical from Goshen College. Epp's publications during the next years included *Whose Land Is Palestine?*, *The Palestinians*, and *The Israelis*.[7]

So while I have not delved deeply into Islam, the Middle East has been a concern for thirty plus years. My particular interest is the religious dimensions of the conflicts. Like Peter G. Riddell and Peter Cotterell,[8] I firmly believe an understanding of historical contexts is essential to understanding Christian-Islam interaction, as well as the Mennonite-Muslim encounter.

A fourth critical incident occurred in April 1995 at a regular meeting of the MCC executive committee. We had as a guest, Sadreedin Sadr, a major administrator with the Iranian Red Crescent Society. MCC had begun some cooperative work with Red Crescent in 1990 following the massive earthquake just south of the Caspian Sea. From Ed Martin and others, Sadr was picking up Mennonite insights. He learned that the two kingdom doctrine of Mennonites—the struggle of the kingdom and church with the world—includes a critique of western culture. In the course of the executive committee's discussion, Sadr suggested that Ayatollah Khomeini's characterization of the

American government as the "Great Satan" may not be that different from Mennonite understanding of worldly institutions.

The executive committee was so dumbfounded by this suggestion of a common cause that they quickly moved on to the next agenda item! A few days ago I received the Toronto Mennonite Theological Centre Newsletter.[9] James Reimer summarized the "Shi'ite Muslim-Mennonite Christians in Dialogue" which took place in Toronto (October 24-27, 2002; see appendix F). Reimer quotes Professor Rahimpour from Teheran who "made the astonishing claim: that on 80 percent of the issues in which Mennonites distinguish themselves from other Christian denominations, they and Shi'ite Muslims agree."

There have been numerous other incidents along the way. One I will long remember was on a visit to Burkina Faso in 1988. At an MCC-sponsored water dam we heard the angry voices of Christian villagers protesting the intrusion of Muslim Falani herdsmen and their cattle. Here along the twelfth parallel north we witnessed in microcosm what Samuel Huntington would soon call a "clash of civilizations."[10]

I will also long remember an intense visit with a Muslim Kadhi in Haifa, Israel, who by day was a judge for Islamic community affairs and by night and on weekends was an active participant in a Plymouth Brethren fellowship. Some local MCC staff in Bangladesh and Jordan call themselves Mennonite Muslims. Can there be Muslim Christians, as well as Jewish Christians?

Last I want to refer to an important book that shapes much of the way I look at Muslim-Christian relations. Arend Theodoor Van Leeuwen was once a Dutch Reformed missionary in Indonesia. After that experience in Asia, he set about to explore how the great world religions have interacted upon one another. *Christianity in World History*,[11] published in 1964, was heady material for a young historian. His contrast between ontocracy, a monistic fusion of religion, economics, and politics in a singular socio-cultural order with the Abrahamic prophetic faith fulfilled in the ever renewing vision of the kingdom of God, had enormous appeal for this two-kingdom Mennonite. Ever since, I have frequently cited Van Leeuwen's notion that the moment Christianity became the official religion of Persia's chief enemy, Christianity lost most of its welcome in Asia. Since then, I've learned that Van Leeuwen may have simplified historical reality. Nevertheless, his suggestion that the radical Christian critique of the Constantinian generation had missiological significance resonated deeply with me.

If the gospel is to have universal appeal, it cannot become captive to a particular power or ideology. Van Leeuwen's insight is certainly not his alone, that Muhammad's protest was to a great degree a counter-cultural movement by marginalized people by the domination of Christian imperial powers nurtured my interest then and now to explore the socio-political contexts of mission endeavor.

Van Leeuwen underscored the urgency of critique, not only of human systems, but also of the church which so often betrays its high calling and best instincts. As Jesus taught us, we ought to search for the mote in our eyes before we presume to locate it in others. On the topic of Islam it is so easy to find weakness and failure. It is so easy to see Islam as at a crossroads, forgetting that Christianity is also at a crossroads.

Van Leeuwen's masterful study opens up numerous questions. Christian-Muslim relationships could have been much different at each step along the way if, rather than rancor and conflict, there could have been a mutual exploration of differences reflected in the other's mirror.

My assignment is the Mennonite engagement with the Muslim community. This, in part, explains my personal story. What I have not sufficiently emphasized are all the individuals who prodded, explained, taught, and corrected me along the way.

Each one of us has our own stories. Incarnational engagement is the meeting of the total persons representing well-developed traditions. These stories all together begin to scratch the surface of the Mennonite-Muslim saga. The label "Mennonite" names only one half of the narrative.

Considerations

There are a number of considerations that strike me as significant for understanding the Mennonite-Muslim engagement. We can only note these as background in this overview.

First, there is the question of scope for this inquiry. I very much like the theme of the consultation that has birthed this book: "The Church Meets the Muslim Community." Yet each of these terms carry heavy freight. "Church." Do we also mean church as communities and at what level? Relatively few North American Mennonite congregations meet their Muslim counterparts. Or do we mean church structures? Which of these? Conferences or agencies? All agencies or only specialized ones?

"Meeting" is also pregnant with meaning. It brings to mind Kenneth Cragg's book, *To Meet and to Greet*.[12] Do we refer to casual encounters or only formal conversation? Do we meet as worshipping communities or as religious power blocs? Are these meetings based on long-term mutual friendship or trendy dialogue? Is faith conversion the first or last item on the agenda? Meeting can be in urban mosques or city churches. They may be the weighty conversation of the school or university or the friendly exchanges of a neighborhood. How much do we need to know about the other for an authentic meeting? Should the parties expect to change in the process of meeting?

We may consider "Muslim" as readily definable. Yet there is the risk of stereotyping. Islam began among Arabic peoples. But very quickly there were Egyptians, Ethiopians, Syrians, Persians, and Indians involved. Today Arabs are a minority within the Muslim community. Southeast Asian Islam has its own style and spirit, as does Islam as it is acculturated in Europe and North America. Muslims are people with all the diversities Christians represent. Andreas D'Souza, the Indian Sufi specialist, once reminded me that Sufi Muslims had more to do with the conversion of Central and South Asia than any military expeditions.

Finally there are the questions of "community." Is it local or global? Is it urban or rural? Is it in West Africa or in Eastern Africa? Is it politically active or Sufi in character? Does it represent one mosque in one place or a great university in Cairo, Damascus, Baghdad, Qom, Karachi, or Jakarta?

Then who are we talking about as Mennonites? Missionaries, academics, or ordinary church members? Students or specialists? Women or men or both together? North Americans or South Asians? Our conference and agency differences are known at least to insiders.

I suspect that one of the problems of many interreligious engagements is that only a few persons are involved and that frequently the well-trained missionary engages less well-trained villagers. Or we may represent institutional authority as much as being gifted by the Spirit.

Even for a relatively small Christian body, Mennonites intersect with Muslim communities on at least four continents. Our story includes Dutch, German, French, and Swiss Mennonites who interact with Muslim neighbors in their towns and cities, as well as in overseas programs at one time or another in Indonesia, Algeria, Morocco, and Chad. Russian and Ukrainian Mennonites since the 1880s have been neighbors to Muslims in the Caucasus and Central Asia, engaging in both evangelization and Bible translation. Russian Mennonites also participated in overseas missions in India and Indonesia. My sense is that North American churches are not as engaged domestically as our European sisters and brothers. In the fall of 2003 David W. Shenk participated in a public dialogue with a Shi'ite spokesperson sponsored by the German Mennonite peace committee. Perhaps we need similar conversations in North America.

North American agencies like Mennonite Brethren Mission and Services have been involved with Muslim communities since the 1890s in India, Afghanistan, Indonesia, and Pakistan. Mennonite Board of Missions (MBM)—now Mennonite Mission Network (Network)—has or has had significant involvements in Israel, Algeria, France, West Africa, Afghanistan, and Dagestan. Eastern Mennonite Missions (EMM) intersects with Muslim communities in Ethiopia, Somalia, Kenya, Djibouti, Israel, Jordan, Central Asia, and Albania (with Virginia Mennonite Mission Board [VMBM]). Rosedale Mennonite Missions (RMM) has been in Cyprus and Turkey. Africa Inter-Mennonite Mission (AIMM) is in Burkina Faso and Senegal. Add to this the sustained involvements with Muslims by large Mennonite churches in Indonesia, India, Ethiopia, and smaller churches in a number of other African and Asian countries. Mennonite Central Committee service ministries have touched most of the Middle Eastern and South Asian countries. In Africa, MCC has cooperated with EMM in Somalia and Kenya. During the past decade MCC has cooperated with European Mennonites in a number of projects in Bosnia and Kosovo.

I mention this long list to impress upon us the large scope of the topic and the enormous research required for fuller understanding. This paper lays out the far-reaching dimensions of Mennonite-Muslim engagement.

A second consideration is to note the abundance of primary sources and the paucity of secondary sources. Chad Bauman and James Krabill's bibliography (see appendix I) lists only twenty published articles or books under the rubric of Islam. One can dig out additional references under specific names or countries such as Bertha Beachy under Somalia. There are also chapter-long studies in larger works on mission, mission history, and religion.

The important point I want to make is that we need a lot of research before we can be very sure about the contours of our total story. We can be very grateful for the short histories we have and significant monographs by David Shenk, LeRoy Friesen, Gordon Nickel, and a few others.

For MCC alone there are dozens of reports to digest, thousands of letters to peruse, and hundreds of individuals who could be interviewed. Similar sources are available in all our agencies. Each of our agencies ought to record our learnings and reflections on involvement in ministry with Muslim communities.

A third consideration is to recognize that the Mennonite story cannot be understood in isolation. John Ruth observes in his long section on European backgrounds in *The Earth Is the Lord's*, "who they were in Lancaster County cannot be understood without some sense of who they had been before they arrived there."[13] In a similar way, Mennonite engagement with Islam cannot be understood apart from the engagement of other Christians with Islam before and since 1525.

Perhaps this is obvious. Most of us received our serious learning about Islam beyond Muslim friends and scholars, from Roman Catholic, Anglican, Presbyterian, and Lutheran scholars. In virtually every case that I am aware of, mission and service agencies have learned much of the art of engagement from the experience of other churches. MCC, which I know best, is deeply indebted to Dutch Mennonites in Indonesia, Roman Catholics in Bangladesh, as well as Coptic, Greek, and Syrian Orthodox, Anglicans, Lutherans, and Presbyterians in the Middle East for sharing their insight on relating to the Muslim community. Mennonite missionaries in eastern Africa learned from Lutherans, Sudan Interior Mission, and Roman Catholics. You can add to this list where you personally or your agency learned to engage the Muslim community.

Who inspired us is as crucial as who called us. In part, disagreements among us on attitudes and approaches flow from the training we received and the authors we read. This, too, must be part of the research.

Yet another consideration is the issue of contexts. It is very difficult to generalize about Mennonite-Muslim relationships because the scope is broad and the time span considerable. The contexts are different both in space and time. Riddell and Cotterell in their recent book, *Islam in Context: Past, Present and Future*, contrast the radical Islamist worldview and the moderate worldview.[14] These worldviews vary from time to time and place to place. Clifford Geertz, a generation ago in *Islam Observed*, noted that traditional Islamic identity flourished from within "scripturalism." More recently he suggests that politicized Islam was "externally stimulated" and religion functioned more as a tool or ideology.[15] A Muslim observer would no doubt detect a similar bifurcation within Christianity. The Mennonite story even in the short twentieth century illustrates remarkable change and remarkable diversity in attitude and practice.

EMM-MCC appointee Bonnie Bergey, in a 1996 report, illustrated the importance of context and memory. "Christians," she said, "are still seen by Somali Muslims as the bearer of the crusade." In fast-paced North American culture we are rapidly losing the capacity to remember even a few months ago. Not so the traditional Muslim community.

Geertz and numerous other analysts make the struggle with modernity a key to understanding the recent history of Islam. We as moderns or postmoderns do well to recognize that cultural diversity has to do with generations, as well as with geography. Bonnie Bergey, in the same report, observed that "Western Christian men are often viewed as nonreligious because Muslims have not seen any evidence of prayer." Indeed, contemporary western culture is not only modern, but also secular in character. While we here express our strong Christian identities, the acids of modernity and secularity are not far away. Our dependence on technology and our conspicuous wealth suggest we easily distort our dependence on both divine empowerment and communal support.

Today it is difficult to ignore the political and diplomatic dimensions of engagement. Mennonites, as late comers, or as Martin Marty once put it, late bloomers, were too late or too recent to interact with classic self-confident religious Islam. We went to Indonesia and India in the imperial epoch, but the churches there flourished after these states became independent.

In my reading of Mennonite-Muslim engagement we cannot avoid the impact of empire, economic status, and intercultural dynamics in our conversations. We cannot avoid the centuries of antipathy and systematic discrimination on both sides. We cannot avoid the significance of two world wars and the repeated conflicts in the Middle East since 1948. Two years ago, Tony Campolo suggested that the American invasion of Afghanistan set back Christian engagement with Islam 100 years. The 100 years may be rhetorical. The impact is not. There is no room in this engagement for complacency, self-satisfaction, or triumphalism. Judgment and repentance begin in the household of faith.

In many places our engagement has been in a crisis atmosphere. This has led to frequent episodic encounters, which in some cases brought promising engagement to a quick conclusion. These considerations are significant for contextualizing the message in an Islamic context.

Windows

First, you will note the sketchy timeline at the end of this chapter, "Some Significant Moments." I am most interested that we see the wide scope, the involvement of multiple agencies and many people. Given my concern that we do not think of our project as unique, I begin with the date AD 380 when Christianity became the religion of the Roman Empire. In spite of our critique of Constantinianism, we need to recall how we are also heirs and participants in that part of the Christian story.

I could not list every significant moment, and others would no doubt include other moments or correct some of the dates. Contextual dates like major conflicts, independence days, establishment of specific projects or congregations could be added. Note three important books cited which represent major Mennonite missiological reflection. The final notations suggest that the story continues.

I can only briefly open these windows. I am very conscious that this is oriented by Mennonite initiative from the north and west. Historians from newer Mennonite communities, or perhaps Muslim historians, will some day be able to demonstrate greater reciprocity than I am able to present.

Don Jacobs recently observed that EMM had a mission in Tanzania with people identified with African traditional religion, a mission in Ethiopia with the Christian Orthodox tradition, and then decided to move into neighboring Somalia where Islam prevailed. Something similar might be said by Mennonite Brethren who went from India to Pakistan. MCC frequently was present or joined mission agencies with relief and development programs.

The important thing is that agencies, like people and governments, cannot simply do one thing. Engagement with Muslim communities is part of our church's missional engagement with other communities. What is consistent is the sophistication of the Islamic tradition, the centuries-long historical interaction and the politicalization of recent interreligious encounter.

It is in these contextual realities that Mennonite engagement with

Muslims has been developing. I highlight five windows that provide insights into the nature of that engagement.

1. Michael Sattler Shaped an Alternative

Recent historical scholarship has strongly emphasized the missionary character of the Anabaptist movement. Wilbert Shenk summarized this well in chapter 1 of *By Faith They Went Out*.[16] Mission is as integral to Anabaptism as discipleship, community, and the ethic of love.

The former Benedictine friar, Michael Sattler, well-known as the convener of the Schleitheim Conference in February 1527, was burned at the stake four months later. The story was recorded by a number of observers. All agree that there were seven or eight charges against Sattler, one of which accused him of saying that "if the Turks come, we ought not to resist them." Hungary had just fallen to the Ottomans whose army was already threatening Vienna. His words were perceived as treasonous.

> If the Turk comes, he should not be resisted, for it stands written: Thou shalt not kill (Matt 5:21). We should not defend ourselves against the Turks or our other persecutors, but with fervent prayer should implore God that He might be our defense and our resistance. As to me saying that if waging war were proper I would rather take the field against the so-called Christians who persecute, take captive, and kill true Christians, than against the Turks, this was for the following reason: the Turk is a genuine Turk and knows nothing of the Christian faith. He is a Turk according to the flesh. But you claim to be Christians, boast of Christ, and still persecute the faithful witnesses of Christ. Thus you are Turks according to the Spirit.[17]

Perhaps we should not read too much into this short statement. Yet it stands in sharp contrast to contemporary Catholic and Protestant leaders who strongly supported military action to protect Christian Europe. Gordon Nickel rightly calls Sattler's words "a remarkable statement" that "summarized a very straightforward mission axiom: you can't tell a Muslim about the love of God in Jesus Christ and bring him into the joy of discipleship by fighting and killing him."[18]

A complete missiology requires a political ethic. Sattler demonstrates an integration that should be a guiding principle for our engagement with Islam.

2. Dutch Mennonites Pioneered the Modern Model

North Americans often forget the European pioneering role. The Doopsgezinde Zengings Raad (DZR) from its beginnings in 1847 was eager to involve Mennonites of other countries. Very early, Russians and Germans joined the Dutch as missionaries who also invited the support of American Mennonites as well. We are all indebted to the first modern Mennonite overseas mission.

Alle Hoekema's essays and Lawrence Yoder's articles and dissertation tell much of this story. One of Alle's articles, "Why the Dutch Were the First Mennonites to Send Missionaries Overseas,"[19] is an important case study of the social, economic, and cultural contexts which nurtured mission enthusiasm. Like many others, this mission program followed the Dutch imperial order and illustrated the cultural and economic energy of a nineteenth-century European Christian community. Would that each of our agencies realize how our ministries benefit from constituent affluence and the interests of public culture.

Like nearly all subsequent Mennonite missions, the Dutch in Indonesia were led by visionary individuals who responded to felt needs on location. Their mission practice followed Reformed and Catholic models. The first missionary sensed the need for scripture in the vernacular, beginning a common mission activity right down to the present.

In private correspondence, Alle Hoekema suggested the Dutch concern was in mission rather than with Islam. Islam simply happened to be the prevailing local faith. It is not until recent decades that Islam has become a focus in any of our agencies. But already in the 1820s a leading Doopsgezinde pastor and seminary professor, Samuel Muller, began writing and speaking on Islam. Like other Dutch pastors and some missionaries, he was also active in the mission board and the Bible Society. One of the recent Indonesian missionaries, Roelf Kuitse, a friend and teacher of many of us, became the first genuine Mennonite Islamicist, later serving with Islam in Africa, and most recently teaching at Associated Mennonite Biblical Seminary.

The Dutch mission began in Java, but soon established a second field in Sumatra next to a Lutheran mission to the Batak people. That field was turned over to a German Lutheran society in 1928. The large Indonesian Mennonite Synods are powerful evidence of God's Spirit at work the past 150 years.

3. Mission Experience with Islam

Mission involvement with Islam did not have a unique identity until recent decades. The Russian Mennonites were the first Mennonites to follow the Dutch in formal mission activity. They began work before 1890 in Central Asia and in 1889 Mennonite Brethren sent their first missionaries to work with American Baptists in Hyderabad, India, a major Muslim principality.

It is not clear when and how Mennonites began to think of intentionally engaging the Muslim community. It probably grew out of MCC experiences with Palestinian refugees, MBM work in Algeria, and EMM work in Somalia. Any interest in Islam per se appears to have followed experience and practice. One milestone was MBM General Secretary J. D. Graber's sabbatical studying with Kenneth Cragg at Hartford in the late 1950s. It was Graber who called the first inter-Mennonite consultation on Islamic ministry in connection with the Mennonite World Conference Assembly held in Kitchener, Ontario, in August 1962. Dutch missionary Jan Matthijssen and Indonesian church leaders S. Djojodihardjo and Herman Tan representing the two synods were present. The report of Djojodihardjo (Pak JoJo) to the World Conference is a fascinating report of vigorous church growth (5,000 new members in ten years) and strong affirmation of the newly independent state. "The churches are convinced that Indonesian independence is a gift of God to the people of Indonesia, including the Christians of Indonesia."[20] Again it is noteworthy that when Pak JoJo refers to Muslims his passion is "to witness within Indonesian society." He does not reflect a particular interest in Islam. At another point he does note the Muslim interest in a theocratic state.[21] Herman Tan's report, although three times as long, reflects a similar stance.

By the 1970s and 1980s the larger North American boards were thinking of explicit engagement with Muslims. The Ethiopian church by this time had a substantial number of former Muslim members. There was a small group of believers in Somalia. The MBM-EMM work in Israel was primarily with Messianic Jewish groups, but also connected to Christian Israeli Arabs in Israel proper. Mennonite Board of Missions seconded workers in Afghanistan and Pakistan before engaging in church planting ministries in Pakistan. In 1978 African Inter-Mennonite Mission (AIMM) began working in Burkina Faso, giving rise to a number of fellowships along with work in Bible translation.

4. Service Ministries in Islamic Contexts

With the Mennonite and Brethren in Christ interest in human well-being there have been few missions which did not engage in social ministries. Missionaries quickly sensed the need for food, medicines, and education in hungry societies. Indonesian missionaries heard these appeals and established schools and a hospital. Peter Jansz's best known writing was entitled, *Land Reclamation and Evangelism in Java,* an early treatise on community development. Missions in India felt the same tug. While mission and service have always been together, there was also constituent interest in specialized ministries for relief and emigration. It was these concerns plus the interest in cooperative work that led to the formation of Mennonite Central Committee in 1920.

During World War II, MCC was assigned the task of coordinating peace work and direction of alternative service camps. This experience plus wartime prosperity unleashed enormous energy in the postwar years, first for relief and reconstruction in Europe, and then beyond. Mission agencies also flourished from these postwar energies. During World War II there was already interest in working in what was then called the nonwestern world. General Conference and Mennonite Church missionaries in India invited MCC to Calcutta in 1943 during the great famine there. Bengal had many Muslims. Famine relief led to a medical program and agricultural projects. With the division of India and Pakistan and the massive conflict along the demarcation line, MCC moved into ministries on both sides of the line in the Punjab. (MCC is still in Calcutta.)

In 1948 some India MCCers reestablished connections with Indonesia Mennonites while Holland was still recovering from the war. In 1949 MCC felt the call to Jordan/Palestine which led to engagement with Muslims throughout the region. Well into the 1960s MCC walked in step with mission boards often as a pioneer activity. MCC began work in Ethiopia and followed MBM into Algeria. The largest single program for MCC with the Muslim community was and is in Bangladesh, begun in 1970. While MCC does not do formal evangelistic work, its ministries are expected to support Mennonite and other mission programs both Catholic and Protestant.

Service agencies find it difficult to limit program to one thing, as do mission programs. In my introduction I noted Palestinian interest in having advocates. They also desired longer-term development programs in education and income generation. What is now called 10,000

Villages was born more than fifty years ago out of Puerto Rico and West Bank. Both the local call and North American interest in reducing violence has led to major interests in peace building.

As is wont to happen with institutions—including mission, evangelistic, and service agencies—they often are inclined to autonomy and insist on their own programs. That has sometimes led to competing visions, even competition for resources and personnel. Sometimes the competition has become ideological with alternative visions like church planting versus local Christian alliances. This sometimes has included alternate engagements with the Muslim community.

5. Developing a Conversation

The window which I perceive to be the newest and quite interesting church engagement with Islam is a sustained conversation with Islamic religious leadership.

Once when visiting with Ignatiius IV, Patriarch of Antioch (Greek Orthodox) in Damascus, he said that if we wanted truly to know him we would need to return again and again and again. Missionaries and service workers have heard that often from Muslim friends. As Cragg observes "we cannot proceed upon convictions of universality without incurring relationships."[22]

But I suspect all readers of this volume would join me in observing that we have not been very good at maintaining a continuing conversation. Fortunately, Mennonites in Ethiopia, Indonesia, and Burkina Faso are demonstrating how this can be done. Individuals with Islamic background like Ahmed Haile of Somalia, Aristarchus Sukarto of Indonesia, Bedru Hussein of Ethiopia, and Siaka Traore of Burkina Faso will take these conversations in fresh and new directions. Indeed, I believe the Mennonite engagement will and should increasingly grow out of the experience of younger Mennonite churches.

One of the fruits of the Somalia Mennonite Mission has been long standing conversations with Somali Muslims. For nearly forty years this took place within Somalia. When the mission was forced to close in 1976 the conversations continued in Nairobi, northeast Kenya, Canada, and the United States. David Shenk deserves much credit for sensing the necessity of long-term commitment to such a process. His book, *Islam and Christianity*,[23] with Badru Kateregga demonstrates the depth and respect necessary for serious engagement.

Other agencies have been inspired by this model. MCC in particular has picked up this model for program in Iran. After seven years of cooperative work between MCC and the Red Crescent Society, an educational exchange was established in 1998. Two couples from the Imam Khomeini Institute in Qom began studies at the Toronto School of Theology. Later the same year, Roy and Marin Hange began study in Qom. Wallace and Evelyn Shellenberger continued this ministry in Qom, later carried forward by Matt and Laurie Pierce.

A notable extension of this is a formal dialogue between Iranian Shi'ite Muslims and Mennonite Christians sponsored by the Toronto Mennonite Theological Center. The first session was held in October 2003 in Toronto and a second session in February 2004 in Qom.

Such conversations require immersion in the other's thought patterns and theological traditions. They also require sustained interaction and mutual trust. Long-term relationships require consistent involvement and significant financial support. I, for one, hope that collectively we can see these conversations as an integral part of the church's engagement with the Muslim community.

I have certainly not touched all the involvements of the Mennonite church with Muslims. These five windows demonstrate authenticity and growth in commitment and understanding. There are two additional windows mentioned in other parts of this paper. One is the mingling of students and neighbors in colleges, universities, and local communities. Another is the witness of Mennonite and Brethren in Christ congregations in Islamic regions, most notably West Africa and Indonesia.

A Case Study

As I was weaving this paper together, the words of the contemporary hymn by Richard Gillard kept ringing in my ears.

> Will you let me be your servant,
> Let me be as Christ to you?
> Pray that I may have the grace
> To let you be my servant, too.
>
> We are pilgrims on a journey,
> We are travelers on the road.
> We are here to help each other
> Walk the mile and bear the load.

I will weep when you are weeping
When you laugh I'll laugh with you.
I will share your joy and sorrow
Till we've seen this journey through.

When we sing to God in heaven
We shall find such harmony,
Born of all we've known together
Of Christ's love and agony.[24]

Does this hymn provide some perspective, even an eschatology for Christian-Muslim engagement? It is not my task to evaluate the successes or the failures of our story. But it does strike me that the sentiments of this great hymn provide a baseline for evaluation.

In reviewing Omar Eby's *Fifty Years, Fifty Stories: The Mennonite Mission in Somalia, 1953-2003*,[25] I was struck by the servant stance of this mission. Like all missions the motivation was evangelistic. But beyond that there was no grand strategy, no considered goal setting. Indeed, oral tradition has it that at the sending service for the first missionaries in late 1952, the suggestion was made that it could be twenty-five years before there would be a congregation of believers. The story since then is a fascinating response of ordinary people who asked, "Will you let us be your servants?"

Even getting to Somalia illustrates the servanthood tradition. An Italian Waldensian civil servant in the United Nation administration told the explorers Mahlon Hess and Merle Eshleman that "You must come" based on his experience with MCC relief workers who served his people in postwar Italy. As soon as they were on location, missionaries responded to the invitation to serve. Former Swedish Lutheran communicants asked for Bibles and then for Bible study guides. Soon requests came for schools and training in the English language. "When are you going to open an English school?" a chief of police asked.

Schools led to medical clinics and eventually to hospitals. There was also agricultural training, demonstration plots, and extension programs. Each action was a response to the invitation to be a servant. Refugees required food, medicine, and housing.

"Will you let me be your servants?" led to building a secondary boarding school. For the first time, youth from multiple tribes would live side by side. Even before the German-funded building was completed, students asked for a prayer room, a mosque within these quarters. Missionaries pondered: is this the result of asking the servanthood question? Even earlier the government decided that the Qur'an must be taught in all secondary schools. Missionaries, the EMM board, and the Lancaster Conference Board of Bishops prayed and asked whether this was the result of asking, 'Will you let us be your servants?"

The winds of revolution came. There was a coup in 1969. The town of Johar wished to celebrate. "Will you be our servants now?" The mission builder was asked to design and build an "eternal memorial to the Revolution." The mission authorized his work. A cholera epidemic threatened. The mission nurses had the only available vaccine and responded to this new call to servanthood.

Throughout the decades the mission worked in the small opening provided by the space between rigid traditionalist Muslims and slightly more open modernizers. In this small space the mission increasingly defined its role as a presence sharing a respectful witness. When other missions may have been confrontational, EMM Somalia missionaries took Islam seriously, respecting Muslim devotion and piety. Local citizens took notice. As recently as a year ago Chantal Logan could write "in a time when Christians and Muslims seem to be in contention, it is worthy to note that Mennonites are greatly honored in this devoutly Muslim country."

There were other notable illustrations. When the mission was forced to close in 1976 the mission administrator wrote a letter of appreciation to the president of Somalia "for the courtesies extended to us during our stay in Somalia."[26]

"Will you let us be your servant?" It was a harsh and difficult path. Merlin Grove was assassinated. There were unpleasant accusations. Some workers were forced to leave. But more than a reputation survived. One of the believers understood what was going on. "Jesus became like us Somalis that we might become like him." Another poet, Mohamud Siad Togane, recalled Merlin Grove singing "Blessed Assurance."

> Singing
> As it was his wont
> The best definition of Islam there is:
> Perfect submission, perfect delight. . . .
> Perfect submission, all is at rest,
> I in my Savior am happy and blest.
> Watching and waiting, looking above
> Filled with his goodness, lost in his love.[27]

The numbers of believers remain small. Some suffered the ultimate sacrifice. Somali was surely not a perfect mission. By asking "Will you let us be your servants?" and responding with some daring risk-taking, we have an instructive story worth remembering.

Harold Reed, longtime Somali missionary and EMM administrator, mused at one of the recent Somalia celebrations, "What unfolded from what the early missionaries did was much broader than what any of us would have imagined." Mohamud Siad Togane agreed with Reed noting that "Mennonites left many things behind."[28]

EMM and MCC have asked Somalis repeatedly since 1976 "Will you let us be your servants?" There have been refugee workers and large food shipments. There have been short-term teachers and continuing relationships in Mogadishu, Nairobi, Djibouti, Hargeisa, Toronto, Minneapolis, and other places. Bertha Beachy living with and listening to Somalis for nearly fifty years has nurtured a women's movement which she believes holds the secret to peace among Somali people. John Paul Lederach has served the powerful factions helping to design processes for conversation and peace building.

> Will you let me be your servant?
> I will hold the Christ light for you
> In the nighttime of your fear.
> I will hold my hand out to you
> Speak the peace you long to hear.

It is a truism that there is a crisis in Christian-Muslim relations. We desperately need new thinking and new models. The mission and missionaries in Somalia had to face all the critical questions of contemporary missiology. I summarized these in the foreword to Omar Eby's book:

> How should the gospel be expressed in a restrictive setting? What does it mean to respect the host people and their culture? Does this respect extend to another religion? How do outsiders relate to local conflicts? How much personal risk should missionary people take? When does the stranger become more of a liability than a helper in a conflictual situation? Can a church representing the peace tradition serve as an alternative to the Christian crusading tradition? How does the contemporary church respond to modern day Nicodemuses? Must "bearing witness" always lead to local houses of worship and groups of

believers? Do women have special opportunities and spiritual gifts for bearing witness in an Islamic environment? Is freedom of religious expression the same in a unified religious society as it is in a pluralistic religious society? [29]

We can add other questions as well. Why should Mennonites highlight the Muslim community rather than the Buddhist or Hindu or Animist or American or Latin communities? Are we sure this is the right priority? How did we decide? Are we trying to be obedient or trying to be with it? My short answer is that it is both a product of obedience to the heavenly vision and a response to our experience.

There are questions of purpose and priority. Some of us look for conversion rather directly, and some of us more indirectly. Some of us want to prioritize the multiple ministries of the church, and others of us prefer not to prioritize. However, I sense that the convening of the 2003 "An Anabaptist Consultation on Islam," the subsequent publishing of this compendium, and after more than fifty years of working together we may now be prepared to affirm the need for different models of engagement, that we can understand how different ministries mutually enrich one another and that we can validate one another's approaches. I suspect that our experiences in places like Algeria and Somalia and the current crisis in Iraq has made us both more humble and more realistic.

The freshest and most positive dimension of our engagement with the Muslim community is taking place in Mennonite churches living among large numbers of Muslim neighbors. On a daily basis they work together in building civil societies as they invite neighbors to consider the significance of Jesus. They are not overwhelmed with the gadgetry and impatience of the north. They do not carry the same onus of the Crusades as northerners and westerners do. If anything has come out of the 2003 Anabaptist consultation on Islam and out of the essays in this book, I would hope that we commit ourselves to support with prayer and training people in these settings for engaging the Muslim community.

Let us not burden these sisters and brothers with our agenda, our zeal for results, and our formulas for communication. Siaka Traore at the Bulawayo Mennonite World Conference Assembly (2003) observed that the prime requisites for engaging the Muslim community are patience, persistence, and transparency. United States people in particular are not noted for these characteristics. Let us be servants.

Conclusion

Mennonite engagement with Muslim communities is extensive and complex. It would be very useful to sense similarities and differences between the engagement in West Africa and the Middle East, between South Asia and East Africa, between ministries where Islam is a majority and where it is a minority, between Mennonite approaches and those by other denominational bodies or indigenous churches.

As I write this paper, material on these topics continues to flow. *The Economist* (Sept. 13, 2003) carried a special feature on "Islam and the West." As to be expected, it dealt with everything but Christianity and the east! That issue was covered in a remarkable review by William Dalrymple of Charles Sennott's *The Body and the Blood: The Middle East's Vanishing Christians* and the "Possibility of Peace" in the September 25, 2003, issue of the *New York Review of Books*. Dalrymple and Sennott lament the emigration of Christian Arabs whose history long predates the advent of Islam.

Dalrymple then puts the issue powerfully for the Christian church, especially in the United States:

> The biggest problem facing the Christians (in the Middle East) is that America is Christian too. Whatever its eastern origins, today Christianity's center of gravity is firmly in the west. The remaining eastern Christians now find themselves caught between their coreligionists in the U.S. and their strong cultural and linguistic links with their Muslim compatriots.
>
> Nothing does more to unite the fractious Islamic world, or to turn it against its Christian minorities, than a U.S. attack on one or another prostrate Muslim state. The U.S. invasions of Afghanistan and Iraq are exactly the sort of adventure that the eastern Christians have learned to dread, and, as at the time of the Crusades, it is they who are getting persecuted for what is seen as the aggression of the Christian west.[30]

This concern highlights the way international conflict becomes a critical ecclesiological and missiological issue. In a world richly intertwined, actions and attitudes in one place impact relationships in another place. Given widespread hostility to Muslim people, including disrespect for the Islamic faith and culture, one of the special missiological concerns for peace-minded people is to explain and interpret how things look from the other's point of view. Striving to explain the humanity and the legitimacy of the other side will not be popular with some of our neighbors, some of our constituents, and certainly not with politicians whose careers are built on bashing presumed enemies. Nevertheless, if we are committed to the great commission and the great commandment we ought to continue to welcome Muslim students, welcome Muslims to our neighborhoods, and insure they are treated according to the golden rule. Only if we act with passionate concern and charity will our missionaries have credibility engaging Muslim communities.

The fullest and deepest involvement of a Mennonite church with Islam is without a doubt in Indonesia. Both Javanese and Chinese Synods have many relationships with their Muslim neighbors and relatives. There have been confrontations and considerable suffering through the years. Nonetheless, Javanese village congregations are growing rapidly amidst Muslim relatives and neighbors. Gereja Kristen Muria Indonesia (GKMI) congregations in Kudus and Solo have been actively involved in cooperative peace building activities with Muslim leaders. The congregation in Solo joined with local Muslim leaders to organize citywide Muslim-Christian prayer services after the Bali bombings a year ago. Christian and Muslim students and faculty at the Christian universities are struggling to overcome a history of confrontation and hostility with joint programs promoting cooperation and reconciliation. A considerable number of former Muslims are joining many congregations, particularly in the Javanese Synod.

Mennonites, thank God, are not alone in engaging the Muslim community. One of the best books I read this year is John W. Kiser's *The Monks of Tibhirine: Faith, Love, and Terror in Algeria.* This is a compelling account of Trappist monks, but also includes White Fathers and Augustinian nuns amidst the civil conflict in Algeria in the 1990s. More than twenty-five died as martyrs in this decade alone. A White Father, Christian Chessel, martyred in 1994 while still in his thirties, preached a sermon in Rome in 1991 which defines a servanthood approach to the Muslim community more profound than any recent Mennonite statement. I conclude with two paragraphs from that moving sermon:

> Our mission in the Muslim world is marked by weakness. This may seem surprising to say. It is not a fashionable term in the missionary lexicon. Weakness is a word with a bad reputation in our world, where strength and vigor—be it physical, psycho-

logical, or intellectual—are synonymous with well-being and success. But in his letters, Paul used the word thirty-three times. In the Bible it is, above all, the weak with whom we are asked to concern ourselves. In Jesus, God becomes man to share in man's inherent weakness. . . .

To accept our lack of power . . . [becomes] an invitation and an urgent call to create with others relationships that are not based on power: when I recognize my weakness, I can accept that of others, and see a way for me to imitate Christ. This attitude of weakness can be misunderstood. Weakness in itself is not a virtue, but rather, an expression of the essence of our nature, one which must be molded and shaped by faith, hope, and love.[31]

That, I believe is what is meant to ask "Will you let me be your servant?"[32]

Some Significant Moments

380   Emperor Theodosius declares Christianity to be the religion for all subjects.

451   Ecumenical Council at Chalcedon strives to define Christology leading to a divided church in the east.

527-565   Emperor Justinian I integrates Christianity into the imperial governing system.

570-632   Muhammad, prophet of Islam.

632-750   Creating the Arab empires from France to Persia.

1086-1400   Age of the Crusades—recurring attempts, some successful for a time—to try to gain control of Palestine by Christian European powers.

1520-1529   Ottoman Turks take over Serbia and Hungary, threaten Vienna.

1527   Swiss Brethren leader Michael Sattler martyred. One reason was his refusal to sanction war against the Turks (Muslims).

1822   Amsterdam pastor and professor Samuel Muller first speaks and writes on Islam.

1851   Peter Jansz, appointed by the Dutch Mission Board, begins work in Java.

1869   Russian Mennonite Heinrich Dirks begins work in Sumatra under the Dutch Board (turned over to Die Rheinische Mission in 1928).

1880	Mennonites in Russia move into Muslim areas as neighbors and sometimes as evangelists, continuing to the present.
1889-1900	Mennonite Brethren (Russia and North America) Mennonite Church, General Conference Mennonite Church establish missions in India. All have a few formerly Muslim members.
1898-1914	MBIC (Missionary Church) works in Turkey.
1948-49	Mennonite Central Committee places relief workers in the Punjab on both sides of the Indian-Pakistan border.
1949	Mennonite Central Committee initiates program in West Bank, Jordan, Lebanon, Iraq.
1953	Eastern Mennonite Missions opens mission in Somalia.
1955	Mennonite Board of Missions initiates work in Algeria joined by Mennonite Central Committee in 1961 until 1978.
1962	(August) First Inter-Mennonite Missiological Consultation in Islam at Kitchener, Ontario, in conjunction with Mennonite World Conference 7th Assembly.
1969	Mennonite Brethren Missions and Service (MBMS) begins work with International Assistance Mission (IAM) in Afghanistan. Mennonite Board of Missions placements begin in 1975.
1970	Mennonite Central Committee initiates its largest programs among Muslim people in Bangladesh.
1972	Mennonite Central Committee places teachers in a variety of church institutions in Egypt, which led to similar placements in Syria in 1989.
1974-76	Somalia government terminates contracts of Eastern Mennonite Missions teachers and orders administration to leave.
1977	Eastern Mennonite Missions establishes a Community Center for Somali Muslims in Eastleigh, Nairobi, Kenya.
1978	African Inter-Mennonite Mission begins an evangelistic and translation program in Burkina Faso.
1980	Badru D. Kateregga and David W. Shenk, *A Muslim and a Christian in Dialogue*.

1980-1993	Eastern Mennonite Missions and Mennonite Central Committee begin cooperative work in Somalia, which continues to the present from a Nairobi base.
1981	Mennonite Brethren Missions and Service sponsors workers in Pakistan. A church planting ministry begins in 1988.
1990	Mennonite Central Committee begins cooperative work with Iranian Red Crescent Society following an earthquake. Beginning in 1998 students and teachers are placed at the Imam Khomeini Institute in Qom.
1991	Mennonite Central Committee makes "strengthening program and placement of people in Islamic contexts" a priority.
1992	LeRoy Friesen, *Mennonite Witness in the Middle East: A Missiological Introduction* (revised in 2000).
1999	Gordon D. Nickel, *Peaceable Witness Among Muslims.*
2002	(Oct.) Toronto Mennonite Theological Center hosts "A Conversation Between Shi'ite Muslims and Mennonites."
2004	(Feb.) A sequel happens in Qom, Iran.

Response: A Mennonite Consensus on Purpose
Gordon D. Nickel

One of the things I like most about John Lapp's historical overview is the way he portrays the wide scope and wealth of involvement which Mennonites have been privileged to enjoy in Muslim settings. John describes Mennonites as "a relatively small Christian body," and yet he finds that Mennonite-Muslim engagement has "far-reaching dimensions." This surely is a reason for praise and thankfulness at this consultation.

Anabaptist Missional Themes
A survey of the writings and stories of Mennonites engaged with Muslims reveals a wealth of reflection on the purpose of Mennonite presence and ministry among Muslims. These writings and stories reveal recurring themes among those Anabaptists who engage

Muslims in an effort to be obedient to Jesus's command to make disciples of all nations, who study Islam deeply, and who establish meaningful faith conversations with Muslims who are similarly zealous for their faith. These themes recur in the literature so consistently that it seems to me that we can think of an Anabaptist consensus.

I highlight only four of these themes.

1. To bear witness to Jesus.

The first aspect of purpose is to bear witness to Jesus. Jesus said, "You will receive power when the Holy Spirit comes on you; and you will be my witnesses" (Acts 1:8). This is a wonderful promise to disciples.

And so, two Congolese women witnesses came to visit Ali El-shariff Abdallah Emmanuel when he was a refugee in Kinshasa, and that visit contributed to the long journey that has brought him to be with us here today. A Christian friend invited Bedru Hussein to a Pentecostal youth meeting in Addis Ababa, and he is here with us today.[33] Herman Jantzen learned Kyrgyzian and other Central Asian languages and led many Muslims into salvation and baptism in the years around the Russian Revolution.[34] Dan and Helen Nickel, working under the Muria Mennonite Church in Indonesia, found a way to make a witness among Muslims in Jakarta.[35] Roelf Kuitse encourages Christians to bear witness with the "gentleness and respect" of 1 Peter 3:15.[36]

The Muslim dimension to this aspect includes an appreciation for the act of verbal witness. Islam has raised confession of faith, *shahada*, to the level of one of the five pillars of practice. Lamin Sanneh singles this out as a lesson Christians can learn from the experience of Muslim missionary work in Africa. Christian experience of Islamic *da'wah* "has shown Christians how seriously the vocation to witness needs to be taken," Sanneh writes. "The devotion and sense of self-sacrifice which Muslims have shown in obedience to the call to spread and establish the faith are a poignant reminder of what lies at the heart of Christian discipleship."[37]

This is not to say that the Muslim friend will welcome the gospel affirmations about Jesus. But Muslims will find the Christian's act of bearing witness both familiar and favorable.

When the promise of Jesus and an invitation from the context come together, you know you have something solid to act on.

2. To imitate Jesus in life.

The second aspect of purpose is to imitate Jesus in life. "Live a life of love, just as [the Messiah] loved us and gave himself up for us as a fragrant offering and sacrifice to God" (Eph 5:2). I remember Siaka Traore telling us at the Mennonite World Conference gathering in Calcutta how he had been attracted to Christ when Christians showed concern for him and valued him for who he was. Reflecting on the work of Henry Martyn in India, Wilbert Shenk concludes that the quality of life of the witness is crucial. "Does that life radiate agape or does it bespeak ulterior motives?" he asks.[38] John Lapp quotes John Derksen, "True Christian witness wins trust through a life of integrity, openness, and compassion which gives authenticity and credibility to the good news." By God's grace we could tell many stories of positive experiences of engagement with Muslims through compassionate ministries, many of them from workers with Mennonite Central Committee.

Roy Hange wrote, after reviewing many of these stories, "Muslims have been willing to acknowledge and accept acts of impartial Christian love and charity."[39] If there is a way of overcoming centuries of misunderstanding between Christians and Muslims, Hange wrote, it will be through such acts.

Some Muslim leaders have accused Christians of using compassionate ministries as an unfair inducement to lead Muslims away from their faith. Mennonites may want to ask whether this accusation attaches to them as they seek to serve people in the name of Jesus. However, if the actual cause of Muslim offense is the name of Jesus, then Christian workers find themselves in a basic Acts 4 spiritual encounter with religious authorities who demanded that the disciples of Jesus cease ministering in the name of Jesus. Given such a situation, would Mennonites answer in the pattern of Peter and John, who clearly declared that they would continue being witnesses for Jesus the Savior?

3. To follow Jesus in the way of peacemaking.

The third aspect of purpose is to follow Jesus in the way of peacemaking. The Christian who seeks to obey Jesus's command to make disciples also seeks to obey Jesus's command to love the enemy by the very same authority. David Shenk has very helpfully shown that though a number of religions use the word "peace," they do not all mean the same thing by it.[40] Is the "peace" of Mennonites solidly grounded in the blood of Jesus shed on the cross?

Creative application of this purpose will include a peaceable manner of witness among Muslims. Will the Mennonite emphasis on nonresistance also mean a readiness to make a martyr witness in Muslim contexts? I was fascinated by the comment of Andreas Christanday, chair of the Asia Mennonite Conference, after the destruction of many churches in Indonesia five years ago. A Muslim leader was telling his community to stop burning churches and to start reading history. Andreas reported, "He told the people that the more they torture Christians . . . the more [the Christian church] will grow."[41]

The Islamic approach to peace and war was clear to the ninth-century Arab Nestorian scholar known as al-Kindi, living as he did under Muslim conquest and domination.[42] But somehow in North America it has become very difficult to tell the truth in this matter. Mennonites who make policy for engagement with Muslims might consider gaining intimate knowledge of the sourcebooks of Islam: the Qur'an, the Sira (the written biography of Muhammad), and the Hadith, and if possible, also Islamic law, or *fiqh* (the science of Muslim law). Secondary sources alone will not bring an adequate foundation for ministry. Is learning classical Arabic too much to ask? Along with this background knowledge, mission leaders could pursue sustained, personal acquaintance with committed Muslims in Muslim majority societies.

I have heard and read a number of stories of Muslims who chose to follow Jesus largely through reading Matthew 5. Do we have a lively estimate of the powerful attraction of the ethics of Jesus? J. Dudley Woodberry has spoken and written about fundamental differences between the Gospels and Sira.[43] What are the implications of this for mission?

4. To love the community of Jesus, the church.

The fourth aspect of purpose is to love the community of Jesus, the church. This aspect is demonstrated in the felicitous framing of the consultation that provided the background for this book. Discipling and gathering believers together have been Anabaptist impulses from the beginning. In the midst of sixteenth-century European society, writes Robert Ramseyer, the Anabaptists sought to recover the New Testament vision of the church "and worked at building a church bound together by love in which members really tried to help each other."[44] There is a deep love for the church. This love has permitted Mennonites to work not only with their own mission agencies and national churches, but also with a variety of other agencies and churches, including the local churches of the Middle East.

The Muslim dimension to this aspect is the situation which develops when Muslims freely choose to follow Jesus. The dynamics of the Muslim ummah and especially the Islamic Law of Apostasy sometimes make it very difficult for the new believer to pursue her choice without cutting off ties to family and friends. The new believer needs a new family to welcome and receive her, and that is the church. The new believer needs to learn everything which Jesus has commanded and to establish her loyalty to Jesus as Lord, and it is the church's joy to disciple her. Mike Brislen has done some good writing on this.[45]

God forbid that Mennonites should be as hesitant and inhospitable to new believers from Muslim background as Lamin Sanneh found the churches in the Gambia to be when he asked to be baptized there.[46]

There are many things which Christians can admire about the strength of the Muslim community, the ummah. But can the ummah also be a prison? Kenneth Cragg once said, in the midst of a remarkable dialogue with Muslims, "A faith which you are not free to leave becomes a prison."[47] Cragg has also written that when a religious system forbids people to see God in Christ crucified, conversion out of that system is "necessary and right."[48]

Foundations for Ministry Among Muslims

This much any observer can learn from reading the writings and hearing the stories of Mennonites engaged with Muslims. What I have cited is just a fraction of what I have seen. These all seem to point toward a significant consensus about purpose. If so, these four themes that I have commented on above would appear to be foundational for Mennonites who have the privilege to serve and minister in Muslim contexts.

As John Lapp rightly indicates, the consensus increasingly includes the voices of those evangelists in the large Mennonite communities of Asia and Africa who are most familiar with living Islam and are most engaged with Muslims on a day-to-day basis.

"In this day of great Middle East unrest and a growing Muslim world," writes Bertha Beachy, "Christians—particularly Mennonites —should give themselves to prayer and fasting to find ways to bring

Muslims, Jews, and western leaders the good news of peace."[49]

There are several practical considerations that we will discover in our calling for faithful presence in the way of Christ.

1. Help from non-Mennonites.

Stepping outside of the circle of Mennonite reflection, John Lapp very candidly says that most of us received much of our serious learning about engagement with Muslims from non-Mennonite scholars. Here again we have much to be thankful for. In addition to wonderful leaders such as J. Dudley Woodberry and Lamin Sanneh, I hope that Mennonites will also include in their circle of guiding lights Hendrik Kraemer and his book, *The Christian Message in a Non-Christian World*. Kraemer's expertise in Islam, his mission experience in Indonesia, and his love for the church surely earn for him a careful reading.

John Lapp and I have referenced Kenneth Cragg. We are so thankful for the wonderful contribution of this Anglican bishop. May we resist the temptation to ransack and proof-text Cragg's writings, but rather take his modeling of sympathetic understanding of Muslim faith and life together with his plea for a strong New Testament Christology in engagement with Muslims.

2. A Mennonite contribution?

Do Mennonites also have something to contribute to the larger engagement of the church with Islam? A recent *Time* magazine article[50] was critical of American missionaries following U.S. troops into Iraq, and gave the impression that most American missionaries among Muslims approved of the military attack. The readiness of some of our Christian friends to link mission with militarism is alarming. Our friends sometimes seem to show an inability to separate Christian engagement with Muslims from an allegiance to American foreign policy.

Might Mennonites say clearly and in love that this is completely inappropriate—not only because the church is international and multicultural and includes many in Iraq, not only because the center of Christian gravity has shifted to Africa and Asia, not only because civil religion represents a particularly pernicious idolatry, not only because Christians must put God's kingdom and righteousness first—but more than anything, because a link between mission and militarism is a perversion of the gospel and a betrayal of the Lord Jesus Christ?

Philip Jenkins recently predicted major trouble ahead between Islam and "the next Christendom," by which he means the growing churches of Africa and Asia.[51] Do Mennonites around the world have nothing to say about this? Surely a church representing the peace tradition can serve as an alternative to the Christian crusading tradition.

3. Human weakness and the power of the gospel.

John Lapp ends his paper with a moving reflection on mission in human weakness. This is a good word. Two responses:

First, any messenger of the gospel working in a majority Muslim environment learns very quickly that she begins in overwhelming weakness. Islam is a strong and self-confident religion with a lively polemical tradition. Mennonites must humbly acknowledge their human weakness, sinfulness, and lack of power. But this must not lead to a loss of confidence in the gospel, because the gospel remains the power of God for salvation for everyone who believes it, whether Jew or Greek or Muslim.

Second, a modesty about human abilities and limits is essential. But, is it not possible that there can also be a false modesty, in which human weakness is used as an excuse for silence and inactivity? Mennonites may well want to be modest about their piety, heritage, good deeds, and many other things. However, Mennonites—as disciples of Jesus—are not called to be modest on behalf of their Lord or on behalf of the gospel.

Here I would like to close with the words of yet another non-Mennonite guiding light, Lesslie Newbigin:

> If, in fact, it is true that almighty God, creator and sustainer of all that exists in heaven or on earth, has—at a known time and place in human history—so humbled himself as to become part of our sinful humanity and to suffer and die a shameful death to take away our sin and to rise from the dead as the first-fruit of a new creation; if this is a fact, then to affirm it is not arrogance. To remain quiet about it is treason to our fellow human beings.[52]

CHAPTER FIVE

The Muslin Nation and the Anabaptist Church: The Indonesian Experience

Mesach Krisetya

The determinative event in the history of relations between Christians and Muslims in Indonesia was the adoption of the Pancasila (five pillars of state ideology) as the foundation of the Indonesian State in 1945. They are: Belief in unitary deity, nationalism, humanitarianism, representative democracy, and social justice for all Indonesians. The formulation of the first pillar avoided giving preference to any one particular religion. As a result, Islam, Christianity, Hinduism, and Buddhism are all recognized as official religions of Indonesia.

The founding fathers and mothers of the country were strongly aware that Indonesia is a pluralistic country, with thousands of islands, hundreds of ethnic groups, languages, religions, and streams of beliefs. They knew that they needed to establish constitutions that have the capacity to regulate the course of life of the country peacefully.

Although Islam is the dominant religion in Indonesia and from its beginning has been deeply involved in the Indonesian nationalist movement, Islam does not have full power over the state of Indonesia. In fact, Indonesia adopted a secular state, rather than an Islamic state. This is perhaps because the Muslims in Indonesia have a lot of division among themselves. If the Muslims were well-organized and less divided, perhaps Pancasila would not have been formed or established at the time of Indonesian independence from the Netherlands.

When it comes to state ideology, one immediately raises a question as to whether there is any Islamic influence at all in the formulations of political ideology. There are many religions in Indonesia, such as Islam, Christianity, Hinduism, Buddhism, and others, that are not the original religions of the Indonesian people. There are also indigenous religions, but the most influential of all is the Javanese traditional religion called the Kebathinan. Most leaders of the country are of the Javanese ethnic group. One prominent leader in preparing the constitution of the country, Roeslan Abdoelgani, said that Pancasila is not based on Islam. For the sake of the unity of the country this was the best solution. Most leaders of the country also realized that the struggles for independence were not the endeavor of the Muslim people solely, but were the struggles of all people of Indonesia, who came from different religious affiliations, and their efforts were not insignificant.

The fact is that the establishment of Pancasila as the state ideology has not been without threat. There were several times that the Muslim groups (the radical-militants) and the communists attempted to abolish the Pancasila. The attempts to demolish it caused damage and bloodshed. For the militant Muslims, Islam is the law of God; they are still not satisfied with Pancasila as the ideology of the state, especially because Indonesia has the largest Muslim population in the world. For them, Shari'a Islam should be the ideology of the state.

The state program of regional autonomy gives opportunity for Shari'a Islam to be implemented in each region-province, even though the central government functions according to the principles of Pancasila. For example, Aceh, in the northern part of Sumatra, is known as the "chamber of Mecca." This province is exercising Shari'a Islam on a full scale. There are only fifty Christians in the Aceh ethnic group numbering 3,500,000. So, the majority of the Aceh people are devotees of a fanatic vision of Sunni Islam. There is a saying that to be Aceh is to be Muslim. The implementation of Shari'a Islam in Aceh resulted in the closing of seventeen churches in the Aceh area in 2002. These were churches of immigrant communities that the local people were opposed to because they insisted that only Muslims could live in their province.

An attempt has been made recently, by several of the Muslim fundamentalist political parties who were in the Planning Constitution Committee, to make Indonesia into an Islamic state. Fortunately, the proposal was rejected by the majority, after having very severe debate. But the attempt to put Shari'a Islam in the state constitution does not stop there; the effort is still in progress.

If it is not possible to go through the "main gate" of the state constitutions, the Islamic parties try to go through the "windows" of the state constitution, namely, through the National Educational System Constitution. After having a lot of debate and rejection from the minority religions, the President (under pressure?) acceded to the Islamists, which of course means that the Muslim groups are benefiting from the new law that tilts toward the Islamists in regard to educational policy. However, the minority religions are anxious about this development.

Another discussion has been going on in relation to the proposed constitution, which will try to spell out the principles of how people from different religious affiliation can live side by side peacefully. Consequently, if this proposal becomes legal law, it will contribute to the disintegration of harmonious relations in this country. In the eyes of the Muslim militants, who are a minority Islamic group in Indonesia, people of religions other than Islam are pagans. Driving them aside from society and even killing them is jihad. If jihadists are killed when engaged in the conflict, they are considered to be *syuhadha* (martyrs). Whether the jihadists die or live, in either case they will win merit. Of course, Christians have also had their holy war theologies. We know how Firmicus Maternus introduced the idea of "holy war" against pagan religions, during Constantine's era.

Theoretically, with Pancasila we can live peacefully side by side among the people, but in practice the feeling of dissatisfaction on the part of Islamic militants creates a lot of tension in the field in terms of territoriality that views the world as divided into territory ruled by Muslims and regions not yet under Muslim rule. An example is the conflict in Poso, which was for sometime peaceful. Then, suddenly in October 9-10, 2003, it erupted with more than eleven Christians killed during a sudden attack by the "Ninja" coming from somewhere, who were shouting "Allah'u Akbar" before they attacked the villages. The government has managed to arrest five persons who are considered as the culprits of all these terrors.

For the last six years, the face of the Indonesian nation has been drastically changed. From a nation that was well known as polite, friendly people, there are those who seek to transform our society to become brutal, wild, and a fatalistic kind of people. Many religious buildings have been destroyed with bombs, fire, or stones. Religious conflicts have spread all over the country. The conflict in Sanggau Ledo West-Kalimantan, Ambon, Halmahera, and Poso were the most brutal and severe of all, because thousands of people were killed, both Christians and Muslims.

It is not just the Muslims who are inclined to think in a territorial mode, but Christians often think in the same way when they are the majority. They also have the tendency to dominate the course of life of the people. During the early development of Christianity in Indonesia, the Dutch government unofficially adopted territoriality among Christian denominations. In the early years the Anabaptist mission was given the Muria area as their mission field, while the Reformed mission was given a wider area of mission. The Anabaptists were not allowed to work or develop their mission beyond Muria Mountain. So the Muslim understanding of territoriality in Indonesia is rooted deep within preindependence history.

So it is not new that fundamentalist radical Muslims are pursuing a territorial model of mission. Actually, all religions that have "missionary" character, including Christianity, are inclined to dominate and regulate whenever they can do so. Missionary religion usually reaches out to get larger followings, and this feeds a strategy that will enable them to "conquer" the land or territory that will make it easier for them to win the people in that area. Religion that believes in war and warfare is in this category.

Actually the church knows that if she wants her presence to be meaningful for the welfare of the country, there is no other choice for her in expressing solidarity with Christ than to express a solidarity with people who struggle for justice and freedom—the first component namely, the masses. Our mission-claim must be the same; we are called to be with the destitute, the outcasts, and the unfortunate group of the mass. The validity of this vision is no doubt convincing. There is no mission call, theologically, which is more accountable than to be with the least of those brothers and sisters of Jesus (Matt 25:40). Besides, there is no legitimacy that is more legal than the legitimacy that is given by honest people, because they are convinced that we are on their side.

However, what are the facts? Generally the church in Indonesia, its organizations and institutions, are still not aligned with the interest and concerns of the masses. The reason why the church and its institutions do not align with the masses is because they do not want to put themselves at risk. To show our solidarity with the masses, the logical consequence is that the church institutions have to put themselves in confrontation with the bureaucrats. This by no means weakens the effort of church institutions to continue to show their solidarity with the masses; in fact it gives credibility to the church. However, if the bureaucrats did not hinder the mission, the small group of militant Muslims do oppose the church's identification with the poor. This condition compels church institutions to find a way of collaboration with the third component, the bureaucrats, so that together we are confronted by the "threat" of Islam, with the risk of losing our solidarity with the masses.

This kind of strategy is fundamentally, theologically, and empirically wrong. It is empirically wrong because recent developments show that Islam and the bureaucrat component have very intimate alliances. Consequently, the present situation with the church is not so good, if we do not want to say it is bad. And this is due to the bad strategy we adopted. Our relation with the masses component is not good, because if we do not show our solidarity with them, likewise they will also not pay attention to us. Our relation with the Islamic component is not good either, because we have the tendency to perceive the presence of Islam as a threat. Finally, our relation with the bureaucrat is not as smooth as what we expected, because we are inclined to be ambivalent, namely, on the one hand we want to maintain our independency, but at the same time we also see that collaboration with the bureaucrat is indispensable.

As I have mentioned above, the strategy we used not only does not work, but it is also fundamentally wrong. Theologically speaking, the strategy is totally wrong, because the orientation is on self—self-existence and self-survival. And empirically, the strategy is also wrong, because it builds on negative assumptions, namely, feeling threatened and helpless in facing the threat.

My concluding statement is that the map of our existence in Indonesia is not so good, and even inclined to get worse, as a result of not having a clear common strategy among Christians. What we have been doing so far is just defensive maneuvers. It is about time that church institutions sit together and formulate a holistic strategy for our mission together.

However, to do that is not an easy matter, because Christian people in Indonesia inherit the bad Protestant tradition, namely, inclining to split. Generally speaking, the sociopolitical accountability of Christians in Indonesia is still divided and it is difficult to unite them into one view and commitment. One group emphasizes a lot of independency from the power structure, a second group collaborates very much with the power structure, and the third and largest group is indifferent.

We must confront the divisiveness of the territorial paradigm nationally rather than just dealing with one particular religion or region. If we focus only on the territoriality of one community of faith, we will fail to see the larger values that unite us all as Indonesians. Furthermore, we will also promote division, injustice, and conflict of interest. A focus on our different doctrines divides us, but if we seek to build understanding through the kind of service we can do together as a nation, then we can be united.

The new paradigm of mission should be developed in such a way, from the older and traditional mandate of mission, which it is now obsolete, to a new strategy of mission that is the "secular mandate." This is an incarnational identification with the aspirations of the people. The church seeks to identify with and join hands together with the Muslims, doing reasonable work together in order to release the country and our nation from the long crises we all have been experiencing.

This approach should be culturally sensitive and within our context, rather than cross-culturally insensitive. However, we must start with our own family, our fellow believers, and with other denominations as well. How can we make peace with Muslims if within our own fellow believers we are so divisive? I hope we can do better. In the words of a popular Christian song, "They will know we are Christians by our love!"

CHAPTER SIX

Revelation and Reconciliation: The Vision of Concord in Abrahamic Traditions

Roy Hange

This chapter will explore the role of reconciliation in the narrative structure of the revelation of the three Abrahamic faiths. This exploration is not an attempt to reduce other themes to reconciliation but to focus on a common theme between the traditions.

We will explore how the ideal mode of knowing the other in the Abrahamic traditions is through reconciliation. The scriptures of the three traditions also deal with the failures of reconciliation and the unbelief of others. The intent of this paper is to move beyond doctrinal comparisons to find parallels in the ways Judaism, Christianity, and Islam value reconciliation.

Reconciliation: Parallel Themes

A summary of these parallel reconciliation themes follows:
The longest story in Hebrew scripture ends with the reconciliation

of Joseph to his brothers in a way that preserved the future of a family and the people of Israel. This story is set in a series of stories and books that end in and idealize reconciliation.

The longest story in the Christian scriptures is about the reconciliation of persons to God and each other in the way of Jesus in a way that created a new community—the church. The church then became a reconciling community among the nations.

The longest sura in the Qur'an (The Cow) is set in the context of the Muslim community's will to be reconciled through a covenant with the Jewish community in Medina. Two of the most significant beginning points for the early Muslim community are this reconciling gesture of a covenant in Medina and the way enemies were dealt with on the return to Mecca in which there is a reference to Joseph's words to his brothers. Both of these events are connected to two significant suras in the Qur'an: The Cow and Yusuf.

The Power of Revelation and Reconciliation

We will also explore how the power of revelation and reconciliation worked together through leaders to enable the formation of new communities:

The Jewish community was the first to break from the idolatrous and imperial structures of their world to acknowledge God as King and form a people and political community whose faith and communal identity out lasted all those other peoples and empires.

The Christian community was the first to break from the ethical exclusivity in the reign of God, setting forth a monotheistic community of worship from many nations that held out an ethic of peace and justice that challenged and transformed those nations.

The Islamic community was the first monotheistic, multiethnic nation of faith (the ummah) bringing to political form a single community of worship and governance from many nations.

Each of these three formations required worship of God and reconciliation with others as the generative principle to combat the denigrating function of idolatry and divisiveness required to maintain the structures of empire. We will see how these three faiths were counter imperial in the way they built communities initially through reconciliation.

In the next pages we will explore how reconciliation is part of the essential structure of the revelation of these three traditions. Much of what follows is well-known but I offer the characterizations in parallel as novel. This chapter will attempt to use the characteristic theological language of each tradition within each section with the acknowledgment that what follows is only an attempt at a fair representation.

Revelation and Reconciliation in Judaism

The Hebrew Bible begins with an account of a peaceful creation that stands in sharp contrast to the violent creation myths of its time. The book of Genesis then follows with a series of conflicts that often end in reconciliation.

Walter Wink shows how in Babylonian mythology creation is portrayed as a battle between the gods:

> Creation is an act of violence. Marduk murders and dismembers Tiamat, and from her cadaver creates the world. As the French philosopher Paul Ricoeur observes, order is established by means of disorder. Chaos (symbolized by Tiamat) is prior to order (represented by Marduk, high god of Babylon). Evil precedes good. The gods themselves are violent.[1]

Wink continues with a commentary on how the Hebrew Bible reverses the meaning of this pagan myth as a kind of polemic and witness to God's nature:

> The Bible portrays a God who creates a good creation. Chaos does not resist order. Good is prior to evil. Neither evil nor violence is a part of creation, but enter later, as a result of the first couple's sin and the connivance of the serpent (Gen 3). A basically good reality is thus corrupted by free decisions reached by creatures. In this far more complex and subtle explanation of the origin of things, violence emerges for the first time as a problem requiring the solution.[2]

Here we have an account of creation that works at reconciling the method of creation with the image of a good and gracious God. What follows the creation story in Genesis and throughout the Hebrew Bible are a series of stories of human folly, tension, and violence that can end in reconciliation showing that it is possible to restore what God intended in creation through reconciliation.

The story of Noah and the flood ends with God's declaration

through a covenant that "never again will all life be cut off by the waters of a flood" (Gen 9:11). This note of reconciliation is a self-limiting of God's power modeling the kind of mercy to be shown by humans in later stories in Genesis (Gen 9:12ff.).

The brothers Jacob and Esau who are alienated from each other for years finally move beyond their mistrust to embrace each other in reconciliation. Briefly before that, Jacob sends family before him out of fear, and struggles so deeply with whether to reconcile with his brother that he is given the name Israel, meaning "one who struggles with God." The name Israel is given in a movement toward reconciliation (Gen 32, 33).

Jacob's son Joseph and his brothers are alienated for years after Joseph's brothers faked Joseph's death and sold him into slavery in Egypt. Joseph's reconciliation with his brothers is the climax of the longest continuous story in the Hebrew Bible and the basis for saving his family from starvation and ensuring the future of Israel (Gen 45).

James Williams in his book, *The Bible, Violence, and the Sacred*, notes how many of the stories of brothers in the Hebrew Bible end up in reconciliation:

> When one looks at all the brother narratives and references in the Hebrew Bible, certain elements stand out and form a pattern. These elements are the younger brother as a shepherd, the younger brother as favored by one or both parents and by God, and the displacement of the older brother followed by the ordeal of the younger and some sort of reconciliation or reintegration of the two.[3]

David repeatedly offers reconciliation to Saul during their rivalry and forgoes two opportunities to kill Saul when given the chance. These reconciling gestures are a mark of David's character as they are featured in two chapters (1 Sam 24, 26) and are finally honored by Saul in an act of reconciliation at the end of 1 Samuel 26. This story may be the first nonviolent, nondynastic transition of power in human history.

Elisha stands as a prophet and makes two reconciling gestures when he heals the enemy, Syrian commander Namaan, of his leprosy (2 Kings 5) and later he feeds enemy captives instead of killing them (2 Kings 6:22 ff.).

At the end of 2 Chronicles we read the narrative of a profound reconciliation between the split kingdoms of Judah and Israel after

Israel had joined with Aram in defeating Judah and taking thousands of Judeans as prisoners. The prophet Oded intervenes and orders the captives sent back (2 Chron 28:8ff.). This act is followed by King Hezekiah organizing a grand, reconciling Passover celebration that intentionally includes persons from both Israel and Judah (2 Chron 30).

The book of Job ends with Job reconciling with his three tormentors by calling for God's mercy on them. In the words of the Lord to Eliphaz, "I will accept his prayer and not deal with you according to your folly. You have not spoken of me what is right, as my servant Job has" (Job 42:8).

The Hebrew prophets, like Oded and Elisha, stood outside of the power structures of Israel, Judah, and neighboring nations and called for true worship, justice, and often reconciliation. The prophet Isaiah represents this call in chapter 11 of his book when he envisions a just and righteous ruler led by the Spirit of God and the reconciliation of even creation when the "wolf will live with the lamb" (Isa 11:6). Isaiah concludes this passage with the words:

> They will neither hurt nor destroy on all my holy mountain, for the earth will be full of the knowledge of the Lord as the waters cover the sea. In that day the Root of Jesse will stand as a banner for the peoples; the nations will rally to him, and his place of rest will be glorious (Isa 11:9-10).

The image of the earth being filled with the knowledge of God comes immediately following a reconciling image of the wolf and the lamb, all seen as a signal to the nations—a signal of a reconciling justice that should cover the earth.

In summary, it could be argued that the Jewish community would not exist today without this whole series of reconciling events. That is, if there were not reconciliation along the way at critical stages of its formation as a community, the Jews would have fallen into the oblivion of history like the other nations. Revelation contains these accounts of how God's reconciling power saved them as a people of faith.

Revelation and Reconciliation in Christianity

Throughout the ministry of Jesus and the formation of the first Christian community, increasingly larger circles of inclusion grow through reconciliation. These growing circles of persons became part of the structure of the revelation as growing circles of reconciliation:

Jesus's disciples come from very different and conflicting backgrounds (tax collector and freedom fighter) yet are joined together through his teachings and the work of the Spirit.

Early followers in the church come from Jewish and Gentile backgrounds yet are served as one and begin to witness as one.

Enemy Roman military officers were welcomed into this community of mercy that then began to grow throughout and beyond the Roman Empire.

A former persecutor of the Christians becomes the foremost proponent of Christianity as the apostle Paul. Paul then described reconciliation as central to the ministry of Jesus and the ministry of the church. Paul wrote that on the cross Jesus broke down the dividing wall of hostility between Jews and Gentiles (Eph 2) and gave Christians the ministry of reconciliation as ambassadors for Christ (2 Cor 5).

For the sake of clarification let us explore the inner logic of this reconciliation through the words of Miroslav Volf who grew up in the conflict zone of the Balkans and is now teaching theology at Yale University:

> Paul's solution to the tension between universality and particularity is ingenious. Its logic is simple: the oneness of God requires God's universality; God's universality entails human equality; human equality implies equal access by all to the blessings of the one God; equal access is incompatible with ascription of religious significance to genealogy; Christ, the seed of Abraham, is both the fulfillment of the genealogical promise to Abraham and the end of genealogy as a privileged locus of access to God; faith in Christ replaces birth into a people. As a consequence, all peoples can have access to the one God of Abraham and Sarah on equal terms, none by right and all by grace.[4]

Volf continues by showing how this reconciliation works not to remove difference, but to remove the enmity that is at the root of destructive divisions:

> Far from being the assertion of the one against many, the cross is the self-giving of the one for many. Unity here is not the result of "sacred violence" which obliterates the particularity of "bodies"

[groups], but a fruit of Christ's self-sacrifice, which breaks down the enmity between them. From a Pauline perspective, the wall that divides is not so much "the difference" as enmity (cf. Eph 2:14).[5]

Volf further shows how differences are not erased in this reconciliation, but how these differences are held in a unity of mutual respect based in the unity of God:

> The body of Christ [church] lives as a complex interplay of bodies—Jewish and Gentile, female and male, slave and free—of those who have partaken of Christ's self-sacrifice. The Pauline move is not from the particularity of the body to the universality of the spirit, but from separated bodies to the community of interrelated bodies—the one body in the Spirit with many discreet members. The Spirit does not erase differences, but allows access into the one body of Christ to the people with such differences on the same terms. What the Spirit does erase (or at least loosen) is a stable and socially constructed correlation between differences and social roles.[6]

The result of reconciliation emerges as a symphony of differences that are now joined together in spite of their differences, whereas before they had been playing different and dissonant notes. Communion and reconciliation transform dissension and conflict.

But, as Rene Girard has warned in his book, *Violence and the Sacred*, this new unity unleashed a new level of power that unchecked can be even more destructive than the lower levels of previously unreconciled conflict.[7] Sadly, elements of history in the Christian world evidence the abuse of this power to reconcile differences in unified, unjust violence against others.

We began the exploration of Hebrew scripture by seeing how the creation story is set against a pagan empire's violent creation myth. Let us observe how the Christian scriptures end with a similar contrast.

In Revelation 22 we have an image of the river of life flowing from the throne of God. Beside this river grow trees and the leaves of these trees are for the healing of the nations.

The image of the river of life flowing from the throne of God in its setting is seen as culturally and politically contrasted to the river of death and captive slaves that flowed regularly into the Roman emperor's throne. This contrast stands as a testament to the fact that an idolatrous empire can never restore the intent of creation. Whereas the death, destruction, and captivity of peoples flowed to the thrones of the emperors in Rome (who often saw themselves as gods), the image of God's throne is of a place where life and healing flow out to all nations.

Revelation and Reconciliation in Islam

Much of the Qur'an can only be fully understood in the context of events the revelation is related to in the life of Muhammad and the community that formed around him. We will explore reconciling events in two of these pivotal contexts: the initial reconciling orientation of Muhammad toward others in Medina, and the reconciling stance of Muhammad toward his former enemies in Mecca.

At the birth of Islam the Bedouin and Arab tribes of the Hijaz were caught in vicious cycles of feuding and vengeance based on codes of honor and the blood price. The Muslim community worked at breaking these cycles of vengeance with an emphasis on the oneness of God (*tawhid*) "based in patient restraint and mercifulness."[8]

Direct references to reconciliation in the Qur'an are related to preferring reconciliation over divorce in marriage relations (2:228; 4:114, 128, 129). Beyond the family level, the power of Islam's early growth lay in the ability of Muhammad to reconcile warring tribes and feuding extended families. The broadest focus of reconciliation is under the principle of tawhid, where all should be unified in submission through worship of the one God. These foci, when combined with the following observations, make clearer the preference toward reconciliation in the teachings of Muhammad and the Qur'an.

We will focus on two actions of Muhammad, mentioned previously, that reveals his orientation to and awareness of reconciliation.

The Entrance to Medina

Following a difficult early period in Mecca, the Muslim community established a presence in Medina alongside of the Jewish and pagan communities already there.

In the early days of the prophet's ministry in Medina the Muslims of Medina were called the Helpers and Muslims who came from Mecca were called the Emigrants. There were tensions between these two groups. The formation of this community depended on a series of reconciling pacts or covenants between the Helpers and the

Emigrants and between this reconciled group of Muslims and the Jews. Martin Lings observes the following about these two movements toward unity through Muhammad's sensitive and accurate moves toward reconciliation:

> In order to unite the community of believers still further, the prophet now instituted a pact of brotherhood between the Helpers and the Emigrants, so that each of the Helpers would have an Emigrant brother who was nearer to him than any of the Helpers, and each Emigrant would have a Helper brother who was nearer to him than any Emigrant. But he made himself and his family an exception for it would have been too invidious for him to choose as his brother one of the Helpers rather than another, so he took Ali by the hand and said, "This is my brother."[9]

It was to be hoped that these two parties would be strengthened by a third, and the Prophet now made a covenant of mutual obligation between his followers and the Jews of the oasis, forming them into a single community of believers, but allowing for the differences between the two religions. Muslims and Jews were to have equal status. If a Jew was wronged, then he must be helped to his rights by both Muslim and Jew, and so also if a Muslim was wronged.[10]

The longest sura of the Qur'an (The Cow) is written in the context of the failing hopes for a reconciled life with the Jewish community in Medina. Various verses in the beginning of The Cow lament the failure of the "deal" or "covenant" and mix images of the failure of the Jews in the past with the present failure of the covenant with the Muslims. Here are two verses that give insights in the lament of a vision for a reconciliation with the Jews that never happened.

"They are indeed those who bartered away good guidance for error and gained nothing from the deal, nor found the right way" (2:16).

"And remember, when We made a covenant with you whereby you agreed you will neither shed blood among you nor turn your people out of their homes, you promised, and are witnesses to it too" (2:84).

The intensity and length of the arguments and lament of the loss of this relationship portrayed in The Cow is evidence of the intensity of the initial hope for good relations with the Jewish community— evidence of the will to be reconciled.

The Return to Mecca

After an initial period of persecution in Mecca, Muhammad went to Medina where his status and community grew and in AD 630 he returned to Mecca with his followers and took Mecca. When Mecca was taken there was a cleansing of pagan religious symbols through effacement and a cleansing of the resentments through reconciliation.

Regarding the cleansing of the pagan religious symbols, Martin Lings relies on the recorded traditions of the life of Muhammad (Hadith) from Waqidi and Azraqi to note Muhammad's respect for the symbols of Judaism and Christianity with these words:

> Apart from the icon of the Virgin Mary and the child Jesus, and a painting of an old man, said to be Abraham, the walls inside had been covered with pictures of pagan deities. Placing his hand protectively over the icon, the Prophet told 'Uthman to see that all the other paintings, except that of Abraham, were effaced.[11]

Lings continued with this account of the prophet's encounter with those Meccan enemies seeking refuge and fearing the command for their death as an act of revenge:

> The Meccans who had taken refuge in the mosque had since been joined by many of those who had at first taken refuge in their homes and they were sitting in groups, here and there, not far from the Ka`bah. The prophet now addressed them, saying: "What say ye, and what think ye?" They answered: "We say well, and we think well: a noble and generous brother, son of a noble and generous brother. It is thine to command." He then spoke to them in the words of forgiveness which, according to the Revelation, Joseph spoke to his brothers when they came to him in Egypt: "Verily I say as my brother Joseph said, this day there shall be no upbraiding of you nor reproach. God forgiveth you, and He is the most merciful of the merciful."[12]

In these two quotes we have Muhammad protecting the picture of Abraham and the icon of Mary and child Jesus, and a while later his own actions honor directly the reconciling tradition of these Abrahamic traditions by mentioning the very words of Joseph's reconciliation with his brothers (12:92) who had also tried to kill him.

I can imagine the affinity in Muhammad's mind: Joseph was

forced into exile in Egypt after his death was faked and his murder was considered just as Muhammad was forced into an exile in Medina by escaping those who threatened his life in Mecca. Both Joseph and Muhammad later took the stance of reconciliation from a position of power that did not require them to do so.

In these two actions Muhammad honors the previous monotheistic traditions and knows and invokes the reconciling conclusion to the longest story in the Hebrew Bible that made the creation of Israel as a nation possible. It could also be argued that Muhammad's gracious echoing of Joseph's words to his own enemies made the creation of the Muslim community in Mecca much easier. Muhammad's gesture of reconciliation overcame the resentments that could have made the establishment of Islam in Mecca difficult.

In the Qur'an, a whole sura is dedicated to the story of Joseph. The sura Yusuf ends with an affirmation of Jewish and Christian scriptures in the context of a discussion of reconciliation: "Verily in their accounts is a lesson for men of wisdom. This is not a fictitious tale, but a verification of earlier Books, and a clear exposition of everything, and a guidance and grace for those who believe" (12:111).

This reconciling and merciful stance is carried on by followers of Muhammad. Ali, as the first legitimate caliph in the Shi'ite tradition and the fourth Sunni caliph, himself echoed these reconciling actions of Muhammad in his instructions to Malik al-Ashtar when Ali appointed Malik governor of Egypt at the time when the rule of Muhammad ibn Abi Bakr was in turmoil.[13]

At this time Egypt was predominately Coptic Christian. These Copts welcomed the Muslims as liberators from the cruel rule of the Byzantine Empire. The Copts could have quickly also turned against their new overlords if the following reconciling stance had not been taken. Part two of Ali's instructions entitled, "Commands and Instructions Concerning Righteous Action in the Affairs of the State," are recorded in the Nahj al-Balaghah and translated by William Chittick as follows:

> Know, O Malik, that I am sending you to a land where governments, just and unjust, have existed before you. They will speak about you as you were wont to speak about those rulers. And the righteous are only known by that which God causes to pass concerning them on the tongues of His servants. So let the dearest of your treasuries be the treasury of righteous action. Control your desire and restrain your soul from what is not lawful to

you, for restraint of the soul is for it to be equitous in what it likes and dislikes. Infuse your heart with mercy, love, and kindness for your subjects. Be not in face of them a voracious animal, counting them as easy prey, for they are of two kinds: either they are your brothers in religion or your equals in creation. Error catches them unaware, deficiencies overcome them, (evil deeds) are committed by them intentionally and by mistake. So grant them your pardon and your forgiveness to the same extent that you hope God will grant you His pardon and His forgiveness. For you are above them, and he who appointed you is above you, and God is above him who appointed you. God has sought from you the fulfillment of their requirements and he is trying you with them.[14]

In summary, these acts of profound reconciliation became the foundation and direction of a nation of faith (ummah) not based on subjugation alone, but based on mutual submission to the one God. In this sense Islam as a nation of faith willed a reconciling, coequal status of "fellow believers" for those who came under Islam's control. We have seen reconciliation in religio-political terms put forward at two critical moments in the formation of the Muslim community in Medina and the beginning of their rule after a victory in Mecca.

Observations and Questions

We have seen revelation bringing into the three Abrahamic faiths new and creative forms of being reconciled to others in a way that was inspiring and life-giving in preserving and building new communities. These scriptures show attempts to restore unity under God of a created order marred by idolatry, divisions, and violence. Reconciliation appears to be the initial intent of the actions of the leaders of the three traditions and sections of each of the scriptures are dealing with the lack of a positive response to the original acts of reconciliation and the tensions and conflicts that result.

We have attempted to see how reconciliation is woven by revelation into the subtle and obvious discord humanity has come to see as normal in ways that create new possibilities beyond the normal. We have also attempted to follow the terrain of hope set forth by revelation toward different paths of relating to others through reconciliation.

May we now imagine together, in line with the prophets of the past, the ways in which our world of faiths can be a place of peace for those who know their faith in the way of torah, gospel, or tawhid. How can we as Abrahamic traditions help each other recover the concord at the core of each tradition's original vision?[15]

CHAPTER SEVEN

Is the Gospel Good News for Muslim Women?

Chantal Logan

The rise of feminism, as the enforcement of principles set in the Universal Declaration of Human Rights in the United Nations charter drafted in 1948, has pressed upon Christianity and Islam a revisitation of the status of women in the light of their sacred texts. Although both Christian and Muslim countries not only endorsed, but actively engaged in the drafting of the U.N. declaration, leaders in neither religion could anticipate how women, some forty years later, would insist on their respective faith traditions granting the rights they were promised in that declaration. However, in Islam and Christianity, the vigor of the feminist movement in the west, as in other parts of the world, has often led paradoxically to the entrenchment of conservative postures.

It might be surprising to some that Islam and Christianity are mentioned together in this context, as if they presented similar views on the issue, especially in times like the present, when political expediency sets one religion against the other. But it might be good, for this very reason, to be reminded that in many instances Islam and Christianity, as religions which believe in divine revelation, have many similarities which place them in the same category for secular observers. When it comes to women, both world religions have been accused of holding a low view of women and of perpetrating discrimination against them. In the same vein, one can find in both assemblies so-called "liberal" and "conservative" theologians who argue the exegesis of their sacred texts. The issue of "contextualization" of texts which deal with the status of women is as hot in Muslim circles as it is for Christians, and the intensity of the debate varies tremendously depending on which part of the world one comes from.

In any case, in this presentation I want to get away, as far as possible, from the paradigms found in Samuel P. Huntington's book, *The Clash of Civilizations*, which puts Islam and Christianity in opposing camps.[1]

Islam is not any more monolithic than Christianity. If people's manner of dress can be an indication, the diversity found in both worlds can be illustrated by the fact that there is as much distance between the woman of Saudi Arabia, who keeps her face covered, and the Tunisian, who wears jeans and no veil, as between Amish women with prayer bonnets and long dresses and modern Mennonite women who wear shorts and halter tops. The stereotyping of Muslim women in Christian countries is as frequent as the stereotyping of Christian women in Muslim countries.

As an academic exercise, to compare the views of women in Islam with those in Christianity, would be a huge but also a fascinating task. My present reflection, besides being brief, is not merely an academic exercise, but it is in harmony with the theme of this book, *Anabaptists Meeting Muslims*. It is an attempt for a Christian community to discern how best to relate to our Muslim neighbors in these troubled times. Therefore, I am approaching this subject, not as a secular thinker, but as a Christian woman who is interested in reaching out to Muslim women.

Yet by asking the question, "Is the gospel good news for Muslim women?," I do not want to take the answer for granted, since it seems that even for some Christian women the message of the gospel has not always been liberating. I also want to show respect for the many devout Muslim women that I have had the privilege to know and who, for the most part, have not answered the invitation of the gospel of Jesus Christ. But I also hope that this presentation will lead us to scrutinize the title question itself, in asking if the claims of feminism have validity when it comes to choosing between Islam and Christianity, or if we might not need to look somewhere else, beyond the categories of gender, to find reasons for a woman to select her guiding faith.

In this essay, I will examine essentially texts from the Qur'an (English interpretation by Yusuf Ali) on one hand, and texts from the gospel (various translations) on the other, although I am aware that there are many other important writings which have contributed to the shaping of current attitudes toward women in both religions. Among the texts, I will concentrate on the ones which deal with praxis rather than general principles, because it is the way relationships between men and women are defined which most accurately reveal how women's worth is assessed. Since marriage is at the heart of those relationships in most cultures, the view of marriage and its meaning will be particularly examined.

Is Islam Good for Women?

Many Muslim women will answer a definite yes to this question. But one has to bear in mind that the question is not inert and can prompt various answers due to the nature of the Muslim community. The ummah is not simply a fellowship of people, but a territorial entity, a specific place where the way of Islam rules. Therefore, in Islamic countries, the teachings of the Qur'an translate into a law (the Shari'a), which affects all aspects of the life of Muslim women. Yet, when Muslim women answer yes to our question, they mainly give two reasons.

First, that before the time of the Prophet, women were not valued and that Islam substantially bettered the situation of women. (An often quoted fact is that daughters were buried alive when they were born, an abomination that Islam condemned. In the Qur'an, 16:58-59 specifically addresses this issue.[2]

And second, that the Prophet himself valued women and was kind to them. Special mention is usually made of his love for his daughters (he did not have any sons) and his respect for mothers. An often quoted *hadith* is the following:

Someone asked the Prophet: "Who deserves my service most after God?"

The Prophet said, "Your mother."[3]

The person asked again, "And who is next?"

The Prophet said, "Your mother."

The man asked further, "And who is next?"

The Prophet replied, "Your mother."[4]

When it comes to the qur'anic text itself, many verses are quoted today to show that in Islam men and women are equal. Muslim theologians will even be prompt to point out that in the Qur'an, there is no mention that man was created first and woman second, neither that it was Eve who disobeyed God first and led her husband to disobedience. They insist that when it comes to piety, women and men are judged by God on an equal footing. The most quoted verses to corroborate these views are the following:

> O mankind! We created you from a single (pair) of a male and a female, and made you into nations and tribes, that ye may know each other (not that ye may despise each other). Verily the most honored of you in the sight of Allah is (he who is) the most righteous of you. And Allah has full knowledge and is well acquainted (with all things) (Qur'an 49:13).
> For Muslim men and women—for believing men and women, for devout men and women, for true men and women, for men and women who are patient and constant, for men and women who humble themselves, for men and women who give in charity, for men and women who fast (and deny themselves), for men and women who guard their chastity, and for men and women who engage much in Allah's praise—for them has Allah prepared forgiveness and great reward (Qur'an 33:35, section 5).

Yet, although men and women are considered equals in the eyes of God, they do not have the same rights. To explain those differences, Muslim theologians emphasize that equality is not sameness and that the relationship between men and women is one of complementarity. Because they are different, men and women do not assume the same roles, which explains the differences in their rights. Men are known to be stronger physically and therefore have the responsibility of protecting and maintaining women, which justifies their having rights over them. The issue of the protection of women is a cardinal point in the Islamic understanding of the relationship between men and women which makes provisions for "protection of woman's chastity" in some Islamic constitutions.

Here are some of the verses from the Qur'an which ascertain men's rights over women's:

> And women shall have rights similar to the rights against them, according to what is equitable; but men have a degree (of advantage) over them. And Allah is Exalted in Power, Wise (Qur'an 2:228).

Men are the protectors and maintainers of women, because Allah has given the one more (strength) than the other, and because they support them from their means (Qur'an 4:34, section 6).[5]

The issue of "men having a degree" over women is a matter of controversy when it comes to decide whether or not it means superiority. As some of their Christian counterparts, who explain that men's headship in the family does not mean that women are inferior, Muslims do the same. But in the case of Islam, legally speaking, the fact that men have a "degree" over women has concrete consequences. It means, among other things, that women inherit only half as much as men, and that two female witnesses are needed where only one man would do. Yet what affects women most is not the inequality in inheritance or testimony, but the rights which are given to men in matrimony: to take more than one wife, to repudiate their wives only by saying the words, and to claim the ownership of the children. Polygamy was described in a document recently as a "specter that demoralizes and haunts every Somali married woman."[6] The fear of repudiation is expressed in many of the *baraanbur* poems that Somali women compose. It would be fair to say that the fear of being divorced, resulting in the loss of her children, and of one's husband taking another wife is one of the most difficult things Muslim women have to face.

The discrepancy between the verses dealing with the equality of men and women and the verses which justify a difference favoring men, has often been noticed by Muslim women, who point to an erroneous interpretation of the qur'anic verses. This has been one of the struggles of the recent Nobel Prize Laureate, Iranian lawyer, Shirin Ebâdi, who considers that since Muslim clerics are always men, they interpret the verses in the sense which gives them the most privileges. She insists on the fact that Islam is one, coherent and homogeneous, and if there are contradictions in Islamic laws it is not because of Islam but because of the interpretation of men. When it comes to the issue of polygamy, many women (but also some men) point out that since the Islamic requirement of treating each wife equally cannot in reality be fulfilled, the Qur'an actually encourages monogamy. Polygamy, it is argued, was only allowed for the sake of protecting widows. Muslim women advocate a reexamination of this and other teachings on the basis that one must "distinguish between the spirit of Islam and the concrete prescriptions valid only for a specific place and time."[7] By doing so they introduce the notion of contextualization which is in hot debate in the Islamic world today, since it touches on the very meaning of the Qur'an as a sacred text.[8]

Yet rights given to men over women is not a simple question of hermeneutics. It reflects a cultural view of the relationship between men and women, not unique to Islam, where the main purpose of a union between men and women is the propagation of a lineage, which is usually the bloodline to which the man belongs. Marriage exists, not for the sake of companionship, but for the sake of producing and rearing children. Although the qur'anic verse "you are a habit for men and men are a habit for women" suggests otherwise, the Islamic right given to a man to take a second wife if the first is barren, illustrates the point.

We see then that when Islam allows men to have more than one wife it does not depart from culture, but only puts limits on it. Muslim theologians, who are virtually all men, continue to justify polygamy on the basis that monogamy leads men to become adulterous, since they naturally will look elsewhere if their wife does not satisfy them for one reason or the other.[9] This view is symptomatic of a much greater issue, which separates Islam from Christianity, and which the teaching of Jesus about marriage brings to light. The issue is the call to radical discipleship. Suffice to say for now that Islam, if it is good for women because it offers her protection and delivers her from many abuses, is definitively better for men. Men's duty to protect and maintain a woman is well overcompensated for by the rights he is given over her.

The Teachings of Jesus: Good News for Whom?

The gospel text found in Matthew 19:3-12, is very much enlightened by the presentation just given of Islam. In the first part of this passage Jesus makes it very clear that a man cannot repudiate his wife:

> Some Pharisees came to him, to test him. They asked, "Is it lawful for a man to divorce his wife for any and every reason?"
> "Haven't you read," he replied, "that at the beginning the Creator 'made them male and female,' and said, 'For this reason

a man will leave his father and mother and be united to his wife, and the two will become one flesh?' So that they are no longer two, but one. Therefore what God has joined together, let man not separate" (Matt 19:3-6).

Then, the right to repudiation, which causes so much heartache for Muslim women, is totally taken away by Jesus. Men are deprived of a privilege that both Jewish and Islamic cultures allotted them; a husband cannot send his wife away just because she displeases him. That this is a great loss for men is confirmed by the reaction of Jesus's disciples when they exclaim, "If this is the situation between a husband and wife, it is better not to marry" (Matt 19:10).

One can then say that if the teaching of Jesus is good news for women, the reaction of the disciples gives us the feeling that it is not so for men.

But the text goes further. It also severs the patriarchal filiation when it states that a man will leave his father and be united to his wife. The wife therefore, does not belong to the husband's family or clan, but she belongs to the husband and he belongs to her, in complete reciprocity. From this statement one can further imply that any children will belong to both. However, the teaching of Jesus is not a rejection of the extended family, but a redefinition of family affiliation. In one single sweep, Jesus gets rid of a major, real, and feared heartache of married women around the world, polygamy, repudiation, and the loss of their children in the event of divorce.

Our focus in this text from Matthew is the fact that Jesus here underscores a notion, unaccepted, or forgotten by the men who questioned him, the concept of oneness between husband and wife. Since Jesus referred back to creation, it is important to notice that in the qur'anic creation narrative there is no mention of men and women being created in the image of God. This omission is very significant because it shows the contrast between the nature of the God of Islam, whose main characteristic is his "oneness" (He does not have any consort) and the nature of the God of the Bible which is relational. In creating two people, rather than one, to reflect his image, God presents himself as the one who exists in relationship.

But we should also note that by bestowing on the married relationship the seal of "oneness," Jesus gives it a dimension which is absent in many cultures where sexual intimacy is the least binding of all relationship (blood relations being the strongest). Jesus asserts an indissoluble tie, not of a contractual nature where one is protector and the other the protégée and therefore justifying a difference of status, but a bond in which both participate of the same nature. Jesus not only sets equality as a principle, but he also details the praxis. The absence of oneness in the marriage relationship in Islam is illustrated by the fact that women can ask for divorce if the husband, whose main role is to provide for the family, ceases to be able to do so. The implication is that marriage is only a contract which becomes void when its stipulations are not met.

Yet, it is also important to see that what Jesus does is not to take rights away from men in order to give them to women. He does not establish some kind of gender equality based on a just repartition of roles. What Jesus does is to create ties which cannot be broken because they are based on the unconditional character of God's love. In that sense, the teachings of Jesus are not just good news for women, but also good news for men, because the man does not run the risk of being discarded by his wife or to lose his worth if he becomes incapable of providing for or protecting his family. A man's ties with his wife are like God's relationship with his people—secure, because they are based on unconditional love.

Maybe the most interesting aspect of this text yet is that it highlights the differences between Islam and Christianity. Jesus explains that the former right to divorce given by Moses was a special dispensation given to men "because your hearts were hard" (Matt 19:8). It is the same assumption that the Qur'an still makes today; since man is weak, one should not expect him to live up to standards which are too high. For this reason, Muslims call Islam the religion of the middle, a religion which does not go against the natural man. It sees the teachings of Jesus in the Sermon of the Mount as impractical.

But Jesus's so called idealism comes for two reasons. One, he is addressing himself to a humanity that he is going to redeem and therefore give the power to live a redeemed life. And two, Jesus is both the messenger and the message, and therefore has authority to issue a call to a radical lifestyle. Since there is no motif of redemption in Islam (no sinfulness, only weakness), or a prophet which claims perfection,[10] such a call cannot be issued in the Qur'an. On the issue of polygamy, even Muhammad himself went beyond the limit of four wives and had to be granted a special dispensation so as not to be living in direct violation of the revealed truth of God.

This, though, does not close the issue of marriage. There remains in this text a very important statement from Jesus which further enlightens his view of the relationship between men and women and which sets it above the cultural values of protection and fecundity. His position was so innovative that Jesus called the option of singleness and celibacy for the sake of the kingdom, a mystery. Such a concept does not exist in Islam, neither for men nor for women. Islam considers denial of one's sexual desire to be unhealthy, but even more, impossible due to the weaknesses of men and women. But by opening the possibility of singleness, Jesus asserts in praxis that to do the will of God is the supreme value in the kingdom of God, and is not dependant on marriage or procreation. This is reemphasized by Jesus's reaction to the woman who exclaimed, "Blessed is the mother who gave you birth and nursed you."

Jesus replied, "Blessed rather are those who hear the word of God and obey it" (Luke 11:28).

The reply of Jesus sounds very much like a rebuke to what was meant as a compliment that should have been appreciated and acknowledged. The woman expressed the common view that to give birth to a good or a successful son is not only a reason to rejoice, but also a sign of being blessed by God. Jesus's refusal to acknowledge her compliment sets him clearly apart from commonly held assumptions about the value of women. Jesus, contrary to Muhammad and almost all cultural patterns, does not sing the praises of motherhood. Yet he does praise women, but on the basis of their character or their faith, not of their ability to produce children. This attitude, which is obviously a cause of scandal for the people around him, is by the same token a clear message that a woman's value is not tied to her ability to give birth. This, indeed, is extremely good news to barren women, the often cursed women of many cultures, as well as to women who due to choice or necessity have remained single.

Is the Church Radical Enough When It Meets the Ummah?

In this brief study we have seen that on the surface, Islam and Christianity hold similar views toward women. They both affirm, at the level of principle, that in the eyes of God men and women are equal, and that on judgment day neither will have any right or privilege over the other. But when it comes to praxis, Islam and Christianity take diverging roads, or it would seem fair to stay, Islam stops when Christianity goes on. Being conscious of the "natural man" who is weak, Islam makes provision for perpetrating a patriarchal order, even though it regulates and sets limits, because it has no authority to challenge culture at its roots. By stretching those limits and challenging the interpretation of key texts, some Muslim women have been able to find a space for personal fulfillment.

On the other hand, Jesus, also aware of our human weakness and fallen nature, has come to redeem humanity with the authority of "The Perfect One" who comes from and is equal to God. It is because of his role as the Redeemer that he cannot only call men and women to radical discipleship, but also enable them to restore the relationship of equality that they had before the fall. Thus, radical discipleship and redemption are intimately linked and can challenge harmful and unjust cultural patterns while a religious worldview without sin or redemption cannot.

Nevertheless, in all fairness we must also point out that the church, like the ummah to which it seeks to witness, has often stopped halfway along the path when it comes to giving women the full measure of grace to which they are entitled. The faithfulness to the radical call to love one's enemy has enabled Anabaptist communities in the past to witness with authenticity to the Muslim community and it continues to qualify them today. Yet by not being equally radical in the area of relationships between women and men, sometimes giving the appearance that women are set against men in a struggle for leadership and power, the church has missed out on the chance to cast a beacon of light into these floundering times. The conservative lifestyle of Mennonite women, including their manner of dress, helped dispel wrong ideas about Christian women. It would have been an even more powerful testimony if the firm emphasis on women's submission could have been balanced by an equally strong emphasis on men's need to yield their power. As a consequence in its work among Muslims, where patriarchal structures are strongly ingrained, the church seems to have missed the opportunity to offer an alternative model for Muslim-background Christians to emulate.

In the name of, or perhaps under the pretext of, cultural sensitivity today, it fails to challenge the biblical exegesis, which gives women a second place in the life of the church and the family and which de-emphasizes the need for men to give up their cultural prerogatives. The church then, which is being born among Muslims, often reinforces the male domination of the culture rather than challenges it. One cannot but wonder if this might not be one of the explanations as to why women married to Muslim-background believers very seldom become Christian themselves.

In any case, the importance of women in Islamic societies should not be overlooked by the church. Today many of the Muslim women who emigrate to the west are becoming more educated and more knowledgeable in their faith. Faced with a loss of identity, they deepen their ties with Islam and for some, the experience is similar to an experience of conversion. One wonders if the church is ready to reach out to these women and converse with them—they represent a powerful group within Islam which can greatly influence the women and societies from which they come and to which they may eventually return.

There are also the women who live in Muslim countries and who need to be cared for. When a woman responds to the invitation of the gospel, she becomes very vulnerable. She is a "double minority" in greater danger, being both "woman and apostate." The church cannot ignore its responsibility to these women's particular needs. If Christianity is to make any headway into Muslim society, it needs to focus its attention on all of those women whose place in society can be prominent but also very difficult.

So after we have addressed some of the shortcomings of the Christian church toward women, the issue of whether or not the gospel is good news for Muslim women remains. In the end, the gospel must be judged by the same standards for men or women, Muslim or otherwise. The response to its message ultimately does not have anything to do with the rights or privileges offered by the church or the ummah. The issue is more basic. It is the answer to the question Jesus asked Peter, "And who do you say I am?"

Is Jesus the Perfect One and therefore the last Revelation of God? Is he our Qur'an, the holy book of God? Or is Muhammad the last of the prophets and the Qur'an he recited the truth about God? Whichever way a woman answers will determine the restrictions and risks to her life she is willing to take. Wearing the veil or not wearing jewelry, being vulnerable to divorce or being severely punished for becoming an "infidel." The good news of the gospel is not a question of rights and restrictions, but of truth.

To the question, "Why have you become a Christian?" a woman from a Muslim background once gave a simple and straightforward answer: "I became a Christian because I met Jesus Christ." Yet, the ordained minister that she has now become values her call to ordination—but as an unexpected gift, a latter discovery of the full equality which exists in Jesus—not the rationale which led her to conversion. Until a Muslim woman meets truth in the person of Jesus Christ, we can only walk her path with her, modeling compassion and love, as prayerful witnesses to the faith we hold dear. Is the gospel good news for a Muslim woman? She will be able to answer yes, but only when she discovers that Jesus is all he claims to be.

∾

Response: My Story
Yakuta Abdo

Every family is distinctive. Not all Christian families function in the same way, and neither are all Muslim families molded over one pattern. So it is impossible and not wise to make general statements. So I will not compare Muslim and Christian attitudes toward marriage and womanhood. However, I will tell my story.

As a teenager I did not welcome the thought of marriage. This was for two reasons. First, I resented deeply that my future Muslim husband could marry other women. Second, I feared divorce and abandonment. For me these were terrible possibilities, and yet I saw no way to avoid this kind of trap, for this was the common pattern of the marriage relationships in my community.

I observed that polygamous marriages were not bonded in love; there was no fellowship and heart-to-heart communication between a husband and wife when there were several wives. I yearned for a marriage bonded in loving commitment. In my dark fears I sometimes contemplated that I might be driven to kill my future husband if he would take another wife. I thought of the possibility of insisting that my future husband sign a contract that he would not marry another woman and that he would never abandon me. But I knew that the contract would be useless because such commitments were considered unrealistic ideals in the Muslim society that I lived in.

I did observe that in some professional urban Muslim families the husband married only one woman. The financial stresses of urban living and the demands for women's rights in modern society brought changes into Muslim family values and patterns that were positive. As a Muslim I hoped for a modern marriage.

However, some years later I met Christ. And the Lord led me to my future husband, Kelifa Ali, who was also a believer in Christ. I treasured the security of our marriage and home. I knew that Kelifa would never abandon me. I knew absolutely that I was his one wife as long as we both lived. In that security we enjoyed good and open fellowship. I loved my husband and he loved me.

Our family life was different than the home I grew up in. Kelifa loved and respected me as an equal. Yet the most significant difference was that Christ was at the center of our lives and home. Meeting Jesus Christ made all the difference.

SECTION TWO

Learnings and Vision

CHAPTER EIGHT

Afghanistan

Mennonite Brethren Missions and Service International

Herb Friesen

Located in what is known geographically as Central Asia, Afghanistan is sometimes referred to as the Crossroads of Conquerors. Alexander the Great, Genghis Khan, Tamerlane and Babur the Great, and others all left their mark, for good or ill, on this isolated mountain-desert former kingdom. The annals of history show a Christian presence in this part of the world even predating Islam. Nestorian and Armenian Orthodox churches had their day even as late as the end of the nineteenth century. We have personally visited the ancient, ornate grave of a Christian in the western city of Herat.

In the middle of the twentieth century a cadre of Christians appeared as engineers and English teachers, most notably Christy and Betty Wilson, who in 1952 held the first service of the Community Christian Church of Kabul. In 1958 the Ahlman (Christian) Academy was opened. In 1965 an eye camp conducted by Dr. Howard Harper signaled the beginning of the International Assistance Mission (IAM) in 1966, which to this day remains one of the oldest and most highly respected aid organizations in the country.

Mennonites Enter Afghanistan

Ruth and I were, as far as we know, the first Mennonites on the scene (1969) with the following workers coming in subsequent years: Carol Erb, Melva and Mabel Kaufman, Daryl and Doris Alwine, Bob and Janie Mullet, Rick Yoder, George Stoller, Richard and Ann Penner, Viktor and Veronika Thiessen, Steve and Sheryl Martin, Alvin and Gladys Geiser, and Clarence and Ferne Hiebert—a total of twenty-one plus children. MCC was involved from 1970-75, and again from 1995 until the present.

Our particular ministry related to specialized medical service for eyes. We developed the eye programs for Afghanistan and also touched communities in Pakistan. We served with Mennonite Brethren Missions and Service International (MBMSI) and IAM for twenty-eight years, and continue to make regular visits to Afghanistan as part of the medical program for eye care and healing. This form of ministry seemed to us to be an expression of the healing ministry of Jesus, who made the blind to see.

The work of IAM has expanded on many fronts, waxing and waning with the exigencies of war and terrorism. At present the major programs are functioning in Kabul, Mazar, and Herat, plus several smaller outposts. Among them: Noor Eye Project, Community Development, Agriculture, Language and Orientation, Mother and Child Health, Physiotherapy School, Renewable Energy Sources and Visual Impairment Services, plus a transit center and guest house in Peshawar, Pakistan.

What Have We Learned from Our Sojourn in Afghanistan?

1. We have learned that Islam is an all-encompassing religious, cultural, and political system affecting every area of life. We as Christians have much to learn from their God-consciousness, devotion, hospitality, modesty, self-discipline, and family values. In Mazar we used to see, regardless of the weather, about fifty pairs of sandals in front of a nearby mosque. Inside were as many boys, faithfully chanting and memorizing the Qur'an and its precepts. How "diligently" are we teaching our children today (Deut 6)?

2. We quickly learned that our western culture and ways of doing things were not always the best; we had so much to learn from them. In the matter of respect for elders and teachers—it was almost disconcerting when I entered the clinic or lecture room to see the doctors stand up. Their generosity—like the time we were invited for

a meal to a humble, squalid tent on the edge of the dry river bed, and having to eat outside on the rocks because the tent was too small. It was very likely they had borrowed money to "properly" entertain us. We made it a practice to take some fruit or candy, and often tried to slip some money to the host on such occasions. Time—we were sometimes gently chided that we were always rushing around and more concerned with projects than people. They always had time for a cup of tea.

3. We learned the power and acceptance of prayer and song. We were sometimes asked, "Do you pray?" Yes, we can pray anytime, not necessarily at prescribed times. We often prayed with and for the sick. Ruth especially prayed with the many widows who came to our door and the many depressed, who had suffered so much hardship as refugees. Although not a singing religion, Muslims very much enjoyed it when we sang, and we often taught them songs, either in their language or sometimes in English. How often their spirits were lifted as we sang.

Onward Vision for a Mennonite Presence in Afghanistan

It would seem that with a strong history of mission, and for many a more austere rural background and simple lifestyle, Mennonites should maintain their presence in the IAM, or similar ministries. As to how our Anabaptist heritage qualifies us more than others, it is difficult to say. However, our commitment to nonviolence was very different than the Afghan experience. A couple of the new converts upon reading the Sermon on the Mount were astonished by Christ's teaching on loving one's enemy. They exclaimed, "This is not what we have been taught; our way has been revenge." They came to convictions to embrace nonviolence through their own searching of the gospel.

Mennonite Mission Network

John F. Lapp

Historical Overview

Mennonite Mission Network—or Mennonite Board of Missions (MBM) prior to 2002—has been in Afghanistan since 1975. Our presence there has been in collaboration with an international consortium agency. We have contributed to the program of our partner agency in a variety of ways: in the placement of workers, in providing project funding, and in filling leadership positions at both administrative and board levels. Workers have served as maternal and child health advisors, mental health coordinators, logistics managers, guesthouse hosts, teachers, secretaries, engineers, and financial consultants and managers. In addition, we have supplied occasional short-term consultants in fields such as worker care, finance, and nutrition, as well as, a few short-term work teams.

Currently two families serve in Afghanistan under the Mission Network. Both live in Kabul. One worker is the finance director for the partner agency. His wife is involved primarily in building relationships with a network of individual women who come for counseling. Another worker is an elementary school teacher for the children of fellow international workers. Her husband serves as manager of a micro-hydroelectric program, harnessing the power potential of villages in the central region of the country.

What Are We Learning?

A mission associate in Afghanistan with our organization wrote in 1980, "In a year when I have seen my co-workers and friends suffer in many ways, I have become more and more convinced that only a change of heart—which is only possible in Christ—can provide any hope. We were reminded in our worship service a few weeks ago that the kingdom of God is here and we are part of it. By the witness of our lives we must stand as lights, revealing his kingdom to those with whom we come in contact. In some ways we experience difficulties, as working in these circumstances is a new experience for us as a team. It has caused me to stop and think about my commitment and how far I am prepared to go" (*MBM Annual Report*, 1980).

Perseverance and patience are the hallmarks of individuals and agencies called to work in Afghanistan. The vicissitudes of the political situation have discouraged and driven away innumerable mission and development agencies since the king was dethroned in 1973. There has been virtually no period lasting more than five years in the past three decades when the nation and its government were "stable." Our partner agency, however, has built an excellent reputation on two central realities: (1) it operates the nation's premier eye-health system, and (2) it has stayed in the country through thick and thin, aside from a few forced evacuations for short periods of time.

We have experienced Afghanistan both collectively as an agency and as individual workers. A significant corporate learning would certainly have to be the joys and sorrows of working cooperatively with a wide range of Christian bodies. As to be expected, differences have sometimes surfaced at the board level and within the worker team. Should workers, for example, put in eight-hour days as development professionals before taking time to build personal relationships? Or, should rare opportunities to share faith take priority over "professional" responsibilities? In terms of strategy, we have sometimes wondered whether we should focus on a few specialty areas, or take on broader responsibilities for social development in many fields.

Christian workers experience relationships with individual Afghans in a more limited range of settings than would be the case in a more tolerant society. Workers learn to appreciate and foster faith expressions in individual people they meet, though this is a constant challenge for Mennonites and others who stress the importance of individuals finding their place in the body of Christ, the community of faith.

Onward Vision

Afghanistan is certainly one of the most difficult countries in which to serve as representatives of the gospel. Not only are some Afghan Muslim religious figures openly and vigorously hostile to other religions, but the culture itself is so conservative and difficult to approach that there is very little practical chance to proactively offer a verbal witness to the good news. Most such opportunities need to be waited for with unending patience. When they do at last occur, they are fondly cherished, and great care is exerted to both respect and protect all individuals involved.

Afghanistan's spiritual and physical needs are of such great magnitude that they are almost unimaginable for most westerners. Mennonite Mission Network remains committed to a ministry of healing and hope in this battered land.

CHAPTER NINE

Turkey

Rosedale Mennonite Missions

Bob Stauffer

In the mid-1970s Rosedale Mennonite Missions (RMM) became more aware of the imbalance of workers among people who have never heard the gospel. There was a new sense in which God was asking Conservative Mennonite Conference (CMC) to prioritize sending workers among such peoples.

The absence of a Christian presence is notable in many eastern cities of Turkey. In some cases there may be a few Christians from Orthodox background, but these groups are quite small. In one city we visited recently, we found remnants of three Orthodox churches that are still functioning. Because they have so few members, they take turns meeting in each others' buildings so as to keep active in all three locations and thus avoid being taken over by the city. This city was once the headquarters for the Eastern Orthodox Church. Most of their buildings today serve as government offices. To our knowledge there are no evangelical believers meeting together in this city of over 250,000. The sobering fact is that almost all of the people living in such cities in southeastern Turkey have never heard the good news about salvation through Jesus. It is in these places that RMM believes God would have us to be a presence for him and a witness for his Son Jesus.

Since 1982 RMM has had workers in Turkey. These workers have for the most part focused on the southeastern part of the country and have been joined by several REACH (discipleship) teams over the past several years. Currently they are working with groups of Turkish believers in three cities. In addition, there are cell groups meeting in a couple of neighboring villages. Local leadership is being equipped to give leadership to these emerging bodies of Christ and to help them start churches in other cities and villages in the region.

We feel that our greatest contribution to what God wants to do in these places is to introduce people to a living Jesus. It is not Christianity as a religion that we promote, but rather we share Jesus as a living hope that can make a difference in one's everyday life. A Bible correspondence course has helped us identify individuals who have a hunger to get to know Jesus. And like Philip with the Ethiopian eunuch in Acts 8, we walk with them helping them understand the gospel and who Jesus is and what he can do for them. Through this, and by simply sharing Jesus with others, a network of family connections and people who express interest in Jesus grows and learns to follow the Good Shepherd.

Persistence is important. There have been times that we have felt like giving up, but God has enabled us to stay and keep on meeting, praying, and worshipping together. We have lost work permits, had workers sent out of the country, had police questionings, and had a meeting place shut down; but we are grateful that now in a couple cities there are places where we can invite individuals to pray and worship Jesus.

As we look to the future, we see these fellowships becoming reproducing churches. We envision that our role will change to more of an equipping role and to helping these precious followers of Jesus share their living faith with others. There are still many cities and villages in Turkey without known followers of Jesus meeting together. We are committed to doing what we can to see the worship of Jesus become a reality for people in these cities and villages as well!

CHAPTER TEN

India

Mennonite Brethren Missions and Service International

Gordon D. Nickel

When Mennonite Brethren missionaries began their work in Hyderabad, India, at the close of the nineteenth century, they found themselves in the midst of territory which had been conquered and dominated by Muslim kingdoms for more than 500 years. The land they purchased for their church, school, and residence was in Malakpet, a neighborhood heavily populated by Muslims. One of the first people in the city to respond to their witness was a Muslim. But when the missionaries wanted to baptize the new believer, local Muslims raised an outcry and also appealed to the Nizam, the rulers of the city. The Nizam then found a property of comparable value in a Hindu neighborhood of the city and relocated the missionaries there.

Missionaries at the time struggled with how to interpret their relocation. If you read the minutes of the missionary meetings, you find that the missionaries understood that God had closed a door to one community, and opened a door to another. And this set the trend for Mennonite Brethren work in India through the 1970s: the open door was to Hindus, actually mainly to low-caste Dalits. A focused witness among Muslims was not subsequently attempted, though the minutes of missionary meetings show that J. N. C. Hiebert repeatedly reminded the missionaries of their opportunity.

A couple of footnotes: when North Americans tell the story of the original witness, they usually mention a U.S. missionary named J. H. Pankratz. But when you interview Indian leaders, they mention a national evangelist named Levi. Levi's descendants and other Indian families had a desire to somehow continue Christian presence and witness in that neighborhood, and when in the wake of Partition a member of the royal family needed to sell the original property around 1950, they urged its purchase. An important Mennonite Brethren church called Bethlehem remains on the original property today, and a number of church families live in the vicinity.

During the seventy years of concentrated Mennonite Brethren mission work in India, missionaries served many Muslims at three mission hospitals and were highly appreciated. Muslims also wrote in to a radio program run by missionaries and national workers in the Telugu language. However, no special efforts were made to learn the language of the Muslims, Urdu, and to make a gospel witness among Muslims.

In more recent years, Mennonite Brethren Missions and Service International (MBMSI) sent Dan and Helen Nickel to work especially in the area of witness to Muslims. Dan and Helen had gained experience in Muslim ministry from working in Indonesia under the Muria Mennonite Church. Arriving in India in 1984, they located in the Malakpet area and began friendship evangelism in their neighborhood.

In addition, Dan taught courses on Muslim evangelism at the Mennonite Brethren Bible College in Shamshabad and began an Urdu Bible correspondence course with the help of a Muslim convert named John Mahboob. Indian church leader R. S. Lemuel supported the work of Dan and Helen from the India conference side. Unfortunately, due to health problems, Dan and Helen had to return to Canada by the end of 1985.

Again in 2000-03, MBMSI sent Gordon and Gwen Nickel to work together with the India Mennonite Brethren Conference in a partnership to encourage the churches and train Indian evangelists in ministry among Muslims. The project, called the Interfaith Ministry, was directed by Indian leader P. Menno Joel. Six evangelists formed an international team and worked together in door-to-door evangelism, leading Bible studies in Urdu, and creative programs for Muslims.

Evangelist Rebecca, daughter of John Mahboob, picked up the Bible correspondence ministry which her father had run before he died. The team cooperated with local Mennonite Brethren churches to challenge members to open their hearts to Muslims and to visit Muslim homes near the church.

The Interfaith Ministry continues today, with local evangelists working under the leadership of R. N. Peter, who has an MA in Islamic Studies from the Henry Martyn Institute.

CHAPTER ELEVEN

Indonesia

Javanese Mennonite Church (GITJ)

Lawrence M. Yoder

When Mennonite missionary, Pieter Jansz, in 1852 applied for a license to establish a school in Jepara, an ancient coastal town along the north coast of Central Java in the then Dutch East Indies, he was also issued a license to evangelize the Muslim population of the Jepara residency. He did not want to accept this license to evangelize because it implied that government also had the authority to revoke it and forbid him to evangelize, a proposition he rejected. Nevertheless, this incident serves to indicate that the primary focus of this first mission of Mennonites outside Europe and North America was to evangelize the large population of Muslim Javanese.

The town of Jepara was situated only about forty kilometers north of Demak, the center of the first Islamic Kingdom of Java founded some 400 years earlier. In fact, for many years Jepara was the seaport for the Islamic Kingdom of Demak. By this time in the mid-nineteenth century the vast majority of the Javanese people had converted to Islam, the process of conversion flourishing in reaction to repressive "Christian" Dutch colonial rule. Only in the highlands of Central and East Java did small pockets of Javanese continue with their Hindu-Buddhist religious practices.

Within forty kilometers of Jepara, high on the southern slope of

Mount Muria, the ancient volcano which dominates the region, are found burial shrines for three of Java's fabled Wali Songo (nine missionaries of Islam)—Sunan Kalijaja in Demak, Sunan Kudus in the city of Kudus, and Sunan Muria in Colo. These shrines serve as goals of religious pilgrimage for Indonesian Muslims who cannot afford the pilgrimage to Mecca.

Javanese Muslims have long been viewed in two groups, the *santri*, those who are schooled in Islam, and the *abangan*, those for whom Islamic practices are more intermingled with pre-Islamic beliefs, understandings, and practices (including elements of Buddhism, Hinduism, and the aboriginal religion of the Javanese). Muslims of Java to this day continue in varying degrees to carry the long-standing Javanese trait of being interested in whatever new spiritual insight or knowledge (*ngelmu*) one may encounter.

In its early stages this first Mennonite mission to Muslims bore fruit that was small in number. By the time of Jansz's retirement thirty years later only about 100 persons had been baptized. Jansz was well-known for being slow to baptize new believers until he was well-satisfied with their grasp of Christian faith.

A parallel effort to evangelize the Muslim population in the same area by indigenous evangelist Kyai Ibrahim Tunggul Wulung (d. 1885) bore far more fruit in the same period of time. He succeeded in gathering more than 1,000 believers into three Christian villages during this period. Tunggul Wulung's primary evangelism strategy through the mid-1880s was to travel hundreds of kilometers the length and breadth of Java sharing his new Christian faith (*ngelmu*) wherever he could get a hearing. He would then gather interested persons and families into new villages, which he founded in relatively remote locations in the larger Jepara area around the Mount Muria.

The remoteness of the location of Tunggul Wulung's Christian villages was to insulate them from the corrupting influences of the Dutch colonial system of forced cultivation of plantation crops, from opium trade, and from the stronger Islamic communities closer to the larger towns. Tunggul Wulung also related liberating Christian faith to an indigenous eschatological vision based on the prophecy of ancient Javanese King Jojoboyo, that in the latter days a "Just Prince" would appear and set straight matters of religion on Java. To Tunggul Wulung the values and spirituality of Christianity were much more akin to the deeper, ancient values and spirituality of the Javanese people than Islam was, in spite of the identification of Christianity with the harsh realities of a long and exploitative colonial rule. For Tunggul Wulung himself, receiving the Bible's Ten Words (or Commandments), beginning with, "I am the Lord your God who brought you out of Egypt where you were slaves, worship no god but me," while he was yet a hermit mystic meditating on the slopes of Mount Kelud, was a profoundly hopeful and liberating message.

Upon Tunggul Wulung's death in 1885, the second generation of Mennonite missionaries succeeded in attracting the majority of Tunggul Wulung's followers into the circle of Mennonite mission churches. The missionaries launched a plan to form a series of Christian agricultural communities partially inspired by Tunggul Wulung's own vision of Christian villages to which new believers would be gathered. A part of the strategy of forming Christian agricultural communities was to provide an environment where new believers and seekers would be more protected from the sometimes harsh reactions of Muslim populations in more established communities and towns.

By the time the Javanese Mennonite Synod was organized under national leadership in 1940, the baptized membership had reached some 5,000 in about seven organized congregations and a number of branches. Virtually all of these believers were either converts from Islam or offspring of such converts. The decade of the 1940s with its occupation by the Imperial Army of Japan and Indonesia's struggle for liberation from Dutch colonial rule after World War II, wreaked havoc in the newly organized Javanese Mennonite Synod, such that membership was reduced to less than half its prewar number.

The most severe hardship was an uprising of radical Muslims based in the area, who in 1942 took advantage of the power vacuum created by the withdrawal of Dutch colonial government functionaries to avoid engagement with invading Japanese forces. The redirection of the Japanese forces in another direction created a vacuum of governmental authority in the Muria area, thus providing the opportunity for radical Muslims to act. The uprising brought with it the physical destruction of the Tayu Christian Hospital, a number of church buildings, including the largest one in Margorejo, the capture and abuse of a number of the church's key leaders, and the slaughter of a Dutch missionary.

Regrouping in the early fifties in newly independent Indonesia under a new generation of Javanese leadership, the church began to grow more rapidly than it had ever grown before. Dozens of new groups of believers sprang up in many locations and eventually became congregations. The old mission focus on creating relatively isolated Christian communities largely dissipated, and was replaced by a residential pattern where Muslims and Christians are much more likely to live next to each other in the same communities. Again, virtually all of the growth of the Javanese Mennonite Christian community was from the Islamic community. Today, more than fifty years later, there are ninety-six congregations with around 40,000 members. When Mesach Krisetya and I were teaching in Wiyata Wacana Theological College twenty-five years ago, where most of the students were training for leadership in the Javanese Mennonite Church, approximately half of the students had grown up in Muslim homes. For some of them, becoming Christian meant being disowned and rejected by their families.

Dynamics of Christian Witness Among Javanese Muslims

What are the dynamics contributing to the growth of these churches in this predominately Islamic environment? A major dynamic is the degree of social and cultural solidarity between Christians and Muslim Javanese. Javanese culture and identity represents a fairly strong point of connection and communication between Javanese people who are Muslims and Javanese people who are Christians. Becoming Christians in the Javanese Mennonite Church does not remove people from social, cultural, and political contact with the larger Javanese Muslim community.

A second dynamic is the long-standing interest of Javanese people in new spiritual insight and knowledge. This means that it is often not difficult to carry on a conversation with Javanese people on religious subjects regardless what religion a person might be identified with. And if one offers substantial and authentic evidence of what one is presenting, Javanese people will be impressed and consider it very seriously. In fact, traditionally speaking, if one is unable to withstand the strength and truth of a person's presentation, she is expected to concede and follow the lead of her interlocutor. This dynamic functions less well among Christians and Muslims, because for both Muslims and Christians a greater emphasis is placed on truth and sources beyond a person's individual command.

Along this same line, Javanese people highly value open and gracious social relationships, so that in the context of personal encounter, people will try hard to avoid offending each other in conversation. Because of this, vigorous debate or confrontation between Christians and Muslims is fairly uncommon. The story goes that if you ask a Javanese Muslim whether he has become a Christian yet, he is likely to answer, "Not yet," even though he has no intention to change religions. He does not want to offend or oppose his interlocutor.

A third dynamic is the awareness many Muslims and Christians have of some special relationship between Christianity and Islam—in contrast to Buddhism or Hinduism, not to mention traditional animistic beliefs. Indonesian Christians use the Arabic word, Allah for *theos* or *elohim* just like Muslims do. All Indonesian Christians worship Allah, not Gott, God, or some other foreign deity. Muslims are in some measure aware that the 'Isa al-Masih, whom most of them know they will meet as judge at the end of the age, is the Yesus Messias (Jesus Messiah) whom their Christian neighbors focus their attention on so strongly. It is not unusual for conversations between Christians and Muslims on religious topics to include references to 'Isa al-Masih.

One Javanese Mennonite pastor frequently invites Muslims to consider what they know about the judge they will face at the end of the age. The Qur'an and Islamic tradition provide minimal detail about 'Isa, Jesus. This minister invites his Muslim conversation partners to just take a look at all the teachings of 'Isa in the Injil (Gospels) of his Al-Kitab (Bible), and all the accounts of 'Isa's life and ministry to be found there. He avoids debate about the authority of the Injil found in the Al-Kitab or whether Isa died or was raised from death. What he finds is that Muslims are often attracted to the mass of material on the life, ministry, and teaching of Jesus, particularly the accounts of his healing and deliverance ministry, such that their regard for the Injil found in his Al-Kitab grows without focusing on the relative merits of the Bible and the Qur'an in a theoretical way.

In fact these very gospel materials provide a sort of "thick description" of the person of Jesus that often attracts Muslims. Sometimes it is the personal moral or ethical vision that one encounters in these accounts of 'Isa that impresses them. Other times it is the remarkable and amazing demonstrations of the wisdom and the power at work in and through 'Isa as depicted in the Injil. Just this week a person who has spent some months in Central Java told me of a young person who was suffering from a certain ailment and was under the care of a physician who also happened to be a Muslim. The illness was serious and medical intervention was of limited effectiveness. Finally the Muslim physician said, "What he needs is a touch from Yesus."

It appears that among some Muslims there is an awareness of power for healing through 'Isa al-Masih through the ministry of Christian believers. It is not unusual that prayer for healing by Christians for Muslims has been an important factor in Muslims coming to claim Jesus as Savior and Lord. I have a very distinct memory of sending students for practical work assignments after one year of study back in the seventies. One student—I think it was Sapinardi—was placed in a new branch congregation on the slope of Mt. Merbabu outside Salatiga. Not long after he was placed there, a delegation of Muslims from a neighboring village came asking the new *pandito* to come and pray for the healing of their father.

This young student felt completely inadequate to do what he was asked. He had never done anything of the sort before, though prayer for healing was a common practice in his church. It soon became clear that he needed to go with them. He went and prayed a prayer for the healing of the old man in the name of Yesus Kristus—that is how Indonesian Christians usually refer to 'Isa al-Masih, Jesus Christ. Remarkably the old man rapidly recovered from the ailment that had so recently threatened his life. Soon, youthful Sapinardi was asked to come to this village and lead a Bible study, which eventually resulted in the conversion of a number of people there and the development of a new group of worshipping believers in Jesus.

One of the more remarkable dramas that has occurred among Christians and Muslims in Indonesia took place in the months following the failed Communist coup in 1965 and 1966. There arose a very powerful and violent action by radical Muslims and the military against suspected Communist Party members and sympathizers in which ultimately more than a half million people lost their lives. Another half million were imprisoned incommunicado without due process.

In this context Christians from the Javanese Mennonite Church and others responded with love and care for suffering people, particularly families of those who were accused of being Communists and had been killed or imprisoned. This was a very dangerous thing to do. Church leaders could not sleep in the same house two nights in a row for a period of time, since they were accused of being communist sympathizers and their names were placed on death squad lists. It appears that tens of thousands of nominal Muslims looked at the actions of radical Muslims in this context, on the one hand, and the actions of Christians to aid the families of missing persons, on the other, and concluded that they would rather identify with Christians than the radical Muslims.

Another motivating factor for them was that in this period there was pressure for people to be religious, since non-religious people were in danger of being accused of being atheist Communists. For a period of time churches were overwhelmed with erstwhile nominal Muslims seeking to find their way into Christian churches. Some became committed believers. Christians who did not have an Anabaptist, pacifist background functioned in similar ways in this period and context. This is a powerful witness to the gospel of love, grace, and peace.

My final comment is to say that people in the Javanese Mennonite Church appear to be more forthright these days about relating to Muslims, particularly in ways that are intended to defuse misunderstandings between Christians and Muslims. In this sense there appears to be a movement beyond an earlier tendency of Christians to isolate and withdraw in some measure of fear. Their challenge is to give witness to whom Jesus is, and to live that belief in the larger circle of their lives in community and society, saying clearly to Muslims in every way, "This is our land as well as yours. We believe that we can learn to live together without hedging the religious obligations we both have to share our faith with others— you Muslims to us, and we Christians to you—without regarding each other as enemies." Javanese Christians and Muslims have resources to help Christians and Muslims elsewhere to overcome their enmity.

Gereja-Gereja Kristen Muria Indonesia (GKMI)

Mesach Krisetya

The GKMI, for a long time known as the Chinese Mennonite Church in Indonesia, began its mission in 1920 during the latter part of 350 years of Dutch occupation. Being of Chinese descent, they were an exclusive-minority-second class citizens of the land, but had several "privileges" from the Dutch colonial power. They had the privilege to collect tax from the "indigenous people" for the colonial power, the monopoly of opium, and being second-class citizens after the Dutch, who were the first. They lived in towns and cities, because their main work was that of trade and commerce. These privileges made them prosperous and wealthy, but at the same time they were hated by the people of the land (indigenous people), who were mostly Muslims.

When the Chinese converted to Christianity, they still inherited the feeling of insecurity and fear of Islam. Furthermore, Islam and Christianity in Indonesia have for many years, been adversaries. This was caused in part by their ignorance of each other, as it was mentioned before that the Dutch colonial policy intentionally kept the two faith communities separate; they didn't really know each other. Due to the largely negative experience of the two faith communities in the Middle East and Europe, which was carried to Indonesia by the Muslims and Christians who came, the Muslim and Christian communities that grew in the archipelago inherited attitudes of antagonism, mistrust, and fear toward one another.

Moreover, the greatest problem facing the Christian community in Indonesia is the impression that Christianity is a foreign element in Indonesian society. Unlike Islam, Christianity was introduced and is perceived to have grown under the umbrella of colonial power (*Agamane wong Londo*). The Muslim rulers in the colonial times did not welcome the coming of Christianity, in the first place.

With that kind of background, the following phenomena commonly happens every decade in Indonesia. Recently, to be exact as early as 1996, Christian people in Indonesia have been confronted by a series of shocking incidents, namely the attacking and destroying of church buildings and properties by some groups of Muslim people.

Besides all of that, they also are attempting to limit Christians' movement and activities; they also instigate, intimidate, and discriminate against minority groups as an effort to diminish them from full participation in the Indonesian society, especially the Christian, Chinese, and the conglomerate. Christians have been cornered and have been accused as betraying the country and the nation. The Christians have been accused of not making any contribution in the fight for independence.

Christians are sometimes mocked as being the followers of the colonial and heathen religion. These instigations have been proclaimed all over the place, in Muslim boarding schools and even in Muslim homes and families. This in turn creates hateful feelings on the part of the Muslim people toward Christians and other minority groups. When the bureaucrats seem to be supporting this idea of segregation, the result is a stronger conflict between Muslims and the other minority groups. How do we then do our outreach in this kind of a situation?

GKMI has a mission board called PIPKA. This mission board is working through cultural outreach. Most of the workers and evangelists are of Javanese, Bataks, and other ethnic groups; almost none are ethnic Chinese. All of the evangelists know the culture of the place where they are sent to.

Therefore, in spite of the social conditions that I wrote about above, the outreach is still going on. God sends us to make disciples. Pray for us in Indonesia, so that God will give us strength and courage amidst the difficulties in our society.

CHAPTER TWELVE

Iran

The Editors

One dimension of Mennonite involvement with Iran is a theological dialogical exchange. The fall 2003 issue of the *Conrad Grebel Review* describes the first dialogue that convened in Toronto, in October 2002. The second dialogue convened in Qom in February 2004. For more information abut this development in Muslim-Anabaptist dialogue, see the joint press release written by A. James Reimer, appendix F.

CHAPTER THIRTEEN

The Middle East

Mennonite Mission Network

John F. Lapp

Historical Overview

Mennonite Mission Network and its predecessor agencies have been involved in the Middle East since the early 1950s. Initial vision included ministry within Jewish society, and particularly support for the germinal Messianic Jewish movement. While that involvement continues into the present, workers also regularly related to various aspects of Muslim society at different times and places.

The longest such relationships were in Nazareth. Mennonite workers held medical, administrative, maintenance, and pastoral positions at Nazareth Hospital (a project of Edinburgh Medical Missionary Society), beginning in 1965 and continuing off-and-on through the present.

The hospital's ministry of healing and compassion for all people, both Arab and Jew, is dramatically portrayed in the 1994 video production "Brother, Brother," which recounts the true story of an Israeli Jewish soldier who was treated there after being stabbed in downtown Nazareth. While making the video, producer Mike Hostetler and his wife, Virginia, became captivated by a vision to create Nazareth Village—a reconstructed first-century village to be located on the land where Jesus matured from childhood into manhood.

Within a few years, the Hostetlers' dream became a reality. The purpose of Nazareth Village today is to introduce the life and words of Jesus to all its visitors. Included here are a large number of Arab Muslim schoolchildren. Most of these have been brought up knowing Jesus only through reference to 'Isa in the Qur'an or through non-religious relationships with Palestinian Christians. The contact at Nazareth Village, however, now offers the remarkable opportunity for these children to experience the uniqueness of the biblical Jesus, portrayed in an appealing and educational way.

Workers with the Mission Network and its predecessor agencies have also served in several other Middle Eastern countries as Mission Associates or as long-term supported workers. One couple is currently working in media production. Another spent several years serving Muslim children at the "Mennonite School" in Hebron.

What Are We Learning?

The founding mandate for the Israel program was encapsulated in the words of J. D. Graber, president of Mennonite Board of Missions (MBM), when he wrote, "We feel it important to seek, pray, and be there as a reconciling presence and witness, amidst the strife and alienation, with our reconciling message."[1] Simple as the words may seem, this mandate has always been a challenge to implement. Workers have over the past fifty years been forced to test a wide range of missiological approaches.

LeRoy Friesen, in his study of *Mennonite Witness in the Middle East* refers to this as "theology on the road."[2] Some of the flexibility required at certain moments was for very practical reasons, to find acceptable means of obtaining visas or other forms of permission. But just as Nazareth Village is rediscovering the innovative character of Jesus's parables, so we too must be ready to make use of innovative techniques in witnessing to the good news of God's kingdom in our time and place.

The reconciling message of the cross—even for those who think of themselves as "experts" in pacifism—is something more than a mere uni-directional activity. We as Mennonites engaged in a variety of ministries continue to learn and grow at least as much as the people with whom we build relationships.

Reconciliation must happen between us and our God, as well as between us and other fellow believers. That has meant for us a commitment to serving and working closely with the already existing churches throughout the region. Our special interest as Mennonite Christians has, not surprisingly, focused particular attention on ministries of dispute resolution in areas of interreligious and political conflict. Even if we believe that reconciliation is God's ultimate goal, we also hold that social justice is an important first step in that direction.

Such fundamental commitments have meant that Mennonite workers did not explicitly seek to found churches in the Middle East carrying the Mennonite name. J. D. Graber stated in 1965 that "building a church and establishing congregations are not considered possible objectives."[3] This decision, though challenged many times over the years, has remained a basic understanding of workers and agency policy up until the present day.

Nurturing a long-term vision of this nature has meant learning another significant lesson, that of patience. We are never finished needing to learn and relearn this virtue, especially we as western Christians who have come to expect speedy results for our efforts. A presence ministry that shows God's love in our words and lives with people seeking healing for the body, soul, and environment is a calling that need neither be measured nor lived out in traditional ways. "Creating opportunities for witness will come along the path of service performed in the manner and spirit of the Master Servant . . . and it must be service given without condition," said MBM administrator, Wilbert Shenk in 1969.[4]

Onward Vision

Mennonites have something unique to contribute to the Middle East environment where civilizations are in constant clash. As Robert Rhodes put it in the October 19, 2003, issue of the *Mennonite Weekly Review*, "The only way to true peace is the true and undistorted gospel, and the peacemakers among us must bring it."[5]

The gospel of God's love is for all people, and missional Mennonite Christians must be there, involved and participating wherever God's ministry is happening at any given moment. Just as God is already present in each Middle Eastern society, so, too, should Mennonites be present in each as well, all the while challenging each to higher levels of performance and accountability. Just as God's mission is holistic, affecting the heart, soul, and body of individuals and communities, so we, too, as ambassadors of Christ, should pursue holistic ministries with emphasis on both social and spiritual dimensions of the human reality.

As described above, Mennonite workers have served in widely diverse communities, among Messianic Jews, Orthodox Jews, Arab Muslims, and Arab Christians. A unified overall vision for "team ministry" has not been easy to craft. In 1998, workers agreed on three foci:

- •to help all people have a new/other view of Jesus;
- •to nurture the kingdom of God in its local expressions/ congregations;
- •to share Anabaptist perspectives on justice/ethics for all the children of Abraham.

These three points emphasize that only God can ultimately conclude God's work. Disciples do help, however, to incarnate God's love, setting the stage in individual hearts and the larger society for God's Spirit to move.

Returning in 2002 to this goal-setting process with a group that included new workers, administrators, and some Mennonite friends, the current Mission Network team working to carry out local ministries has boiled down their vision to this single affirmation: "[We as] Mennonite Associates are committed to being agents and models of reconciliation within the region."

We have learned much in this first fifty years of ministry in the Middle East, but we still come back to this essential goal of our Christian ministry: to proclaim and participate in God's mission, the *missio Dei*—the "already" and "not yet" of human-to-human and human-to-God reconciliation!

CHAPTER FOURTEEN

North Africa and the Middle East

Eastern Mennonite Missions

Jewel Showalter

An Overview

Jordan: One couple works with a Baptist church outside Amman. This church has a vision to open a small clinic and offer English classes to serve the community. They are involved in leadership training of Arab Christians, and have a vision for church formation in neighboring communities that have no Christian witness. One single woman spent two years studying Arabic and relating to women in Amman. She is taking time to listen to and write up the stories of Iraqi refugee women who work with Karis Krafts, an income-generation project.

Eastern Mennonite Missions (EMM), and Meserete Kristos Church (MKC) of Ethiopia, have begun to partner with an Eritrean-Ethiopian man who heads up a network of African immigrant fellowships in the Middle East. He helps to lead African congregations in Amman and Dubai, and has also been helping with church development and leadership training in Iraq.

Egypt: One family has helped teach both Catholic and Protestant church workers from all over the world who come to Egypt for training in Arabic and Islamic studies at Dar Comboni for Arabic Studies, a Catholic institution. They taught on the Christian experience in the Islamic world and looked at history, theology, spirituality, and law in Islam. The man served as the assistant supervisor of Islamic studies at Dar Comboni, and taught at the Coptic Evangelical Theological Seminary. The woman taught religion in the German school their children attend. Both have completed advanced degrees in Islamics and are involved in various teaching and dialogue situations outside Egypt. (In 2004 this family transferred to Beirut for an assignment at Near East School of Theology. EMM continues as a partner, but with Network carrying primary responsibility.)

Israel: One young couple is studying Hebrew and works with the Bible Society. They are involved with Messianic believers and in outreach to Jews and Arabs. EMM also contributes to the financial support of Network workers in the country.

Morocco: One young woman is studying language in preparation for working at a center for handicapped children. She is part of a team working among the indigenous people of Morocco in one of the least-reached regions. EMM also facilitated the visit of Mennonite leaders from Chile and Honduras who have interest in work in North Africa.

Discipleship Ministries Involvement in the Middle East

The past two years there have been Youth Evangelism Service (YES) teams serving in north Galilee. These teams also took service and learning trips into Lebanon, Cyprus, and Turkey as part of their training and exposure to the region.

The last two years EMM has had three YES teams working in Spain and France among North African immigrants. These teams have also worked with port ministries that distribute Christian literature to North Africans. The teams have taken learning and exposure trips into Morocco and Tunisia.

As part of the new GO! program that facilitates short-term prayer and exposure assignments for up to a year in length, EMM has facilitated three short-term GO! teams to Morocco. GO! has also placed two young women for nine-month assignments in Israel and Morocco.

From 1995-99 EMM had four YES teams serving in the West Bank at the Bethlehem Bible College. In 1996 a team served in Jordan. In 2000 a team served in Turkey in earthquake relief and rebuilding.

Learnings and Vision

In our sojourn in the Middle East we have learned that it takes long-term commitment to language and culture learning, creative ways of "tentmaking" to maintain a long-term Christian presence, and unusual sensitivity and openness to the work of the Holy Spirit in connecting Christian witnesses with God-fearing Muslim seekers who are hungry to know the Word made flesh.

EMM's most fundamental commitment is to share the gospel of Jesus Christ in places of spiritual darkness, especially where the church is weak or nonexistent. To this end we aim to continue placing teams of North Americans in long-term "tentmaking" roles throughout the Middle East, to send complimentary short-term teams for prayer, service, and learning, to partner with African immigrant groups in the region for their training and encouragement in a common mission, and to facilitate the training and placement of missionaries from partner conferences in the International Missions Association (eight mission groups from Asia, Africa, Latin America, and North America) in order to see the strengthening and encouragement of resident Christian communities in the Middle East and the beginning of new fellowships of Muslim background believers.

CHAPTER FIFTEEN

Albania and Kosovo

Virginia Mennonite Board of Missions
Eastern Mennonite Missions

Tom Yoder

Whereas four Mennonite/Anabaptist mission-service agencies are engaged in the Albania-Kosovo region, this report will mainly attempt to address the journey and discoveries of two of these, namely Virginia Mennonite Board of Missions (VMBM) and Eastern Mennonite Missions (EMM). However, we also recognize the significant contribution of Mennonite Central Committee and Cornerstone Church and Ministries. All four of these agencies have cooperated together in the ministries in this region. Throughout the 1990s these agencies and their constituent churches have worked cooperatively among a wide variety of Albanian peoples, a portion of which claim Islam as their religion. This report focuses especially on what our VMBM-EMM team has learned, as well as gleanings from other evangelicals with whom we've enjoyed precious fellowship and counsel.

Background

The present Albanian cultures were shaped by a fascinating variety of influences, many of which, as they are aware, were to a degree forced upon them. From their likely ancestors, the Illyrian tribes, Albanians retain remnants of pagan, animistic roots, as well as a tradition of communal life organized around loyalty to familial clans. From earliest collective memory the concept of blood relationships has stirred deep passions and loyalty.

Islam first came to the southern Albanian area in the Bektashi Sufi form, ironically as a variant form of Orthodoxy. This syncretistic sect remains a major factor in central and southern Albania, as well as western Macedonia. In fact, Tirana, Albania, is the official world center of Bektashiism. Most predominant in the 400-year Ottoman rule of the Balkans, however, was Sunni Islam. The Albanians, who had been basically divided between Catholics in the north and Orthodox in the south, nominally converted to Islam for political and financial benefit. Under the Ottoman millet system, the Empire divided its population not along ethno-linguistic lines, but by religious affiliation. The result was an entwining of national and religious identities in the Balkans, which produced a modern legacy of a confusion of concepts of citizenship, religion, and ethnicity.

The Albanians' conversion to Islam and frequent mingling of Christian rites, points to a tolerant, pragmatic attitude toward religion still quite evident today. Thus, while the evangelical Christian community constitutes a tiny religious minority in Albania (approximately 10,000 active believers), it has by far the most consistently, day-by-day practicing members.

Mission History and Program

Anabaptist missionaries entered Albania in 1991, participating in evangelistic efforts in Tirana and Lezhe at the peak of the nation's economic collapse and political revolution. Within two years, leaders of three organizations: EMM, VMBM, and Cornerstone Church and Ministries formed a working partnership to coordinate their efforts and to interact with the many other evangelical agencies working cooperatively in Albania. Each partner shared a commitment to make disciples and form small groups and congregations of believers. Contextually, this often seemed like yet another religion trying to compete with the three historical and governmentally recognized religions. The missionaries resolved, however, to share the life and truth of the living Christ, and to cultivate the fellowship of his body. To this end, three church planting teams of four to six adults settled in different regions of Albania. Three small congregations have emerged in two of those locations, all yet under missionary leadership, with Albanians engaged in all areas of church life and ministry. Social and economic chaos, as well as the transitory nature of relationships and commitments in the nation undergoing such traumatic transition, have challenged these efforts.

From the beginning the witness to God's love also found expression through a variety of service and development projects, involving both the long-term workers as well as dozens of short-term teams representing the partner organizations. Albania's staggering unemployment, decaying infrastructure, backward medical services, and general sense of hopelessness begged a response. Extended efforts have included agricultural microcredit and development, English language and computer skills courses, and physician services. Empowering local Albanians, while avoiding favoritism and dependency, stretched missionary faith and creativity, and provided natural opportunities to model and disciple.

The Mennonite fellowships and missionaries plunged unanimously into the service mode for several months in 1999 when ethnic Albanian refugees from the war in neighboring Kosovo province flooded the country. These "Kosovars" held staunchly to a Muslim identity, and speak a quite different dialect than most Albanians, some enclaves still speaking Turkish from the Ottoman era. The needs and the openness of these profoundly wounded families impacted the entire evangelical community so much that many, including the Mennonite missionary team, launched efforts to contact Kosovar friends after their return from exile to continue witness and blessing. This has led to Mennonite funding of several reconstruction projects, and the recent placement of long-term workers in Kosovo.

Learning and Vision

We have learned that cultivating authentic Christian community among persons steeped in wounding, distrust, and unforgiveness is not only difficult, it's humanly impossible. All of our attitudes, relationships, and ministries must be conceived, birthed, and developed through prayer that releases heaven's resources.

As we listen to hear their hearts, we must enter into the lament of the aching heart of the Father God who has known and suffered with every injustice, every atrocity, every point of brokenness, and whose unending, loving kindness wills exactly the reverse of every curse unleashed upon his precious children. We give voice to the lament of these who, by no means innocent victims, need intercessors to bring their complaint, their anguish before the throne of grace on their behalf, lamenting with and for them all that has been, is yet lost or pain-filled, and seems to promise only despair for the future. Until we grieve with them and for them, we've no right to attempt to persuade them.

Further, we must intelligently and passionately engage the spiritual forces of darkness that have bound individuals, towns, and nations, and veiled their understanding of the revelation of the glory of God in Christ Jesus. Historical wounds of abused authority, bloodshed, falsehood embraced as truth, and iniquity that has opened doors for evil to enter and become entrenched in the land and in the minds of the people of the land—these must be confronted in concerted prayer that their transmission from generation to generation be cut off. Heaven must be implored, "God, please show us the keys!" for individuals, families, and communities. Only then will community transformation be released.

The Albanian Muslims also need Christ's servants to ask God on their behalf for unique and powerful revelations of the living Jesus and his love for them. Such divine encounters are known to often cut through layers of confusion and spiritual slumber, awakening an appetite and receptivity for the truth of Jesus. Perhaps we've not seen much hunger for God among Albanians because we've not asked more for such miracles.

A few particular elements of leadership development have emerged as critically important. First, we recognize that the Balkan peoples are born and raised in an atmosphere of strife and division. Their instincts and formation are bent toward distrust, and especially in Kosovo, toward hatred and vengeance. Just as Paul strove to help the Corinthians and Cretans (Titus) to wrestle with issues arising from weaknesses in their surrounding cultures, so we must address the Balkan spirit of division as we develop leaders. They need to learn from our example and from the scriptures how to handle gossip and slander, how to receive rebuke, and how to resolve conflict.

Secondly, in societies where positions of authority mean personal enrichment, combined with a tradition of tapping into sources of funds from abroad, we must keep our leadership and multiplication anchored on the eternal, and on heart issues. Emerging leaders ought to be learning to appreciate walking in honest accountability. They should be growing in worship, character (i.e., embodying the two great love commandments of scripture), and in applied love, which is tested and refined in the context of close relationships. Such relationships, we've found, take much time. However, delegating authority prematurely (or not delegating at all), and relying on a person's displayed abilities or ambition will bear unpleasant fruit down the road. In Albania and Kosovo, where few church members are even employed (not to speak of giving faithfully to the church), the trend has been to drift toward the "position equals vocation" view of leadership. This seems to have caused many believers to miss their unique yet common calling to walk with Jesus in full-time relationship ministry.

Finally, we've found that walking with Albanians and Kosovars in friendship tends to flow better and go deeper if we have roles in the community that locals understand. Suspicion and misunderstanding have often followed foreign missionaries for whom folks have no categories other than CIA agent, or rich American. Service roles have not only fostered better understanding of our workers, but genuine appreciation for their empowering of persons to earn a living or educate their children. This opens doors for the gospel message.

CHAPTER SIXTEEN

Central Asia

Eastern Mennonite Missions

Jane Hooley

With the breakup of the Soviet Union in 1991, Central Asian republics came into being. Opportunities for mission began to emerge. In 1998 the hearts of several young people were stirred as they began to pray, learn, and travel in Central Asia to discover what ministry opportunities were available.

Since 1999 several short-term (six month) YES teams from Eastern Mennonite Missions (EMM) served in Central Asia. These young people have had an impact in the communities where they served as they taught English classes, built relationships, worked with other young people, and lived with families. Meanwhile, EMM's relationships have grown and vision for longer-term ministry has continued to develop. Places to work have been identified.

In the last half of 2001, David Shenk, who is Global Consultant for EMM, traveled with his wife, Grace, in Eastern Europe and Central Asia, representing Lithuania Christian College and Eastern Mennonite Missions. David was an encourager and resource for many mission workers, promoted Lithuania Christian College, and provided counsel to Eastern Mennonite Missions.

As members of the Global Discipleship Training Alliance, the YES program has partnered with a group of Central Asian congregations to launch a discipleship training and mission program.

EMM short- and long-term representatives have made several trips and built relationships across the region. As they traveled and prayed, they sensed the time had come to place longer-term workers and that collaborative partnerships with congregations and other organizations would be needed.

In God's timing, a couple who had a heart for the people became available, a partnership of congregations developed, and an organization with which to work was identified. In January 2001 EMM approved entering Central Asia. An administrator recommended: "That EMM enter Central Asia in a ministry . . . to the whole person, soul, and spirit with personnel and eventual program commitments."

In January 2002 one couple began language study and joined a registered NGO doing development. Additionally, after the Afghan war supporting congregations provided funds to rebuild several elementary schools.

What Is the EMM Vision?

1. Continue to move in the direction the Lord leads as those with a call to the region become available.

2. Continue to build relationships throughout the region.

3. Consider long-term ministry when appropriate in other locations.

CHAPTER SEVENTEEN

Canada

Mennonite Church of Eastern Canada

Mary Mae Schwartzentruber

Introduction:

Mennonite Church of Eastern Canada (MCEC) and its Mission and Service Commission have not articulated a philosophy of relationships with our Muslim neighbors. Rather, we have responded to the gift and the challenges of welcoming them, newcomers to Canada, as described in the reports below.

Post-September 11 has brought new awareness and opportunities to Mennonite congregations in Eastern Canada. It has been reported that Muslims in the Waterloo, Ontario, region seem to feel a certain safety and protection through having a Mennonite constituency as "neighbor," especially in the heightened fears after the tragedies in the U.S. Mennonite leaders in social service agencies have contributed in creating this atmosphere over the years. In addition, several MCEC congregations and pastors have had contact with a group of Iranian Muslim clerics visiting Canada, but that story can be told better by Mennonite Central Committee people who have been more directly involved (see appendix F).

What is our vision? What is our future direction? Since we cannot provide many details in these areas as yet—except for what we have tried to do in extending hospitality—we offer therefore the following stories.

Doug Amstutz, Pastor of Grace Mennonite Church in St. Catharines

Following the events of September 11, the local mosque in St. Catharines was firebombed and a number of churches offered responses by way of flowers or encouragement cards. I asked our Mennonite churches to provide such a response and appreciated the few that joined us in this endeavor.

At the end of an open house at the mosque, I met Murtaza, a well-educated Muslim man, whom I asked to be a resource person for a "Study in Islam" that I was planning for Grace Mennonite Church. With Murtaza's help, the course went well. Murtaza and his wife guided the church on a visit to the Al-Noor mosque.

After we had finished the study, Murtaza and I met to plan a seminar (that, unfortunately, never materialized) and then decided to continue meeting on a regular basis. Our families have gone out together and hosted each other in our homes. Recently, Murtaza has shown interest in the Bible and so we plan to study the Bible together. He gave me a wonderful book entitled, *The Muslim Jesus*, which explains how Muslims have viewed Jesus for the past fourteen centuries. While Murtaza and I have had our own moments of tension in trying to understand each other's religious praxis, particularly in its sociopolitical application, we have affirmed out loud our desire to continue to walk together.

Gord Alton, Pastor of Community Mennonite Church in Stouffville

Following the tragedy of September 11, Community Mennonite Church initiated a relationship with the Islamic Society of York Region. I met with their imam, Zafar Bangash, and this led to reciprocal speaking appointments—I spoke at the mosque and Zafar at Community Mennonite.

The relationship between our two communities continued with exchanges of gifts, books, and videos, and times of fellowship and religious dialogue. The Mennonites were treated to an awesome meal prepared by the Islamic community at the mosque followed by speeches and questions. The Muslim people articulate their faith very well and are quite direct with questions and responses. A follow-up gathering was held at Community Mennonite where Zafar Bangash and I shared responses to five basic questions based on their respective religions. On another occasion our church shared through video and personal stories what it means to be a Mennonite. This fall we will visit the mosque for a time of Islamic storytelling.

Our church's goal in having these encounters with the Islamic community is twofold. With the increased tension between Christians and Muslims around the world, our church wants to model a healthy relationship with our Muslim brothers and sisters, one of trust and mutual respect. Hopefully, other churches will see our modeling and do something similar. Secondly, our people have a desire to share our Christian faith, but also to learn from our Muslim friends. Our goal in these encounters is not Christian conversion, but rather increased understanding of both the Muslim faith and of our own. As we face the questions and issues raised by the Muslim people, we are forced to dig deeper into our own Christian faith, and thus know it and appreciate it even more. At the same time, we gain deeper appreciation of our Muslim brothers and sisters and the faith they are trying to live.

Clayton and Amy Kuepfer, Jane Finch Ministry in Toronto

"We have wonderful neighbors next door to us who welcomed us the day we moved here five years ago. They helped us unload our moving van, shared garden produce with us, suggested a mechanic for our automobile, and invited us to their home for an ` Id celebration. In this extended family, the older parents live in the basement, and the man is an imam in the Muslim faith. Their daughter, Lila, and her husband, Abdul, live with their three teenage children on the main floor. Abdul is a local high school teacher, and Lila is a receptionist at Sick Kids Hospital. The entire family is active in their faith walk. Our exchange in conversation about faith and various issues is rich. Abdul has just agreed to serve on an initial board for the chaplaincy in the Jane Finch Ministry."

This is the experience of Clayton and Amy Kuepfer, pastors of the Black Creek Faith Community (Toronto, Ontario), as they minister to a small emerging congregation meeting in a subsidized high-rise apartment building at Jane and Finch Streets, one of the most infamous sections of the city. Clayton and Amy serve not only as pastors for this group, but also as chaplains in the high-rise, following twenty years of Mennonite-Christian presence in the building. A congregation began to take shape after about sixteen years of presence there, but the chaplaincy role has continued throughout this time and is now being organized more clearly with a charitable board.

In the past five years of ministry, the demographics of this building have continued to undergo dramatic change. Among great diversity of cultures and faiths, about one third of the residents are now Muslims, mostly newcomers to Canada. What is the role of a Mennonite chaplaincy or Christian presence in a setting that is now strongly interfaith?

At first, very few adult people of color or Muslim residents participated in any of the long-established structures and social programs in the community rooms on the building's first floor. The hiring of a staff person from Trinidad and the help of a Muslim woman in children's programs were the first steps in welcoming all persons into full participation. Two years ago, the Muslim community wished to celebrate ` Id. Since only staff is allowed to book and supervise activity in the community rooms, Amy and Clayton facilitated and supervised the ` Id party. Now the Muslim adult residents are much more fully involved in the social and educational life of this community.

One woman in particular, Ruqia, has offered her leadership skills to the community at large. She is establishing a program where she will teach basic sewing and mending to women who live on the economic fringe. She has also agreed to serve as a mentor and social coordinator for the small, but stable group of students in the community. It will be important to form healthy relationships as a part of this activity. While some of Ruqia's Muslim neighbors are a bit suspicious of her close relationships with "the church people," she has not backed off.

Amy and Clayton, as chaplains, want to build bridges of trust which lead to the mutual sharing of struggles and faith. They have succeeded to a large degree in lowering the level of fear and apprehension. They have struggled with questions about their role as Christian ministers, but they are clear that they have no desire to either violate or pressure their Muslim friends and neighbors they have grown to love. They are ready to both *share* and *listen to* faith stories. Amy was greatly relieved when a speaker at a recent conference she attended suggested that sharing the story of Jesus in order to convert others is the wrong track. Sharing Jesus because one loves them is the right track.

Victor and Viola Dorsch, MCEC Mission and Service Commission's Somali Reference Council

The Mission and Service Commission of Mennonite Church Eastern Canada has worked with Somali refugees in southern Ontario since 1991. The relationship began when Victor and Viola Dorsch, missionary teachers in Somalia (1956-1970), were contacted by several of their former students, now adult refugees in Toronto. From these initial contacts, the Dorsches discovered that there were more than 40,000 Somali refugees living in the Toronto metropolitan area.

In December 1991, the Dorsches, with the help of Maple View Mennonite Church, hosted twenty-seven former Somali students. This led in 1992 to the formation of the Canadian Somali Friendship Association (CASOFA). When the work became more than the Dorsches alone could handle, the Mission and Service Commission became involved. The CASOFA continued functioning for five years, until 1997, when no Somali could be found to provide leadership to the office in Toronto.

Through this network, the first biennial reunion of former missionary teachers and Somali students was held in Toronto in 1993. One hundred people from across the U.S. and Canada participated in the event. Included among them were Baptists, Mennonites, Sudan Interior Mission personnel, and many former students.

Appreciating in particular the Mennonites' "moral standards," one of the CASOFA board members moved to Kitchener, and in 1993 formed the Somali Canadian Association of Waterloo Region (SCAWR). Ahmed Geddi Mohamud served as director of the Association. The Mission and Service Commission helped to fund the SCAWR office, and in 2001 created a Reference Council to work with the organization in the development of relationships and program. Alfred Heinrich serves as Council chairperson.

Areas of focus for the Somali Reference Council include:

• Assisting SCAWR with immigration matters (e.g., legal issues pertaining to multiple wives, etc.);

• Assisting with settlement matters (e.g., housing, furnishings, etc.);

• Assisting with an advocacy program (e.g., help with integration, letters of reference, etc.);

• Assisting Muslim women;

• Assisting with the Homework Tutorial Program, designed to help children from grades five through high school. The program, open to everyone, operates two evenings a week with the help of two Somali supervisors, two retired teachers, university students who tutor the children, and volunteer drivers. Eastern Mennonite Missions contributes funds for the program.

• Assisting in the potential development of joint humanitarian aid for Muslim neighbors—a suggestion proposed by Sheik Kishki, a member of the Reference Council.

Alf Heinrichs, Chair of MCEC Mission and Service Commission's Somali Reference Council

The Somali Reference Council has helped to build a sanctuary where the mostly Mennonite-Christian community relates to and serves the Somali Muslim community by:

• Relating to the multicultural Canadian government services so that these can better accommodate the specific needs of the Somali community;

• Connecting Somali Muslims to various available services in order to build their sense of community and equip them to more adequately help each other;

• Assisting Somalis in building their own services to strengthen the internal structures of the community and increase a sense of ownership and empowerment;

• Helping Somali Muslims understand how they fit in as a minority group within the larger secular society as they attempt to practice and live out their faith.

We are committed to serving the Somali community as we believe Jesus would do. Offering our services in this manner has gained us the trust and credibility to speak candidly on various issues, and when we have done so, it has been well accepted. This approach creates an atmosphere of collaboration and partnership. Once friendship at this level has been established, we believe all other "agendas" will more smoothly and naturally fall into place.

CHAPTER EIGHTEEN

Burkina Faso

Africa Inter-Mennonite Mission
Mennonite Mission Network
Mennonite Church Canada Witness

Donna Entz

The journey in Burkina Faso began long before my husband and I arrived in the country. Africa Inter-Mennonite Mission (AIMM) was originally called the Congo Inland Mission, and it sent out missionaries from a variety of Mennonite denominational conferences across the North American continent. My husband, Loren, saw firsthand the work of some of these amazing workers in the Congo. During our engagement period before our wedding, he took me on a grand tour across the Congo to meet many of these people. Jim and Jenny Bertsche modeled for us the critical necessity of learning the language and its deeper cultural significance. Ben and Helen Eidse showed us the importance of working with groups by villages or families, and not simply with isolated individuals.

Other mentors in this journey were Mennonite Board of Mission (MBM) workers, Ed and Irene Weaver. They taught us in their own faithful, but rebellious way that God may work outside mission agencies, and that, "Just because nobody else has done it, doesn't mean you shouldn't." From their work with African independent churches, we saw that there were ways for people to be Christian, yet fully African. The importance of ritual in these churches has been of particular fascination to us over the years.

History of the Work in Burkina Faso

It was Jim Bertsche's vision for Burkina Faso that got the present AIMM involved in this new country. Loren and I went with the blessing and support of the General Conference Mennonite Church's Commission on Overseas Missions. Today that body has become Mennonite Church Canada Witness and, in the United States, the Mennonite Mission Network. (The ministries of the former Mennonite Church's Mennonite Board of Missions were also folded into the work of these two new agencies.)

Arriving in Burkina Faso, our work was in many ways exploratory, beginning with our commitment to learning the trade language of the region in which we were living. The best speakers of this language were those of a larger town who had become separated from their village roots and had in recent years embraced Islam for its sense of community.

It soon became clear to us that we would follow our elder colleagues from the Congo in focusing on learning local languages, and eventually doing linguistic and Bible translation work. So we began by placing two teams in as many of the language groups as possible in the province of Kenedougou. The plan for each location was to have one team focus on church planting and evangelism, and the second on linguistics and translation. After six years in the country, Loren and I also accepted an assignment as church-planters/evangelists in an ethnic group that was entirely Muslim in composition.

Teams have, over the years, been placed in four language groups and today ministry continues at various stages in each of them, carried out by both expatriate and national workers. Where fellowships have emerged from the missionaries' work, new believers have become a part of the Evangelical Mennonite Church of Burkina Faso. This emerging national church has a radio spot on the local FM station, popular with Muslim people, and has initiated a new outreach effort with a vibrant young man working sensitively among another people group. With the help of Mennonite Central Committee (MCC), the church has worked diligently at AIDS consciousness-raising through-out the province. And together, as both mission and church, we work in partnership to provide leadership training, offer seminars, and facilitate the building of church sanctuaries for newly-formed fellow-ships.

So What Have We Learned from the Journey in Burkina Faso?

We have observed that once a group or individual becomes Muslim, they do not readily change to some other religion. This is especially true as it relates to individuals. And so it is far better to find ways of working within village or family structures, than to pull out or isolate individuals. Our historic group identity as Mennonites is strong. We have emphasized the importance of the church as a redeemed community, not simply a group of disconnected or unrelated individuals. Rather than extracting individuals from their culture, we believe it is better to engage the entire group with the biblical message. The truth is that in a society where many important decisions are made as groups, the decision to follow Christ could also be made in this manner. Many peoples are more group-oriented than individually-focused, and the Anabaptist vision of embracing group movements could, indeed, be a very appropriate and effective means of evangelism.

One of the most dramatic encounters of Mennonites with a group movement outside of Africa took place among the Toba people in northern Argentina. We would do well to learn from this experience in creating indigenous theology. Ben Eidse, AIMM worker in the Congo, reflected on his experience there by saying, "Although we realized that the indigenous people in Africa make many decisions as a group, we knew that they are keenly aware that group decisions also involve personal commitments to the words that they decide to study together."

For those of us in Burkina Faso, the next steps toward a group movement are getting the word out in whatever way possible. This is what some might refer to as saturation evangelism. We are currently researching the expansion of our cassette ministry into some kind of radio-diffused message, since this is one of the least invasive forms of media for Muslim audiences. It could well be that once the whole people group has understood the good news message in this manner, God will choose to send dreams that will call the entire group to take that radical step toward belief in Jesus.

Once the connections between all the "Holy Books" referred to in the Qur'an were clear to our Muslim neighbors, the Bible took on a particular fascination for them. We were delighted to learn, for example, that because "oldest is always best," the Torah held authority, even over the Qur'an.

Aspects of African traditional religion and certain Muslim names are also important bridge-builders to the gospel, bringing to life much of the biblical message. Virtually no persuasion or argument is needed when the biblical message is clearly presented in a people's own language. God's word is infinitely more powerful than human words. The Psalms, or Zabur, as they are referred to in our region, are among the most inspiring texts for new Muslim background believers, longing to learn how to relate directly to God in their own language and develop the basis of a ritual for worship.

It seemed wise to us to take on a clear and unapologetic religious identity among Muslims, rather than a strictly detached secular one cultivated by many development agencies. Certainly, it is extremely difficult for Anabaptists coming out of the North American scene to adopt a strong religious profile in such a context. This only indicates that we have accommodated ourselves to the prevailing attitudes of our culture, where sensitive people do not push their religion on someone else. The result is that we as Anabaptists, in our desire to be especially respectful of other faiths and cultures, are often far less confident than our fellow evangelical missionary colleagues at verbally proclaiming our faith. The challenge for Mennonite mission agencies and for our mission education work in the constituency is to remember that in working with Muslim people, it is best to embrace a confidently intentional spiritual and religious identity. This is what will gain the respect of Muslims who are themselves a very religious group of people.

Challenges for the Future

Among the language groups where we have only a few Christians, the greatest challenge is to be a catalyst for contextualizing the good news message. This requires (1) being committed to researching the local traditional religious worldview with its overlay of Muslim beliefs and practices, and then (2) allowing the biblical message to bear light on whatever issues might emerge from the particular context. The next step (3) is to pray for the Holy Spirit to bring forth a synthesis that is both respectful of the local phenomenon, and faithful to the biblical message. Finally, and perhaps most importantly, is to (4) find ways of infusing present ritualistic practices with the new content and message that comes from the gospel story.

The oldest man in our village is, in this way, changing some of the traditional rituals of the village for which he holds responsibility. He has become convicted to do so through hearing the Old Testament stories about idolatry. Thus, last year, when the traditional ancestor-land ritual was held, this old patriarch began to see the importance of offering his chicken sacrifices in the courtyard to the Creator God, rather than carrying out the traditional practice over the ancestral stones.

Ultimately, we as Mennonites may need to examine our own attitudes about the use and importance of ritual in worship. It is interesting to note that many of us in North America are slowly redis-covering the power of story, ritual, symbol, and liturgy, and the role they play in building community. A Burkina Mennonite leader of Muslim background critiqued the comments I was preparing for this conference by saying, "I see that the Muslims have ritual, and so do the Catholics, yet we as Protestants do not. I'm wondering now if we are in the right or the wrong."

Many of us as foreigners living in Africa have watched for years as Muslim people who do not even understand Arabic go through their seemingly empty ritual of five prayer times a day. But the group loyalty that we also know well in Islam has its very roots in the power of that same ritual to form community.

Several years ago, a translation consultant told us that the book of Leviticus is often the first choice of the African church once expa-triates no longer figure prominently on the scene. This book is rich in describing the delicate contextualization process, showing us how God led Israel in developing a ritual life that spoke loudly in its context, all the while remaining at odds with it. This was confirmed for me recently again by a Muslim background believer who thought Leviticus had "a lot to say to Muslims."

I have myself been convicted in a new way of the power that the Lord's Supper holds for becoming the ritual foundation of our newly emerging Mennonite faith communities. Africa's covenant traditions, so strong in our local context, can build a rich basis for this central ritual of the Christian faith.

The Anabaptists believed in the "hermeneutical community." They believed that God spoke to them through other members of "the body." We must sadly admit that in today's North American context, this sense of community functions in little more than a very informal way. Mission agencies have the exciting opportunity of helping the North American church recover the "priesthood of all believers" by telling the stories of how this is being experienced and lived out in cross-cultural contexts!

Among the most important examples to reference here are the "base communities" found widely across Latin America. This model of teaching, whereby each person is given the opportunity to respond to God's word, has inspired even what we teach about how to do evangelism. A person who encounters the gospel by being given a chance to share and explain their own ideas to others is one who is automatically active once they choose to become a part of the community of faith.

Muslim seekers with strong social ties particularly appreciate this hermeneutical community. This shifts our primary emphasis off of right doctrine and onto the community discernment process as the Holy Spirit is sought for guidance in each context. This, in turn, increases our dependence on the Holy Spirit, and makes us less culturally-bound and more adaptable to a wide variety of cross-cultural ministry settings.

As Anabaptists we have said that Jesus is the norm for how we interpret the scriptures. This has sometimes led to a disregarding or devaluing of the Old Testament and an emphasis on the New Testament as being the more important of the two. The use of the Old Testament, however, is an excellent way of connecting to Muslims worldwide.

During our visits as a family to congregations in North America, I have frequently used African cultural explanations to help bring life to many of the Old Testament texts. Perhaps we could use some good African Old Testament teachers to help enlighten us North Americans about the Bible! I have noticed that our Sunday school study hour in many North American Mennonite churches has often been more focused on discussing issues than on studying the Bible. Pastors I have met were often struggling with how to get their North American church members to read the Bible. This is a crucial issue for us, because if there is little interest in the message of the scriptures in North America, why would we be interested in the power of God's word to change lives in other places?

We need to learn from those who have worked at Old Testament storytelling, rather than New Testament preaching, as a primary evangelism strategy. Some have discovered that believers introduced to God's word in this way are less legalistic than those whose first encounter came through the New Testament.

The tendency toward legalism is a very crucial issue when working with Muslim people. This may be difficult for Mennonites who see the Old Testament as law (i.e., legalism) and the New Testament as gospel. How do we get out of these ruts we are in? Perhaps we need to first understand why we are in such ruts. My suspicion is that this reading of the Old Testament comes from a certain way of understanding the Pauline epistles. I do know that we need to learn to see and understand "gospel" in the Old Testament before we can truly minister cross-culturally, especially to Muslims, for whom the Torah is held in such high esteem.

With our Anabaptist emphasis on justice and peace, it would also seem fitting that the preserving of languages and traditions, such as music, folklore, and artistic expression, might figure among our ministry priorities in the world. Radio may in fact be one of the most powerful ways of preserving language and identity in our province of very small languages. This ethnosphere, as some call it, composed of a group's language and customs, is disappearing at an alarming rate, much faster than the biosphere that sparks worldwide concern.

This is especially true for small groups like ours, where in order to be connected to a larger reality—in this case, Islam—one's own cultural identity is put at risk. By using only the Arabic language, there is a strong push to conform and do away with cultural distinctiveness. Is this a problem in other countries, I have wondered, where Arabic is not the first language among the Muslim population? And in the context of our world's cultural wars today, which powerful influence, modernity or Islam, is more effective in snuffing out minority peoples? Perhaps it is in keeping with our own strong Mennonite ethnic identity to be concerned when other ethnic groups are losing theirs, so long as developing ethnic ministry does not contribute to interethnic strife and conflict.

One last comment about new developments in our ministry: AIMM as a mission agency is presently undergoing a restructuring process of rather massive proportions. Our challenge will be to find ways of working in an international partnership council with new and old North American members, European partners, MCC, and the Mennonite church here in Burkina Faso. We have longed nonetheless for this day when decision making would be rightly placed on Burkina soil.

Conclusion

There is "something" about being Anabaptists that those of us working for Mennonite mission agencies need to understand. This "something" is difficult to describe. I noted it in David W. Shenk's book describing the East African revival. This revival, we should remember, encountered considerable opposition from the larger European and North American missionary community. Yet Shenk writes, "Only the Mennonite mission gave official endorsement to the Revival, possibly because of the Revival Fellowship's apparent affinities with Anabaptism, particularly in its emphasis on the Church as being a redeemed and reconciled community of believers." Even David wasn't sure why the Mennonites could or would endorse this movement.

This same "something" inspired AIMM's Jim Bertsche to demonstrate a deep sense of respect in his research on the language and customs of the people he had grown to love. A similar empathic quality has also been referenced in connection with the various Mennonite mission agencies that have worked tirelessly to affirm and encourage the believers of Africa's independent churches, all the while taking great care not to proselytize them by planting Anabaptist churches among them.

Now this "something" that I can't describe, is probably what fits us especially well, in these troubled days, to connect with Muslims in ways that others may not be able to. In relation to Islam, I encourage us to engage, influence, and teach Muslims wherever openness permits. Our primary concern is not whether or not people convert. It may even be that we will be seen by some, as we are in Burkina, as a renewal movement within Islam, rather than a new "foreign" religion disconnected to the current local spiritual realities. Only God's Spirit, I believe, will someday reveal the true difference.

Maybe the reason we have this gift is that we are, as Walter Klassen has suggested, "neither Catholic nor Protestant." Perhaps, this "something" we are describing is the ability to sense where the Spirit is at work drawing people closer to God and to meet people exactly where they are, despite their official religious affinities or denominational affiliations. It is perhaps this approach to others that permits us, in partnership with the Spirit, to throw our energy into empowering people as groups and individuals to move forward in their faith pilgrimage, no matter what their starting point.

When the work in Burkina Faso first began, I was energized by a sense that what was happening was something new and creative.

Now I see both continuity and discontinuity with the past. Anabaptist mission agencies in the future need to empower North American congregations to take the legacy that has been handed down to them, and begin moving across new frontiers to apply it in new contexts.

I have a sense that a key frontier to which we as Anabaptists are being called and perhaps uniquely prepared is the Muslim world. Some of the gifts we bring to this challenge were honed in the fires of the sixteenth-century Reformation. Other gifts simply sprang up because some Anabaptists descending from these early years of trial and persecution were sensitive to what the Spirit was saying, sometimes as faithful representatives of the mission agencies they had created, sometimes in spite of those same agencies.

Muslim Tribe Celebrates Publication of Bible Portions
April 2, 2004

SARABA, Burkina Faso (AIMM/Mennonite Mission Network)— Last month, seeds planted over three decades blossomed and bore sweet fruit when people from various parts of the West African country of Burkina Faso gathered to dedicate two books of portions of the Bible in the Samogho language.

The event celebrated God's written word and the Samogho culture in Saraba, a remote village where only a handful of people read and write. Representatives from the national Mennonite Church, *Eglise Evangélique Mennonite du Burkina Faso*, and governmental authorities attended the festivities.

Burkina Faso has been home for the Donna and Loren Entz family since the 1970s, where they minister with the support of Africa Inter-Mennonite Mission and Mennonite Mission Network.

The three Entz children learned to work alongside Burkinabé friends in fields and mud-walled courtyards, while their parents learned the Samogho language and gained the confidence of the village elders.

"Before our arrival in Burkina Faso, we were told that we might be obliged to do some sort of development work in order to earn a hearing for the gospel message [among a Muslim people]," Donna Entz said. "What we experienced was that people loved to talk about their religious beliefs, and we could be very open in talking about our relationship with God. Had we gone with the idea that it was wrong to share our faith with these brothers and sisters, we would almost certainly have been cut off from any deep relationship."

Entz said there is a connection between the Qur'an and the biblical material. "The Qur'an refers to Christians and Jews as 'the people of the book,' and says that their holy books are good counsel. Many proper names of people and places are also common to the Qur'an and the Bible. Building on these connections helped us to be sensitive in our proclamation."

The Entz family often gained insights into biblical material from their Muslim neighbors whose culture was, in many ways, more similar to Hebrew culture than the North American world in which they grew up.

From the beginning of their ministry in Burkina Faso, the Entzes were opposed to mass evangelistic campaigns because they felt the here-today-gone-tomorrow approach inoculated people against radical discipleship. They chose instead an incarnational strategy emphasizing deeply-rooted relationships and the powerful impact of God's word shared in a people's native tongue.

Working as a team with educated Muslim translators, Donna and Loren Entz began to translate Bible stories. During the translation process, the translators decided to become followers of Jesus and founded the first Samogho church.

Over the years, the biblical story of salvation has been shared around evening fires—the Samogho schoolroom—where traditional stories pass on values to subsequent generations. To further extend the impact of the story of Jesus, solar-powered cassette players have been given to village elders in neighboring villages.

"[The cassettes] tell the story of how God worked with his people," Entz explained. "We envisioned people learning to know God in a natural way with the cassettes, like a friendship enfolding."

The twenty-two, one-hour cassettes feature eighty Old Testament narratives, the gospel of Luke, and the story of the early church found in the first chapters of Acts.

Last month's gala celebrated the publishing of these Bible portions in two books. "[Samogho Christians] felt these should not be sold without a dedication service," Entz said.

The service included traditional music from each Samogho village; newly composed music by Samogho Christians; speeches given by visiting government officials, national Mennonite church leaders, and the Samogho translators; a traditional fable followed by a biblical parable; and a prayer for the upcoming rainy season.

Certain speakers lauded the event for its role in strengthening Samogho culture. Others told how God had given peace and new understanding through the translated word.

"The most exciting [part of the celebration] was the non-preachy attitude of the Christians, who got up to dance while traditional songs were sung. Not only did they talk of their appreciation for the richness of the Samogho culture, they also showed it by their actions. We were deeply touched," Entz said.

Several influential Samogho people living in Ouagadougou, the capital city, told the Entzes they had been quietly supporting their work but now wanted to become public advocates. A village neighbor said, "[Christians] are the only ones who can do what all of us try to do: live lives that honor God and keep from doing evil."

After the festivities ended, the head of the Muslim community came to visit. The Entzes apologized for the celebration running overtime into Friday prayers. The imam responded that it was not at all serious because the community had been worshipping God.

"It sounds like we finally, after all these years, took part in an evangelism campaign that we are very comfortable with, because we were both respectful and yet very open about our relationship with God," Entz said.

"We pray that God would allow us to remain among these people that we love. But, we sense that the Samogho church people have understood that they are called to live exemplary lives in faithfulness to God. They also see the importance of living lives intertwined with the rest of their people, as trailblazers to the many who are searching for meaning, all during these times of very rapid cultural and social change. We are not as crucially needed as we once were."

CHAPTER NINETEEN

Senegal

Africa Inter-Mennonite Mission
Mennonite Mission Network

Jonathan Bornman

"After this I looked and there before me was a great multitude that no one could count, from every nation, tribe, people and language, standing before the throne and in front of the Lamb. They were wearing white robes and were holding palm branches in their hands. And they cried out in a loud voice: 'Salvation belongs to our God, who sits on the throne, and to the Lamb'" (Rev. 7:9).

These verses paint a picture of the culmination of all history. Worship in heaven is rich, encompassing all the families of the earth. With such an end in mind, life has deep purpose and meaning. This is our motivation for our relationship to the Muslim Wolof people of Senegal.

Historical Background

The Wolof Partnership (composed of Friends of the Wolof, Africa Inter-Mennonite Mission (AIMM), and Mennonite Mission Network (Network) works in Senegal to fulfill this vision statement: "partnering for a movement to Jesus among the Wolof people." There is a team of five adults and five children who live and work in Senegal as part of the Wolof Partnership.

How did this come to be, ten North Americans living in a small, predominantly Wolof city in Senegal? From the mid-1980s until the mid-1990s, AIMM explored ministry possibilities in Senegal. The Mennonites from the Congo were exploring this as well. AIMM contacted my wife and me in 1996, at the same time that our home church, Communion Fellowship (based in Goshen, Indiana) was making five and ten year goals. One of these goals was to plant a church among an unreached people group. When AIMM's Garry Prieb told us of the Wolof people, "our hearts burned within us," to use the Emmaus road analogy. This ministry possibility eventually led me to seminary training at Fuller Theological Seminary where I was privileged to study under Dudley Woodberry and others.

In 1997 we put together an exploration team of five people and visited Senegal. Church leaders and mission workers alike indicated that the northern cities of Senegal had little or no witness of Jesus in their midst. When we visited the city that is today our home we went unannounced with no known contacts. We asked for a hotel and moved into the rooms, but had no specific plan for what to do next.

But God is mighty, working way ahead of us and preparing the way. We met a young Wolof man playing with children by the pool and started a conversation. Maktar (not his real name) offered to take us to a friend's home and we had cold drinks together. He then arranged for us to eat in his family courtyard the next day. There we had *ceebu jënn* (rice and fish), the national dish, and our first taste of *ataaya*, a tea ceremony that is the national pastime. There was joy and laughter as we ate fresh, locally grown watermelon, with juice running down our chins. This was friendship born in the Spirit of God and we reveled in it. God had spoken in friendship and watermelon, in *ceebu jënn* and *ataaya*, and in other ways. We decided we would place our team in this city.

Unknown to us, Maktar would not turn out to be our primary contact in the city. In a village some fifty kilometers away was a Wolof man named Ibu (not his real name) who had just heard the gospel and had chosen to reject it. Then, in a dream, Jesus visited Ibu and called him to follow. Ibu eventually responded and began to pray that God would send other followers of Jesus to his home city to assist him in telling his city about Jesus.

Ibu's return to his home city and our arrival there coincided and a relationship began, with Ibu teaching me Wolof language and culture, and with me teaching him from the Bible. Ibu's personal witness of real change in lifestyle through his encounter with Jesus has led many people to take notice and ask questions. Through his testimony about Jesus a number of other men and women now follow Jesus.

Our Approach to Ministry

Our approach has been one of respect with an eager desire to understand and embrace Wolof culture and language.

1. We take our context seriously. We have made conscious choices to speak Wolof, rather than French. We attempt to dress in traditional clothing and to be conscious of the local customs (their ways of greeting, for example). We use the Muslim names for the prophets, Adama, Ibrahima, Noé, Yahkya, and 'Isa. We talk of the Taurat, Zabur, and Injil when referring to the Bible.

2. We believe that Jesus lives in us, thus when we eat, play, go to market, attend baby-naming ceremonies, funerals or weddings, when we attend Islamic celebrations . . . Jesus is present. This is incarnational living; who we are is much more important than our words. At the same time we often have opportunities to clearly talk of the reason for the hope that we have.

3. Prayer walking teams have made a considerable contribution.

4. We have made it clear that we are Talibe 'Isa, disciples or followers of Jesus. This is a new idea for most persons. This term doesn't fit in any of their boxes and so they ask questions to find out what this means. The word Christian carries negative connotations for most persons in our community. However, it is important to be known as people of faith. While in Dakar doing some language learning we hired a taxi driver to take us to and from school each day. He had a stomach ulcer and could not work one week, and my colleague, Jim Hanes, and I went to visit him and offered to pray. God answered our prayer and he was back at work the next morning. We also hired him to help us move from the capital to our home three hours away. While we unloaded our belongings, Ousmane was next door telling the neighbors about his healing.

5. We are committed to being a blessing to our community, both in how we live, act, and speak, and in how we respond to needs in our community. This has resulted in launching a cyber café that shows our community that we are making a tangible contribution to the well-being of our city. Investigation is underway on getting involved in drip irrigation.

6. We are committed to building a Wolof church that embraces all that is good about Wolof culture, one that Wolof Muslims will be

attracted to join. A development in the past year has been bringing together Wolof believers from all of northern Senegal every two months for times of fellowship, teaching, and worship. Out of this is emerging a sense of belonging to a new community of faith. It is this group that is beginning to experiment with Wolof forms of worship. There is a spirit of unity among missionaries of many different organizations.

7. We are building ties with the evangelical churches in Senegal. We participate in a fraternity of evangelical churches and missions. More importantly, we are increasingly getting help from an indigenous mission agency, Mission Inter-Senegal, for discipling new followers of Jesus.

What Have We Learned?

It seems foolish to speak of learnings after four short years, especially when we consider the contributions at this consultation of Woodberry, Sanneh, and Lapp who have provided us with sweeping, long-view assessments, or the 150 years of history that we have heard about from the church in Indonesia. Yet, we too have learned much.

We have learned that this kind of love is costly. It has not been easy to live cross-culturally, honoring our host culture above our own. We have been tired and discouraged as often as we have felt encouraged. Huge questions remain as we consider how best to live in our area of calling.

We have learned that God has been working to prepare hearts and lives to hear the message of salvation. The Holy Spirit orchestrates things in ways we can never imagine and this gives us expectant hope.

We have learned that Wolof people are more open to receiving the gospel when it is presented by other Wolof persons.

Future Vision

Prior to going to Senegal I had heard that the Wolof Muslims were resistant to the gospel. I went expecting many years of patient witness. I went ready to spend years in culture and language learning. It was somewhat unsettling to begin discipling new followers of Jesus when I was still learning to speak with the proficiency of an average child.

Yet God provided resources and people to make that possible. I think now that perhaps the Wolof people are considered resistant primarily because they have not had real exposure to our living Lord Jesus through his followers. The apostle Paul was speaking of people like the Wolof when he wrote, "How, then, can they call on the one they have not believed in? And how can they believe in the one of whom they have not heard? And how can they hear without someone preaching to them? . . . As it is written, 'How beautiful are the feet of those who bring good news!'" (Rom 10:14-15).

A significant part of the good news for me is that one day there will be Wolof men, women, and children standing before the throne, worshipping the Lamb!

CHAPTER TWENTY

Djibouti

Eastern Mennonite Missions

Mike Brislen

An Engagement with People, Not with a Religion

The literature on Islam and Christianity often gives the impression that in Christians meeting Muslims we engage a religious system. We have learned that we are not witnesses to Islam. Our ministry is not to a religion, but among people. These people are in fact Muslims, and Islam permeates every area of their life, yet Islam still does not totally define each person as an individual. They are also fathers and mothers, sons and daughters, teachers and students, employed and unemployed, rich and poor, and so forth. These other relationships and situations can have as much defining power upon a person's life as their religion. Our engagement is therefore with a variety of people within a group, rather than with a monolithic system.

Losing Instead of Winning

We have been blessed with years of education. We have read and learned much about Islam. Many of us have some theological and biblical training. We can win religious debates with our cleverness and acquired skills. However, I've seen Jesus receive more glory when I've lost these debates. A Muslim sheikh came to my house one afternoon accompanied by a few trainees. He wanted to discuss faith and religion in hope of converting me to Islam. He asked me if I would go to paradise when I died. I told him yes that I was certain of that. He then asked what I thought about his eternal salvation. I said that God was a God of love and this man seemed like a good and sincere man. Perhaps God would save him, even though he didn't believe in Jesus. He jumped on my answer declaring that he knew I would be condemned, because I wouldn't acknowledge Muhammad's prophethood. He'd won the debate, yet his trainees had found greater sympathy for me. Later I met the trainees on the street, and they had abandoned their training. Perhaps we should develop a theology of losing.

Fasting at Ramadan

Several people with Eastern Mennonite Missions (EMM) in Djibouti have chosen to fast during the month of Ramadan in solidarity with their Muslim friends and colleagues. I've personally fasted during several Ramadans. Our children have even fasted. Fasting has usually enabled us to grow closer to our Muslim friends. Spiritually-oriented conversations have more naturally occurred. We've been able to share more authentically in *aftuur* (daily breaking of the fast at sunset) and Eid (end of Ramadan feast) celebrations. Fasting has also brought us times of deep spiritual experience. We've learned to appreciate the spirituality of Muslims. The Ramadan fast should not, however, be thought of as a certain method to greater witness. One worker in particular had a very negative experience of fasting during this month, holy to Islam.

Transformed by Christ?

We firmly believe that Jesus Christ not only saves us for heaven, but also transforms our lives in this world so that we might be his servants, living out the fruit of the Spirit. But how do we wrap our thinking and our theology around the fact that some of our Muslim friends are among the best people in the world? Their lives consistently shine with what we would consider the fruits of the Spirit. They have dedicated themselves to their understanding of God. Where has this transformation come from? What can we say about their eternal salvation?

For answers to these questions we try to listen to the responses of Djiboutian Muslims who learn to know of Jesus of the New Testament gospel. We listen to their responses to the question: what difference does Jesus make?

CHAPTER TWENTY-ONE

Algeria

Marian E. Hostetler

I am presenting this paper as a summary of the research I have done in preparation for a book released this year entitled *Algeria: Where Mennonites and Muslims Met, 1955-1978*. I personally spent nine years in Algeria during the period treated in this study.

The Beginning of Mennonite Presence in Algeria

It was in the fall of 1954 that Algeria experienced two earthquakes. The first one struck in September of that year, lasted only twelve seconds, killed 1,000 people, and destroyed many homes. In contrast, the second "quake" began two months later, lasted seven and a half years, and killed nearly one million people. This was the struggle of the Algerian people to gain independence from France.

The idea of having a group of young Mennonite men go to Algeria to help in rebuilding after the September earthquake came from John Howard Yoder, who was at that time living in Europe as a coordinator for Mennonite Board of Missions (MBM). In the spring of 1955, the first PAX men arrived in western Algeria in an area afflicted by the quake, and began to construct housing. Prior to this assignment, the men had been working with Mennonite Central Committee (MCC) in Europe. But when they were transferred to Algeria, they worked instead under MBM's Relief and Service Committee.

The first assignment for the workers was not too successful, but soon they moved to the nearby village of Flatters, where they stayed until the spring of 1959. There they built a village of thirty-two cement block houses.

The PAX volunteers were mostly young men, not long out of high school, arriving in a country at war and in an area devastated by natural disaster. They had to contend with the presence of the French army, while learning to know the Algerian people—Muslims who spoke mostly Arabic or one of the Berber languages, though some also knew French.

These young men were far away from Europe and their homes in North America. They needed to depend on their own leadership in the midst of this unfamiliar culture and religion. Equally challenging was their assignment in construction work, for which some of them were ill-prepared. But their enthusiasm and willingness to learn and work hard, coupled with the warm empathy they demonstrated for the local people, made them popular wherever they went.

The workers who came later during the twenty-three-year period of Mennonite presence in Algeria were mostly better-prepared in language skills and cultural orientation than the first wave of volunteers. And these, like their predecessors, also endeared themselves to the people they had come to serve. When asked recently for her thoughts on the work the Mennonites had done in Algeria, veteran Methodist missionary, Sue Robinson, who was present during these years, commented, "Your willingness to live simply and work hard, to become friends with the people whom you had come to serve was, I believe, a much more effective witness than simply preaching about God as manifested in Christ. 'They knew you were Christian by your love.'"

The Relief Effort Is Intensified

As a result of four years of continuous fighting against France's rule, hunger, hardship, and bloodshed had increased dramatically, and thousands of displaced people had become refugees within their own country. MBM therefore requested the involvement of MCC to do relief work in cooperation with two other agencies already at work in Algeria: Church World Service and CIMADE (a French Protestant organization).

MCC responded quickly with a shipment of blankets and canned meat, and began looking for personnel. The first MCC workers, Vern and Marion Preheim, arrived in September of 1960. They were followed by several PAX men who worked in CIMADE locations, alongside the two or three remaining MBM PAX men who were eventually transferred to MCC. By this time MBM had recruited longer-term mission personnel who were working in Algiers—Miller and Carol Stayrook, Robert and Lila Rae Stetter, Annie Haldemann, and Marian Hostetler.

Early in 1962 the war for independence reached a crucial stage. The French colonials, seeing they were losing the fight, formed a terrorist group, the Secret Army Organization (OAS), which embarked on a reign of terror that included machine-gunning clinics, burning down schools, planting hundreds of plastic bombs, and randomly shooting any Algerians brave enough to leave their homes. Illustrative of this type of hatred was the French Protestant pastor who told Vern Preheim that his son had gone out and shot several Algerians, adding, "I just wish that he could have done more."

I had a chance to reflect on this experience again this past summer (2003) during an extended stay in Israel/Palestine. When I returned home, people asked me, "Weren't you afraid?" "Didn't you see terrible things?" I could only observe to myself that anything that I experienced there was *nothing* in comparison with the situation we lived through in Algiers in late spring and early summer of 1962.

The Postindependence Era

The conflict ended, finally, and the six-year-long curfew was lifted. Fear turned to joy as we participated with our Algerian friends and neighbors in the celebration of the birth of their new nation on July 3, 1962. For the first time we could drive wherever we wanted to, and the neighbor ladies enjoyed riding along with us through the crowded streets. Our landlord's wife looked at the mass of people and said, "They killed a lot of Arabs, but there are still a lot of us left!"

Before the war's end, churches were gearing up to be able to meet some of the stupendous needs of the country. The churches came together and formed a new organization called CCSA (Christian Committee for Service in Algeria). MCC became part of this organization and worked through it, all the while continuing good relations with MBM personnel.

An influx of MCC workers and programs beginning in the fall of 1963 brought the total number of Mennonites in Algeria to a high of thirty-one adults and ten children. Most of these were located in eastern Algeria in the Constantine area. MCCers were doing a wide variety of assignments, including:

• relief distributions and construction of housing;
• farm programs with crops, gardens, cattle, artificial insemination, raising poultry and rabbits;
• educational programs for girls and training of mechanics;
• medical work in clinics and a hospital.

After four or five years, many of these programs changed, were phased out, or were turned over to the government. CCSA also modified its personnel criteria, clarifying that it no longer wished to receive "unskilled or semiskilled PAX men." MCC therefore began sending only high school teachers, mostly for English-teaching assignments. MBM's long-term personnel, the Stetters, Mary Ellen Shoup, and myself, were also working by then as high school English teachers.

Expatriate Workers Are Expelled

The few Algerian Christians who existed were beginning to make some progress in trying to form a church, and Robert Stetter was an elder in the group that was taking shape. A sudden change in the attitude of the government toward Christian foreigners, however, brought that to a halt.

On December 27, 1969, government officials raided a youth meeting sponsored by the Methodists, arresting all thirty-five people in attendance, and expelling from the country the seven Methodist foreigners involved. They then confiscated the extensive church property and accused the Methodists of proselytizing and carrying out subversive political activity. Beginning in 1970, other organizations such as CARE and Catholic Relief Services were expelled, and many people were questioned by the secret police.

Our mission policy had never been to form a Mennonite church in Algeria, but to be there as a Christian presence. From the time of the very first PAX men, we sought to work in cooperation with Christians and church groups like the North Africa Mission (now Arab World Ministries) and the United Methodists, already present in the country.

As the third and last phase of Mennonites' presence in Algeria was beginning in 1970-71, both MBM and MCC personnel were diminishing in numbers. I left after nine years at the end of 1970, and in 1971, the Stetter family returned home following a thirteen-year ministry.

A Handful of Teachers Is All That Remains

MCC was by then assigning only TAP teachers (Teachers Abroad Program), usually four or five of them at a time. These workers lived isolated from one another, each couple or individual on their own, scattered in schools across Algeria. At one time or another there were TAP teachers in thirteen different locations, including the Sahara Desert.

Many of these volunteers had little knowledge of what had gone before. They worked in extremely difficult teaching situations, and often experienced a great deal of loneliness. MBM's Mary Ellen Shoup, living at the time in Algiers and in her fifth year of teaching, was the only person remaining with background and experience from the earlier days of the ministry.

In early 1974, representatives of MBM, MCC, and the Methodist mission met and formulated an agreement for working together. Later that year, MCC discontinued its partnership with CCSA when the word "Christian" was dropped from the name. (CCSA retained the same initials, but instead of "Christian Committee for Service in Algeria," the group now went by the name "Center of Cooperation and Service in Algeria.")

During the summer of 1975, MCC administrator Peter Dyck wrote a letter to a group of former Algeria workers having a reunion in Iowa. He informed them that there would be no MCC workers in Algeria for the 1975-76 school year, but that he hoped to have new personnel entering language school in preparation for the following year.

Mary Ellen Shoup was at that point the only Mennonite personnel remaining in Algeria, aside from Annie Haldemann, a French nurse who came to Algeria early on when the Flatters program was being launched. Annie was still in Algeria in 1975, partially supported by MBM, but "doing her own thing." So far as we know, Annie is today still in Algeria, living out her retirement years.

The next year, Mary Ellen Shoup was on leave in the U.S., preparing for her retirement. Hugh Johnston from the Methodist mission helped find jobs and housing for the two MCC couples from Canada—Len and Phyllis Redekop and Walter and Anne Friesen—who arrived after language school. Neither they nor anyone else realized they would be the last Mennonites sent to Algeria. Mary Ellen returned from the States for one more year, worked as a translator at an oil company, and then left for good in 1977 after eleven years in

Algeria. The Friesens and Redekops completed one term of service, leaving Algeria in 1978.

The Work Comes to an End in 1978

Why no more Mennonites? It's not very clear. Peter Dyck, MCC administrator, and Wilbert R. Shenk, administrator for MBM, each claim that their organization never made a decision to formally discontinue work in Algeria.

In 1978, Peter Dyck wrote to Wilbert Shenk, saying, "We are not actively recruiting workers for Algeria. While in practice this means that we have terminated MCC's presence in the country, in fact we have not made that an official MCC decision." Wilbert wrote back to Peter affirming the same, "Like you, we have taken no formal decision to withdraw workers from Algeria, but through attrition we are virtually finished. . . . I share with you a sense of uneasiness over this failure." As recently as 2001, while doing research on my book about Mennonites in Algeria, Wilbert responded to my query by confirming, "I am confident that MBM never did take a formal decision to withdraw from Algeria."

Was This Really the End?

A total of some 165 adult Mennonites and Brethren in Christ lived in Algeria during the twenty-three-year period from 1955-78. In addition to these were the sixteen babies of workers born in Algeria, and the many other children old enough to have been influenced by their encounter with the country.

Here are some recent reflections from a few of the workers about their time in Algeria, now many years ago:

Paul Gentner (Germany): "I met Muslims who helped me to understand better their religion and at the same time, they opened my eyes to see what is really important and what is secondary in my own Christian faith. . . . From the Catholics I learned to meditate in silence; from the Mennonites, stewardship and nonviolence; from the Muslims, spontaneous hospitality . . . what I learned strongly influences my life."

Steve Gerber (Pennsylvania): "I was fortunate to work with many wonderful people, both Algerian and American. They have forever changed my life. Almost daily I will think of something connected to my Algerian experience."

Ron Denlinger (Indiana): "It's a beautiful country. I think it began a closer walk with God for me. It gave me a burden for Islamic people."

Mary Leatherman (Pennsylvania): "We learned to listen to the evening news with a different slant. We now have an understanding of the North African culture and of the Muslim religion."

Don Litwiller (Illinois): "We learned a lot about another very important culture and religion. Hopefully, we react differently now about wealth and fairness issues, and we are more tolerant about people who are different."

So the influence Algeria had on us continues right up until the present day. Did we, in turn, have any influence there, and if so, did it perhaps continue as well? We don't know for certain. But news about the growth of the church in Algeria today indicates that such may well have been the case.

During the years of the Mennonite presence in Algeria, there were at most perhaps a few hundred national Christians in the entire country. Today, it is thought there are between thirty and forty thousand believers, scattered about in small groups, with a majority being located in Berber areas.

The recent unrest in Algeria between Islamic fundamentalists and the government has purportedly killed about 100,000 people. It has apparently also stimulated, however, some measure of church growth. An article in an Algerian newspaper, written in December 2000 to describe the growing strength of the church in the country, stated, "The deterioration of the image of Islam during the crisis has played its part in the rise of conversions to Christianity. . . . Killings in the name of Islam have led many to declare, when asked what was the difference between the two religions: 'Christianity is life; Islam is death.'"

I offer you in closing these words from Albert Schweitzer, "None of us knows what effect our life produces and what we give to others. That is hidden from us and must remain so, though we are often allowed to see some little fraction of it, that we may not lose courage."

CHAPTER TWENTY-TWO

Somalia

What's in a Name?

Chantal and Mark Logan

It might be good to reflect a bit on why God chose to send conservative, Lancaster County Mennonites to the Somali people in 1953. There may be some lesson we can learn to guide us further along the way. We can only speculate on the mind of God, but using the rational minds he has given us, we see missiological wisdom in this plan. It is perhaps ironic that what is sometimes amusing to the newcomers and sometimes interpreted as Mennonite exclusiveness could be seen as a positive point of commonality for Mennonites in the land of the Somali. The Mennonite understanding of identity is somewhat akin to that of the Somalis, as illustrated in the famous "Mennonite name game." The way Mennonites who meet for the first time start reciting family names in search of a close family relationship is not unlike what Somalis do when they meet at the well or at the crossing of trails in the bush.

Adding to a communal sense of identity, and playing the family names game, a conservative way of life was also a point of unity. With the abstinence of drinking alcohol and a modest dress for the women, the early Mennonites stood in sharp contrast to other "infidels" from the west being observed by the Somali people. The expatriate community in Somalia, as in most parts of Africa, has never been known for its high moral standards. Among the Italian colonizers in Somalia, only priests and nuns made any effort to observe the strict moral standards required of Muslims or to live a life of service. Mennonites, however, who while striving for a radical discipleship to their Prophet Jesus, were allowed to marry and have families if they so chose, and were seen as a religious people to whom the Somalis could relate. This lifestyle approval helped Mennonites overcome the obstacle of skin color, which at first sight identified them as *gaal* or infidel.

Even more, it was their allegiance to one particular teaching of their Messiah which made Mennonites well-suited for the call of God laid upon their lives. A theology of peace and nonviolence placed Mennonites in a position "to give the reason for the hope that you have" (1 Pet 3:15) in a gentle and respectful way. The Anabaptist belief that peace is the very heart of the gospel prepared Mennonites to witness in nonaggressive ways to a Muslim people, a people for whom the Christian message has always been tainted by the blood of the Crusades. That same belief gives us credibility even today, in the aftermath of the September 11 attacks in the U.S. and October 7, 2001, attacks in Afghanistan,[1] which have brought the Crusades mentality flying back at us with vengeance.

And loyalty to the Anabaptist heritage gave Mennonites the will and courage to stand firm under hardship and testing in the Horn of Africa. A knowledge and understanding of the history and beliefs of their "founding ancestors" informed the Mennonite clan on how to react when challenges came from governing authorities. Faced with first a government restriction on preaching their faith, then with a government mandate to permit Islam to be taught in their schools, Mennonites found in their past a model for remaining present in society and true to their faith, despite adverse government require-ments.

In the world, but not of the world. The Anabaptist experience and understanding of being a witnessing community in submission to, but not in agreement with, ruling authorities, presented Mennonite missionaries with a viable alternative to leaving Somalia when others decided they could not stay. We have been told by Somali friends that it was then that true colors were shown. Mennonites indeed had come to educate and to serve. Their main concern was to be a faithful witness, not to proselytize, and therefore could be trusted. Again we see how God provides for the people he sends, this time with events centuries ahead of the time they were called to be in—the right people in the right place.

Yet, surely if the whole story were to be told, one would discover that the Mennonites who served in Somalia were no less sinners than others. They were not devoid of prejudices and misconceptions about African people, and if they were indeed a community, there was plenty of grumbling and bickering in their midst. But as the story is told and the book is written, it becomes clear that it was God's grace which prepared them, it was God's grace which carried them through, and it is God's grace which has today given Mennonites the harvest of a known and respected name in the land where they lived as missionaries of Light.

It is, however, unfortunate that the harvest of a respected name is not what captures the attention of people in the western world these days. Even Mennonites can be influenced by the prevailing values of the culture around them, and many tend to see numbers as being all important. Yet, for it to be an honor in an Islamic state to be introduced as a representative of the Mennonite Mission, and for the Mennonite Mission to be blessed in the poetry of a society that sees itself as 100 percent Muslim is a gift which cannot be taken lightly, and especially, when it is so clearly a gift from God. God may have given us this gift in reward for the obedience and faithfulness of our predecessors, but we believe, in all humility, the real gift is to the Somali people, and it is a gift that has not yet been fully received.

As many who have not had Muslims as neighbors are just now discovering Islam, it might be significant to point out that there is a category worse than the infidel in Islam: the hypocrite, someone who pretends to be something he is not. A hypocrite calls himself by a false name or disguises his true identity. Mennonites in Somalia have never hidden their identity. We don't make a point to introduce ourselves as Christians, since Christianity has many connotations today which do not represent the teachings of Jesus, and using these terms can be offensive to Muslims. Yet, Somalis know we are followers of Jesus. They sometimes say, "Yes, we know Mennonites are Christians, but they are the good kind." We have always been thankful that Mennonites have had the wisdom and fortitude to be open and transparent about who they are, and even under the pressure to produce numbers, have not sold their birthright for a plate of beans.

What about the future? Any Somali, or any African, will tell you that the worst thing that can happen to a name is for it to disappear. And your name is only forgotten when you cease to have descendants who carry your name. Being forgotten by your descendants is worse than death, for time is more than a few short life spans. Polygamy is allowed, as fathering many children will keep your name alive for many generations. So, as we stand at the threshold of this jubilee year, 2003, we look around us and we wonder: where are our descendants who will carry the torch for the next fifty years? At this moment we don't see a long line of people waiting to give their lives to God in Somalia, but we believe that God, as before, is preparing workers for his harvest. Is it that we can't see them because they have not been challenged to come forward, or could it be that we are looking at the wrong places?

Still one last thing remains for us to learn from the stories of clans and founding ancestors. According to some Somali experts (Gunther Schlee and Abdi Mohamed Mohamed), the very notion of clan is not only a biological affiliation. A weaker clan can join a stronger one and then adopt its name. It is called *sheegad*, which means that one accepts to tell the names of the ancestors of the stronger clan when asked to give the names of his own forefathers.

One thing this practice shows us is that to be part of the Mennonite clan one does not necessarily need to be white, North American, or to come from Lancaster County. It is not a question of ethnicity; it is a question of claiming a name. But something more in *sheegad* strikes a deep chord in our understanding of the Christian faith. For what is the name of our founding ancestor, the name which gives us life? What is the name that makes us part of the clan of the redeemed? No, it is not the name Victor Dorsch, neither the name Menno Simons, but it is the name Jesus Christ.

It is our hope and our prayer that the name Mennonite Mission will live long in Somalia, not for the sake of Mennonites, but for the Somali people. It is our yearning that they will have an enduring signpost pointing to that other name, the Name above all names, the ancient name of the One whose return we await together. A road marker leading to that only name by which we can ever be saved from the chaos and conflict of this world and that name which will open, to Mennonites and Somalis alike, the way into the world to come.

CHAPTER TWENTY-THREE

Ethiopia

The Meserete Kristos Church (MKC)

Bedru Hussein Muktar

Although Ethiopia is only a short boat ride south of Arabia, the motherland of the Islamic movement, it was not until the twelfth century that Islam became a serious challenge to Ethiopia. There are several factors that prevented Islam from penetrating and spreading quickly in Ethiopia. (1) The Christian emperors of Ethiopia formed its Christianity and defended it against Muslim attacks. (2) Its elevated tableland served as a natural fortress. (3) When the country was surrounded by the forces of Islam, Ethiopia was forced into an independency that was later reflected in its religious life and its cultural, economic, and social structures. Consequently, the Ethiopians developed a strong sense of national and Christian identity. These realities enabled the Ethiopians to defend their country against Muslim invasion.[1]

Those Muslims who were able to penetrate Ethiopia's borders entered first within the low lands of Ethiopia as traders and they settled by marrying Ethiopians and Islamizing their families. Then in the twelfth century a famous Islamic leader by the name of Mohammed Grange (the leftist) began a war of conquest, starting from the south-eastern part of Ethiopia to northwestern regions. At that time a lot of Ethiopians were forced to embrace the religion of Islam.

Today, Islam is growing fast in the country because of the freedom of religion that the democratization processes support. Many mosques are being built throughout the country. Arab money is pumped into the country through many channels. The poverty in the country has assisted the speedy growth of Islam in the country. The Muslims have access to petro-dollars that they use to open Islamic schools and offer free education for poor families. They have many orphanages where the children are taught Islam. Poor people receive help from the Muslims and that encourages people to become Muslims.

What is MKC doing towards reaching the Muslims? So far there is no direct evangelization of the Muslims. However, churches are continuously being formed within Muslim communities. The interest of Muslims in the gospel has been part of the Mennonite experience in Ethiopia right from the beginning of the missionary presence. This is because half a century ago the first North American Mennonite missionaries were given the mandate from the Emperor Haile Selassie to start schools and clinic work in Muslim dominated areas. Nathan Hege writes, "The Ethiopian Government has designated open areas of missions among the non-Orthodox people, where missionaries could evangelize; and closed areas where it was strictly forbidden to convert an Orthodox person."[2]

As a result, clinics, hospitals, and schools were opened. There were chances for Muslim students to hear the gospel in those schools. Some of the converts are very dedicated Christians serving the Lord in different capacities within the country and outside the country.

One experience MKC has is the evangelization among the Muslims in the Shone area. An evangelist, Tesfaye Makango, was led by the Lord to go and preach the gospel of peace in this region. Today there are many Muslim converts. In that area, there are eight churches that are planted and six more church planting centers.

The following are what the church has been doing toward reaching the Muslims with the gospel in Ethiopia:

1. Provide awareness of Islam for key leaders of the church.

2. Give a course on Islam to students at the Bible College of MKC.

3. Have intercessory prayer to break down strongholds that resist the gospel (2 Cor 10:3-6).

4. Proclaim the gospel through radio. There is a new radio ministry that has begun preaching in the language which most Muslims use. These programs are developed in ways that relate especially to Muslim understandings and interest. The gospel is being preached

every day in these radio broadcasts, and this has become an effective way to bring the message home.

5. Become a Christian presence in Muslim communities. This is one of the most important ways that evangelization happens. When you are living within the Muslim community it is much easier to be available to bring the message and pray for the people. Through presence, MKC has planted many churches in Muslim dominated areas.

6. Live with patience. The commitment to wait for God's timing is very essential currency in evangelizing Muslims.

God has blessed this six-dimensional approach to witness among Muslims. We thank God that many are coming to faith in Jesus Christ and many churches are being formed. Here is a statistical table of the MKC churches that have developed in regions within Ethiopia where there is a significant Muslim population.[3]

	Established Churches	Church Plantings
Harregieh	13	51
Bale	1	12
Nazareth and Arrsi	24	60
Jimma/Illubabur	24	85
Wollo	7	16
Williso	8	22
Total	101	306

MKC is also reaching out into regions beyond Ethiopia. The church seeks to equip young people for outreach in neighboring countries like Djibouti, Somalia, Sudan, and even Yemen and Saudi Arabia. Already there is a large presence of Ethiopian Christians in those countries who have gone in search of jobs or for political reasons. MKC attempts to follow up with these believers in diaspora and seeks to encourage and equip them for faithful witness.

SECTION THREE

Issues and Themes

CHAPTER TWENTY-FOUR

Presence and Patience

Topic One
A Theology of Presence and Patience

Calvin E. Shenk

When my wife, Marie, and I were teachers at the Nazareth Bible Academy, a secondary school in Ethiopia, in the 1960s we were privileged to have students from Muslim background, though the majority of students were from the Christian tradition. At the Academy we were candid in teaching Christian faith, but the quality of our Christian presence either reinforced or detracted from our witness. Some Muslims became believers; others did not. Sometimes it seemed that students from Muslim background were exploring belief in Jesus, but one needed to be patient lest too much encouragement on our part be counterproductive.

Kelifa Ali was one of those students from Muslim background who publicly acknowledged his faith in Jesus. Kelifa later became a church worker and leader in the Meserete Kristos Church. During the Marxist period in Ethiopia he was imprisoned for four years. Upon his release he didn't hesitate to again assume leadership in the church. Later, suffering from cancer, Kelifa traveled to Nairobi and the United States for specialized care. While undergoing treatment he studied at Eastern Mennonite Seminary. Students and teachers will recall his favorite phrase, "He is faithful." This phrase is on his tombstone at Lindale Mennonite Church in Harrisonburg, Virginia.

Often Christians in witnessing to Muslims become impatient for results. But where the language of the church is a foreign language in Islamic contexts it is vitally important that Christians give attention to Christian presence. Words are often ineffective because they are misunderstood. Presence means to share the lives of people where they live in their struggle with life's meaning. Without meaningful presence witness can be interpreted as a posture of over-againstness or even confrontation.

Presence is preparation for witness, as well as having its own witness dimensions. Presence expresses concern for the whole person, not just one's soul. Presence sees Muslims as persons, not as objects to whom one bears witness. Meaningful presence cultivates love and openness in contrast to imposition of one's convictions. Presence is especially important for westerners at this time in world history. Christian presence stands in contrast to the assertion of western power. Presence is foundational for any kind of witness, but particularly important where mission in the traditional sense is not allowed. Sometimes presence is the only possible way to witness. But presence is not second-rate witness.

Christian presence demonstrates the gospel. Presence helps people to discover the meaning of Jesus. I asked one of my students from Muslim background why he became a Christian. He replied, "The God I knew as Allah came close in Jesus." People have opportunities to discover the deeper dimensions of the gospel. Presence seeks to be among people in love and openness. Presence is not just "being on the scene." Presence implies involvement, being present with and for others. Presence is not merely silence. But presence insists on being and doing before speaking.

Christian presence attracts the attention of others as the Jerusalem community (Acts 2) drew seekers to itself. Believing persons and the believing community model presence as they are "salt of the earth," "light of the world" (Matt 5:13-14), "a royal priesthood, a holy nation" (1 Pet 2:9), and a community which spreads the fragrance of God (2 Cor 2:14). When we model a community of reconciliation and peace our presence is a "missionary presence." Presence must be undergirded with prayerful intercession. We re-present God in Jesus among the Muslim people.

Presence can't be programmed. It is a work of the Holy Spirit. Presence models openness to Muslims, attention to Muslims.

Presence is incarnational and foundational to all witness. Presence is often more difficult than word. Without meaningful presence other forms of witness are less effective.

In the Muslim world, Christian witness is often associated with the political and economic aggression of the west. We need to acknowledge that our ecclesiastical record is marred with misunderstanding of Islam and an uncritical acceptance of western culture. In countries where religious pluralism is not tolerated, the church can easily be accused of proselytizing for conversion or giving inducement for people to change their religion. In spite of these misunderstandings, we do not refrain from witness; we seek to witness differently. We don't have to insist on our right to use a particular method of witness.

Presence needs to rely on the Holy Spirit. The Spirit blows where he wills. The Holy Spirit energizes presence in relationship. A Christian friend of mine who lived in Egypt frequently went to the mosque for meditation. He said, "I witness and let the Holy Spirit do his work." Presence has intrinsic value. It is not merely pre-evangelism. Presence is like salt, light, and leaven. Presence insists on visualization before verbalization. It incorporates being and doing. When we commit ourselves to be involved in Muslim cultures we are an "active presence," not just a "passive presence." Christian presence is God-centered and person-centered.

Being present as Jesus was present is to express solidarity, self-emptying, and sacrifice for others. Presence means to live transparently in the world by living with people in non-paternalistic or non-patronizing ways. Sometimes a silent presence raises curiosity, stimulates questions, and invites response. In some situations it is more Christian to be silent than to speak, especially when Christian witness is experienced as harshness and aggressiveness. If we are not present as Christians we have opted for absence. Decisions to be present should not be made on the basis of freedoms we are permitted. Lack of freedom might even help to illuminate the gospel as one is forced to give more attention to the quality of Christian presence. Powerlessness may have its own potency. We discover again that witness is more than organized activities.

We must avoid the temptation to disguise our identity, but we don't need to advertise it in an obnoxious way. Deceptiveness of any kind destroys the integrity of presence.

How can we overcome antagonism between Christians and Muslims? Are Muslims enemies to be conquered or friends to be won? We can't share faith when we are afraid or intolerant of Muslims. Is our relationship with Muslims characterized by love or fear? Paranoia develops when we don't have Muslim friends. One of the most successful ways to break down walls of suspicion is to meet the person on the other side of the wall—to be present with Muslims. Roelf Kuitse, a Dutch Mennonite missiologist who worked with Muslims in Indonesia and West Africa, noted that in Islamic contexts "Suspicion is lived away, not talked away." How we treat the other will affect the response of the other to us. Bridges of understanding need to be built. We should regard Muslims as God-fearers and truth-seekers.

Presence refuses to use militant language, for example, "target Muslims," or "reclaim enemy lands for Christ." Christian presence cares for people; we don't target people. Witness is not imposition. Jesus stands at the door and knocks. We commend faith; we don't coerce faith. We have often talked about Muslims. Then we've talked to Muslims. But we must spend more time living with and talking with Muslims.

Christian presence can help us get rid of ignorance, bias, fear, prejudice, stereotype, hostility, or distorted images of Islam. Christian presence helps us to avoid false witness against our Muslim neighbor. We need to describe Muslims in a way that they recognize themselves. Our attitude should be characterized by empathy more than judgment. How can we get rid of mistrust and mutual antipathy?

We don't enter conversation empty-handed. We need to give attention to the content and quality of conversation. But Muslims are not persuaded by the quality of Christian arguments alone. Islam is too often presented in negative terms (i.e. fear, or the enemy to be conquered). Engaging in "spiritual warfare" against Islam as enemy can fill us with fear and hostility toward Muslim people. The Crusades should teach us that Muslims do not respond to the gospel of coercion.

St. Francis of Assisi modeled a passionate nonviolent alternative to the dominant militant culture of his time. Crusaders used a sword with the cross. Francis sang hymns that spoke of Christ and peace. Francis modeled the presence of Christ and ministered Christ's love to Muslims. St. Francis sought to direct Muslims to Christ by few words and loving service.

Aggression should not be used to express spiritual realities.

Samaritans in the New Testament were perceived as enemies. The disciples wanted to call down fire on the enemy. But Jesus loved the Samaritan enemy and rebuked the disciples. Jesus did not allow his disciples to project the battle in the spiritual realm on the people who opposed or rejected him. Is it love or fear that drives us in our relationships with Muslims? Our task is to beam light, to build bridges of understanding, and to model Christian presence with patience.

Topic Two
The Somali Journey: Presence and Patience

Bertha Beachy

It was nearly ten years after Somalia Mennonite Mission (SMM) arrived in the southern part of Somalia that special new challenges began. In March 1962, ten months before independence in neighboring Kenya, all activities were closed down. In July permission to reopen was granted, but on July 16, Merlin Grove was assassinated. By June 1963, after twelve years of religious freedom, the national assembly changed the constitution to no "propagandizing of religion other than Islam." By September 1963 all private schools recognized by the government had to allow the teaching of Islam and Arabic in their curriculum. A coup took place October 21, 1969, which related to Russia and Marxist ideology.

It was Orie Miller who was the first Mennonite to envisage mission in Somalia. That was at the beginning of the 1950s. At that time he served as secretary for Eastern Mennonite Board of Missions and Charities (EMBMC) now known as Eastern Mennonite Missions (EMM). In his international travels he was impressed that all United Nations trusteeships had religious freedom; he therefore urged that EMBMC explore entrée into Somalia as a Mennonite commitment to mission among Muslim people.

Somalia became the first country that was over 99 percent Muslim for EMM to enter. After due investigation, the first mission family arrived January 16, 1953. The mission was registered as Somalia Mennonite Missions (SMM). Somalia became independent on July 1, 1960, and the British-administered northern region and the Italian-administered southern region joined together that day as the Somali Republic.

The Swedish Lutheran Mission (SLM) had worked with Somalis from 1896-1925 under shifting colonial powers and borders. The Catholic mission came with the Italians. From 1954-1974 the Sudan Interior Mission (SIM) worked within Somalia, and at present they continue to have many areas where they relate to Somalis in diaspora. Though the Somali language was not written officially until 1972, SIM completed a Somali translation of the Bible in 1976.

How should Mennonites relate to a Hamitic people with mostly one religion, language, and a camel culture? There were several other minority groups in coastal towns and along the two main rivers. All of these groups had their own languages, but they normally understood and spoke Somali as well. In the mind of most Somalis, Christianity was connected with the Crusades of a thousand years ago, as well as with the twentieth-century colonial masters who had divided the Somali people into five parts: The Ethiopians in the Ogaden, the French in Djibouti, the English in northeastern Kenya and northern Somaliland, and the Italians in southern Somalia. Islam was the core of Somali unity and identity with Arabic the religious language.

Through careful listening and exploring the land, English language schools and health concerns became priority for SMM. By the end of 1963 SMM was developing programs in four locations. Within one decade of SMM being registered as a mission agency in Somalia the following were staffed and functioned: two adult schools; one primary and one intermediate boarding school for boys; two health clinics; one twenty-five bed hospital; one day school; and two agricultural projects, one of which closed and another in process for a remote clan in the interior along the Juba River.

Christian worship services were open to Somalis and international people. In the far south services were held in two villages with former SLM believers. Somalis early on requested Bible classes to increase their English. There were a few private Bible classes as well with individual Somalis. Though SMM always had conversion as a given priority, by 1961 there were less than ten believers. New believers faced ostracism, ridicule, were often rejected by their families, and some even received death threats. In these ten years, there had been warnings from Italian officials, Somali Islamic leaders, and government officials at various times for different issues. But the greatest suspicion centered on possible conversions to Christianity with young students in our schools. However, many government officials sent their sons to our boarding schools. SMM was constantly challenged as to whether they actually came to help Somalis or to convert them.

A shift toward a focus on mission as presence began early in the 1960s. Developments in the society pushed SMM in the direction of a missiology of presence. The changing realities included the closure of the mission for several months, a violent attack against Merlin and Dorothy Grove, new regulations that restricted religious freedom, and the requirement that Islam be taught in SMM schools. The mission team developed a written statement on a theology of presence that formed the basis for discussion and reflection.

A stance of presence and patience brought changes into the way we served and shared. These changes included the following. A person interested in a Bible study had to write a request stating his interest and assuring that this was a voluntary request with no inducements by the mission. Bibles were always sold from the SMM offices and not from the more public SMM bookstore downtown. Believers began baptizing believers without missionary participation. Somali believers also carefully screened requests for Bible studies to ascertain whether the inquirers were sincerely interested. Persons who wished to attend worship services with the believers were also interviewed to determine whether they were sincere.

It was mostly young men and students who attended the worship gatherings and fellowships. There were no women for many years. In order to develop Somali leadership, Bible schools took place during the vacation times at the boarding school. It was difficult to disciple this young group without developing dependencies. SMM provided several scholarships for secondary training for believers and others to study at Nazareth Bible Academy in Ethiopia.

The general government and public noted that when the government demanded that Islam be taught in SMM schools, the mission allowed this to happen. This was in contrast to the SIM that closed its boarding schools when the government mandated this requirement. In 1972, when the government declared an official script for written Somali, all private schools were nationalized. The plan was that all classes would eventually be taught in Somali instead of English. All SMM properties were nationalized. In the capital city of Mogadishu this meant that we had to move out of the housing on the mission compound and find rental homes in different parts of the city. We offered our teachers with degrees to the Ministry of Education (MOE). Persons with Bible in their degrees were asked to leave, but the MOE assigned ten of us very important positions. Several remained at the SMM secondary school. However, by May of 1976 all of us were asked to leave. We surmise that the reason was the preparations for war with Ethiopia that was moving forward; the government did not want possible distraction by western foreigners.

The believers in Mogadishu shifted the gathering place for worship to the Catholic cathedral where they were warmly received.

We also invested in a house where believers could live, but this became very divisive.

A calamitous war with Ethiopia ensued. After the war and four years after SMM had to leave Somalia, Mennonite Central Committee (MCC) was invited to help the UN with the drought in 1980. That was the beginning of a nine-year involvement in Somalia for MCC. SMM teachers were also invited to return by the leading officer in the MOE, who had been a former teacher in SMM schools. So from 1981-1990 SMM teachers were again engaged in teaching in government schools. By this time the country was falling into chaos under the army general, Siad Barre. He was violently pushed out of power in 1991 and clan warlords have reigned ever since. A Somali MCC-EMM office developed in Kenya in 1991 that remains connected to believers, refugees, educational, development, and social and peace issues with Somalis.

Meanwhile, the Catholic bishop was assassinated, the cathedral burned, and many Somalis have died including believers. Sometimes it happened because they were not in their clan areas, or worked for international agencies, and other times because they were believers.

For Somalis some pivotal points seemed to be (1) the decision of the SMM to continue in Somalia after the assassination of Merlin Grove, (2) the teaching of Islam in our schools, (3) our openness to teach where they placed us in their schools, and (4) our return in the 1980s and our ongoing connections via the Nairobi office. The Somalis always comment that the Mennonites have an understanding of, and a commitment to, Somali people. Both the American and Russian government help has come and long gone in these fifty years. But the Mennonites have remained committed.

In 1978, former missionaries in Lancaster, Pennsylvania, began meeting on a monthly basis to pray for Somali believers and other concerns. There are Muslim Somalis that know about this and are grateful for these prayers. The Nairobi office reports on special concerns and joys.

Nairobi, Kenya, is a gathering place for Somali refugees and a weekly worship service takes place on Saturday. There are young women attending, as well as entire families. In the mid 1970s EMM and the Nairobi Mennonite Church built a community center across from the mosque in Eastleigh, which is in the Somali section of Nairobi. It has been a place of dialogue and trust-building, a place where Muslims and Christians can and do meet. It is the home of the

People of God Bible correspondence course written for Muslim seekers, which has been or is being translated into more than forty languages. The Sudan Interior Mission team has partnered with the center in developing English classes and sports for Somalis from this center. Even though we cannot at present live in Somalia because of the political anarchy, members of our team visit regularly as encouragers for life-giving efforts such as schools or women's groups advocating for peace. This includes keeping in touch with believers. Recently, I received word that a woman from my classes in 1960 had become a believer. We rejoice when the streams of life touch persons who have lived within the devastation of Somalia's interclan wars.

The presence ministry among Somalis living outside of Somalia is multifaceted. For example, EMM has begun a presence ministry in Djibouti. SIM and others connect with some of the estimated one million Somalis in North America. Probably fifteen Somalis have graduated from Mennonite colleges. One of these graduates has developed a peace program that touches many parts of Africa through his teaching at Daystar University near Nairobi. Currently there are two Somalis at Goshen College, one a believer and one a Muslim. Both had Mennonite connections that brought them to Goshen.

During a 2003 reunion with North American Somalis and SMM missionaries at the EMM headquarters in Salunga, Pennsylvania, these former SMM students met to work at peacemaking across clans. (They tell me that Toronto Somalis alone have thirty-nine divisions in that city.) They also report that no former SMM students participate in fighting with the warlords. The 14th Somali Peace Conference began in December 2002 and continues in Nairobi. Probably the biggest issue is the destructiveness and trauma of the clan connections.

Today to say you represent the Mennonites, in this war-torn society, opens doors and opportunities for ministry. We are recognized as followers of Jesus who are committed to his way of peace. In that spirit the team in Nairobi working with Somalis have developed booklets in the Somali language on peacemaking that have been very well received by Somalis who want to wisely and helpfully work at peacemaking in their troubled country. There is great appreciation for the Mennonite commitment to encouraging such efforts at peace-making.

Fifty years ago the journey of Mennonites with Somalis began. Today there are many opportunities to connect with Somalis, but

EMM-MCC often find it difficult to find people. It is not a typical "mission" connection of church growth. No one can report a thriving church or how many Somali believers exist around the world. But it is a journey of call, of incarnational presence, of prayer and fasting, and of patience—God does the converting.

Topic Three
Incarnational Witness Among the
Samoghos of Burkina Faso

Donna Entz

The stance that most clearly describes our witness in Burkina Faso is "incarnational." In John 1:18 we are told, "No one has ever seen God. It is God the only Son, who is close to the Father's heart, who has made him known" (NRSV). Now in this period of time since Christ returned to heaven, who else is there to make God known to Muslim people if not Christ's body, the church, empowered by the Holy Spirit? The people in Jesus's day could not see God without Jesus. The Muslims of our day cannot see God without us.

It was seventeen years ago that we told the elders in the West African Samogho village where we were living that our elders in North America had sent us with a message from God. But we would have to live among them, we said, and learn their language so we could communicate that message in the Samogho language. An incarnational ministry requires taking seriously the issue of identification. For us, that meant learning to eat the local food, wearing African dress, and of even greater importance, setting up our family courtyard in a semi-traditional way so that we would be comfortable with people, and they with us.

Identification for us meant participating in most village activities and allowing village people to help raise our children. In fact, we specifically chose a small village so that participation would be manageable for us socially. We depended on the elders to help us find workers to get our work done.

Islam was strongest in West Africa during the Middle Ages. Ethnic groups like the Samoghos and others held out, some violently, against Islam. One can still find traces of Muslim theology in the folklore and in conversations with isolated Muslim individuals who have been attached to Islam for many years.

The majority of Samoghos, however, only became Muslim some fifty years ago. For that reason, Samogho society has a much more African flavor than an Arabic one. Only a few scattered individuals have studied some Arabic. That being the case, we have not used Muslim forms of prayer in our worship or gone to pray at the mosque. We sensed that in a country less than half Muslim, there is some religious tolerance, and therefore we would focus on living our faith most genuinely for us, instead of engaging in some form of radical contextualization.

As our family lived in the village, we have attempted to model a daily time of worship, prayer, and study, anticipating the need for daily group worship in a future church. But perhaps the most important thing we did was to learn the local language, our son being the first white person ever to have developed fluency in the Samogho language. The real significance of this only became clear to us with time.

Islamic teachers in our area adopted early on the regional trade language for communication and instruction. This has meant that the local, indigenous languages are being quickly swallowed up, preserved only by the women who hang on tenaciously to their mother tongues.

We took on for ourselves the roles of religious teachers, not development workers, largely because we wished to gain the respect of our friends and neighbors who were themselves very religious people. But both my husband and I also have interests in village development needs. Loren is involved with the economic and agricultural issues in the village. He counsels in those areas and also serves as a bank for people. I have interests in the medical and nutritional needs of the village. I visit the sick to offer counsel on health issues, blessings for healing, and prayers for family problems.

As our Wycliffe colleagues were busy in analyzing and writing an alphabet for the Samogho language, we were busy in cultural study, working to preserve the traditional folklore, proverbs, and music of the people. The ethnic funeral music was banned by Islam, remembered only by those who grew up in the pre-Islamic period.

Instead of preaching with use of fear tactics or strictly emotional appeal, our chosen form of proclamation was storytelling from the Bible. We wrote a lengthy script of Old Testament stories, covering in great detail the entire narrative, much like an extensive children's Bible story book. Our colleagues went to work, with the help of two French-educated Muslims, in translating these stories. Finally, with the addition of stories from the Luke-Acts account, the "evangelism series" we had developed formed a total set of twenty-two audio-cassettes recounting the biblical narrative.

In the West African context, many of the Bible stories linked by historical connectors are understood without explanation. Unlike some missionary colleagues we had encountered at work elsewhere in the country, we have refrained from preaching the appropriate Christian doctrine at the end of each Bible story. If true African faith and theology were what we were envisioning growing out of the study of God's word, it seemed counterproductive for us to teach doctrinal formulations that had emerged from the northern hemisphere. In our setting, an added bonus was that in contrast to Muslim teaching that took place in the regional trade language, the Bible stories we were developing and recording had special appeal, being recounted in the people's own local, indigenous language.

We placed a particular emphasis on a full treatment of Old Testament stories before turning to the New Testament. Covenants between people and groups have been important in the Samogho traditional worldview, and consequently this theme is better understood among many of them than among most North American Christians.

In our setting, many people have Muslim names, but don't know the meaning of their names. The meaning of names, however, is very important in Samogho tradition, and for this reason, people often find a particular appeal in the Old Testament stories.

We also make connections with what Muslims refer to as the Holy Books: the Torah, the Zabur (Psalms), and the Injil (Gospels). Different, no doubt, than in settings influenced by more orthodox Arabic teaching, we were surprised and delighted to discover that the Christian holy books were considered more authoritative than the Qur'an because "they are older."

In order to maintain the existing social structures, we have worked hard to build relationships with the elders. We presented the Bible stories first to the older people, both men and women. By working with the elders, we were at least leaving open the possibility of a group movement toward acceptance of the gospel. Of course, one does not create a group movement, God does. But this approach has helped to keep our focus on the whole village as a collectivity, rather than on the ostracizing and isolation of individual group members. The use of recorded cassettes also made it easy for illiterate elders to capture the stories. We were concerned not to speed up the already rapid westernization process in the village that favors youth over elders and individuals over community.

Though our colleagues, both expatriate and national, do the

actual work of translation, our role has been to help with the testing process. The oldest tester we work with is an elder who has led the village in making some changes in the rituals of the village. The village as a whole has not always supported his stance, not being as aware of the biblical message, nor of his reason for the changes.

A church of ten baptized members has formed around the first Samogho Christians who were Bible translators in the neighboring village. Several Christian families have joined them from other areas of the country. It is a faithful group, using primarily the Samogho language, but also a translation of the regional trade language. One of the most exciting aspects of seeing the church develop is watching how the translation of the Old Testament Psalms has become the basis for church worship music, accompanied by musical styles and instruments deeply rooted in Samogho culture and tradition.

∾

Response: Historical Perspectives

Walter Sawatsky

The essays on presence and patience by Donna Entz, Bertha Beachy, and Calvin Shenk are rooted in the fact of the Mennonite experience of ministry over the past three to four decades, not only in Muslim settings. The essays provide narratives on the way that living with Muslims, without explicit intentions of starting churches or stressing immediate conversions, have resulted in two things: (1) some remarkable conversion stories, often as a journey of responses to various encounters with living Christians while God did the converting; and (2) in a history of relationships of trust and authenticity, Muslims see God within us! This becomes exceedingly practical and specific. For example, a commitment to presence and transparency impacted how the Entz's built their home in the village in Burkina Faso where they live.

In what ways are we still consciously following a "relevant theology of presence" as articulated in a small *Mission Focus* publication of 1982. At that time Calvin Shenk had written a composite of five papers presented at a Council of International Ministries (CIM) consultation. Several assertions from that consultation over twenty years ago illumine and illustrate the experiences of Anabaptists in Muslim settings. Calvin Shenk wrote that a missiology of presence is "preparation for witness," "demonstrates the gospel," "shares the lives of people," and "cannot be programmed." In negative language, deceptiveness destroys the integrity of presence, and presence ministry "refuses to use militant language."

These three essays especially prod us to personal reflections on witness through presence, mostly in African and Middle Eastern settings. However, the same principles have applied to a missiology of presence in socialist countries, national security state settings, and Muslim contexts, more than twenty years ago.

When presence leads to proclamation, does a missiology of presence set limits to what is good and what is an improper application of proclamation missiology? For example, the negative experiences of post-Soviet massive proclamation is undercutting the seedbed provided by the long patient witness of believers. It is instructive to emphasize how vital a missiology of presence as authentic incarnational witness is, not just as a possible method under restricted settings, but as central missional mode anywhere.

It seemed fitting that one of the participants in the discussion of these essays told how a thirty-year witness by a sister who converted had finally resulted in the conversion of her father and mother, as well as the sister's conversion who participated in our seminar. She also shared the way in which her sister's witness shaped her expectations of where her life of faith and witness might lead her after college.

CHAPTER TWENTY-FIVE

Justice and Reconciliation

Topic One
Justice and Reconciliation in
Muslim-Christian Encounter:
Perspectives from Israel/Palestine

Dorothy Jean Weaver

If anyone had told me ten years ago that I would be contributing an essay to a volume, *Anabaptists Meeting Muslims*, I would have been vastly amazed. Ten years ago I don't think I had ever even met a Muslim face to face, let alone developed a friendship with one. And I had only the most rudimentary awareness of who Muslims are and what they believe.

A lot has happened in the last eight years to change all that. I have not become a scholar of Islam, to be sure. While I now have a few pertinent books sitting on my shelf and have listened to a handful of lectures here and there, I am still a basic newcomer to the ethos and the teachings of Islam. But eight years ago, in the fall of 1995, I made my first sojourn to the Middle East. And ever since then I have been finding my way back there with increasing regularity and out of a growing sense of personal call. During these visits I have worked in a variety of locations and been engaged in a range of activities. I have spent three semesters in short-term Mennonite Central Committee

(MCC) assignments teaching New Testament courses in three different settings: Beirut in 1995, Bethlehem in 2000, and Cairo in 2002. I have spent two semesters studying and writing at Tantur Ecumenical Institute in Jerusalem in 1996 and 2003. I have co-led two three-week Middle East study tours from Eastern Mennonite Seminary (EMS) in 1998 and 2000. In 2001 I joined a two-week Christian Peacemaker Teams (CPT) delegation to Hebron. And in 2002 I co-led a twelve-day delegation from EMS to Christmas Lutheran Church in Bethlehem shortly after the forty-day siege of Bethlehem had ended.

Throughout these experiences I have witnessed several different majority-Muslim cultures up close and personal, encountered many individual Muslims in their ordinary, everyday worlds, and developed strong personal ties to a growing handful of Muslim acquaintances. It is from these personal experiences, and specifically my experiences in Israel/Palestine, that I will be drawing as I reflect here on "Justice and Reconciliation" as viewed through the lens of Muslim-Christian encounter.

A couple of general observations may be helpful for starters:

1. In Israel/Palestine the prominent dividing walls are not above all between Muslims and Christians, but rather between Palestinians, *both Muslim and Christian,* and the community of Israel, *"the Jewish,"* as the Palestinians refer to them. So while I have had many conversations with Palestinian Muslims, the focus of these conversations was most often on Israeli-Palestinian issues and very seldom on Muslim-Christian issues. There are surely Muslim-Christian issues that emerge within the daily life of Palestinians, but these issues tend to play a secondary role vis-à-vis the far more prominent Israeli-Palestinian issues.

For example, in the fall of 2000 I taught a course on the life of Jesus for Palestinian Muslim and Christian tour guides. The venue for the class was the Christmas Lutheran Church in Bethlehem. In that class, in that church, Muslims and Christians did talk with one another about faith. I asked the pastor, Mitri Raheb, whether Muslims and Christians talk about their faith with one another in other circumstances. He responded, "This is the *only* place in which they *do* talk with each other about such things!"

2. While there are clearly religious militants on each side of the dividing line, the Israeli-Palestinian conflict is not fundamentally a religious conflict focused on the theological differences between Muslims, Jews, and Christians. Rather, it is an ideological conflict

focused on differing political visions concerning the ownership and management of a prime bit of real estate in the Middle East. Key evidence supporting this view lies in the fact that Muslims, Christians, and Jews, Palestinians, Israelis, and internationals regularly work together *across religious lines* in opposing the Israeli occupation of Palestine.

3. While I myself am not personally acquainted with Palestinians from the radical Muslim factions such as Hamas and the Palestinian Islamic Jihad, I am aware that these groups have significant support in the Palestinian community. And they clearly do espouse violence as a response to the evils and the injustice of the Israeli occupation of Palestine. But there are at the same time many Muslims who do not subscribe to the violent strategies of the radical factions and many Muslims who are working diligently and nonviolently day by day, sometimes (or is it always?) at great personal cost, for the cause of peace and justice.

4. Any present-day Muslim-Christian encounters in Israel/Palestine will be taking place within the shadow of several major geopolitical events or realities that significantly color the perspectives of Palestinian Muslims: (1) The Crusades of the Middle Ages, carried out by Christians *against* the Muslims of the Holy Land; and (2) the current political commitments of the United States, above all other western nations, to support the state of Israel far in excess of any support for the nascent state of Palestine.

Where then is the potential for fruitful Muslim-Christian encounter in the search for justice and reconciliation between warring groups and enemy factions within Israel/Palestine? And what are the concerns or the cautions that come into play? Out of my own personal experiences I would offer a few very simple observations and share a few stories:

1. In the arena of justice and reconciliation work the door is wide open for fruitful encounter between Christians and Muslims on the personal level. Wherever personal relationships of friendship and mutual respect are established, there will be opportunity to engage in serious and open discussion about issues of justice and reconciliation. And there will also be opportunity for genuine trust levels to grow up between individuals in place of suspicion.

I think here of a conversation that I had one day this past spring with Ahmad, the front desk clerk at the Star Hotel in Bethlehem. Ahmad had been the solitary staff person on the premises at the Star

Hotel during four days of curfew back in the spring of 2002, when our Bethlehem Delegation was lodged at that hotel. So we had developed strong personal ties to him as we assisted him in setting out the breakfast and washing the dishes and as we visited with him downstairs in the reception area. And before we left, we collected a money gift and gave it to him for a medical procedure that he needed but could not afford.

So this past spring when I returned to the Bethlehem area, I reestablished those personal ties with Ahmad and visited with him regularly on my Sunday trips down into Bethlehem. Our conversations almost always focused on "the situation," and the specific events of the week. One day as we sat in the lobby of the Star Hotel, visiting over pita sandwiches and tea, we found ourselves in a conversation that seemed to go round and round in circles, from one pole to the other. My pole was the observation that violence only begets violence, an observation that appeared to me absolutely unassailable, given the everyday context of the Israeli-Palestinian "tit for tat" attacks and counterattacks. Ahmad's pole was that "if they hadn't done 'x' to us in the beginning, there would be no problem." And then it was my turn again; and I was back with my observations about the obvious futility of violence. And so it went, back and forth.

That day we did not arrive at any neat conclusions to our discussion. But the important aspect of that conversation for me is the fact that it took place at all, that I had an open opportunity as a Christian to share with Ahmad, a Muslim, my deeply-held beliefs about violence and to do so in an entirely natural and nonthreatening context. And that opportunity was enabled above all by the simple but crucial factors of friendship and mutual respect.

I think as well of Majdi, my shopkeeper friend from Manger Street in Bethlehem. I first met Majdi one night in the spring of 2000 when Kevin Clark, my tour coleader, and I were walking along Manger Street past Majdi's shop. Majdi called out to us, invited us into his shop, and served us tea. I have visited Majdi's shop many times since then, bought numerous souvenir items from him, witnessed his deep concerns for my personal safety during dangerous times in Bethlehem, taken my friends to buy in his shop, received souvenir gifts from him, and had many conversations with him over cups of tea or coffee. Most recently, and at Majdi's request, I have collected orders here in this community for olive wood items from Majdi's shop. Through these encounters Majdi and I have built a sturdy friendship based on mutual respect, each for the other.

Just recently, then, in a phone call from Bethlehem, Majdi expressed his gratitude for my assistance with the olive wood sales and assured me that I will always have a welcome in his home when I come to Bethlehem. And somewhere in the midst of all these expressions of gratitude he made an intriguing and totally unsolicited comment, only partially spelled out, that I think might be completed as follows: "People say bad things [about Americans]. But I disagree with them. I tell them that I know people like you and your friends, [Americans who are goodhearted and compassionate]." What I find striking here is that simple acts of friendship and mutual respect have created a context within which Majdi, a Palestinian Muslim, is willing to counter the prevailing sentiments of his Palestinian neighbors and to work proactively to break down stereotypes and walls of suspicion and hatred between people groups.

2. In the arena of justice and reconciliation work the door is likewise wide open for fruitful encounter between Christians and Muslims on the institutional or group level. Here again friendship and mutual respect are essential components. But in this case the crucial credentials for fruitful engagement in justice and reconciliation work are above all the commitment to live vulnerably and nonviolently in the midst of a world of violence, the willingness to stand in active solidarity with those who are the victims of violence and oppression, and the ability to reach out simultaneously to those who perpetrate that same violence and oppression.

I have participated in two very different sorts of Muslim-Christian encounters at the level of group or institution. The first of these I referred to above, when in the fall of 2000, I taught a "Life of Jesus" course for Palestinian tour-guiding students at Bethlehem's Christmas Lutheran Church. Because the tour-guiding course was for Palestinian students, it included both Muslims and Christians. Because it was a "Life of Jesus" course, it necessarily focused squarely on the Gospel portraits of the life of Jesus. And because this course was running in the fall of 2000, I found myself teaching about Jesus and his life of peacemaking right in the midst of the outbreak of violence that we now know as the Second Intifada. The significance of these converging factors did not at all escape me. On Sunday, October 1, 2000, I sent the following e-mail reflections to family and friends:

I was pondering this morning just what it means for me that I am here to teach about the life and teachings of Jesus (to tour guides, no less!) precisely in these days and in these moments. It seems like an amazing opportunity! Please pray with me that my teaching will be fruitful in ways that I can't even begin to imagine. My students are very eager to learn, and it seems just an incredible opportunity for me to portray to them (and, as the case may be, to the tour groups that they guide) a Jesus who is not a violent Crusader coming to burn down the Middle East and annihilate his enemies, but someone who conquers by loving his enemies. I myself don't know what all it is going to mean for me to teach this course here right in these moments. I know that I can't come with any glib answers. Nor do I intend to. But I do intend to communicate the story of Jesus as I understand it from the Gospels. Please pray with me that I will be an effective communicator.

I do not and may never know the long-term impact of my teaching that fall on the thoughts and perspectives of the students in my class, some of whom were Muslim. I do know, however, that one of the Muslim students, Ibrahim, came to me in great distress when I gave them the assignment to identify the central themes of the Sermon on the Mount. "I can't do this assignment," he said to me. "Jesus is a very important prophet for us. And everything that he said is important." And as a result Ibrahim turned in the longest paper of any of the students, a paper far longer than those of his Christian colleagues in the class. And in spite of Muslim teachings that claim that Jesus was never crucified, another of the Muslim students, Nimer, gave a powerful and moving account of the crucifixion of Jesus as his final project in the tour-guiding class. Above all, I am deeply grateful to God for that astonishing opportunity to teach a course about Jesus the peacemaker right in the midst of a social context rapidly exploding into ugly and brutal warfare.

The other significant Muslim-Christian encounter that I participated in was the summer 2001 CPT delegation to Hebron. Here I witnessed firsthand the faithful, patient, creative, and very risky work being done by the CPT corps members and reservists in Hebron as they literally "get in the way" of ugly conflicts and violent confrontations between Israeli soldiers and settlers on the one side and Palestinian residents of Hebron on the other. And here the encounter with Palestinians is by definition an encounter with

Muslims, since, except CPT members, there are no Christians in Hebron.

The engagement of the Hebron CPT team with the various parties in conflict is striking on several fronts. On the one hand they have a strong, public, and uncompromising commitment to nonviolence at all times and in all places. At critical moments when their own lives have appeared to be at special risk, they have published statements reaffirming their commitment to nonviolence and making it clear that they wish no one to engage in violence on their behalf.

On the other hand they spend their days specifically seeking out trouble spots and getting in the way wherever things are ugliest and most violent. This draws them into actions carried out in solidarity with the occupied Palestinian community. They walk the streets of Hebron on the lookout for incidents of harassment carried out on the Palestinian population by Israeli soldiers or settlers. They assist Palestinian schoolchildren get past soldiers or settlers on their way to school. They advocate with soldiers on behalf of Palestinians detained at checkpoints. They assist Palestinian families harvest their crops in the face of harassment and violence by Israeli settlers nearby. They stand with Palestinian families whose houses are threatened with demolition by the Israeli military. And their regular involvement in these sorts of activities gives the CPT Hebron team, with their red hats and armbands, enormous credibility among the Muslim population of Hebron and even beyond.

But at the same time the CPT Hebron team works diligently at the task of "un-demonizing" and thereby "re-humanizing" the occupying Israelis, soldiers and settlers alike, whom the Palestinians clearly view as their enemies. CPT has published a statement affirming the commitment of CPTers to resist all expressions of anti-Semitism. And as the CPT Hebron team gets in the way between belligerent factions, they find it essential to nurture the best possible relations with people on all sides of the conflict. This means that they work to establish solid lines of communication and good relations with the Israeli soldiers posted in Hebron, and, where possible, with the Israeli settler communities as well. And they nurture whatever Muslim-Jewish connections are possible within their context. They often join Israeli Jewish groups, such as Rabbis for Human Rights, in actions on behalf of Palestinian Muslims. Several years ago, when they were engaged in a time of fasting, one or all of them determined that they would break their fast only when they could sit down at a table together with Jews and Muslims. So while the CPT Hebron team spends its days getting in the way between people who fear, hate, and frequently abuse each other, they are also reaching out on both sides, where possible, to nurture dialogue and ultimately reconciliation between these groups of people.

3. In the arena of justice and reconciliation work within a Muslim context, there will be times when crucial discernment needs to take place concerning which activities are appropriate and which are inappropriate for Christian peacemakers. And in such moments it is essential to be clear with all parties about the meaning of the Christian message of reconciliation.

One such defining moment came to us during our CPT delegation to Hebron back in the summer of 2001. And our defining moment was our demonstration.

It happened on day five of our delegation, at a crucial juncture. We had spent the previous days in Jerusalem learning to know each other, doing nonviolence training, and hearing from human rights activists, both Israeli and Palestinian. And now we were in Bethlehem, sitting in the home of a Palestinian Christian and listening to another such presentation. From here, Plan A was to drive the short distance over to Beit Jala to begin our first real CPT action, a Human Shield operation, spending the night in houses endangered by nightly gun battles between Palestinian gunmen in Beit Jala and the Israeli military across the way in Gilo.

But in Palestine Plan A often gives way to Plan B. It did so this day with very little warning. Right in the middle of our group processing session the phone rang. One of our group leaders took the call. And when she returned, she had a major change in plans to announce. Due to an especially violent act carried out by the Israeli military that day, an assassination that had killed a number of Palestinians, including a young child, an emergency committee was planning a demonstration starting from Manger Square. If we wanted to connect with the man arranging our homestays in Beit Jala, we would have to go to the demonstration, since he would be there.

And now the question was put to us: "What do you want to do?" We needed to decide, and to decide very fast. There wasn't much time. One member of our group needed no time at all. She spoke up with great passion: "What are we waiting for? This is exactly what we came here to do, to support our Palestinian friends. And that's what they want us to do. So I think we should go and support them!" There were nods of approval at a number of places around the circle.

I myself had deep reservations about the whole thing. I had vivid memories of the many demonstrations I had witnessed from the roof of Christmas Lutheran Church in Bethlehem only months before. And I had never once considered joining such a demonstration. They were always marked by the chanting of some seven-syllable slogan which I felt sure was a kind of angry statement or ugly threat. And the group power evident in such marches frightened me, even as a bystander. I made known my reservations. But my voice did not carry the day. Even our host assured us that the demonstration would be peaceful and encouraged us to go. So it was decided: We would go to Manger Square.

Once we arrived on the scene, highly visible as we were in our fire-engine red CPT hats, I took stock of the situation. Men (no women!) were milling around. There was a small stage set up in the middle of the square, with a sign posted above it in Arabic. I asked someone to tell me what the sign said. The answer was a chilling one: "Death to the collaborators!" And then I noticed that there was also a noose hanging from the sign. This was all the information I needed. I knew that this was no demonstration in which I could take part under any circumstances. I managed to find our group leader in the crowd and tell her what I had learned. And she called another group caucus. "Sixty-second decision making" is what they call it in CPT.

We had to go around the circle and declare ourselves. There was still a majority of persons who wanted to go, who thought that we could express our own peaceful agenda in some way that would maintain our integrity. By this time I was literally in tears. Feeling the call to stand against group sentiment is never an easy thing, and surely not in such pressurized circumstances. But I knew I couldn't go. All I needed to do was to think of my Christian friends in Bethlehem, the folks at the Lutheran church just up the street from where we were standing. I knew, I just knew, that this was nothing that they would ever have considered. And I knew that I couldn't break faith with them. I said I could not go. Several others said the same. The rest of the delegation group headed on up the street with the demonstration, leaving the three of us and the CPT Hebron team members standing in the square.

For our part we got a ride back to Beit Jala. We assumed it would be a long wait until the others came back. But we were surprised. Only a short while later, there they were. And then the story came out. They too had left the demonstration. Part way up the street they had discovered, by talking with some of the demonstrators, that the event had in fact been sponsored by the Palestinian Islamic Jihad and Hamas. And when they learned this, they pulled out of the demonstration and did yet another round of sixty-second decision making. This time they also knew. This was not an action for CPT. There were still several journalists in the group who wished to stay on with the demonstration. They were told that they could do so, if they took off their CPT hats and armbands and went incognito. But they decided not to stay.

Important lessons in life often come through difficulty. This was surely one such lesson. In recounting their experiences after the fact, a number of persons acknowledged that they too had known all along, that they had in fact acted against their own better instincts in joining the demonstration. For us as a group the incident became a prime lesson on how (and how not) to make corporate decisions and what it meant for us to be and to act as a Christian peacemaker team. I am profoundly grateful that there were no media cameras out that night. But the entire event was, in the end, a gift to us all, a lesson we could probably have learned in no better way.

These, then, are my observations about Muslim-Christian encounter within the arena of justice and reconciliation work in Israel/Palestine, and here as well are a few of the personal experiences that lie behind them. I believe that the opportunities are wide open for us in Israel/Palestine and elsewhere as we follow Jesus's example and invest our energies in the work of peacemaking in a world hell-bent on war. May God give us courage and wisdom for the task!

Topic Two
Justice and Reconciliation in the Somali Experience

Ahmed Haile

My first relationship with Mennonites was having a mashed potato meal in the home of Bertha Beachy and Naomi Smoker in Mogadishu, Somalia. I didn't have a clue what I was eating, and wasn't sure that I liked this mushy food, but it was the beginning of my journey with Mennonites. That was in 1970, and in 1973 I moved to Nairobi and joined the team with David and Grace Shenk at the Eastleigh Fellowship Center. In time my sojourn took me to North America where I enrolled in a Mennonite high school, then a college, and finally peace studies at Associated Mennonite Biblical Seminary. Today I invite you to consider three dimensions of peace and justice as it relates to reconciliation (restoration). First we will look at the Somali traditional culture, secondly we will explore briefly the Islamic contribution, and finally the biblical faith roots and the gift of the grace of reconciliation we experience in Jesus Christ.

I begin with two myths, one from the Nilotic Turkana people of Northern Kenya, and the other from the Somali people. These two myths demonstrate a basic truism: peace brings life. It is not the other way around. Life does not bring peace, but rather a fruit of peace is abundant life.

The first myth comes from the Turkana. A long time ago, the heavens were very close to the earth. In those days, there was much rain in Turkana land. Rain came down every day, and everywhere there was green pasture. The livestock and wild animals had plenty to eat. God was very close to the Turkana. God talked with them, especially through the seers (diviners) who were the intermediaries between God and men. Then the Turkanas began to complain about the goodness of God, because there was too much rain and water. The days were so cold that the people covered themselves with animal skins and during the day warmed themselves with fire. They could not enjoy life because there was no sunshine at all, and the sky was close to earth. Then the women, in answer to these problems, came together, gathered sticks and pushed the sky away from the earth.

The second myth comes from the Somalis. In the beginning, the sky and the earth were very near to one another. But the transgression of humankind caused the sky (*waaq* or god) to move away from the earth.

Almost all the people of the world have the myth of a one-time warless world in a lost age of gold, whose recovery was the object of desire and endeavor.[1] Basically, both of these stories that are cited tell about God's close relationship with humankind from the beginning times, but human transgression caused the separation.

The name for sky in the Somali language is *waaq*. This is also the name for God. In ancient times *waaq* was very near to earth. And there was blessing. But then there was a broken relationship between humankind and *waaq*. Consequently *waaq* has gone away: the sky is far above us. Consequently we have heat and drought and the perennial blessing of *waaq* is a distant memory.

So for both the Turkana and the Somali people the separation between sky and earth, between God and humankind, brings drought and hardship.

However, within the Somali worldview, peace is linked to the cultivation of renewed relationships between earth and sky, between humankind and God. The term for peace in Somali is *nabad*. Very frequently *nabad* is linked with another word *barwaaqo*, so a common greeting is *nabad iyo barwaaqo*. *Bar* means place, location. *Waaq* means sky, or in the traditional culture, God. So this greeting, *nabad iyo barwaaqo* means, "May you have the peace which God gives to your place or to the earth." So peace is intimately linked to a renewed relationship between God and place.

If the rains are adequate, the grass is green, your cattle are doing well, then that is *barwaaqo*, namely the place of God, and that is peace, *nabad*.

We observe that in both the Turkana and Somali myths about the primal state of humankind, there was peace and abundance when God was near. However, a separation has taken place between humankind and God. Consequently there is drought and suffering. However, when there is a renewal of the relationship between God and place, then there is blessing and peace.

These two myths have some similarities to the biblical worldview which describes Adam and Eve in the garden enjoying fellowship with God and abundant provision. When the relationship with God was broken because of their sin, they were sent from the garden. Separation from God and separation from the garden go hand in hand.

Islam has a similar understanding. Adam and Eve were in paradise, and when they sinned they were sent from paradise to earth. In this case, disobedience to God means separation from paradise. Although there are differences within these various understandings, there are also convergences.

As mentioned above, in the traditional Somali culture blessing and peace are related to God's favor and presence. Peace is also grounded in justice. The Somali term *gar* literally means a chin, but when it is used as a verb it refers to lead a person or an animal to the water hole or place. This suggests that justice is a journey. It is a journey linked to God. Justice is referred to as *garwaaq*—that is to say that justice belongs to God and not to humans, thus justice proceeds from God.

If justice proceeds from God, then justice is not determined by the individual. Neither is it determined by the community. Justice has a transcendent quality. It is rooted in God. So if I am in conflict with my colleague, I will say to him, *garwaaqso*. That is, take God's justice, not my justice. This is to say that God's justice transcends my judgment and my justice, as well as the judgment and justice of my community.

However, God's justice affects the community. There is a social contract known as *xeer* that binds the community together in submission to God's justice. So when there is conflict between two individuals, the whole community is involved in discerning the nature of God's justice in relationship to this broken relationship. When that is determined, then the two communities unite in making a *xeer*, a social contract, a covenant which is binding not only upon the two individuals but also upon the two communities. So you have not only reconciled two individuals, but justice has brought the reconciliation and restoration of two communities as well. The reconciled communities surround the two individuals assuring that they will submit to the justice, God's justice that has been determined by their respective communities.

The consummation of the covenant of reconciliation requires that the community of the person who has been found guilty (the offender) will meet with the aggrieved (the victim) community and place in their midst a person as a symbolic sacrifice. The community of the guilty party will proclaim to the aggrieved community that this person is given as a sacrifice in order that the *xeer* (covenant) of reconciliation be established. The aggrieved community will accept this sacrificial victim, but both communities will then agree that an animal will be offered as a substitute for the human who has been offered.

This reminds one of Abraham who was prepared to sacrifice his son Isaac, and God's intervention with a substitutionary sacrifice. Within life in the Somali traditional society the human is redeemed from sacrifice by a sacrificial animal. The *xeer* is consummated as the aggrieved and guilty communities join together in eating the sacrificial animal. In this way the covenant of reconciliation is established.

Of course, the procedure for discerning the justice of God and applying his justice to the situation at hand requires careful counsel. This gathering for counsel and discernment is known as the *shir* and is foundational to the whole justice and reconciliation process. At the conclusion of the process, justice (*garwaaq*) is served and *barwaaqo* (the place of God) is created, peace and the blessing of God.

Barwaaqo is also grace (*nim'a*). Wherever the blessing of God is experienced, that is the gift of grace, a favor that we do not merit. There are many signs of grace as, for example, the gift of rain is a sign of God's grace.

Peace and reconciliation must be seen within the context of culture. Culture involves the social capital of a society, that is, the institutions, practices, and values of a people. Within the Somali context the social capital is very much informed by the traditional culture, as well as Islam. The influence of Christian presence has also in some ways influenced Somali social capital.

There is an interrelationship between the Somali social capital and the faith of Islam that all Somalis have traditionally embraced. This includes a dialogue between the different approaches to peacemaking and reconciliation within Somali traditional culture and that of Islam. The fundamental divergence between Islamic justice and Somali traditional justice and peacemaking is that within the Islamic understanding justice is retributive and Somali justice is restorative. For example, within Islamic justice the thief must have his hand cut off. The murderer must be killed. However, the Somali traditional justice systems work quite differently. If someone is involved in murder, he can flee to a safe place and he is protected until the matter is investigated. And in all likelihood a restorative process will be put in place with the payment of blood wealth and the murderer's life will be preserved. So Somali restorative justice is based not on an eye for an eye, but rather restitution. For example, the restitution price for a murdered man is 100 camels, and for a woman it is 50 camels.

Within the traditional Somali culture all of this is based on the principle of *xeer* (covenant). If the clan of a man who has been murdered demands that the murderer die, it is impossible to establish *xeer*. Killing the murderer does nothing to restore relationships. But the payment of wealth, which is mutually agreed upon with the affirmation of *xeer* between the clan of the murderer and the victim, contributes to breaking the cycle of violence and grievances. This makes it possible for relationships to be restored within the context of covenant. In this way the social capital of the Somali society is preserved thereby enabling people to continue functioning as a healthy society with a network of intercommunity and interclan relationships being preserved.

However, the Islamic approach to justice is retributive and one of the consequences is the fragmentation of society rather than the preservation of social capital. Retributive justice does not preserve the delicate bonding of covenantal *xeer*. It is for this reason that the instinct of the Somali people is to fall back upon traditional approaches to justice and peacemaking rather than to look to Islamic systems of justice. Furthermore, in modern times the Somali people are not only engaged in the dialogue between an Islamic approach to justice and peacemaking and that of the traditional culture, but also with postmodern globalization and all that this has meant for the integrity of the Somali clan and *xeer* system. These various streams of influence are very much present within the current peacemaking conversations as the Somali people seek to find a way to break the cycle of interclan violence that has bedeviled the country during the last several years. There are voices that are reaching for United Nations intervention, which is a quest for outside power that has no connections with the traditional grassroots processes based upon trust building and *xeer*. Those who look for outside United Nations intervention believe that justice needs the imposition of external power, a power that circumvents traditional processes.

One of the reasons that the traditional processes seem so inadequate to the present-day crisis is the devastating influence of the Cold War upon Somali society. The fragile political systems that emerged as Somalia moved into the modern community of nations were ruthlessly torn apart as the Horn of Africa became an arena for the cold war struggle between east and west. Even after the collapse of the Soviet empire, polarization still persists, pulling Somali society in different directions. Dimensions of that struggle are alluded to in

Samuel Huntington's thesis: *The Clash of Civilizations.*[2] Somalia is affected by the global responses to the events of September 11.

There are divergent peacemaking perspectives between the western world and the Islamic world, and Somalia is caught within those tensions. The roots of these divergences go right back to the Roman empire and the emergence of the Muslim empire. The *Pax Romana* of the Roman empire perceived that all regions under its political and ecclesial control were the regions of peace. Barbarians lived beyond the borders of the empire. Likewise, the vision of the Muslim empire was that all regions under Muslim control are the region of peace and those areas outside of the Muslim nation were the regions of confusion and war. And both systems developed theological justifications for war in order that the peace might be established according to the systems of political and military power. Although the *Pax Romana* is no more, the west still lives within the shadow of that worldview, that Europeanized cultures are the regions of peace. That is a very different vision of peace than the Muslim nations proclaim. Those different visions assure conflict; Somalia is one of the border regions where this conflict is joined.

However, New Testament biblical faith brings to the table an alternative vision, that of restorative justice, a justice that is established through forgiveness, covenantal relationships, and reconciliation. This justice nurtures peace that is voluntarily embraced, and is covenantally and communally sustained. That vision is in tune with the Somali traditional understandings of peacemaking. It is for that reason that the Mennonite commitment to walking alongside the Somali people in the peacemaking journey is received with such appreciation by Somalis who are committed to an approach to peace-making that is rooted within their traditional culture. Both the biblical and Somali approaches to peacemaking preserves the social capital by nurturing *xeer.*

∽

Response: Israel/Palestine and Somalia—Signs of Hope
Barbara Witmer

Dorothy Jean Weaver and Ahmed Haile in their respective papers described peacemaking and reconciliation situations in the

Middle East and Somalia. Both are areas of a large Muslim population, but with very different dynamics. Israel/Palestine involves Palestinians of both Muslim and Christian faith against Jewish "occupiers." In Somalia, which is essentially 100 percent Muslim, opposing factions fight each other in a civil war.

In both Israel/Palestine and Somalia, there are indigenous voices for peace, as Weaver and Haile related. Weaver refers to "many Muslims who do not subscribe to the violent strategies of the radical factions and many Muslims who are working diligently and nonviolently day by day, sometimes (or is it always?) at great personal cost, for the cause of peace and justice." Haile identifies ways in which the Somali culture embraces restorative justice and reconciliation. Clearly, the church does not have a monopoly on reconciliation.

In addition, at times the church has been, or has been perceived as being, against peace. Most Muslims look to the Crusades as an example of Christian aggression against Muslims (as well as Jews and eastern Christians). The colonial experience in both Israel/Palestine and Somalia has also reinforced that image. Haile related the destructive effect that colonial policies had on indigenous traditions of reconciliation. Although the colonizers may not have been practicing Christians, they were certainly perceived to be Christians by the Somalis.

At the same time, as Christians we know that the church does have a witness in situations of violence and conflict. When asked about the role of the church in these areas of conflict, both presenters affirmed a special contribution of Christian believers. Weaver pointed out the leading role that the indigenous church has in peacemaking efforts in Israel/Palestine, and named Christmas Lutheran Church in Bethlehem as an example. Haile referred to the impact of Mennonite missionaries on himself personally, as well as on Somalis who attended mission schools. Haile, who became a Christian from the influence of missionaries, is now an advocate for peace in East Africa. Somali alumni of Mennonite Mission schools see themselves as members of a different group (some even call themselves Mennonite Muslims) and their loyalty is to each other and Somalia first and their clans second. Many are involved in peacemaking even on a small scale, and interact with members of other clans freely.

Reconciliation is not an easy or safe vocation. Both Weaver and Haile have found themselves in dangerous situations because of their commitments to peace. But especially in the context of Christian-Muslim relations, the church needs to join with peace-loving

Muslims, overcome negative perceptions of Christianity, and add her own perspective, following her Master who came to reconcile.

CHAPTER TWENTY-SIX

Pacifism Among Muslims in Africa

Mike Brislen

Since September 11, 2001, Islam has often been characterized as either a religion of war, or as a religion of peace, with very little reference to historical reality in either case. This chapter looks at two examples of pacific values and commitment among African Muslims. The first example comes from West Africa, and we rely on the research and writings of Lamin Sanneh. The second example comes from the Republic of Djibouti in northeastern Africa. It grows out of my experience of teaching in the public schools and living in Djibouti the past fourteen years.

Before we begin our look at West Africa and Djibouti, a short comment on values is in order. Values are behaviors, ideas, and attitudes that are highly desirable and important. They are socially acquired, and therefore often differ from one society to the other. In reality there is usually a gap between the expressed values of a people and their actual behavior. However, socially and personally internalized values encourage people to strive to live up to their ideals. In this essay we explore pacific values that are an influence within Islamic societies in West Africa and Djibouti.

Jakhanké Clerics in West Africa

The influence of the Jakhanké clerics has been subtle, similar to that of yeast in a mixture of dough, rather than through a program of growth. In fact, the clerics are a sort of clerical clan, in which the sons of the clerics receive intense religious education to prepare them for their future as clerics. One is then born into the community rather than converted into it. The mode of influence of the clerics is therefore limited to their educational programs at various *majlis* spread throughout West Africa.[1]

In the thirteenth century Al-Hajj Salim Suwaré founded an order of Muslim clerics which became known as the Jakhanké clerics (or sometimes as the Suwarians). Centers for the Islamic education of the local people, especially the training of children to become religious leaders, were opened originally in the area now known as Senegal and the Gambia. In the ensuing centuries educational centers have been founded as far away as northern Nigeria.[2]

Al-Hajj Salim rejected political and military coercion in religious matters. Professional clerics were forbidden from holding secular political office.[3] This rejection of the political differed from the Muslim tradition in most other parts of the world. Salim's ideas arose from a different reading of the Muslim tradition in which he emphasized the pacific elements of Islam. As Sanneh observes, Africans were "mediators in a fluid, dynamic intercultural process,"[4] rather than passive receptors of Islam. African values and institutions interacted creatively with Islam's tradition.

There are also practical considerations in Salim's, and the Jakhanké pacific stance. Present-day clerics have said that when you use violence against your neighbors, you will eventually use violence on yourselves. These Jakhanké clerics also maintain that violence has done more harm to the spread of Islam and Muslim community than any benefit due to the expansion of Muslim political control. They have characterized the various Muslim-led wars as *musibah*, catastrophes with no redeeming value, and blamed these wars for the *fitnah*, division of the Muslim community.[5]

As mentioned above, clerical/educational centers have been established throughout West Africa. Sanneh writes that the *majlis* have been "centers of influence" among a wide variety of ethnic groups and populations. In every *majlis* students, and by extension the local population, receive teaching in Islam and Arabic, as well as the pacific counsel of the Jakhanké clerics. Local populations, having been influenced by this pacific tradition, have not historically accepted the theocratic rule of various jihadist campaigns. West Africa saw several attempts at theocratic rule in the nineteenth and twentieth centuries, often in reaction to colonialism. The ultimate failure of these movements was due to the "prevailing unfavorable quietest climate of opinion." The people preferred pluralism to a monocultural, monoreligious theocracy.[6]

The Jakhanké clerics have also been directly involved in encouraging their nonpolitical understanding of Islam. Secular rulers were traditionally barred entrance to the clerical centers, except for a yearly pilgrimage in which the ruler would pay respect to the clerics and participate in a ceremony of repentance. Within the clerical center the secular ruler held no authority.[7] However, the presence of the clerics within a ruler's territory conferred a certain religious and spiritual legitimacy on the government. During the various jihadist movements the clerics would simply move their clerical center out of jihadist-controlled territory, thus denying them the spiritual legitimacy they needed in the eyes of the population.[8]

The Jakhanké clerics demonstrate a wonderful example of 700 years of commitment to a pacific view of Islam and life. Their influence is still felt in modern West Africa, as the *muftis* of Senegal and Burkina Faso have come from the ranks of the Jakhanké clerics.[9]

Emerging Pacific Values in Djibouti

In contrast to the long Jakhanké tradition of West Africa, pacific values are still evolving among the Somali clans of Djibouti. Time will tell if these emerging values will find the long-term commitment of the Jakhanké clerics. However, peace is a deeply cherished value among the Muslims of Djibouti. I'll examine this in the following paragraphs, then comment on how these values are practiced.

Somali traditional laws intended to hold society together and provide justice are called *xeer*. Ali Moussa Iye writes that the primary goal of the *xeer* is establishing peace among the various Somali clans.[10] It calls for equality among clans and individuals: no one is above the law. In the case of violence, whether accidental or intentional, compensation is paid to the victim and his clan. The guilty party's clan is held responsible for providing the compensation as fines are generally too large for one person to assume. Cycles of revenge are thus blocked; reconciliation rather than punishment is sought. The collective fines place immense social pressure upon perpetrators to never repeat such violence. The outcome is generally the reestablishment of peace among clans and families.

The *xeer* system is remarkably effective in establishing and maintaining peace. John Drysdale observes that an increase in the practice of traditional values has lead to a virtual absence of interclan fighting in Somaliland.[11] This is remarkable, for Somaliland was horribly embroiled in interclan civil wars before separating from Somalia and emerging as a region under separate governance based upon traditional clan systems. In other words, within Somaliland the *xeer* system works. The same is true in Djibouti where the *xeer* continues to play a prominent role in both official and nonofficial judicial systems.

Anthropologist I. M. Lewis states that Somalis have also traditionally separated religious authority and political authority.[12] The Muslim clerics known as *wadaads*, or sheikhs, are ideally above clan politics, and therefore often function as "go-betweens and peace embassies" during conflicts. A man who knew Arabic, therefore enabling him to read the Qur'an, and knew and practiced Islam faithfully was commonly considered to be a *wadaad*. In the modern urban context many men and women learn Arabic and the Qur'an.

The knowledge of Islam and a more stringent following of Islamic rites and tradition have blossomed in the urban setting. This urban context is fertile soil for producing faithful and knowledgeable Muslims. These men and women, though not ordinarily called sheikhs, are seen as very religious people and, therefore, inescapably men and women of peace. The modern situation has transformed society from a *wadaad* minority and a *waranle* (warrior) majority to something approaching its opposite. Society as a whole has become more predisposed toward peace than fighting. This transformation of the order of society should not be underestimated.

Taking into account the state of affairs in Somalia where warlords and interclan conflict have largely destroyed the modern national infrastructures, we are justified in asking how the Somali people of Djibouti have come to value peace highly while the Somali people of Somalia have not seemed to acquire the same value. More than a century ago the history of these Somali peoples strongly diverged in the "scramble for Africa." Somali territory was divided between four foreign powers: England, Italy, Ethiopia, and France, which colonized Djibouti. We won't speak of the benign nature of French colonialism. The colonization of a people is never benign. However, Djibouti found itself in circumstances that made it different from these other regions. We will look at these circumstances and examine how they contributed to the value placed upon peace in Djibouti.

Somalis, of the Issa clan and Afars, have lived for centuries in the land that France claimed for itself in the 1880s. These two groups, who had interacted primarily as rivals for watering holes and pastures, were now brought together for a common political and economic future. In 1917 the railroad between Djibouti and the Ethiopian capital, Addis Ababa, was completed. Additional groups, Yemeni Arabs and Ethiopians, came to Djibouti to fill roles as merchants and workers on the railroad. Individuals and families from other northern Somali clans, Issaq and Gadabuursi, also arrived to work in the growing port city. Later, after independence in 1977, wars in neighboring Somalia and Ethiopia brought thousands of refugees into Djibouti. The Somali people of Djibouti have thus developed in a multiethnic atmosphere. In this way the Djibouti-Somali identity has evolved differently from that of Somali people elsewhere.

According to theologian Miroslav Volf, identity and the exclusion of the other are at the root of violence.[13] I propose that the Somali people of Djibouti, through the above historical events, have been including the other into their own identity. Openness to the other, even those outside of the historical others, Afar, Ethiopian, Yemeni, and French, is becoming a part of the Djibouti-Somali identity. This developing identity lends itself toward peace rather than war.

This entire process was significantly aided by the policies of Djibouti's first president, Hassan Gouled Aptidon. He very intentionally courted good relationships between the Somali and Afar peoples. Ethnic composition became an important part of the political process, assuring that each ethnic group felt included. Additionally, as wars ravaged Ethiopia and Somalia, Djibouti considered itself a haven of peace.

So far I've said very little about Islam. Islam, itself, does have much to say about peace and war. Islam's position could be compared to that of the Christian just war tradition. War should be fought only in self-defense. Noncombatants should not be harmed. The physical infrastructure that assures a people's livelihood and existence should not be destroyed. This would include livestock and agricultural fields. The Somali war tradition is similar to this Islamic just war position.[14]

The tendency in Somali society is to identify every good quality of Somali culture with Islam. For example, women generally have a more open role in Somali society than they do in Arab societies. Most Somali people claim that it is because they are following the teachings of Islam and the Arabs are following Arab tradition. As Djibouti-

Somali identity has moved in a more pacifist direction, the traditional Islamic just war position is being stretched, yet this emerging peaceful identity is consistently stated to be part of Islam.

I have tried to show that four processes, *xeer*, separation of religion and politics, a developing identity of openness, and Islam, have interacted to produce a situation in Djibouti where peace has become an important value. I would like to now give a few examples of how this value is working itself out in real life.

First, as a teacher I have the opportunity to assign and read compositions. Over the years I've asked students to comment on a text concerning a man who saves the life of his enemy. A vast majority of students write that peace and forgiveness are better than revenge and war. I've challenged many of these students with concrete situations, and most stick to their peace conviction.

Physical violence, itself, is rare in Djibouti. In a high school of over 2,500 students I've seen two or three fights in six years. Whether in school, on the street, or in a neighborhood, when a heated argument begins people come to cool tempers and prevent a fight. In one recent year no murders occurred in the capital city of over 300,000 people.

Several years ago Djibouti suffered a three-year civil war. While this incident would seem to contradict my thesis, some events during the war seem to confirm it. Rumors are that the Djibouti army went outside of Djibouti to recruit Somali Issa soldiers. The story was that Djiboutian soldiers just weren't vicious enough. They didn't like to fight and kill. Though I can't confirm or invalidate this rumor, even if it is false, it shows the self-image and identity that the people of Djibouti are developing.

A story will show how these values are integrated into Islam. A friend told me the following *hadith* to illustrate the Islamic value of love for enemies.

As Muhammad, the prophet of Islam, would go to the mosque to pray, each day a young Jewish boy would throw garbage, sewage, or other types of unclean matter in his way. This would cause Muhammad to become unclean, therefore needing to redo his full ablutions. One day the young boy was not there to disturb his way to the mosque. Muhammad went into the boy's house to inquire about him, and learned that he had fallen ill. Muhammad then went immediately to the market and returned with fruit for the young boy.

I conclude this section with the words of a student answering the question: Is it truly good to save the life of your enemy?

> In this life we aren't living to hate someone and to love someone else. But, in this life, we are living to love the ones and the others. Then if someone decides to kill his enemy, this act is bad because if this person really kills his enemy, what will he gain? Nothing. And when your enemy's life is in danger and if you let him die instead of saving him, what will you gain? Nothing.
>
> And in life we must save the enemy because your enemy could be your best friend if you save his life.
> —*Fatouma Ali Hassan*

Conclusion

These two examples of pacifism among Muslims from West Africa and Djibouti contain some significant differences.

The Jakhanké clerics form a pacific community within a larger non-pacific society, though with some influence upon that society. In this way the Jakhanké clerics may be said to resemble an Anabaptist-type group within Islam—they are pacifists within a larger religious milieu that is nonpacifist. In saying this we must remember that the founding of the Jakhanké clerics predates Anabaptism by over two centuries. The Jakhanké clerics have also demonstrated a true commitment to peace and nonviolence over a period of more than 700 years.

In Djibouti pacific values persist in a fragile emerging state. These values are also territorially defined, rather than being the teachings of a community-defined group. They are much more vulnerable to the vagaries of political situations or manipulations.

Both examples illustrate that Africans can and have interpreted Islam on their own terms, through their own cultural and social values. Each example also shows that some Muslim societies have engendered movements toward nonviolent expressions of peacemaking.[15]

༄

Response: Muslim Peacemakers

Susan Kennel Harrison

In his essay, Mike Brislen has explored two case studies of pacifism among Muslims: the Somalis of Djibouti and the Jakhanké Muslim clerics in Senegambia. These two streams of pacifist inclinations among Muslims were explored in a seminar at the Anabaptist consultation on Islam by Mike Brislen from Djibouti and Lamin Sanneh from Yale University (whose roots are West African). Brislen's essay probes these themes that emerged in the seminar with helpful insights.

Within the Republic of Djibouti the Somali Muslim society is cultivating peacemaking themes within their traditional culture. This is in a region notorious for endemic violence and interclan warfare. Building the peace has led the Somalis to embrace the value of *xeer*, which is traditional Somali laws that call for equality among clans and individuals. This peace advocacy takes form in leadership, laws concerning compensation when violence has been done, and an immense social pressure not to enact revenge between clans, but rather, reconciliation that leads to an absence of interclan fighting. The peacemakers are those who function as go-betweens, the *wadaad*; those who can read the Qur'an and provide respected religious advice.

Since Somalis have traditionally separated religious authorities and political authorities, the person knowledgeable of Islam has been able to work outside the secular political law as an arbiter of clan disagreements. As the Djibouti society has become more educated, there is more widespread knowledge of Islam as well and this tradition is blossoming in the urban setting. In the seminar Brislen observed, "The modern situation has transformed society from a *wadaad* minority" into a majority, thus transforming the order of society into one more "predisposed toward peace than fighting." In this society there is an increased openness and embrace of the *other*, which is providing a sense of inclusion as the ethnic composition of the country expands. The increase in knowledge of Islam, and the separation of religion and politics, has facilitated the ability for the religious tradition to resource a reconciliatory approach between people groups creating an Islamic society that values peace.

In his essay, Brislen has drawn from the scholarship and research of Lamin Sanneh in his discussion of a little-known Muslim clerical group called the Jakhanké Muslim clerics. In the seminar Sanneh enlivened the discussion with his description of these clerics who have been located in Senegambia, West Africa, since AD 1250. Of particular interest is the originating impulse of this clerical group to refuse to participate in political office. By their strict separation between religious and political leadership they were able to carve a way for an Islamic based pacifism. Over time their choices have led them to live in communities that are separate from mainstream society, but not in an unprogressive way.

CHAPTER TWENTY-SEVEN

Secularization and Democracy in Christian-Muslim Relations

Beyond Modernity Toward Transforming Encounter

Roy Hange

In the west our evolved wisdom for dealing with religious differences is secularism, and the evolved method for dealing with abuses of power is democracy. The West has had a number of centuries of working with these two elements in politics to the degree that some see secularization and democracy as the solution for current political struggles in the Muslim world.

The following exploration will consider these following questions: What are the historical and theological factors in Islam's encounter with secularism and democracy? How can Muslims and westerners understand secularization and democracy in a postmodern, post-September 11 context?

One of the paradoxes in the Muslim world is that the nations that are the most secular are often the least democratic (e.g., Iraq and Syria), and the nations and movements that are the least secular are often more democratic in elements of their internal structure (e.g., the Islamic Republic of Iran and various Muslim Brotherhood organizations).

One of the paradoxes in the western world is that even though their conceptions of secularism and democracy (as a synthesis of Greek and Christian traditions) have internal balances against the abuse of power, the Nazi government was democratically elected in the secular state that was one of the most educated nations of the time.

Within these parallel paradoxes we will explore the history of Islam and the west's journey together. Before doing so we acknowledge that secularization and democracy are western terms, while similar conceptions in Islam are a constitutional respect for religious minorities and the principle of *shura* (consultation). The west and Christianity are not being defined as the same, yet there are significant overlaps especially from a Muslim perspective.

Historical Backdrop

In our postmodern and post-September 11 context, it may be helpful to explore September 11 in the context of Islamic renewal as a countermove to secularism and democracy and a move to capture the soul of the Islamic world which is pulled by some forces toward western business and political models and by other forces toward restoring original, Islamic structures. Yet other Muslims want to form a synthesis of these forces. This survey is presented to show a view of history that is the context for the acts of militant Islam and the deep resentments behind them often created by secular and democratic western states. The next few pages will set a historical backdrop for critical reflections on our current situation.

Islam's Initial Conquest: 600-1600

Islam spread quickly after its inception in the seventh century until the unsuccessful siege of Vienna in 1683. The Muslim Ottoman Empire, which held power in the Middle East until 1918, was for the previous 600 years almost continually either trying to expand into Europe and Russia or responding to European or Russian counterattacks. This state of chronic tension and conflict became the foundation of the deeply held fears, suspicions, and prejudices that are emerging now.

Political Contraction of Islam: 1600-1900

Although most of the peoples conquered in the initial Muslim military expansion of the seventh and eighth centuries eventually became Muslim, the carpet of Muslim political domination was rolled back with the growing military power of Europe and Russia. Some European states and Russia began to colonize the Muslim world beginning in the sixteenth century. By the end of World War I, of the forty-five or so current members of the Organization of the Islamic Conference only four countries (Afghanistan, Turkey, Saudi Arabia, and Yemen) were not under European colonial rule.

The European powers established educational, cultural, and political institutions of western character in most Muslim countries. These institutions formed and trained the postindependence leadership who maintained the western structures of governance begun by the colonial powers. A further affront to Muslims was that Christian missionaries ran many of these colonial institutions like schools and hospitals. The role of missionaries meant that colonialism was not perceived as a secular enterprise and there were few, if any, attempts by colonial powers to establish democracies.

Islam's Political Independence: 1900 and Beyond

The twentieth century has witnessed the nations of the Muslim world moving through three stages of independence: (1) political independence, (2) nationalization, and (3) Islamization. All Muslim countries have obtained political independence from European powers and the nationalization of political and religious institutions. Muslim countries are at various stages of Islamization given the various degrees of success of the Islamicists in a given country.

Political Independence

The majority of Muslim countries obtained their independence from colonial rulers within the three decades following World War II. Divisions of the Muslim world that became independent nation states were often contrived sections or mandates of the Ottoman Empire that the European colonial powers deemed logical for their own interests.

Nationalization

Islam was denied an integral role in the political and social formation of its own people during the colonial era. After political independence, most Muslim nations maintained western governance patterns and institutions in a nationalized form. Initially the prime political loyalty of the citizens was formed to be national rather than Islamic in the pattern of the western nation states. There were also attempts at Pan-Arab nationalism that resulted in temporary unions of various countries. Most of the new nationalist leaders had western-oriented political or military education. Through the nationalization process most Islamicists were thwarted in their attempts to bring more Islamic character to their nations (for example, Nasser's suppression of the Muslim Brotherhood in Egypt).

An Egyptian diplomat, Hussein Ahmed Amin, offers the following reflections on the identity crisis in Islam following colonialism. He describes the need to find a central, Islamic focus for Egyptians often results as a reaction to aspects of secularization and democracy:

> For a century Egypt has flirted with a variety of beliefs and ideologies. Each phase was greeted with great fanfare, each new belief adopted with conviction, each new sacrifice accepted without question. Egypt in the past has tried liberalism, military rule, democracy, fascism, one-party rule, and pluralism. It has flirted with capitalism and socialism, it has talked Arabism and Africanism, and then befriended the East. . . . We made war with Israel, and then peace. We were united with Syria and then not on speaking terms. We fought American domination, and then surrendered to it. We made a friendship treaty with the Soviet Union and then tore it up. And throughout all of this, Egypt's intellectuals have watched and become increasingly disenchanted; Egypt's young people have watched and become incredulous. Against this background is it surprising that people have come to search for an immutable doctrine, for some constancy in the values they are asked to support? Why, they ask, since everything else has resulted only in corruption, in economic disaster, in the repression of civil liberties, and in military defeat, should we not embrace an Islamic rule, in accordance with the decrees of the Qur'an and Sunna.[1]

Islamization

The final stage of political independence in many Muslims' view is the current re-Islamization of the Muslim world. This spiritual, social, political, and occasionally military struggle (all viewed as jihad) is a comprehensive reclamation and redefining of Muslim's life together in terms of Islam. If necessary, at times this process can include violence but most often it need not. Some Muslims see this process as the final stage of independence when the "west-toxification" of cultural and political life has been removed. Some Islamicists have a vision of a transnational, regional Islamic union that would do away with the nation state divisions left over from European colonial history. I was shown a map of such an envisioned union by a member of the Muslim Brotherhood. This map covered most of the Middle East.

The end of the colonial era left dictatorships or monarchies in most Muslim countries. Many Muslims see as residual colonialism the close relationship these leaders often have with former colonial powers. A Muslim told this author in the mid-1990s "the violence in Egypt and Algeria is a natural reaction by Muslims to not being allowed free and fair democratic expression of their will to bring an Islamic order to society."

Within this context the attacks of September 11, and related attacks, were an attempt to instigate a globalization of these Islamizing sentiments by a radical wing of the Islamicist movement through symbolic attacks on the centers of economic and military power in the United States, which is seen as the current world power.

The Solution as a Threat: The Paradox of the West's Great Hope

The solution the west, especially the United States, sees for the tensions revealed by September 11 is to promote freedom (to be read as secularism) and democracy in Islamic contexts. The greatest efforts in this area so far are those in Afghanistan and Iraq where freedom and democracy are being imposed in a direct attempt to rebuild those nations' political structures as models for the rest of the Muslim world.

These efforts approach both ends of the Muslim world's paradoxes referred to at the beginning of this paper, with Afghanistan's government having been Islamic and Iraq having been very secular. The success of these efforts is still in the balance. Even though democracy would bring about more autonomy and control for many Islamicist forces, these efforts are generally seen as a new kind of colonialism given that control over the outcome is still in western hands. What are the deep fears generated by this control?

Many Muslims see secularism as cloaking a moral freedom that would threaten their social fabric and diminish the role of Islam in forming all of their life including politics. Some also fear that what happened to Christianity in the west would also happen to Islam.

William Cavanaugh, in an article entitled "The Wars of Religion in the Rise of the State," gives an account of what happened to Christianity in the west:

> In the medieval period the church was the supreme common power; the civil authority, as John Figgis put it, was "the police department of the church." The net result of the conflicts of the sixteenth and seventeenth centuries was to invert the dominance of the ecclesiastical over the civil authorities to the creation of the modern state. The chief promoters of this transposition . . . were Martin Luther and Henry VIII and Philip II.[2]

Cavenaugh continues his comments on the results of the Reformation and Enlightenment in the west:

> The concept of religion being born here is one of domesticated belief systems which are, insofar as it is possible, to be manipulated by the sovereign for the benefit of the state. Religion is no longer a matter of certain bodily practices within the body of Christ, but is limited to the realm of the "soul," and the body is handed over to the state.[3]

When the European colonization of the Muslim world followed soon after these developments in western Europe, the colonial powers brought to the Muslim world this perceived need to de-emphasize religion through state control and nationalism. To this day secularization and democracy are seen in the Muslim world as an imposition of the west's domestication of religion.

The drama of this tension is being played out this very day in Iraq where a western power is proposing secularization, democracy, and freedom as the solution alongside of multinational Muslim militants fighting for the protection of Islam and Shi'ite militants and scholars working and fighting for a religiously oriented governance model.

The Search for "Consensus Between Secularity and Religious Ideology"

There are many Muslim scholars who affirm that Islam is not inherently opposed to incorporating new ideas nor opposed to aspects of democracy.[4] Both the lands of Islam and the west are respectively facing theological and political challenge as they face each other.

Douglas Streusand, in a speech before the Center for the Study of Islam and Democracy, has noted how adaptive Islam has been.

> Islamic civilization is a composite, like Western civilization. Islam is the crucial, defining component, but the customs of pre-Islamic Arabia; the heritage of the civilizations of the Fertile Crescent, refracted primarily through Sasanian Iran; and Greek philosophy all contributed to the formation of classical Islamic civilization. Each transmitted its own set of norms; the interaction of these norms created lasting tensions within Islamic civilization, which affected its political and social order as well as its intellectual traditions. But historians, Western and Muslim, have frequently treated Islamic civilization as a normative, rather than descriptive, term, and depicted much of Islamic history as a struggle between "true" Islamic norms and outside impurities and distortions. The dialogue on Islam and democracy reflects this perspective. It holds that Muslims will accept democracy only if they recognize it as Islamic, a part of Islamic civilization rather than a borrowing or distortion. The concept of Islamic civilization as a composite, however, makes what would otherwise be impurities natural parts of the composition. I shall demonstrate, in a preliminary and incomplete way, that Muslims themselves perceived a fusion between Islam the religion and the other traditions they encountered and developed a composite set of political norms in pre-modern times.[5]

Aziz Sachedina, also in a speech before the Center for the Study of Islam and Democracy, has shown how Muslims have not reacted to democracy as an idea but to the western presentations of liberal democracy. He also shows how there can be an overlap between secularity and religious ideology without falling into the trap of secularization:

> I do not want to convey that (the) Muslim public is religiously oriented and, therefore, we need to make democracy appealing to them by fictitiously "Islamizing" this discourse. Rather, my major concern is to show to the learned and the lay in Muslim societies that democratic ideals are very much part of the Islamic ethical culture that speaks about human responsibility and accountability in this and the next world. Instead of prescribing a shortcut to secularism as a guarantor of liberal democracy, our

intellectual endeavors need to be geared towards demonstrating that at the core of Islamic belief system is relationship at all levels of human existence. Since Islam is existentially to be preserved in nurturing and maintaining relationships, then it is to be expected that Islam will grant humanity its basic freedom in negotiating as well as maintaining all social relationships with a sense of equality of human dignity and freedom of human conscience. This is the area where one can show the overlapping consensus between secularity and a religious ideology without falling into the trap of all out support for secularization, which appears unacceptable to the traditional religious leaders.[6]

Re-examining Theology in Search of Concord

Moving beyond these observations, it is my contention that the concepts at the core of secularism and democracy are not the most critical for transforming Islam, Christianity, or the west toward more peaceful existence and encounter called concord. The critical factor is the nature of power used in whatever social and political situation as the nature of the paradoxes noted at the beginning of this paper reveal. In that sense part of the solution is theological and rests on a theological exploration of power.

In an article entitled "Theology and the Clash of Civilizations," Jack Miles, a senior advisor to the president at the J. Paul Getty Trust, has argued for a theological solution saying, "Peace will come not when any one terrorist and his network of secret agents have been 'surgically' excised, but when an authentic alternative vision has emerged within the House of Islam." Miles continues later implying that secularization and democracy are not the main solution.

> Americans argue over whether Harry Truman or Ronald Reagan deserves more credit for defeating the Soviet Union. Osama bin Laden, to American astonishment, thought that the *umma*, rallying to a *jihad* in Afghanistan had won the real victory and would now proceed with the second victory over the United States itself. American astonishment at the grandiose claim and American horror at the lethal ambition may stand as a measure of the chasm that separates Western and Muslim civilization. Unless this chasm can be bridged, the world may slide into a war of terrorist reprisal and counter reprisal with no end in sight. Where should we begin? In my judgment, it should begin with theology, a term that naïve enthusiasts for globalization tend to use as a synonym for that-which-may-be-dispensed-with or,

worse, that-which-gets-in-the-way. The real theology is more than that, and the moment may be at hand for religion and for theology as its intellectual dimension—to come in from the cold as a topic in international diplomacy.[7]

In the beginning of this new millennium both the western and predominately Christian nations and the Muslim nations are at a point of profound identity crisis whereby there is a convergence of a parallel reformation within each community toward discerning new and different roles for religion in shaping the social and political context of our lives. A major issue is how their theologies and practices of power intersect. Secularism has its own theology of power called "realpolitik."

How then can we encounter, or need, each other in this time of transformation? Given the paradoxes and imbalances in each community, how can we find a compensating wisdom in the theology of the other? Kenneth Cragg describes the needed symmetry in an article about prophethood and God.

> If, in the immediate foregoing, while mediating impartially between faiths in common, we have been looking through a Christian lens, it remains to fulfill a promised acknowledgment of Islam. May it be we should conclude that two great faiths serve to keep always in perspective a characteristic accent which, sensitively, the other needs to hear. That stance will not resolve all our tensions. It may at least set them in kinder light. If, as said, we cannot survive in a world where no love carries sins, a world where no one rejects violence or learns to be vicarious, a world where no one wills to suffer and forgive, a world where we cannot root these patterns in God Himself, in a word, a world without Christology and Christians in Christ, then, too, we cannot well survive in a world bereft of power-structure, of the means to order and some rule of law. If in some measure, we have need of a faith born in Gethsemane, we may also salute of faith characterized in Hijra.[8]

Cragg continues with an expression of his envisioned mutual enrichment between Islam and Christianity.

> We might say that it was the genius of Islam, and the fact and symbol of its Hijra into Medinan politicization, to have grasped this truth and effectuated it in its venture after "all things under

God." Such vindication, however, if we read it well, must by the same token be balanced by another truth, a truth that Christianity has at the heart of its Gethsemane. It is that power will always pass into guilt, will always overreach itself, always foul its ends by its means, and always tend to demand a false absolution in the interests of its own perpetuation. That being so, it will always need alongside its pride and its assurance the witness of a faith born of the God of wounds, the wounds of power's excess and folly.[9]

Cragg here expressed the nature of power within the vision of the Christian tradition to both form and transform our spiritual, social, and political relationships. Without such power the political process in either a secular democracy or, to the degree that the pitfalls of power are universal, in an Islamic government would lose value to maintain concord.

I cannot speak for Islam's side of the balance Cragg is referring to, but I offer here an example of how this Christian perspective on power can work in dialogue with Muslims and secular systems. This formulation came to me as gift of encounter with Muslims while participating in a dialogue between Mennonites and Shi'ite Muslims at the Toronto School of Theology on October 25, 2002. The following response was to a paper on "Modernity and Contextualism" by Imam Mesbah Moosavi of Toronto, Canada:

> Imam Moosavi, I wish to thank you for the insightful comments and questions in your paper. Your survey of Christianity's struggle with modernity was impressive and helpful to me as a Christian. I saw in your portrayal a kind of Christian "*Ijtahad*," a continual reinterpretation of a tradition and theology for the sake of giving glory to God. I appreciated your insight into the struggles within Christian theology.
>
> I am limiting my responses to your direct questions in section 3 on the nature of the glory and power of God in relation to human responsibility; and, whether God's power or powerlessness can be a source of hope. I, like you, do not believe that God is powerless but that God is all-powerful. I have to affirm this of the Creator of so great universe and so beautiful a planet.
>
> I will focus my response to your question, "What can be expected from a society that views its God as weak or humiliated? How is it possible for such a society with such a belief to have hope or courage to reject humiliation, weakness, or suffering

whereas its Master, the Creator of the world, in its view is subject to suffering, oppression, and humiliation? Does such a belief not discourage that society from gaining power and struggling against its oppressors? Does such a theology not promote weakness, humiliation, and the acceptance of oppression?"

Following I will attempt to present a model of overcoming oppression and suffering not with a kind of revolution, but in transforming oppression and suffering toward creating a new kind of relationship, a new kind of community and a new kind of.politic.

Responsibility is necessary and power is a component of responsibility. The necessity of power in creating and sustaining just and peaceable structures and society in politics requires contention. In shaping social and political life power, responsibility and contention are all necessary. Therefore, the nature of that necessary power held makes all the difference in the quality of the responsibility and the kind of contention.

As Christians we confess that in the broken power of the cross there can be found a kind of power for the transformation of nations, persons, and evil in the world. There is the place where lords are called to become servants. In the nature of the cross's power there is a grace and reconciliation that breaks cycles of violence in family systems, social systems, and political systems leading toward a new kind of community.

Paradoxically, then, in the inversion of power seen in the cross responsibility and contention can be held in a creative tension that serves the greater good.

In the course of human events contention is inevitable but the disposition and nature of power will determine a course toward transformation toward peace or destruction through cycles of violence. This was the choice of the cross for which Jesus became the originator of a new way in human history. I believe that Jesus chose a new stance in his willingness to move toward the cross. In this way God changed history through this bold act and changed hearts through the way this act reveals human evil and the need for each of us to change.

In this sense the way of God becomes weak so that a greater human good may be known. In this greater good God is seen as being glorious for God's willingness to associate with our human suffering to show us a way beyond suffering in resurrection. Can we see God as powerful enough to intentionally become weak? How this all happens, we Christians say is a mystery.

I readily acknowledge Islam's hesitance to associate anything or anyone directly with God as *shirk*. But I ask the question: Does it not give greater glory to God for God to be seen as powerful enough to be able to associate with humanity? If God could not associate with anything, then why should God have created in the first place?

Within the prophetic tradition then, can we not see God in the witness of Jesus as upsetting the pretensions and the pride of the powerful whose *al-Kibr* (great arrogance) so often stands up against God's ways of peace and justice. Was not this great arrogance in the hearts of the political and religious leaders who along with the people intended to kill Jesus?

The differences between our traditions may be in how to understand the nature of power and glory. And, whether that power and glory is great enough to also include a kind of weakness that calls forth change from human beings. Our main differences as faith communities may be within our conceptions of how power and glory are related to our image of God and our understanding of human responsibility.

Augustine caught this difference in the value of redemptive suffering versus redemptive violence to transform society and politics in his Letter 138 to Marcellenus.

"Therefore he who conquers evil with good patiently forgoes temporal convenience in order to teach how such things, the excessive love of which made the evil man evil, are scorned for the sake of faith and justice. In this way the wrongdoer might learn from the very person whom he wronged what sort of things they are for the sake of which he did wrong. Repenting, he is overcome, not by ferocious violence but by the benevolence or forbearance and thus brought to concord which is more beneficial to the city than anything else."[10]

Conclusion

Maybe this kind of concord is what secular democracies, Christianity, Islam, Islamic governments, and the west are looking for. The question is how to get there together while respecting each other. Such a process requires encounter within and between these communities to form a new synthesis that can move us beyond "a war of terrorist reprisal and counter reprisal with no end in sight" as Miles warns.

One of the ways to get there is through faith-based encounter and diplomacy.[11] Anabaptists have engaged Muslims around the world in creative and peacemaking encounter. With regard to the nature of power in political settings, the early Anabaptists were profoundly modern in this sense of their rejecting the church-state synthesis of medieval Europe, yet they were also not modernists in the sense that they still willed to have faith at the core of determining their spiritual, social, and political relationships. Many were killed for their prophetic stances in relation to the abuses of power around them.

In this sense Anabaptists have a deep affinity with Muslims who criticize the modern, secular world for making a profound separation between one's faith and one's social and political relationships. This affinity has enabled Anabaptists to encounter Muslims around the world with this sense of deep respect and connection even though major theological assumptions differ and the way social and political energies are expressed in their contexts are radically different. The search for concord in the midst of radical difference continues.[12]

CHAPTER TWENTY-EIGHT

Theology of Economic Development: Calling or Strategy?

Topic One
Transformational Development: Our Calling, God's Strategy

Mark Logan

Jesus charged his followers to communicate the good news about him to all nations. The church has taken that mandate seriously and has spread the story about the life and death of Jesus across the globe. Yet still today there are ethnic groups which know nothing of this Jesus, and there are nations that have never heard his message in a way they can understand. Followers of Jesus today, as before, are eager to bear witness to the unique truth of his way for people everywhere. Nevertheless, in this age of rapid transit and high mobility, the path of the news bearers is often blocked by the nations they seek to reach.

Many countries around the world today routinely deny visas to any who seek to enter as missionaries. Others place restrictions on foreigners who are allowed to enter forbidding them to verbally share their beliefs. As the church views physical presence as a major strategy for sharing the message, the question of gaining access to closed countries naturally arises. Many approaches for securing entry have been suggested, but development work is one of the most prevalent and is the topic this chapter will address.

In this brief paper I present one basic argument in support of transformational development[1] as a valid ministry of the church, and then several short observations about how development work should be done in missions.

Mission starts with God. God created, loves, and cares about all people. He desires an intimate relationship with us and when we betrayed his friendship soon after our creation, God unveiled a plan to remedy our disloyalty. In his compassion God sent Jesus to seek and bring back all who were apart form him. Jesus then commissioned those who repented and were reconciled to continue the search and rescue operation which he modeled. This seeking and saving is the central mission of the church.

However, even before our sin separated us from our Creator, God had given us a mission. On the sixth day of creation, when God brought humanity into existence, he charged the people into whom he had just breathed his Spirit, to rule, have dominion over, care for, and in other words develop, the earth. Their first task was to "name the animals." From our beginning, taking care of and developing earthly resources, in accord with God's design, was central to our existence—something that God chose for us to do. It is an awesome responsibility to take part in creation.

In the beginning, when we were in close communion with God, we were capable of doing development in a way that benefited the whole earth and all of its people. But instead of being God's emissaries and following his instructions, we desired to be in God's place, knowing in ourselves the right and wrong thing to do. And so we became wise, but at the cost of a broken linkage between us and the God who understood, loved, and had the plan for the development of the earth. Humanity gained a knowledge of good and evil, but lost the motivation to make right choices. Our own individual and personal gain became the focus of our work and we sought to develop this earth for our own satisfaction, disregarding God's love for all people and ignoring the needs of our neighbors or the well-being of the earth.

God tried again and again to rescue us from our selfishness, speaking through prophets and giving written rules to a chosen people. Finally, he sent us Jesus. Through the life, death, and resurrection of Jesus, God lifted us back into our proper relationship with him, assuring us of eternity with him, but also restoring us as earthkeepers. As we experience the warmth and depth of God's love, our motivation to do right things returns. As we focus on Jesus, we see compassion and selfless concern for the needs of others. It is in the light of Jesus that the church can resume the work of development that humankind was called forth to do.

So then we have the God-given task to develop the earth, the mandate of Jesus to reconcile all people to their correct relationship with the Creator, and the example of Jesus as motivation for our doing transformational development. The question then is not, do missions and development go together, but how do we carry out the integral work of bringing people into a proper relationship of obedience out of love with God, so that through redeemed people, God can develop his kingdom on earth?

Since development is rooted in Christian theology, what about the issues surrounding the use of development work as a means of securing visas or as a cover to gain access to a closed country? Most countries grant visas, even invite, humanitarian aid workers and there is no doubt that the need to improve human living conditions is great in many parts of the world where the gospel is not known. Transformational development is a worthy pursuit for any Christian and the church is more than justified in sending out development workers. The question is motive. Are we doing humanitarian development work in response to God's calling and our love for him? Or is there a hidden agenda? Is development just a clever strategy to gain access to a closed people or a hook to entice them to become Christians?

For some the distinction may be small. We care about the physical needs of our neighbors and we want them to know the truth about Jesus. We rightly care about the whole person, and we do missions and development together in order to address needs both physical and spiritual. The problem generally arises when secular governments or religious regimes do not allow evangelism or the propagation of new religions. Church agencies will be barred from entry if their purpose is perceived to be preaching and aid workers who openly demonstrate a desire to share their faith may be asked to leave.

Mission agencies have taken different approaches. Some church planting groups have put development programs in front of their regular mission work. Others have registered as secular nongovernmental groups (NGOs), disclaiming any church affiliation. While both of these techniques raise the question of motivation, the second is the more serious, bordering on denying Christ.

Jesus taught that our thoughts, motives, and intentions are important (Matt 5) and it is clear that honesty, sincerity, and integrity are fundamental to our restored relationship with God. Jesus also told us that our enemy, the devil, is a liar and the father of lies (John 8:44) and that our yes should be yes and our no, no (Matt 5:37). If this is the gospel we preach, our methods must not contradict our message. We cannot use deception in our witness to truth. In mission via development, it is our actions that speak. We hope our conduct will attract attention as we seek to model the way of Jesus. In this glass house our motives cannot be hidden and that is our intention.

We want people to wonder about what we do and to reflect on our motivation. The reason for our doing development work is our message. We have a renewed relationship with God and so we love and care about all his children. In that relationship there is no room for duplicity. Deception, mistrust, and untruth were at the heart of the separation from God from which we have been rescued. The use of any deceit, coercion, or trickery is contrary to who we believe God to be and must be shunned in all we do.

For us who follow Jesus, transformational development is inspired by our love for God, our desire to please him, and our belief that he loves and cares about all people. We seek to help and share our wealth with others in an attempt to model the life and teachings of Jesus. Our desire to do humanitarian assistance comes from the compassion God blew into us when he created us in his image, the image Jesus restored in us. That everyone can know God's love and enjoy a wholesome relationship with him and his creation is the good news we preach. And we believe that it is from this healing relationship that all people from all nations will learn to live together in mutual love and respect while sharing and developing the earth in accordance with God's purpose. This is what we are called to share and what we are sent out to proclaim with action and voice.

When we do humanitarian or development work in the name of Jesus, we are confessing the faith he commissioned us to present to all the world in a comprehensible, credible, and convincing manner. This, I believe, is God's strategic plan for the extension of his kingdom on earth and the task to which he has called his church. As God's creatures and creation are nurtured and developed in his love and in accord with his goodness, all that he has made will find it normal and fitting to give honor to his holy name. "May your kingdom come, your will be done on earth" (Matt 6:10).[2]

Topic Two
An Internet Café in Senegal:
An Experiment in Development

Jonathan Bornman

I want to use our experience in starting an Internet café in a small city as the point of departure. Our team moved into a small city of 80,000 in 1999. This city is 99 percent Muslim and is a religious center. Most people work in the informal sector in a combination of marketing, farming, and a variety of other jobs. All white-collar workers are government employees. There is no expatriate community of westerners. However, practically every family has a son or sons in Italy, Spain, France, or the United States. This is the main source of income, the economic force that drives the city.

We came into this complex city as language learners and students of the culture. We struggled to learn Wolof, we made friends, and we learned the cultural rules. After a year of grace, the community began to put pressure on us, asking "Why are you here? What is your real purpose?" We freely acknowledged that we were followers of Jesus and that we were students and teachers of the Holy Books—the Torah, the Psalms, and the Gospels. For those who were our friends this was sufficient. For the wider community this was not. It became apparent that we needed a publicly acceptable and understandable raison d'être.

At the same time, we were surprised when a group of seekers and believers in Jesus sprang up, seemingly overnight, centered on the testimony of one dynamic man in our network of relationships. Suddenly we were being asked to disciple a group of newly born followers of Jesus. We asked ourselves and our mentors many questions, "How do we do this? What is discipleship? What is the best place for this to take place? What do sharing and generosity mean between rich and poor followers of Jesus? How do we respond to our brothers' and sisters' economic needs?"

The Internet café was birthed out of this context. We felt a pressing need to define ourselves more clearly to the community, and at the same time we were compelled to look with our local community of believers for ways to respond to physical needs in that community. We started the Internet café in April of 2002. It is run entirely by members of the local church in its day-to-day operations. The primary business is simply providing people with Internet access. There is also a photocopier and a laminating machine. Coffee and soft drinks are sold. Limited computer courses are offered, as well as training in Internet use for e-mail and research. The business has yet to turn real profit, but it is headed in the right direction. Demand for our services is high, and the expenses for utilities and telephone are also high.

Our primary goals for starting the business are being met. The community appreciates the services that are available. Half of our computers and our copier are more recent models than others available in town. We are the only Internet café that offers air-conditioning and that sells soft drinks. Above all, we have qualified, friendly, and courteous staff who are there to serve the customer. The business is also a place for discipleship in a real life context for the local church. We are not interested in simply interacting with people in a time of Bible study, but we are interested in discipleship that trains for real life. The staff members take turns hosting a weekly meal in their homes for the other staff. There we have a time of biblical input, which is usually centered on a parable of Jesus, followed by agenda related to the issues of the Internet café.

Our theology of economic development emerges out of this real life experience. It is not that we had no convictions about economic development beforehand, but that in our situation the real life pressures and events of our context influenced us to take actions that ultimately tell us about our emerging theology. The title of this chapter "Theology of Economic Development: Calling or Strategy?" poses the question, "Are we involved in economic development because it is part of the call of God for the church?" or "Are we doing economic development as a strategic means to evangelism?" I believe we are involved in economic development primarily for strategic reasons, yet those are not divorced from a sense of calling.

Desiring to live in our city with the favor of all, we needed a raison d'être that the community could appreciate. From the inception of our team, we wanted to be a blessing to our community. The Abrahamic call, "I will bless you and you will be a blessing" is fundamental to how we see ourselves as a team. Faced with pressing questions of discipleship and the conviction that this should not happen in a sterile setting, the Internet café business meets a strategic discipleship need. At the same time, starting the business was in part a response to human need. None of the persons in this group were formally employed. The good news, according to Jesus, is that the kingdom of God is near. As preachers of the good news, we must do our best to meet the physical needs of others, especially the needs of a close friend, a brother or sister in the Lord with whom we worship each week.

Another strategic issue for us was helping the believers avoid persecution. There was a study of Muslim background believers in Senegal that indicated that those who had jobs and contributed to the family's economic needs faced much less persecution than those who were unable to contribute.[3] We wanted to offer something in terms of job creation and training to help new followers of Jesus to be strong contributors to their family's economic needs.

Ultimately, the question of calling or strategy is not easily separated. We started an Internet café in our city in response to a variety of needs and pressures. Some of these were strategic and some more related to our calling as followers of Jesus, namely, that being messengers of the kingdom means that we work for the kingdom, even if we know that we may not succeed. We work each day in the Internet café with the realization that many such enterprises fail in this type of setting. Yet, whether the business succeeds or fails financially, it is our best attempt at being faithful in the situation we find ourselves at the present time.

∾

Response: God's Reconciliation Strategy
Ronald J. R. Mathies

Jonathan Bornman, and Mark Logan provide case studies from Senegal and Somalia. The emphasis in both of these essays is on transformational development, which is holistic and thus broader than economic development. This expanded understanding and practice of development is part of the Christian calling and provides legitimacy and integrity to a Christian witness, both locally and globally. This type of involvement is a part of God's strategy in reconciling God's creation.

CHAPTER TWENTY-NINE

The Challenge of the Muslim Critique of Christianity

Topic One
The Trinity: A Response to the Islamic Critique

Jon Hoover

The central Islamic criticism of the Christian doctrine of the Trinity is that it violates God's unity: three is three, not one (see Qur'an 5:116, 4:171, 112:1). Moreover, Muslims often credit the influence of Greek polytheism for corrupting primitive Christianity's pure monotheism. Church leaders, compromised by their alliance with imperial Roman power, formulated the Trinity as Christian orthodoxy at Nicea in AD 325. For Muslims, the Trinity not only violates the unity of God, it is also an unnecessary irrationality foisted on Christians by unscrupulous leaders.[1]

The Enlightenment has withered western Christian confidence in the doctrine of the Trinity with similar assertions: the doctrine is irrelevant to Christian life and a corruption of primitive Christian monotheism. My brief interaction with the Islamic perspective here is indebted for its basic insights to the modern trinitarian response to the Enlightenment point of view[2] and reflects traditional Anabaptist-Mennonite concerns for biblical foundations.

When faced with Muslim bewilderment at the Trinity, Christians often turn instinctively to analogies to show how one can be three. One analogy Muslims might appreciate is that of the sun with its light and its warmth. However, Christians may be uncomfortable with this analogy's impersonal character. Then there are psychological trinitarian analogies such as the mind, its knowledge of itself, and its love of itself (Augustine). In a similar train of thought is the modern notion of God as the absolute and perfect subject who appears in three different modes or aspects (e.g., revealer, revelation, and being-revealed). Such explanations, which portray God as a single subject, might also make some sense to Muslims, but they may rightly ask what is so special about the number three. Finally, there is the social analogy of the Trinity as community, which tries to make sense of the biblical witness that God is love. This has its roots in the Cappadocian Fathers and appears in sophisticated forms in some modern theology, as in the work of Jürgen Moltmann. However, social analogies are especially difficult for Muslims because they quickly suspect tri-theism.

Analogies are never completely adequate to the task, and we do well to acknowledge that God is in some sense unseen and beyond description (1 Tim 6:16). However, there is a deeper problem: trinitarian analogies show only *how* God might be one and three, but they do not tell Muslims *why* Christians came up with this doctrine in the first place. Even our best trinitarian philosophical theology may only confirm Muslim suspicions that the doctrine is superfluous and perversely complex. Overcoming this problem requires a shift in focus from the ontology of one and three to the history of God's interaction with humankind. In this way, the Islamic critique of the Trinity gives Christians opportunity to clarify the biblical and soteriological foundations of this doctrine.

The Islamic critique returns us to the beginning of the Christian doctrine of God in the Jewish confession, "Hear, O Israel: The LORD is our God, the LORD alone" (Deut 6:4, NRSV). Christians, like Jews and Muslims, confess and worship only one God, and we find this not only in the Old Testament but also in the New Testament (Mark 12:29; 1 Cor 8:4-5). Beyond this, there are hints in the Old Testament and clear evidence throughout the New Testament that the Father,

Son, and Holy Spirit are involved in an extensive reconciling mission with humankind and the rest of creation. Thus, the biblical witness to one God and to Father, Son, and Holy Spirit is the fundamental reason Christians face a puzzle of one and three, and it is why we do not talk about two, four, or even infinity. Philosophical theology might fruitfully investigate the significance of one and three, but it cannot indicate, as scripture does, that one and three are numbers pertinent to the Christian doctrine of God.

As Muslims point out, the word "Trinity" does not appear in the Bible. It only goes back to the late second century. Muslims often assume that the development of trinitarian doctrine implies its corruption, in this case out of love for obscurity and concession to Roman power. From the Christian perspective, however, the doctrine confirms, or even better, safeguards, the soteriological impulse central to primitive Christianity. Trinitarian doctrine emerged out of the early Christian conviction that the salvation experienced in Jesus Christ was fully an act of God himself. Only the Creator could save creatures, which he did in the incarnate Christ. The deity of the Holy Spirit was justified on similar grounds: the Spirit was found doing only what God could do.[3]

Explanation of the biblical and soteriological rationale for the Trinity offers Muslims the central reasons Christians persist in holding this doctrine. Having come this far, we might try again to find an apt analogy for God's tri-unity, especially one that will illumine rather than obscure the biblical story. Muslims may now better understand the grounds for this exercise. Additionally, Sunni Muslims who believe that the Qur'an is God's eternal speech may be able to comprehend the Christian problem insofar as they face a similar question: how does God's unity square with God's eternal attributes of speech, power, knowledge, and many others?

However, difficulties remain. While the analogical task is vital for Christian theology, Muslims are often inhibited to explore the mystery of God's unity analogically because of their belief in God's radical incomparability with anything in creation (Qur'an 42:11). The traditional Anabaptist-Mennonite reticence to speculate beyond the immediate witness of scripture might help those in this tradition empathize with the Muslim reserve. Nonetheless, I believe that a bit more can be said, but along a different tack.

Muslims may be able to acknowledge an important protective and balancing function that the Trinity performs in Christian faith. Revivalist Muslims usually take pride in Islam as a moderate and balanced religion: Judaism focused on law alone and Christianity on grace alone, but Islam perfectly combined law and grace.[4] The point here is not to evaluate this claim but to illustrate how Muslims hold moderation and the golden mean in high esteem (cf. Qur'an 2:143).

The Trinity may be understood as a set of rules that help Christians maintain balance by avoiding errors that arise through exclusive focus on one trinitarian member. First, the danger of limiting God to the Spirit is pantheism—pure immanence—where everything is God and all desires and culture are deemed good. A second error is confining God to transcendent Father or Creator. Here, the great distance between God and creation opens the door for other gods to rush in to fill the vacuum. Third, the peril of restricting God to the Son is idolizing the particular and neglecting the linking and mediating role that the Son/Word plays between the transcendent and the immanent. This occurs when Jesus is turned into an exclusive friend, or creeds are worshiped more energetically than the God to which they refer.[5]

In the Bible, Father may not always connote transcendence, the Spirit immanence, and the Son mediation and linkage. However, these senses are sufficiently strong to make the point, and trinitarian doctrine thus serves to remind Christians that God is greater than either transcendence or immanence or the link between the two taken alone. Although Muslims by no means subscribe to any kind of trinitarian doctrine, they should be able to appreciate the moderating influence the Trinity can exercise on Christian faith. With some thought, they might also recognize their own attempts to hold these elements in balance as they discuss God the Creator (transcendence), God's preservation of the Muslim community (immanence), and God's revelation in the Qur'an (link between the two).[6]

In conclusion, Christians have a story about what God has done in history that the doctrine of the Trinity seeks to secure. Thus, we cannot simply discard the doctrine because it does not meet criteria of unity that are foreign to its character. This needs to be explained to Muslims so that they can see that we are not being intentionally obscure and irrational. To the Christian, God's unity is not a simple, numerical unity, but a rich narrative unity. The God who is Father, Son, and Holy Spirit is the *only* source and end of the divine love story of creation and redemption. The whole of history comes under this one God, and it is this one God that we love, serve, and adore.

Topic Two
Why Don't Muslims Like Christians?:
A Response from Indonesia

Mesach Krisetya

Before I wrote this article, I invited my former Muslim student to meet me to have dialogue with him at my office. He is a quite open person and has been studying at our graduate department as a religion and society major, and he graduated last year, with a thesis on the topic, "The Role of China in Spreading Islam in the Northern Part of the Island of Java in the Eighteenth Century."

Resentment Against Christians in Indonesia

My intention of meeting with this former student was to ask him why Muslim people in Indonesia don't like Christians. We live in a situation where some Muslims have resorted to so much violence in their goals and their opposition to the Christians. I asked this student to respond to my question without being afraid of insulting me as his professor and his thesis guide. I encouraged him to be himself and say whatever Muslim people don't like about Christians in Indonesia. And these are some of his responses to my question.

1. There are Christianization efforts that are obtrusive, confrontational, and offensive. Some of the independent denominations use big and very demonstrative slogans like, "Christianize Indonesia in the year of 2000," and "Win Indonesia for Christ." This causes the Muslim community to feel threatened with that kind of movement.

2. Christianity is viewed as being the religion of the former colonial power. The greatest problem facing the Christian community in Indonesia is the impression that the Muslims have of it as a foreign element in Indonesian society. Unlike Islam, Christianity was introduced and is perceived to have grown under the umbrella of colonial power. That is the perception.

(Here I make a parenthetical comment. The reality is that Islam also grew under Dutch colonial power. The Muslim rulers did not welcome the coming of Christianity. Not wanting religious problems to interfere with the Dutch rulers trading interests, initially the Dutch authorities for the most part prohibited missionary work that might threaten intercommunity harmony. For example, Christian missionaries were allowed to come, but their work was generally limited to areas where indigenous religion, rather than Islam or Hinduism, was dominant. The Muslim community benefited from this policy because it allowed Islam to expand unopposed into the interior sections of Java and Sumatra.

Nowadays, as the society is highly stratified and Islam is more sophisticated, the ruling powers see in Islam a means of preserving order, an order that can protect their position. Therefore, they "manipulate" Islam by no means cynically, they too believe in it. They give lots of concessions to Islam that make other religions, particularly Christianity, feeling left out and experiencing unjust actions on the part of the ruling power.)

3. Muslims are offended by the aggressiveness of western politics and the cultural arrogance. There is a perception among many Muslims that the church especially identifies with a wealthy minority in a world of much poverty.

4. Muslims and Christians in Indonesia have, for many years, been adversaries. This was caused in part by their ignorance of each other, an ignorance fostered by the Dutch colonial policy that kept the two faith communities separate. However, in some regions they lived side by side peaceably, when external pressures did not interfere. Due to the largely negative experience of the two faith communities in the Middle East and Europe, which was carried to Indonesia by the Muslims and Christians who came, the Muslim and Christian communities that grew in the archipelago inherited attitudes of antagonism, mistrust, and fear toward one another. The "we-they" attitude grew sharper and more negative in the Moluccas, North Sumatera, and Kalimantan. The same thing happened on Java. Thus the Republic of Indonesia began its life with a substantial heritage of negative feelings between Christians and Muslims.

5. From the Muslim point of view, Christians were the favorites, at Muslim expense, of the colonial government, and after independence by the national governments as well. This happened in spite of these governments' declared neutrality with respect to religions.

Muslims resented this pro-Christian favoritism and consequently during the first fifteen years of the Old Order, fanatical guerrilla forces in West and Central Java and in South Sulawesi waged terrorist attacks with the aim of establishing an Islamic state in the new republic.

Since Islamic political parties did not repudiate these efforts, though they did not support them either, the clear impression was given to those non-Muslims, that a militant Muslim community committed to changing the foundations of the Indonesian state threatened their future.

Relationships Between Christians and Muslims

In spite of the fact that the relationships between Christians and Muslims in Indonesia have been strained, if we Christians are committed to a holistic strategy with the orientation toward the welfare of all people, we must take a good look and engage in clear thinking concerning our relationship with the Muslims. Do we see them as friends in a common struggle to uplift the life of the people? Or do we see them as a threat to our existence?

It is clear that if our orientation is on our self-existence, Islam becomes a threat or at least our rival. However, if our orientation is toward the interest of the masses, we do not have another choice, except that we must see Muslims as friends in a common struggle who are very important and a determinant movement. The Muslims are one of the largest social forces in this country besides the military. It is, therefore, impossible that our fight for democracy, commitment to overcoming poverty, and struggle for freedom can be successful without the participation of the Muslim people.

But how can this joint effort be achieved? It is not as simple as it sounds. As it was mentioned above, the reality is that many Christians experience the feeling that their presence in Indonesia inclines them to be oppressed and marginalized. It is very interesting to note that many Muslims, when they are asked, express having the same feeling Christians have of being marginalized, if not even more so. Even if it is true that they threaten us, this happens as a result of their feeling that they are being threatened first by us. This concern that is touched with deep feelings cannot be overcome with rational argumentation. What both sides can do is to show their good intentions so as to address the elements that are felt as threatening to the other side.

We are also aware of the presence of the extremist groups that confirm our impression that we are under the threat of the Muslim community. However, we should also realize that within Christianity we have several extremist groups that make the Muslims feel threatened as well. The most important part of Islam that needs to be taken into our consideration is that Muslims in Indonesia are undergoing fantastic changes and enormous development. Their power is not on the ground of their big numbers alone, but their self-confidence, their sense of identity, their intellectual capability, their clear vision, and their strong commitment to develop their communities. In this situation, it is very natural that they demand a role in the power structure that is more determinant and proportional. If the result of this demand makes us feel threatened, removed, and marginalized, we have to work hard so as to oppose the process of any community being removed or marginalized because of religion. The marginalization of any one religious community is dangerous and threatens the national unity, which is required for our nation building.

We as Christians must stand with people, whoever they are, who search for a fair and proportional role in the society. One's position in society should be determined by competence and hard work, not on the basis of the community from which one comes. If Christians are to avoid marginalization, we must demonstrate our quality and the unique gifts we offer the culture and society. The days when Christians had an advantage because we were Christians is rapidly vanishing.

In this fluid and evolving Indonesian context, our Mennonite church is looking for a way where we can be a peacemaking agent in Indonesia. Twice we have been involved in peace rallies as part of an interfaith dialogue program in Solo (Surakarta). These efforts are led by our pastor, Paulus Hartono, who is pastor of the GKMI church in Solo. He has been very instrumental in doing these peace rallies. In both rallies I was invited as one of the orators, representing the Mennonite community. The first rally was called, "Tumpengan Perdamaian," January 2002, and then we had another one called "Deklarasi Perdamaian 2003." I thought that this was a small gesture we could do, hoping to invite people to be disciples of Christ, through proclaiming Christ as the Prince of Peace. This is not the end of our effort to work for peace. There will be more work and more plans for obtaining peace in Indonesia. The Mennonite community is also able to contribute something for the peace we are longing for.

Response: Careful Theological Reflection Is Required

Lindsey Robinson

Jon Hoover dealt with the doctrine of the Trinity because this doctrine is one of the major theological obstacles for Muslims. In attempting to explain the Trinity, analogies are inadequate. Instead of trying to explain *how* God is one in three, refer to the biblical witness to explain *why* God is Father, Son, and Holy Spirit. Explain salvation history and that salvation experienced in Jesus Christ is fully an act of God himself. The biblical revelation of the one God who reveals himself as Father, Son, and Holy Spirit is the reason why Christians believe in the doctrine of the Trinity.

Mesach Krisetya reflected on theological dialogue with Muslims in the Indonesian context. He said that many Muslims in Indonesia have a majority complex. They fear the Christianization of Indonesia and advances that the church makes are viewed as evidence of Christianization. Conversely, many Christians have a minority complex and are afraid of the Islamization of Indonesia. He also related the traumatic experience of Christians living with violence and their response. Christians in Indonesia know that there is always the threat of violence from radical Islamists. He went on to say that we must approach dialogue with Muslims through cultural awareness and sensitivity. We should use the pluralistic approach recognizing that we are not losing our identity as Christians and they need not lose their identity as Muslims, but we must be willing to talk to each other.

CHAPTER THIRTY

Incarnation:
Obstacles and Bridges

David W. Shenk

All Muslims believe in revelation. So do Christians. What is the nature of revelation? That is the question Muslims and Christians repeatedly encounter in dialogue.

In the book, *A Muslim and a Christian in Dialogue*, I wrote, "In all of the biblical scriptures the personality of the different writers is evident."[1] Badru Kateregga, who was my dialogue companion responded, "Gifted personalities as the prophets were, their lives and histories did not form part of the divine message."[2]

The Islamic understanding is that revelation is *tanzil* (sent down) and therefore suspended above history and the human dimension. The biblical understanding is that revelation is incarnational, that is, all revelation is clothed within the human. This is supremely so in Jesus the Messiah. In this essay we explore these differences, with a special concern for building understanding between Muslims and Christians.

A conversation with Ibraihim, a Muslim student in Somalia, illustrates the challenge. He asked for a Bible, and the very next day returned it to me saying, "This is corrupted scripture, because it is a history book."

Muslims believe that the Qur'an as sent down revelation is

noncontingent with history. Events in history are not revelation. Of course, the Qur'an impacts history powerfully as people submit to its revelation. However, the mainstream of Islamic theology insists that there is no authentic contingency between qur'anic sent down revelation and history.[3] Christian scholars sometimes raise questions about this prevalent theology of noncontingency that so significantly forms Muslim understanding of the Qur'an. Noteworthy is Bishop Kenneth Cragg who has invested years of scholarly reflection on the Qur'an and exegetes contingent themes within the Qur'an.[4] For example, the Qur'an by its own admission is an Arabic Qur'an so that the Arab people might understand (Qur'an 41:44).

In the biblical understanding, the very soul of revelation is God's encounter with people within our history. So the core of biblical revelation is the acts of God within history. That means that all revelation has an incarnational quality—God meeting us within our history and our response.

I encountered this Islamic and Christian divergence in the spring of 2000 when I was engaged in a series of formal dialogues with a Muslim theologian in the United Kingdom, sponsored by the Muslim Students' Association. The very first evening our dialogue turned to Adam and Eve. The next day my Muslim dialogue companion counseled, "We Muslims are offended when you say that God entered the garden seeking Adam and Eve!"

I responded, "I know that is true. However, that is the gospel. God seeks us sinners wherever we might be hiding. That is the whole drama of biblical revelation—God in suffering love pursuing us so that we might be redeemed and reconciled to him."

This conversation illustrates that an incarnational or tanzil understanding of revelation forms different understandings of God and his relationship to us. In Islam God does not encounter us. He reveals his will and attributes, but God does not meet us in person-to-person encounter. In biblical faith encounter is the very center of the drama of revelation.[5]

Recently I was in Jakarta, Indonesia. Often when our car would stop at an intersection, beggar boys knocked on the window. Usually the driver rolled down the window a crack and gave 100 rupia without comment. Then we were on our way. It struck me that this is the Muslim understanding of revelation. God in his mercy gives us the gift of revelation, but there is no personal encounter. However, in Christ God has opened the car door, entered the street, and invited the beggars to join him in a feast and fellowship, in fact invited the beggar boys and girls to become his adopted children!

Incarnation has a breadth of meaning. It is not only that revelation is clothed within human idiom, personality, and culture. It also means that God enters into the midst of the mess in which we live in order to redeem us. It means that God is personally acting within history as he seeks us and meets us and redeems us. God is the good Shepherd who seeks the lost sheep in the dangerous wilderness. All these themes are intertwined within the biblical theology of incarnation. However, these themes are a perplexity within a theology that views revelation as a mercy that God sends down, but a mercy that preserves the majesty of God from ever being affected by the human situation.

Yahweh and Allah

The biblical account of Moses at the burning bush further highlights the convergence and divergence between Islamic tanzil revelation and biblical faith. The Qur'an alludes to this event. However, most Muslim theologians have the stance that it was the angel Gabriel who met Moses, not God. This is in harmony with the Muslim belief that Gabriel met Muhammad from time to time bringing the revelations of the Qur'an to him. Therefore, an angelic appearance rather than an encounter with God is the direction most Muslim theologians will choose when commenting on this event.

Nevertheless, in the biblical account, God meets Moses at the burning bush.

"What is you name?" Moses asks.

"I AM," God responds.

Later theologians have expressed this nameless name of God as Yahweh. This is the God who encounters, who meets us personally, yet who is beyond naming. He is the righteous covenant God: I WAS; I AM; I WILL BE.

Muslims trace their understanding of God to Abraham, in fact, to Adam. They believe that they are the worshippers of the God of Abraham. Although not all scholars are agreed on this, it seems to me likely that the Muslim name for God, Allah, is etymologically linked to El or Elohim, the name for the Creator that Abraham used.[6] This is to say that Jews, Christians, and Muslims all worship the God of Abraham: El or Elohim within the biblical scriptures and Allah within the Qur'an.

However, the event at the burning bush is a theological development that takes the community of biblical faith far beyond Abraham's understandings. We read, "God also said to Moses, 'I am the LORD [I AM or YAHWEH]. I appeared to Abraham, to Isaac and to Jacob as God Almighty [El or Elohim], but by my name the LORD I did not make myself known to them" (Exod 6:2-3).

People very frequently ask, "Do Muslims and Christians worship the same God?" I believe that both communities do worship the same God, the God of Abraham, Ishmael, and Isaac. However, Muslim theology has not comprehended God as the one who encounters personally. The I AM of the burning bush within biblical revelation invites us into a personal covenant relationship with our Creator. God incarnate in Jesus the Messiah is in continuity with God's revelation to Moses at the burning bush.

However, there are the Sufi mystics within Islam who do seek to experience God. They are encouraged in their quest by the qur'anic assertions that God spoke with Moses and that Abraham was a friend of God. These hints of divine-human relations are an encouragement to the Sufi quest for the touch of the divine in their experience. In this quest, Sufis might be a bridge for understanding between Islamic orthodoxy and Christian experience. I say that with some caution, because the quest of the Sufis is not encounter with God. Rather it is absorption into divinity with the subsequent loss of personal identity, rather similar to Hindu Brahmanism.

The biblical God who encounters never disparages the significance of the person. I-Thou encounter is a call to repentance. It is also the invitation to know God as our loving heavenly Father.

Objection to the Incarnation

In Islam God sends his will down in the form of books. He is merciful and compassionate. But he is never affected by what we do.[7] Although God is closer to us than our jugular vein (Qur'an 50:16), he does not meet us and he is not affected by our experiences. We can learn of God's attributes and rejoice in his mercy, but we cannot know God personally, for he is the unknowable one.

This, then, is the primary reason for the Muslim objection to the incarnation of God in the Messiah. God sends his revelation down and he bestows his mercy, but he never becomes personally involved. For revelation to be incarnation would make God vulnerable.

The name for Jesus in the Qur'an, at least symbolically, reveals that the theological understanding of an incarnational revelation is not worthy of the majesty and transcendence of God. The Messiah is 'Isa, not Jesus. What does 'Isa mean?—Nothing.[8]

Jesus means Yahweh Saves. The God who encounters redeems! The angel announced to Joseph: "You are to give him the name Jesus [Yahweh Saves], because he will save his people from their sins" (Matt 1:21). However, in Islam Jesus is 'Isa. He is not redeemer. He is not God with us. Jesus as 'Isa carries no hint of Savior. It is impossible to find space theologically for incarnation or redemption in a theology of tanzil. I will comment further on this.

Revelation as Tanzil

Muslims believe that throughout the eras of human history God has always revealed his guidance to humanity by sending down his instructions through prophets. The Arabic Qur'an is the final and clarifying revelation, and, of course, it is tanzil revelation just as has been true of all other revelations. That is the foundational belief of the Muslim ummah (community).

This understanding is consistent with the Islamic belief that there is the Mother of Books in the heavens inscribed on Golden Tablets. That heavenly book is Islam, God's unchangeable and eternal will. Adam was the first prophet upon whom God sent down guidance. That guidance instructed Adam on the ways he should live as God's vicegerent on earth. Later God sent other portions of that guidance down in books: the Taurat (Torah) through the prophet Moses, the Zabur (Psalms) through the prophet David, the Injil (Gospels) through Jesus the Messiah, and finally the Qur'an through the prophet Muhammad. God also sent down the Suhuf (Scrolls) through the prophet Abraham, but that book has been lost.

The doctrine of tanzil demands that believers preserve revelation from corruption. What is corruption? It is the human dimension. Although Muhammad sought the counsel of others, the doctrine of the inimitability of the Qur'an means that the Arabic Qur'an that he recited had no imprint of human influence. Muslims believe that the Qur'an was uncorrupted; it transcended all human influence. It is a miracle that can never be replicated. That is the reason why the Qur'an cannot be translated into other languages. It is only Qur'an in the sent-down Arabic language. When the Qur'an is referred to in any language other than Arabic, this is considered an interpretation of the Qur'an. The Qur'an is sent down upon humanity; it is not influenced by humanity.

Badru Kateregga comments, "Revelation which is contained in scriptures or divine books is the true guidance sent down (tanzil) directly from God. It is God's Word revealed to chosen prophets."[9]

Revelation as Incarnation

Incarnation is a biblical understanding of revelation and is in contrast to tanzil. Incarnation means "in the flesh." It refers to revelation that is clothed in the human.

When Muslims consider the human dimension of the Bible, the inclination is to conclude that these scriptures are corrupted, just as Ibraihim stated in the beginning of this chapter. If corruption means anything that pertains to the human, then indeed the biblical scriptures are corrupted. All biblical revelation includes the imprint of the human; it is clothed in human idiom, personality, culture, and thought patterns. It is in-history revelation.

In biblical faith it is the advent of Jesus the Messiah who is the fullest expression of God's in-history revelation. God sent his one and only Son into the world. That Son was Jesus of Nazareth, a Jewish carpenter. God in the Messiah is clothed within the "corruption" of humanity. In the Gospel according to John, the eternal truth of God is called the Word. This refers to God's full self-expression—the Word through which he created the universe. Jesus of Nazareth, the Messiah, is the incarnation of this Word.

In John's Gospel we read,

> In the beginning was the Word, and the Word was with God, and the Word was God. He was with God in the beginning. . . . The Word became flesh [in Jesus of Nazareth] and lived for awhile among us. We have seen his glory, the glory of the one and only Son, who came from the Father, full of grace and truth (John 1:1-2, 14).

In Shi'a-Mennonite dialogues in Qom, Iran, in February 2004, one of the mullahs very perceptively observed, "In the Gospel we never read that Jesus said, 'Thus says the Lord.' Rather Jesus always said, 'I say to you!' This is in contrast to Moses who proclaimed, 'Thus says the Lord!' And everything in the Qur'an is 'Thus says the Lord.'

"The reason for the difference in the biblical accounts between

Jesus and the other prophets is that in the Gospel, Jesus is proclaimed as the person who is the Word of the Lord; in fact he is the Lord. However, Muhammad and Moses are prophets who are spokespersons for the Lord. In the Gospel, Jesus the Messiah is not a spokesperson for he is the Lord."[10]

Implications for Mission

The incarnational quality of biblical revelation and the incarnation of God in Christ is the reason the church in mission translates the Bible into the idiom of the people. Wherever the gospel is heard, people seek to incarnate that gospel within their own culture. That is the driving inspiration for translating the Bible. Today portions of the Bible are translated into over 2,000 languages. That reality is enormously empowering to the local churches and encourages emerging churches to take deep root within local culture.

In contrast, a tanzil understanding of revelation means that the Arabic Qur'an cannot be authentically translated into any language —it can be interpreted, but never translated. Consequently Arabization always accompanies Islamization. The devout person who knows Arabic best and uses that gift in the study of the Qur'an, he is the one who moves most readily into the centers of authority within Muslim communities everywhere.[11]

These understandings form the nature of the Muslim ummah (community) and the Christian church, and the mission of these two communities. Even leadership roles are formed by these understandings of the nature of God's revelation. God in Christ is the good Shepherd who seeks the lost sheep and, in fact, lays down his life for the sheep. This reality inspires congregations to view their leaders as pastors, shepherds who seek the lost and comfort the distressed.

On the other hand, Muslim congregations do not have pastors. The leaders of Muslim congregations are imams whose primary responsibility is to lead in worship and instruct the congregation; of course this does not exclude caregivers. The life and ministry of the Muslim or Christian congregation is formed by its understandings of God and his relationship to humanity.

Interpreting Jesus

How, then, might Christians respond to Muslim perplexity or objections to incarnational theology? How do we interpret Jesus when the questions come? Here are some suggested approaches as we seek to bear witness to Jesus the Messiah within an Islamic context.

Clarifications

First, there are several points of clarification and comment.

1. There is a persistent conviction among Muslims that Christians believe that Jesus is the progeny of God and his consort, Mary. This notion is nurtured through several qur'anic references (3:55; 9:30; 19:34-35). No Muslim will ever consider the Christian faith as long as this misunderstanding persists. Christians need to be forthright in insisting that we do not believe that God had a consort and fathered a son. That is rank polytheism, and has no place in Christian or biblical understanding.

2. Christians should resist comparing Jesus to Muhammad. This is because Jesus occupies a very different position in Christian theology than does Jesus and Muhammad in Muslim theology. Muslims believe that Jesus, like Moses, David, and Muhammad, was an apostle (*rasul*) through whom a divine messenger (angel) has revealed a book of God. So the book of God known as the Gospel (Injil) has been sent down through the Messiah just as the final revelation, the Qur'an has been sent through Muhammad.

3. However, the witness of the New Testament is that Jesus the Messiah is himself the Gospel; he did not bring the Gospel. The Gospel, who is the Messiah, came through the Virgin Mary. The Gospel did not come through Jesus the Messiah, for he is the Gospel.

4. Muslims are often confused by the presence of four Gospels in the New Testament. Since the Gospel of Jesus the Messiah does not seem to be present in the Bible, a common notion among Muslims is that people rejected the Gospel that Jesus revealed, and therefore he took the Gospel with him when he ascended into heaven. So there is no Gospel available.

5. It is helpful for Christians to clarify that Jesus himself is the Gospel; he did not bring the Gospel. Actually, the Qur'an refers to the Messiah as the Injil (good news or gospel; Qur'an 3:45). Thus the four writers of the Gospel accounts in the New Testament are witnesses of the person, Messiah, who is the Gospel, meaning the good news or the Injil.

6. Muslims believe that the Qur'an is the criterion of truth and that it clarifies all previous revelation. Jesus the Messiah occupies that place in Christian theology. He is the truth and the fulfillment of the

scriptures. It is important in conversation with Muslims to remember that in Islam, the Qur'an occupies much the same place of authority that Jesus occupies in the Christian faith.[12]

7. In the Asharite stream of Islamic theology, which dominates much of contemporary Muslim philosophy, the Word is uncreated, co-eternal with God, and of one essence with God. Of course, the Asharites believe that the Qur'an is the Word.[13] However, it is noteworthy that the Qur'an also refers to Jesus the Messiah as the Word of God—*kalimatullah* (4:171).

Jesus is a mystery

1. There is an aura of mystery in regard to the qur'anic 'Isa. He is, for example, honored as the Messiah. What does that mean? The Qur'an does not provide much light on that question. And why is it that 'Isa the Messiah will return at the end of history to establish truth throughout the world? I will not elaborate on the etchings that comprise the qur'anic 'Isa, except to list dimensions of the mysterious qualities that adorn this beloved prophet.
   - Messiah (3:45)
   - Good News (3:45)
   - born of a virgin (19:16-35)
   - the Word of God (kalimatullah; 4:171)
   - the Spirit of God (*ruhulah*; 4:41)
   - Miracle Worker (3:49)
   - established the former scriptures (5:49)
   - brought the Gospel (5:49)
   - pure and without sin (19:19)
   - predicted the coming of Muhammad (61:6)
   - not the Son of God (9:30)
   - a servant (43:59)
   - limited mission (13:38)
   - nevertheless, a sign to all creatures and an evangel for all people (21:91; 2:253)
   - rescued from death on the cross (4:157)
   - taken to heaven without dying (3:55-58)
   - returning at the end of history to get the world ready for the final judgment (in seventy different Traditions and the Qur'an 43:61).

2. Muslims have developed a deep reverence for 'Isa. In fact, there is so much eulogistic poetry for 'Isa that one can refer to a

Muslim Gospel of 'Isa the Messiah.[14] This is not to say that there is a book by that name, but rather that there is a whole body of lore about 'Isa that inspires Muslim admiration and devotion. However, the 'Isa of the Muslim gospel and of the Qur'an is on the margins of real life. The Muslim gospel of the traditions and popular lore portrays 'Isa as a wondering ascetic who is devoted to his mother and whose teachings and life are for monks on the margins of society. So it is with the qur'anic 'Isa as well.

3. Although some Muslims would view Jesus as having a universal mission commensurate with Abraham or Moses, for most he is a beloved saint who is an impractical idealist with a limited mission for a small group within Israel for a particular time (13:38).[15] Although honored within the Qur'an, Jesus is marginalized. Only fourteen suras mention Jesus, out of the 114 that comprise the Qur'an. Abraham, Moses, and above all Muhammad are the most prominent prophets.[16]

4. There are, however, significant areas for exploration in dialogue. Both Muslims and Christians believe that Jesus is the Messiah, the Word of God, the Good News, and that he will return at the end of history. Consequently, there is often intrigue and persistent questions that Muslims and Christians meet in their conversations with one another.

- What is the meaning of Jesus as the Messiah?
- What is the meaning of Jesus as the Word of God?
- What is the meaning of Jesus as servant?
- What is the meaning of Jesus's return at the end of history?
- What is the meaning of the cross? Why do Muslims deny the cross and why do Christians embrace it? What difference does this make in our understanding of God and his kingdom?

Who Is Jesus?

In a dialogue in the Central London Mosque with 400 people packing the basement hall, an usher put this question on the podium, "Do you believe that Jesus is the Son of God?"

This is how I responded. "I do not believe that God took a consort and fathered a child! Never! That is polytheism, which Christians as well as Muslims totally reject. However, the name 'Son of God' is given to Jesus the Messiah by God himself. When the angel announced his birth to the Virgin Mary, he exclaimed that the child will be called 'the Son of God.' Furthermore, twice in the ministry of

Jesus the Messiah, God spoke from heaven declaring, 'This is my beloved Son.' What does God mean by proclaiming that Jesus the Messiah is his beloved Son?

"Perhaps there is a hint in the Qur'an that helps us understand what this means. We read that Jesus the Messiah is kalimatullah (the Word of God). I realize that Muslim theologians explain that this means that God spoke and Jesus was created miraculously in the womb of the Virgin Mary, just as Adam was created miraculously through the Word of God. However, bear with me as I give witness as to what the gospel reveals about the meaning of Jesus the Messiah as the Word of God.

"The Word of God is the expression of who God is. He speaks, and the universe is created and sustained. Since God cannot tell a lie, his Word is the full revelation of who he is. In the Gospel according to the apostle John we read, 'In the beginning was the Word, and the Word was with God, and the Word was God' (John 1:1).

"In Jesus the Messiah the Word of God is fully revealed. We read, 'The Word became flesh and lived for awhile among us. We have seen his glory, the glory of the one and only Son, who came from the Father, full of grace and truth' (John 1:14).

"Since it is impossible to separate God from his Word, when we meet Jesus the Messiah we are meeting the fullness of the revelation of God. If we want to know God, we discover that revelation in Jesus the Messiah who is the incarnation of the Word of God. That is what it means for the Messiah to be the Son of God; he is the presence of the Word of God in human form.

"Those who read the New Testament will discover that there are four accounts of the life and ministry of Jesus the Messiah: Matthew, Mark, Luke, and John. This is because a book from God called the "Gospel" was not revealed through Jesus the Messiah. Rather, Jesus the Messiah who is the Word of God *is* the book from God. So there are four biblical witnesses concerning this One who is the Word of God. Each of these four witnesses give testimony about his life and ministry, so that we can have confidence in the truth of the witness.

"Son of God also means that Jesus the Messiah had a perfect relationship with God the Father. Jesus said, 'I and the Father are one' (John 10:30). One of the greatest surprises of God's grace is that through the ministry of Jesus the Messiah, we are also invited to begin to know God as our loving heavenly Father. We are invited into the family of God as his daughters and sons. Jesus the Messiah is the

Son, but we also are invited to become sons and daughters who experience the grace and joy of knowing God as our loving heavenly Father."

Later my dialogue companion, Shabir Ally, commented, "You are sharing the gospel with clarity, and they are listening with respect. Of course, one reason is that you respect us."

That has always been my experience. Whenever I respectfully present the incarnation as I have described above, my Muslim friends are greatly interested, and in fact, generally enormously relieved that I do not believe that God had a consort through whom he fathered a son. I do not mean that Muslims automatically embrace an incarnational theology when I give witness to Christ in this manner, but I sense that obstacles have been addressed that enable a true engagement in regard to the core realities of incarnation or tanzil understandings of revelation.

Transcendence and Power

Muslims are fearful that accepting that scriptures have an incarnational quality or considering the incarnation of God in the Messiah will subvert the sovereignty, transcendence, and power of God, as well as the integrity of his revealed will. Muslims believe that a tanzil understanding of revelation protects the sovereignty, transcendence, and power of God. Incarnation is impossible for that would subvert the authority of God.

Is genuine power invulnerable transcendence? Or is genuine power suffering love? Is the vulnerability of the incarnation and the cross weakness? The witness of the church is that God incarnated himself and that suffering is the power of God within and among us, offering new and abundant life that transforms people and renews and sanctifies all creation. The incarnated Gospel is always vulnerable. God in Christ invites, he does not force the truth upon us.

The faithful church is the community of incarnation, in which the life of the Messiah is present for grace, ministry, and confrontation against the powers of evil. Muslims might never read the Gospel accounts. However they do read the church. God's intention is that the church be the presence of the body of Christ, the "letter from Christ" who Muslims read (2 Cor 3:3)—the life-giving sacramental presence.

In the sura in the Qur'an called The Table, the disciples pled with Jesus to bring a table of food from heaven in order that their hearts may be satisfied.[17] And through Jesus, God did indeed send the table down (5:115-18). This is a revelation of a longing for fellowship with God, a sign within the Qur'an of the eucharistic table, which within the gospel is a sign of the new life offered in the sacrificial self-giving of the Messiah for the sins of the world. In this qur'anic vision God generously provides the feast, it is a celebrative feast, an abundant feast, a feast touched with eschatological hope, a feast wherein "our hearts are satisfied." The Christian calling is to bear witness that indeed the feast has come from heaven, and all are welcome to participate.

This feast is given through the vulnerable serving and suffering of the Messiah for and because of the sins of the world. Bishop Kenneth Cragg commented in a Hartford Seminary assembly of Muslims and Christians some years ago, "It is urgent that communities of faith be present in our violent and troubled world who give witness that God is most fully revealed in the vulnerability of the baby in a manger in Bethlehem, in a refugee child in Egypt, in a carpenter in Nazareth, in an itinerant teacher of the good news of the kingdom of God, in a man crucified between two thieves at Golgotha who, as he died, cried out in forgiveness for those who have crucified him."

However, this Jesus of the gospel, as the Muslim scholar Tarif Khalidi observes, cannot be possessed by either Muslims or Christians. He is the "one who easily, almost naturally, rises above two religious environments, the one that nurtured him [Christian] and the other that adopted him [Muslim]."[18] We can never possess Christ; it is he who possesses the believer.

Yet although we cannot possess him, he meets with us and shows us his wounded hands, feet, and side, and then blesses us with these words of commission, "Peace be with you! As the Father has sent me, I am sending you. . . . Receive the Holy Spirit" (John 20:21-22).[19]

∾

Response: How Much Does God Love?

Jeanne Sahawneh

The Muslim understanding of revelation is tanzil, meaning God has sent his word, via the angel Gabriel, to his prophet, Muhammad. The Qu'ran is a word-for-word dictation from the Mother of Books in heaven. Muhammad is like a conduit through which God's message is sent. Nothing of Muhammad's personality or culture corrupted that message.

The Christian understanding of revelation is incarnational. God has revealed himself through his interactions with humans in history. This started with God seeking Adam and Eve in the garden after the first sin. To Abraham, Isaac, and Jacob, God revealed himself as El, Elohim (God). The Arabic word for God, Allah, is linguistically equivalent and is used by both Christians and Muslims in the Arabic-speaking community. In the burning bush, God revealed himself to Moses as I AM (Yahweh). Islam has no equivalent personal I-thou encounter with reference to God.

Christians confess that the fullest revelation of God is in Christ Jesus. He is the message, the Gospel. The four Gospel accounts in the New Testament are witnesses to Jesus, the good news. Muslims think that Jesus is the prophet through whom the Gospel, the book, was sent. The four Gospel accounts must therefore, according to this view, be corrupted versions of the original book.

Christians believe the Holy Spirit inspired the writers of scripture, using their gifts, language, and cultural settings. This is hard for Muslims to understand, because to them God is completely transcendent; yet in Islam God is also imminent, closer than the jugular vein. Nevertheless, nothing humans do affects God. Yet it really is good news when they understand that God does choose incarnation to reveal the extent of his love for us.

CHAPTER THIRTY-ONE

Islamic Intercession and Christian Atonement: Stumbling Blocks and Bridges

Timothy Bergdahl

But we proclaim Christ crucified, a stumbling-block to Jews and foolishness to Gentiles" (1 Cor 1:23, NRSV).

Introduction

I have known Muslims and studied Islam for the better part of my life. In that time I have had the opportunity to consider many things about my understanding and the understandings of others. Some of these understandings have taken the form of an enigma, and perhaps the greatest of these is how peoples who desire the same thing could be so at odds. I have never believed that Muslims desire to hope in any but the one God. Their desires are similar to my desires including closeness to God, meaning and direction in life, help in times of trouble and success, and a place with God in eternity. Many of us even hold in common a will to see our traditions reformed and brought in line with the unadulterated teachings of our origins.

My Muslim friends clearly see the divide that remains as being mostly my fault. They complain to me that though they revere my prophet Jesus Christ, I do not honor their prophet Muhammad—why is this? I often respond by asking if to honor Muhammad one must know him as a Muslim does and honor him for what Muslims believe he is. Invariably they reply, yes! To which I add that to truly honor Jesus one must know him as a Christian does and honor him for what Christians believe he is. My Muslim friends are wont to do this for fear of committing *shirk*, associating God with another, by identifying Jesus as God's Son.

This leaves us at something of an impasse, unable to even approach the work of God in Christ known as the atonement. Because of their understanding of what God can and cannot be, a Muslim may honor Jesus for many things, but not for the Christian perspective of his sacrifice on our behalf, his victory over sin and death, and his place at the right hand of the Father.

A Basis for Discourse

Long ago God spoke to our ancestors in many and various ways by the prophets, but in these last days he has spoken to us by a Son, whom he appointed heir of all things, through whom he also created the worlds (Heb 1:1-2, NRSV).

Do we then just agree to disagree? That hardly seems proper for people who believe that God has revealed himself and his will for us in distinctive and compelling ways. Also, Christianity has a unique relationship with Islam in that these two world religions officially claim Jesus Christ as an intermediary of their distinctive revelations. We recognize that Muslims believe that the Gospel (book of revelation) was revealed through Jesus Christ; Christians believe that Jesus Christ in his person is the revelation of the Gospel.

Both Muslims and Christians share in the first half of the Hebrews 1:1-2 quoted above: God has spoken to the ancestors through prophets. However, Islam does not own the Christian understanding of the second part of the passage: Jesus as the Son through whom God created the world. Christians are often quite surprised that in the development of Islamic theology, Muhammad is believed to be the one appointed as intercessor, as authority, and in fact, creation itself is associated with Muhammad.

A significant stream of Muslim theological consensus refers to the *noor* (light) of Muhammad as predating creation and giving cause to it. Ghulam Hussain Osto observes, "The Prophet is reported to have said that what God created first of all was my light (noor)."[1] This perception has its roots in Muslim Sufi mysticism, but cannot be seen as solely Sufi. Common practice among most Muslims has exalted Muhammad so that his attributes may be profitably dwelt on in the same way as the ninety-nine names of Allah, names which firmly place Muhammad as essential and accessible. Nevertheless, Jesus Christ holds a place of esteem in Muslim understanding only surpassed by the family of the prophet Muhammad and by Muhammad himself.

While our discourse may be about many things, it at least (and even at most) must be about Jesus Christ. Since Islam holds a special place as a post-Christian religion in having formed Islamic scriptural perspectives on Jesus, our concerns will be both who Muslims say he is not and who they say he is in the light of whom they say God is. Specifically, what role does Jesus Christ play in the plans of a merciful and compassionate God?

The Nature of Islam

Indeed, under the law almost everything is purified with blood, and without the shedding of blood there is no forgiveness of sins (Heb 9:22, NRSV).

Both Christians and Muslims revere Jesus Christ and see him as instrumental in God's activity in the world. For the Muslim, Jesus's failed mission, picked up and accomplished by Muhammad, will be vindicated in the last day. For Christians, however, there is a centrality to the work of God in Christ that trumps and precludes all else. Christians commonly refer to this unique work as atonement.

The gospel message unites the atoning sacrifice of Christ as the Lamb of God with his ministry as intercessor for all believers (Heb 4:14–10:18). Atonement and the ministry of intercession are united in the ministry and mission of Christ.

Within Islam, Muhammad or the saints of Sufism cannot atone for sin, yet there are broad streams of Muslim piety that venerate both the Prophet and the saints as intercessors.

The theology of atonement and intercession is rooted in the sweep of Old Testament and New Testament revelation. We discover that, through Adam and Eve, sin not only entered the world, it entered the make-up of all humanity after them. All humanity participates in the turning away from God, sinfulness, and death of the first parents. In our sinfulness, all humanity experiences alienation from God our life-giver, alienation from others, alienation from ourselves, and alienation from creation.

Yet even in the midst of the primal turning away from God, God clothed Adam and Eve with the skins of an animal (Gen 3:21) and promised that a son would be born to the woman who would confront and triumph over evil and sinfulness (Gen 3:15). Interestingly in the Qur'an we read that God gave Adam and Eve the raiment of righteousness (Qur'an 7:26). Christians and Muslims might consider together the meaning of these acts of mercy from God to cover the shame of Adam and Eve, acts that both the Qur'an and the Bible mention. Is this not a sign that God has revealed within the biblical scriptures (and that the Qur'an alludes to) in the descriptions of the dawn of human history—we need the clothing of righteousness that only God can provide.

Christians confess that Christ, who is the Lamb of God, is the fulfillment of this sign of the need for the clothing of righteousness that only God can provide. Our sinfulness separates us from God, but Christ crucified is our atoning sacrifice for our sin, he has taken our place, he becomes our righteousness, and in him we are clothed with the righteousness of God. In the atoning sacrifice of Christ the demands of justice for the sins of the whole world are fulfilled (Rom 3:22-26). In Christ, God has taken our place. The righteousness of God becomes our righteous clothing.

Throughout the Old Testament animals were offered to atone for sin. Christians believe these sacrifices were signs pointing to the Lamb of God, Christ, who is the atoning sacrifice for the sins of the whole world. In the New Testament a person took the place of animals and other valid sacrifices to become the one sacrifice for all. That person was Jesus Christ, who was able to serve as the Lamb of God due to his fully divine, fully human status.

The Four Spiritual Laws, The Roman Road, and many other simple written statements, survey basics of these biblical understandings and present an invitation for accepting Christ's atonement as the means of salvation. These simple statements, while apparently quite effective in communicating the gospel within some worldviews, are not well honed to Muslim understandings of reality. Because these presentations are both simplistic and aimed at helping a non-Christian understand the essence of God's work in Christ, a number of questions are raised. One cluster of questions concerns the extent of the atonement's effect, the other concerns the model(s) used. This brief essay cannot explore these questions adequately, but I do want to comment very briefly on the models used in describing the nature of the atonement.

A number of themes characteristic of Islamic intercession and Christian atonement commend themselves as either stumbling blocks or bridges to the Christian presenting the promise and challenge of the atonement to Muslims. A major stumbling block that cannot be dismissed or ignored is that the atonement in Christ crucified and risen is normative and defining for a Christian experience of God's work in the world and his purpose for humankind.

The church has attempted to interpret this normative and definitive act of God in the atoning sacrifice of Christ in a variety of ways. Our understandings include a range of models from the church fathers' focus on ransom, the medieval scholastic focus on satisfaction, the reformers' emphasis on meeting the demands of justice, to recent emphases on the victory of God (with variations and combinations of themes of every sort). These descriptions all have in common that they, like Karl Barth recommended, try to hold the Bible in one hand and the newspaper in the other. They attempt to connect biblical expression to current understanding and circumstance. They provide viewpoints that, in spite of what some of their advocates might think, provide a glimpse at, rather than the full picture. They are especially, and reasonably, tied to the situation in which the church found itself historically, confronting paganism and then existing within imperial, feudal, or otherwise western societies.

However, the church today is predominantly nonwestern and it is mostly nonwestern Christians who are engaged on a daily basis with Muslims. Perhaps a way forward in discovering proper Muslim metaphors for atonement is to (1) look at such nonwestern metaphors as already exist in the Christian community and (2) encourage nonwestern churches in a "voyage of rediscovery" where the western models have been inappropriately imposed. Ironically, it is outside the west that the biblical ideas of substitutionary sacrifice and a God empowered triumph over death and evil are most readily accepted without modification.

Appealing to a God of Mercy and Compassion

Since, therefore, the children share flesh and blood, he himself likewise shared the same things, so that through death he might destroy the one who has the power of death, that is, the devil, and free those who all their lives were held in slavery by the fear of death. For it is clear that he did not come to help angels, but the descendants of Abraham. Therefore he had to become like his brothers and sisters in every respect, so that he might be a merciful and faithful high priest in the service of God, to make a sacrifice of atonement for the sins of the people. Because he himself was tested by what he suffered, he is able to help those who are being tested (Heb 2:14-18, NRSV).

Muslims believe that God is a God of mercy and compassion. So do Christians. What an amazing point of unity and separation. "In the name of God, the merciful, the compassionate!" How many times have I heard that? Every trip, every letter, every newscast, began with that assertion while I lived in Pakistan. On several occasions I tried to press the point by asking how God's mercy and compassion was understood. I was told that God gives us all we need according to our obedience. This raised additional questions. How is such action different from the expectation of idol worshippers? Wouldn't compassion be more a giving in spite of disobedience?

More to the point, wouldn't compassion require a level of "fellow-suffering," of "walking in my shoes"? My Muslim friends are troubled by this. On the one hand, God in no way stoops to our level to share in our sufferings. On the other hand, compassion by definition requires that very thing. Usually my friends and I agree that the compassion of the God they know is something quite different from the compassion they have experienced or shared elsewhere.

However, the most gospel-like verse in the Qur'an describes the mercy of God as inscribed upon God himself, that is of his very essence. We read:

> And when those who believe in Our revelations come unto thee, say: Peace be unto you! Your Lord had prescribed for Himself mercy (or inscribed upon himself the rule of mercy), that whoso of you doeth evil and repenteth afterward thereof and doeth right, (for him) lo! Allah is Forgiving, Merciful (Qur'an 32:4).

The Christian witness is that Christ as our atoning sacrifice and his intercessory ministry is the ultimate revelation of the love of God who has inscribed upon himself the rule of mercy. How I wish that the Holy Spirit would make the hearts of our Muslim friends tender to the one who emptied himself, taking the form of a servant, and acted in a way of unparalleled compassion.

> Since, then, we have a great high priest who has passed through the heavens, Jesus, the Son of God, let us hold fast to our confession. For we do not have a high priest who is unable to sympathize with our weaknesses, but we have one who in every respect has been tested as we are, yet without sin. Let us therefore approach the throne of grace with boldness, so that we may receive mercy and find grace to help in time of need (Heb 4:14-16, NRSV).

The intercessory ministry of Jesus Christ is rooted in his atoning sacrifice for our sins. Although Islamic orthodoxy teaches that there is no atoning sacrifice for sin, within Islamic orthopraxis there is much interest and involvement in sacrificial rites, and especially so within the Sufi mystical streams of Islamic piety. A key dimension of the phenomenon of sacrifice is the qur'anic assertion that a son of Abraham was ransomed from death by God intervening and providing a "tremendous" sacrifice. Here is a profound convergence between the biblical accounts and the Qur'an. Muslims and Christians jointly give witness that God providing a substitutionary sacrifice when Abraham was prepared to offer his own son in obedience. To this day Muslims commemorate this sacrifice of Abraham during the annual pilgrimage to Mecca. What would it take to help our Muslims friends discover that while their focus remains on goats and camels offered as reminders of the sacrifice that redeemed a son of Abraham from death, there is a much greater and ultimate sacrifice that God has provided for the redemption of all people?

We read:

> But when Christ came as a high priest of the good things that have come, then through the greater and perfect tent (not made with hands, that is, not of this creation), he entered once for all into the Holy Place, not with the blood of goats and calves, but with his own blood, thus obtaining eternal redemption. For if the blood of goats and bulls, with the sprinkling of the ashes of

a heifer, sanctifies those who have been defiled so that their flesh is purified, how much more will the blood of Christ, who through the eternal Spirit offered himself without blemish to God, purify our conscience from dead works to worship the living God

For this reason he is the mediator of a new covenant, so that those who are called may receive the promised eternal inheritance, because a death occurred that redeems them from the transgressions under the first covenant (Heb 9:11-15).

Stumbling Blocks and Bridges

What can be concluded from this? I have sought to identify a few stumbling blocks and bridges. Sometimes we stumble over something unexpected we encounter in the dark, and sometimes we stumble over realities we wish were otherwise. The former can be revealed and removed, while the latter are the nature of reality and therefore immovable. If the individual persists in tripping over them is it not their own responsibility?

A number of unnecessary barriers have stood between the Muslim and the opportunity to accept or reject the work of God in Christ Jesus. One unnecessary barrier is the perception that the message of the atonement is alien and un-Islamic. This idea is generated in part by the fact that the atonement as such is presented as an idea outside of Islamic revelation and teaching promulgated by outsiders, most specifically, westerners. So long as witnesses to the atonement draws firmly from the philosophy and politics of western contexts, particularly legal descriptions, in generating argument and description for the atonement, it will be difficult for Muslims to comprehend. The real stumbling block of the atonement must not be obscured. Muslims must be able to accept or reject the atonement in its biblical foundations, not in the clothing of western theologies.

Another unnecessary barrier has been the focus on the work of the atonement as being more an idea than an act of love and righteousness. Christians tend to focus on belief at the expense of practice. I do not mean to imply that the church in the Muslim world is not known for its acts of service, rather that, in my opinion, orthodoxy remains far, far more important to most Christians than orthopraxy. By example, consider two Christians. One rejects the virgin birth, the other refuses to turn the other cheek. Who will be placed under church discipline? Christians are often satisfied by professions of faith rooted in assent to a concept, rather than an altered allegiance that calls for a new way of living.

One way forward is to utilize the best of anthropology and other sciences in order to understand how gospel is always contained within culture, but never owned by a culture. Communication of the atonement to a Muslim means a disconnection from alien contexts and a seeding (and husbandry) within Muslim contexts. What are some of these Muslim contexts?

1. Prayer in Jesus's name has the authority to cast out demons, heal the sick, and bring other petitions before God.

2. Obedience through walking and talking with Jesus brings blessing.

3. Participation in the communion of Jesus is equitable with and fulfilling the promise of sacrifice in Islam.

4. Acknowledgment that the Qur'an stipulates that only God can appoint an intercessor and that the Injil states that God has appointed Jesus as intercessor.

5. Celebrating the assurance that in the atoning sacrifice of Christ we receive the forgiveness of sins.

6. Living the way of the cross in all our relations.

7. Understanding that the greatest mercy is found in God's work through Jesus.

Especially connected to this last point, I believe a way forward is found in a core Anabaptist commitment that the atonement and the empowerment of the Holy Spirit should lead to following Jesus in gratitude for the work God has done through him, a work that in fact enables us to do our work.

From the beginning the qur'anic rejection of the cross and atonement has been the essential barrier between Christians and Muslims. We recognize that the cross is the universal stumbling block, not only for Muslims, but for all people. The gospel is the proclamation of the universal necessity of the cross as central to God's atoning work in Jesus Christ. For the Christian, there is no compromise in Jesus Christ (not Muhammad) being God's final message to, and most important act among, humanity. It is not my intention to argue the point here, only to point out that this has been a core proclamation of Anabaptists, and at least as much a distinctive as concerns for peace and justice. This stumbling block persists with the understanding that for many Muslims it provides a solid reason for rejecting the atonement.

The Muslim rejection of the cross is consistent with the Muslim understanding of the nature of God who is unaffected by humanity. Although compassionate, God never suffers with us or for us. How can a God who is wholly other be involved in a work such as the atonement? This reminds me of discussions I've had with Muslims about their experience of Allah, the Merciful, the Compassionate. My friends conceded that mercy and compassion from Allah is unique to him, and not the kind of mercy or compassion we expect from human beings who, by definition, are relational in exhibiting these qualities, even sharing in our suffering.

The high position given to Muhammad is also problematic. He has always been venerated and has provided the opportunity for relationship with the divine so lacking in direct correspondence with Allah. However, as the ummah has had ever increasing contact with the outside world there has been a concerted effort to apply any good thing found in other faiths to their own beloved prophet, sort of a "anything your prophet could do, ours could do better" attitude that has led to, among other things, a Christmas like focus on the birthday of Muhammad.

As I mentioned earlier, it seems to me that among the probable bridges are the experience of Muslims as to humanity's true inclinations as wicked and in need of salvation. Something that has been explored by many is the apparent high esteem of Muslims in literature and practice for the person of Jesus Christ. His work on behalf of God is not wholly rejected by the Muslim, rather there are many things Muslims expect from him. Finally, the felt need for relationship at the center of religion and so for an intercessor needs to be considered.

Where can we go from here? I have several broad suggestions and a few specific ones for future emphasis. These factors should be kept in mind by Christians seeking to give Muslims opportunity to respond to the atonement of Jesus Christ in as unencumbered a way as possible. They are:

Cherish the necessary. If the atoning work of God in Jesus Christ is necessary for all (and I believe it is), than it serves neither Christians nor Muslims to emphasize similarities while denying or trivializing its distinctive power.

Set aside the unnecessary. Occam's Razor is an excellent tool to use. If it is unnecessary, it is by definition out of place. If it is unnecessary, history has already shown us that it hasn't been part of the answer, but part of the problem. Insistence on western forms of worship, even the semi-sacredness of western forms of commerce, have not served the cause of the gospel.

Recognize that God is at work within the Muslim worldview. Just as the gospel has taken root within the worldview of other cultures, including the traditional religions of Europe, so the gospel can also take root within an Islamic culture and worldview.

Appendix: Verses from the Qur'an in regard to intercession.

Take heed of the day when no man will be useful to a man in the least, when no intercession matter nor ransom avail, nor help reach them (2:48).

God: there is no god but He, the living, eternal, self-subsisting, ever sustaining. Neither does somnolence affect Him nor sleep. To Him belongs all that is in the heavens and the earth; and who can intercede with Him except by His leave? (2:255).

Warn those who fear, through this, that they will be gathered before their Lord, and they will have none to protect or intercede for them apart from Him (6:51).

Leave those alone who have made a sport and frolic of their faith, and have been seduced by the life of this world. Remind them hereby lest a man is doomed for what he has done. He will have none to help him, or intercede for him, other than God; and even if he offer all the ransoms they will not be accepted from him (6:70).

"You have come before us all alone," (God will say), "as when you were created first, leaving behind all that We had bestowed on you. We do not see your intercessors with you who, you imagined, had partnership with you. Shattered lie your ties with them now, and gone are the claims you made" (6:94).

The day that (Reality) is unravelled, the people who had lost sight of it will say: "The apostles of our Lord had indeed brought us the truth. Do we have any one to intercede for us? If only we could go back to the world, we would act otherwise." Indeed they have caused themselves harm, and the lies they concocted did not help (7:53).

Your Lord is God who created the heavens and the earth in six spans, then assumed His power, dispensing all affairs. None can intercede with Him except by His leave (10:3).

Say: "God's is the intercession entirely; His is the kingdom of the heavens and the earth; then to Him you will return" (39:44).

Those they invoke apart from Him have no power of intercession, except those who testify to the truth and have knowledge (43:86).

Many as the angels be in heaven their intercession will not avail in the least without God's permission for whomsoever He please and approve (53:26).

So, the intercession of intercessors will not avail them (74:48).

∽

Response: A Poem in Memory of Merlin Grove
Mohamud S. Tagane

In his essay on intercession and atonement, Timothy Bergdahl explores the yearning among Muslims for an effective intercessor. He confesses his conviction that Christ is both our atoning sacrifice for sin and our intercessor. He pleads with Christians to reveal this reality in orthopraxis. I have written this poem in grateful memory of a North American Mennonite missionary in Somalia who practiced the life-giving orthopraxis of the way of the cross and who rejoiced in the salvation offered in Christ his intercessor and atoning sacrifice.

We Somalis have failed
to listen,
to learn
the lesson the Mennonites have been trying to teach us
for the last fifty years:
to love God and to love each other.
That is why today the Somali nation is homeless;
that is why we Somalis have made our home
Somalia
into a hell to flee from
Not only have we Somalis failed
to listen,
to learn that lesson,
we Somalis have also killed
on July 16, 1962
one of the Mennonite teachers
who came to teach us Somalis that lesson:
Merlin Russell Grove.
Right now,
in my friend's eye,
in the village of Mahaddei Uen

I can see Merlin
I can even hear Merlin
singing
as it was his wont
the best definition of Islam there is:
"Perfect submission, perfect delight,
Visions of rapture now burst on my sight;
Angels descending bring from above
Echoes of mercy, whispers of love.
Perfect submission, all is at rest,
I in my Savior am happy and blest;
Watching and waiting, looking above,
Filled with His goodness, lost in His love.
This is my story.
This is my song,
Praising my Savior all the day long."
This is the message of the World of Love
This is the message of the Prince of Peace
This is the message of Jesus
That Merlin and his fellow Mennonites
have been trying to
teach us Somalis
for the last fifty years.[2]

CHAPTER THIRTY-TWO

Dialogue and Witness

Topic One
Precious Friendships in the Middle East

Jewel Showalter

From 1982-89 my husband Richard, our three school-age children, and I served in the Middle East with a Rosedale Mennonite Mission (RMM) team, commissioned to share the gospel in culturally sensitive ways that, by God's grace and in the power and leading of his Holy Spirit, would result in the formation of reproducing fellowships of believers among persons, most of whom had never even met a Christian, and most certainly had never heard the gospel.

The constitution of the country where we served guaranteed freedom of religion even though the country is almost 100 percent Muslim. This freedom of religion did not include, however, freedom to proselytize or to serve as missionaries in the traditional sense. Open Christian witness, although technically not illegal, was unacceptable, and sometimes an invitation for deportation.

We obtained residence through my husband's English teaching jobs in three different universities, and quietly engaged in "friendship evangelism" among numerous neighbors and friends.

In the very first worship service we held in our home we focused on Acts 10 and the story of Cornelius. "Connect us with devout, God-fearing people who are truly seeking you in the only way they know," we prayed. And indeed we were inspired by the faith and zeal of many of our Muslim friends.

Informal dialogue and discussion was a common, almost everyday experience as we encountered people who had never met Americans or Christians before. Assuming that all Americans are Christians, just as all nationals are Muslims, common sidewalk, grocery store, or neighborly conversations often went something like this.

"So you're a Christian. Is it true that Christians do not accept the Honorable Muhammad as a prophet? We accept the Honorable Jesus as a prophet. Why don't you accept the Honorable Muhammad?"

Or, during Ramadan, "Christians don't fast, do they? What are the responsibilities of your religion?"

Witness and dialogue on that level came easily. Our Muslim friends were glad to instruct us in the practices of Islam, and we were eager students of language, culture, and religion in this setting where we were a decided minority. In curiosity and exchange they asked frequent questions about our beliefs and practices. In these exchanges, we encountered common misconceptions about Christianity, and had opportunities to explain what we really believe: No, Christians do not believe in three Gods—God, Jesus, and Mary. No, the Bible does not speak of the coming of Muhammad. In John 14 Jesus is talking about the coming of the Holy Spirit, not about the coming of Muhammad. No, we do not believe the original Christian scriptures have been corrupted. Yes, Christians do believe in fasting, and so on. We never got into more formal, scholarly dialogue settings.

In our home city of half a million people, our children were required to take Muslim religious education classes in the local public school they attended. When we asked for an exemption from religion classes the teacher insisted that the classes were not religion, but values and morals that all religions hold in common.

We permitted our children to attend, but carefully monitored the situation. One day our daughter came home saying she'd been assigned to write a paper on why Muhammad is a superior prophet to Jesus. We wondered if she had specifically been assigned the topic, but learned it had been assigned randomly. So we suggested that she ask the teacher if she could write on something else, explaining that she did not really believe that topic. The religion teacher was most apologetic and obliging, suggesting instead that she write her paper explaining to the class what Christians believe. So even our children were involved in dialogue!

The environments in the university settings where Richard taught and the elementary and high schools where our children attended were quite secular. For example, no female teachers or public servants were permitted to wear scarves while on the job. Secularity was the national religion. Politicians were far more worried about the influence of Islamic fundamentalism than of Christianity.

People frequently commented about how good and devout our family was. I often wore a scarf when I went out and for times of public worship. We did not drink or smoke. We were seen as upright, moral people who were very friendly and hospitable. In fact, we were frequently asked if we had become Muslims. We certainly did not fit the stereotype they had of "Christians" from popular American TV shows like "Bay Watch" and "Dallas."

So what was the impact of this informal witness and dialogue?

Four of the first seekers who came to us as Nicodemus did, came in response to a newspaper ad for a Bible correspondence course. Several of the more liberal, secular newspapers in the country ran the ads.

After seekers from our region completed the course, the course directors put them in touch with us. We then followed up with visits and Bible studies which led to Christian commitments, baptism, and incorporation into a small house fellowship.

There were also two miraculous healings which took place. One healing of a child impacted a whole extended family of about thirty people. Another healing changed the course of a young radical who had infiltrated our fellowship for the purpose of exposing us to the police. This Saul became Paul and instead of persecuting Christians was himself arrested and interrogated by the police for his Christian commitment. (He is currently studying for a doctorate in missiology in Korea.)

One of the believers had a vision of a ball of light (*noor*) resting on the Bible after he placed the Bible and the Qur'an beside each other and asked God to reveal which was really his word.

Another believer discovered a Bible hidden high on a shelf in his work place. He began reading in Matthew, and when he got to the Sermon on the Mount was so gripped with the radical nature of the message he sensed immediately it had to be the word of God. No one else would say anything as preposterous as "love your enemies"!

One day when I heard a young believer sharing his testimony with another seeker, I was impressed with his use of scripture. He said Jesus asked his disciples, "Who do people say that I am?" to which Peter replied, "You are the Christ, the Son of the Living God." Then Jesus replied, "Flesh and blood did not reveal this unto you, but my Father which is in heaven."

The young man testified, "I was attracted to Jesus, but knew I could never cross the huge chasm that exists between Muslims and Christians. No human being [flesh and blood] could ever have convinced me to cross that divide, but God did."

This same brother shared a vision he had while in prison for his faith. He said, "I saw a large multitude of my countrymen streaming toward someone who was preaching." Then he turned to my husband and said, "I looked more closely, and I saw that the preacher was not you. The preacher was not me. The preacher was Jesus." It is impossible to measure the importance of divine revelation in the midst of all our human dialogue, witness, and discussion.

The number of national "Followers of Jesus" in the country of our service has grown to around 2,000 in the last twenty years since Christian "tentmakers" like ourselves have worked at business development and English teaching. But there are still many large cities that do not have residential Christian witness or fellowships of believers. A generation of young national Christian leaders from Muslim background is emerging. They are seeking legal recognition and the right to change their identity cards from Muslim to Christian, the right to have legalized houses of worship. The evangelical church is still very weak and vulnerable, a fragile crocus pushing up through the frozen earth—but a harbinger of spring—God's spring.

Topic Two
Peaceable Dialogue with Muslims

Gordon D. Nickel

What sort of dialogue is most appropriate for Anabaptist engagement with Muslims? "Dialogue" in ordinary speech simply means conversation or discussion. This certainly is something which Anabaptists should welcome with any group inside or outside of their circle. But in the area of contemporary interfaith relationships, the word "dialogue" has come to be associated with certain specific philosophical commitments. Some of these commitments would be unfamiliar—and indeed would be found unfaithful—to the majority of Anabaptists in the world.

So what sort of dialogue would be authentic to Anabaptist faith and life? The following notes are suggestions toward an answer. Dialogue for Anabaptists must emerge from the teachings and example of Jesus, the New Testament pattern of witness, the Anabaptist mission heritage, the global missionary wisdom of contemporary Mennonites and Brethren in Christ, and the experiences of actual faith conversation with Muslims.

Dialogue must take into account the earliest Christian uses of the term in its Greek form in the ministry of Paul as recorded in the book of Acts (17:2, 17; 24:25).[1] Paul's concept of dialogue is clearly dissonant with some common modern definitions of dialogue. We may also look for help from the records of the first conversations which Christians (often from the Nestorian and Monophysite streams) held with their Muslim conquerors.

Friendly Faith Conversation

Dialogue begins with friendly faith conversation with Muslims and the conviction that the gospel is God's power for salvation to everyone who believes it.

In spite of political trends in the world, Anabaptist Christians do not consider Muslims their enemies. And if Muslims should think of Christians as their enemies, the words of Jesus in Matthew 5:43-48 becomes the rule for Christians: love your enemies. Christians believe that friendly faith conversation with Muslims is desirable and possible.

When Christians and Muslims talk together, Christians are not looking to argue with their partners in dialogue, but rather to converse with them in an authentic way. Christians are not looking to disagree. They freely affirm what they can. They do not hesitate to acknowledge Muslim achievements, and to confess Christian failures. Christians in dialogue do not participate as representatives of countries or cultures, they do not participate to defend Christendom or even the Christian religion. They participate as representatives of Jesus Christ, and this gives them a great freedom to treat the dialogue partner with love and compassion in the Spirit of their Lord.

Faithful to Jesus

Christians carry out their dialogue and witness under a prior commitment to Jesus. They are entrusted by God with a message "of first importance" (1 Cor 15:3), and they are accountable to pass it on to others. The gospel—that is, the good news message of God's love through the birth, life, teachings, death, and resurrection of Jesus—is not theirs to include or not include in the dialogue as they see fit. The gospel is not their opinion, or philosophy, or spirituality. It is the good news of God's love through a historical event.

The lordship of Jesus has implications for all of life, including Christian dialogue and witness. When Christians involved in dialogue with Muslims seek to leave out the name of Jesus and the claims he made for himself, they raise the question of disloyalty. Jesus himself spoke of the possibility of people being ashamed of him and his words. By God's grace many of the first Anabaptists left an example of remaining faithful to Jesus.

Realistic to Actual Conversations

Christians approach the conversation with Muslims with an informed estimate of Islam, rather than with what Calvin Shenk has called a "library version."[2] Here Anabaptist evangelists in countries of Asia and Africa where there is a living Muslim tradition can be of great help. These evangelists know that there are very few Muslims in the world who approach dialogue with people of other faiths with the assumptions of relativism or philosophical pluralism.[3] Those assumptions are largely a product of western culture.

Though the Christian participant may make no effort to argue, and may be careful not to say anything to provoke or offend, a frequent experience is that the Muslim partner will make some pointed denials of central gospel truths, and may challenge the Christian to account for Christian beliefs which Muslims find repugnant. Denial of crucial New Testament teachings is not an accidental part of conversation with Muslims, but rather is embedded in the source books of Islam themselves.[4] Frequent targets of Muslim polemic are the integrity of the Bible, the divinity of Jesus, and the historical truth of his crucifixion.

At this point, the Christian must decide how to respond peaceably. She must resist the temptation to fight back (the literal meaning of "debate"). At the same time, she must take seriously her responsibility to represent Christ faithfully. Some Anabaptists in dialogue with Muslims have found room in friendly faith conversation for making a strong case for the truth of the gospel.[5] Eastern Christians who participated in early dialogues with their Muslim rulers tended to speak forthrightly. In one of the first recorded dialogues between a Christian and a Muslim, the Christian Arab al-Kindi described his debate with a Muslim opponent in front of the Caliph Ma'mun as "our friendly strife."[6]

Listening to the Dialogue Partner

The first step in meaningful dialogue is to listen carefully to the Muslim partner. In order to better understand the beliefs that the Muslim is expressing, the Christian must become familiar with the source books of Islam, including the Qur'an, the Hadith, and the Sira. The Christian may want to consider learning the language of the Muslim so that she can hear the expressions of the Muslim's heart. In addition to solid academic knowledge of Islam, the Christian needs to listen to and observe its living expression. All of these things the Christian does to show respect for the partner, and they are well within the realm of possibility.

Listening in dialogue does not mean hearing what we want to hear. Christians tend to err in two main directions: they may hear the justification of a negative prejudice on the one hand, and they may hear echoes of their own idealized view of Islam on the other. Both of these are unhelpful. Rather, Christians listen carefully to earnest, authentic expressions of Muslim faith and appreciate what they mean in the light of the gospel.

Bearing Witness to Jesus

After listening carefully, Christians take the freedom to put words to the gospel. They bear witness to Jesus. Without this essential element, Christian encounter with Muslims becomes somehow strange and artificial. The New Testament pattern of witness and the Anabaptist mission heritage both recommend an open verbal witness. And Muslims themselves have raised witness—or confession of faith (*shahada*)—to the level of one of the five main pillars of Muslim practice. This is an invitation to Christians to share the gospel freely.

Jesus's word that his disciples will be witnesses to him when the Holy Spirit comes upon them (Acts 1:8) has, as Lesslie Newbigin notes, more to do with overflowing joy than with obligation.[7] It is indeed a privilege to bear witness to Jesus. And that witness is sorely needed. Study of the sourcebooks of Islam, and fellowship with Muslims in parts of the world where Islam is a living tradition, reveals that the gospel and Islam are different in many of their most basic affirmations.[8] The blessings of salvation through belief in the redemptive death and resurrection of Jesus, as described in the New Testament, are not on offer in Islam.

Trusting the Holy Spirit

Christians wish for all Muslims to know the joy of discipleship to Jesus. They work toward that end in the knowledge that no human can convert another human to discipleship to Jesus. First of all, they know that discipleship must be a free choice on the part of the seeker. Second, conversion is a work that only God can do. Christian evangelism is perverted when coercion, manipulation, deception, or inducement are used.[9] The pattern of Jesus and his first disciples was rather proclamation, invitation, and gentle persuasion. God then can be trusted to bring about a new birth by the power of the Holy Spirit. And the command of Jesus to the church is to be prepared to make disciples for Jesus of all those who believe and are converted. It is true that in the midst of dialogue Christians hope and pray for the conversion of their Muslim partner. But they relax in the knowledge of their own human limitations and of the limitless power of God.[10]

Personal Experiences

It is a great privilege to be in contact with Muslims who take their faith seriously and believe it to be the truth from God. Dialogue with such people sharpens the mind and strengthens faith. My personal experiences in dialogue have been mainly in South Asia among Urdu-speaking Sunni Muslims. Some of this dialogue has taken place in the context of the ministries of the India Mennonite Brethren Church, when local evangelists and I have visited Muslims in their homes in villages of south-central India where there is a church presence. Other conversations have been initiated by Muslim friends, who invite me to accept Islam.

During the past three years in India I greatly enjoyed taking part in a hastily-set-up dialogue in an Arabic school in Gadwal—an important Mennonite Brethren centre. One morning I asked the director of the school if I could talk with him, and he responded by organizing a formal meeting in the afternoon. The young students at the school were gathered in a circle, the teachers were looking in at the windows, and the director began the meeting by saying in Urdu, "There is one truth here. It is yours or it is ours. Now let's talk."

Another life-stretching experience was being challenged by a young Muslim preacher named Imran to partner with him in a public "open dialogue" in the city of Hyderabad. The theme we agreed on was "The Word of God." I prepared carefully and prayerfully to explain what the Bible and the Qur'an say about the word of God. Young Imran, however, could not resist speaking in a combative style. His presentation consisted of attacks on the integrity of the Bible, on the divinity of Jesus, and on American culture!

I was determined to respond peaceably to his fighting words. But when questions to me from the audience consisted mainly of standard stumpers, I began to wonder whether I would get a chance to say something meaningful about the gospel. The chance came unexpectedly at the very end of the dialogue, when a questioner asked me, "Why does God need a sacrifice for sin?" Our intercultural Mennonite Brethren witness team had worked at exactly this question in the course of our training. I was only too glad to share with the audience the many benefits of Jesus's death on the cross.[11]

Topic Three
The Internet and Dialogue Boxes

Ali El-shariff Abdallah Emmanuel

In this essay, I will focus the light on certain issues of dialogue and witness to Muslims. First I will give a brief set of meanings and boundaries for the word dialogue, and then I will try to see what the intentions are of both Muslims and Christians when they come together in a dialogue setting. Furthermore, I will attempt to give some highlights of my experience of dialogue and witness to Muslims and what we can learn from it. Finally I will look at the influence of the Internet and how it shifts the dialogue with Muslims and how it affects the Christian strategies to witness. I will conclude with some lessons we might learn through exploring issues related to dialogue and witness among Muslims.

Meanings and Boundaries

Dialogue is both an old and new word. In ancient thinking it refers to a method of question and answer to arrive at a better understanding of truth. However, in theological discussion, dialogue is quite a new word. Some understand the concept more literally as "conversation" and suggest that it is only an initial step in the development of positive relations between the religious traditions of the world.[12] I believe the concept of dialogue covers more ground in theological dimensions in an interfaith relation that supports a theology of mission as well. Therefore, I enter into Christian-Muslim dialogue as a means to witness.

However, dialogue is a word that is used in common speech with a variety of meanings. Dialogue can mean simply "chatting." It can refer to a very formal process of conversation at an official level between representatives of different groups. It also can refer to purely linguistic exchange between the dialogue partners. It can also mean an encounter that goes far beyond the merely verbal level. The dialogue with the Islamic faith and Muslims has always taken all these various meanings. However, my commitment to dialogue is consistent with my understanding of mission and witness. This leads me to ask this question: Why should I conduct a dialogue with a Muslim or a group of Muslims?

Dialogue for Witness

I initiate dialogue with Muslims, not because I feel that I have to defend Christianity against the attack of Muslim scholars, but because the Bible tells me to. The apostle Paul writes, "To the weak I became weak, to win the weak. I have become all things to all men so that by all possible means I might save some. I do all this for the sake of the gospel, that I may share in its blessings" (1 Cor 9:22-23). Therefore, I believe dialogue is one of the possible means to help the Muslims understand who Jesus Christ is, that they might be saved through him.

In addition, the biblical passages in Matthew 11:27, Acts 4:12, John 14:6, Philippians 2:10-11, Ephesians 1:21, and Matthew 28:19-20 are clear invitations to an exclusive understanding that there is no other road to salvation than through Jesus Christ. I can proclaim this, however, at the same time that I accept the dialogue with Muslims in order to understand them better so that I would be able to witness to them effectively.

Furthermore, I believe that in each religion there are fingerprints of God. For example, in the Qur'an, Jesus Christ is described as the Word of God and as the Spirit of God (Suras 3:45, 4:171, 66:12). When I was a Muslim, through this fingerprint of God in the Qur'an I came to know Jesus Christ. However, that does not mean that I believe that the Qur'an is the word of God. Yet in dialogue I use these fingerprints of God in the Qur'an to help Muslims understand the truth about Jesus Christ.

There have been many regular meetings and gatherings between Muslims and Christians held in various places in the world. The result has been declarations, recommendations, and clarifications, as well as many books. But as a disciple of Jesus Christ my hope and prayer is that the result of such dialogue should be that many Muslims would encounter Jesus Christ because they discovered the truth, the truth that has been unveiled to them in the dialogue.

Dialogue Intentions Between Muslims and Christians

Muslims are sometimes cautious about dialogue, feeling that the Christian approach is a veiled means of evangelism. They are concerned because they believe that Islam is the true and final religion and they do not feel a need to hear what Christians believe. However, some Muslims welcome dialogue hoping for conciliation between Christians and Muslims. A Muslim scholar writes,

> So if the intentions of both sides are good, and dialogue is free from tendencies to sow doubt or evangelize, if it is reserved for those who are qualified for it, and the participants concentrate on exchange of information and cooperation over what can be agreed together, such as acts of charity, kindness, and those which relate to the general benefit of humankind . . . then we may hope that it will lead to the spread of friendship and a spirit of conciliation between followers of the two religions.[13]

Some other Muslim theologians support dialogue hoping that both sides will agree on certain principles that would help us together to fight those who do not know God at all (atheists). Others view dialogue as a quest for understanding or cooperation. While it is true that one dimension of dialogue is cultivating understanding and respect, it is also true that both Muslims and Christians believe they have a witness to give. I believe it is helpful and honest for both the Muslim and Christian participants in dialogue to be open and truthful about this reality. So, as a Christian I am open with my Muslim dialogue participants that a conciliation that requires us to ignore the different truth centers of Christianity and Islam is not the intention of my commitment to dialogue.

If my intention in dialogue is different than that of the Muslims, how can we arrange to make an agreement with Muslims to start a dialogue? Should I have my own conditions and intentions? Should I disclose my intentions of evangelization, as I know that Muslims would not like it? Of course, many Muslims also enter dialogue with an intention to evangelize, for giving witness to Islam and inviting people to believe in Islam is a universal commitment of the Muslim community.

Thus we see that different intention is one of the challenges we encounter in the dialogue between Muslims and Christians.

Dialogue to Understand

The legacy of a sometimes bitter history between Muslims and Christians does not serve the cause of truth and understanding between Muslims and Christians. Rather they do serve the cause of political and religious forces that would maintain the long legacy of bitter relations between the two. The past must be overcome.

My yearning is that Muslims might acknowledge Jesus Christ as Lord and Savior. I enter into dialogue as a means to bear witness to Jesus Christ. It helps me to understand the Muslim as a human being. What are his worries? What are his questions? How does he understand the gift of salvation that God has prepared for him? Also, dialogue allows me to determine his deepness in Islam and how aggressive or soft he is in dealing with people who believe in Jesus Christ.

The dialogue helps the Muslim to define himself to me and helps me to define myself and my beliefs in Jesus Christ. It will help each side to move beyond the stereotypes and misconceptions of the past and the present circumstances. It is very crucial to listen to the Muslims and understand them in their own terms. Even though I come from a Muslim background I try to empty my mind of all I know about Islam and prepare myself to learn from the Muslim dialoguing with me and try to understand him as a person.

In my one-to-one encounter and dialogue with Muslims, I first have to listen to his testimony as to what Islam means to him. This will help me to understand his reasons for believing in Islam and his journey as he seeks to know the way of God. Telling and listening to our different testimonies would allow us to discover our shared concepts about God, and this will constitute a ground on which we can stand together and understand each other.

Dialogue to Witness (Kinshasa case study)

In 1995 I came to accept Jesus Christ in Kinshasa, Congo (formerly Zaire). A year later I was baptized and I received the call from God to go back to my people, the Muslims, and proclaim the gospel. I started a radio program in the Market of Kinshasa (60 percent Muslim). After a year and a half we wanted to check and see how the three times weekly broadcasting had influenced the Muslims. We did what we called "Operation Table to Table." We trained fifty-one Christians and divided them into a group of four to five in which each person had his own major role. Within three days we shared the gospel throughout the whole market. Twenty-eight persons came to faith in Christ.

Our approach in this outreach was to focus on a major question within a five-minute dialogue: Are you sure that God has forgiven your sins? This question came to the attention of the Muslim religious leaders. They found us and they asked to debate us, but we asked for a dialogue rather than a debate.

We started some dialogue groups on Fridays in the houses of the leaders. We chose only one subject and we started the dialogue. We had about five small dialogue meetings. Then the Muslims asked for a bigger meeting. That was to be held in the hall of the Zoo in Kinshasa. We strategized for this meeting very well. First, we backed this meeting in long prayer and fasting sessions. Second, we trained the Christian people who would participate. We gave them very clear instructions about the appropriate questions, where they should sit, and how they could initiate friendship, and what kind of clothing they should wear. Third, only those Christians who took the training were allowed to enter the hall. Fourth, we agreed that the subject was to be: Who is Jesus Christ?

We agreed on a neutral person to lead the meeting. The meeting began with five Muslims and three Christians on the stage. Each group representative could speak for forty-five minutes. Then we had fifteen minutes to ask each other questions and respond. Then the dialogue opened to the public participants. There were about 560 people. Only sixty were Christians, all the rest were Muslims. The dialogue lasted for five hours.

This was a sophisticated intelligent, organized, and spiritual strategy. Very early on in the dialogue one of the Muslim leaders on the stage was persuaded to commit his life to Christ. Three other leaders came to Christ later. We made about 300 new friendships to be followed up with after the dialogue. And we had an opportunity to witness to about 500 hundred Muslims at the same time. Even today that dialogue has its effect on the Muslim people in Kinshasa.

Dialogue with Muslims Today

Today when we look at the opportunities that we have for dialogue, we find many types and settings in which the dialogue can take place. I would mention some forms of dialogue without making any restrictions to other forms:

1. Dialogue in written essays and books. (The book, *A Muslim and a Christian in Dialogue,* written by Badru D. Kateregga and David W. Shenk is an excellent example of Christian-Muslim dialogue.)[14]

2. Dialogue in a public meeting. (The gathering in the Zoo Hall in Kinshasa, Congo is an example.)

3. Dialogue in meetings aired on TV.

4. Dialogue one-on-one through writing letters, telephone, and even emailing.

5. Dialogue in family gatherings or through arranged meetings for certain occasions.

6. Dialogue through an Internet conference.

7. Informal dialogue, friend with friend.

Today the Internet touches our private life, coming even into our bedrooms. I have found the Internet an amazingly open door for Christian witness and dialogue with Muslims. Today through the Internet we can make these kinds of dialogues with Muslims and Muslim leaders without moving from our place. Therefore, the question to us would be: How can we benefit from the technology to improve and enlarge dialogue? Now it is time to bring something new. There are many benefits of conducting dialogue through the Internet:

1. Security: anyone can enter into these chat rooms using only his nickname. There is no need to identify someone in the room, because it is not about people personally, but it is about principles and positions.

2. Reach the heart: We can chat openly about questions that a Muslim might hesitate to talk about in a public forum. For example, questions could be asked about Muhammad or the Qur'an and its validity. We can bring into the dialogue any question and communicate with candor.

3. Access: The Internet has an extensive database with excellent Muslim Web sites, as for example, Alazahr University's Web site.

4. Global audience: Through the Internet we can touch a large number of people from anywhere in the world. A multilanguage team can use the language that suits the person. Therefore, we can reach interested people right in the privacy of their homes.

5. Provide testimonies: Witness can be expressed through testimonies and the real stories of the people. This year I told my testimony more than 137 times in the Internet.

Types of Virtual Internet Dialogue

In order to meet the theological challenges of the Muslims, we have to conduct what I call here the virtual dialogue. This dialogue would meet the Muslims according to their types and interests. We open various rooms to serve this purpose. In the following subtitles I will try to explain and illustrate this.

Islamic Only Room. In these rooms we present some searching questions that are almost impossible to discuss in face-to-face dialogue. I will not elaborate here on some of the questions and issues that we raise for our Muslim friends to consider.

Private Rooms. For those who wish to discuss the issues and questions, or desire more information, we invite them into one of our many private chat rooms. The Islamic only rooms are always backed up by private rooms, which are equipped with friendly and spiritual people who give opportunity and the space for Muslims to speak, ask questions, and express themselves. Many Muslims have these questions but they cannot find any opportunity elsewhere to ask them or to seek answers. When these questions are answered we see that many are open to abandon Islam and consider the gospel.

Rooms for Theological Challenges. These rooms offer dialogue opportunities with Muslims to deal with the theological question, the similarities, and the differences between Islam and Christianity. Here the questions are mainly about the doctrinal differences between Islam and Christianity. These differences are:
• The incarnation and God as Trinity.
• Death and resurrection of Jesus.
• Atonement and forgiveness of sin through the sacrificial death of Jesus Christ.
• The Prophet of Islam.
• The validity of the Bible.

This room is also backed up with many other private rooms to meet the needs and interest of those who express their desire to continue the dialogue.

Sometimes we encounter unanticipated developments. For example, January 2003, some Muslims scholars invited Christians in a dialogue through the Internet about the person of Jesus Christ. This included scholars from a number of the respected Islamic institutions. It was a remarkable event with a surprisingly positive response on the part of at least one of these scholars.

Christian Rooms for Witness. In these rooms, Islamic issues are not allowed. The dialogue is only about the Bible and Jesus Christ. The intention is to complement the other rooms by providing personal testimonies and witness. We coordinate together very well between these rooms. Those who have entered the private rooms and who show an interest in the gospel, are invited into the Christian rooms to hear testimonies and ask further questions.

Results

As a result of these coordinated activities of virtual dialogue and witness through these rooms, there are hundreds of Muslim people coming to accept Jesus Christ as Lord and Savior every month. The Internet has opened doors for Muslims and gives them freedom to listen and ask questions about their own faith.

Conclusion

What have we learned of this experience? First, we have to continue praying and fasting to God that he may open our eyes to see where he is working and join him. Second, we have to obey the call of God and follow his step wherever he leads us and journey with him to be witnesses in this earth. Third, dialoguing and witnessing among Muslims is not and could not be an affair of one church or one denomination. All the Christians of the different confessions of faith should agree together and partner together in order to bring the good news to Muslims. Fourth, we see through this experience that dialogue is not an end for itself, but it is an expression of faithful witness.

∽

Response: Context Informs Our Approach

Lydia Harder

Powerful experiences were shared about instances of dialogue and witness in three different contexts: (1) India and Pakistan, in which there are already existing churches, (2) Turkey, where Christians are almost unknown and ministry begins by being a Christian presence among people, and (3) ministry via the Internet throughout the Muslim world. Clearly context makes a difference in the shape that witness takes. Some saw dialogue as a means to witness while others acknowledged that both dialogue and witness are instruments of the Holy Spirit's work. The nature of dialogue includes a more mutual interaction, while witness understands that it is a secondary role to the actual event that it is witnessing about. There was some disagreement about the nature of dialogue and how it related to debate and prosyletizing.

The keen interest in this particular workshop testified to the fact that we need more discussion and work on how these two "strategies" of dialogue and witness relate to the work of God in the world and our relationship to Muslims in the various contexts.

CHAPTER THIRTY-THREE

Suffering

Topic One
God Makes a Way for Me

Yakuta Abdo

I was born into a Muslim home in Deder, Ethiopia. My father had six wives, three of them at one time. My siblings and I are the children of six mothers. My father brought most of his children to my mother so they could go to the Deder School near where my mother lived. My mother kept everyone together and raised us. She often told us that she did not know what the next day would bring—that another mother might come and raise us. So she wanted to be the best mother possible.

My mother has strong beliefs. She faithfully prayed and told us the stories of Abraham and Joseph according to the qur'anic version. She taught us the value of prayer. She knew that God would answer her prayer when something was not right. She would go into the garden and cry out to God—not like a Muslim, although she prayed those prayers as well.

Our father traveled about to the various farms he owned and spent only a few days with us about once a month. When we needed clothing or school supplies, we would ask him for money. He was often absent, as were most fathers.

My relationship with my mother was much closer. She taught us about the Muslim religion, how to pray, how to clean, and how to do handcrafts. She taught us to respect ourselves and others. Other Muslim children in our community, especially the girls, did not go to school, but my mother sent us. She was convinced that if we got an education we would have a better life. That gave us the opportunity to study with Orthodox Christian children. In fact, a few Christian children of my father's employees lived in our home. We had no friction between us. This greatly helped me to accept people of other faith traditions and enabled me to explore the Christian faith.

My mother constantly asked, "How can I get to heaven?" Her friends and relatives told her to do good and to obey God and the Qur'an, and that when she died God would weigh both her good and evil deeds and determine her destination on the basis of which was the greater. Yet she lived in the fear that her good deeds may not out-weigh the evil.

My own life was like a yo-yo as I swung back and forth with the same uncertainties my mother had. Then I got the opportunity to study to be a nurse's aide at the Mennonite-run hospital in Nazareth, Ethiopia. Here they taught the Bible along with our nurse's training. I studied the Bible, but I was sure the other students did not know the truth because they called the human Jesus "God" and I was certain that could not be true.

After a year, the Holy Spirit started working in my life and I started to compare the two religions. I was drawn to Christ because he offered salvation without my having to pay for it or work for it. However, I soon discovered that while believing was easy, living out my faith was difficult. I learned there was a cross for me as well, and that I had to pick up my cross to follow Jesus. At that time my cross was my family. I knew that when they found out I was a Christian, they would reject me. But I decided to show them love and try to be with them as much as possible.

After my training I went home. It was difficult to live with my family on a daily basis, but when I went to work at the Mennonite hospital in Deder I had opportunity to pray, to talk about Jesus, and read my Bible. God gave me an opportunity to be strong. When I went home I was very quiet. My mother wondered why I was different. She knew I had studied the Bible in nursing school and that I was now working at a Christian hospital. She had told me many times not to believe as the Christians do. She knew that I had become a Christian although I had not told her. She began to blame my father for not teaching his children the Muslim religion.

Finally, my father called me aside and told me that he had the right to kill me if I became a Christian, but he didn't ask me whether I had become one. I assured him that I understood this. To myself I said, "Even if I die, I know where I am going. This is my cross." I knew that if I'd start talking to my parents about Jesus my life would be short and I did not want to break off relationships with them.

One day my uncle came to the hospital and noticed that I was wearing a necklace. Without greeting me he pulled it off, only to discover that it held a map of Africa and not a cross as he had expected. I asked him what he intended to do if it was a cross. He replied, "I would cut off your neck."

I knew I was in danger and I knew I had to do something. I prayed that the Lord would either take me out of the Deder community or find a Christian husband for me. It didn't take him long to find one. When I reported to my mother that Kelifa had asked me to marry him, she felt her prayers had been answered. For her, Kelifa was from a Muslim family; for me, he was a Christian. I went back to Nazareth to plan for our wedding. We did not want to disappoint our families, nor did we want to disappoint the Lord. So we decided to call several church elders to perform the ceremony privately and not invite our families to a large wedding celebration. This would spare them the embarrassment of seeing us married in a Christian church.

As we pondered this, we had misgivings. "Are we glorifying God by hiding our faith? Jesus did not hide himself. He died for our salvation in the presence of everybody." So we went to tell our parents that we would be having our wedding in a church. My mother was devastated. My father covered his face and went to bed. I believed we needed to glorify God by having a public wedding, but I knew there would be a price to pay. At that time I thought this would mean losing my whole family. I prayed, "Jesus, be my Dad, be my Mom, be my brothers and sister."

On our wedding day my oldest brother arrived with a lot of money and promised to give it to us if we would only cancel the church ceremony. When we refused, he left saying he could not attend. I thought there would be no further contact with my family.

After several months my mother called us to her home at Deder and prepared a reception dinner for our extended family and neighbors. That helped me to reconnect with my relatives. My father was not present, but I did meet him briefly en route back to Addis Ababa where we then lived. One of my brothers completely avoided me.

After about two years, my father came to visit and stayed with us a while with one of his brothers. He said little, but he watched us. Eventually he tried to make peace between my brother and me. We have little in common, but now when we meet we at least greet each other.

Since those days during the 1970s, Islam became more militant in Ethiopia. But I was surprised to experience hostility in the States. Once in a store I spoke with a man who appeared to be Ethiopian. When he learned my name, he assumed I was Muslim. I explained that I had been, but was now a Christian and started to witness to him. He stopped me and said, "I won't report this, but please don't talk about your religion to anyone; they will kill you."

I don't feel at ease around my family. We don't have much in common. Our cultures and the way we act are different now. For example, I don't pray as they do, or keep the Muslim fast.

The Marxists took over in Ethiopia in 1974 and after about three years they started to persecute evangelical Christians. The Holy Spirit began to work in a mighty way in the churches; people were healed of their ailments. The Marxists began to harass Christians because many were flocking to the church and miracles were happening that they could not deny.

One evening my husband came running home to tell me that he was okay but that things were not. A government edict had gone out banning public meetings with a threat to imprison and confiscate the goods of anyone who had more than two people visiting his house. Kelifa warned me not to take the children to church.

I replied that we knew these things would come when we accepted Christ and that with his help we were ready, not only to lose our things, but to give our lives as well. The one in whom we believed was able to save us and if not, as in the case of the three Hebrew children, we would not deny him. Kelifa was surprised at the firmness of my faith. Soon after that Kelifa was put in prison.

The church tried to help us understand what the Marxists might do by making us aware of the persecutions which had happened to Christians in Russia. I knew the stories of torture to get people to deny their faith. So my one request to the Lord was that he would grant me the favor to see my children killed before the authorities killed me, rather than my children having to witness my death and they being spared to perhaps return to Islam.

The support of the church was overwhelming—much more than

I expected. From all over the world people started helping us, so that I had all I needed and was able to share with other people. My mother stayed with me six months and watched everything that happened—how people contributed to our needs and how they came to my home to pray for me and Kelifa. It was a great testimony for her to see the love Christians have for each other. My mother could hardly believe what she was observing.

But I had a problem at work. Every Friday we had to listen to Marxist indoctrination for two hours. I'd sit in a corner and silently pray. A Marxist front of a Chinese variety began opposing the government which retaliated by killing the rebels. Authorities would come to our meetings and call the names of suspected supporters of this front and take them off for execution. This was known as the red terror. The authorities reported to us that they would soon start the yellow terror—when the government would start to harass evangelical Christians. I assumed that one day they would come for me, tie my hands, blindfold me, and take me off for execution. I prayed that when given the opportunity to speak my last words, the Lord would give me strength and grace to tell the people that I knew where I was going when I died, that I would see Christ in heaven, the place where there is no sickness, no fear, the place where I could live forever and ever. I asked the Lord for the chance to invite others to join me. I wanted to preach this word and then die. Since I did not pass through that experience I can't say today how I would have responded.

The authorities never took me. As you know, it did not come to this. My husband was released from prison after four years and we began to live normally again except that he was constantly under surveillance by plainclothesmen. They tried to trap him into speaking something against the government, but God gave him wisdom.

Next the church asked Kelifa to be an administrator as before, this time working underground. This was difficult for me to accept. I asked the Lord if this really was what he wanted Kelifa to do. The Lord said to me, "Remember the time I rode into Jerusalem on a donkey? I did it to glorify God. And I want to take you with me to Jerusalem. Be my donkey. I want to glorify my name through you. Why don't you accept?"

I started shouting, "Lord if this is you speaking, let come what may. I want to be in your will."

Kelifa worked only a few months until he became ill with cancer. He came to the States for treatment and here he died. Before his death

God spoke to me at three different times as I was praying for Kelifa's healing. The Lord asked me a question, "Do you know you are my servant? A servant does not have the right to ask his owner 'Why did you do this?' or 'Why did you do that?'" The second question was, "Do you know you are my lover and that a lover gives everything he has? Do you know that Kelifa is not yours and the children are not yours?" The third time the Lord spoke to me was here in the States on Good Friday before Kelifa died on Monday, the day after Easter. I didn't know where to turn. It felt as though the weight of the whole world had fallen on my back.

I told the Lord that I did not know why Kelifa was dying, but that I was sure he knew what he was doing. The Lord reminded me of a promise I had made when Kelifa was in prison. I had told the Lord that I wanted his anointing, that I did not just want a sprinkling, but that I wanted to swim in his anointing. The woman praying with me at the time told me that this would be very costly. "Are you willing to pay the price?" she asked. I replied that I didn't want to pay the price if it meant physical torture for my faith. Yet I had no peace. For several months I struggled with this question. Finally I said, "Yes, Lord, I'm willing to pay the price. Death holds no fear. Anoint me for your mission."

After Kelifa died, this came to my mind. I remembered my promise, but I did not know that it would cost me Kelifa's life. I have not seen that anointing yet. I have not served him yet as I hope to. I don't know how he is going to fulfill his purpose in me. Perhaps it will be through my children who have a heart for mission and a concern for the lost. At this point I am not sure what God is planning for my life. I only know that he will carry out his purposes according to his will.

Topic Two
Muslim Background Believers and the Price They Sometimes Pay: Two Case Studies

Richard Showalter

Mehmet Ali

Mehmet Ali was born into a lower middle-class family in a small Middle Eastern provincial capital. When he was eight years old, a paternal uncle came home from work one day and reported his conversations with some Italian engineers who had come to town to install a new electric system.

In the course of their conversations, Mehmet's uncle reported, they had traded stories about their religions. He had told them about Islam; they had told him about Christianity. He went on to describe how the Italians had said that God had sent Jesus to be the Savior of the world, and that anyone who believed in him would be saved.

Young Mehmet Ali listened to his uncle's stories with rapt attention, and when the uncle told the part about Jesus, Mehmet felt something deep within him saying, "This is true. Jesus can save you." Mehmet was powerfully impressed, and from that time, he began to search for more information about Jesus. When he was in elementary school, he told his religion teacher that he would not memorize the Muslim prayers because he was not a Muslim.

"That's impossible," declared the teacher. "All our people are Muslims. If you are not a Muslim, what are you?"

"I don't know what I am," Mehmet replied, "but I am not a Muslim." He failed his religion class.

He learned that the Bible is the holy book of Christians, and he searched for a Bible in his hometown, but none was to be found. As a young adult he went to the national capital and looked for a Bible there. Had he looked in just the right shop, he might have found one there, but he didn't, and again he failed.

Serving his compulsory military service, he looked for a Christian in the army. But though he found one or two persons who said they were Christians, he soon understood that they knew little of the Jesus who could save him.

Still later, and married now, he traveled to Germany to visit a relative who worked there. Surely, he thought, I will meet many Christians in Europe. But he spoke only one language, and though he smiled and hung around religious-looking people, he found no one able to talk with him about Jesus.

One day he went into a large German cathedral. Suddenly, unexpectedly, the most wonderful peace he had ever experienced flooded his soul. He sensed it came from God. It was as though God was speaking to him and saying, "Mehmet, the answers you are looking for have something to do with the church and they have something to do with Jesus. Keep looking." But there was still no one to talk with. He enjoyed the peace for a long time, but then left. Soon afterward, he returned home.

Back in his home country he discovered the address of a Bible correspondence course printed in a national newspaper. Excitedly, he wrote for information and received two small tracts which explained the way of salvation. He felt that this was the answer he had been looking for. He wrote back, inquiring whether any Christians lived in his region.

Some time later, two foreign Christian families and a single woman moved to his city as Christian witnesses. Within a few months, Mehmet Ali made contact with them. It was now twenty-five years since he had first heard the Christian story from his uncle as an eight year old. Before six months had passed, he and his wife were baptized. Coming up from the water, Mehmet Ali described how ten years before he had had a dream about being baptized, and that in his dream it had happened very much like what he had just experienced.

He was exuberant in his new-found faith. He shared eagerly with others, and he tore out a wall between two rooms in his home to make space for a small Christian house fellowship. He began to make plans for building a Christian meetinghouse in his city. Other members of his extended family became Christians.

But the opposition was soon to come. Another man who attended the emerging fellowship asked him for financial assistance to buy a television. Mehmet shared the needed money quickly. "We are brothers," he said. But the other man sold the television, pocketed the money, and left him holding the bag. Mehmet was disillusioned.

But he pressed on.

Then came another blow. The foreign Christian who had been discipling him was taken by the police, interrogated, and tried in court. He lost his job. Mehmet was questioned by the police, and though not intimidated, he began to realize that there was a price to pay for following Jesus. Within a year, his foreign friend was deported with his family. Tears flowed freely, but there seemed to be nothing anyone could do.

But the worst was still to come. Three years after his baptism, Mehmet himself was taken by the police and interrogated with torture for six days. He himself had been a sergeant in the army, and there was little that could break him, but when they brought his beautiful wife in and insulted her and struck her before his eyes, he broke. She suffered a brain concussion, and he was placed in solitary confinement.

A month later he was released from prison, now physically a shadow of what he had once been. He had almost died from the torture.

But meeting with a Christian friend, he prayed, "Father, I just want you to know that though I suffered terribly, for your sake I am willing to go through it again. Please, though, don't make my wife face the torturers again."

As for his wife, she was adamant. When asked by a friend whether she now regretted her decision to follow Christ, she shot back, "How could you even dare think that? I wouldn't give up Jesus for any amount of suffering."

Her friend pressed in, "What then gave you courage in your suffering?"

She replied, "It was the words of Jesus when he said, 'Blessed are you when men revile you, and persecute you, and say all kinds of evil things about you. Rejoice, and be exceedingly glad, for great is your reward in heaven.' I remembered my reward in heaven."

After his imprisonment, Mehmet Ali was closely watched by the police. He lost his job as an electrician in the city and was reassigned to a distant rural post. He was branded as a traitor. His children were teased unmercifully.

A few years later, he bought a used car and placed it in his courtyard, rarely driving it. A friend, surprised at this new extravagance, asked him why he bought a car—knowing that he could scarcely afford such a luxury.

"I bought it for my wife and children," he said. "If I am taken by the police again, they can get in the car and drive away to another city where they will be safe."

Still later, more than a decade after his imprisonment, he sought

. refugee status in another country. "It's not for me," he explained. "There's no future for me here. But I want a life for my children."

Today, Mehmet Ali lives with one son as a refugee in a foreign land, working to bring his family to religious freedom. The current fellowship of Christians in his hometown continues to struggle for existence.

Questions for reflection:

1. What should new believers in Mehmet Ali's situation do? Tough it out in a community that rejects them? Find shelter in another community, even if it means moving to another country?

2. How should the international Christian community respond? Work through diplomatic channels to reduce persecution in Mehmet's home country? Assist him in leaving? Encourage him to "take up his cross and follow Jesus," staying where he was born?

Enver Hasan*

When he was a child, Enver Hasan lost his father, and he was reared by his mother. A bright young man, he passed his university exams against heavy competition from children who possessed many advantages he did not have and enrolled as an electrical engineering student. He was not a particularly devout Muslim, but a strong nationalist.

In university, though, his life was to take an unexpected turn. One of the teachers was a foreign Christian, and Enver decided to make a closer acquaintance in order to make it difficult for him to stay at his post. He didn't like the thought of having a Christian teacher in his university, and he hated Christianity as far as he understood it.

Visiting the home of the Christian teacher, Enver presented himself as a new Christian who had been converted through a Bible correspondence course. He said some Christian prayers, and convinced the teacher that he was for real.

Simultaneously, however, Enver began to be attracted by the love he experienced in the new Christian fellowship. He was warmly received, and though he was still not attracted to the Christian faith, he felt strangely drawn back to the fellowship again and again.

The next spring he was invited to be baptized with others, but he

*A pseudonym

found a way to avoid it. Increasingly he was drawn toward Jesus, but he found himself in a spiritual no-man's-land. "Am I a Muslim, or am I a Christian? Or am I neither?" Enver Hasan no longer knew.

That summer he attended a camp for Christians with other members of the fellowship. Here again several persons suggested that he be baptized. Enver went to his Christian teacher friend who was also at camp and asked, "Am I ready to be baptized?"

His friend responded, "I don't know whether you are ready. Why don't you ask God?"

Enver took the counsel to heart and went to his tent. Simply and fervently he prayed, "God, please tell me whether I'm ready to be baptized." And in that moment he heard a voice saying clearly, "You're not ready."

He went back to his friend and reported what had happened. "Was that really God?" he asked.

His friend answered with a question, "Who were you asking?"

"It was God," he said.

"Then," said his friend, "I believe it was God who answered."

Enver received that word from God and went back to the capital city where he was spending the summer vacation. There he took some medication for a passing illness he was experiencing, and suddenly, at home alone, discovered he could scarcely breathe. His throat was swelling. Terrified, he remembered the stories of Jesus the healer, and he cried out, "Jesus, heal me."

A moment later the swelling subsided, and Enver wondered, "Was that Jesus?" Soon he forgot.

But a couple weeks later it happened again. Only this time he was with friends when the swelling began. His friends were frightened and rushed him to the hospital. There, sometime later, he regained consciousness and found himself looking up into the eyes of a doctor.

"Young man," the doctor said, "has anything like this ever happened to you before?"

"Yes," he said. "Once."

"Well, what did you do?" the doctor inquired.

"Oh, nothing," he said. "It just went away."

"This doesn't just go away," the doctor said. "You have a severe allergy to that medication. If you had arrived here twenty minutes later, we couldn't have saved you."

As if to prove his point, this time it took a couple weeks for Enver to recover. And now he knew that Jesus had indeed healed him.

During his recuperation he immersed himself in the New Testament, and he met Jesus in a powerful, personal way. That fall, back at the university, he was baptized—now certain that he was ready.

Enver thrived in the young fellowship of believers. Mature beyond his years, he encouraged and counseled others, emerging as a leader. Knowing English, he began to read the writings of Watchman Nee, the Chinese Christian.

But the way ahead was not to be easy. When his Christian teacher was forced to leave the university, Enver encouraged him. When the teacher was deported, he suggested that Enver take responsibility for nurturing the little group of believers. Enver agreed.

Enver, however, was taken by the police and tortured. A sensitive soul, he suffered terribly and felt that he would die in prison.

But one day in solitary confinement, he cried out to God, "God, why do I have to suffer so much?"

The words in response were almost audible. "You have to suffer so that others of your people know that some of your people are Christians."

Enver was encouraged. Little did he know then that at that very time the news of his arrest and imprisonment was being carried in the pages of the major newspapers of his country. Though the stories were negative and even hostile, everywhere across the country people were learning that there were at least a few of their people who professed to be believers in Jesus.

Later he was sitting in his cell when he saw a vision. There was a man preaching, and hundreds of his people were pressing around him, listening. Many of them were becoming Christians.

When Enver told his Christian teacher about the vision, he smiled and said, "The preacher in that vision was not you." He added, "And it was not me."

Then with sober, intense, yet somehow joy-filled eyes, he said quietly, "The teacher was Jesus. I saw him."

Enver went on with Jesus. Marrying a foreign Christian who visited his country, he has lived for nearly a decade in his wife's home country, getting academic degrees in theology and missiology. He is currently pastoring a church of immigrants from his country to that nation, and his vision is to start a mission society among his people for taking the good news not only to his country, but to other parts of the world as well.

Question for reflection:

1. What is the place of suffering in the effective proclamation of the good news in highly resistant societies?

CHAPTER THIRTY-FOUR

Apologetics

Topic One
Experiences in Defending Christ

Abd el Rab
Adana Abd el Rab

Much attention has been given recently to the terrorist attacks by radical Muslim militants, but there are also Muslims that are peace-loving, friendly, and truth-seeking people. As some Muslims become disillusioned with their faith and/or become more interested in Christianity, it can—at the right times and using a friendship approach—be considered good discipleship to share Christ with them.

This essay focuses on answering Muslim challenges to the Christian faith. There are a plethora of questions and challenges from Muslim believers in Islam. We will present some of the core beliefs of Islam, as well as Muslim misconceptions about Christianity. We will then present experiential advice from our many years of experience in the field and from supporting materials.

Christian Perspectives of Muslims

What are some Christian viewpoints on Muslims and Islam?

Listen to what Del Kingsiter, a missionary to Muslims in the Middle East, writes:

> Many Christians are afraid of getting too close to Muslims; some even believe Muslims are all terrorists or, somehow, evil people. I would like to say that as a general rule, I have found Muslims are very God-conscious people. Conversely, in my dialogue with Muslims I find the same fear and suspicions. I have also found that these people are asking some very fundamental questions which need to be answered.[1]

What are some Muslim misconceptions about Christianity? What do you think is the most profound misconception about Christianity? (e.g., Muslims believe that the Bible mentions Muhammad).

Many Christians think that the Muslims' view of Christianity as a polytheistic system (i.e., belief in the Trinity means worshipping three gods) is the most pressing misconception. In practice, however, we have found that the greatest stumbling block is the Muslim belief of a corrupted Bible. If this is true, then establishing the authority and integrity of the Bible as holy scripture is the single most important step in overcoming challenges to the majority of Muslim misconceptions.

Responding to Muslim Challenges

There are many issues which Christians must address in their ongoing conversations with Muslims. Here are a few of the most important ones:

Issue #1: "Your Bible Has Been Corrupted."

A Muslim Viewpoint

Muslims believe that the Bible is not holy or divine since it never says it is "the holy word of God." They believe the Bible was composed by man. They also question why Christians have four "gospels" (Matthew, Mark, Luke, and John).[2] Another reason they refute the authority of the Bible is because of differing accounts of the same event.

Muslims reject the Bible as the only authoritative book on which to base all matters of doctrine, faith, and practice. They believe that the recorded sayings of the prophets such as Moses, David, and Jesus are holy books. However, they believe these are not exactly like our scriptures because the real sayings have been lost or corrupted over the centuries by Jews and Christians. Only the Qur'an and the words of Muhammad, they believe, have been preserved free from error.

A Christian Viewpoint

Christians believe that the Bible is an authoritative, divinely inspired book. The apostle Paul wrote, "All Scripture is God-breathed and is useful for teaching, rebuking, correcting, and training in righteousness" (2 Tim 3:16).

An interesting way to approach this issue with Muslims is to point out that Muhammad firmly believed in the authenticity of the Bible as it existed in his day. There are many verses in the Qur'an which demonstrate his confidence in the Holy Books that came before him. Here are two examples of references from the Qur'an that affirm the authority and reliability of the biblical scriptures.

"Say people of the book! Ye have no ground to stand upon unless you stand fast by the law, the gospel and all the revelation that has come to you from our Lord" (Sura 5:68).[3]

"Believe in God and His messenger [Muhammad], and the Scripture which He revealed to His messenger [the Qur'an] and the Scripture which He revealed aforetime [the Bible]" (Sura 10:91).

If the Bible was corrupted, did this take place before or after Muhammad? Archaeological discoveries have unearthed ancient Old Testament manuscripts dating back more than 2,000 years. These contain no major changes from the Bible we know today. It is unreasonable that Jews and Christians would both conspire to change the Old Testament to support the views of a common opponent, the Muslims.

Furthermore, by the time of Muhammad, the Old Testament had been in circulation in many regions and collaboration to corrupt the text uniformly would have been impossible. In terms of the New Testament, there are over 5,000 manuscripts of the New Testament dating from the second century AD to the fifteenth century that confirm the same substantial text of the whole New Testament before, during, and after the time of Muhammad.

When confronted by a Muslim on this issue, one should ask when, who, what, where, and how was the Bible corrupted or changed? Where is the proof of these changes? In general, it does not help to use the Bible to prove the Bible. So, you can turn to history, archaeology, verses in the Qur'an, and the effects of the Bible on people who read it. Muslims do not have answers to these questions. The

Qur'an, in fact, supports the authenticity of the Torah, the Gospels, and the "People of the Book," before, during, and after the time of Muhammad.

Issue #2: "What About the Predictions of Muhammad in the Bible?"

Muslim Viewpoint and Christian Responses

Muslims have insisted that some verses[4] in the Bible also point to the coming of Mohammed. Here are some examples of prophesies concerning the coming of Muhammad that Muslims often quote.

"The sceptre will not depart from Judah, nor the ruler's staff from between his feet, until he comes to whom it belongs and the obedience of the nations is his" (Gen 49:10).

Muslims assert that this passage refers to Muhammad, since Judah comes from a Hebrew verb signifying "to praise"—the same meaning for the Arabic name Muhammad. The context of Genesis, however, shows that the promised king was to be born among the descendants of Judah. However, Muhammad, we know, came not from Jewish ancestry. He descended rather from the Arabian tribe of the Quraish.[5]

"The Lord your God will raise up for you a prophet like me from among your brothers. You must listen to him. I will raise up for them a prophet like you from among their brothers; I will put my words in this mouth, and he will tell them everything I command him" (Deut 18:15-18).

Muslims assert that the prophet predicted in Deuteronomy is Muhammad. Since "from your midst" does not appear in either the ancient Greek Old Testament (the Septuagint) or the Samaritan Pentateuch, the original text, they say, must state that the prophet would come from the relatives of the Israelites, the descendants of Ishmael, the Arabs.

There are earlier ancient Hebrew manuscripts, however, supporting the customary reading. In addition, "brethren" naturally and commonly refers to one's closest relatives (e.g., the Israelite tribes). A qualifier would be needed to indicate less close relatives (e.g., the Ishmaelite tribes).

There is yet another scriptural passage which Muslims believe refers to Muhammad. This is the New Testament text in Matthew 17:10-13 where Jesus states, "To be sure, Elijah comes and will restore all things." Verse 13 here, however, explicitly says that "Elijah" has already come, over five centuries before Mohammed, and that he is John the Baptist! Thus, any possible reference to Muhammad here simply does not make sense.

Christian Viewpoint

It seems strange that Muslims would appeal to the Bible as an authority on Muhammad, implying that the Bible is divinely inspired and uncorrupted. This is in direct contradiction to their more fundamental charge that the Bible is humanly composed and corrupt in the content it contains. It is not possible to have this argument both ways.

While Christians do not hold to the authenticity and holy qualities of the Qur'an, we have still demonstrated above how, based on the Qur'an and Muhammad, the Bible is a holy text from God. These biblical texts seem to make it clear that the promised prophet would be sent to the children of Israel, not to the Arabs. Muhammad cannot, therefore, be the prophet who would perform miracles or know God intimately.

Issue #3: "Is Jesus the Son of God?"

Muslim Viewpoint

Let us examine what the Qur'an teaches about Jesus in Suras 3:59; 4:171; 5:17-18; and 9:30. (Quoting from the Qur'an does not indicate our agreement with the content of these statements. We are simply trying to understand what is said about Jesus from the Muslim perspective.)

The Qur'an states that Jesus is both a prophet and the Messiah. Jesus is a word from Allah, but not The Word. In the Qur'an, Adam is also a word from Allah. There is no one who can claim to be the son of God or child of God. This is blasphemy in Islam, since it reduces God to the level of humans.

Muslims believe Jesus will return again as the Messiah, but his role will be minor compared to that of Muhammad. Islam denies the deity of Christ, his crucifixion, his resurrection, his atoning sacrifice, and his unique relationship with God the Father. Muslims often discount the miracles Jesus performed and compare them with the miracles of other prophets. They look at the individual miracles, but overlook the larger issue of the person and life of Christ.

Christian Viewpoint

In terms of nonbiblical evidence, there are a couple of key points to be made regarding this question about Jesus.

First of all, the Jews in the first century of the Christian era possessed a unique memory tradition for preserving statements made by their religious teachers. Something akin to this today would be the Maori tribesmen of New Zealand, some of whom can recite the four-thousand-year-old history of the tribe, and they do so in a ritual that can last up to several days. Making use of memory techniques, Jewish believers remembered with high precision the statements of Jesus and recorded them in the early writings.

In addition, other writings about Jesus appear from non-Christian sources during the first centuries after Christ. Although these are admittedly somewhat few in number, their existence is of particular importance, since to the Romans and pagans of this early era, Jesus was little more than a marginal Jew leading a marginal movement.[6]

With regards to the larger question of "Jesus as the Son of God," one can of course answer briefly and simply saying that it is impossible to fully understand the divine relationship between God and Jesus. The Bible teaches it, and we as Christians believe it. To fully understand God is beyond our mental capacity. Colossians 2:2-3 states that Jesus Christ is God's "mystery," so we cannot pretend to fully comprehend him until God reveals him to us!

It may be better to concentrate on the differences between Islam and Christianity concerning Christ. The Qur'an says Jesus did not die on the cross for our sins, but the Bible insists repeatedly not only that he did die, but that he rose again from the dead. Finding a way to look with Muslim friends at what the Bible actually says about Christ's death and its meaning is an important first step in conversations with them. Verses found in John 1:1-14 are particularly good ones for explaining the significance of Jesus as God's "Word," a key expression used for Jesus in the Qu'ran.

In terms of the title, "Son of God," it is important to explain that this is not a literal term limited to the physical reality as we know it. The Bible does not teach that God and Mary were physically intimate and produced a son. Even to Christians this would be blasphemy. God is Spirit, so the term Son of God is used in this spiritual sense. The birth of Jesus to the virgin, Mary, is considered a divine miracle.

Issue #4: "Jesus Was Never Crucified."

Muslim Viewpoint

Muslims do not believe, of course, that Jesus died on the cross.

They think that somebody who perhaps looked like Jesus was crucified, somebody like Judas, Simon of Cyrene, or yet another person unknown to us today. Some Muslims believe God was involved in this act as "it was made to appear so" (Sura 4:156-158), that God raised the crucified one up to himself, perhaps mistakenly. Others believe that it was in fact Christ on the cross, but that he did not die. One of the qur'anic passages that makes reference to the death of Jesus is Sura 19:33.

Christian Viewpoint

We must realize it is not only Muslims, but also Jews and many non-Christians, who may stumble over the fact that God could allow his prophet, much less his son, to be crucified. Superficially, to our fallen hearts, God allowing such a thing to occur would seem blasphemous. We must realize that the atonement is not a natural or human event. We must realize that it is indeed offensive, something even the Bible recognizes: "For the message of the cross is foolishness to those who are perishing. . . . The man without the Spirit does not accept the things that come from the Spirit of God, for they are foolishness to him, and he cannot understand them, because they are spiritually discerned" (1 Cor 1:18; 2:14).

Here are some points to consider in discussing the crucifixion of Christ with Muslims:

In terms of support from outside the biblical text, we can again refer to the memory capabilities of the Jews and writings from Roman and pagan authors from that time period.

We certainly do not believe that evil men can do anything without God's permission! The death of Jesus on the cross was God's plan and purpose. This is why Jesus came into the world—in order to die for us (see Matt 26:28.)[17]

A theological discussion about atonement and the necessity of blood sacrifice to cover sin may be helpful. For a Muslim, sin is an occasional act of disobedience to Allah. Muslims, therefore, do have a sense of sinfulness and of the need for redemption. For the Muslim, humans sin by act only, not by nature. Muslims also do not believe that sin against God is hurtful to God in any way.

It may be useful to refer to the prophecies about the crucifixion, "but he was pierced for our transgressions, he was crushed for our iniquities; the punishment that brought us peace was upon him" (Isa 53:4-8).

The plethora of scriptures that refer to the crucifixion is an indicator that this was a monumental and real event in the life of Jesus and was witnessed by many (1 Cor 15:3-8). The biblical teaching on this is clear and simple: Christ went to the cross to pay the penalty for human sin, he died, was raised from the dead, appeared to the disciples, and ascended to heaven (2 Cor 15:3-6, 17; 1 Pet 2:24; Heb 9:26-28).

Approaches to Apologetics

Relationships

There are different philosophies and approaches to when and how to deal with questions from our Muslim friends. We should not just go recklessly into confrontation and debate. Yes, we should depend on the Holy Spirit, but in addition, we need to seek counsel from our Christian leaders, focus on our own spiritual disciplines and biblical study, and most importantly, build strong and confident relational bridges with Muslims in a sincere context of love and respect.

When is the right time? In our experience, it is not ideal to get into apologetics on the first meeting. A first step is required of developing a relationship and building trust. We prefer to show our Muslim friend Christ through our life and actions. The best time to discuss Christ is when our Muslim friend initiates the conversation. The saying "live your life so it demands an explanation" comes to mind here.

What is the right approach? This is a delicate issue. One must be careful not to insult Muslims personally through insensitive comments, and always attempt to use a peaceful tone of voice and nonthreatening body behavior. It is also a good discipline not to denigrate or show disrespect for Muslims privately, as this attitude is completely contrary to a spirit of love and fellowship. Culture is quite important to a Muslim. We must thus respect their culture, all the while sticking to the core gospel message. We should also not attempt to delve into parts of the Bible or theology that we have not examined properly. It is important to be prepared intellectually for any conversation, because in the Arab culture, a simple question is sometimes used as fuel for many more.

New Media

New technologies also allow us to communicate and build bridges as never before straight into the heart of the Muslim world.

One example is http://inarabic.org/ and various television broadcasts into the Muslim world. Through broadcasts and the Internet, we are able to engage Muslims, develop relationships through the Holy Spirit, and help guide Muslims to Christ.

Our Commitment

In our commitment to Muslims, we follow the example of the apostle Paul. He writes, "I have become all things to all men so that by all possible means I might save some. I do all of this for the sake of gospel" (1 Cor 9:22-3). We listen, we identify, we befriend, we pray, we serve, and we commend Christ.[8]

Topic Two
May We Not Also Confront?

Jay Smith

Since the events of September 11, 2001, there has been a dilemma in missionary circles concerning the correct missiological methods to use with Muslims, especially with the more radical fringe groups whose violent acts have brought death and destruction to so many innocent people.

On the one side, there has been a push to continue using only the more irenic, traditional method of "interfaith dialogue" with Muslims, some of whom have been violently targeted by their western neighbors. Most missiologists from the Anabaptist community today would likely fall into this camp. This is due to their deep convictions about peace and reconciliation, and their desire to define Islam along the lines of many westernized Muslims as a religion of peace and tolerance. This group believes that the violence we witness today is not representative of true Muslims as a whole, but by only a small, disillusioned, and irrelevant minority, who live far away. The irenic approach is also a response grounded in the perceptions that the roots of Muslim anger against the west need to be heard and addressed, and that a listening and repentant spirit is needed in times like these, not confrontation.

On the other side is another group who believes that interfaith dialogue, while proven adequate in bringing about mutual under-standing between the two faiths, can no longer cope with today's more aggressive and growing radical element within Islam. This second group believes that the roots of radical Muslim anger against the west is not due necessarily to western materialism, or nineteenth- and twentieth-century colonialism, or even American imperialism, but that Islam, throughout its history, has contained within itself a channel of violence, legitimized by certain passages of the Qur'an, and exem-plified by their prophet Muhammad himself.[9] This group, therefore, sees the need to incorporate new approaches to deal with such a par-adigm, ones which confront the foundations of the more radical ele-ments within the Muslim community, particularly those theological and historical foundations rooted in Islamic scriptures and the Islamic

Hadith (traditions) to which the radicals look for authority in substantiating the actions they carry out.

This group contends that the desire for peace and tranquility between the two faiths does not reflect present reality. They believe that we now live with a newly invigorated and increasingly militant Islam which is no longer distant, but has brought their "battle" to the west in an attempt to seduce young and impressionable minds to their way of understanding Islamic scriptures and traditions.

Many pundits in the west seek to dismiss these militant elements as irrelevant extremists, representing only a small minority of the Muslim community. Recent research shows, however, that they are rapidly growing in numbers and importance, and are prepared to die for what they believe.

In the United Kingdom, the mood among resident Muslims is becoming ever more negative with regards to the west, particularly against the governments of the United States and Great Britain. According to BBC (Gallup) and *Q-News* polls, taken in 2001 immediately following the September 11 incident, radical Muslims made up roughly 15 percent of the Islamic community within the United Kingdom. By 2002, however, the radicals had gained up to 25 percent of the U.K. Muslim population.[10] Following the recent Iraqi war that figure has probably moved even higher; and this, in a strong western environment, situated outside the traditional world of Islam.

If one were to look to traditional Islamic societies where people are fed anti-western views regularly, with little recourse to alternative opinions, the statistics are even more disturbing. According to a recent poll of four mainly Muslim nations, taken in March 2004, by the *Pew Global Attitudes Project*, of the Pew Research Center, around 31 percent of Turks now support the radical movement of Osama bin Laden, while in Morocco it is 45 percent, and in Jordan it is 55 percent. Of particular interest, according to this poll, support for Osama bin Laden in Pakistan, one of Islam's largest countries, has risen to 65 percent of the population, or roughly 80 million people![11]

Fortunately, there are still a few Christians willing and equipped to work among these more radical Muslims. Yet virtually none of those Christians come from within the Anabaptist community. This is troubling, since today it is the radical Muslims who are attacking the foundations of the Christian faith more vociferously and more comprehensively than any other Muslim group. Their literature, in the form of books, tracts, tapes, videos, and the Internet, is filled with

material attacking Christianity, focusing in particular on our foundations, the Bible, as well as the person of Jesus Christ. Their passion,
though misguided, is indeed amazing, even impressive.

How, then, might these more radical Muslims be approached? Is
there any way, not only to grab their attention, but to address the
issue of their deep anger and to keep it from spreading to other sectors
of the Muslim community?

Many politicians, and a growing number of Christians in the
west, believe that the only way to deal with this growing radical
threat is to either ignore it, or even worse, to eradicate it through the
barrel of a gun. There is, however, little evidence that a philosophy, or
a belief, perceived by its adherents to have its source in divine revelation, can be removed by the use of violence. History has, in fact,
shown that movements such as Islam have thrived and even expanded
when attacked violently from without.

A better solution, I believe, is the "tough love" practiced by Jesus,
his disciples, and the early church in the first century. This solution is
one which employs confrontation against those who choose to challenge our foundations: our paradigm—the Lord Jesus Christ, and our
revelation—the scriptures which speak about him. However, not with
the use of a sword, but instead, with the use of one's mouth, mind,
and volition. In order to do that we will need to begin by confronting
the very foundations of Islam: their paradigm—the prophet
Muhammad, and the revelations which speak about him—the
Qur'an. For those of us from within the nonviolent Anabaptist tradition,
this stance is one we should be able to accept, adapt, and apply well.

It might be wise here to ask whether it is possible to find a case
for a confrontational model of evangelism in the New Testament.
Most Christians would likely reply "no," making reference to the classic
text in 1 Peter 3:15-16 which stipulates that Christians should be
prepared to defend their faith with "gentleness and respect."

However, defense or apologia against an accuser should not come
as a surprise as it is mentioned five times in the New Testament: Acts
22:1, 25:16; 1 Corinthians 9:3; 2 Corinthians 7:11; and 2 Timothy 4:16.
Twice Christians are asked to defend the gospel (Phil 1:7, 16; and 1 Pet
3:15). A strong defense of our beliefs is thus not foreign to New
Testament teaching at all, and it was practiced by the early church.

Jesus was a Jew from the Mediterranean world, an environment
similar to those who birthed Islam. When approached by those who
came to listen and to learn, he treated them with respect by listening

courteously and engaging them in friendly dialogue. Nicodemus, a Pharisee who came to Jesus at night (John 3:1-21) is a fine example of such an approach. We, too, are asked to follow the example of our Lord, and respond to the Nicodemuses of our world, answering their questions and sharing with them the truths of the gospel in a spirit of "gentleness and respect."

Yet, when approached by those whose sole purpose was to confront, Jesus met them with a similar mode of conversation they understood. Take, for example, Jesus's exchange with the rich young ruler (Matt 19:16), or his confrontation with the Pharisees and Herodians (Mark 12:13), or his dispute with his Pharisee host at a dinner party (Luke 7:36-50).

Perhaps the best example of a confrontational response is that found in Matthew 23:13-33, where Jesus referred to the Pharisees who came to challenge him as "hypocrites," "blind fools," "whitewashed tombs," and as "snakes" and "vipers." He was equally confrontational with the money-changers at the temple (Matt 21:12-13; Luke 19:45), not seeking in any way to "discuss their positions in an atmosphere of mutual understanding," but by storming in and overturning their tables.

We do not have the authority of Jesus and it would be ill-advised to literally "upset the tables" of those who stand in opposition to the church. Jesus's example and resolve, however, can be a model for us as we seek resolutely to confront opponents to the kingdom of God in our day as well.

Paul is another example of a person who used confrontation in his ministry. Like Jesus, Paul was multifaceted in his methodology. At times he contextualized his message, such as when he met dispersed Jews on their territory across the Mediterranean world and read the scriptures with them (Acts 13:13-15), or when he borrowed ideas from Greek philosophy when formulating a response to the thinkers of his day at the Areopagus in Athens (Acts 17:22-31).

Paul was not adverse, however, to confrontation, and was, in fact, remarkably proactive in his apologetics and polemics, venturing into the synagogues and the market places to reason with some, and to speak boldly, refute, debate, and argue with others (Acts 13:46, 17:17, 18:28, 19:8-9; 2 Cor 5:11, 10:5). The treatment he received by both Jews and Romans in the form of flogging, riots, imprisonment, and stoning hardly suggests he was interested in little more than "mutual understanding."

Paul's resolute and non-compromising stance can be traced

throughout his ministry in the book of Acts. There were times when he went outside his Jewish community to the Greeks in their territory, reasoning with them from within their traditions (Acts 17:1-2, 17). In the pagan city of Ephesus, he began first by "arguing persuasively" in the Jewish synagogue for three months (Acts 19:8). When forced to leave, he went on to the lecture hall of Tyrannus, a secular institution, where he continued his discussions with both Jews and Greeks for two more years (Acts 19:9-10). Later, in Rome, Paul pursued his ministry in his rented apartment, from morning till night, for another two years, where he "boldly tried to convince" those who came to talk to him about Jesus (Acts 28:23-31).

Through it all, Paul preached unremittingly the gospel (Rom 1:16; 15:20; 1 Cor 1:23). Uppermost in his mind was the need to persuade people of the truth of Christ's gospel. As he himself wrote, he sought to "demolish arguments and every pretension that sets itself up against the knowledge of God, and take captive every thought to make it obedient to Christ" (2 Cor 10:5). As a consequence, Paul obtained results using both irenic and confrontational methods (Acts 11:34; 13:32; 17:4, 32; 18:6).

The examples given here often involved Paul ministering to people who were Gentiles, living outside the Jewish community. This stands against the popular criticism held by some that the early church challenged only those within their own community of faith— the implication being that we in like fashion should refrain from challenging those who are not "of our kind," such as our Muslim friends and neighbors.

Other New Testament apostles also employed confrontational approaches with those from outside the faith community. Stephen, for example, when challenged by members of the Synagogue of the Freedmen (i.e., the Jews of Cyrene, Alexandria, Cilicia, and Asia), held his ground and returned their arguments, so much so, in fact, that "they could not stand up against his wisdom" (Acts 6:9-10), and finally decided to execute him (Acts 7:57–8:1). One does not get executed, of course, for merely "agreeing to disagree"!

Philip was likewise comfortable when confronting the Ethiopian (Acts 8:26-40). Why then do we consider this proactive and resolute form of witness, often addressed to people outside of the Christian community, detrimental to the gospel, when it was this very model that was used so often by the earliest believers who gave us the gospel?

In my ministry in the U.K., I have often used a confrontational approach, many times challenging the historicity of what Muslims claim concerning the Qur'an and the prophet Muhammad. I have used both formal debates with Muslim scholars (around thirty to date), as well as more ad hoc, informal debates (i.e., every Sunday afternoon, leading a team from All Souls Church, to take on the local radical Muslims, from a ladder, at the notorious Speaker's Corner in Hyde Park).

We have seen results from both these debates, as well as the material engendered by these debates. Recently, two Muslims with status, one a high ranking doctor in a Middle Eastern country, and the other a champion martial arts fighter, have both given their lives to the Lord after reading a polemical paper I wrote on the prophet Muhammad, and then comparing him with the Lord Jesus Christ. Another Muslim, a graduate with honors from Al-Azhar University in Cairo, having studied videos of me there in order to attack my ideas and tactics, has now met the Lord in a remarkable almost Pauline like vision, and has recently joined our team at Speaker's Corner. He believes it is one of the most effective arenas to not only train Christians to learn how to publicly define and defend their faith (something we are poor at), but conversely to publicly confront and confound the foundations of Islam as well. These are the men like Paul that we are looking for, men and women who had status to begin with, and so can go back into their own communities and make a greater impact on those communities than any of us from without.

Many of us from an Anabaptist missiological background have been at the forefront of dialogue with Islam. Few have sought to confront its foundations, perhaps out of fear, or perhaps due to our methodological restraints. We have tended to sit on the sidelines and watch from a distance the discussions and debates which have ensued within secular academic circles.

This is unfortunate since our tradition has equipped us to take on such a challenge, not only because we refuse to resort to violence, but because we, like the radical Muslims, start from a similar presuppositional framework, the efficacy of revelation as a source for all we believe and practice. Therefore, we can best debate the truth of these different claims to revelation.

The situation post-September 11 has brought into focus a need to reassess whether there is room for some of us to return to the early church models of active engagement, to confront the more radical elements of the Muslim community today, especially with regards to their theological and historical foundations, since it is to these foundations that they derive their authority in substantiating the actions they carry out.

I believe it is time for some of us to move away from the sidelines and look beyond our fear and restraints. We need to learn from those who have been at the forefront of this debate, and ascertain whether we can benefit from the materials and methods that have been employed in this approach to the Muslim community. Perhaps these, then, could be applied to a healthy ongoing public debate with our Muslim brothers and sisters who far too often see us as a threat to much of what they hold true and dear.

Both Muslims and Anabaptists believe that ultimate truth can only be known through revelation. That is what Muslims hold dearest to their hearts—a passion for revealed truth. So do Anabaptists! So we, both Muslim and Christian, enter the debate, not to destroy one another, but rather to acknowledge that the intention of the debate is to destroy falsehood, and uphold the truth.

Jesus and Paul gave us an example of this kind of confrontation in the first century which I believe is just as applicable for those of us today in the twenty-first century. May we not then, like them, also choose to confront?

∾

Response: Stand Firm in the Truth of the Gospel
William Sahawneh

Apologetics has been descried in these two essays, not as a defense, but rather as a readiness to "give a reason for the hope that is in us" (1 Pet 3:13-17). This is a commitment to give witness to our faith without apologies or excuses, but with meekness, love, and humility. Apologetics is a commitment to cultivating a "relational approach" with Muslims, as this is what works best.

In order to do this effectively we will need to know our faith well enough to give a witness, and the Muslims' faith in order to be able to speak reasonably and accurately. Muslims seek validation for their faith. We dare not compromise the truth of the gospel by simply agreeing with Muslims about their beliefs.

It is important to carefully define the terms we are using in conversations with Muslims, since we often mean very different things with the words we use. Ultimately, the question that needs to be asked is this one: Is the God of the Bible one and the same with the God presented in the Qur'an? Discussions surrounding these two essays are not in total agreement on this matter. We need to do our homework, for that question is exceedingly basic to all that we are about in apologetics.

We are called to give witness to our faith without apologies or excuses, but with meekness, love, and humility. There are basic principles that are mandatory for informed apologetics. Know your faith well enough to give a witness. Do not muddy the faith with untruths. Know the Muslims' faith so as to be able to speak reasonably accurately. A relational approach to the Muslim is most fruitful—you cannot defend the gospel if you are hostile or do not have a trusting relationship.

We do not dare to compromise the truth by agreeing with the Muslim about his beliefs when those beliefs are contrary to the gospel. Muslims desperately seek validation of their faith. However, the Muslim and Christian understandings of God are different. That is what you will discover if you examine the respective Muslim and Christian scriptures. Who is God in the Bible and who is God in the Qur'an? Are they the same? No. Any revelation of God that is not centered in Jesus Christ is incomplete and distorted. God as revealed in Jesus Christ loves even the sinner! That is different than the qur'anic understanding of God. Define the terms early on in your conversation and dialogue with the Muslim.

CHAPTER THIRTY-FIVE

Literature and Media

Topic One
Mass Media Presence and the
Middle East Market

Wayne and Jeannie Larson

In 1985 we visited the country where we currently live in the Middle East for the first time. We had received our instructions about what to do at the airport and how to get where we were going, in case no one arrived for us. But the first thing we noticed as we were getting off the plane was the heaviness that hung in the air. I remember my Jeannie and I looking at one another, as if to say, "This is serious business here." You see, we had never been overseas in this region before, but we were smart enough to realize from the outset that even the atmosphere—spiritual or whatever you wish to call it—was something totally different from what we were accustomed. Thus, our first taste of realities with which we have wrestled over the past eighteen years in regard to this area of the world.

I am a media producer not a theologian. At the time when we began with Middle East Media (MEM), the field organization we work with, we also met Ron Yoder and Ken Weaver of Mennonite Board of Missions (MBM), now Mennonite Mission Network, and thus began our relationship with the Network. Shortly thereafter, we were taken on as Associates and currently are Long Term Workers with the Network.

To introduce you to MEM, let me say that we as an organization have been in the media marketplace for the past twenty-six years. We are team-based with seventy plus members, the great majority of whom are Middle Easterners. We are a field-based ministry, meaning that the work started in the Middle East and it is administered from there as well. Our areas of media cover print, Internet, television, film, and music.

A long-time pastor friend of mine who works in our country expressed to me his passion for what we are doing. He shared that when he walks out in the street, he knows that at least nine out of ten persons around him have no understanding of the gospel and Jesus's desire for them to spend eternity with him, and that my friend can do nothing about it. He is convinced that media must be used to help fill the gap. He went on to say that he has dabbled in video production, but it has to be done by professionals to do it right. This is the vision of MEM—to take the truths of the gospel story into the marketplace where they can be seen and heard and read by everyone, without the barriers which are automatically erected by the label, "Christian." Our material has to be good enough so that no station can afford to turn it down. Yet at the same time, by its witness and presence there, it can change the marketplace from the inside out.

Methods and Approach

Dual Contact Points

A. Mass Media Product—Types

1. Print: We have a number of publications. The front runner is a popular monthly magazine, sold on the newspaper stands. It has been published for more than twenty-six years. In addition to this, there are other magazine-type booklets, used for even more direct interaction. These include *Ultimate Questions*—for the seeker; *Kitabi*—meaning "my book"; and *Believer's Feast*—for the new believer. The first two of these have been produced in quantities of 25,000 to 90,000 per year.

2. Internet: One of the newer ventures is the use of Web sites. There are five different Web sites with various aims generating thousands of contacts.

3. Visual: The video-television production team started with a focus toward children and the use of puppets. It expanded into transliteration of other children's shows into Arabic, including animation and live action. Next we produced our own live action and drama pieces. More recently we have broken into animation and women's issues, with a feature-length film ready to go into the market.

4. Music: Our music studio produces music "albums" with lyrics that draw people to God. In addition they create the lyrics and music for the songs within the programs. Music can inspire other productions, as we have seen in the production of some music clips which then led us to a feature-film project.

B. The Individual—The Second of the Two Contact Points

1. Training and Equipping: Our training team works to develop professional level skills in believers and to pass on a vision to use the media to open dialogue whether via programs or other ways. One of our training projects was held in a more agricultural region of a Middle Eastern country with smaller cities. A group of young people who attended the video production course decided to use their skills in a community outreach project with their church. They went out on the street to interview women in all types of professions, from the corner kiosk selling cigarettes to the woman physician or teacher. Then they invited all the women who had "starred" in the video along with their families and friends to the church, to a seminar on "Women in the Workplace." Of course it included a showing of the video production! For many from both communities, this was a first opportunity at direct interaction, especially from within the church context.

2. Personal Contact in the Course of the Business Day: During the shooting of the film, one of our producers walked with an elderly actress back to her car. The woman shared how touched she was by the persons she was working with and the story of the film. She told how she had erred in marrying a majority religion person. (In the Middle East this would mean that the children must be trained up in that religion.) However, her children had both moved to the United States and married Christian spouses. Now, she was feeling the desire to come back to God herself.

3. Business Practices: As believers, we must do business in ways which are morally and ethically responsible. The media business can be very cutthroat. Thus, when media people work with us, and see

that the way we do things is different from the rest of the market-place, this speaks quite clearly about Christian values in a place where direct statements are not always appropriate.

Audience

A. As Mass Viewer

We are aiming for that major mass audience which would never seek to watch a Christian program. For instance, would you choose to watch a qur'anic sermon? Probably you might if you were trying to understand what "the other half" was thinking, but you likely would not choose to do so for your own enrichment or enlightenment. Likewise, if we label our media products Christian, it automatically cuts out perhaps upwards of 75 percent of the listening audience. The point is to get the programming and life-changing media content into the commercial marketplace for the largest number of viewers and the ones who would never try to find out about Christ on their own.

B. As Business Community

Our hope is that the marketplace itself will begin to be changed by the "salt and light" of both our products and the way we deal within it. One example is that a number of people on our team are taking courses in local film institutes. The individual professionals have the opportunity to rub shoulders with those in the industry and to impact these "up and coming" artists.

Distribution

As already stated, the market is the commercial, or what we would in the west call secular. However, in the Middle East—though this seems to be changing—traditionally, nothing is secular.

A. Product and Message

1. Standard: The standard we keep must be market driven, competitive, and professional. Two weeks ago we received a phone call from a regional TV station. The representative expressed how proud they are of the quality of our programs, since we are home-grown in the Arab world. They asked that we produce programs for them. So we are currently negotiating a substantial contract with this station. This sort of commercial work serves not only the purpose of giving us operating funds, but helps us to stay competitive in the

market, and more importantly another avenue of dialogue with the community we work within.

2. Message: We share the message through stories. How many of us remember the sermon content from three weeks ago? But what about a movie from three years ago? How did Jesus communicate? Largely through parables or stories, he "sowed" the truth, piece by piece. The Middle Eastern audience, to whom he spoke, knew exactly what he was preaching about.

While speaking recently to an audience of young people in Dubai, I asked, "What would Jesus be today?"

Some of the answers were: writer, TV producer, and actor.

B. Four Concepts That Focus Our Ministry—GPPC

1. Grace: Forgiveness is not a developed concept within the local cultures. Yet we introduce these understandings. One issue of our magazine dealt with reconciliation. We received the story about how two young women who were angry with one another had both read the same issue of our magazine. The one tried to call her friend to apologize for their fight. While she was phoning and unable to get through to her, the friend rang her doorbell to come to ask *her* forgiveness, with a copy of the magazine in her hand!

2. Power of the Holy Spirit: We can have access to God's Spirit and power in our lives.

3. Personal Relationship with God: God is not the vague, distant, and capricious god which has been taught. He desires a personal relationship with us.

4. Certainty of Heaven: One can be sure of heaven. We can know where we are going. Funerals here are very serious affairs. Though in Islam there may be a theological hope of heaven, practically there is little or no real hope or assurance of seeing a loved one again.

As a result of a survey printed in our monthly magazine, more than 30,000 young people responded to an open-ended question about what concerns they had in life. The single largest concern voiced was forgiveness of sins with over 20 percent of the responders listing this issue on their own initiative.

Balance

No one episode of a program or issue of a magazine tells the whole truth of the gospel. The process of giving bits of truth is like digging up the soil and adding fertilizer, along with a few seeds. It is about trusting the Holy Spirit to work in someone's heart and bring him or her to the next step on the path.

In summary, the goal in a media interaction is to not attack or confront, but to challenge beliefs. We seek to introduce a potential for attitude change. Visual media is powerful at the heart and emotive level, more than the intellectual level. If viewers begin to seek who is the true and living God, he will answer. Yet we continue to have much to learn.

To Learn/Discover

We conclude with several summary observations and questions.

1. Mass media tends to be most effective on the ends of the Engels Scale. In other words, those persons who are farthest away from a decision point or most "clueless" can be moved toward a softer or more open place. And those farthest along with the Lord can be encouraged by a non-direct approach.

2. How can we build adequate feedback mechanisms or opportunities that do not jeopardize the delivery method? How do we listen to audience response without alienating the audience?

3. Personal contact is always critically important. Our commitment to media does not in any way obviate the need for direct contact. Media is only one piece of the picture in the total movement of God in a person's life. It is like the double-panned scale with a weight equal to ninety-nine sugar cubes on one side. This represents the Muslim's life and need for input about the Lord. As he watches one TV program, perhaps a couple of cubes are placed onto the opposite pan. As someone prays for him, several more. As his Christian neighbor acts out of love toward him, another and another and so forth. But which sugar cube was the most important, when the one hundredth one has been added and the scales of his life are finally tipped toward Christ?

4. Dialogue and relationships are very significant. However, we do have stories of persons coming to the Lord with little or no human contact. Why? Because, with God, nothing is impossible! Though the situation looks impossible, God sees and answers the seeking heart according to his promise.

Topic Two
The Veil and the Vision:
Bible Stories for Middle Eastern Muslims

Bruce Heckman

Leaders from the Bible Society in the Middle East asked me to join them in Bahrain for the annual international book fair. We resided in California at the time, and it truly seemed like another world from the life we had lived in the Middle East. In California we attended an Arabic fellowship at times, enjoying the intense relationships and hoping to keep some familiarity with Arabs alive in our children's lives. This was an odd time of transition for our family. My wife Joyce and I had lived in a Middle Eastern nation for the past seven years. The last three and one half of those years were in the Bible House in the capital city of our adopted nation. During those years we witnessed many Jordanians and Palestinians grow in their respect for the authority of the word of God. Some carried Bibles into neighboring nations.

We had the privilege of involvement in the early 1980s with placing a Bible Society stand in the International Book Fair in Bahrain. During those early book fairs many Bibles were sold to nationals of most Arabian Gulf States. The book fairs were a forum of interaction, in their language, on the validity of the Bible and the life of Jesus. What a very special encouragement it was when the Bible Society in the Middle East asked if I could travel from Los Angeles to Bahrain to join them for the International Book Fair in November of 1987.

Visitors to the book fair asked questions about the Bible, others voiced objections to our very presence there. This book fair seemed very much like previous ones. Then a veiled woman approached the Bible display booth. She had several children all following her in descending order of age. I remember thinking it looked like a human train. Her veil had only a slit for her eyes. Her voice was slightly muffled behind her veil. *"Matha 'indakum lilulaad?"* ("What do you have for children?") This question troubled me and would not go away. We had nothing. Some of our literature had a few random stick figures, but nothing that could attract children. I shook my head slightly, giving her the sad news that we could not help her request.

This woman's haunting question stayed with me upon my return to the Los Angeles area. The vast number of children's Bibles available in English struck me as a treasure that many other languages, especially among those in our world who have little or no opportunity to hear the gospel, are lacking. Christian bookstores in the United States, I discovered, had Christian literature for tots to teens. I looked through several of the children's Bibles, looking for Genesis to Revelation books that would give a proper chronology of the work of God.

Bible Stories Are Fascinating to Muslims

Through our years in the Middle East it was evident the Muslims had little understanding of biblical chronology. In order for people to understand God's revelation in the Bible they need to be introduced to the history of God dealing with people. The Qur'an gives chronological confusion in terms of the work of God through specific people. The following example is taken from Surat Al-Anaam, verses 81-86.

> Those that believed and did not wear their faith with darkness will be granted safety and proper guidance. This is our evidence we gave to Abraham against his people: We raise up through ranks whom we will. Your Lord is wise and filled with knowledge. And we gave to him Isaac and Jacob and guided both of them as we previously guided Noah and from his descendents were David and Solomon and Job and Joseph and Moses and Aaron— in this way the righteous are rewarded. And Zechariah and John (the Baptist) and Jesus and Elijah: all were among the just. And Ishmael and Elisha and Jonah and Lot: all of these we exalted over common people.[1]

The eighteen men listed in these five verses represent an order that buries Jesus in "among the righteous, rewarded, and exalted." The accounts of biblical salvation history are not comprehendable in this cocktail of names and exhortations.

A requirement of bearing witness is communicating in a way that the receptor understands. Pictures will communicate a great deal in a society that claims all forms of art to be idolatry. In other words, Muslims will say they detest pictures, and that placing pictures of prophets in a book is unspeakable. That is what they say, but I know they love pictures and would devour a book with colored pictures depicting the work of God. Granted, it is necessary for a children's Bible storybook to depict modesty in the artwork. It must be suitable for a Middle Eastern audience. Pictures that depict western faces or take too much liberty in describing the story line would not be acceptable. I chose two children's Bibles that would be readily translated into Arabic and wrote the publishers, asking for permission to put their books into another language.

Translation Efforts—Overwhelming

Translation projects are overwhelming. The question that came repeatedly to my mind was, "Who are you to write to major publishing houses and advocate the translation of their book?" When I wrote the publishers, I explained that I worked previously for the Bible Society in the Middle East, and would work the project through them. Both companies answered back, both willing to have their work placed into Arabic. Both required approximately $11,500 for a copy of their colored plates to print the pictures.

I approached the Bible Society in the Middle East during one of their joint meetings, and presented the project and the willingness of the two publishers to work with us. At first the Bible Society was a little reluctant, explaining that they were considering printing booklets on individual Bible characters. They would have a booklet for Moses, for Daniel, and for Jesus. My contention with this plan was that anyone could shuffle the booklets and tell you of the life of Jesus, Moses, and Daniel. Order and chronology are important because they are part of the story. "For the law was given through Moses; grace and truth came through Jesus Christ" (John 1:17). This verse tells us that the law came before grace and truth. Disregarding the order will confuse the message.

There is tremendous confusion that comes to anyone, especially a child, when the message of grace, mercy, and forgiveness is superceded by a message of law and personal responsibility. It is not just a matter of confusing Moses and Jesus. The message of the Qur'an is that law and personal responsibility for maintaining the proper balance on one's "scales" abrogates the message of grace and substitutional sacrifice. Order is important. One book is required to give the needed chronology. The Bible Society leadership agreed.

My heart was elated that they agreed to consider the project. And also very quickly my heart sank with the news that they had reservations with the one book, and rejected the other. The one book had beautiful artwork, but the text was far too western to translate. The other book was rejected because of the style of artwork. They chose *The Children's Bible in 365 Stories*, published by Lion Publishing in England. But the text for a western audience took too many freedoms, slightly embellishing the text for children.

Lucian Accad, director of the Bible Society in Lebanon and the Middle East told me, "What we call Bible in the Middle East needs to be Bible."

This book was not to be one quickly translated and on the shelves in six months. We would take the time to rewrite the entire text, using *Today's Arabic Version* as the basis for writing the stories. There were three new items to work around. One was now finding a primary writer to form the text. The second challenge was that the text for *Today's Arabic Version* was not yet published, and would not be for another four years. The third hurdle to cross was drawing together a review committee to carefully examine the text.

My secretary went through the entire English text, listing every scriptural reference made in the entire book. These references were given to the Bible Society in Lebanon who then printed out the texts available in the Old Testament to begin the process. A Lebanese professor was chosen for the project, and given the assignment of placing the Bible texts into a twelve-year-old's comprehension level. His background in children's literature gave him the rare ability to see the text through a child's eyes. Committee members were picked that represented Jordan, Lebanon, Palestine, and Egypt. Some feedback from Bahrain was included occasionally. A translation consultant joined our team, and I was asked to be the general editor for the project.

Manuscript Challenges

The Middle East is not an easy area of the world to coordinate an international Christian project. Borders, unending questions, and legalities make a project like this challenging. The Lebanese professor wrote his manuscript on yellow legal pad paper. The normal twenty pages were inserted into a brown envelope in Beirut labeled "Bible Society," and sent by *servis* taxi to Amman. The need was to find a "Christian" *servis* driver in Beirut, explain the importance of this packet reaching the Bible Society in Jordan, and pay the appropriate fee to insure the package made it past the Lebanese, Syrian, and Jordanian borders. I then received a telephone call from the Bible

Society in Amman, "A package has arrived," after the driver delivered the envelope.

My secretary typeset the manuscript, arranging the story sequence. The manuscripts were sent Fed Ex overnight to each nation involved with the review. Upon receiving the typed manuscript, committees met in each nation, reviewed the stories and made suggested textual changes. These suggested changes were e-mailed back to our office, where they were compiled in columns representing each review committee. Each story and each paragraph was scrutinized. Every three to four months, heads of the review committees met in neutral locations (outside the Middle East) with the translation consultant to discuss every suggested change to the text. For me, this work was exhausting; as a foreigner, my eyes were nearly crossed by the end of each day, reading and rereading texts and changes. Yet each time our textual committee met, another twenty or twenty-five stories passed the scrutiny of many, and entered the finished work category.

Editing Challenges

We faced several challenges forming the text that all could agree upon. One man pushed repeatedly for a more proper Arabic. The language to him seemed silly and childish. He commented at one point, "I never hear this type of language coming from the pulpit!" How important it was that the text was readable to those outside the church. Our purpose was not to get a nice storybook into the hands of Christians that had grown up with a background in Bible stories. Our goal was to make a text simple enough for the common young person outside of church and, to be honest, a text that a parent could read to her child without the embarrassment presented by most cryptic religious literature. We all had to think repeatedly of our target, not our background.

The words of the prophets needed to foretell the coming of the Christ. The prophets could not be understood as unrelated messengers, each with their righteous warning as the Qur'an suggests. We found a way for Isaiah 6, 7, and 53 to come out of the prophet's mouth, and remain true to the text. The "holy, holy, holy" Isaiah heard is followed by the Lord sending him with a message: "The virgin will conceive and bear Emanuel, God with us. He will carry our pain and all our sin and wipe away death forever."

Linguistic Challenges

We approached the completion of the Old Testament portion of the project. This had already become a two-year investment, and we were far from a finished product. I took the Old Testament text to a grammar specialist. This was a Muslim lady that taught high school level Arabic grammar. She was not only from outside the church, but would be able to look at the text without the background of someone partial to one particular translation of the Bible. The result of her grammatical check was embarrassing for the entire review committee. She asked me if a foreigner wrote the text! (I was too ashamed to tell her that a Lebanese professor wrote a manuscript that was edited by many Arabs.) Her red pen of scrutiny covered each page. She offered the same grammatical check for the New Testament. Although our committee faces were quite pink in light of her red pen, all agreed to each change suggested. Her work took us from a childish attempt into a correct piece of Arabic children's literature.

Publishing

Four years into the project, *The Bible for All Ages* was published in Arabic. Eastern Mennonite Missions (EMM) contributed an enormous amount to this project. EMM covered the cost of office space and secretary's wages in Jordan. They covered the grammatical reviews of the entire book. The name of EMM is not listed in the book, which I personally believe is commendable. It remains a book without denominational ties or western recognition. The Bible Society covered the cost of manuscript writing, flights, hotels, and meals for numerous review sessions.

We risked printing ten thousand copies, wondering how this book would be received. Anyone reading this paper must realize that literature in the English-speaking world has an ocean of readers in several nations. The numbers printed in one language cannot be compared to the numbers in another language as proof of accomplishment. The ten thousand quickly were distributed. Twenty thousand more were printed within months. To date a conservative estimate of 120,000 copies of *The Bible for All Ages* have gone out. The primary nations of interest have been Iraq, Lebanon, Jordan, and Syria.

Results

When we enter the home of a Muslim and find *The Bible for All Ages* on their coffee table, it is evident that everyone in the family has access to a book that does not appear to be a religious book, or one threatening to them. Yet it has the message that does transform lives into the image of Christ. A neighbor of ours in Jordan took a copy home. I saw the man the next day with dark circles under his eyes. He read the book from cover to cover, finishing at 2:30 in the morning.

The Bible Society in Lebanon reported that a completely veiled woman approached their stand in Beirut at an international book fair. She began to thank God aloud and call blessings down on the heads of those running the stand. "I have looked everywhere for this book and have found it. God bless you for making this book available!"

One sobering story came from a Palestinian refugee camp. A woman with children had received a copy of *The Bible for All Ages* and placed it on the coffee table of their multi-purpose living-sitting-dining-bedroom. A neighbor came to their house, saw the book and began to read. He asked if he could take the book home. The woman was afraid to give the book up, not knowing if it would come back and if she could get another.

In a telephone conversation with Lucian Accad, general secretary of the Bible Society in Lebanon, he told me that the most effective tool in sharing the gospel they have is *The Bible for All Ages*.[2]

Personal Note

Shortly after *The Bible for All Ages* was published, the director of Living Bibles International in Egypt told me my work had just begun. He told me that the illiterate and partially literate would never handle such a large book. "The book must be placed on cassettes that can go anywhere," was his advice. Others said the same. In January 2003 the same cry was raised for this children's Bible to be placed into audio media, onto compact disks (CDs) that could be easily reproduced and distributed. *The Bible for All Ages* entered a new phase, placing the text, background music, and sound effects onto eleven audio CDs. A foundation grant made available from New Jersey, along with donations from DOVE Christian Fellowship churches, covered the production of the audio CD's. The project was completed in September 2003, and is currently ready for duplication and distribution.

An added blessing is found in this book going into other Middle

Eastern languages. The thinking process into Arabic paved the way for other Middle Eastern people to have the same book placed into their language in relatively short order.

I have several words of encouragement to those entering sizeable projects.

1. It takes people with vision to contribute financially to a project as it begins. Contributions for secretarial wages and flights for review committees are more difficult to raise than funds to print or distribute a completed project. Fundraising requires solid goals and timeline to encourage contributions.

2. Dealing with a committee requires so much more work than working with a few individuals. However, the result of a committee is so much farther reaching and shares the ownership with many people. Never sidestep the committee to get a quick result from a few individuals, especially in translation projects.

3. The joy of partnering with many groups and people is that all can rejoice. No individual gets a pat on the back. Everyone can rejoice together.

Topic Three
The People of God (POG)

Darren Schaupp

Had you been a missionary in the scrub lands of Somalia in the mid-1970s, you might have answered the door to a late-night knock. Eastern Mennonite Missions (EMM) missionary David Shenk answered such a knock and invited in the cautious Muslim inquirer he found standing there.

This young Muslim's search for simple Bible study materials instigated the creation of what is known today as the *People of God* (POG) course. During the next few years after the visit, David, along with a team of reviewers from many different backgrounds, developed four booklets that take a seeker from Muslim background through the Bible from Genesis to Revelation: *The Beginning of People, God's Covenant with People, God Loves People*, and *The People of Faith*.

Booklets for Study

Designed for use in areas where people don't have background knowledge of the Bible, the POG course tries to use simple and culturally appropriate language to develop the major themes of the good news. The material is written with a Muslim religious worldview in mind. So instead of turning to the book of Genesis, readers are referred to the "first book of the Taurat,'" or to the "Zabur" instead of Psalms.

Understandably, this culturally sensitive, invitational approach has made the POG course popular among Muslim inquirers. In Eastern Africa, where POG is headquartered, these materials are used as a correspondence course and for group studies. The Bible society has worked with POG in providing the relevant scripture portions, for example, for the first course, *Genesis: The First Portion of the Taurat of the Prophet Moses.*

POG Director Bishop Joash Osiro, a ten-year veteran of POG work who recently completed a master's degree in Islamics in England, reports, "Concerning readership, there is an average of a thousand students per year [in Eastern Africa]. A substantial number of inquirers have, according to their letters, come to the Lord. Many more write to the office seeking more information."

Exciting news indeed! But that is only a portion of the story. The POG books continue to be in high demand internationally, having been translated, or being translated, into languages around the world—primarily in predominantly Muslim societies where the church is a distinct minority.

Here is the list of forty-four languages that we know of that the course has been or is being translated into: Afar, Arabic, Albanian, Aringa, Bambara (Dioula), Bengali, Bulgarian, English, French, Fulani, Hausa, Indonesia, Kalgan, Kazak, Kyrgyz, Liberian, Maderuse, Manguindanao, Malagasy, Malayalam, Malay, Maranao, Orma, Oromo, Philippine English, Pulaar, Russian, Sama, Sindhi, Somali, Spanish, Swahili, Tagalog, Tajik, Tamil, Tausug, Thai, Turkish, Urdu-Indian, Urdu-Pakistan, Uzbek, Yakan, and Yoruba.

This course often becomes a bridge building trust and respect between the Christian community and the Muslim society. Though it's impossible to get accurate data on how many POG students there are worldwide each year, the number is definitely in the tens of thousands, and the demand for the materials continues to grow.

The POG office in Nairobi has its hands full. Aside from overseeing these international requests and issues, and managing their Eastern African students, they also work with churches in Eastern Africa to follow up with the students, give seminars on Islam to church leaders, and work on new POG initiatives.

In fact, on one trip to "the field" to meet with students and other ministry leaders, the idea for POG's latest project was birthed. Muslim women were expressing significant interest in learning more about the Bible. Unfortunately, in Eastern Africa, many women are not literate and have no way to study such materials on their own. So, the vision to put the POG materials in audio format was born.

POG on the Air

With the vision of reaching millions of nonliterate Muslim women in particular, the POG study materials have been developed into brief radio programs. The four POG books have been condensed into twenty-five easy to understand lessons of fifteen minutes each. The simplified English radio script has been broken down to include four voices, notations for inserting local music, and the POG Radio

Program signature tune to be played at the beginning of the program. The POG Radio Program is ready for translation and use in any language, on the radio or even as a cassette tape series.

Lord willing, these materials will also be available soon for downloading from the Web. It is exciting to have the potential to share with many people, literate and non-literate alike, a simple and clear study of the Bible. Praise the Lord for what he has done and will continue to do through the People of God materials. Continue to pray for all those who work to share the good news.

For further information on the written POG course materials or the POG Radio Program, please write: pogradio@emm.org

ᆨ

Response: *Amazing Creativity*

Sara Fast

These essays on media and literature are excellent and elicit creative ideas for those interested in media ministries. The presentations provide a variety of approaches to media ministries to the Muslim world.

Bruce Heckman's essay reveals how he, together with a team, joined with the Bible Society in the Middle East to create and publish a book entitled *The Bible for All Ages*. Bruce's vision for creating a Bible specifically for children emerged after speaking with a veiled Muslim woman who asked for books for children, and he had nothing to offer her. Today there have been 120,000 copies of this Bible printed and distributed in the Middle East. The creation of this book is a testimony to how nothing is impossible for God. I am impressed with the steps Bruce took to make this vision a reality. Noteworthy was his strong commitment to working with an international team of Middle East Christians.

Darren Schaupp's essay gives a brief description of the *People of God* program. This is a Bible correspondence and radio program presenting books written by a team of writers and Islamic specialists led by David Shenk. It provides Muslims with the opportunity to learn about the truth of Jesus Christ in a contextual way.

Wayne and Jeannie Larson of Middle East Media have presented an insightful essay on their program. In the seminar the essay was supplemented with video clips from some of their high quality productions. One of their goals is to reach an audience that would not normally watch Christian television. They desire to provide programs and literature that begin to gradually change people at a heart level. By teaching biblical principles such as grace, Holy Spirit empowerment and transformation, forgiveness, and certainty of heaven, their hope is that people's hearts will begin to be softened to God. One question that lingered in my mind was "How would Jesus relate to our culture today?" Surely, media would be one of his main tools.

These essays are most informative as each presenter writes about learnings they have discovered while living and witnessing among Muslims. A common theme that is interwoven into each presentation is the intentional use of creativity through media in the proclamation of the truth of Jesus Christ. God is at work, and the kingdom of God is growing as many seeds are being planted and nurtured through media and literature.

CHAPTER THIRTY-SIX

Fellowship Formation

Topic One
Believers Fellowships:
The Somali Experience

Harold E. Reed

Traditionally a nomadic pastoral people comprising a nation of few material resources, Somalis have been largely unknown except as they have recently appeared on North American newscasts or become our neighbors (approximately 30-40,000 in Minneapolis and 20,000 in Toronto). Further, the two major identifying characteristics of the Somali people are their universal religion (Islam) and language (Somali). The commonly-held belief is that there are no exceptions: "To be Somali is to be Muslim," was the response of a Somali policeman who interrogated several believers, and to whom they joyfully responded, "We have been changed."

How did a Mennonite witness and fellowship begin and develop among a people such as this? In this essay I review this half-century journey reflecting on four chronological eras. The commitments to Mennonite presence and witness in Somalia was first initiated by Eastern Mennonite Missions. (EMM at that time was known as Eastern Mennonite Board of Missions and Charities.) Later Mennonite Central Committee (MCC) also became involved in Somalia.

1. Colonial Era—Early Mennonite Missionaries Arrive in Former Italian Somaliland (1953-1959)

After articulation of the initial vision and exploratory visits by experienced overseas personnel, early missionaries began, in 1953, to learn the Somali language in Mogadishu (the capital), followed by further exploratory work at other locations. At about the same time Sudan Interior Mission (SIM) also entered Somalia.

Program: Early programs were selected by listening to what was valued by Somalis and EMM. Included were: adult English language and commercial classes (women were included later), elementary schools (boarding and day, male and female students), medical clinics, and small-scale agricultural projects. Shortly before independence a hospital was opened in Lower Juba, complementing the already existing elementary day and adult schools.

Worship: Christians, though very few in numbers and mostly expatriates (U.N., Italian government, commercial and military personnel), were already present in Somalia. Of these, the few Somali Christians included riverine Swahili-speaking families who had become Christians before the Swedish Lutheran Mission departed from Lower Juba about 1935. Missionary teams at each location met regularly in their homes, including Eritrean families in Mogadishu, and several of the Bantu families in Lower Juba.

Suffering: Somalis attribute both tragedy and blessing to the will of God (*Ilahhi amarkiis*). Nor did suffering bypass the mission family. We experienced the death of an infant and a nighttime attack on one of the missionary women, with additional losses following in subsequent years.

Observations:

• The permission for two Christian missions (EMM and SIM) to be present in an almost exclusively Muslim Somalia seems miraculous. Developing mission programs which responded to felt needs of the people was essential to continuing missionary presence. They contributed to further openness of the Somali people to a Christian missionary community with public influence.

• A few small groups of believers met together for regular worship, in a society which held mostly negative perceptions of western Christians. Although a few Somalis had become Christian, historically there was no expression of a viable Christian community among the dominant Somali people in Somalia. The missionary team living and working together in Christian community would provide an essential model for indigenous fellowship formation.

• A confessional but sensitive approach was attempted regarding (1) Christ as the core of faith and life, and (2) Christian mission rooted in a church community. When the U.S. ambassador challenged the late Orie Miller, the initial EMM visionary, regarding the EMM's stance on evangelism, Orie responded, "We want to be respectful and careful, but if anyone inquires about our Christian faith, we are ready to share it with them."[1] Our Mennonite Church and mission (EMM) community identities were clear from the beginning.

• The vision and commitment of EMM, including the Somalia Mennonite Mission (SMM) team, was to "bear witness" to "the true light" "coming into the world" (John 1:8-9).

Jesus said, "For where two or three of you are gathered in my name, I am there among them" (Matt 18:20, NRSV).

"Let each [builder] who comes on the job take care to build on the foundation! Remember, there is only one foundation, the one already laid: Jesus Christ (1 Cor 3:10b-11, The Message).

2. Independence and Nation-Building—Former Italian and British Somalilands Become the Unified and Independent Somali Republic (1960-1969)

Among competing ideologies, Somalis tilted toward modernity. They were proud to be Somali while devoutly Muslim. Politicians and religious leaders aspired to develop a national ideology and political model beyond what had been developed during the U.N. Trusteeship. Students, confident in a newfound national identity, were inspired to explore options from a worldwide perspective. It was hoped that Somalis in northeast Kenya, Djibouti, and the Ogaden (in Ethiopia) would be joined to the Republic, completing all five points of the star on the new flag of the Somali Republic. As relationships developed with Somali people serving among several missions (Roman Catholic, SIM, and SMM), awareness of a "new community" emerged and was viewed as another model for consideration.

Program and Government Intervention: Most earlier SMM programs continued and others were begun—intermediate schools, a nursing school, a bookstore, and Mennonite Economic Development Associates (MEDA) funded several microenterprises. However, the government closed all SMM programs in March 1962, following rumors in the pervasive Somali "grapevine" of proselytizing by SMM and Somali believers. After extended prayer and negotiation, SMM activities were allowed to resume in July 1962, provided (1) there not be any non-Muslim teaching to Somali children or students, and (2) that children be prohibited from attending SMM religious services.

As students were registering for the reopened schools, a zealous militant killed Merlin Grove and severely wounded his wife Dorothy in Mogadishu. The Prime Minister expressed his sincere regrets, and while assuring us that the government would not tolerate such actions, he challenged SMM to function in ways that would not be offensive to religious and political sensitivities.[2] Dorothy, although still suffering some medical implications today, joyously shares her testimony of joy, peace, and goodwill. In more recent years she has returned to Somalia for a brief term of service.

The national constitution was altered in June 1963, to ban "propagandizing any religions other than the True Religion of Islam," with the Somali ambassador to the U.N. declaring, "The amendment underscores Islam as the State religion but does not impinge on internal activities of other religions."[3]

The Somali government ordered all schools to permit teaching of Islam in September 1963. Following extended deliberation and prayer by believers, missionaries, the EMM board, and Lancaster Mennonite Conference leadership and constituency, there was agreement to move ahead with implementation of this directive. A year later Paul Kraybill, EMM overseas secretary, noted, "This action has not compromised our witness. In fact, it has helped to break down negative attitudes that hindered."[4]

Worship: Several small fellowships of committed Somali believers began arising mostly from the one-to-one Bible studies personally requested by young men and a few women. The national constitution initially provided freedom to choose one's religion, and was perceived, especially by young men, as opening an unprecedented window of religious opportunity. At the same time, however, government restrictions were tightened and the state constitution was then revised.

Some Somali believers met regularly for periods of fellowship and chose leaders in the mid-sixties. One of the Bantu believers was chosen as a wise senior leader—a "father figure"—for counsel and wisdom, and as a model of Christian family life. Since the Bantu riverine Swahili-speaking people were commonly regarded as slaves among ethnic Somalis, respecting this brother as a senior leader was a very noticeable expression of nondiscrimination and cross-cultural fellowship. Steps toward development of Somali faith communities were often initiated among themselves, with missionaries being invited to activities. From the mid-sixties onward, EMM-SMM regularly offered a few educational scholarships, mostly in nearby African countries. Translation of the New Testament into Somali was completed.

Famine, flooding, and disease frequently threatened health and the main food supply around the two major rivers; suffering and death continued to affect the Somali populace at large. In addition, high aspirations for nationhood had begun to erode by the late sixties. "The 1960s," according to Omar Eby, "boomed for the Mennonites." Yet these "Golden Years," as the Somalis call this decade (the decade begun for the SMM with the death of Merlin Grove) ended for the Somali nation with "a political assassination and a military coup."[5]

Observations:

• Quality educational and medical programs provided an arena for developing positive relationships and perceptions of SMM and local believers. The resulting respect and trust were enhanced by taking the local context seriously. For example, we affirmed the Ministry of Education (MOE) curriculum in their struggles to develop a nationally effective educational program, even when SMM was ordered to include the teaching of Islam. Boarding schools provided in-depth involvement with students and parents, who came from all parts of Somalia, and day schools and evening classes provided opportunities for women and girls. Additionally, the nursing school provided an opportunity for young women and men to train at a post-intermediate level.

• SMM council members were all missionary men, which was not an example of mutual respect. Missionary women and Somalis were incorporated into central decision making of the SMM disproportionately little in contrast to their unique and indispensable contribution.

• The SMM team developed a theology of presence—of "being" as primary over "doing."

• Modeling a lifestyle of vulnerability was essential for meaningful identification with Somalis, whether by giving up our right to determine school curriculum, or sharing food and medical assistance with our Somali neighbors. In such a context, western missionaries can only live victoriously and joyfully by walking the way of the Lord, of the cross, and of peace. Otherwise our presence becomes an intolerable threat to a Muslim government and people, or we make our exit when demands contradict our terms.

> In your hearts sanctify Christ as Lord. Always be ready to make your defense to anyone who demands from you an accounting for the hope that is in you; yet do it with gentleness and reverence. Keep your conscience clear, so that, when you are maligned, those who abuse you for your good conduct in Christ may be put to shame. For it is better to suffer for doing good, if suffering should be God's will, than to suffer for doing evil. For Christ also suffered for sins once for all, the righteous for the unrighteous, in order to bring you to God (1 Pet 3:15b-18, NRSV).

3. Military/Marxist Revolution—The President Major General Mohamed Siad Barre Era (1969–1991)

October of 1969 brought an armed, socialist-Marxist revolution by the military. Although in the name of development and virtue, nepotism and violence finally overruled. Shortly thereafter, U.S. aid was terminated, and when Somalia declared war with Ethiopia in 1977 the Russians sided with Ethiopia, thereby ending aid from either superpower. A step forward during this time was the writing of the Somali language, which was done by government order in 1972. The Roman script was chosen, thereby establishing a preference for the academics over the Arabic script preferred by the most conservative clerics. Drought, increasing clannish warfare, and erosion of national leadership in the late 1980s led to the eventual overthrow of the military government in 1991, leaving a state of anarchy.

Program: Two additional mission institutions were begun—a sizeable secondary school[6] and a community development program. All nongovernment programs and properties were nationalized in 1972 except the bookstore, which was previously sold to the Somali manager. At nationalization SMM schools were the only private schools operating under MOE curriculum, calendar, and administrative policies. The MOE was favorably impressed with teacher dossiers when presented for consideration for further employment. However, all SMM personnel were terminated by 1976, although the MOE Director General first gave official words of appreciation for the decades of fine work by SMM teachers. In the early nineties, these and most of the earlier SMM programs and buildings were destroyed in the anarchy following the collapse of central government authority.

From 1976 to 1980, EMM maintained limited contact with Somali fellowship leaders and a few contacts with MOE personnel and friends. Somali friends in the U.S. and Canada provided another connection.

In 1980 Mennonite Central Committee (MCC) sent personnel for refugee and drought assistance, as well as a ship load of corn. During the early 1980s one of the believers also worked for World Vision in Somalia. EMM teachers returned by official invitation in 1981, but MCC withdrew its final six workers in 1989 due to escalating civil war. EMM workers, following consultation with believers and friends, left the next year.

Worship: The scarcity of available jobs, especially for believers, led to a few of them working for National Security Service (NSS) at a time when believers were under constant surveillance. This had the effect of eroding trust among believers who had already been affected by fierce clanism. Following the departure of SMM personnel, believers in Mogadishu found space to meet for worship in the Catholic cathedral, although it was later destroyed by looting and burning (January 1991). In other locations, believers met together when and wherever possible.

A Somali "shepherd" was chosen and commissioned for the fellowships before EMM departed. He specifically appealed to God and the group for help and prayer support. After his death in 1994, no one was appointed to replace him.

Translation of the Old Testament was completed in 1977, thus making the entire Bible available in the Somali language.

Observations:

•Through the development of a new nation state and international relationships, Somalia became more aware of the need for education, the writing of the Somali language, and giving leadership and direction to the entire educational enterprise. Nationalization was not seen by SMM as a deterioration of relationships with the Somali people, and freed up mission personnel from running programs to relate more with people.[7]

•Boarding students from different regions, clans, and socioeconomic levels learned mutual respect, thereby establishing an alternative community which would contrast in later years with the fracturing of Somali life along clan lines. Character was further developed and evidenced by the level of respect for teachers, including women, and missionary families. Parents of students showed a high level of interest in the best possible education and character-building for their daughters and sons. Today, twenty-five years after SMM teachers have left and students have scattered to many parts of the world, many still view their boarding school or even day school friends as a primary community. What unfolded from the efforts of early missionaries far surpassed what any of us would have imagined.

•Learning even a "fair" level of Somali language has been a contributing factor to developing relationships.

• A pamphlet, *Mennonite Witness Among Muslims,* was developed by EMM conjointly with Lancaster Mennonite Conference in 1982. This statement endorsed a theology of presence, and also covered issues of vulnerability and guidance for engagement with Muslims. This EMM board-approved document expressed renewed support and commitment to missionaries for building and sustaining in-depth, longer-term relationships in predominantly Muslim communities.

•A correspondence course was translated linguistically and theologically into a variety of languages. Having been developed in consultation with Muslims and Christians from throughout eastern Africa, it has been received as a step toward a fuller understanding of God and the biblical scriptures.

> "Now to [God] who by the power at work within us is able to accomplish abundantly far more than all we can ask or imagine, to [God] be glory in the church and in Christ Jesus to all generations, forever and ever. Amen" (Eph 3:20-21, NRSV).

4. Christian Peacemakers Among a Noble But Desperate Muslim People (1991-2003)

The anarchy following the deposing of the military junta has made it largely inadvisable for EMM to place personnel in Somalia. The instability continues in varying degrees to the present time, being fueled by various warlords. In the north (Somaliland), there has been a modicum of stability, with a national, separatist government slowly establishing control, but struggling without international recognition. Given the state of violence, travel is generally not safe except with "technicals"—vehicles with .50 caliber machine guns bolted in back. Hopefully, the covenant for peace affirmed by clan leaders in Nairobi in 2001 will lead Somali to a stable state.

Program: From 1990 to the present there has been a joint EMM/MCC Somalia concerns office in Nairobi, Kenya, which attends on a limited scale to ongoing Mennonite-Somali relationships and activities—refugee and humanitarian assistance, peace initiatives, community development, and contact with believers. Included are brief periodic trips into various parts of Somalia which, in addition to assessing potential projects, have developed meaningful relationships with Somali organizations and families during this disastrous era.

In 1990 EMM began work in Djibouti, and has also briefly placed people in nearby Somaliland, where MCC workers had previously lived and where there is a standing request for more Mennonite teachers.

Because of the anarchic violence in Somalia, humanitarian agencies such as Church World Service and World Vision have requested armed protection by U.N. forces for their service teams. MCC and EMM have not, though our people do accept the protection of "technicals" on a less formal basis when personnel visit Somalia. The "technicals" are the armed escorts that our Somali partners provide when their Mennonite friends visit to discuss program commitments such as assisting in developing elementary schools. Mennonite theologians have debated this. How does the church live and serve faithfully within the kingdom of God in a violent world?[8]

In 1991 MCC International Conciliation Service, in conjunction with Somalia Peace and Consultation Committee (*Ergada*), found little interest from the warlords in the earlier Djibouti peace initiatives.[9] In 1991, a Somali believer trained in peacemaking responded to the call of *Ergada* and his own people to facilitate peacemaking. Currently he teaches peace studies at Daystar University in Nairobi, and from there relates to Somali concerns, especially in Kenya and Somalia.

Former missionaries and Somalis associated with SMM gather biennially for a time of renewing friendships. At the 2003 gathering some encouraged an initiative fielded by Somali participants to begin schools in Somalia according to the Mennonite Mission model. Also, former SMM missionaries meet monthly for a time of prayer for Somalia concerns.

The lack of security in many areas has opened the door for random revenge by the more zealous elements of Somali society, with reinforcement by powerful outside resources and influence. North American Mennonite response to Somali requests for teachers, including peacemakers from the Mennonite community seems hampered by fear and concern about serving under protection of "technicals."

Worship: Prior to the mid-sixties, most songs used by Somali believers had translated texts but used western tunes. Thereafter an increasing variety of original Somali songs (music and words) was written, including during the years of Marxist ideology and devastating war and drought. A Somali songwriter expressed his testimony in a much-loved song (with Somali music and words). The refrain: "Immortal God, Creator of the world, I promise you, I will never fear. I will never deny my Savior."

Observations:

•The Nairobi administrators, though not overseeing long-term programs, continually hear Somalis express their respect toward SMM. "When will the Mennonites return?" is a common question.

•A Somali woman from pastoral background, as managing director of Horn Relief Organization says, "Mennonite volunteers and workers visit civil society organizations inside Somalia, risking their lives for solidarity and visualizing the real happenings on the ground . . . Mennonites are culturally sensitive and humble. They eat with us from the same plate and sleep with us on the same floor."[10]

•Somali women have made stronger movements for peace than men, so that specific ways to bolster women's initiatives are being pursued.

•Among Somalis of the diaspora a number of believers fellowships have emerged.

5. Conclusion

For further reflection, including historical, sociological, and theological perspectives, see "Afterword: What's in a name? Of clans and ancestors: lessons to be learned from the Somali-Mennonite story."[11] This is found in Omar Eby, *Fifty Years, Fifty Stories: The Mennonite Mission in Somalia.* Following are a few "one-liner" examples from Eby's Afterword:

•"Somalis and Mennonites will agree on the importance of identifying themselves in the broader context of community" (119).

•"It was God the Gardener who tended Mennonite life and death in Somalia, and from that seed brought forth the fruit of the ancestral name of Mennonite in Somalia" (120).

•"A conservative way of life was also a point of unity" (121).

•"A theology of peace and nonviolence placed Mennonites in a position 'to give the reason for the hope within them' (1 Pet 3:15) in a gentle and respectful way" (121).

• "The Anabaptist experience and understanding of being a witnessing community, in submission to, but not in agreement with, ruling authorities, presented Mennonite missionaries with a viable alternative to leaving Somalia" (122).

• "If the whole story were to be told, one would discover that the Mennonites who served in Somalia were no less sinners than others" (122).

• "Mennonites have always had the wisdom and fortitude to be open and transparent about who they are, and even under pressure to produce numbers, have not sold their birthright for a plate of beans" (123).

• "As we stand at the threshold of this jubilee year, 2003, we look around us and wonder: where are our descendants who will carry the torch for the next fifty years?" (123).

I conclude with a word from John's Gospel,

> The hour has come for the Son of Man to be glorified. Very truly, I tell you, unless a grain of wheat falls into the earth and dies, it remains just a single grain; but if it dies, it bears much fruit. Those who love their life lose it, and those who hate their life in this world will keep it for eternal life. Whoever serves me must follow me. (John 12:23b-26a, NRSV).

Christian witness among Muslims lives by the faithful prayers and surrender of God's people![12]

Topic Two
Church Formation in a Muslim Community:
Meserete Kristos Church (MKC)

Bedru Hussein Muktar

The southern peoples region in Ethiopia is part of a district called Badawacho. Islam came to this region. However, Islam has not been established in Ethiopia without a struggle.

From the twelfth century the Christian emperors of Ethiopia supported Christianity as the national faith and defended it against Muslim attacks. The elevated tableland of Ethiopia served as a natural fortress when the forces of Islam surrounded the country. However, Muslim traders settled along the northern frontier of Ethiopia. Some Arab traders penetrated the lowlands of Ethiopia all along the borders in the name of trade.[13]

This penetration took root among peoples in the border lands of Ethiopia, including a tribal group south of the regions being Islamized; these people were known as Hadiya. According to Paul Balisky,[14] Islam was introduced by a Muslim leader by the name of Grange Mohammed, a left-handed person who led invading forays into many parts of Ethiopia. He started from the east and went north and northwest of Ethiopia forcing people to accept Islam.

The Hadiya people, because they were tolerant, accepted Islam, which they merged with their traditional cultural practices and traditional religion, ancestral worship, charms, medicines and magic, witchcraft, and sorcery. All these were practiced until the light of the gospel came to the area.[15] The chief local gods like Golfa, Sole, and Bugecho were being worshipped in the area, and the Muslims added Allah. These religions and practices that were a mixture of Islam and traditional religion oppressed the people and they suffered for a long period of time. It was the gospel of Jesus Christ that finally brought them relief and freedom.

Evangelist Tesfaye Makango, a graduate of the degree program of Meserete Kristos Church (MKC) College, received a vision from the Lord in 1995 to go and evangelize the Muslim Hadiya region. According to Tesfaye, in his vision he saw two fighting tribes. He comments, "I saw myself right in the middle of the fighting and was preaching the message of peace and reconciliation to both sides. A voice came, which said, 'Go to Korga.'" The place where they were fighting was in a locality called Korga, an area which was dominated by Muslims.

Tesfaye explains, "When I woke up from the dream, I just took my clothes and a big Ethiopian shawl (gabi) and determined to go to plant a church among the Hadiya Muslims of Korga. A Christian brother confirmed to me that there was local war that was going on in the locality, Korga."

Actually the Korga area connects with Showa, Arrsi, and Wolayta. The locality has been affected by draught and local wars for many years and there is inadequate water for the people to drink.

The Christian brother warned Tesfaye of the difficulties saying, "If you go you will die."

However, Tesfaye said, "It is the Lord who gave me this call, and so I have to go anyway."

Tesfaye shared this call with the MKC regional office chairperson. He told Tesfaye to take a person who knows the area very well. So a team of two brothers went together to Korga. According to Tesfaye's description, the area was wicked and rebellious. Illiteracy and ignorance were in control. Furthermore, spirit worship, continuous tribal conflicts, killing of many people, robbery, theft, murder, adultery, and destruction of houses were common every day experiences.

Within the MKC there were devoted Christians who were praying continuously that Muslims would hear and receive the gospel. They were also praying that God would send workers into Muslim areas with the gospel. Even before Tesfaye and his companion arrived, small groups of Christians were already meeting for prayer and ministry in the Korga area. Muslim persons in the area who had been frustrated in their crisis were bringing their demonized children and relatives to these Christians where the Spirit of the Lord was actively working. The demons were cast out, but in spite of these demonstrations of the power of the gospel, many Muslims remained loyal to their inherited religion, which was Islam. However, the Holy Spirit was preparing many for the preaching of the gospel in the area.

Tesfaye, as instructed by the Lord, made the journey with his companion to Korga. They went straight to a place where believers were meeting in prayer at the home of a Christian sister. The Lord brought a family of Muslim people to them whose daughter was delivered from demonic possession, but still had a problem with her sight. Tesfaye preached to the whole family that came, along with the sick daughter, and consequently the whole family believed in Christ and the child was completely healed. The news spread around throughout the village. As a result, forty to sixty Muslim people accepted the Lord in the house of this formerly Muslim person. Later a preaching conference was held in the place where fighting had been going on for many years. From that day until now there has been no war. Many have turned to Christ. Even mosques are now used to worship the Lord.

As reported by one of the evangelists, Samuel Bateno, from the regional MKC conference of Shone, among these communities where Islamic and traditional religious practices, such as the occult, prevailed there were adverse problems for years, such as (1) children were disappearing, (2) men were dying and the communities were having many widowed women, (3) among new couples the bride and the bridegroom were sometimes getting mad or the brides were dying for no known reason, (4) cattle were giving premature birth or if calves were born they died immediately, (5) the cows did not seem to give milk, (6) there was constant draught in the area and the land lost its fertility, (7) people were poor and living in dire conditions, (8) some became blind and lame, and (9) people were drawn into local wars easily.[16] However, as people repented and believed the gospel message, the curse that had entrapped the region was lifted. This testimony is like that in the book of Deuteronomy 28:1-6 where God himself removes the curse that was in the area because they had turned their face toward him.

Repentance has transformed the life, and the environment. It is indeed a great testimony for those who knew the area before. A lot of people have witnessed a drastic change after they accepted the gospel. Prosperity came to the region. The locality has become very attractive for communities that live in distant places. When they come to Korga they, too, receive the message of the gospel and become Christians. As a result there are over twelve churches that have been planted in the area. Recent membership roles reveal that membership in these churches range from 67 to 671. Most churches have more than 200 baptized members.[17]

One remarkable story is of a Muslim sheik, Hajji Hussein. He had a dream some six years ago. He saw that a footpath came from the center of revival to his house and saw that path spreading to different places from his house. One time a lady from his family got married and became a Christian. He came to her house and he remembered the dream he saw. He said, "The Lord has spoken to me, please come and witness to me." As a result, he accepted the Lord. At this time he is facing persecution, yet through his witness the gospel has already crossed into another predominately Muslim region. Just as was revealed to him in his dream, his home has indeed become a center from which paths of revival move outward in many directions into the community.

For those who, like Sheik Hajji Hussein, come to receive new life, then what? Many suffer ostracism and sometimes even persecution, as has been true of Hajji Hussein. In most cases the strong bonds of the Islamic ummah entwine the person. Usually there is resistance to the notion that a person has the right and ability to choose a faith other than Islam. It can be exceedingly challenging to move from the ummah to a commitment to Christ and the church. The challenge is so great that some might elect to remain in the ummah, attempting to live as Muslim disciples of the Messiah.

However, most often Muslims who meet Christ desire to move into the full and visible fellowship of the church. Gordon Nickel from his India and Pakistan sojourn and Mike Brislen in Djibouti describe five ways that the church needs to be present for the new disciples of Jesus Christ.

1. The disciple needs a church that provides them with security and rest in the midst of their anxiety-driven society and the added stresses which persecution brings.

2. The church must also nurture a new sense of identity and worth in the disciples because society rejects their decision to follow Jesus.

3. The disciple needs the church to help them, wherever possible, to maintain ties with their families.

4. The disciple also needs healing and practical help; perhaps the disciple will lose his job or be put out of his home. The church must be present as a new family of support in such circumstances.

5. The new disciple also needs guidance through the Holy Spirit and "solid culturally relevant Bible teaching" along with a quality of worship, which allows disciples "to celebrate their new creation."[18]

The church must be present with the new disciples, lest we as church become an obstacle ourselves to their growth in Christ.

In conclusion, it is high time for Mennonites to develop a training center to equip people for mission among Muslims. I recommend that we develop together a Summer Institute of Muslim Studies. I would suggest that David Shenk take leadership to organize such a school. My conviction is that Anabaptists are uniquely positioned in taking the gospel to our Muslim friends, and we need to develop ways to equip people for this calling.

ဏ

Response: Interesting Differences
Joe Showalter

These two essays explore ways that the body of Christ is forming in Muslim contexts in the Horn of Africa: the Somalis of Somalia and the Hadiya of southern Ethiopia. The Somali people have been Islamized for many centuries. The islamization of the Hadiya is in process, and for most, their beliefs and practices are a mixture of traditional religion and Islam. The approach to church formation in these two regions has been quite different.

Harold Reed describes the development of church in Somalia as a fruit of a long-term ministry of presence by North American Mennonites. Service such as schools and medical institutions were well received signs of the fruit of the gospel. Although there has been occasional and sometimes severe opposition, yet long-term presence has provided much good will that opened the hearts of some for the good news to be warmly received. Some became disciples of Christ and formed fellowships.

In a quite different approach, Bedru Hussein describes how Meserete Kristos Ethiopian Christians are establishing fellowships among the Hadiya. This ministry is characterized by prayer-backed power encounter against demonic spirit possession. He also describes the role of visions, as well as miracles of extraordinary healings. Not only are individuals being redeemed form the oppression of the demonic and occult, but the whole region is being transformed as churches develop that are centers of new life.

The different approaches are intriguing and merit reflection. The North American Mennonites were communities of prayer who developed institutions and the Ethiopian Meserete Kirstos were communities of prayer who confronted demonic manifestations in power encounters. Both were expressions of the presence of the kingdom of God that demonstrated the power and fruit of the gospel in ways that attracted at least some people to embrace the good news of Christ. In both settings the Holy Spirit has been at work forming believers into fellowships.

CHAPTER THIRTY-SEVEN

Contextualization

Topic One
A Contextual, Incarnate Jesus

Ed McManness

The declaration *"Kontekstualisasi itu sama dengan sincretisme!"* ("Contextualization is the same as syncretism!") woke me from daydreaming during a morning chapel at the Bible college where I was a part-time teacher in a Southeast Asian country. I wasn't being the best listener that morning until the translated guest speaker, an American pastor, rocked my world. He went on to declare contextual ministry was "watering down the gospel" and "falling prey to religious and cultural elements against the word of God." This was contrary to what I had been teaching.

As an adjunct teacher at the Bible school, in this predominately Muslim country, I was asked to teach a class each semester called Contextual Ministry in Islamic Contexts. Of the 400 or so students in the chapel that morning, seventy-five attended my class that focused not only on the biblical, theological, missiological, and anthropological understanding of contextualization, but also on the practical, "roll up your shirtsleeves" and "get your hands dirty" interactive side of contextualization. Part of the curriculum (forty percent of class time) was spent in mosques, in Muslim homes, on the streets, and in relationship building. My mind drifted back to my journey among Muslims, which had begun nearly eight years earlier.

Our Story

When my wife and I arrived in this Southeastern Asian country in 1988 we asked our sending organization not to pick us up at the airport, nor did we want housing with missionaries to be arranged. As a student at Fuller Seminary, I was exposed to "bonding" and its biblical counterpart, incarnational ministry. In the incarnation the greatest example of love was demonstrated to humankind. Wasn't his life the perfect model, "the Word became flesh and lived for a while among us" (John 1:14), for us to follow? So, armed with only enough stuff that would fit into the baggage allowed by the airline, we flew to this Southeastern Asia paradise without greeters at the airport nor an idea where we would stay. In fact, we didn't know a single word of the language of the people who God had put on our hearts, only the name of the city where God was leading us. We hired a taxi and five hours later arrived to our new "home," a city of three million. We found the cheapest hotel in the city, in the Muslim majority section of town, and used that as our base for the next three days until we found a Muslim home to live in for several months, which God provided on the third day!

"Bonding" with the people of that city was one of the greatest joys we have experienced. To live incarnationally among them demonstrated that we cherished and valued their worldview and customs. Yet we didn't know the first thing about life among Muslims, their dress, language, food, how they greet one another, or anything else. It seemed hilarious telling our friends back home that we were "living cross-cultural" when very little was known up close about their religion, culture, or worldview. We were learners. We wanted to model the Spirit of the One in whom the "Word became flesh and lived among the people." So we, too, moved into the neighborhood and began learning all over again. We entered a phase of deprogramming and deconstructing of our "previous ways of life," seeking to model the way as the Son of Man who "made himself nothing, taking the very nature of a servant . . . found in appearance as a man, he humbled himself" (Phil 2:6-8).

Don't get me wrong here, our attempts at Jesus's style of incarnational ministry were feeble at best, yet they were huge jumps across our cultural and religious chasms for this half-Arab, half-Irish Christ follower raised in a Catholic home and my wife of Swiss-German Mennonite roots. The Muslims in our neighborhood welcomed us, though, with open arms.

Incarnational Presence

We wrestled with what it meant to live authentically among these Muslims. I have never felt comfortable with the word "contextualization" because it can sometimes be used to explain a "theological option" or slick strategy instead of the loving, biblical reality that Paul exhorted believers to live by with the words, "I have become all things to all men so that . . . I might save some" (1 Cor 9:22). Paul pleads for a Jesus-style incarnational life among those seeking God so they see the real Jesus in their cultural context, without the baggage that builds walls and barriers. Paul demonstrated this while keeping the Word of God as his ultimate authority (read 1 Cor 9:19-23).

So, in our context, I stopped using the word contextualization because it was a misunderstood term. When asked about our style of ministry we explained that we were attempting to present Jesus without hindrances that can so easily creep into our sharing of the true essence of the gospel. Hindrances like presenting the gospel in foreign ways and forms, using only Greek-formed terms and western customs, have crept in some of the cultural interpretations of God's transcendent word. This can build barriers between Muslims and Christians. I have often wondered, "Could it be that hindrances, additions, and denominational patterns create the real syncretism here?"

Syncretism?

In 1979, Phil Parshall, who has pushed the frontiers of evangelical thinking in regard to contextualization, wrote the following guidelines to help us avoid syncretism while engaged in witness among Muslims. The Bible, along with these principles, guided our team of Indonesians and westerners in living incarnationally among Muslims.

1. We must be acquainted with biblical teaching on the subject of syncretism. New Testament passages on the uniqueness of Christ should be carefully observed.

2. Islam as a religion and culture must be studied in-depth.

3. An open approach is desired. Careful experimentation in contextualization need not lead to syncretism as long as one is aware of all the dangers.

4.Contextualization needs constant monitoring and analysis. What are the people really thinking? What does the contextualized communication convey? What do specific forms trigger in the mind of the new convert? Is there progress in the grasp of biblical truth? Are the people becoming demonstrably more spiritual?

5. Cross-cultural communicators must beware of presenting a gospel which has been syncretized with western culture. The accretions to Christianity that have built up over the centuries as a result of the west's being the hub of Christianity should be avoided as far as possible.[1]

So, how did this play out in our lives, and the lives of the twenty plus gifted teammates (western and Indonesian) that we had the privilege of serving with among Muslims? What essential ingredients opened our eyes to an incarnate approach to sharing Jesus with Muslims? There are several keys.

Keys to Contextual Ministry Among Muslims

1. Be a Learner. From our bonding experience in 1988 to this day we are under the conviction that to learn from others is to truly honor them.

Phil Parshall once asked a group of us missionaries, "How many years have you spent in language learning?"

"Two," I replied.

Then he asked, "How many years in culture learning?"

I was stumped because I had focused so intently on learning the language that I had almost forgotten to have the same commitment to digging into, participating in, and learning culture at a deep level. I was observing the culture, but wasn't giving it the same level of ethnographic interpretation and reflection as I should have. Some culture can be understood in the vernacular, but not completely. So, we regularly attended and engaged in cultural events like weddings, funerals, circumcisions, and Islamic religious festivals. We developed strong friendships with "culture insiders" who assisted us with the interpretation of what we were learning in the religious and cultural aspects of these events. We learned so much at these events for they were windows into culture and Islam, and showed us what was meaningful to the community.

The community included us in their most precious moments, and allowed us to cry with them during hardship. Living among Muslims was not a strategy, but rather an embracing of their life, culture, and community where God desires to bring Jesus as the true transforming reality. It was our hunger to see Jesus incarnate in this event that led us to seek redemptive ways where Jesus was at work and God's word was touching their lives, which leads to the second key to contextual ministry.

2. Be a Participant. Among the people group where we served, there are sixteen various stages in their life cycle. One such event takes place during a woman's seventh month of pregnancy. The event is rich in cultural and religious elements too numerous to mention in this paper, yet contain many Islamic and non-Islamic forms. It culminates in a ceremonial washing where the woman is "bathed" (with a sarong covering her) by all the older women in the community while prayers of blessing are pronounced.

As we prepared for the birth of our third child my wife and I decided we wanted to hold a similar celebration at our home in her seventh month. As in all celebratory ceremonies we held at our house, we began the planning process months in advance by studying the religious and cultural elements through a christological filter, while relying heavily on Parshall's guidelines as mentioned above. Culture informants assisted tremendously with the planning of the celebration, many of whom were Muslims while others were Muslim background followers of Jesus. It was amazing how long it took to plan and analyze and pray through a Jesus-centered cultural-Islamic celebration in our Muslim neighborhood! Our hope was that Muslims would look beyond our foreignness and see a relevant Jesus who can enter into their worldview. Of course the ceremony would have elements of quirkiness to the Muslim on-looker (usually 100 plus Muslims attended the events in our home) because some of the elements essential to this particular life cycle ceremony were slightly altered. In addition, our American faces, our less than perfect pronunciation of their language, as well as the reading from the Taurat, Zabur and Injil (Bible) would strike them as odd. But not entirely! The events were always successful and our desire for them to see Jesus in a different light than had been previously portrayed to them was realized.

Our neighbors commented how wonderfully honored they felt by our choosing to respect their customs, and how close they felt to us. The elder members of the community declared me a son, while men my age called me brother. My wife included her Muslim friends who to this day write and e-mail her with questions about life and

God. It was not uncommon for some to be in tears at the end of such events and would express how surprised they were by Jesus's words, which we read, the prayers we prayed to God, and the peace the evening brought to them.

After the ceremonial bathing of my wife where we asked the women to pronounce blessings and praises to God, I commented to my local teammate that the beauty of this ceremony closely resembles baptism (water, cleansing, reconciliation, etc.). Just several weeks before we had baptized five people in a cold, dirty river high in the mountains and it was not a good experience for anyone involved, I am sad to say. Rivers are used for toilets and washing clothes and sometimes bathing, but rarely, if ever, seen as a place for "cleansing." A few weeks later we baptized three new believers with key elements from the cultural ceremonial "bathing" style my wife had experienced, and it was greatly received. In fact, one of the women baptized in the river a few weeks earlier sobbed during the entire ceremony and finally confessed, "I was baptized in a cold and dirty and unholy river, can I be rebaptized in this cultural fashion that I know and love?"

This is just one example of how we sought to bring Jesus into the faith and fabric of an Islamic community. Participating in such events led to a greater understanding of how the emerging community of believers can retain certain biblically acceptable cultural and religious elements. Practitioners could move forward confidently knowing that the learning and participation process had been filtered through the guidelines designed to avoid syncretism.

3. Be a Practitioner. This new style of baptism was one of the cultural-religious elements that found their way into the Muslim followers of Christ community in our ministry. As we learned essential elements of culture and religion, and participated in their many functions, we prayed for God's insight into other ways the good news might be proclaimed and demonstrated to these precious Muslims. The slowly growing community of Muslim followers of Christ commented that the Jesus ('Isa al-Masih) we proclaimed to them and they were reading about in the Injil (Gospels) was not as offensive as they had imagined. 'Isa had an Arab face and feel to him, he was on their side, and they were comfortable with the way we prayed (both our style and our words) with and for them.

The Word had indeed moved into the neighborhood, and it was a Muslim neighborhood! Serious seekers began coming to our fellowship meetings where meals were shared, worship and prayer styles were familiar, and the word of God was proclaimed in ways not foreign to them. Our meeting place was arranged very similar to that of a mosque where the Holy Book is placed on a prayer stand, believers sat on the floor, and prayed with their hands open and lifted to heaven. Music (of cultural origin) was sometimes played on traditional instruments and liturgies were chanted in Arabic style. These forms were key, but the essential elements that we prayed for were worldview changes at a heart level, which we believed would demonstrate Jesus incarnate in their lives. That became a reality when Acts 2 type of sharing began to take place between the new believers. Muslim followers of Christ regularly cared for those in need within their fellowship, broken lives were reconciled and burdens were shared when persecution took place. One of the weekly "tithes" was when each person brought a cup of dry rice to deposit into a common bag to be taken home to the neediest member of the group. True caring was taking place.

In summary, by living incarnationally we learned the language, culture, worship forms, and religious identity of our Muslim neighbors. We discovered in those forms ways the core elements of the gospel could be shared and address the enormous diversity which exists throughout the Muslim world. This diversity means that a myriad of approaches are needed to successfully share the gospel and plant Christ-centered communities among the world's 1 billion followers of Islam; ours represents just one of many.

It seems rather arrogant on my part to begin this paper with my own journey as a learner among these Southeastern Asian Muslims, and then draw the conclusion that from our humble beginnings several fellowships of Muslim followers of Christ resulted. Ultimately, God causes growth and multiplies our feeble efforts for his glory and honor. Our journey was not an individual one but was shared on three different teams consisting of Asians, Americans, Dutch, and British nationals. Many of these wonderful people continue to share Jesus in practical ways that Muslims understand.

Topic Two
Living Jesus's Peace Message Among Muslims: Rethinking the Motives of Contextualization

A. Christian van Gorder

In act 4, scene 1 of Eugene O' Neill's *Long Day's Journey into Night*, the young Edmund tells his wearied father that he has no answers but only questions about the storms of an uncertain future. While Edmund's statement that, "stammering is the native eloquence of us fog people"[2] may not serve Christian enthusiasts at our Urbana's and our mission conferences as well as Francis Xavier-esque statements about giving up "small ambitions," perhaps we would be better served by more confidence in mature uncertainty and more emphasis on humility in the face of so much ambiguity. Anabaptist mission among Muslims must be characterized by what Gordon Nickel[3] calls a "heritage of defenseless witness" marked by patience, persistence, and humility.

We have been asked to examine the questions of missiological contextualization in a Muslim context. In one sense this might seem like asking the question, "How can Christians be effective among Muslims?" I will frame my remarks so as to avoid covering the same "territory" that Ed McManness covers with his excellent reflection on this topic. Ed responds to the accusation from some that syncretism is the inevitable result of contextualization.[4] Instead, I will begin at the other end of the spectrum and ask Christians among Muslims to consider how an overemphasis on contextualization might result in the breeding of "stowaway rats" able to transmit a deadly bubonic plague of arrogance from the decks of our ministry "caravel's."

The apostle Paul, and Christ himself, have been presented for our consideration as master contextualists[5] so often in the past three decades that we may be forgiven for thinking that a certain chameleonic character was the centerpiece of their ministries. The phrase, "I have become all things to all men so that I might win some"[6] is in particular fashion as proof of a host of Willie Lomanesque strategies to "close the" evangelical "deal." In actual fact, Paul's words must be understood out of his life of tremendous vulnerability and suffering.[7]

The message of mission is the gospel of peace. The presentation of that message must come in peaceful means. The primary call of the great commission is faithful witness and not a perpetual and elastic effort toward adaptation with the primary agenda of being efficient and successful. The results of our witness are with God alone. They may result in developments that we had not foreseen. God's word is leaven. It may be surprising and may result in Muslims coming to know God in a positive and passionate way while remaining Muslims. We cannot approach Muslim "spirituality" as simply points of reference to an ultimate more Christian or more North American or even a more Anabaptistic experience of "our" God.

Regrettably, the frequent motivation for Christians employing methodologies of contextualization has often been triumphalistic, even while claiming to "love" those that they approach with condescension and paternalism. But that might only be what we might call "Triumphalism Lite," the real villain, that widely perceived to be normative by Muslims, is clearly seen to be dishonest and manipulative.

Seamus Heaney in his poem "At the Well-Head" offers us the following lines, "She was our blind neighbor Rosie Keenan/But also just our neighbor/Being with her was intimate and helpful/Like a cure that you didn't even know was happening."[8] Perhaps it should be Heaney and not result-impatient missiologists to whom we should look for direction. As Christians among Muslims can it be said that we are "intimate and helpful"? A sense of what Kosuke Koyama calls "neighborology" in his masterpiece on contextualization; *Water Buffalo Theology*[9] is a compelling example of this approach. Koyama calls us not to worship a God who is first and foremost the "Great Efficient and Efficiency," but to be people who are willing to go into the entire world as neighbors and friends.

Much has been made of Islamic exclusion of non-Muslims from Mecca, but Christians must ask if Muslims are not also excluded from conferences and missionary programs out of fear that they might learn information that they might find disagreeable. Anxiety often parades as expediency or even respect for Christians among Muslims who might face persecution. These views forget that many of those Christians among Muslims that we are seeking to "protect" have actually functioned for centuries as neighbors among Muslim communities. For Muslims, being with us should be in Heaney's words "intimate and helpful" even like a "cure" that Muslims may not recognize as happening.

Sharing the gospel of a God who gives in Jesus Christ will mean the sharing of every aspect of our lives. Sensitive Christian presence among Muslims will include embracing fears about our presence, as well as walking beside them together toward our mutual threat: God's majesty and greatness in the face of our human frailty and weakness.

Can the message of Philippians 2 suggest that one of the primary results of Anabaptist witness among Muslims will be their betterment and encouragement? In the parables of Jesus, metaphors of salt and light may speak of our pervasiveness.[10] They are not allusions to our hidden agendas and subtle intrusiveness. If this seems like an unfair characterization or a "straw-man" rendering of everything called contextualization it would be fair to say that this is also exactly how many Muslim clergy would describe evangelical Christian efforts at contextualization among their communities.

Again, sitting in this climate-controlled environment nestled in the Shenandoah Valley, I am not going to lecture "fish on how to swim" or advise Anabaptists among Muslims how to robe the gospel in Kazakh or Malay or Nigerian cloth. What I am saying is that as we do that, we need to make sure that any and all our efforts and even our thoughts should be able to be understandable and explainable and defensible before our Muslim hosts.

In a real sense, builders of God's kingdom must not be a "threat" to anything but injustice, inhumanity, and violence. We are often a threat to much more than that. Paul called Christians to be "living letters read by all people" with an almost blinding honesty and authentic transparency. Living Letter Christians will be approachable and welcomed and even easy to taste, cups of water if you will, among Muslims. We will be blessed peacemakers and not suspicious troublemakers. Indeed, the fact that Christian (often western) missionaries are not "welcome" in so many Muslim communities may say as much about the nature of an intrusive expression of Christianity as it does about well-known Islamic intolerance.

Invariably the message of Christ and him crucified will be a stumbling block to Muslims as it is for most honest Christians. But J. Denny Weaver reminds us in his recent book, *The Nonviolent Atonement*[11] that we must not present a violent cross in a violent manner if "Christ and him crucified" is as much about "Christ" as it is "him crucified." Christians need not provide additional stumbling blocks, and an emphasis on methodology and tactical strategy invariably clouds relational dynamics. Muslims become "targets" and "souls" needing strategies in a "spiritual battle." They become Canaanites.

Many Muslims do not trust us. Christians need to ask why some Muslims view many missionaries as dishonest. Once at the Pine Ridge Indian Reservation in Pine Ridge, South Dakota, when asked by a Native American what I, as a European-American Christian could "do" he simply replied "try being quiet for the next two hundred years."[12]

When I ask religion students how long was the earthly ministry of Jesus, I often get the answer "three years" although, if most of them were honest, they actually believe it was only the three days or even the six hours that Jesus spent on the cross. Instead, Christians need to embrace the "30/33rds" of Jesus ministry that was "hidden" in relationship and trust building, in carpentry and eating bread with family and friends.

Christians among Muslims need to root our work in the historic Christian commitment to discipleship instead of being focused on an immediate event-oriented conversion. This kind of "Zacchaeus come down out of the tree!" conversion may be different than what some Christians expected but it will, over generations, establish not only individuals, but also corporate communities of Muslims who love God "with all of their heart and mind and soul" and can also fully embrace the life and heart of Jesus.

And here, in North America, where religious persecution is far less likely, it is important to ask where are the Muslims in our midst and why are they absent in so many of our gatherings, even those gatherings designed for their benefit and because of our "love" for them? Their absence and lack of participation in the formation of our missiological thinking strips us of our accountability as we go to work in their communities. Muslims must be our teachers and not our targets. Why have Christians not decided to always speak as if Muslims are genuinely and dynamically in our midst and even to wish, as peacemakers, that we could eagerly learn and listen from them and honor them and nurture their hopes and longings for God's work in the earth? The theological implications of this question need to be explored in depth.

In speaking of the "mission of the Jewish prophets," Abraham Joshua Heschel stressed that the prophets had always to remember that results are always with God.[13] The primary concern of the prophet was faithfulness. Listeners may not like or admire the prophet, but there is the clear sense in their audience that the prophet is inevitably motivated by a deep compassionate agape love that breaks down barriers of entrenched difference. Peacemakers do not seek to dominate or defeat, and in these shadings of the term even to convert. God sends the prophet Jonah to Nineveh not to reach "Ninevites" as much as he does to reach human beings living in a place called Nineveh. Jonah is reminded that he has no reason "to be angry" or surprised at the results of God's word among the Ninevites.[14] In mission, the "I and You" relationship becomes the "I and Thou" dynamic where the Christian servant is the debtor to the Muslim.

Along these same lines, in Matthew's Gospel we see this same power at work when Matthew speaks of his own conversion in a very different way than Mark and Luke who talk about Matthew as "the tax collector." Instead, Matthew records that Jesus saw the man, and not the outcast, and this seeing allowed him to leave his money-table altar and follow Jesus.[15] To use Heschel's understanding of the prophetic life of Jesus we could say that Christ Jesus transformed Matthew not because he addressed his "category," but because he looked beyond it and spoke to his humanity.

Many of us have heard, as I first did from David Shenk,[16] accounts of how Anabaptist missionaries in Somalia were required by government officials to invite Muslim teachers to teach Islam in Somalia Mennonite Mission (SMM) schools. The supporters of SMM in Lancaster County probably did not envision their task as facilitating the teaching of Islam accurately and sympathetically to make better Muslims of East Africans, but this was what happened. Because Islam was taught in SMM schools in the context of Mennonite presence, a presence that was like "leaven," to this day the graduates of SMM schools are nicknamed by fellow Muslims as Mennonite Muslims. And in fact, this request is the clearest indication that these missionaries had successfully accomplished the heart of their calling: to gain mutual trust and build a threat-free relationship living the peace of Jesus and bearing witness to his life. These Christians were not seen as a threat to social cohesion; they were seen as a valued part of the Muslim community.

There have been references in this volume about the Mennonite Central Committee (MCC) response to requests from Iranians to come to the ancient religious city of Qom and join in that academic and religious community. Common "us-them" logic rooted in the assumptions of adversarial hostility (contextualization as warfare) would say that it is "impossible" for Christians to go to Iran and live openly as Christians. Uncommon genuineness fosters uncommon opportunity. What Christian missiologists can learn from these two (among many other) instances is that Muslims are more than capable of welcoming faithful peacemaking Christian witnesses who bring blessing instead of cursing.

Muslims in countless contexts express their confidence in their relationships with Christians who are not "crusaders" (a synonym for missionaries) as much as witnesses and peacemakers intent on building God's holy kingdom in this world. Whatever else is happening in Somalia or Iran, the Christians are not being seen as arrogant or triumphalistic. They are defenseless and not a threat. It can also be observed that Muslims in these settings do not feel threatened by the obvious fear that these Christians in their midst will misuse their hospitality. Theirs is a confident and mature relationship.

Perhaps most importantly, it is people within the Muslim community who are setting the "agenda," making the requests and plotting the strategic goals for the Christians. Dare I say it, these Christians are as much Muslim missionaries as they are Christian missionaries in this trust-enhancing stage of their relationship. And why is that problematic to confident people worshipping the Creator of all the worlds? Seeing Christ's great commission mandate to faithful witness in its actual Jewish context reminds us that Jesus came not to abrogate the category of historic Judaism, but to invigorate and transform humanity to a dynamic spirituality of intimacy with God.

Peter began with a vividly triumphalistic motivating awareness that his way as a Jew was much better than the spirituality of the Gentile Cornelius.[17] Peter "knew" that Cornelius was lacking and deficient and "lost" and in need of Peter's enlightened assistance. A more "Jewish" rendering of this lesson would be that God first intended to change Peter through Cornelius and only after that was done, to begin to change Cornelius. Christians among Muslims are in the same situation today. Methodologies, especially when they calcify into assumptions (e.g., contextualization) can easily become vehicles for presumption and arrogance. What happened in Iran and East Africa (and many other places) is not the "result of a strategy" as much as it is the fruit of faithful Christian witness.

In the 1930s Dr. E. Stanley Jones had something of an epiphany in his mission career among Muslims and Hindus in India when he stopped trying to "win" them and allowed them to win him. In learning and listening he showed those with whom he related something of the meek and lowly character of Jesus. Similarly, for twenty-two years in Afghanistan, Dr. J. Christy Wilson Jr. worked with amazing straightforwardness. All knew his purpose for being with them. Now, I recognize that this might be a "Generation X" recasting of figures who lived much earlier in the alphabet of missionary generations, but the fact remains that Jones' methodologies (e.g., ashrams and sadhu garb) could just as easily be seen as a model for a Christian-Taoistic "effortless effort" as much as it could be for those adherents who use him to illustrate the need for contextualization *uber alles*.

In actual fact, in settings where Muslims and Christians live together any activity done with a hidden or secretive agenda seems fundamentally problematic. Peacemaking is transparent. It is vulnerable and honest. We need to be simple, direct, and forthright while also embracing culturally sensitive vessels in creative and flexible ways. The question then is not the validity of contextualization per se but its limitations, possible abuses, and above all else, its motives. Any expression of a methodologically driven contextualization that is not acceptable to our Muslim hosts should not be pursued. Christians among Muslims should be able to answer any and all questions about our methods and our motives. We need to be "open letter" Christians read by Muslims.

Bishop Stephen Neill long ago reminded us that when a Christian enters a Muslim community they should come with "bare-footed reverence"[18] to all that Muslims take seriously. In October 2003, Neil Postman, author of the book *Amusing Ourselves to Death* passed away. In his writings he leveled the critique that North American society had shifted the focus of the public arena away from content to presentation and away from substance to technique. Is it possible that some North American missiologists are also guilty of contextualizing themselves to death? Have we like the first apostles, been fishing all night in the shoals of contextualization when we should be letting down our nets in waters that are less murky on the other side of the boat? In this journey toward greater authenticity, insight, and more meaningful Christian service in relationship with those who call themselves Muslims, let our Muslim sisters and brothers be our teachers.

∾

Response: True Listening Is Authentic Contextualization
Loren Horst and Joe Bontrager

What are appropriate models for contextualization? The essays suggest that contextualization should not be understood as a delivery system for "our" message to the Muslim community, in which we look for ways to share "our wine in their bottles." Rather, contextualization is building bridges between the Muslim and Christian communities so that new wine and new wineskin emerges.

The greatest danger of syncretism, for western Christians, may be approaches to ministry that are shaped by secular, materialistic, results-oriented western culture. This approach, with its focus on strategies and methods, is viewed and resented by Muslim communities as crusade. The biblical model is the incarnation. Christian disciples are called to witness as salt and light, leaving the results to God. Our primary calling is faithfulness, rather than effectiveness.

Contextualization as bridge building results in transformation of those on both ends of the bridge. God needed to change Peter before he could use his witness to change Cornelius (Acts 10). Our engagement in incarnational witness does not leave us untouched.

Contextualization is not a strategy for change, but is an attitude of learning through participation in the community. The result is new understandings and practices that transform both the Christian disciple and the Muslim community.

CHAPTER THIRTY-EIGHT

Building Peace with Muslims

Patricia Shelly

This essay is a reflection on a journey of peace building with Muslims that Ron Kraybill reported about at the Anabaptist Consultation on Islam. Kraybill's sharing comes from learnings from the Conflict Transformation Program (CTP) at Eastern Mennonite University, where nine to twelve Muslims participate each year in the program, either during the summer term or during the regular academic year. CTP staff members have also traveled to the Philippines, to India, and to other locations around the world to work with programs in Muslim contexts.

Kraybill listed thirteen learnings from the Mennonite mission and service experience over the past seventy-five years that inform Mennonite peace-building efforts today:

1. identity—know and be who we are;
2. networking—work where we have natural relationships and connections;
3. relationships are the foundation for everything;
4. trust is essential for relationships;
5. a long-term time frame for involvement and planning should be expected;
6. mid-level and grassroots levels of the social pyramid are the primary focus;

7. priority should be given to empowering the voiceless;

8. our *modus operandi* as outsiders should be quiet and low-key with accountability to local people;

9. recognize the need for and employ multifaceted approaches to problems (social, economic, political, religious);

10. honor local resources;

11. recognize pedagogy as fundamental—a high priority on empowerment of the people being taught;

12. build collaboratives, not monopolies, among multiple partners;

13. priority should be given to structural change by building alternatives, rather than reforming the center.

Kraybill discussed the dual importance of identifying ourselves as Christians, deeply rooted in a commitment to Jesus Christ and transparent about our faith, while at the same time acknowledging our human limitation in claiming to discern definitively where God is and is not at work. We need to be willing to recognize that God may be at work in Islam and that we may learn to be better Christians through a respectful engagement with Muslims. We may find ourselves seeking to make Muslims "better Muslims"—"better" being very much influenced by our being followers of Jesus.

Kraybill emphasized that we work at relationship and trust-building between Christians and Muslims in a context that is, unfortunately, characterized by suspicion and mistrust. How best do we convey the good news of Jesus Christ in this context? CTP does not evangelize Muslims and asks others associated with CTP not to evangelize in the context of CTP programming. The emphasis is on exploring the ways to reduce violence and hatred in the world and to be aware of how religious competition can play a role in the hatreds and misunderstandings currently polarizing our world.

Part of the seminar discussion centered on our awareness that at this consultation there are at least two different circles of assumptions about what our approach to Muslims should be as Anabaptist Christians. This division is very much apparent in our plenary meetings. While recounting our experiences with culture and diversity abroad, as a consultation group we have not been able to discuss the diversity in our midst. This would seem to be an important issue to engage with openness and candor. Perhaps we need another consultation: "The Church Meets the Church."

SECTION FOUR

Observations, Witness, and Counsel

CHAPTER THIRTY-NINE

Open Doors Through Walls

Bedru Hussein Muktar

May we be humble yet bold as we serve as Christ's ambassadors and as ministers of reconciliation. Paul writes, "God was reconciling the world to himself in Christ, not counting men's sins against them. And he has committed to us the message of reconciliation. We are therefore Christ's ambassadors, as though God were making his appeal through us" (2 Cor 5:19-20).

The call of God for disciples of Jesus Christ to live as ambassadors of reconciliation is an invitation to be present among Muslims in the way of Christ, as the title of this book states. There are walls that divide Muslims and Christians. Our calling is to be a reconciling presence, a presence that opens doors, not a presence that builds walls.

Yet there are walls. First I look at some of these walls, and then look for doors through the walls that ambassadors of Christ will enter as they seek to become a reconciling presence in the way of Christ.

Walls

Some walls are built by the Muslims. Other walls are created by Christians. Sometimes both communities build walls together. Here is a survey of some of these walls that separate Muslims and Christians. Several of these challenges are described in greater detail by Abd al-Masih who lives a life committed to presence among Muslims.[1]

1. Islam and Christianity Are Both Missionary Religions

Many Muslims are "evangelistic" about their faith. They proudly proclaim that in Islam they have a complete way of life. A Muslim missionary will usually come into a new place unannounced and uncelebrated. Many come as merchants and settle down to a normal life, identifying with the local people. Soon enough one sees a mosque going up! They are wiser in their witness than many of us Anabaptists.

Of course, Anabaptists are also committed to mission. In Ethiopia over half a century ago the first Mennonite missionaries began schools and development work in Muslim areas. Why? They yearned to share the good news of Jesus Christ with Muslims. The Mennonite missionaries believed that in Christ God reconciles the world to himself, just as the scriptures above state.

Anabaptists and Muslims go about mission in different ways and the message is different, yet both communities, the church and the ummah, believe they have a mission—to give witness to the gospel for Christians or proclaim the *shahada* of Islam. Often Muslims feel threatened by the missionary commitments of the church, and Christians likewise can feel threatened by the mission of the Muslims. This can raise barriers as each community seeks to protect themselves from the missionary outreach of the other community.

2. The Goal of Islam Is to Extend the Dar al Islam Throughout the World; the Goal of the Church Is to Extend the Kingdom of God Throughout the World

Many Muslims are committed to a worldwide Islamic empire wherein Muslims would have the power and authority to be a witness over the nations. Although the New Testament vision of the kingdom of God is very different than that of Islam, nevertheless Jesus Christ commanded his disciples to "make disciples of all nations."

Through its long and amazing history, Islam has born witness to its inherent urge for an empire; the church has also too often been engaged in empire building, although the kingdom of God as proclaimed by Jesus is very different than either the Christian or the Muslim empires. Throughout history and in our generation we have seen a collision between these two empires, the Islamic empire and the Christian empire. That collision builds walls. Yet it is important to recognize that the kingdom of Jesus Christ is not an empire, for it is totally based on love and voluntary commitment. Empires use force; not so the kingdom of Jesus Christ. However, empires build walls for they control territory and people forcefully.

3. Islamic Orthodoxy Refuses to Dichotomize Between the Sacred and the Secular, the Religious and the Political

In contrast to the Islamic ideal of the union of the religious and the political, there is a deep conviction among many Muslims that the separation of church and state in the west has contributed to secularism and moral decline in western societies. For Muslims, communism, of course, is a classic example. Yet the same applies to the liberal democracies of the west and to the capitalist system. They believe that Islam is the cure to all political ills and social decadence. To this end, there are some movements in the Muslim world that pursue Islamic political dominance and control wherever possible.

However, it is important to realize that not all Muslims support the Islamic political agenda. In fact, some states with majority Muslim populations have embraced secularist or pluralist constitutions that resist the goals of political Islam, as for example Indonesia or Turkey. Nevertheless, there are movements that champion the Islamic political mission.

The politicized expressions of Islam is often a concern for the church and western societies, for separation of church and state and liberal democracy are core values of the west. The Islamic political agenda seems to challenge those core values. These tensions are global, not just a tension between the Euro-American west and Islam. For example, this tension touches almost every African country, for some expressions of the Islamic political agenda are present throughout the continent. Of course, many African nations and communities strongly resist the Islamic political agenda. These divergent visions build walls! Sudan is a tragic example of how high those walls can become.

4. The Rich Arabic Countries Are Determined to Spread the Islamic Faith and Culture Throughout the World

Arab petro-dollars are invested in spreading Islam. In an earlier era there were finances from the west that supported the growth of Christian missions and churches in many parts of the developing world. Today it is Arab-Islamic wealth that is being invested in Muslim mission.

Though we Africans have been liberated from western imperialism, there is concern that a new challenge to our freedoms and national identity is at hand. We may still face an Islamic economic imperialism, as well as religious and cultural imperialism. From time to time political leaders rise that want to exploit the opportunity of money from the Arab countries by even declaring their countries to be Islamic states. These political forces pushing in various directions can sow mistrust and build walls.

5. Theology Is an Obstacle

Muslims are perplexed and often dismayed by the Christian confession that Jesus is the Son of God, the belief in God as Trinity, and the crucifixion of Jesus Christ. These core beliefs of the church are in deep divergence with Muslim beliefs that God is utterly unitary and that the sovereignty and power of God mean that the crucifixion of the Messiah is an anomaly and impossible. Part of the Muslim objections is rooted in misunderstandings, to be sure. Yet even after the misunderstandings have been addressed, the Christian theology of the incarnation and atonement is a very different understanding of God and salvation than that of Islam.

The Muslim conviction that God is utterly unitary and transcendent is impressed deep within the soul of Muslims in the daily prayers. Every Muslim is required to recite their creed five times a day as they repeat their liturgical prayers. The prayers require seventeen daily prayer rounds (*rak'ah*) wherein a Muslim will prostrate himself before Allah thirty-four times. During each of the five prayer times he repeats the testimony of the Islamic creed: "There is no god but Allah, and Muhammad is the apostle of Allah." This fills his deepest subconscious mind and impresses upon the heart of Muslims a strong wall of resistance for accepting anything except what Muhammad and the Qur'an has prescribed for them.

These different theologies that form these two communities, the Christian church and the Muslim ummah, can become a wall that divides us from one another.

6. The Many Divisions Among the Christians (Denominations)

Muslims believe that they have a mission to help the church acquire unity by providing a clear and simple theology. The divisions in the church convinces many Muslims that they really do have an important mission to help Christians find the truth and become a unified community under the authority of the one true faith: Islam.

Of course, Muslims also have their divisions: Sunnis, Sufis, or Shi'ites, and many other tensions within the Muslim communities as well. Nevertheless, divisiveness within both the Muslim and Christian communities can create barriers of misunderstanding, hostility, and confusion.

7. Muslims Have Never Forgotten the Crusades

Of course the word *crusade* is derived from the cross. The Crusades distorted the cross turning it into a sign of violence. This is one reason that the cross is so offensive to Muslims. It strikes terror in the mind—a sign of Christian violence against Muslims. The current American-led war on terrorism strikes many Muslims as a repeat of the eleventh-century crusades when the Christian west invaded Muslim territory.

Equally serious is the rise of Islamic jihadism in recent times. Occasionally the jihad movements target the church in regions such as northern Nigeria or Indonesia. The violence that Islamic jihadists champion and the violence of the war on terrorism inflame a cycle of violence and is a serious challenge to peaceable Muslim-Christian relations. The violence increases mistrust, and anger and hostility becomes a wall that divides and distorts Muslim-Christian relations.

8. The Muslim and Christian Approach to Scripture

Sometimes Christians handle the Bible very disrespectfully, even placing it on the floor. No Muslim would ever show such disrespect for the Qur'an. In fact, the Qur'an must be the highest object in the room, never on the floor. Not only do Muslims sometimes observe that Christians handle the Bible disrespectfully, but they are also perplexed as to why there are so many translations of the Bible. The Qur'an is only authentic in its Arabic original.

Many Muslims believe that the Bible is corrupted, and that notion becomes a barrier. How can Muslims and Christians dialogue if Muslims assume that the Bible is not a trustworthy authority and that the Christian scriptures are a corruption of the original uncorrupted revelation?

Of course, Christians view the Bible and the Christ whom the Bible reveals as their authority. In dialogue Muslim always base their approach on the authority of the Qur'an. The challenge arises in this that a Christ-centered biblical commitment and a qur'anic-centered commitment can take the Muslims and Christians in rather different directions.

Open Doors

I have briefly described eight walls. What are the doors through these walls? Are the doors locked or open? If the doors are locked, how should we knock on those doors so that the doors will open? I will not address each form of wall and the quest for open doors through each wall. Rather I highlight one door: presence in the way of Christ, which, as mentioned above, is the theme of this book. That door is authentic for every wall, and it is a surprisingly open door.

Tokumboh Adeyemo describes various nuances that characterize the commitment to presence:[2] identification, accommodation, toleration, conversation and dialogue,[3] open friendship, love and charity, doing good, maximizing the areas of common belief and commitment, prevailing prayer,[4] simplicity in communication—and we recognize that authentic presence opens the door for heart to heart sharing.

Christians have developed many approaches in a quest to find open doors through the walls that separate Muslims and Christians. The essays in this book reveal that for many of us Anabaptists we join hands with other evangelical Christians in seeking approaches that authentically gain an audience for the gospel among Muslims. There is a diversity of approaches that the essays in this book have described or that we are aware of. These include approaches such as Christian radio or television programs, the Internet, videos, literature, Bible correspondence courses, Bible translation work, contextualized commitments to theology, witness, and church life, moving into Muslim communities for employment, films such as "Jesus," ministries of compassion such as hospitals or development work, intercessory prayer and prayer against the powers that seek to destroy and deceive, and careful theological scholarship sometimes done with Muslims. In amazing ways God is using all such approaches.

Occasionally we are surprised by the open doors. I am finalizing this essay several months after the Anabaptist Consultation on Islam—who would have imagined at that consultation in late 2003 that in early 2004 a film made in Hollywood (*The Passion*) would elicit an outpouring of interest in Muslim societies around the world who after seeing that film want to know more about Jesus. We need to be alert to the open doors and steward these "welcomes" in ways that glorify God, minister blessing, and bear faithful witness to Christ.

Presence in the Way of Christ

However, although we seek open doors through the walls, and give thanks for all the doors that are open before us, our central calling as Anabaptists is to become present in the way of Christ. For example, a Muslim might be intrigued by a Christian radio program, but a Christian friend will be so much more helpful in answering her questions and modeling the Christian life that she has only heard about on the radio.

Presence in the way of Christ means that we listen. We remember that God gave us two ears and only one mouth. It means that we do not see Muslims as targets for evangelism, but rather as friends whom we love. Presence means respect for the other person. Presence means prayer. It means faithfulness and patience. Presence means that we welcome hospitality and service from our Muslim neighbors. Presence means that we serve and receive service. Presence means that we love and seek to serve those who seek to harm us, even enemies. Presence does not retreat in times of suffering or hostility. Presence means becoming friends with Muslims.

Christian presence in the way of Christ is the only Bible most Muslims read. However, it is not just the physical presence of the disciples of Jesus that is a vitally significant open door through walls. The praying ministering presence of the church is complemented by the work of the Holy Spirit in revealing Christ; very often indeed this happens through visions and dreams.

Two Stories of Open Doors

Here are two accounts of ways that the presence and witness of the church and the acts of the Holy Spirit in revealing Christ through visions and dreams has opened doors for Muslims to believe in Jesus Christ.

A Story from Niger

A certain Muslim government official was sent to prison. As he was asleep he saw a beautiful person with fine linen clothes. He asked the person who he was. The person responded saying that he is Jesus who died for his sin. Jesus told him that he would have his freedom at the end of April. In the morning a friend of his gave him a small transistor radio. On that day as he was trying to turn on his radio he came across a program where the gospel was being preached. He was captivated by the message. He went on thinking about what he heard. He remembered the dream he saw about Jesus. He accepted the Lord in his prison cell.

Then on April 30, he gathered all his belongings and was waiting to be freed from the prison. His friends made fun of him. He forgot his freedom was from the bondage of sin, but still was sure that he would be free to go out of prison. The day passed. The next day the prison officials called him and told him that he could go home. He remembered that the Person he met in his dream had told him that he would get his freedom. That promise was fulfilled in two ways. He was freed from sin and he was freed from the prison! Today, this brother is a very strong witness among his country fellow Muslims.

A Story from Ethiopia and Yemen

Rehana was born into a very devout Muslim family. Her father was a Yemeni by nationality but living in Ethiopia. Rehana was given qur'anic study by a well-known teacher before she joined government school. She was also hearing about Jesus from Christian students. One day she went into her bedroom to pray, performing her Muslim *salat*.

As she was preparing herself, from behind her, she heard a beautiful and attractive voice which said, "Rehana, I love you. You do not seem to get time to come to me."

She was intrigued by these words. She asked, "Who are you?"

The voice responded, "I am Jesus."

Then she went and confronted her father, "Father I have never heard you say to me that you love me, but this Jesus said he loves me."

Her father was very angry at her and tried to advise her that what she heard was not true. He suspected that she had become a follower of Jesus. He wanted to punish her by not talking to her. He brought several elderly people to give her advice. She could not change. And the only punishment he thought was to send her to Yemen to his relatives and get more qur'anic education. She was sent to Yemen, but could not leave the Christian faith. There in Yemen she found Christian sisters and became a very strong believer. She is now living by herself, renting a house and having fellowship with other Christians.

The Holy Spirit Opens Doors

These accounts are only illustrations of the work of the Holy Spirit in opening doors through the walls as Christians meet Muslims. It is the Holy Spirit who leads the way in opening the doors. The calling of the church is to follow the leading of the Holy Spirit and heed the calling to become present in the way of Christ. The Holy Spirit cannot open the doors alone; neither can the church in its own power and strategizing open doors through the walls. The walls are too thick and strong and resistant for us in our own power to go through. However, the Holy Spirit does not despair, and wherever the church heeds the mind of the Spirit, doors open through the walls, and behold there is a welcome for the church to become present among Muslims in the way of Christ, bearing witness to new life.

"These are the words of him who is holy and true, who holds the key of David. What he opens no one can shut, and what he shuts no one can open. I know your deeds. See, I have placed before you an open door that no one can shut. I know that you have little strength, yet you have kept my word and have not denied my name" (Rev 3:7-8).

As the Holy Spirit opens doors, we need to be committed to cooperating with the Holy Spirit in entering those doors and in the servant spirit of Christ, invite our Muslim friends to the new life in Christ.

"The Spirit and the bride say, 'Come!' And let him who hears say, 'Come!' Whoever is thirsty, let him come; and whoever wishes, let him take the free gift of the water of life" (Rev 22:17).

CHAPTER FORTY

Questions Muslims Address to the Church: An Anabaptist Response

David W. Shenk

In the Mennonite journey among the Somali Muslims we were always guests—usually honored and appreciated guests. We were welcome because we were present as servants, and the ministries we shared were greatly appreciated. The Somalis provided a home, a place in their hearts and land for their Mennonite guests because we sat and walked and ate and worked together with them. We drank tea in their kiosks, traveled in their buses, visited in their homes, and hosted them in our homes. We became friends.

We developed friendships that both Somali Muslims and Mennonite Christians treasure. Within those friendships, our Muslim friends often presented pertinent questions. We Mennonites also asked questions of our Muslim friends as we sought to understand the inner soul of Somali Islam. Such questions persist wherever Christians and Muslims meet in trusting relations. Recently I have been reading early Muslim-Christian dialogues.[1] The same questions persisted in the first centuries of the Muslim movement that engage Muslims and Christians today.

The questions are exceedingly pertinent, certainly because

Muslims deserve and want response to their questions, and because it is essential that Christians understand Islam and their Muslim friends. However, at least equally significant is that the probing nature of the Muslim questions calls for reflection and response within the soul of the Christian. The Muslim questions, when deeply heard, can clarify within the Christian soul the nature of the gospel as well as the meaning of Islam. I believe we need to receive the Muslim questions as a gift to the church.

This essay focuses especially on persistent questions that Muslims bring to the "tea shop" when Christians and Muslims meet. It is not an exploration of the questions and concerns that Christians bring to the table when they engage Muslims in dialogue.

I highlight seven core themes that are persistently present within the Muslim questions to the church: (1) witness and conversion, (2) faith and the secular, (3) church and state, (4) place and diversity, (5) Jesus and Trinity, (6) power and the cross, (7) the Bible and revelation.

1. Witness and Conversion

Perhaps on a crowded bus, or in tranquil tea-drinking on our veranda, a Somali would ask, "Why are you here?"

Behind that question, we always knew that there was a touch of concern, perhaps suspicion or even fear, that our ultimate motivation was to convert Somalis to the Christian faith. They suspected that the friendships and sacrifice and service were really a front—they feared that the real reason for our presence was to turn Somalis from Islam to Christianity.

Within the Somali worldview, any notion of a Somali being anything other than Muslim was unthinkable. In their genealogical legends, every Somali traced his family line to the Prophet Muhammad. "The blood of Muhammad and of Islam flows in the veins of every Somali," friends often reminded us.

Surely the Mennonites could not have come with any delusional ideas that Muslims might become Christians! Nevertheless, some Somalis did become believers and disciples of the Messiah. That was a seismic shock when the homogenously Muslim Somali nation became aware that some of their fellow country-persons were entering the fellowship of the church.[2] A self-styled jihadist traveled many miles to Mogadiscio, the capitol city, to attack the Mennonites who had contributed to this debacle. A consequence was the death of Mennonite missionary Merlin Grove.

The government and most Somalis were appalled and made it clear that there was strong opposition to such atrocities. Nevertheless, the constitution was amended to make it illegal to propagate any religion except the true faith of Islam.

"We aren't pagans! Missionaries may convert pagans, not God-fearing Muslims!" a government official emphasized.

"However, why have you come to our country? We appreciate your service, but what is behind the service? What is your ultimate motive? Is your service an enticement for Muslims to become Christians?"

Such concerns are always present, often explicitly, always lingering within the matrix of Mennonite presence and service among Muslims wherever that might be. How do Anabaptist Mennonites respond to such questions? What is our motive for ministries of service?

Some of us responded along these lines. We have come to Somalia because of the call of God. We are grateful for the welcome we have received and for the privilege of serving the Somali people who have become dear friends. We seek to live and bear witness as people who walk in the way of Jesus the Messiah. As we all know, conversion is the work of God.

However, trust was earned not so much in our verbal responses to these questions of motivation as through a spirit of servant ministry. The great trust-building watershed came in the mid-1960s when the government required that Islam be taught in Mennonite Mission schools by government appointed teachers. The Eastern Mennonite Missions constituency invested time in prayer and fasting as they sought to discern the mind of Christ. By this time there was a small fellowship of believers in Somalia. All urged that the Somalia Mennonite Mission accept this requirement. The North American supporting constituencies heard and accepted this counsel. From that time onward Islam was taught in all Somalia Mennonite Mission schools. That trust-building decision contributed to a legacy of goodwill that receives with appreciation a Mennonite presence that bears witness to Christ.

Ministries of service, quite frequently not only provide space for Christian presence, but also open the door for faith-centered conversations, questions, and bearing witness.

2. Faith and the Secular

In 1969 Somalia was embroiled in a Marxist revolution. The leaders of the revolution wanted to embrace an Islamized form of Marxism. That was difficult! The secularization of the society was creating a theological crisis for many Somalis, as is always true in secularizing Muslim societies. As the revolution strengthened its hold on the country, one night Muhammed, a high school student, stopped in our home for a cup of tea. As we chatted he queried, "I want to be a secular man, but I do not want to become an atheist. Is Christianity the faith for a secular person?"

"Why do you think that might be true?"

"Because the Somalia Mennonite Mission is influencing our country in secular ways, yet you are a people of deep faith. The Muslim missions are starting Arabic schools to teach the Qur'an and they are teaching the students to be very religious, but in your schools there is emphasis on secular knowledge such as history, geography, and science. You are pioneering agricultural development, girls' education, and health services. I think all that has to do with your Christian faith. That is attractive to me."

Muhammad's comments came at a time when I, as a missionary in my late twenties, had just read Lesslie Newbigin's, *Honest Religion for Secular Man*. Coming from his India sojourn Bishop Newbigin argued that there is a fundamental relationship between the Christian gospel and the secularization process.[3] By secular, both Newbigin and Muhammad meant a commitment to authentic development within the secular present. They did not mean secularism, which is an ideology that ignores or disparages God and our accountability to God.

Muhammad's whimsical question revealed intrigue with the secular commitments of the Mennonite Christian way; he liked that kind of faith. On the other hand, some Muslims view the church as being the harbinger of dangerous inclinations to secular ideologies that detract from faithful submission to revealed religion. It is obvious to most Muslims that faithful Mennonite Christians are far less engaged in religious rituals than are faithful Muslims. Wherever I have lived among Muslims, I am usually snugly asleep at 5:00 a.m. when my Muslim neighbors slip out of bed and down the street to the mosque to perform *salat*.

Divergence between a Muslim and a Christian in regard to faith and the secular may be seen in the different accounts of Adam and Eve in the garden. In the biblical account they were created in God's image with the responsibility to name the animals. In fact, God's first commands to Adam and Eve were all secular commands: have children, have dominion, till the ground, trim the trees, name the animals. However, in the qur'anic account Adam is the *khalifa* (caretaker), and God teaches Adam the names of all creation. God also sends the religion of Islam down to Adam. Thus in the biblical accounts God entrusted and empowered humankind with astonishing authority, while in the Qur'an we are informed that God taught and instructed Adam on his responsibilities as caretaker of the good earth.

The Qur'an of Islam is understood to transcend history and the secular. Although the message is intended to impact human relationships within the secular, the Qur'an as such is not affected by the historical or the secular. Of course, Muslims are committed to the unity of the religious and the secular under the will of God, and they frequently accuse Christians of dividing the two. Yet in the New Testament secular and the sacred are surprisingly united, in fact, scandalously so from a Muslim perspective.

In the Christian faith the incarnation of God in Christ is an astonishingly secular event. God in Christ is clothed within the material and secular. The material bread and wine of the communion service are signs of God in Christ present and suffering and dying and resurrecting within the secular. Christians confess that the future kingdom is beginning now within the secular. All of this means that Christ and the faithful church is the harbinger of authentic secular development: good news for the poor, sight for the blind, release for the captives, food for the hungry (Luke 4:18-19). Church is the primary, often the only, development community in the developing world. Governments or agencies might initiate development projects, but communities of development are principally church communities.

Muhammad's question is not an isolated quest. One of the most perplexing arenas of turmoil within modern Muslim communities is exactly the issue of faith for a modernizing secularizing world. Muslims believe that Islam is the perfect *diin* (religion). Yet for multitudes of Muslims the requirements of religion and religious law is experienced as burdensome. That is one of the reasons for intrigue about the Christian faith.

A Muslim theologian, international leader, and teacher among Muslims commented to me not long ago, "For me as a Muslim, it would be enormously freeing to become a Christian."

How should Anabaptist Mennonites respond to that yearning for a faith that frees? How do we respond to Muhammad's question: Is the Christian faith the faith for a secular person? Should an encouragement of the secularization process be an authentic intention of Mennonite presence among Muslims? How should Mennonites relate to the tensions that modernizing and secularizing forces bring into Muslim societies? When secular forces champion irreligion or atheism, can Muslims and Mennonites work together in confronting atheistic ideologies?

3. Church and State

Islam is committed to *tawhid*, the oneness of God. Muslim theologians insist that tawhid also applies to God's will and the unity of all things under his sovereign will. Ali Sahri'ati is an Iranian Muslim sociologist-theologian who has been a leading conceptualizer for the Iranian Muslim revolution of the last twenty-five years. Tawhid is the bedrock of his philosophy. He insists that there is one God and one will of God and any deviation from full submission to God's one will is *shirk*, a sin as pernicious as polytheism.[4]

Islam resists any notions that God's will is divided, with one will for the public order and the other for the private life, with one will for the sacred and another for the secular. Thus it seems to Muslims that the separation of church and state that has increasingly characterized modern western societies is because of the rejection of the ethics of Jesus within the public arena. A state does not function on the principles of nonviolence. That is one reason Anabaptists have always insisted on the separation of church and state. But the Muslim question is this: Don't Anabaptists abandon responsibility for the actions of the state? Isn't the theology of separation and abandonment of the vision that all things must come under the rule of God?

There have been several references in some of the preceding chapters about the Iranian Shi'ite and Mennonite dialogues. In the October 2002 dialogue at the Toronto School of Theology, my presentation reflected on the ethics of the way of the cross. Jesus even freed the betrayer, Judas, to continue on his treacherous way. I insisted that the way of Jesus does not coerce; rather, the kingdom of God breaks into our experience in the suffering love revealed in Jesus who forgives his enemies who have nailed him to the cross.

The Iranian respondent commented, "This is a very wonderful ethic for monks. But what does this have to do with those of us who have political power and responsibilities?"

In his address at An Anabaptist Consultation on Islam, Lamin Sanneh mulled over the dilemmas of attempting to organize a state or a society on the ethical foundations of Jesus. He alluded to colonial Pennsylvania as an example of the special challenges that Anabaptist-Quaker nonviolence encounters in the centers of political power. In pacifist William Penn's Pennsylvania, the dilemma of commitment to peaceful nonviolence when confronted with the real-politic of the state created enormous perplexities for the Quaker representatives in the early Pennsylvania legislature.

Alas, the Quaker nonviolent commitment unraveled in mid-eighteenth century when atrocities escalated on the borderlands between European settlements and Indian hunting grounds. It was one thing to be a member of a local Quaker pacifist congregation. It was another reality to be thrust from their local congregations into political responsibilities, especially when settlers such as the Irish born on the frontiers were demanding war against the Indians. By the time the Revolutionary War erupted, Quakers and Anabaptist Mennonites were totally marginalized and in fact sometimes persecuted. The experiment in nonviolent governance for Pennsylvania was dead.[5] Muslims consider this development normal and fully understandable.

The Anabaptists have historically insisted that the state is the state and the church is the church and any attempts to merge the two leads inevitably into the quandary Sanneh described. Anabaptists claim to be committed to tawhid just as fervently as any Muslims, but within that commitment they insist on the separation of church and state. The church will influence the state for justice and righteousness, like salt, yeast, or light influence. The church influences but does not coerce, for truth revealed in the cross never needs the assistance of coercion. Whenever the two kingdoms clash, the Anabaptist theology insists that the church takes the rap rather than compromise their commitment to the eternal kingdom of Christ.

That is not theoretical; the Anabaptist movement was birthed in martyrs. As noted several times in this volume, one reason they suffered was their refusal to participate in the military campaigns against the Turks. Muslims appreciate the consistency of that stance, for impractical as it may seem to be, it is, nevertheless, a commitment by the community of faith to live within the tawhid of God's will as taught and modeled by Jesus. By way of example, during the height of the Iranian hostage crisis (1979-81), a Southern Baptist acquaintance of mine, Charles Kimball, accompanied a church delegation to Iran. They met Ayatollah Kohmeini who proclaimed a message for all American Christians: Follow Jesus. If the American Christians would follow Jesus, this crisis would be quickly resolved.

"Why are Christians fighting in Vietnam? Doesn't Jesus command Christians to love their enemies?" Somali Muslims sometimes asked me in the 1960s.

"The Mennonites are not involved in the fighting, but rather are attempting to serve within both sides of the conflict ministering to the wounds of war with medicines and other assistance. Some are also engaged in trying to facilitate peacemaking conversations between the battle lines."

"Ah that is good! You are following the way of Jesus," was their response.

Yet there is persistent Muslim perplexity about the practicality of the way of Jesus. Muslims observe that Christians who go to war really agree with Muslims that Jesus is not realistic. So why don't these Christians become Muslims and join the community that has a realistic ethic?

"Be consistent," Muslims plead. "Either follow Jesus, or admit that his ethics are best suited for monks. In that case why not become a Muslim, for Islam is practical and realistic. It is the religion of the natural man."

We recognize that much of the church in the United States really agrees that in a violent world, the way of peace demands the violent liquidation of "the bad guys." That has become the overwhelming U.S. government response to the tragedy of September 11. What is the calling and mission of the U.S. and Canadian Anabaptists in meeting the Muslim community at a time when much of the church in United States has embraced a nationalist agenda? Or when much of the Muslim world nurtures deep grievances against the west? What is our Anabaptist vocation within North American Christendom and within the Muslim world in times like these?

4. Place and Diversity

"Muslims are united, for all Muslims pray in the same way and face toward the same place in worship," the imam in the central mosque in Nairobi exclaimed. "But as I see it, Christians are very diverse, and that is a weakness of the church. Why are Christians not united like the Muslims?"

One in our group commented, "Next week we will visit the Ismaili Shi'a mosque. They are different than your Sunni congregation, aren't they?"

"Please do not visit them, because the Ismailis are not Muslims!" the Sunni imam pled with vehemence. Of course, not all Sunni Muslims cut the difference between Shi'a and Sunni Muslims that sharply.

However, the global Muslim movement does encompass diversity, and especially the Shi'a–Sunni diversity. Nevertheless, it is true that the universal Arabic Qur'an and a Ka'bah-centric worship pattern do create a Muslim movement with a homogeneity that is remarkable. Consequently, a persistent perplexity by Muslims is the diversity of the Christian movement.

However, Christians view the diversity of the church as an enrichment and strength. For example, all across the African continent the very first book printed in vernacular languages has been the Gospel of Matthew. This is because the church believed that the Gospel should be clothed (incarnated) in local culture and idiom. That assures diversity! The Muslim movement, on the other hand, does not participate in that kind of diversity, for Islamization requires the progressive Arabization of culture. This is because the final revelation is sent down from heaven in the form of an Arabic Qur'an.

Christian diversity is also nurtured because the church has no geographic center. The Anabaptist understanding is that the church is wherever two or three or more meet in the name of Jesus. There is no Ka'bah toward which Christians must turn in prayer or take a pilgrimage. Yet the church does enjoy symbols that reveal a unity of faith, as for example the broken bread and wine of the communion table. But there is no geographical or cultural locus for the universal church.

The church is the people of God who are the temple of God. Within Islam the House of God is the Ka'bah, the place. This need for place is a core reason for the Muslim-Jewish conflict over Jerusalem. The Jewish Temple Mount and the Muslim Al-Aqsa are at the same sacred place. The current intifada is called by Palestinian Muslims the Al-Aqsa intifada; this at its core is a conflict about a sacred place.

A Muslim friend asked me, "Why don't Christians fight for their sacred places in Jerusalem, like Muslims and Jews are doing?"

Of course, we are aware of Christians fighting for their sacred places, as in the recent war in Kosovo wherein Serbian Orthodox forces violently demanded control over their sacred sites. Nevertheless, what is an Anabaptist-New Testament response to conflict over sacred places?

I shared with my Muslim friend that in the Christian journey the place is wherever believers gather in Jesus's name, for the temple of God is the people of God. For Anabaptist Christians there is neither a Christian Ka'bah nor a Temple Mount.

Is the absence of a geographical place in the Christian movement a weakness when compared to the Muslim movement? Missiologist Andrew Walls observed in a consultation at the Overseas Missions Study Center in New Haven (December 6-8, 2002) that the Christian movement with no geographical center has waned in strength in the regions of its origin and has gained strength on the peripheries, whereas the Muslim movement, with its geographical center in the Ka'bah, has always maintained its greatest strength close to its center.

An analogy for Mennonite Anabaptists is that the only region in the world where the movement is declining in membership is within the regions of the European origins of the movement, and the regions of greatest growth are within the younger churches, and especially Africa. Walls' question is whether the absence of place within the Christian movement contributes to malaise at the places of origin with strength on the new peripheries.

How do Anabaptists respond to that observation? How do we respond to the Muslim need for place? Christ himself had no place. He was born on the periphery, in a cattle stall. In a quite astonishing way the Christian movement is revitalized again and again throughout its journey as a movement energized within the placeless margins. In fact, within the current Palestinian-Israeli impasse, the Palestinian Christians have become a people on the margins. Although they are a miniscule community, they have a stubborn vitality that does not suggest the malaise that Andrew Walls speaks about. Decline in numbers does not necessarily suggest a decline in vitality.

What is the Anabaptist-Mennonite vocation within this conflict? What is the Anabaptist calling at a time when there is a deepening alliance between much of the mainstream North American evangelical community and Israel? How do we respond to Muslim and Palestinian concerns and frustration in regard to that alliance? Do Anabaptists, who are marginal to mainstream Christendom, have a vocation to identify with and encourage those marginalized minority Middle Eastern Christians who are committed to be a reconciling presence and witness in a tragically volatile situation?

5. Jesus and the Trinity

After an afternoon of very energetic conversation with Muslim student leaders in the Islamic Center in the heart of Sarajevo, I commented, "A guest joined our circle this afternoon and he persisted in making his presence felt."

All participants agreed. The guest was Jesus.

Tarif Khalidi of Harvard University observes that with remarkable persistence Jesus occupies the conversation when Muslims and Christians meet. Who is Jesus? That question unites and divides Christians and Muslims as no other theme.[6]

"Do you believe Jesus is the Son of God?" shouted a passenger above the pop music in a bus wending through the bush in Somalia. He addressed that question to me when he learned that I was a Christian.

Certainly a dimension of the question is nurtured in distortions of the incarnation that are embedded within the Qur'an. Here are several pertinent examples of the distortions. To many Muslims, Christians believe that God begot a son through a consort. God takes unto himself associates. Christ is one of two gods. God is Christ. (New Testament theology proclaims that Christ is God, not that God is Christ.)

Christian theological jargon often does not help to clarify the muddle. Facing the Dome of the Rock Mosque in Jerusalem is a church with this inscription: To Mary the Mother of God. And Muslims observe that Christian prayers sometimes sound as though we are addressing a gentle Savior God called Jesus beseeching him to implore an angry Creator God to forgive us.

Equally perplexing is the Christian confession of God as Trinity. Although the Qur'an does refer to God as creator and to the Holy Spirit and to Jesus the Messiah as the Word of God and Spirit of God, Trinity is construed in the minds of many Muslims as meaning a tritheism of father, mother, and child divinities. Such misperceptions must be addressed if Muslims are to ever give any credence to the gospel.

How do Anabaptist Christians live by this counsel from the pen of Peter? "But in your hearts set apart Christ as Lord. Always be prepared to give an answer to everyone who asks you to give the reason for the hope that you have. But do this with gentleness and respect" (1 Pet 3:15). We recognize that the Muslim objections to Jesus as Son of God and God as Trinity are significantly formed by misinformation. However, we also recognize that there are persistent theological reasons for the objections as well. (The incarnation and Trinity are explored in some depth in chapters 28 and 29.)

In Islam God sends his will down, but he does not personally seek us. Absent in the Qur'an are the images of God as the Father in the account of the prodigal son described in Luke's Gospel, who abandons his dignity to redeem his lost son or God as the Good Shepherd of John's Gospel who seeks and rescues his lost sheep in the wilderness. In Islam God is transcendent, he is merciful, but he is never affected by what we do. So there is very little theological space for the God who seeks us, encounters us, and who enters our history in Christ as redeemer.

In the book, *A Muslim and a Christian in Dialogue*, Badru Kateregga and I comment in our concluding paragraphs that the core divergence we have experienced in our dialogue is this question: How much does God love? In Islam the merciful and compassionate Allah sends his will down to us. In the gospel God in Christ enters our history and experience so fully that he suffers for us, because of us, and with us.[7]

One afternoon I heard a loud, "Hodi," at our door. We were living in Eastleigh, Nairobi, within the Somali-Muslim part of the city and across the street from a mosque. I met Abdulgani at the door, and he blurted in anger, "Your teaching that there are three gods must stop!"

He refused my offer of tea and a chat.

He persisted, "You are teaching about the Trinity!"

I responded, "The Trinity is not about three gods. Rather Trinity means that you and I should love each other!"

He was quite surprised.

I continued, "If the word Trinity is not helpful, we can disregard the term. It is not a biblical term, although most Christians find it to be a helpful way to express in human language the way we experience God.

"We experience God as the one who loves us totally. This means that within God there is loving, self-giving fellowship. But God does not keep his love within himself. No indeed! God reaches out to all humanity in loving commitment. He has revealed his love for us fully in Jesus the Messiah, who had a prefect relationship with God. When we meet the Messiah we are meeting God's full loving presence among us. And through the Holy Spirit, we are invited and empowered to love one another in the same way that the Messiah loves us. So Trinity means that God the Father and Creator of us all has revealed his love for us fully in the Messiah and through his Holy Spirit he empowers us to love one another as God loves within himself. Indeed you and I should love and serve one another!"

Abdulgani responded, "If that is what Trinity means, it is very good!" Ever after that he referred to me as brother Daud.

Miroslav Volf, in his book *After Our Likeness, the Church as the Image of the Trinity,* explores how our understanding of God forms our communities of faith. His perception is that an Anabaptist theology of Trinity is relational and egalitarian rather than philosophical or hierarchical. He believes that a relational, loving, self-giving, serving understanding of God as Trinity forms communities of faith as fellowships. A self-giving Trinitarian theology forms church governance that is best described as servant leadership.[8]

Volf does not explore Muslim theology, but my perception is that the unitary oneness of God in Islam projects brittleness into the community of faith that makes diversity a theological conundrum. As for leadership, the primary role of the imam is to inform and lead in worship.

God as Trinity has enormous practical implications for the community of faith. However, an understanding of God as the one who relates with us in self-giving, loving service means that congregations that gather in the name of Jesus are pastoral. A primary role of a leader is pastoral, that is to emulate the Good Shepherd by visiting the ill, serving the needy, encouraging the brokenhearted.

Most Muslims never read a Bible, but they do read the church. The pastoral, loving, serving ministries of the church are signs of God as Father, Son, and Holy Spirit that is a more fruitful witness and response to Muslim perplexity about Christian understandings of God, than is possible through theological discourse alone. For example, Pastor Lucian Accad told me about his church in Beirut, Lebanon, that ministered to their Muslim neighborhoods during the civil war by visiting apartments and asking if there were any needs that they could pray about. There was much appreciative response to this expression of the church as good shepherd. In fact, some Muslims were attracted to the fellowship of the church and became disciples of the Messiah.

God as Father, Son, and Holy Spirit is God as the self-giving one. Whenever the church ministers in the spirit of the self-giving God, that will elicit questions. These are the kinds of questions Somalis often asked. "Why do Mennonites serve among us faithfully? Why are you engaged in peacemaking? Why did the Mennonite Mission continue in Somalia after Merlin Grove was killed? Why do Mennonite teachers dialogue and respect the opinions of students rather than enforce their ideas on students?"

Then there is one further question that takes us right into the very center of the conversation: "Who is Jesus?" How do each of us personally and we as a community of faith respond to this question that persists whenever the church meets Muslims? In what ways can the church commend Christ?

6. Power and the Cross

Muslims believe that Jesus is the Messiah. That is why Muslims deny the crucifixion. The denial of the crucifixion is an Islamic affirmation that he is the Messiah, for Muslims believe that it is impossible for the Messiah who is anointed with the power of God to be crucified. Without elaborating, I share several accounts related to this theme of the Muslim perplexity in regard to the cross.

At the Toronto dialogues with the Iranian theologians, I observed in an aside with one of the participants, "It seems to me that it is possible to interpret the qur'anic passages related to the death and crucifixion of Jesus in a way that would open the door to the possibility that he was crucified."

This Shi'ite theologian responded, "You might be right that exegetically there might be space in the Qur'an for the crucifixion of Jesus. However, theologically the cross is impossible. Remember, glory cannot suffer!"

That is the same objection we heard some years ago when my wife and I were enjoying breakfast in our home with three Somali Muslim friends. The respected elder among them asked, "Why are Mennonites involved in peacemaking in Somalia?"

I responded, "Because that is the way of Jesus the Messiah. When he was put on the cross between two thieves, he cried out in forgiveness for those who had crucified him. He died forgiving."

Our friend responded, "But that cannot be! The Messiah was anointed with the power of God, and power cannot suffer."

On another occasion I was engaged in a four-day formal dialogue with an Iranian woman Shi'ite theologian in Germany. When I shared the journey of Jesus to the cross she responded with some zest, "I have never before known that the cross has anything to do with love or forgiveness. We Muslims experience the cross as an instrument of violence. The Christian movement as we experience it is a violent movement."

In my response I said, "I ask your forgiveness, and may God forgive the church for masquerading a false Jesus." I was touched with tears as I tried to absorb the awful reality of the distortions of the gospel she has experienced.

After lunch she commented, "The last two hours have been the most significant minutes of my life, for never before have I experienced a Christian asking a Muslim forgiveness. This has opened my eyes to a Jesus I never knew existed."

As noted above, it was just over forty years ago that Merlin Grove was killed by a sheikh who believed he was doing the will of God. Merlin's wife, Dorothy, was critically wounded in the attack as well. At the trial, Dorothy, who was hovering between life and death in the hospital, sent a letter to the judge which was read to the court. The letter said: I press no charges. I have forgiven the assailant.

The court and all throughout the Somali nation who heard this were astounded. That statement is present within the quiet lore of the Mennonite mission legacy in Somalia to this day.

Of course, the Muslim perplexity or objection to the cross is not only related to the Muslim conviction that the cross is a denial of the sovereignty and power of God, but it is also related to perplexities about redemption.

Shabir Ally pressed that question in a dialogue with me in the Central London mosque a few years ago.

"Why," Imam Shabir asked, "would God choose to sacrifice his Son? Does the sacrificial death of Christ redeem you from Satan or from an angry God?" This question is very pertinent within current North American Mennonite theological discourse as well.

In the most gospel-like verse in the Qur'an we read, "Your Lord had prescribed for himself mercy" (32:4). The verse is sometimes expressed in this way: God has inscribed upon himself the rule of mercy. The Christian witness is that the cross is the ultimate revelation of the rule of mercy. That rule of mercy is inscribed upon God himself. In that cross we experience God in Christ with outstretched wounded hands seeking to embrace us and redeem us from Satan, from the justice that rightfully condemns us, and from our own sinfulness and rebellion.

"Oh, but remember, no one can ever take our place. Each of us must suffer the consequences of our own sins. That is the way it is in every court of law!" exclaimed the imam at the Germantown Road Mosque in Philadelphia.

One of us responded, "Unless the judge himself enters the courtroom and takes our place. In that case we are genuinely free. In the Messiah crucified the Judge has entered the courtroom and taken our place. That is the reason that in Christian experience we give witness that we know that our sins are forgiven."

The Christian confidence that in Christ crucified there is forgiveness of sins is a winsome witness among Muslims for whom forgiveness is an illusive hope.

"Why have you become a disciple of the Messiah?" I asked a Muslim friend from Sudan.

He explained, "A Mennonite friend working with Mennonite Central Committee Sudan gave me a copy of the Gospel of John. I read in the first chapter that Jesus the Messiah is the Lamb of God who takes away the sin of the world (John 1:29). I connected that statement with the annual pilgrimage to Mecca when Muslims all over the world offer animals in sacrifice as a remembrance that God ransomed Ishmael from death at the hands of his father Abraham by providing a ram as a tremendous victim (37:107). When I read that the Messiah is the Lamb of God, it came clear to me that the ram offered as a ransom for Ishmael is a sign pointing to the ultimate sacrifice of Jesus the Messiah."

"Surely someone explained that to you," I suggested.

"Yes, it was the Holy Spirit who explained that to me!" Mekki rejoined with a dance of merriment in his eyes.

The Christian confession is that in the cross we see most fully revealed what it means for mercy to be "inscribed" upon God himself. How do Anabaptist Christians bear witness to that conviction? How do Anabaptists bear witness to the redemptive, reconciling suffering of the cross? How do we express the Christian witness that God in the Messiah crucified reaches out to us in forgiveness and reconciling embrace? How do we express the conviction that Christ crucified is the power of God (1 Cor 1:23-4) who is the foundation of the kingdom of God?

7. The Bible and Revelation

Although the Qur'an has high regard for the biblical scriptures, and in fact commands Muslims to ask counsel from those who possess the former scriptures (Torah, Psalms, and Gospel), nevertheless there is a persistent suspicion that the Bible is corrupted and not reliable. This is in contrast to the Qur'an that Muslims believe to be a verbatim duplicate of the heavenly book. There are various reasons for the charges that Christians have corrupted their scriptures. However, a core reason is that the Bible is a history book.

Muslims have their history. It is the Hadith (Traditions) that describe the life and sayings of Muhammad, but these writings are not in the Qur'an. As Muslims understand it, the Qur'an transcends history for it is God's sent down revelation. On the other hand, within biblical revelation the acts of God in history are the core of revelation, and supremely the revelation of God in Jesus the Messiah.

How do we respond to this concern that the Bible is corrupted because it is a history book? This, of course, is the core divergence between an incarnational understanding of revelation, and a Muslim sent down understanding. In Islam God does not reveal himself and he does not meet us. Rather it is his will and attributes that he sends down in a revelation that is suspended above and transcends history. Andrew Rippin, a contemporary Islamics scholar, refers to this understanding of revelation as noncontingent. The historical never affects God or revelation.[9]

In dramatic contrast in biblical faith God enters right into the midst of our history where he meets us personally. The acts of God in his self-disclosure is the very soul of biblical revelation: God meeting Adam and Eve in the garden, meeting Moses at the burning bush, meeting Israel at Mount Sinai, transforming Israel in the exile, and his full and definitive revelation of himself in Jesus the Messiah.

Why does God reveal himself? His intention is to call forth a redeemed and forgiven people who will be his sign of blessing among the nations. This is to say that God not only acts in history throughout the unfolding drama of biblical revelation, but he continues to work within history calling forth a people who are witnesses to his grace and redemption among the nations.

When we developed the *People of God*, a Bible correspondence course for Muslims in East Africa,[10] Muslims appreciated the course. But they sometimes wrote notes saying, "We do not know if the Bible and this course are true, until we meet you." So members of our team would travel to meet those Muslims taking the course.

I am not confident that it is possible to win the debate on the corruption questions with Muslims. However, the letter from heaven which is most convincing is the life of the church. As noted above in regard to the christological questions, the church is the "letter from Christ" (2 Cor 3:3) read by Muslims wherever the church is present. How does an Anabaptist presence express the calling to be a "letter from Christ"?

These are some of the most persistent questions Anabaptist Christians meet in the journey with Muslims. There are many other questions as well such as salvation, marriage, family, women, ethics, heaven, attitudes toward Muhammad or the Qur'an, decadence in western Christian nations, or whether Jesus predicted the coming of Muhammad.

Finally, here is one more question that Muslims sometimes ask that I thoroughly enjoy, "Why does Christian worship sound as though the worshippers are having a party?"

Key Summary Questions for Anabaptists Meeting Muslims:

1. What is our stance in regards to Muslims converting to Christ?

2. What is the role and mission of an Anabaptist presence in Muslim societies that are secularizing and modernizing?

3. What is the calling of the Anabaptist community meeting the Muslim community at a time when much of the church in North America (especially the United States) has embraced a nationalist agenda? What is our mission within North American Christendom?

4. What is our Anabaptist-Mennonite vocation within the Palestinian-Israeli conflict and our role in relationship to the minority Middle Eastern churches?

5. How do we as Anabaptist Christians respond to this question that persists whenever the church meets the Muslim community: Who is Jesus?

6. How do we as Anabaptist Christians bear witness to the redemptive and reconciling suffering of the cross?

7. How does an Anabaptist presence express the calling to be a "letter from Christ"?[11]

CHAPTER FORTY-ONE

What Difference Does Jesus Make?

My Journey: Now I See

Ali El-shariff Abdallah Emmanuel

As the blind man said when Jesus opened his eyes, "One thing I do know. I was blind, but now I see!" That is what I can also say.

I am from Sudan. I was raised in a devout Muslim family. My father was one of the Muslim leaders in Sudan. One of the things he had in his mind when I was born was that I would carry forward in the leadership roles he had within the Muslim community.

My father sent me to qur'anic school when I was three years old in order to learn the Qur'an. By the age of six I had already memorized three-fourths of the Qur'an. My father died at that time. However, I continued in the study of the Qur'an.

Nevertheless, in my youth I began to ask unintentional questions. These questions eventually led me to Jesus Christ who has changed my life. There were three questions that led me to think a lot about the truth in Islam.

The first question came when I prayed in a wrong direction. In Islam when you pray in a wrong direction you must go back and repeat your prayer. I asked this question to my religious teacher,

"Why doesn't God recognize our prayers if they are not done toward the Ka'bah in Mecca? Is God limited?" The teacher was angry and he chased me away from school for one week. I had that question all the time in my mind, but I feared to ask it again in a loud voice because I knew what the consequences would be.

The second question came when I was in the University of Khartoum. I had a friend and one thing we had in common was that we wrote poems in Arabic and hung them on the walls of the university. My friend wrote a poem where he described some of the punishments for crimes that happened in Sudan when they applied the Shari'a laws from 1982 to 1985. At that time the authorities demanded that hands or legs of thieves must be amputated. Some violations of the law required the death penalty. My friend described this in a descriptive poem in a way that criticized the application of Shari'a law. For this reason he was killed, being accused of blasphemy and mocking Islam. This led me to feel that God and his laws are revengeful. That troubled me a great deal, but I did not know who I could talk with about these feelings in my soul.

The third question developed in my mind when I was teaching the Arabic language in one of the Iranian schools. I also assisted in a mosque to help newcomers to practice Islam. One thing I noticed was that these newcomers to Sudan didn't know Arabic, but they had to pray in the Arabic language. The five daily prayers had to be said in Arabic. This began to trouble me. Why must even old people learn to pray in Arabic? Why does God require this?

I did not doubt the truth of Islam. Yet I felt that I really am more merciful and compassionate than God. I knew that such thoughts were very wrong, but I sometimes felt I was more capable than God for I knew three languages yet God only hears our prayers of *salat* in Arabic. I was very troubled by my wrongful thoughts about all of this. These terrible thoughts left me feeling very insecure, and finally led me to the decision to leave my homeland and immigrate to Congo (Zaire). I intended that this would be only a short time away from my homeland.

Then I met a Christian. We started a dialogue for three months reading the Qur'an and the Bible exploring who Jesus Christ is. Then two women also began to share the gospel with me.

I thought, "These two women are Christians and they want to talk to me about God! What do they know about God, and they are ugly. They are blasphemous. They don't know anything about religion and yet they come to talk to me."

However, they persisted and I asked them many questions which they answered for me. These conversations led me to discover two dimensions of Jesus Christ in the Qur'an that I never noticed before. In the Qur'an, Jesus Christ is the Word of God and Jesus Christ is the Spirit of God! It was, therefore, the Qur'an that helped me to gain an increasing interest in Jesus Christ.

Then these friends gave me a Bible. As I was flipping the pages of that Bible my eyes fell on John 1:1: "In the beginning was the Word, and the Word was with God, and the Word was God." I was surprised to discover that the Bible, as does the Qur'an, described Jesus Christ as the Word of God. That realization led me to accept Jesus as "the one and only Son, who came from the Father" in whom God has fully revealed himself (John 1:14). I went to the church after that. I called myself a Muslim Christian and declared that I believe that Jesus Christ is God.

I was attending the church for two months when the pastor preached on Matthew 11:28, "Come to me, all you who are weary and burdened, and I will give you rest." He explained how Jesus Christ could give rest and how he takes my burdens of sin. In that place I stood up and accepted the Lord Jesus Christ as my Lord and Savior. Things changed in my life as I experienced the transforming grace of Jesus Christ.

With my conversion came a great love and concern for my people and my country. Before believing in Jesus Christ as my Lord and Savior, I felt that I would sometime return to my country and help to give leadership to transform my nation politically, socially, and economically. However Christ transformed my vision. I began to understand that true change happens as hearts of people are transformed and they have a change of mind. I realized that this change comes about as people receive the grace and love of Jesus Christ and are thereby empowered to forgive and to reconcile with each other. That is how rest and new life comes. So my life goals have been changed. I now want to give priority to sharing the gospel, just as three Christians shared with me when I moved to Kinshasa.

I also found the answers for my questions that I had during the years that I was questioning God. I found that God is merciful and loving, even to the point that he doesn't even kill the people, but to the extent of becoming incarnate in a human being in order to die in my place to forgive me and to give me eternal life. And I found that God is not only waiting for me to open his door five times a day, he is always on line with me. I can dial his phone at any time and he always answers me in prayer through his Holy Spirit.

Another realization is the freedom we have in Jesus Christ to worship God in our own language and cultural forms. When Jesus Christ came into my life he filled me with the Holy Spirit who witnesses that God is my loving heavenly Father. The Holy Spirit enables me to discern my ways in this life for every step that I take. I also know that I am free from the guilt of sin. Before I met Christ I did not know what my fate would be and where I would spend eternity. However, Jesus Christ said, "I am the way and the truth and the life" (John 14:6). He also proclaims, "I am the resurrection and the life. He who believes in me will live, even though he dies; and whoever lives and believes in me will never die" (John 11:25-26). Jesus has promised that "whoever believes in him shall not perish but have eternal life" (John 3:16).

Indeed, Jesus Christ has met me. This is what has happened in my life and changed my life.

My Experience: Power in Prayer

Yakuta Abdo

Jesus taught his disciples to pray. We need to be taught the power of prayer. That is power that no one can take away from us. Authority in prayer is the gift of God available to all who believe in Jesus Christ. That is the source of power that can change the face of the earth. That is the power that can change a human being's heart. We have the key for all that we need in prayer.

Here is a picture of what I mean. God gave us a car with a key. The car is our existence as a human being. Everybody says how beautiful the car is, the details, the motor, everything. However, I don't hear people recognizing that the car needs a key in order to take us on our journey. We need to use the key in order to go anywhere. The key is prayer, and we receive that gift from Jesus Christ who promised us, "If you remain in me and my words remain in you, ask whatever you wish, and it will be given you" (John 15:7). The key for the car is the power of prayer; the key for our destiny as human beings is being in touch with God through prayer.

God taught me and my church the gift of prayer. God taught me to pray personally; he put me in a corner where I could not go anywhere from him. I learned a lot and benefited a lot by this. I can share hundreds and thousands of stories of what God did in my life through the power of prayer. But I have chosen only three of them.

The first story is when I was in my country during the communist regime when everybody said there was no God. Everywhere you read and heard there is no God. The government killed people like chickens, in fact chickens had more value than human life in my country at that time. Everywhere you went you saw death. People asked, "Where is God, where is God?" Even in my church at that time there were only a few signs of life. There was no healing ministry; the church was just normal.

One night I was doing my duty in the hospital. There I met the wife of an army general who had served in Eritrea. He was killed by his own bodyguard. His wife was a registered nurse. Her son was sick. I don't know what happened, but he had trouble breathing, so they brought him to the hospital and he had a tracheostomy. This child got shortness of breath. So we called the emergency medical team doctor and pediatric doctor. They told us they could not help the boy.

The mother was desperate, just pacing up and down saying just one word, "As soon as this child dies, I will throw myself from this stair, and I will die. I will not live after him. I lost my husband whom I loved and now to lose my child! I don't have any future or any life."

Inside of me I heard God say, "Pray for this child!"

I protested, "Are you kidding me God? Pray among these people who don't believe who you are and who proclaim atheism! No! I am not going to do this."

Yet God persisted to command me to pray. So I went to the bathroom and I said, "Lord, do you want to heal him? Okay, I am praying here. Heal him!"

So I prayed in the bathroom. However God said, "No! Go lay your hand on the child and pray for his healing."

I said, "Okay, I will do that if the mother agrees."

I hoped that the mother would say no. So I went to the bed where the child was receiving oxygen, because there was nothing more the doctors could do. The sister-in-law of the mother was also there; she was also a nurse. I said, "There is nothing I can do, but if it is alright with you I will pray for your son."

She said, "Yes."

So I did not have any choice then. I asked the mother to lay her hand on the child. I wanted her to know I don't have any power, I just pray. So she laid her hand on that child. I laid my hand on her hand. I prayed for ten minutes. I felt the power of God. I never experienced such power before, nor since then. I knew God had done a miracle, but I didn't say it. In ten minutes I had to give him medication. I went in and the child was calm and sleeping.

Three years later I met that mother in front of my church. She told me surprising news. Not only did God heal her son that day in the hospital, but God also touched and healed her. After her husband died she needed medication to be able to sleep. She was taking a lot of medication and then was addicted to it. This was a secret habit and she kept the drugs hidden. That day when I lay my hand on the hand of that woman in prayer, not only did God heal the child, but he also healed her of her drug addiction. She was a high-class woman. Now she was going from home to home telling what God did for her!

The second story I share happened after my husband Kelifa died.

That was a deep valley for me, and I prayed, "Lord, I know you answer prayer. But my husband has died. So I don't know if you answer my prayer anymore."

I was struggling with this question. Then, one night my little girl got sick. She had the same problem with shortness of breath that the boy in the Addis Ababa hospital had. I considered calling for emergency services. Then I remembered there is the power of prayer.

I prayed, "Lord, you told me these children are yours and I am yours too. When Kelifa died you promised that you will take responsibility for me and the children. Now take charge! I know you can do everything. I am not going to touch this child. I just want to see you."

I turned my back and laid down there and in ten minutes my daughter calmed down and started breathing.

I said, "Yes! You answered my prayer."

A third story is when a hurricane was threatening the coastal regions of the mid-Atlantic states. This was in 1994 when I was working at a retirement community, the Mennonite Home in Lancaster, Pennsylvania. A very dangerous hurricane was threatening to roar inland across the Carolinas.

I said Lord, "You give us power. Why don't Christians come together and pray about the hurricane?"

Then I felt inside of me, "Why don't you pray?"

Yet I felt that for this kind of challenge we needed a group of people who knew how to pray and who could pray together. But God brought Elijah's prayer in my heart. He was one person and he prayed and the rain started.

I started to pray and I heard the Lord say, "Take a map and kneel down on that map."

However, I could not find a map so I drew an imaginary map and placed the location of the hurricane on the map. I knelt on the map in prayer asking God to send the hurricane away. The next morning when I checked the weather reports that hurricane had gone back to the sea.

Of course I realize that hurricanes do not always go out to sea when Christians pray. In fact, although I prayed so much, God did not remove the hurricane of cancer in my husband's body. Yet as I knelt in prayer on the map asking God to send this hurricane out to sea, and that is exactly what happened, this answer to prayer was an assurance from God that, although there is much I do not understand about the ways of God, he does answer prayer. He invites me,

Yakuta, to pray and he hears me! Isn't that amazing!

So I want to emphasize that a difference that Jesus makes is the realm of prayer. In Jesus's name we have power and authority in prayer, for we are in touch with the power of God who can control everything, who can do that which we as human beings cannot do.

I conclude with a verse that describes my relationship with God and shows why God delights in answering prayer. "I belong to my lover and his desire is for me" (Song of Songs 7:10).

CHAPTER FORTY-TWO

Counsel to the Anabaptist Community

J. Dudley Woodberry

I have three points. But I have a lot of sub points in looking at the big picture of God's plan for Muslim-Christian relations and where the Anabaptists fit in.

The first major point: remember God's work and plan. We find this in 2 Corinthians 5:18, "God, who reconciled us to himself through Christ and gave us the ministry of reconciliation."

Now three sub points. First, reconciliation has a vertical dimension between God and humans and a horizontal dimension between humans. Second, Jesus and his death are the means of forgiveness and reconciliation; that is the context of this scripture passage. And then the third sub point: here we have a ministry of reconciliation and in the next verse we have a message of reconciliation based on God's forgiveness; therefore deed and word are both involved. We experience reconciliation through Christ and we are witnesses to that reality.

The second major point: note the major challenges and opportunities for Muslim reconciliation with God and within and between the Muslim and Christian communities. However, most Muslims fit Kenneth Cragg's description in regards to reconciliation centered in the cross of Christ. They believe that the crucifixion did not happen historically, need not happen theologically, and should not happen morally. The invitation to reconciliation is further challenged by western and especially American cultural and economic globalization, military and political invasion of Afghanistan and Iraq, and support of Israeli expansion. These developments have created Muslim hostility to the west and by association to Christianity.

That's the challenge. Here is the opportunity within that challenge. Whenever the Islamist resurgence against secularization have taken a militant form and tried to impose Shari'a law and there has been a friendly Christian presence there, in these settings there has been a Muslim responsiveness to the gospel. There has also been interest in the gospel when Christians have been involved in reconciliation or relief and development in situations of political or ethnic strife and natural disasters. So the challenges and the opportunities turn out to be in very much the same places.

The third major point: see how Anabaptists are uniquely equipped and positioned to meet the challenge and opportunities by your Christian commitment, peace orientation, history of suffering and martyrdom, experience of working in troubled areas, reputation for integrity, values of humility and patience, vulnerability and teachable-ness, cordial relations with Muslims, even Islamists, and incarnational witness. So you are equipped as perhaps no other group to minister in the present state of the Muslim world and Muslim-Christian relations if you can corporately hold together the vertical as well as the horizontal dimensions of the ministry and message of reconciliation that God is accomplishing in Christ.

Donna Entz

A strong theme as Anabaptists meet Muslims is the call to walk in weakness, humility, and servanthood. For many that means language learning. Simply taking the stance of language learner in a culture sets up a system of reciprocity where both parties contribute, and, therefore, fruitful ministry is possible. A woman serving in West Africa from an English mission, World Horizons, recently told me about a new recruit who wanted to learn language, meaning make her mistakes, in one village and then move to another for ministry. The more seasoned missionary had replied with horror, "Of course not! That would defeat the whole purpose."

Humility for westerners gets really practical when we have to decide whether to do it ourselves our way, or to depend on the local people to help us with it and make the decision about it. In Burkina Faso this has meant that we decided to depend on the counsel of the village elders on how to get our work done and the village elders also found our workers for us. They even had to watch our house for termites while we were gone.

It is impressive to learn of several ministries that were begun through the prayers of congregations who prayed for God to show them what unreached people group to serve among. Truly we are becoming a missional church! Part of engaging the people among whom we serve in relevant witness may also be advocating for them as a minority or oppressed community when that is their experience. The reports from the Middle East show us the need to empower and support those like the Palestinians who are oppressed. Some places we need to be helping to preserve or restore identity, as in Albania, or helping to preserve a culture being taken over by Islam.

We have heard about situations where the local churches were unprepared to welcome Muslim background believers, as in some Hindu settings. I believe North American Anabaptists serving internationally within a Muslim environment have a calling to not only learn to relate with integrity to Muslims, but there are also churches who welcome help in ways to overcome the barriers that separate them from their Muslim neighbors, and ways to integrate Muslim background believers into the fellowship of the church.

There are churches that welcome help in how to relate in presence and witness among their Muslim neighbors. In Burkina Faso there are even Muslim background believers who have said they are not happy with their current evangelism approaches and are looking for new direction. I have felt called to respond to this demand. At a rather important meeting recently, Mennonite Central Committee (MCC) Middle East made a policy change to give priority to connecting local churches with Muslim agencies, instead of only the expatriate MCC team being connected to these Muslim organizations. This is the same principal. North Americans should not only engage ourselves with Muslims, but help to empower local Christian minorities for engagement with Muslims.

We heard a comment at this Anabaptist consultation on Islam, "Divisions show we don't have the truth." That is a challenge indeed! I share from the perspective of Burkina Faso. Last week we attended a first for us—an intermission meeting in Burkina Faso of mostly American-based groups. The facilitator asked if these meetings were important, and we told him we thought the effort he was making was worth it. At the same time, I had just heard the distress from my daughter's Jamaican teacher at the international school, about the very young missionary children who are all excited about the Americans beating the Iraqis. Yes, we need to work to bring unity among Christians.

"But, Lord, do you really know how difficult that is right now?"

As Anabaptist Christians we remind ourselves that we need to firmly take a step against nationalist Christianity. However, can we really do both, preserve the unity of the church and distant ourselves from the nationalistic patriotism that permeates so much of North American Christianity?

Presence is a recurring theme when Anabaptists reflect on ministry among Muslims. Calvin Shenk has given us a great perspective on that. Let us remember, however, that where presence is done in sensitive ways, the door is then often open to proclamation as well. We need to steward the opportunity to proclaim when the invitation is present to do so.

However, in the three years I recently spent in North American churches, I sensed a great unease among many with proclamation. It seems internationally we work in many fields that are development, mediation, and other areas of Mennonite commitments, and that is great. However, I am troubled when we leave the ministry of proclamation to those whose methods we cannot endorse. We are uneasy as Anabaptists with coercive means of proclamation, so we just don't do it at all. Instead I would encourage us to pray together for creativity to proclaim the message in ways that are consistent with our faith. The first worship team shared with us this need for a third way between weak pluralism and confrontational evangelism.

For me the most helpful words in these essays describing our stance in relation to Muslim people is "Incarnational Engagement" from John Lapp. I believe this means meeting individual Muslims and whole communities of Muslims exactly wherever they happen to be in their faith journey, including the perplexing questions many of them face today, and according to their openness and with the help of the Holy Spirit, leading them to know more fully the God, Allah, they follow in all sincerity.

Lord, are we wrong to desire that in your time, they meet, appropriate the blessing of, and experience the joy of serving, the Lamb, who intercedes for them in the complexities of their particular struggle, because he shares their humanity? I conclude with the words of a favorite song, "To God who sits upon the throne, we sing eternal praise. To the Lamb for our salvation, our song of joy we raise. All blessing, and glory, wisdom, thanksgiving, honor and power and might belongs to our God forever and ever."

Ahmed Haile

In Somali society, when the elders speak the young should be sitting and listening to what they say. So I am younger than some who have written essays for this volume, yet I am invited to contribute one of the concluding essays in this tome!

After the September 11 catastrophe in the United States, when I was in my office at Daystar University in Nairobi, Kenya, one of the Kenyan Christian pastors came and said, "I hate the Muslims."

I told him, "You just told me you hate my mother."

That woke him up!

This book is about Anabaptists meeting Muslims. For me, that means meeting my mother. What does the meeting mean for you?

There are various ways that we express ourselves in our relationships with Muslims, just as the people of Israel in Jesus's day had varied approaches in their relationships with non-Jewish people. We can relate as the Pharisees: self-righteous in our piety and true faith. Or as Sadducees: enamored with philosophical engagement and debate. We could become Zealots: resorting to violence against those whom we fear or who oppress us. Others might take the Essene path of retreat from engagement so as to practice pure religion and piety. Or we can hear and obey the call of Jesus, a call that takes us in different directions than that of Pharisees, Sadducees, Zealots, or Essenes. Those options are available, but in the essays in this volume I have met anew the call for a commitment to presence and witness in the way of Jesus the Christ

I illustrate with a story, not from Somalia, but from India. A mother was concerned because her child was addicted to sugar. So she asked Ghandi if he could help her son break his excessive sugar-eating habit.

So Ghandi said, "Let the son stay with me."

For two weeks the son stayed with Ghandi and when the mother came back he said, "Your child is not eating sugar."

The mother asked, "What did you do to him?"

Ghandi said, "I just didn't eat sugar."

This story describes our calling as Anabaptists for whom peace is a way of life. It is not peace at the macro level that we pursue, but a micro level peace. We show people that we don't eat sugar, we can abstain. We abstain from that which destroys the peace, and seek to embrace that which makes for peace. We can show people this way of peace if they stay with us.

In conclusion, let us remember that our calling to mission among Muslims is rooted in the way of peace described in Ephesians 2:14-17.

> For he himself is our peace, who has made the two one and has destroyed the barrier, the dividing wall of hostility, by abolishing in his flesh the law with its commandments and regulations. His purpose was to create in himself one new man out of the two, thus making peace, and in this one body to reconcile both of them to God through the cross, by which he put to death their hostility. He came and preached peace to you who were far away and peace to those who were near.

Christ is our peace. Christ came to bring peace for us. Christ came to reconcile us with the Muslims and other communities and other Christians. Christ came to proclaim peace. Our mission is to go out to proclaim the peace of Christ. Our mission is not to refrain from eating sugar, but share the sugar so that all may have.

Gordon D. Nickel

In this remarkable compendium of essays each one of us has read something which will stay with us for some time, and will influence our thinking on the theme of this volume: a calling to presence in the way of Christ. This volume is a rich feast of essays and reports. Two especially priceless insights connected with me in the essay by Chantal Logan on the theme: "Women in Islam and the Gospel."

Chantal writes, "There is no redemption in Islam. Therefore, there is no call to radical living." The first part of this statement is a matter of academic fact.[1] The second part of the statement, and its shrewd connection to the first, was worth the trouble of coming across the North American continent to attend the Anabaptist Consultation on Islam.

Thinking of the church as the community of the redeemed seems especially appropriate. Redeemed means purchased—"bought back." It is not a matter of human goodness or intelligence. There is no room for human pride. Rather, redemption is something which God alone has done out of his grace. Peter wrote that we were redeemed, "with the precious blood of Christ" (1 Pet 1:18-19). Paul wrote, "You are not your own; you were bought at a price" (1 Cor 6:19-20). This raises an important question about the shape of Anabaptist witness among Muslims: For what purpose were we bought?

When we think about Anabaptist witness among Muslims, we need to be alert to three areas. The first is witness. Are we agreed about what it is, or more properly to whom is it, that we bear witness? Have we accepted the witness to Jesus contained in the New Testament as the truth from God? Are we committed to both the life and teachings of Jesus as portrayed in the gospel, and the good news of the redemptive death and resurrection of Jesus as explained in the epistles?

My counsel is that we choose to commit ourselves to the New Testament witness to Jesus Christ, and to pass on that witness faithfully to other people in both word and deed.

The second area of concern is Anabaptism. What do we have in mind when we use the term Anabaptist? Have we studied the history of the Anabaptist movement? Are we willing to accept the whole package of the discipleship portrayed there? Or do we simply use the term as a kind of cipher to justify our personal inclinations?

My counsel is that if we choose to use the name Anabaptist, we commit ourselves to what it stands for, including the texts of scripture which the Anabaptists are reported to have cited most frequently when tried and tortured for their faith by European authorities: Matthew 28:19-20, Mark 16:15, and—when questioned about entering Catholic, Lutheran, and Reformed domains to preach the gospel—Psalm 24:1, "The earth is the Lord's and everything in it!"

The third area of concern is Islam. Have we done our homework to gain a realistic knowledge of the faith of Muslims? Have we possibly sometimes settled for what Calvin Shenk has called a "library version"? Have we been able to steer clear of both the polemical approach and the politically correct version? The degree to which we are realistic about Islam will determine the accuracy of our discernment of the significance of the gospel for Muslims and our role as the community entrusted with the gospel.

My counsel is that we commit ourselves to learn Islam deeply—both from the sourcebooks which Muslims continually indicate as authoritative for them, and from meaningful relationships with lively, practicing Muslims. Let us do this as a way of showing love and respect to the Muslims with whom we are engaged.

There is a great need in the world today for humble, faithful, vulnerable, peaceable gospel witness among Muslims. Is this perhaps one purpose for which God has bought us?

I conclude with another simple yet profound statement in Chantal Logan's essay when she describes what women converts identified as the main difference between Islam and Christianity. These women had told her, "I met Jesus!" This reality is echoed in Yakuta Abdo's testimony in her response to Chantal's presentation.

Can it really be this simple? Have we met Jesus? Are we jealous for his glory? My counsel is that we meet Jesus, commit ourselves to him as Savior and Lord, and live our lives in his service.

The Listening and Discernment Committee Report

"The Church Meets the Muslim Community"

October 23-26, 2003
Eastern Mennonite Seminary, Harrisonburg, Virginia

Mesach Krisetya
Martha Yoder Maust
Gordon Nickel
Peter Rempel
Jewel Showalter
Ervin R. Stutzman, Chair

Committee Assignment
- Listen for what God is doing among us
- Pay attention to the spirit and sense of our group
- Provide a place for persons to share concerns

•Identify the challenges before us
•Write a confessional statement of our commitment for broader discernment in the churches

Not the Assignment
•Capture details, take minutes, keep the record

What is God doing among us?

God has granted us a spirit of compassion for our Muslim neighbors that continues to grow in intensity and scope after 150 years of engagement. At this consultation we are hearing a renewed call from God to extend a united witness through various means to the Muslim peoples of the world.

God is moving among us. . . .

The consultation began with presentations on the more theoretical and academic level. We heard concerns that we were not openly engaging each other in conversation about our theological and missiological differences.

God is moving among us. . . .

On Saturday afternoon, we heard a call to "get our act together," to openly address our differences and find ways to work together in the mission task.

God is moving among us. . . .

In the Saturday evening session, we sensed a clear movement from a theoretical discussion to a confessional stance. We sensed a growing desire among participants for unity in the midst of our diversity.

God is moving among us. . . .

We heard a strong desire to be present in Muslim communities as representatives of the church of Jesus Christ around the world. We cannot all do everything, but we can have a common sense of what God is doing in the world and we can bless each other with the incarnational role that God has given us—through relief and development, introducing people to Jesus, Bible teaching and discipling, peacebuilding, etc. Together we are followers of Jesus in word and deed, and we thank God for all the ministries that participate in this calling.

Themes that emerged
•The post-September 11 realities in the world have only served to heighten the importance of the questions we are addressing in this conference.

•The wars waged by the United States and its allies in Afghanistan and Iraq create strong reaction against Christians by Muslims around the world, who view it as a crusade against Islam as a religion.

Process concerns expressed
In the course of our meeting, we heard requests for:
•more time for questions and group discussion
•less narrative in agency reporting with more discussion of actual learning/vision
•the inclusion of Muslim voices in the conference itself

Theological concerns expressed
We heard:
•concerns that missionaries have sometimes been insensitive in Muslim contexts
•a concern that we have not always had a good balance between judgment and grace
•concerns that we continue to grow in our understanding of Muslims, both through formal education and personal interaction

What is the main question in this consultation? (What we believe is actually at stake)
What is our Anabaptist "calling" in relation to the Muslim community?

Our commitments
To witness to Muslims in one or more of the following ways that are faithful to Christ's call and example:
•to love our Muslim neighbors as we love ourselves
•to demonstrate God's compassion for the Muslim community through relief, service, and/or development projects

•to address conflicts and tensions through peacebuilding activities

•to engage Muslims in respectful and transparent dialogue about our respective faiths

•to give witness to our personal and corporate relationship with God through Jesus Christ

•to invite Muslims to become disciples of Jesus Christ

•to invite Muslims into the fellowship of our Christian communities

•to repent of beliefs and actions that pose unnecessary barriers to our witness to Muslims

The challenge

To ask ourselves: How can we change so that God can best use us?

The Proposal for "An Anabaptist Consultation on Islam"

In many regions of the world there is dismay concerning relations between the *ummah* and the church that together comprise over
half the world's population (1.2 billion Muslims and 2.1 billion
Christians). In the wake of September 11, 2001, these tensions are
increasingly informed by a "clash of civilizations" (Samuel Huntington)
mentality.

The complex and sometimes paradoxical issues include:

• Western cultural, military, and economic systems that under-
mine Islamic aspirations.

• Regimes governing Islamic societies that are in certain cases
anti-democratic, corrupt, repressive, and in collaboration with the
West because of oil.

• A Dar al Islam (Muslim political order) that is counter to the
core values of Western democracies, pluralist cultural aspirations, or
the vision of emerging nations.

• Church growth in some regions that Muslims have considered
to be the suzerainty of Islam.

• Conviction among Muslims that Islam has a mission to save
Western culture from decadence.

• Grievance among Muslims at perceived injustices, especially in
relation to the Israeli-Palestinian conflict.

•Militant Islam that is expressed in polemical jihadism or violence; crusade-spirited Christianity that views the Muslim world as an evil to be confronted with all means necessary.

•Search for identity among Muslims in the face of the challenges of modernity and globalization—a search that is present within the soul of Muslim communities everywhere.

•Fear of theological engagement between Christians and Muslims who often do not know how to meet one another in constructive theological discourse and dialogue. This impasse can encourage silence with regard to faith matters or, alternatively, confrontational polemics when we meet one another.

•A Muslim understanding of the finality of Islam that creates for Muslims a perplexity as to why any one would want to embrace the Christian faith.

•A Christian perplexity on the part of the church as to why Muslims are so resistant to the good news of salvation.

Current Positions

Within this milieu, different themes inform Christian thinking. Here are three examples of current positions:

•The belief that Islam and the Gospel are co-equal truths. At the core, both Islam and the Gospel are about peace. Therefore any missional engagement is misplaced. The only valid mission for the church is to cultivate mutual respect.

•The notion that everything Islamic is false and diabolical. Therefore, confrontation is the only right path.

•The conviction that church is called by God to engage in a ministry of respectful presence, listening, and witness among Muslims. This is an Anabaptist stance that is committed to being an authentic sign of the presence of the kingdom of God within a Muslim context.

Focus of the Consultation

To explore the theological and missiological foundations and implications of faithful Anabaptist Christian presence and witness among Muslims in the light of our experience.

Purpose

To provide a forum for exploring Anabaptist learning as we have served and lived among Muslims and reflect on our "calling" to a continued engagement with Islam. The conference will be confessional with a commitment to discerning how to serve as faithful witnesses to Jesus Christ as Lord and Savior. This forum will provide opportunity to listen to the experience and learning of a variety of persons who have served within a Muslim context. It will provide an opportunity for the wider church to hear about the pilgrimage of presence and witness among Muslims and reflect on God's call to the Mennonite and Brethren in Christ churches in relationship to Muslims.

The Forum

Presenters will be invited to write papers for discussion and discernment. The papers will be publishable in a compendium to be a resource for the wider Anabaptist family and the global church as well. (It might be that some of the writers of reports will choose not to have their papers published. Those requests will be honored.)

Planning Team

James R. Krabill (Mennonite Mission Network), Linford Stutzman (John S. Coffman Center—Eastern Mennonite Seminary), David W. Shenk (Eastern Mennonite Missions), Convenor.

All other North American Anabaptist groups engaged with Islam will be included in the consultative network as plans for the forum develop, e.g., MCC, RMM, MBMSI, BIC, GD, AIMM, Witness Canada. The planners will also seek to involve representation from Mennonite and Brethren in Christ colleges and seminaries.

Cost

It is anticipated that registration fees will cover the costs. Primary sponsoring agencies (John S. Coffman Center, Eastern Mennonite Missions, and Mennonite Mission Network) will backstop. There will be no honoraria or travel costs paid by the conference for agency sponsored presenters, for the expectation is that the agencies will cover the costs for persons who make presentations who are agency appointees.

Program

Each day begins with a brief time of worship. There will be eight major sessions: Thursday evening, Friday morning, afternoon, evening, and Saturday morning, afternoon, and evening, and worship Sunday morning. Agencies will present brief regional reports on the theme: "Learning as We Journey."

Presentations

This forum is a reflection on our pilgrimage as Anabaptists among Muslims. The purpose of each presentation should be a reflection on what we are learning as we walk and witness among Muslims. This is not a time for triumphalism, but rather a time for humble reflection, listening, and discernment. The seminars and reports will be informative, but with an emphasis throughout on "learning as we journey." What are we learning? What should we be learning?

Announcement and Invitation to Participate in the Consultation

The Church Meets the Muslim Community
An Anabaptist Consultation on Islam

October 24-26, 2003
Hosted at Eastern Mennonite Seminary,
Harrisonburg, VA

A forum that explores, from an Anabaptist perspective, the calling and challenges of the church meeting the ummah in trust-building relations and witness.

In many regions of the world there is growing dismay concerning relations between the ummah (Muslim community) and the Christian church. Together these two groups comprise one half of the world's population. In the wake of September 11 and the war in Iraq, these tensions are increasingly characterized by a "clash of civilizations" mentality described by Samuel Huntington.

Within the complex, volatile, and perplexing developments of the recent past marked by conflicting political, economic, and social agendas of Western and Muslim nations, Christian responses range from an affirmation of Islam as co-equal truth with the Gospel, to a denunciation of Islam as false and diabolical.

This consultation will provide a forum for exploring Anabaptist learnings through the experience of serving and living among Muslims, and for reflecting on God's call to engage in a ministry of respectful presence, listening, and witness among Muslims. The forum will be an opportunity to listen to distinguished guest speakers, as well as a variety of experienced persons who have been engaged within Muslim communities over many years. It will provide an opportunity for the wider church to hear about the pilgrimage of presence and witness among Muslims and reflect on God's call to the Christian church in its relationship to Muslims.

Letter to the Participants

October 23, 2003

The Church Meets the Muslim Community
An Anabaptist Consultation on Islam

Dear Participant,

Welcome to Eastern Mennonite University for these days of reflection on the Mennonite/Anabaptist journey with Muslims.

We are convening during the fiftieth anniversary year of Eastern Mennonite Missions commencing a journey with Muslims in Somalia. That was one of the first North American Mennonite engagements with the Muslim community. However, in this last half century there has been considerable expansion in Mennonite presence, service, and witness among Muslim peoples.

So some two hundred of us have come for this gathering from across North America and with representation from Africa and Asia to tell our stories of what we have been experiencing and learning in the journey with Muslims. We have come to discern what the Spirit is saying to the churches as we continue the journey.

We also meet fully aware that as North American Anabaptist Christians we are part of the wider global church encompassing a variety of denominations and theologies. We extend a special word of thanks to those who are meeting with us these days who come from other traditions. Your counsel is welcome!

Quite occasionally we meet as Christians with Muslims to reflect on our journey together (see appendix F). At other times it is necessary to gather only as Christians to hear the counsel of the Holy Spirit and discern the way together. That is the nature of this gathering. This is an Anabaptist Christian retreat to listen in the spirit of discernment and counsel.

The schedule is very full. We had not originally planned it this way. However, as the planning commenced, agencies and individuals would contact the planning team asking whether there could be space in the program for yet another story. So there will be about seventy presenters. This should be a full and enriching several days.

In the concluding hours of this gathering, we will hear from a listening and discernment team. They will commend to us and the wider church a statement in regards to our onward journey with Muslims. As a community gathered we will have opportunity to comment and counsel that team as they refine that statement.

This meeting convenes on the eve of the Muslim month of fasting, when Muslims remember in a special way God's gift of revelation to them. As we gather let us join with Muslims in prayers of thanksgiving for God's gift of revelation. In these disturbing times let us in this gathering remember and embrace the words of our risen Savior who, after showing his disciples the nail prints in his hands, raised those wounded hands in blessing upon them and exclaimed, "Peace be with you! As the Father has sent me, I am sending you. Receive the Holy Spirit."

In the Peace of Christ,
The Planning Team

David W. Shenk
James Krabill
Linford Stutzman

Program for An Anabaptist Consultation on Islam

Schedule

THURSDAY, OCTOBER 23, 2003
EVENING   Chairperson: Linford Stutzman
7:00   *Welcome*   Linford Stutzman
       Worship   Calvin and Marie Shenk
7:25   *"The Kingdom of God in Islam*   J. Dudley Woodberry
       and in the Gospel"
8:10   *Respondent*   Bedru Hussein
8:25   *Discussion/questions*
8:45   *Adjourn*

FRIDAY, OCTOBER 24, 2003
MORNING   Chairperson: James Krabill
8:00   *Worship*   EMU students
8:15   *"Peacemaking and Territoriality:* Lamin Sanneh
       The Muslim Nation and the
       Anabaptist Church"
9:00   *Respondent*   Mesach Krisetya
9:15   *Discussion*
9:30   *Break*

10:00	*"A Global Perspective on The Current Status of Christian-Muslim Relations"*	J. Dudley Woodberry
10:45	*Respondent*	Jonathan Bonk
11:00	*Discussion*	
11:15	*Learnings/Vision: Afghanistan*	Mennonite Missions Network (Network) Mennonite Central Committee (MCC) Mennonite Brethren Missions and Service International (MBMSI)
11:45	*Discussion/Prayer*	
12:00	*Lunch*	

AFTERNOON   Chairperson: Nancy Heisey

1:30	*"A Historical Overview of Anabaptist Engagement with Muslims"*	John A. Lapp
2:30	*Respondent*	Gordon Nickel
2:45	*Discussion/Prayer*	
3:00	*Break*	
3:30	*Learnings/Vision:*	
	3:30 Turkey	Rosedale Mennonite Missions (RMM)
	3:45 *Pakistan*	MBMSI
	4:00 *India*	MBMSI
	4:15 *Iran*	MCC/Network
4:45	*Discussion/Prayer*	
5:00	*Adjourn*	

EVENING   Chairperson: Jewel Showalter

7:00	*Learnings/Vision:*	
	7:00 *Indonesia*	Lawrence Yoder, Mesach Krisetya
	7:20 *Dagestan*	Network
	7:40 *Middle East*	Network/Eastern Mennonite Missions (EMM)/MCC
	8:10 *Albania/Kosovo*	Virginia Mennonite Board of Missions/EMM/Network/MCC
	8:25 *Uzbekistan/Central Asia*	EMM
8:40	*Discussion/Prayer*	

9:00   *Adjourn*

SATURDAY, OCTOBER 25, 2003
MORNING   Chairperson:
                                               Richard Showalter

8:00   *Worship*   Mesach Krisetya,
                                               James Krabill
8:15   *"Women in Islam and the Gospel"*   Chantal Logan
          Moderator: Bertha Beachy
8:45   *Respondent*   Yakuta Abdo
8:55   *Discussion*
9:10   *Break*

       SEMINARS
9:25   Session One   Presenter(s)   Chair

       • *Secularization*   Roy Hange   *John F. Lapp*
         and Democracy
       • *Suffering*   Yakuta Abdo,   *Tim Bergdahl*
                                Richard Showalter
       • *Contextualization*   Ed McManness,   *Loren Horst*
                                Chris van Gorder
       • *Presence*   Donna Entz,   *Walter Sawatsky*
         and Patience   Bertha Beachy,
                                Calvin Shenk
       • *Pacifism among*   Lamin Sanneh,   *Susan Harrison*
         Muslims   Mike Brislen
       • *Apologetics*   Abd el Rab and   *William Sahawneh*
                                Adana Abd el Rab,
                                Jay Smith approach
       • *Conflict Mediation*   Ron Kraybill   *Patty Shelly*
       • *Incarnation: Obstacles* David Shenk   *Jeanne Sahawneh*
         and Bridges
10:35 *Break*
10:50 Session Two   Presenter(s)   Chair

       • *Literature and Media* Darren Schaupp   *Sara Fast*
                                (written),
                                Carl Wiebe,
                                Bruce Heckman

- *Reconciliation and Justice* — Dorothy Jean Weaver, *Barbara Witmer* / Ahmed Haile
- *Theology of Econ. Development: Calling or Strategy? Church Formation* — Ed Martin, *Ron Matthies* / Mark Logan, / Jonathan Borman / Harold Reed, *Joe Showalter* / Bedru Hussein Muktar, / Tim Bergdahl
- *The Challenge of the Muslim Critique, of Christian Theology* — Jon Hoover *Lindsey Robinson* / Mesach Krisetya / (Comments: Elias George / and William Sahawneh)
- *Dialogue and Witness* — Jewel Showalter, *Lydia Harder* / Gordon Nickel, / Emmanuel Ali
- *The Cross, Atonement, and Intercession: Obstacles and Bridges* — Tim Bergdahl *Mohamud Siad Togane*

12:00	*Lunch*

AFTERNOON   Chairperson: Ed Martin

1:30	*Brief Reports from Each Thematic Group (two minutes each)*	
2:00	*Learnings/Vision:*	
	2:00 *North America*	MBMSI
	2:15 *Canada*	Mennonite Church of Eastern Canada (MCEC)
	2:35 *Burkina Faso*	Network/Africa Inter-Mennonite Mission (AIMM)/ Canada Witness
	2:50 *Senegal*	Network/AIMM
3:05	*Break*	
	3:25 *Djibouti*	EMM
	3:40 *Algeria*	MCC/Network
	3:55 *Somalia*	EMM
	4:15 *Ethiopia*	Meserete Kristos Church
	4:30 *Pan Africa*	Nzash Lumeya
4:45	*Discussion/Prayer*	
5:00	*Dinner*	

EVENING   Chairperson: Ron Flaming

7:00   *"Questions and Concerns*   David W. Shenk
        That Muslims Address to the
        Church: An Anabaptist
        Reflection and Response"

7:30   *Group Discussion:*   Linford Stutzman, facilitator
        "What is our Anabaptist 'calling'
        in relation to the Muslim
        community?"

        (Listening committee prepares summary statement)

SUNDAY, OCTOBER 26, 2003
MORNING   Chairperson: David Shenk

8:00   *Worship*   Richard and Jewel Showalter

8:30   *Two Personal Reflections:*   Yakuta Abdo
        "What Difference Does   Emmanuel Ali
        Jesus Make?"

8:50   *This Is What We Have Heard*
        • *"This is our counsel to the*   Lamin Sanneh
          Anabaptist Community"   J. Dudley Woodberry

        • *"This is our counsel from*   Gordon Nickel
          within the Anabaptist   Donna Entz
          Community"   Ahmed Haile

9:15   *Statement from the Listening Committee and Open Mike*

9:30   *Sermon: "Walls and Doors"*   Bedru Hussein Muktar

9:50   *Communion*   Roy Hange and Patty Shelly

10:10   *Concluding Comments*   James R. Krabill
        and Benedictory Prayer

10:20   *Adjourn*

Revelation, Reason, and Authority

(A joint news release by Imam Khomeini Education and Research Institute (Qom) and Toronto Mennonite Theological Centre)

Shi'ite Muslim-Mennonite Christian Dialogue in Iran

Qom, known as the most "religious" city of Iran, was the location of phase two of an academic Shi'ite Muslim-Mennonite Christian dialogue, February 15-16, 2004, as part of a two-week visit. Eight North American Mennonites joined a similar number of Muslim scholars for an intensive but cordial two-day discussion at the Imam Khomeini Education and Research Institute in Qom, on the topic of "Revelation and Authority." Scholarly papers were presented on both sides on a variety of topics related to this overall theme, with video cameras recording the entire event.

This unusual scholarly interchange of ideas is the culmination of an exchange program between Mennonites and Iranian Muslims, initiated by Mennonite Central Committee (MCC) and the Imam Khomeini Institute, in 1997. This exchange was the consequence of MCC's relief work following a severe 1990 earthquake in Iran. As part of the exchange the two institutions sponsor a Mennonite couple living and studying in Qom (Matthew and Laurie Pierce) and two Iranian doctoral students studying at the Toronto School of Theology (Mohammad Farimani and Yousef Daneshvar). The Toronto Mennonite Theological Centre (TMTC) helps to oversee the academic aspect of the exchange in Toronto and organizes the academic dialogue together with the Khomeini Institute.

Part one of the academic dialogue, sponsored by TMTC, MCC, and the Imam Khomeini Education and Research Institute, took place in Toronto, October 24–26, 2002, on the topic: "Muslim, Christians and the Challenges of Modernity." Four Iranian scholars, including a translator, flew in from Iran to Toronto for that event, including in their stay not only intellectual discussions, but also a visit to a Mennonite church service (Tavistock), a modest Old Order Mennonite Farm, an upscale Niagara Mennonite home, and Niagara Falls. The proceedings of the first dialogue were published in *The Conrad Grebel Review* (Fall 2003).

On this occasion (part two of the dialogue) a group of North American Mennonite scholars were invited to Iran, and were treated to typical Iranian hospitality and generosity over a two-week period, February 11-22, 2004, under the able leadership of Professor Aboulhassan Haghani of the Imam Khomeini Institute. This was religiously and politically a propitious time for such a visit: with the dramatic twenty-fifth anniversary celebrations in Teheran of the 1979 Islamic revolution on February 11, the day of our arrival, an event widely reported in the Western press, and the elections for Parliament on February 20, also extensively reported on by Western media.

Still tired from the flight, our group was probably the only Western delegation to be ushered into the stands to observe the twenty-fifth anniversary celebrations, together with politicians, Muslim clerics, representatives from various religious groups, media, and other dignitaries to see the parachutes, fireworks, musical and oral tributes, and listen to the President of Iran address the people. An estimated two million were thought to have been out on the streets of Teheran on that day. At the end of the two-week visit, on election day, two of us were briefly allowed into an election polling booth to observe the carefully monitored and orderly voting procedure.

The Imam Khomeini Institute generously paid the entire cost of hosting our group over the entire two-weeks, including tours of a model prisoner of war camp which is now a museum, the former

American Embassy grounds, palaces of the former Shahs and the simple dwelling place of the revolutionary leader Ayatolla Khomeini (highlighting the contrast in lifestyle between the two), visits to the beautiful Iranian cities of Kashan with its lavish pre-revolutionary homes, and Esfahan and its world famous seventeenth-century square and market, exquisite ancient mosques, the old Armenian Christian Church, and the Zoroastrian "Temple of Fire."

Particularly memorable was a visit to the home of the late Murtada Mutahhari, an internationally known Islamic thinker whose many volumes of writings are currently in the process of being published as collected works. Drafter of the constitution of the Islamic Republic, and personal confidante of the Ayatollah Khomeini, he was assassinated only three months after the revolution by a faction not in agreement with his views. An international twenty-fifth anniversary commemorative conference on his thought is taking place at the University of Teheran in April 2004. The friendliness of the Iranian people was reflected in numerous ways, especially by the hospitality of the extended families and relatives of the two Muslim doctoral students studying in Canada.

Participants were carefully chosen from both sides. Most of the Muslim scholars had received doctorates from Western universities—McGill, Canada; Manchester, England; Innsbruck, Austria—and spoke English well. The Christian participants all had some knowledge of Islam, some like David Shenk, Jon Hoover (Cairo), and Roy Hange, having spent a major portion of their professional careers studying and writing about Islam and Christianity.

Christian participants from the Toronto Mennonite Theological Centre were A. James Reimer, (director and professor); Lydia Harder (adjunct professor); Phil Enns (doctoral student); Susan Harrison (advanced degree student). Ed Martin, Director of Central and Southern Asian Program, MCC, and Matthew and Laurie Pierce (current MCC exchange students studying in Qom) also participated in the dialogue. With the exception of Yousef Daneshvar, doctoral in Toronto, all Muslim participants were professors at the Imam Khomeini Institute: Dr. Legenhausen, Dr. Twofiqi, Dr. Shomali, Dr. Sajedi, Dr. Shameli, Dr. Fanaei, Dr. Namazi, and Prof. Haghani.

Themes dealt with by the formal presentations included revelation, reason, authority, law, conscience, canonical texts, religious experience, and Islamic and Christian views of God. The dominant motif throughout was the relation of revelation to reason. Islam sees no fundamental contradiction between a high view of human reason (a gift from God) and a high view of revelation (the divine will as revealed through Gabriel to the Prophet Muhammad in the Qur'an).

This is related to their positive Islamic anthropology, what Yousef Daneshvar, referred to in his paper as the "human theomorphic nature (Fitrah)"—human beings are naturally oriented toward the divine. The Christian doctrine of "original sin," the result of the fall of Adam and Eve in the Garden of Eden, which has corrupted human nature, including reason, and requires a sacrificial atonement, has no equivalent in Islamic theology.

The Qur'an mentions the forbidden eating from a tree which has negative consequences for Adam and Eve, but it is not identified as the tree of the "knowledge of good and evil" as it is in Genesis 3. In Islamic thought the knowledge of good and evil is not negative but rather a positive, natural knowledge planted within the human conscience by God. All human beings have a tendency to sin but this is not an inherited condition. While human beings are not perfect, there is no excuse, God expects them to use their reason to the fullest extent in determining what is right and what is wrong and to follow the path of obedience to Allah. God, the all merciful and all compassionate One, is ready to forgive directly those who repent, without any need for sacrificial mediation. In their high view of reason, freedom and human responsibility and their rejection of the more severe Protestant notions of original sin, Mennonite Christians have something in common with Shi'ite Muslims.

Most remarkable in the course of the dialogue was the respect which both sides showed toward each others' texts. Both have a high view of the authority of the sacred book—one reason why the theme "Revelation and Authority" was chosen. Perhaps the most dramatic example of this is the wise, senior Muslim scholar, Professor Towfiqi, who has taught Christianity to Muslim students for some forty years. He knows the four Christian gospels for memory and referred to Jesus as "our Lord Jesus Christ" on a number of occasions. Towfiqi's expression did not imply the divinity of Jesus but represents the respect Muslims have for Jesus as a great prophet. Jesus is for them not God who died on the cross, but one who ascended and will return with the twelfth Imam (presently hidden) to establish an earthly kingdom of justice.

There are of course substantive and methodological differences in how Muslims and Christians interpret their respective texts.

Muslims manage to achieve a much greater consensus on the fundamental meaning of the Qur'anic text than do Christians (including Mennonites) in their interpretation of the Bible. Rather than applying the Western tools of historical-criticism to the Qur'an, Muslims "let the text stand" as God's literal, revealed Word, and then find a rich variety of mystical and spiritual levels of meaning in the text.

Apparent throughout the visit and the theological discussions was the growing level of trust between our two communities of learning. Pivotal to this trust is the sincerity of the dialogue, the common search for truth, and the firm conviction on both sides that the life of the intellect ought not to be separated from devotion, piety, and moral integrity. This was mentioned a number of times, also in the concluding session with the head of the Imam Khomeini Institute, Ayatollah Mesbah.

Ayatollah Mesbah, himself a leading Islamic scholar and writer, belongs to the most important council of Iran: the seventy-member elected Council of Experts responsible for choosing and overseeing the Grand Leader of Iran. He has the ear of the Grand Leader and gives his official sanction to the Mennonite-Shi'ite Dialogue. In his closing address to our group he called on all religions to join forces in the struggle against secularism and the moral decay of values, especially among the youth.

My own appreciative response to his comments included the following: "At that first phase of the dialogue [Toronto, October 2002] . . . we very quickly realized that our two traditions have some very important commonalities: first, we both have a strong conviction that the intellectual life should not be separated from faith and devotion to God; second, both of our traditions emphasize the importance of an upright moral and ethical life.

"The second phase of our discourse has reinforced these initial impressions. We sense a growing spirit of community and solidarity between us as we together search for truth and greater faithfulness and righteousness. There are, of course, also, some serious theological differences, but we believe that before we dwell on these we need to develop a spirit of trust between us. We sincerely hope that our exchange and the community of trust that we have already developed may continue to grow and be a sign of hope for much greater mutual understanding between our two traditions and also between our countries."

Gifts were exchanged—we presented Ayatolla Mesbah with the

three-volume *History of Mennonites in Canada* by Frank H. Epp and Ted Regehr, the *Confession of Faith in a Mennonite Perspective,* and the Fall 2003 issue of *The Conrad Grebel Review* with the conference proceedings of the first dialogue. The final session ended with a prayer by David Shenk, to which the Muslims said "Amen."

The proceedings of this second dialogue will also, *Insha' Allah* ("God willing" in Arabic), be published in a future volume. The hope is that the dialogue will continue, perhaps with part three back in Toronto in two years time.

—*A. James Reimer*

News Reports of "An Anabaptist Consultation on Islam"

(A joint news release of Eastern Mennonite Seminary, Mennonite Mission Network and Eastern Mennonite Missions.)

Seminary Hosts Major Church-Islam Consultation

The original plan was to hold a small meeting of people who live and work among Muslims to talk about trust-building relationships and what constitutes an appropriate witness to them.

But as word spread about plans to hold such a forum, more groups and organizations who have been engaged within Muslim communities over the years asked to come and to be involved in whatever would be presented.

The result: more than 220 registrants gathered at Eastern Mennonite Seminary for an Anabaptist Consultation on the Church and Islam, October 23-26.

Representatives came from across North America, Africa and Asia and from a variety of denominations and theological traditions. Attendance at some sessions went over the 300 mark.

The forum was jointly sponsored by Eastern Mennonite Seminary, Mennonite Mission Network and Eastern Mennonite Missions, with participation from more than 15 other global agencies, groups and organizations.

"Christians and Muslims have gathered in various settings to reflect on their journeys together," noted Linford L. Stutzman, associate professor of culture and mission at EMU and planning team member. "But this meeting has been designed as an Anabaptist Christian retreat to hear the counsel of the Holy Spirit and to listen to each other in a spirit of discernment.

"You see before you an incredibly full program schedule, with more than 70 presenters over these four days," Dr. Stutzman told the assembly at the opening session. "It's feeling at times like taking a drink from a fire hose," stated James Krabill of Mennonite Mission Network later in the conference.

The consultation coincided with the 50th anniversary of Eastern Mennonite Missions' involvement with Muslims in Somalia and also convened on the eve of Ramadan, the start of a month-long of fasting on the Muslim calendar.

Fact: The "ummah" (Muslim community) and Christian church together make up a little over one half of the world's population. Yet relations between the two groups have grown increasingly tenuous, especially since the events of September 11, 2001, and the Iraqi war.

In a keynote address, Dudley Woodberry, professor of Islamic studies and dean of the School of World Mission at Fuller Theological Seminary, Pasadena, Calif., summarized the current status of Muslim-Christian relations with the opening line of Dickens' *A Tale of Two Cities*: "It was the best of times, it was the worst of times."

The "worst of times," according to Dr. Woodberry, is evidenced by the anger of many Muslims against the West and, by association, against Christianity, which came onto the world stage with the Iranian Revolution of 1978-79 and into everyone's living room on September 11, 2001. It has intensified with hostilities in Afghanistan, Iraq and Israel/Palestine," he said.

The "best of times," Woodberry continued, "is seen in the reaction of many people in churches and mosques who see the necessity of people of goodwill getting to know each other and cooperating on the grassroots level in peacemaking and conflict transformation . . . After 9-11, both churches and mosques opened their doors to those of the other community."

Woodberry went on to recite a list of specific events and actions that have helped strengthen intercommunal relations in countries around the world.

John A. Lapp, former executive secretary of Mennonite Central Committee, gave an extensive overview of Mennonite engagements with the Muslim community. He noted that one of the founders of the Anabaptist movement, former Benedictine prior Michael Sattler, was burned at the stake in 1527 for his religious beliefs, including his call—seen as treasonous—not to resist the Turks of the Ottoman Empire if they were to invade Germany.

"Sattler's statement summarized a straightforward mission axiom—you can't tell a Muslim about the love of God in Jesus Christ and bring him into the joy of discipleship by fighting and killing him," Lapp stated.

Noting that "it's not clear when and how Mennonites began to intentionally engage in dialog with the Muslim community," Lapp believes it likely grew out of MCC experiences with Palestinian refugees, Mennonite Board of Missions work in Algeria and Eastern Mennonite mission work in Somalia. In each case, the Mennonite emphasis on servanthood and peacebuilding led to the establishment of schools, clinics, hospitals, and extension programs.

Major input sessions were supplemented with "learning/vision" presentations by church agency personnel working with Muslim peoples in North America and abroad. Special interest seminars were also offered, ranging from "literature and media" to "pacifism among Muslims" to "dialog and witness."

David W. Shenk, considered a leading Mennonite voice in Christian-Muslim conversations and global consultant with his wife Grace with Eastern Mennonite Missions, raised questions and concerns that Muslims address to the Christian church.

"The chief question that unites and divides Christians and Muslims as no other theme is, 'Who is Jesus'?" he said.

"In Islam, God sends his will down. In Christianity, God enters our history and suffers for us," Shenk said, adding: "How much does God love? That is the core divergence we experience in our conversation."

Following Shenk's presentation, participants broke into small groups and were asked to reflect what they had been hearing in the various sessions. They then worked to come up with several summary sentences and then to share these statements with the total group.

Because of the massive, almost overwhelming amount of input from speakers and variety of convictions represented among participants, a five-member listening and discernment committee took up the assignment to pay close attention to the voices, issues, and challenges that came to the fore and to write a "confessional statement" for broader consideration and discernment.

The listening group sought "to identify ways that God is moving among us," themes and theological concerns that emerged and common commitments to the Muslim community.

The consultation ended with worship, a message on "Walls and Doors" by Bedru Hussein, vice president of Meserete Kristos College in Ethiopia, and a communion service.

"The ability of a widely diverse group of participants to listen to each other and to the voice of God, and to respond with a unified voice to the question, 'what is our Anabaptist calling in relation to the Muslim community,' was an amazing example of the hermeneutical community in action," Stutzman said later.

Added David Shenk: "I was deeply stirred by the depth, breadth, insights, commitment, and diversities of the Anabaptist journey among Muslims."

Richard A. Showalter, president of Eastern Mennonite Missions, echoed the sentiment: "The consultation was a heady mix of academics, missionaries, farmers, administrators, students, and international church leaders from a wide cross-section of the North American Mennonite community and beyond. There was hardly a dull moment with a rare blend of heart and mind—testimony, analysis, worship, debate and discernment—one of the finest inter-Mennonite meetings I've ever attended."

A book with the major papers and other materials growing out of the consultation will be published by Herald Press, Scottdale, Pa., with projected release date in mid-2004.

Cassette tapes from the consultation and videotapes of the main presentations are available from the Learning Resources department at EMU. For more information, call 540-432-4231; e-mail: kingmg@emu.edu

—Jim Bishop, EMU Public Information Officer

Outreach to Muslims Seen as Vital Today

EMU Event Looks at Interfaith Encounters

by Robert Rhodes
Mennonite Weekly Review

HARRISONBURG, Va.— With more at stake in Christian-Muslim relations than ever before, Christians may have a rare opportunity to overcome age-old stereotypes.

"Most Muslims never read a Bible, but they do read the church," said David W. Shenk, a longtime missionary to Muslim countries and one of the organizers of a consultation on Islam at Eastern Mennonite University, October 23-26.

Recognizing different approaches to the Christian encounter with Muslims—seeking converts or building mutual understanding—was a key focus of the conference. Shenk, an author and former mission director with Eastern Mennonite Missions, said Muslim confusion about many aspects of Christianity makes dialogue difficult at times. "The pastoral, loving, serving ministries of the church are signs of God as Father, Son and Holy Spirit [and are] a more fruitful witness and response to Muslim perplexity about Christian understanding of God than is possible through theological discourse alone," he said.

The conference, attended by about 200 people, included assessments of Christian-Muslim relations as well as accounts of the challenges and hazards faced by Mennonite mission and aid workers in predominantly Muslim countries.

Differences in viewpoint and terminology often contribute to the difficulty of mutual understanding, Shenk said. "Islam believes that Jesus is the Messiah," Shenk said. "That is why Muslims deny the crucifixion. The denial of the crucifixion is an Islamic affirmation that he is the Messiah, for Muslims believe that it is impossible for the Messiah who is anointed with the power of God to be crucified. . . .

"In Islam, God never reveals himself and never meets us. Rather it is his will and attributes that he sends down in a revelation [the Qur'an] that is suspended above and transcends history."

Among those at the conference with direct experience in the Muslim world was Dudley Woodberry, an authority on Islam at Fuller Theological Seminary at Pasadena, Calif.

In the months since the September 11, 2001, terrorist attacks, Woodberry said, the West's encounter with Islam has grown increasingly complex and volatile.

"Although there was considerable empathy for Americans at the time of the [Sept. 2001] tragedy, once the war on terrorism started, [Muslim leaders] saw non-Muslims killing and imprisoning Muslims, and they became angry," Woodberry said.

Yale Divinity School professor Lamin Sanneh, a native of Gambia who is an authority on the two religions, detailed the long history of Christian interaction with Islam, and their varying views on war and nonviolence.

"Islam as such is not a pacifist religion, which is not to say that there have not been pacific Muslim voices, including the Sufi masters who repudiated the 'smaller jihad' of holy war and instead adopted the so-called 'greater jihad' of personal purification," Sanneh said October 24.

Sufism is the largely tolerant, mystical branch of Islam—a movement often repudiated and suppressed by fundamentalist Muslims.

John A. Lapp of Akron, Pa., presented a review of Mennonite involvement in Muslim countries, from the efforts of Dutch Mennonites 150 years ago in Indonesia to modern mission and aid programs.

"Today it is difficult to ignore the political and diplomatic dimensions of engagement," said Lapp, who served in Jerusalem for several years as head of the Mennonite Central Committee peace section. "There is no room in this engagement for complacency, self-satisfaction or triumphalism. Judgment and repentance begin in the household of faith."

Lapp also called for greater openness and charity in exploring links between Christians and Muslims. "It is so easy to see Islam as at a crossroads, forgetting that Christianity is also at a crossroads," Lapp said. "Christian-Muslim relationships could have been much different at each step along the way if rather than rancor and conflict there could have been a mutual exploration of differences reflected in the other's mirror."

Woodberry explored some of these differences, and similarities between the two religions. "The roads that Jesus and Muhammad walked started in very similar circumstances," Woodberry said. "Both were born in humble homes but had prominent ancestors."

Key differences in the two faiths can be found in the outlook of their holy books, he noted. "For the Bible and the Qur'an, the world starts with creation and a garden," Woodberry said. "The Qur'an, however, does not see the problem of sin as being as serious as the Bible teaches. So Muslims believe that by the habit of following the law, humans actualize the kingdom and can return to the garden."

Also at the conference, Chantal Logan—who with her husband, Mark, has served with EMM in Somalia—discussed the roles of women in Christian and Muslim cultures. "Islam is not any more monolithic [when it comes to women's issues] than Christianity," she said. "If people's manner of dress can be an indication, the diversity found in both worlds can be illustrated by the fact that between the women of Saudi Arabia, who keep their faces covered, and Tunisians, who wear jeans, there is as much distance as between Amish women with prayer bonnets and long dresses and modern Mennonite women who can be seen in shorts."

Chantal Logan also reacted to what some at the conference saw as a reluctance to call for the conversion of Muslims. She said the church needed to "get its act together" on this issue.

Other organizers of the consultation included EMU professor Linford Stutzman and James Krabill of Mennonite Mission Network.

Abbreviations for Proper Names

AIMM	Africa Inter-Mennonite Mission
AMBS	Associated Mennonite Biblical Seminary
BIC	Brethren in Christ
CIM	Council of International Ministries
CPT	Christian Peacemaker Teams
EMBMC	Eastern Mennonite Board of Missions and Charities (former name of EMM)
EMM	Eastern Mennonite Missions
EMS	Eastern Mennonite Seminary
EMU	Eastern Mennonite University
GC	Goshen College
GKMI	Muria Synod of the Mennonite Church in Indonesia (Gereja Kristen Muria Indonesia)
GITJ	Evangelical Churches of Java (Mennonite) (Gereja Injili di Tanah Jawa)
IAM	International Assistance Mission
MB	Mennonite Brethren
MBM	Mennonite Board of Missions (now Mennonite Mission Network and Mennonite Church Canada Witness)
MBMSI	Mennonite Brethren Missions and Service International
MC	Mennonite Church (now integrated with the General Conference Mennonite Church)
MCC	Mennonite Central Committee

MCEC	Mennonite Church of Eastern Canada
MKC	Meserete Kristos Church (Ethiopia)
MOE	Ministry of Education
MWC	Mennonite World Conference
Network	Mennonite Mission Network
PIPKA	The mission and service agency of the Muria Synod in Indonesia
RMM	Rosedale Mennonite Mission
SIM	Sudan Interior Mission
SLM	Swedish Lutheran Mission
SMM	Somalia Mennonite Mission
TMTC	Toronto Mennonite Theological Centre
TST	Toronto School of Theology
VMBM	Virginia Mennonite Board of Missions

Bibliography of Anabaptist Writings Concerning Islam

James R. Krabill

Beachy, Bertha. "Reflections on Mennonite Mission Experience in Somalia." *Mission Focus* 10/4 (December 1982): 52.

———. "Mennonites and Muslim Somalis." *MCC Peace Office Newsletter* (April-June 2003): 10-12.

Bergen, Kathy. "The Uprising (in the West Bank and Gaza)." *MCC Peace Office Newsletter* (November-December 1988): 5-6.

Bergen, Kathy, David Neuhaus, and Ghassan Rubeiz, eds. *Justice and the Intifada: Palestinians and Israelis Speak Out.* New York: Friendship Press; Geneva: WCC Publications, 1991.

Bergey, Bonnie. "The 'Bottom-Up' Alternative in Somali Peacebuilding." In *From the Ground Up: Mennonite Contributions to International Peacebuilding,* Cynthia Sampson and John Paul Lederach, eds., 149-64. New York: Oxford University Press, 2000.

Bertsche, James. *CIM/AIMM: A Story of Vision, Commitment and Grace.* Elkhart, Ind.: Fairway Press, 1998.

Bradshaw, Bruce. "Integrity and Respect Are Keys to Muslim Witness." *Evangelical Missions Quarterly* 24 (1988): 358-62.

Brislen, Mike. "A Model for a Muslim-Culture Church." *Missiology* 24 (1996): 355-67.

Byler, J. Daryl. "U.S.-Iraq Policy: Has the Die for War Been Cast?" *MCC Peace Office Newsletter* (July-September 2002): 3-5.

Charles, J. Robert. "Post-September 11 Peace Theology: A Handful of Challenges for U.S. Mennonites." *MCC Peace Office Newsletter* (April-June 2002): 8-9.

Checole, Alemu, with Samuel Asefa. "Mennonite Churches in Eastern Africa." In *A Global Mennonite History: Africa*, John A. Lapp and C. Arnold Synder, eds., 220-89. Kitchener, Ont.: Pandora Press, 2003.

"Christian Conduct in Situations of Conflict." Elkhart, Ind.: Council of International Ministries, 1980s.

Davidson, Rose (pseudonym). "Ethiopia: The Church in a Revolutionary Context." *MCC Peace Office Newsletter* (June-July 1980): 4-5.

Driedger, Leo, and Donald B. Kraybill. *Mennonite Peacemaking: From Quietism to Activism.* Scottdale, Pa.: Herald Press, 1994.

Dyck, Cornelius J., ed. *The Lordship of Christ: Proceedings of the Seventh Mennonite World Conference* (including a report on the First Inter-Mennonite Missiological Consultation on Islam, August 1962). Elkhart, Ind.: Mennonite World Conference, 1962.

Dyck, Cornelius J., Robert S. Kreider, and John A. Lapp. *Responding to Worldwide Needs: In Europe, the Middle East, Africa, Asia.* The Mennonite Central Committee Story, vol. 1. Scottdale, Pa.: Herald Press, 1980.

Eastern Mennonite Missions staff and partners. *Learnings from the 1998 Ethiopia Mission Study Trip* (20-30 July 1998). Salunga, Pa.: Eastern Mennonite Missions, 1998.

———. *Indonesia 2000: Bridging Cultures, Changing Lives* (6-15 May 2000). Salunga, Pa.: Eastern Mennonite Missions, 2000.

Eby, Omar. *Sense and Incense.* Scottdale, Pa.: Herald Press, 1965.

———. *A Whisper in a Dry Land: A Biography of Merlin Grove, Martyr for Muslims in Somalia.* Scottdale, Pa.: Herald Press, 1968.

———. *Fifty Years, Fifty Stories: The Mennonite Mission in Somalia, 1953-2003.* Telford, Pa.: Cascadia Publishing House; Scottdale, Pa.: Herald Press, 2003.

Entz, Donna Kampen. "Personal Reflections on Language Ministry in Burkina Faso after Two Decades." *Mission Focus Annual Review* 9 (2001): 33-61.

————. *From Kansas to Kenedougou . . . And Back Again.* In the *Missio Dei* series, no. 3. Elkhart, Ind.: Mennonite Mission Network, 2004.

Entz, Loren. "Challenges to Abou's Jesus." *Evangelical Missions Quarterly* 22/1 (January 1986): 46-50.

Epp, Ed. "Images." *MCC Peace Office Newsletter* (March-April 1991): 11.

————. "Lighting a Candle or a Fuse (Middle East Peace Accords)." *MCC Peace Office Newsletter* (January-February 1994): 1-2.

————. "Rebuilding Together Builds Reconciliation." *MCC Peace Office Newsletter* (January-February 1994): 5.

Epp-Tiessen, Esther. "Please Go and Tell the Truth (about the Sanctions in Iraq)." *MCC Peace Office Newsletter* (July-September 2002): 8-9.

Epp, Frank. *Whose Land is Palestine?* Grand Rapids: Eerdmans, 1970.

————. *The Palestinians: Portrait of a People in Conflict.* Toronto: McClellan and Stewart, 1980.

Fast, Alfrieda. "Four Muslim Women." *MCC Women's Concerns* 120 (1995): 2-4.

Fast, Deborah, and Menno Wiebe. "MCC's Involvement in Iraq." *MCC Peace Office Newsletter* (July-September 2002): 2-3.

Franz, Delton. "Prospects for Palestinian Autonomy and Middle East Peace." *MCC Peace Office Newsletter* (May-June 1981): 1-3.

Friesen, Duane. "The Church's Response to September 11." *MCC Peace Office Newsletter* (April-June 2002): 7.

Friesen, Herb. *A Reluctant Surgeon,* 1996. Published privately in Pakistan.

Friesen, LeRoy. "An Appeal on Behalf of the Palestinian People." *MCC Peace Office Newsletter* (September 1976): 1-2.

————. *Mennonite Witness in the Middle East: A Missiological Introduction.* Elkhart, Ind.: Mennonite Board of Missions, 1992; rev. ed., 2000.

Gerber, Hansulrich. "Former Yugoslavia—On Peacekeepers and Forgiveness." *MCC Peace Office Newsletter* (April-June 1996): 5-6.

————. "Europeans on Terrorism and the U.S. Response." *MCC Peace Office Newsletter* (April-June 2002): 6.

Gish, Peggy. *Iraq: A Journey of Hope and Peace.* Scottdale, Pa.: Herald Press, 2004.

Good, Merle. "Bedru Hussein: Gentle and Intense." *Festival Quarterly* (Winter 1994): 12-13.

Habib, Gabriel. "Mission or Renewal in the Middle East." *Mission Focus Annual Review* 6 (1998): 25-30.

Hange, Maren Tyedmars, compiler. *Sisters, Friends: Middle East Reader on Women*. Akron, Pa.: Mennonite Central Committee, 1996.

Hange, Maren Tyedmars, and Roy Hange. "Dislocated for Service (in Iran)." *MCC Peace Office Newsletter* (July-September 2001): 3-6.

Hange, Roy. "Rebuilding Old Walls: A Survey of Religious Violence in the Middle East." *Mission Focus Annual Review* 2 (1994): 9-24.

———. "Healing 'Holy Hatred': Biblical and Practical Reflections." *Mission Focus Annual Review* 4 (1996): 63-73.

———. "Report on MCC's Presence in Iran in 1998." *Mission Focus Annual Review* 7 (1999): 45-52.

———. "Give Us This Day...." *MCC Peace Office Newsletter* (July-September 2001): 11.

Harder, Lydia. "No Longer Innocent!" *MCC Peace Office Newsletter* (April-June 2002): 11-12.

Harvey, Dona. "How Does Peace Theology Affect Our Encounters with Islam?" *The Conrad Grebel Review* 14 (1996): 119-23.

Hege, Nathan B. *Beyond Our Prayers: Anabaptist Church Growth in Ethiopia, 1948-1998*. Scottdale, Pa.: Herald Press, 1998.

Herr, Bob. "Iraq Sanctions: Immoral from the Very Beginning." *MCC Peace Office Newsletter* (July-September 2002): 10-11.

Hiebert, Paul. "The Gospel and Culture." In *The Gospel and Islam: A 1978 Compendium*, D. M. McCurry, ed. Monrovia, Calif.: MARC, 1979.

———. "Power Encounters and Folk Islam." In *Muslims and Christians on the Emmaus Road*, J. Dudley Woodberry, ed., 45-61. Monrovia, Calif.: MARC, 1989.

Hiebert, Paul G., and Frances F. Hiebert. *Case Studies in Mission*. Grand Rapids: Baker Book House, 1987.

Hildebrand, Art. "Some Concepts in Understanding the Conflict (in the Middle East)." *MCC Peace Office Newsletter* (November-December 1988): 11.

Hoekema, Alle. "Why the Dutch Were the First Mennonites to Send Missionaries Overseas (Indonesia)." *The Conrad Grebel Review* (Winter/Spring 1997): 23-34.

———. *Dutch Mennonite Mission in Indonesia: Historical Essays*. Elkhart, Ind.: Institute of Mennonite Studies, 2001.

Hoover, Jacqueline. "Two Discussions on the Status of Non-Muslims under Islam in the *Journal Institute of Muslim Minority Affairs.*" Unpublished MA thesis. University of Birmingham, England, 2000.

Hoover, Jon. "Theological Foundations for Dialogue with Islam." *MCC Peace Office Newsletter* (September-October 1994): 1-2.

———. "Proselytism in Contemporary Egypt." *Mission Focus* 6 (1998): 85-95.

———. "September 11 in the Egyptian Press," *MCC Peace Office Newsletter* (April-June 2002): 3.

———. "Christianity and Islam." Two parts in the *Canadian Mennonite* 6/16 (26 August 2002): 6-7; and 6/17 (9 September 2002): 6-7.

———. "Rooting Dialogue with Muslims in Love." *The Mennonite* 5/22 (19 November 2002): 12-13.

———. "An Islamic Theodicy: Ibn Taymiyya on the Wise Purpose of God, Human Agency, and Problems of Evil and Justice." Unpublished PhD dissertation. University of Birmingham, England, 2002.

———. "A Typology of Responses to the Philosophical Problem of Evil in the Islamic and Christian Traditions." *The Conrad Grebel Review.* Special issue on "The Challenge of Modernity: Shi'ah Muslim-Mennonite Christian Dialogue," Toronto, 24-27 October 2002 (Fall 2003): 81-96.

Hostetler, Marian E. "I Cannot Follow Two Paths." In *The Mennonite Encyclopedia*, vol. 5, 457-58. Scottdale, Pa.: Herald Press, 1990.

———. *What Is Islam? Who Are the Muslims?* Elkhart, Ind., 2002. Available from the author, 57717 Seventh Street, Elkhart, IN 46517.

———. *Algeria: Where Mennonites and Muslims Met, 1955-1978.* Elkhart, Ind.: Marian E. Hostetler, 2003.

"Iraq and Sanctions: An MCC Comment." Excerpted from a statement adopted by the MCC executive committee, June 26, 1998. *MCC Peace Office Newsletter* (April-June 1999): 9.

Jantzen, Mark. "Case Study (on Peacekeeping): Bosnia/Serbia." *MCC Peace Office Newsletter* (May-October 1997): 6-7.

Janzen, Bill. "Canada's Iraq Policy Since 1990." *MCC Peace Office Newsletter* (July-September 2002): 5-6.

Jibrell, Fatima, with Chantal Logan. "Trying to Convince Men and Women to Make Peace (Somalia)." *MCC Peace Office Newsletter* (April-June 2003): 8-10.

Kern, Kathleen. "From Haiti to Hebron with a Brief Stop in Washington, D.C.: The CPT Experiment." In *From the Ground Up: Mennonite Contributions to International Peacebuilding*, Cynthia Sampson and John Paul Lederach, eds., 183-200. New York: Oxford University Press, 2000.

Klassen, Mary Lou and Dave. "Allowing the Peace to Flow." *MCC Peace Office Newsletter* (September-October 1994): 11-12.

Koontz, Gayle Gerber. "The Meaning of Feminism for Egyptian Islam." Unpublished paper. Boston University, 1977.

Koontz, Ted. "Reflections on a (Short) Middle East Trip: Symmetry and Asymmetry." *MCC Peace Office Newsletter* (August 1975): 1-2, 5-8.

Kraybill, Donald B., and Linda Gehman Peachey, eds. *Where Was God on September 11?* Scottdale, Pa.: Herald Press, 2002.

Kraybill, Paul N., ed. *Called to Be Sent: Fifty Years in Mission*. Scottdale, Pa.: Herald Press, 1964.

Kraybill, Wanda. "Letters from Baghdad." *MCC Peace Office Newsletter* (April-June 1999): 10.

Krisetya, Mesach. "Suffering Discipleship." In *Asia Mennonite Conference: Report Book*, 49-53. Taipei: Asia Mennonite Conference, 1986.

———. "The Situation of the Church in Indonesia." *Mission Focus Annual Review* 7 (1999): 37-40.

Kuitse, Roelf S. "Islam in Africa Project Ghana Survey." *Bulletin of the Christian Institute of Islamic Studies* 3/3-4 (1970): 34-51.

———. "When Christians and Muslims Meet." *Mission Focus* 9/1 (March 1981): 1-4.

———. "Islam." In *The Mennonite Encyclopedia*, vol. 5, 456-57. Scottdale, Pa.: Herald Press, 1990.

———. "Christology in the Qur'an." *Missiology: An International Review* 20/3 (July 1992): 355-69.

———. "Islamiya: Islamic Fundamentalism or Renaissance?" *Mission Focus Annual Review* 2 (1994): 25-34.

Kumedisa, Eric. "Burkina Faso." In *A Global Mennonite History: Africa*, John A. Lapp and C. Arnold Synder, eds., 296-99. Kitchener, Ont.: Pandora Press, 2003.

Lambert, Rose. *A Brief History of Our Orphanage and Mission Work in Hadjin, Turkey*. Hadjin, Turkey: United Orphanage and Mission, n.d.

———. *Hadjin and the Armenian Massacres*. Chicago: Fleming H. Revell Company, 1911.

Landis, Marian. "The Horn of Africa: World's Worst Refugee Problem." *MCC Peace Office Newsletter* (June-July 1980): 5-6.

Lapp, John A. "The New Environment for Mission/Service in the Middle East." *MCC Peace Office Newsletter* (April-May 1979): 1-8.

————. *The View from East Jerusalem.* Scottdale, Pa.: Herald Press, 1980.

Lapp, John F. "Can a Foreigner Understand?" *MCC Peace Office Newsletter* (January-February, 1993): 1-2.

————. "Israeli-Palestinian Peace and MCC Plans." *MCC Peace Office Newsletter* (January-February 1994): 2-3.

Lapp, John F., interviewer. "Lapp Interviews an Islamic Jihad Activist." *MCC Peace Office Newsletter* (January-February, 1993): 6-7.

Lederach, John Paul. "Mennonite Central Committee Efforts in Somalia and Somaliland." In *From the Ground Up: Mennonite Contributions to International Peacebuilding,* Cynthia Sampson and John Paul Lederach, eds., 141-64. New York: Oxford University Press, 2000.

Logan, Chantal. "Somalia, Somalia: What Has Happened to the Beloved Country?" *MCC Peace Office Newsletter* (April-June 2003): 1-4.

Lybarger, Loren Diller. "Defining Presence: The Formation of Mennonite Agency Approaches and Attitudes Toward Muslims and Islam, 1949-1995." Unpublished MA thesis. Lutheran School of Theology, Chicago, 1995.

————. "Response: Mennonite Engagement of Islam." *Mission Focus Annual Review* 6 (1998): 31-36.

Martin, Ed. "MCC and Iran." *MCC Peace Office Newsletter* (July-September 2001): 1-3.

Martin, Steven. "Islamic Fundamentalism and Economic Development: Can the Two Co-Exist?" Unpublished paper for course on "Kingdom of God." Eastern College, St. Davids, Pa., 2001.

"Mennonite Witness Among Muslims." Salunga, Pa.: Eastern Mennonite Board of Missions and Charities, 1983.

Miller, Edward. "Halting the Free Fall (in Iraq)." *MCC Peace Office Newsletter* (July-September 2002): 11-12.

Miller, Joseph S. "A History of the Mennonite Conciliation Service, International Conciliation Service, and Christian Peacemaking Teams." In *From the Ground Up: Mennonite Contributions to International Peacebuilding,* Cynthia Sampson and John Paul Lederach, eds., 3-29. New York: Oxford University Press, 2000.

"Ministry in an Islamic Context." *Beyond Ourselves*. Elkhart, Ind.: Mennonite Mission Network (Spring 2004).

Nafziger, Dale. "Religion and Emerging Economies: The Case of Islam." Unpublished paper for MBA course on "Emerging Market Economies." Eastern College, St. Davids, Pa., 2000.

Narimalla, Vidya J. "Christian Faith and Persecution in India." *MCC Peace Office Newsletter* (October-December 1998): 4-6.

Nickel, Dan. "A Witness to Muslims in Indonesia." *Mennonite Brethren Herald* 19/3 (1 February 1980): 6-7.

————. "Muslim Ministry Comes Full Circle." *The Christian Leader* (24 December 1985): 14-15.

Nickel, Gordon D. "Making a Gospel Witness to Muslims." *Mennonite Brethren Herald* 33 (11 November 1994): 6-8.

————. "How Does Peace Theology Affect Our Encounters with Islam?" *The Conrad Grebel Review* 14 (1996): 115-18.

————. "Jesus Reveals His Glory." *Mennonite Brethren Herald* (19 July 1996): 6-7.

————. "A Cross and a Dove." *Witness* [MBMS International] (May-June 1997): 1-2, 4.

————. *Peaceable Witness Among Muslims*. Waterloo, Ont.; Scottdale, Pa.: Herald Press, 1998.

Nickel, Randel. "So Close, Yet So Far." *MCC Peace Office Newsletter* (January-March 2001): 4.

Nikkel, Walter. "Northern Sudan: Opening Windows in the Walls." *MCC Peace Office Newsletter* (September-October 1994): 3-4.

Osborne, David. "Islamic Resurgence: Something New or Something Old?" *Mission Focus* 7/4 (September 1979): 68-69.

Peachey, Paul, George R. McLean, and John Kromkowski, eds. *Abrahamic Faiths, Ethnicity and Ethnic Conflicts*. Washington, D.C.: The Council for Research in Values and Philosophy, 1997.

Peachey, Urbane. "Negative Autonomy (West Bank and Gaza)." *MCC Peace Office Newsletter* (May-June 1981): 8-10.

————. "A Good Will Visit to the Middle East: An Analysis." *MCC Peace Office Newsletter* (July-August 1983): 3-6.

Peachey, Urbane, compiler. "A Reader on Islam: A Sample of MCC Experience." Unpublished collection of MCC position papers and experiences, July 1984. Available in MCC library, 21 S. 12th St., Akron, Pa.

Penner, Carol. "MCC Exchange Program Brings Iranian Muslims to Toronto to Study Theology." *MCC Peace Office Newsletter* (July-September 2001): 9-10.

Peters, George W. "An Overview of Missions to Muslims." In *The Gospel and Islam*, Don M. McCurry, ed., 390-404. Monrovia, Calif.: MARC, 1979.

Quiring, Paul. "Israeli Settlement in the Occupied West Bank: *Fait Accompli* as a Political Tactic." *MCC Peace Office Newsletter* (March-April 1978): 3-6.

Reimer, A. James. "Shi'i Muslims and Mennonite Christians in Dialogue: Two Religious Minority Groups Face the Challenges of Modernity." *The Conrad Grebel Review*. Special issue on "The Challenge of Modernity: Shi'ah Muslim-Mennonite Christian Dialogue," Toronto, 24-27 October 2002 (Fall 2003): 3-14.

Rempel, John. "Iraq Before and After the Gulf War: Some Broad Brush Strokes." *MCC Peace Office Newsletter* (April-June 1999): 1-4.

———. "Iraq: A Looming Invasion?" *MCC Peace Office Newsletter* (July-September 2002): 6-8.

Rempel, Ruth. "The Superpowers and the Horn of Africa." *MCC Peace Office Newsletter* (September-October 1987): 1-3.

———. "Making Peace (in Sudan)." *MCC Peace Office Newsletter* (September-October 1987): 11-12.

Rempel, Terry. "Palestinian Refugees: 'We Will Return.'" *MCC Peace Office Newsletter* (January-March 2001): 5-6.

Ruth-Heffelbower, Duane. "Post 9-11 Reflections on the Response of Indonesian Muslims." *MCC Peace Office Newsletter* (April-June 2002): 4.

Samatar, Said S. "Marxism, Islam and Tribalism in the Horn of Africa: The Improbable Triumvirate." *MCC Peace Office Newsletter* (June-July 1980): 1-3.

Sawadsky, Hedi. "Meeting the Enemy Face to Face (in Jordan and Iraq)." *MCC Peace Office Newsletter* (March-April 1991): 7.

Schlabach, Gerald W. "Working Notes on the Question of Policing, Post 9-11." *MCC Peace Office Newsletter* (April-June 2002): 10-11.

Siemens, Mark. "Why Did Hussein Give Up the West Bank?" *MCC Peace Office Newsletter* (November-December 1988): 12.

Shellenberger, Wallace and Evelyn. "Conversations with Muslims after September 11." *MCC Peace Office Newsletter* (April-June 2002): 5.

Shenk, Calvin E. *A Relevant Theology of Presence*. Elkhart, Ind.: Mission Focus Publications, 1982.

———. *Who Do You Say That I Am: Christians Encounter Other Religions*. Scottdale, Pa.; Waterloo, Ontario: Herald Press, 1997.

———. *Understanding Islam: A Christian Reflection on the Faith of Our Muslim Neighbors.* In the *Missio Dei* series, no. 1. Elkhart, Ind.: Mennonite Mission Network, 2002.

Shenk, David W. "The Path to Faith." In *A Kingdom of Priests,* Wilbert Shenk, ed., 24-37. Newton, Kan.: Faith & Life Press, 1967.

———. "A Study of Mennonite Presence and Church Development in Somalia from 1950 through 1970." Unpublished PhD dissertation. New York University, 1972.

———. "A Study of Mennonite Presence and Church Development in Somalia from 1950 through 1970." *Mennonite Quarterly Review* 47/1 (January 1973): 62-63.

———. "The (Sufi) Mystical Orders in Popular Islam." *Mission Focus* 9/1 (March 1981): 5-9.

———. "The Muslim *Umma* and the Growth of the Church." In *Exploring Church Growth,* Wilbert R. Shenk, ed., 144-56. Grand Rapids: Eerdmans, 1983.

———. "Muslims and Christians: Finding Doors Through the Wall." *Mission Focus Annual Review* 1 (1983): 39-44.

———. *Global Gods: Exploring the Role of Religions in Modern Societies.* Scottdale, Pa.: Herald Press, 1995.

———. *The Holy Book of God: An Introduction.* Salunga, Pa.: Eastern Mennonite Missions; Achimota, Ghana: Africa Christian Press, 1980; rev. ed., 1995.

———. "Christian Witness and Muslim Witness: The Issues of Personal Freedom versus Community Integrity." *Mission Focus Annual Review* 6 (1997): 75-84.

———. *Journeys of the Muslim Nation and the Christian Church, Exploring the Mission of Two Communities.* Scottdale, Pa.: Herald Press, 2003.

———. "Pluralist Culture and Truth." *The Conrad Grebel Review.* Special issue on "The Challenge of Modernity: Shi'ah Muslim-Mennonite Christian Dialogue," Toronto, 24-27 October 2002 (Fall 2003): 67-80.

Shenk, David W., and Badru D. Kateregga. *Islam and Christianity: A Muslim and a Christian in Dialogue.* Grand Rapids: Eerdmans, 1979; Scottdale, Pa.: Herald Press, 1997.

Shenk, David W., and team. *The People of God.* Nairobi: Evangel Press, 1976.

Shenk, Gerald. "Questions on Bosnia." *MCC Peace Office Newsletter* (April-June 1996): 1-4.

Shenk, Phil L. *"The Greatest of These Is Love:" A Story of Dagestan.* In the *Mission Insight* series, no. 8. Elkhart, Ind.: Mennonite Board of Missions, 1999.

Shenk, Wilbert R. "Authoritarian Governments and Mission." *Mission Focus* 5/5 (May 1977): 6-8.

Smith, Jay. "Courage in Our Convictions: Debating Muslims." *Evangelical Missions Quarterly* 34 (1998): 28-35.

———. "Reaching Muslims in London: Is It Time to Confront?" *Urban Mission* 15 (March 1998): 37-46.

Sukarto, Aristarchus. "Christians and Muslims in Indonesia." *MCC Peace Office Newsletter* (September-October 1994): 6-7.

Swartz, Merlin. "The Position of Jews in Arab Lands Since the Rise of Islam." In *Reflections on the Middle East Crisis*, H. Mason, ed., 17-37. The Hague: Mouton, 1970.

———. *Studies in Islam.* New York: Oxford University Press, 1981.

———. "Rules of the Popular Preacher in Twelfth-Century Baghdad." In *Prédication et Propagande au Moyen Age: Islam, Byzance, Occident*, 223-39. Paris: Presses Universitaires de France, 1983.

———. "Al-Ash'ar," vol. 1, 93; "Hadith," vol. 2, 18; "Hanbalis," vol. 2, 24-25; "Hanafis," vol. 2, 24; "Malikis," vol. 2, 476-77; "Mu'tazilis," vol. 3, 66-67; "Shafi'is," vol. 3, 418-19. *Encyclopedia of Asian History*, 4 volumes, Ainslie T. Embree, ed. New York: Scribners and Sons, 1988.

———. "Preaching, Islamic." *Dictionary of the Middle Ages*, 12 volumes; Joseph Strayer, ed., vol. 10, 70-74. New York: Charles Scribner's Sons, 1982-1988.

———. "A Hanbali Critique of Anthropomorphism." *The Arabist: Budapest Studies in Arabic* (Budapest University, 1999): 26-37.

———. "Arabic Rhetoric and the Art of the Homily in Medieval Islam." In *Religion and Culture in Medieval Islam* (*Levi Della Vida* volume dedicated to G. Makdisi), R. Hovannisian, ed., 36-65. Cambridge: Cambridge University Press, 1999.

———. *A Medieval Critique of Anthropomorphism: Ibn al-Jawzi's Akhbar as-Sifat.* A critical edition of the Arabic text, with translation, introduction and notes. Leiden: E.J. Brill, 2002.

———. "Hanafi(s)"; "Hanbali(s)." *Encyclopaedia Iranica*. New York: Columbia University Press, 2003.

Swartz, Merlin, co-editor and contributor. *Humaniora Islamica*, vol. 1. The Hague: Mouton, 1974.

————. *Humaniora Islamica*, vol. 2. The Hague: Mouton, 1974.

Toews, John E., and Gordon Nickel, eds. *The Power of the Lamb.* Winnipeg: Kindred, 1986.

Van Gorder, A. Christian. *No God But God: A Path to Muslim Christian Dialogue on God's Nature.* New York: Orbis Books, 2003.

Voth, Susan. "'Mixed Blood' in Hebron." *MCC Peace Office Newsletter* (January-February, 1993): insert, between pp. 6-7.

Wagler, Jane. "Why Should Coptic Christians Dialogue with Muslims?" *MCC Peace Office Newsletter* (September-October 1994): 5-6.

Wagler, Trenton. "To See Jerusalem." *MCC Peace Office Newsletter* (January-March 2001): 8-9.

Weaver, Alain Epp. "Martyr Cards and Lost Childhoods (West Bank)." *MCC Peace Office Newsletter* (January-February 1994): 11.

————. "Mission and Dialogue in Palestine: A Case Study." *Criterion* 38 (Spring 1999): 26-34.

————. "Oslo's Failure and Beyond," 1-4; "Resisting Closure," 7-8; "Settlements Are Incompatible with Peace," 9-10. *MCC Peace Office Newsletter* (January-March 2001).

Weaver, Alain Epp, and Sonia K. Weaver. "Fighting with Olive Branches," 6; "Students March with Drums and Trumpets," 6. *MCC Peace Office Newsletter* (January-February 1994).

————. *Salt and Sign: Mennonite Central Committee, 1949-1999.* Akron, Pa.: Mennonite Central Committee, 1999.

Weaver, Sonia Epp. "Stories of Jerusalem." *MCC Peace Office Newsletter* (January-March 2001): 6-7.

Wenger, A. Grace. *A People in Mission, 1894-1994.* Salunga, Pa.: Eastern Mennonite Missions, 1994.

Wenger, Martha. "Learning to Hate Iraqis." *MCC Peace Office Newsletter* (March-April 1991): 4-5.

Widjaja, Paulus S. "Religious Persecution and Political Bargaining in Indonesia." *MCC Peace Office Newsletter* (October-December 1998): 6-8.

Wiebe, Elsie. "Baghdad Weeps." *MCC Peace Office Newsletter* (July-September 2002): 1-2.

"Who Is My Neighbor?" *Missionary Messenger.* Salunga, Pa.: Eastern Mennonite Missions (June 2002).

Yoder, Lawrence McCulloh. "The History of the Java Evangelical Christian Church." Unpublished MDiv thesis. New York Theological Seminary, 1970.

————. "The Church of the Muria Christian Church of Indonesia—GMKI." Unpublished MA thesis. Fuller Theological Seminary, 1981.

————. "The Introduction and Expression of Islam and Christianity in the Cultural Context of North Central Java." Unpublished PhD dissertation. Fuller Theological Seminary, 1987.

Notes

Foreword

1. Mark Juergensmeyer, *Terror in the Mind of God: The Global Rise of Religious Violence* (Berkley: University of California Press, 2000).

2. Ian Buruma and Avishai Mergalit, *Occidentalism: The West in the Eyes of Its Enemies* (New York: Penguin Press, 2004).

3. Owen Collins, ed., *2000 Years of Classic Christian Prayers: A Collection for Public and Personal Use* (Maryknoll, N.Y.: Orbis Books, 1999), 160.

Preface

1. Fra Ignacije Gavran, *Fellow-Travelers of Bosnian History* (Sarajevo, 2001) and Enes Karic, *Essays on Behalf of Bosnia* (Sarajevo: El Kalem, 1999).

Introduction: Three Journeys

1. Comments written when Linford Stutzman was leading a Middle East student study group from Eastern Mennonite University in February 2004.

2. Excerpt from Art and Leona DeFehr's Christmas 2003 greeting card. Art is president of Palliser, an international furniture enterprise. He and Leona are Mennonite Brethren globalists. Art's comments about the exchange on peacemaking and violence at Davos (2003) are pertinent to the Anabaptist vocation in the journey with Muslims within the context of western culture and global religious pluralism.

3. Comments made in a forum on "Islam and the Gospel" with Central Asian church leaders, January 27, 2004.

4. Subsequent to "An Anabaptist Consultation on Islam" at Eastern Mennonite University, I presented the main themes of this introduction as part of a dialogue in Indonesia. The theme was peacemaking in Islam and the Christian faith. The Muslim presenter was Rahmawati Hussein from the Universitas Muhamadiah Yogyakarta. The venue of the dialogue was at the Universitas Hristen Satya Wacana, Salatiga. The sponsors decided to have the presentation published in the *Journal WASKITA, A Journal on Religion and Society*. There is considerable convergence and duplication between these two essays, but the journal editors have given permission for use in this introduction.

521

5. N. T. Wright, *The Challenge of Jesus: Rediscovering Who Jesus Was and Is* (Downers Grove, Ill.: InterVarsity Press, 1999), 123.

6. Jean-Michel Hornus, *It is Not Lawful for Me to Fight: Early Christian Attitudes Toward War, Violence, and the State*, rev. ed. (Scottdale, Pa.: Herald Press, 1980), 86-87, from Origen, *Contra Celsum*, 33.

7. Hornus, 160, from Origen, *Contra Celsum*, 8:73.

8. Hornus, 160, quoted from Cyprian, *AD Donatum*, 6-10.

9. W. H. C. Frend, *The Early Church* (London: Hodder and Stoughton, 1971), 136-37.

10. Ibid., 313.

11. J. W. C. Wand, *A History of the Early Church to A.D. 500* (London: Methuen & Co. Ltd., 1965), 128.

12. *Demonstratio Evangelica*, vii, 2 as quoted in Frend, *The Early Church*, 138.

13. Frend, *The Early Church*, 138.

14. Firmicus Maternus, *The Error of the Pagan Religions* (New York: Newman Press, 1970), 77-78.

15. "Oration on Habib the Martyr," in *Cureton, Ancient Syriac Documents, 95* as quoted in Samuel Hugh Moffett, *A History of Christianity in Asia*, vol. 1 (Maryknoll, N.Y.: Orbis Books, 1988), 138.

16. Theodoret, *Ecclesiastical History* 1:24, quoted in Moffett, *A History of Christianity*, 144.

17. Eusebius, *Life of Constantine*, 4:56, quoted in Moffett, *A History of Christianity*, 138.

18. Arend Theodoor van Leeuwen, *Christianity in World History: The Meeting of Faiths East and West* (New York: Charles Scribners Sons, 1964), 210.

19. Moffett, *A History of Christianity*, 288-323.

20. Ibid., 211.

21. Internet.

22. Kenneth Cragg, *The Call of the Minaret* (Maryknoll, N.Y.: Orbis Books, 1985), 189.

23. Bernard Lewis, *The Political Language of Islam* (Chicago: Chicago University Press, 1988), 29.

24. Bernard Lewis, *What Went Wrong: Western Impact and Middle Eastern Response* (New York: Oxford University Press, 2002), 9-11.

25. John Howard Yoder, trans. and ed., *The Legacy of Michael Sattler*, Classics of the Radical Reformation, vol. 1 (Scottdale, Pa.: Herald Press, 1973), 72-73.

26. Ibid.

27. Helmut Isaak, "Menno's Vision of the Anticipation of the Kingdom of God in His Early Writings" and Marjon Blok, "Discipleship in Menno Simon's Dat Fundament: An Exercise in Anabaptist Theology," in *Menno Simons: A Reappraisal*, ed. Gerald R. Brunk, 57-79, 103-30 (Harrisonburg, Va.: Eastern Mennonite College, 1992).

28. Howard John Loewen, *One Lord, One Church, One Hope, and One God* (Elkhart, Ind.: Institute of Mennonite Studies, 1983), 79-84.

29. "The Challenge of Modernity: Shi'ah Muslim—Mennonite Christian Dialogue," *The Conrad Grebel Review* 21:3 (Fall 2003).

Chapter 1: The Kingdom of God

1. A. Miguel in *Encyclopedia of Islam*, CD-ROM ed., vols. 1-11 (Leiden: E.J. Brill, 2003), s.v.

2. Bassam Tibi, *The Challenge of Fundamentalism: Political Islam and the New World Disorder*, rev. ed. (Los Angeles: University of California Press, 2002), 20.

3. George Elden Ladd, *The Gospel of the Kingdom* (Grand Rapids, Mich.: Wm. B. Eerdmans , 1959), 219.

4. John Bright, *The Kingdom of God in the Bible and the Church* (London: Lutterworth Press, 1955), 219.

5. Herman N. Ridderbos, *Matthew's Witness to Jesus Christ: The King and the Kingdom* (New York: Association Press, 1958), 60.

6. Ibid.

7. A. Guillaume, trans., *The Life of Muhammad* ([Ibn] Ishaq's *Sirat Rasul Allah*) (Oxford: Oxford University Press, 1955), 79-81.

8. "Masih," *Encyclopedia of Islam*, s.v.

9. A. Yusuf Ali, *The Holy Qur'an: Text, Translation, and Commentary*, 57:27, n. 5321.

10. Larry Poston, *Islamic Da'wah in the West* (New York: Oxford University Press, 1992).

11. Qur'an 20:8; 22:30; 6:103; 7:180; 7:163; 17:23; 6:151; 24:2; 5:38; 4:112; 4:32.

12. Robert Roberts, *The Social Laws of the Qur'an* (London: Williams and Norgate, 1925).

13. Allama Muhammad Baqir al-Majlisi, *The Life and Religion of Muhammad*, Hiyat al-Qulub, vol. 2, trans. James L. Merrick (Cambridge: Cambridge University Press, 1982), 292.

14. Ibid., 289.

15. See references in Neal Robinson, *Christ in Islam and Christianity* (Albany: State Universities of New York Press, 1991), 120-22.

16. Mahmoud Ayoub, *Redemptive Suffering in Islam: A Study of the Devotional Aspects of 'Ashura' in Twelver Shi'ism* Religion and Society Series (Hague: Mouton Publishers, 1978).

17. *Sahih al-Bukhari*, trans. M. Muhsin Khan (Beirut: Dar al-Arabia, 1975), v. 4, bk. 55, ch. 44, trad. 657 (p. 437).

18. Badru D. Kateregga and David W. Shenk, *Islam and Christianity: A Muslim and a Christian in Dialogue* (Ibadan, Nigeria: Daystar Press, 1985), 81.

19. Ibid., 79-80.

20. Abdo Shemsudin, "Christian and Muslim Relationships" (unpublished paper, 1985).

21. Abd al-Masih, *The Main Challenges for Committed Christians in Serving Muslims* (Villach, Austria: Light of Life Publications, 1996).

22. Ibid.

Chapter 2: A Global Perspective

1. *Gulf News* (Dec. 12, 2003): 1.

2. Ovey N. Mohammed, S.J., *Muslim-Christian Relations: Past, Present, Future* (Maryknoll, N.Y.: Orbis Books, 1999). Hugh Goddard, *Christians and Muslims: From Double Standards to Mutual Understanding* (Richmond, Surrey: Curzon Press, 1995). Stuart E. Brown, ed., *Meeting in Faith: Twenty Years of Christian-Muslim Conversations Sponsored by the World Council of Churches* (Geneva: WCC Publications, 1989). Jutta Sperber, *Christians and Muslims: The Dialogue Activities of the World Council of Churches and Their Theological Foundation* (Berlin: Walter de Gruyter, 2000). *The Middle East Council of Churches News Report* 14:1 (Summer 2002). Kate Zebiri, *Muslims and Christians Face to Face* (Oxford: Oneworld, 1997). Colin Chapman, *Islam and the West: Conflict, Coexistence or Conversion?* (Carlisle, Cumbria: Paternoster Press, 1998). Jorgen S. Nielsen, "Is there an escape from the history of Christian-Muslim relations?" in *A Faithful Presence: Essays for Kenneth Cragg*, ed. David Thomas with Clare Amos (London: Melisende, 2003). Rollin Armour, *Islam, Christianity, and the West: A Troubled History* (Maryknoll, N.Y.: Orbis Books, 2002).

3. *Christianity Today* (Oct. 2003): 21.

4. *Economist* (June 5, 2003).

5. *New York Times* (Oct. 1, 2003): A1.

6. http://www.ciar-net.org/asp/crr2003.asp

7. Irshad Mauji, *The Trouble with Islam* (Toronto: Random House Canada, 2003). Clifford Krauss, "An Unlikely Promoter of Islamic Reform," *New York Times* (Oct. 4, 2003): A4.

8. "Iran Exchange," *Peace Office Newsletter* (Mennonite Central Committee) 31:3 (July-Sept. 2001): 2-3.

9. Survey directed by John Green of the Ray C. Bliss Institute of Applied Politics, University of Akron, Ohio.

10. Laurie Goodstein, "Seeing Islam as 'Evil' Evangelicals Seek Converts" (May 27, 2003), http://www.nytimes.com/2003/05/27/national/27ISLA.html.

11. Akbar S. Ahmed, *Islam Under Siege: Living Dangerously in a Post-Honor World* (Cambridge: Polity Press, 2003).

12. www.ird-renew.org/muslimdialogue; Mark Stricherz, "Evangelicals Advise on Muslim Dialogue," *Christianity Today* (July 2003): 21.

13. For example, Tony Carnes, "Kosher Cooperation: Jewish elites broker new relations with evangelicals," *Christianity Today* (Oct. 2003): 20-21.

14. *New York Times* (Nov. 9, 2002).

15. Craig S. Smith, "Minarets and Steeples: Can France Balance Them?" *New York Times* (Oct. 1, 2003): A4.

16. *Economist* (Feb. 7, 2004): 24-26. *New York Times* (Feb. 11, 2004): A3.

17. *New York Times* (Jan. 15, 2004).

18. *Time* (Sept. 15, 2003): 33-34.

19. *BBC News* (Jan. 17, 2002).

20. For example, "Egypt's Christians Seek Answers After Deadly Riots: At least 21 Christians killed in clash with Muslims," *Christianity Today* (Jan. 10, 2000). *Ecumenical Dialogue* by the Evangelical Church in Germany, Hamburg (April 2002).

21. *New York Times* (Oct. 12, 2003).

22. *New York Times* (Oct. 4, 2003).

23. For example, "Egypt's Christians Seek Answers."

24. *Barnabas* (Jan.-Feb. 2004): 9, www.barnabasfund.org; http://www.copts.net/index.asp.

25. *Time* (Sept. 15, 2003): 37.

26. Ibid., 24.

27. Ibid., 20.

28. *Khaleej Times* (Dec. 12, 2003): 9. *New York Times* (Dec. 24, 2003): A8.

29. "Interview with Mr. Muhammad As-Sammak," *The Middle East Council of Churches (MECC) News Report* 13:3-4 (Autumn 2001).

30. Editorial from Syrian newspaper *Ad-Diyar* by Nazir ?Abd ul-Qadir, *MECC News Report* 13:2 (Summer 2001).

31. "The Arab Working Group on Muslim-Christian Dialogue," *MECC News Report* 14:1 (Summer 2002).

32. "Interview with Mr. Muhammad As-Sammak."

33. Kevin Begos, "Other Baghdad battles ahead for Christians," *Christianity Today* (Sept. 2003): 35-36.

34. "Iran Exchange," 1-3.

35. Johann Haafkens, "Christian Muslim Relations in Sub-Saharan Africa," in *Christian-Muslim Encounters*, eds. Yvonne Yazbeck and Wadi Z. Haddad, 305-6 (Gainesville, Fla.: University Press of Florida, 1995).

36. See Omar Eby, *Fifty Years, Fifty Stories: The Mennonite Mission in Somalia, 1953-2003* (Scottdale, Pa.: Herald Press; Telford, Pa.: DreamSeeker Books, 2003).

37. Tom Michel, S.J., "Christian-Muslim Relations: Are We Missing the Real Story?" *National Catholic Reporter* (June 25, 2003).

38. Samuel Huntington, *The Clash of Civilizations* (New York: Simon and Schuster, 1996).

39. *New York Times* (Oct. 18, 2003): A6.

40. *Khaleej Times* (Dec. 12, 2003): 4. *Gulf News* (Dec. 12, 2003): 11.

41. Fr. Thomas Michael, S.J., "Terror and Hope in Indonesia," edited transcript of Woodstock Forum, May 2, 2003, cosponsored by Georgetown University's Center for Muslim-Christian Understanding.

42. See Mark Juergensmeyer, *Terror in the Mind of God: The Global Rise of Religious Violence* (Berkeley, Calif.: University of California Press, 2000).

43. Jonathan Glover, *Humanity: A Moral History of the Twentieth Century* (New Haven, Conn.: Yale University Press, 2000).

44. See also John M. Drescher, "War has psychological essentials," *Mennonite Weekly Review* (July 29, 2002), for a survey of the seven elements essential to conditioning people to both legitimate and require war.

45. See David E. Stannard, *American Holocaust: Columbus and the Conquest of the New World* (New York: Oxford University Press, 1992); or Ronald Wright, *Stolen Continents: The Americas through Indian Eyes since 1492* (Boston: Houghton-Mifflin, 1992).

46. Clyde Prestowitz, *Rogue Nation: American Unilateralism and the Failure of Good Intentions* (New York: Basic Books, 2003), 6.

47. Ibid., 33, 36. Clyde Prestowitz is the president of the Economic Strategy Institute in Washington, D.C.

Chapter 3: Islam—the West—Anabaptists

1. "Qaeda Grocery Lists," *New York Times* (Mar. 17, 2002): 18.

2. "The Challenge of Peace: God's Promise and Our Response" (Washington, D.C.: United States Catholic Conference, 1983).

3. Ibid., 74.

4. William Barclay, *Thou Shalt Not Kill: War and the Church in the Past* (New Malden, Surrey, UK: The Fellowship of Reconciliation, 1966), 24. Emphasis in original.

Chapter 4: The Mennonite Engagement with Muslims

1. Bruce Bradshaw, *Change Across Cultures: A Narrative Approach to Social Transformation* (Grand Rapids, Mich.: Baker Academic, 2002), 245-47.

2. Arend Theodoor Van Leeuwen, *Christianity in World History: The Meeting of the Faiths of East and West* (New York: Charles Scribner, 1964), 344.

3. John Duerksen, "Monthly Report from Egypt to MCC" (Akron, Pa.: Mennonite Central Committee, June 1982).

4. Kenneth Cragg, *Christianity in World Perspective* (London: Lutterworth Press, 1969), 65.

5. Edward W. Said, *Orientalism* (New York: Vintage, 1977), 325-26.

6. Bradshaw, *Change Across Cultures*, 21.

7. Frank H. Epp, *Whose Land is Palestine?* (Grand Rapids: William B. Eerdman Publishing Co., 1970); *The Palestinians* (Toronto: McClelland and Stewart, 1976); *The Israelis* (Toronto: McClelland and Stewart, 1980).

8. Peter G. Riddell and Peter Cotterell, *Islam in Context: Past, Present, and Future* (Grand Rapids, Mich.: Baker Academic, 2003).

9. *The Conrad Grebel Review* (Summer 2003).

10. Samuel P. Huntington, *The Clash of Civilizations* (New York: Simon and Schuster, 1997).

11. Arend Theodoor Van Leeuwen, *Christianity in World History.*

12. Kenneth Cragg, *To Meet and to Greet: Faith Meets Faith* (London: Eppwoth Press, 1992).

13. John Ruth, *The Earth Is the Lord's: A Narrative History of Lancaster Mennonite Conference* (Scottdale, Pa.: Herald Press, 2001).

14. Riddel and Cotterell, *Islam in Context.*

15. Cliford Geertz, *Islam Observed: Religious Development in Morocco and Indonesia* (New Haven, Conn.: Yale University Press, 1968).

16. Wilbert R. Shenk, *By Faith They Went Out: Mennonite Missions* (Elkhart, Ind.: Institute of Mennonite Studies, 2000).

17. John Howard Yoder, *The Legacy of Michael Sattler* (Scottdale, Pa.: Herald Press, 1973), 72-73.

18. Gordon D. Nickel, *Peaceable Witness Among Muslims* (Scottdale, Pa.: Herald Press, 1999), 92.

19. Alle Hoekema, *Dutch Mennonite Mission in Indonesia: Historical Essays* (Elkhart, Ind.: Institute of Mennonite Studies, 2001).

20. Cornelius J. Dyck, ed., *The Lordship of Christ: Proceedings of the Seventh Mennonite World Conference* (Elkhart, Ind.: Mennonite World Conference, 1962), 271.

21. Ibid., 482.

22. Kenneth Cragg, *Christianity in World Perspective*, 65.

23. Badru Kateregga and David W. Shenk, *A Muslim and a Christian in Dialogue* (Scottdale, Pa.: Herald Press, 1977).

24. Richard Gillard, © 1977 Scripture in Song. Used by permission.

25. Omar Eby, *Fifty Years, Fifty Stories: The Mennonite Mission in Somalia, 1953-2003* (Scottdale, Pa.: Herald Press; Telford, Pa.: DreamSeeker Books, 2003).

26. Ibid., 61.

27. Ibid., 43.

28. *Mennonite Weekly Review* (Sept. 15, 2003): 6.

29. Eby, *Fifty Years, Fifty Stories*, 7.

30. William Dalrymple, review of *The Body and the Blood: The Middle East's Vanishing Christians and the Possibility of Peace*, by Charles Sennott, *New York Review of Books* (Sept. 25, 2003): 16.

31. John W. Kiser, *The Monks of Tibhirine: Faith, Love, and Terror in Algeria* (New York: St. Martins Press, 2002), 199.

32. There are a number of specialists that are basic. Each has several books and multiple articles. These include: Kenneth Cragg, John Esposito, David Kerr, Lamin Sanneh, David W. Shenk, and J. Dudley Woodberry. Solid current articles are found in such quarterlies as *The Muslim World*, *International Bulletin of Missionary Research*, and *Mission Focus*.

The following authors also have additional recommended writing:

Armour, Rollin, Sr. *Islam, Christianity, and the West: A Troubled History.* Maryknoll, N.Y.: Orbis Books, 2002.

Bauman, Chad Mullet, and James R. Krabill, eds. *Anabaptism and Mission: A Bibliography, 1859-2002*. Elkhart, Ind.: Mennonite Mission Network Publication, 2002.

Bradshaw, Bruce. *Change Across Cultures: A Narrative Approach in Social Transformation*. Grand Rapids, Mich.: Baker Academic, 2002.

Chapman, Colin. *Islam and the West: Conflict, Co-Existence, or Conversion*. Carlisle, UK: Paternoster Press, 1998.

Cragg, Kenneth. *Christianity in World Perspective*. London: Lutterworth Press, 1969.

Daniel, Norman. *Islam and the West: the Making of an Image*. Oxford: One World, 1993.

Eby, Omar. *Fifty Years, Fifty Stories: The Mennonite Mission in Somalia, 1953-2003*. Scottdale, Pa.: Herald Press; Telford, Pa.: DreamSeeker Books, 2003.

Hoekema, Alle. *Dutch Mennonite Mission Indonesia: Historical Essays*. Elkhart, Ind.: Institute of Mennonite Studies, 2001.

Kimball, Charles A. *Striving Together: A Way Forward in Christian-Muslim Relations*. Maryknoll, N.Y.: Orbis Books, 1991.

Lybarger, Loren Diller. "Defining Presence: The Formation of Mennonite Agency Approaches and Attitudes Toward Muslims and Islam, 1949-1995" (master's thesis, Lutheran School of Theology, 1995, available at MCC, Network and EMM).

Mennonite Encyclopedia. Vols. 1-5. Scottdale, Pa.: Herald Press, 1955-1959, 1990.

Nickel, Gordon D. *Peaceable Witness Among Muslims*. Scottdale, Pa.: Herald Press, 1999.

Riddel, Peter G., and Peter Cotterell. *Islam in Context: Past, Present, and Future*. Grand Rapids, Mich.: Baker Academic, 2003.

Shenk, Calvin E. *Who Do You Say That I Am: Christians Encounter Other Religions*. Scottdale, Pa.: Herald Press, 1997.

Shenk, Wilbert R. *By Faith They Went Out: Mennonite Missions, 1850-1999*. Elkhart, Ind.: Institute of Mennonite Studies, 2000.

Stassen, Glen H., and David P. Gushee. *Kingdom Ethics: Following Jesus in Contemporary Context*. Downers Grove, Ill.: InterVarsity Press, 2003.

Van Leeuwen, Arend Theodoor. *Christianity in World History: The Meeting of the Faiths of East and West*. New York: Charles Scribner, 1964.

Yoder, John Howard, Michael G. Cartwright, and Peter Ochs. *The Jewish-Christian Schism Revisited*. Grand Rapids, Mich.: Eerdmans, 2003.

33. Merle Good, "Bedru Hussein: Gentle and Intense," *Festival Quarterly* (Winter 1994): 12-13.

34. Herb Klassen, "A small remnant engaged in a big work," *Mennonite Brethren Herald* (June 27, 1997): 19.

35. Dan Nickel, "A Witness to Muslims in Indonesia," *Mennonite Brethren Herald* 19:3 (Feb. 1, 1980): 7.

36. Roelf S. Kuitse, "Witness: 'Accounting for the Hope in Us' (1 Peter)," *Mission Focus* 13 (1985): 42.

37. Lamin Sanneh, "Christian Experience of Islamic Da'wah," in *Christian Mission and Islamic Da 'wah* (Leicester, U.K.: The Islamic Foundation, 1982), 64.

38. Wilbert R. Shenk, "Editorial," *Mission Focus* 9 (1981): 20.

39. Roy Hange, "Rebuilding Old Walls: A Survey of Religious Violence in the Middle East," *Mission Focus: Annual Review* 2 (1994): 23. See also Hange, "Healing 'Holy Hatred': Biblical and Practical Reflections," *Mission Focus: Annual Review* 4 (1996): 63-73.

40. For example, in his *Journeys of the Muslim Nation and the Christian Church: Exploring the Mission of Two Communities* (Scottdale, Pa.: Herald Press, 2003), 153 et passim.

41. Laurie L. Oswald, "Persecution fuels church growth," *Canadian Mennonite* 2:6 (Mar. 16, 1998): 21.

42. Anton Tien, trans., "The Apology of Al-Kindi," in *The Early Christian-Muslim Dialogue: A Collection of Documents from the First Three Islamic Centuries (632-900 A.D.)*, ed. N. A. Newman (Hatfield, Pa.: Interdisciplinary Biblical Institute, 1993), 429-32, 439-40, 448, 478-83, 513-14.

43. The most recent examples are, "Muslim Missions after September 11th," *Evangelical Missions Quarterly* (January 2002); and "Terrorism, Islam, and Mission: Reflections of a Guest in Muslim Lands," *International Bulletin of Missionary Research* (January 2002).

44. Robert Ramseyer, "Sixteenth-Century Insights and Contemporary Reality: Reflections on Thirty-five Years in Mission," *Mission Focus* 18:2 (June 1990): 23.

45. Mike Brislen, "A Model for a Muslim-Culture Church," *Missiology: An International Review* 24 (1996): 355-67.

46. Lamin Sanneh, "Christian Missions and the Western Guilt Complex," *Evangelical Review of Theology* (1995): 393-400. Also "The Defender of the Good News: Questioning Lamin Sanneh," interviewed by Jonathan J. Bonk, posted October 1, 2003, at http://christianitytoday.com/ct/2003/010/35.112.html.

47. Kenneth Cragg, "On Religious Freedom," *International Review of Mission* 65 (1976): 450.

48. Kenneth Cragg, "Conversion and Convertibility—With Special Reference to Muslims," in *Down to Earth: Studies in Culture and Christianity*, eds. John R.W. Stott and Robert Coote (Grand Rapids, Mich.: Eerdmans, 1980), 197.

49. Bertha Beachy, "Reflections on Mennonite Mission Experience in Somalia," *Mission Focus* 10:4 (1982): 52.

50. *Time* (June 30, 2003).

51. Philip Jenkins, *The Next Christendom: The Coming of Global Christianity* (New York: Oxford University Press, 2002), 163-90.

52. Lesslie Newbigin, "A Sermon Preached at the Thanksgiving Service for the Fiftieth Anniversary of the Tambaram Conference of the International Missionary Council," *International Review of Mission* 78 (1988): 328.

Chapter 6: Revelation and Reconciliation

1. Walter Wink, *The Powers That Be: Theology for a New Millennium* (New York: Doubleday, 1998), 45.

2. Ibid., 46.

3. James Williams in William Chittick, trans., *A Shi'ite Anthology* (Albany: State University of New York Press, 1981), 60.

4. Moroslav Volf, "Distance and Belonging" in *Abrahamic Faiths, Ethnicity and Ethnic Conflicts*, ed. Paul Peachey, George F. McLean, and John Kromkowski (Washington, D.C.: The Council for Research in Values and Philosophy, 1997), 222.

5. Ibid., 224.

6. Ibid., 225

7. Rene Girard, *Violence and the Sacred*, trans. Patrick Gregory (Baltimore: John Hopkins University Press, 1981).

8. Marshall G. S. Hodgson, *The Venture of Islam: Conscience and History in a World of Civilization*, vol. 1. The Classical Age of Islam (Chicago: The University of Chicago Press, 1977), 174.

9. Martin Lings, *Muhammad: His Life Based on the Earliest Sources* (Rochester, Vt.: Inner Traditions International, Ltd., 1983), 128.

10. Ibid., 125

11. Ibid., 300

12. Ibid., 301

13. Chittick, *A Shi'ite Anthology*, 68.

14. Ibid., 68-69.

15. For further reading see the following:

> Chittick, William, trans. *A Shi'ite Anthology*. Albany: State University of New York Press, 1981.
>
> Hodgson, Marshall G. S. *The Venture of Islam: Conscience and History in a World of Civilization*. Vol. 1. The Classical Age of Islam. Chicago: The University of Chicago Press, 1974.
>
> The Holy Bible. *New Revised Standard Version*. New York: Oxford University Press, 1989.
>
> Lings, Martin. *Muhammad: His Life Based on the Earliest Sources*. Rochester, Vt.: Inner Traditions International, Ltd., 1983.

Al-Qur'an: A Contemporary Translation. Interpreted by Ahmed Ali. Princeton: Princeton University Press, 1994.

Volf, Miroslav. "Distance and Belonging" in *Abrahamic Faiths, Ethnicity and Ethnic Conflicts.* Edited by Paul Peachey, George F. McLean, and John Kromkowski. Washington, D.C.: The Council for Research in Values and Philosophy, 1997.

Wink, Walter. *The Powers That Be: Theology for a New Millennium.* New York: Doubleday, 1998.

Chapter 7: Women in Islam and the Gospel

1. Samuel P. Huntington, *The Clash of Civilizations and the Remaking of World Order* (New York: Simon & Schuster, 1997).

2. Yusuf Ali, *The Holy Qur'an: Text Translation and Commentary* (Beirut: Dar al Arabia, 1968), notes 2082, 670.

3. Ibid.

4. Quoted by Muhammad Abdul-Rauf, *The Islamic View of Women and the Family* (New York: Robert Speller and Sons, Publishers, 1979), 25.

5. One should note here that the whole verse includes a part which is not often quoted in books written for a western readership because it is an embarrassment to Muslims in the west. The verse suggests that the husband can beat his wife (lightly) as a last resort if she is disloyal to him. To face the criticism which can be prompted by the verse, some Muslim scholars in the west suggest that it needs to be understood in the context of the times. Here is the rest of the verse.

> Therefore the righteous women are devoutly obedient, and guard in (the husband's) absence what God would have them guard. As to those women on whose part ye fear disloyalty and ill-conduct, admonish them (first), (next), refuse to share their beds, (and last) beat them (lightly); but if they return to obedience, seek not against them means (of annoyance); for God is Most High, Great (above you all) (Qur'an 4:34).

6. Quoted in *Rebuilding Somalia: Issues and Possibilities for Puntland* (WSP Somali Program, 2001), 262.

7. Farhad Khosrokhavar, "Islamisme et féminisme," in *Iran: comment sortir d'une révolution religieuse* (Paris: Seuil, 1999), 228 (my translation).

8. For a book which deals with the issue, see *Les musulmans d'occident et l'avenir de l'islam* (Tariq Ramadan, Arles, France: Sindbad, Actes Sud, 2003).

9. This view is expressed by Hammudah Abdalati in *Islam in Focus* (American Trust Publications, 1993), 168.

10. It is important to clarify here that Muhammad never claimed to be perfect, neither did the Qu'ran, which only said that he was of "noble nature"

(68:4), nevertheless, he is revered as such by most Muslims. As Annemarie Schimmel states in her book, *And Muhammad Is His Messenger: The Veneration of the Prophet in the Islamic Piety* (Chapel Hill, N.C., University of North Carolina Press, 1985), 4: "He (the non-Muslim) will find that Muhammad indeed constitutes the exemplar and model for every Muslim believer, who is called to imitate him in all, even seemingly insignificant, actions and habits, and he will likely be amazed by the way in which the mystics developed the theory of Muhammad's primordial light and accorded to him, in his position as The Perfect Man, an almost cosmic status and function."

Chapter 13: Middle East

1. Quoted by Marie Shenk in *Mennonite Encounter with Judaism in Israel: An MBM Story of Creative Presence Spanning Four Decades, 1953-93*, Mission Insight Series 15 (Elkhart, Ind.: Mennonite Board of Missions, 2000), 3.

2. Leroy Friesen, *Mennonite Witness in the Middle East: A Missiological Introduction*, rev. ed. (Elkhart, Ind.: Mennonite Board of Missions, 2000), 77.

3. The Graber quote comes from Marie Shenk's master's thesis, "Mennonite Encounter with Judaism in Israel, 1953-1993" (Eastern Mennonite University, 1998).

4. Ibid., 4.

5. Robert Rhodes, "In Iraq, chaplain helped soldiers deal with death," *Mennonite Weekly Review* (Oct. 20, 2003): 15.

Chapter 22: Somalia

1. On September 11, 2001, commercial airliners were hijacked and deliberately crashed into three large office buildings in two American cities. On October 7, the United States and Great Britain attacked thirty targets across Afghanistan. As the U.S. is generally considered to be a Christian nation and Afghanistan is an Islamic state, many voices from around the world have identified these related attacks as a renewal of an old religious conflict between Christianity and Islam.

Chapter 23: Ethiopia

1. Peter Falk, *The Growth of the Church in Africa* (Congo, Kinshasa: Institut Superieur Theologique, 1985), 71-72.

2. Nathan B. Hege, *Beyond Our Prayers: Ethiopia* (Scottdale, Pa.: Herald Press, 1998), 45-46.

3. "MKC Statistical Data: Regional Conference Reports," (Addis Ababa: MKC Headquarters, August, 2003).

Chapter 25: Justice and Reconciliation

1. Roland Bainton, *Christian Attitudes Toward War and Peace* (Nashville: Abingdon, 1980), 20.

2. Samuel P. Huntington, *The Clash of Civilizations* (New York: Simon and Schuster, 1997).

Chapter 26: Pacifism among Muslims in Africa

1. Lamin Sanneh, "Pacifism among Muslims" (seminar, An Anabaptist Consultation on Islam, Eastern Mennonite University, Harrisonburg, Va., October 2003).

2. Ibid.

3. Lamin Sanneh, *The Crown and the Turban: Muslims and West African Pluralism* (Boulder, Colo.: Westview Press, 1997), 214.

4. Lamin Sanneh, *Piety and Power: Muslims and Christians in West Africa* (Maryknoll, N.Y.: Orbis Books, 1996), 1.

5. Sanneh, "Pacifism among Muslims."

6. Sanneh, *The Crown and the Turban,* 214-15.

7. Sanneh, *Piety and Power,* 15.

8. Sanneh, "Pacifism among Muslims."

9. Sanneh, *Piety and Power,* 18.

10. Ali Moussa Iye, *Le Verdict del'Arbre* (self-published: n.d.), 145-57.

11. John Drysdale, *Stoics without Pillows* (HAAN Associates, 2000), 13.

12. I. M. Lewis, *Saints and Somalis* (HAAN Associates, 1998), 63.

13. Miroslav Volf, *Exclusion and Embrace* (Nashville: Abingdon, 1996), 72-92.

14. Mohammed Abdillaahi Riraash, et al., *Spared from the Spear* (ICRC: 1997).

15. For further reading see:

> Abu-Nimer, Muhammed, *Nonviolence and Peace Building in Islam, Theory and Practice.* Gainesville: University Press of Florida, 2003.
>
> Drysdale, John. *Stoics without Pillows.* London: HAAN Associates, 2000.
>
> Lewis, I. M. *Saints and Somalis.* London: HAAN Associates, 1998.
>
> Riraash, Mohammed Abdillaahi, et al. *Spared from the Spear.* ICRC, 1997.
>
> Sanneh, Lamin. *Piety and Power.* Maryknoll, N.Y.: Orbis Books, 1996.
>
> Sanneh, Lamin. *The Crown and the Turban.* Boulder, Colo.: Westview Press, 1997.

Chapter 27: Secularization and Democracy

1. Hussein Ahmed Amin, "Associations of Religion, Violence and Despair," *Al-Ahram Weekly* (June 18-24, 1992): 7.

2. William Cavanaugh, "'A Fire Strong Enough to Consume the House': The Wars of Religion and the Rise of the State," *Modern Theology* 11:4 (Oct. 1995): 398-99.

3. Ibid., 405.

4. Khaled Abou Al Fadl, "Islam and the Challenge of Democracy," *Boston Review* (April/May 2003). http://www.bostonreview.net/BR28.2/abou.html

5. Douglas E. Streusand, "The Historical Muslim City: Lessons for the Discourse on Islam and Democracy" (speech at the Fourth Annual Conference at the Center for the Study of Islam and Democracy, Washington, D.C., May 16, 2003).

6. Aziz Sachedina, "Why Democracy and Why Now?" (speech at the Fourth Annual Conference at the Center for the Study of Islam and Democracy, Washington, D.C., May 16, 2003). http://www.islam-democracy.org/4th_Annual_Conference-Sachedina_address.asp

7. Jack Miles, "Theology and the Clash of Civilizations," *Cross Currents* (Winter 2002). http://www.crosscurrents.org/mileswinter2002.htm

8. Kenneth Cragg, "'My Tears into Thy Bottle': Prophethood and God," *The Muslim World* 88:3-4 (July-October, 1998), 252.

9. Ibid., 255.

10. Michael Tracy and Douglas Kries Hacket, trans., *Augustine: Political Writings* (Indianapolis: Hackett Publishing, 1994), 206-7.

11. R. Scott Appleby, *The Ambivalence of the Sacred* (Lanham, Md.: Rowman & Littlefield, 2000); Douglas Johnston, ed., *Faith Based Diplomacy: Triumphing Realpolitik* (New York: Oxford University Press, 2003).

12. For further reading see:

> Appleby, R. Scott. *The Ambivalence of the Sacred*. Lanham, Md.: Rowman & Littlefield, 2000.
>
> Cragg, Kenneth. *Call of the Minaret*, 2nd ed. New York: Daystar Press, 1989.
>
> Johnston, Douglas, ed. *Faith Based Diplomacy: Triumphing Realpolitik*. New York: Oxford University Press, 2003.

Chapter 28: Theology of Economic Development

1. As defined by Bryant Myers, *Walking with the Poor* (Maryknoll, N.Y.: Orbis Books, 1999), 3.

2. For further reading see:

> Myers, Bryant L. *Walking with the Poor*. Maryknoll, N.Y.: Orbis Books, 1999.
>
> Sen, Amarty. *Development as Freedom*. New York: Random House, 1999.
>
> Sider, Ronald J. *Good News and Good Works*. Grand Rapids, Mich.: Baker Books, 1993.

3. The study was undertaken by Adama Diouf, funded by World Vision and commissioned by the Fraternité Evangelique du Senegal.

Chapter 29: The Challenge of the Muslim Critique

1. See Hugh Goddard, *Muslim Perceptions of Christianity* (London: Grey Seal, 1996), index entry "Trinity." Of the many Muslim theological critiques, that of Ibn Taymiyya (d. 1328) is particularly incisive. For this, see Thomas F. Michel, *A Muslim Theologian's Response to Christianity: Ibn Taymiyya's Al-Jawab Al-Sahih* (Delmar, N.Y.: Caravan, 1984), 255-325.

2. Especially Jürgen Moltmann, *The Trinity and the Kingdom* (San Francisco: Harper, 1991), and James Wm. McClendon Jr., *Systematic Theology*, vol. 2, *Doctrine* (Nashville: Abingdon Press, 1994), 280-323.

3. On the theology involved in the forging of trinitarian doctrine, see Jaroslav Pelikan, *The Christian Tradition: A History of the Development of Doctrine*, vol. 1, *The Emergence of the Catholic Tradition (100-600)* (Chicago: University of Chicago, 1971), 172-225.

4. For Ibn Taymiyya's version of this thesis, see Michel, *A Muslim Theologian*, 350-69.

5. These thoughts are based on Nicholas Lash, *Easter in Ordinary: Reflections on Human Experiences and the Knowledge of God* (Notre Dame, Ind.: University of Notre Dame, 1990), 254-85, and Victor A. Shepherd, "The Trinity Against the Spirit of Unitarianism," in *The Trinity: An Essential for Faith in Our Time*, ed. Andrew Stirling (Nappanee, Ind.: Evangel Publishing House, 2002), 179-96.

6. See David B. Burrell, *Freedom and Creation in Three Traditions* (Notre Dame, Ind.: University of Notre Dame Press, 1993), 161-84, for an application of Lash's insights to Judaism, Christianity, and Islam.

Chapter 30: Incarnation

1. Badru D. Kateregga and David W. Shenk, *A Muslim and a Christian in Dialogue* (Scottdale, Pa.: Herald Press, 1977), 142.

2. Ibid., 50.

3. Andrew Rippin, *Muslims: Their Religious Beliefs and Practices*, 2nd ed. (New York: Routledge, 2002), 240-41.

4. Kenneth Cragg, *The Event of the Qur'an: Islam in Its Scriptures* (Oxford: Oneworld Publications, 1994).

5. A. Christian van Gorder, *No God But God: A Path to Muslim-Christian Dialogue on God's Nature* (Maryknoll, N.Y.: Orbis Books, 2003), 25-50.

6. Philip K. Hitti, *History of the Arabs*, 10th ed. (London: MacMillan, 1973), 100-1.

7. Ibid., 141-45.

8. Kenneth Cragg, *Muhammad and the Christian: A Question of Response* (Maryknoll, N.Y.: Orbis Books, 1984), 10.

9. Kateregga and Shenk, *A Muslim and a Christian*, 150.

10. Oral comments by a mullah at a Shi'a-Mennonite dialogue, February 14-15, 2004, convened at the Imam Khomeini Research and Education Institute, Qom, Iran.

11. Lamin Sanneh, *Translating the Message* (Maryknoll, N.Y.: Orbis Books, 1989).

12. Ibid., 9.

13. Murtada Mutahhari, *Understanding Islamic Sciences* (London: Islamic College for Advanced Studies Press, 2002), 69-74.

14. Tarif Khalidi, *The Muslim Jesus* (Cambridge: Harvard University Press, 2001).

15. Ibid., 17-21.

16. van Gorder, *No God But God*, 90-91.

17. This was the text of a sermon by Bishop Kenneth Cragg at a conference, "Christian Presence and Witness," at the International Baptist Theological Seminary, Prague, February 2-6, 2004.

18. Khalidi, 45.

19. For further reading see:

> Cragg, Kenneth. *Muhammad and the Christian.* Maryknoll, N.Y.: Orbis Books, 1984.
>
> Kateregga, Badru D., and David W. Shenk. *A Muslim and a Christian in Dialogue.* Scottdale, Pa.: Herald Press, 1997.
>
> Khalidi, Tarif. *The Muslim Jesus.* Cambridge: Harvard University Press, 2001.
>
> Mutahhari, Murtada. *Understanding Islamic Sciences.* London: Islamic College for Advanced Studies Press, 2002, especially 69-74.
>
> Sanneh, Lamin. *Translating the Message: The Missionary Impact on Culture.* Maryknoll, N.Y.: Orbis Books, 1989.
>
> Shenk, David W. *Journeys of the Muslim Nation and the Christian Church: Exploring the Mission of Two Communities.* Scottdale, Pa.: Herald Press, 2003.

Chapter 31: Islamic Intercession and Christian Atonement

1. Ghulam Hussain Osto, *The Cause of Creation: A Biography of Prophet Muhammad* (Karachi: Shah Nawaz Osto, 1997), 10.

2. Omar Eby, *Fifty Years, Fifty Stories: The Mennonite Mission in Somalia, 1953-2003* (Scottdale, Pa.: Herald Press; Telford, Pa.: DreamSeeker Books, 2003), 43-44.

Chapter 32: Dialogue and Witness

1. Martin Goldsmith, *Islam and Christian Witness* (Bromley, Kent: OM Publishing, 1982), 116-17.

2. "Who do you say that I am?" *Gospel Herald* (Sept. 8, 1992): 7.

3. On realism in actual Christian-Muslim faith conversation, see Michael

Nazir-Ali, *Islam: A Christian Perspective* (Exeter: Paternoster, 1983), 148; Goldsmith, *Islam and Christian Witness*, 116-18; and C. M. Naim, "Getting Real about Christian-Muslim Dialogue," *Word & World* 16 (1996): 179-83.

4. Hendrik Kraemer, *The Christian Message in a Non-Christian World*, 2nd ed. (Grand Rapids, Mich.: Kregel, 1956), 354.

5. Jay Smith, "Courage in Our Convictions: Debating Muslims," *Evangelical Missions Quarterly* 34 (1998): 28-35.

6. Anton Tien, trans., "The Apology of al-Kindi," in *The Early Christian-Muslim Dialogue: A Collection of Documents from the First Three Islamic Centuries (632-900 A.D.)*, ed. N. A. Newman (Hatfield, Pa.: Interdisciplinary Biblical Research Institute, 1993), 486.

7. Lesslie Newbigin, *The Gospel in a Pluralist Society* (Grand Rapids, Mich.: Eerdmans, 1989),116.

8. Arne Rudvin, "Islam—An Absolutely Different Ethos?" *International Review of Mission* 71 (1982): 59-65.

9. Paul Varo Martinson, "Dialogue and Evangelism in Relation to Islam," *Word & World* 16 (1996): 188.

10. George Brunk III, "The Exclusiveness of Jesus Christ," in *New Directions in Mission and Evangelization 2: Theological Foundations*, eds. James A. Scherer and Stephen B. Bevans (Maryknoll, N.Y.: Orbis, 1994), 52.

11. For further reading see:

Accad, Fouad Elias. *Building Bridges: Christianity and Islam.* Colorado Springs, Colo.: NavPress, 1997.

Borrmans, Maurice *Guidelines for Dialogue Between Christians and Muslims: Pontifical Council for Interreligious Dialogue.* New York: Paulist Press, 1990.

Brewster, Daniel R. "Dialogue: Relevancy to Evangelism." In *The Gospel and Islam* (a 1978 compendium), edited by Don M. McCurry, 513-22. Monrovia, Calif.: MARC, 1979.

Bryant, M. Darrol, and S. A. Ali. *Muslim-Christian Dialogue: Promise and Problems.* St. Paul, Minn.: Paragon House, 1998.

Christian Mission and Islamic Da'wah: Proceedings of the Chambesy Dialogue Consultation. Leicester, UK: The Islamic Foundation, 1982.

Christian Witness Among Muslims. Achimota, Ghana: Africa Christian Press, 1971.

Friesen, LeRoy. *Mennonite Witness in the Middle East: A Missiological Introduction.* Rev. ed. Elkhart, Ind.: Mennonite Board of Missions, 2000.

Glasser, Arthur F. "Is Friendly Dialogue Enough?" *Missiology* 4 (1976): 261-66.

Goldsmith, Martin. *Islam and Christian Witness.* Bromley, Kent: OM Publishing, 1982.

Guenther, Alan. "Christian-Muslim Apologetics in the 'Abbasid Period." *McGill Journal of Middle East Studies* 3 (1995): 1-16.

Guillaume, Alfred. "Theodore Abu Qurra as Apologist." *The Muslim World* 15 (1925): 42-51.

Haddad, Yvonne Yazbeck, and Wadi Zaidan Haddad, eds. *Christian-Muslim Encounters.* Gainesville, Fla.: University Press of Florida, 1995.

Hoover, Jon. "Theological Foundations for Dialogue with Islam." *MCC Peace Office Newsletter* 24:5 (1994): 1-2.

Jeffery, Arthur, trans. "Ghevond's text of the correspondence between 'Umar II and Leo II." *Harvard Theological Review* 37 (1944): 269-332.

Kimball, Charles. *Striving Together: A Way Forward in Christian-Muslim Relations.* Maryknoll, N.Y.: Orbis Books, 1991.

Kraemer, Hendrik. *The Christian Message in a Non-Christian World.* Grand Rapids, Mich.: Kregel, 1938.

Kuitse, Roelf S. "When Christians and Muslims Meet." *Mission Focus* 9 (1981): 1-4.

Martinson, Paul Varo. "Dialogue and Evangelism in Relation to Islam." *Word & World* 16 (1996): 184-93.

Mingana, A., translator, with introduction by Rendel Harris. "The Apology of Timothy the Patriarch before the Caliph Mahdi." *Bulletin of the John Rylands Library* 12 (1928): 137-46, 147-226.

Naim, C.M. "Getting Real About Christian-Muslim Dialogue." *Word & World* 16 (1996): 179-83.

Nasr, Seyyed Hossein. "Islamic-Christian Dialogue—Problems and Obstacles to Be Pondered and Overcome." *The Muslim World* 88 (1998): 218-37.

Nazir-Ali, Michael. *Frontiers in Muslim-Christian Encounter.* Oxford: Regnum, 1987.

Newbigin, Lesslie. *The Gospel in a Pluralist Society.* Geneva: WCC Publications, 1989.

Nickel, Dan. "A Witness to Muslims in Indonesia." *Mennonite Brethren Herald* 19:3 (1980): 6-7.

Nickel, Gordon. "How Does Peace Theology Affect Our Encounters with Islam?" *The Conrad Grebel Review* 14 (1996): 115-18.

———. *Peaceable Witness Among Muslims.* Scottdale, Pa.: Herald Press, 1999.

Rahbar, Daud. "Urgent Issues in Christian-Muslim Encounter." Paper for the Division of Studies of the World Council of Churches, 1961.

Rousseau, Richard W., ed. *Christianity and Islam: The Struggling Dialogue.* Scranton, Pa: Ridge Row Press, 1985.

Rudvin, Arne. "The Gospel and Islam: What Sort of Dialogue is Possible?" *Al-Mushir* 21 (1979): 82-123.

Schimmel, Annemarie, and Abdoldjavad Falaturi, eds. *We Believe in*

One God: The Experience of God in Christianity and Islam. London: Burns & Oates, 1979.

Shenk, Calvin E. "Conversion in Acts: Implications for Witness to Religions." *Mission Focus* 14:1 (1986): 1-4.

Shenk, David W., and Badru D. Kateregga. *A Muslim and a Christian in Dialogue*. Scottdale, Pa.: Herald Press, 1997.

Shenk, Wilbert R., ed. *Anabaptism and Mission*. Scottdale, Pa.: Herald Press, 1984.

Siddiqui, Ataullah. *Christian-Muslim Dialogue in the Twentieth Century*. New York: St. Martin's Press, 1997.

Smith, Jay. "Courage in Our Convictions: Debating Muslims." *Evangelical Missions Quarterly* 34 (1998): 28-35.

———. "Reaching Muslims in London: Is it time to confront?" *Urban Mission* 15 (March 1998): 37-46.

Tien, Anton. "The Apology of al-Kindi." In *The Early Christian-Muslim Dialogue: A Collection of Documents from the First Three Islamic Centuries (632-900 A.D.)*, edited by N. A. Newman, 381-545. Hatfield, Pa.: Interdisciplinary Biblical Research Institute, 1993.

Voorhis, John W. "The Discussion of a Christian and a Saracen." *The Muslim World* 25 (1935): 266ff.

Vroom, H. M. *No Other Gods: Christian Belief in Dialogue with Buddhism, Hinduism and Islam*. Grand Rapids, Mich.: Eerdmans, 1996.

Watt, W. Montgomery. *Muslim-Christian Encounters: Perceptions and Misperceptions*. New York: Routledge, 1991.

World Council of Churches. *Christians Meeting Muslims: WCC Papers on Ten Years of Christian-Muslim Dialogue*. Geneva: World Council of Churches, 1977.

Zebiri, Kate. *Muslims and Christians Face to Face*. Oxford: Oneworld, 1997.

12. David Lochhead, *The Dialogical Imperative: A Christian Reflection on Interfaith Encounter* (Maryknoll, N.Y.: Orbis Books, 1988), 46.

13. Izz al-din Ibrahim, "Islamic-Christian Dialogue: A Muslim View," in *Muslim-Christian Dialogue: Promise and Problems*, ed. M. Darrol Bryant and S. A. Ali (St. Paul, Minn.: Paragon House, 1998), 25.

14. Badru D. Kateregga and David W. Shenk, *A Muslim and a Christian in Dialogue* (Scottdale, Pa.: Herald Press, 1997).

Chapter 34: Apologetics

1. Del Kingsiter, *Questions Muslims Ask* (Center for Ministry to Muslims, 1991).

2. Ahmad Dedat and Anis Schoros, *Published Debate* (Islamic Society Library, 1992).

3. Translation here was done by Dr. M. Al-Hilali and Dr. M. Khan. See also Suras 4:136; 5:43, 44, 46, 68; 10:91; and 15:9.

4. Also Deuteronomy 33:2, Isaiah 21:7, and Matthew 17:11.

5. Anis A. Shorrosh, *Islam Revealed* (Nashville: Thomas Nelson Publishers, 1988).

6. Grant R. Jeffrey, *Jesus: The Great Debate* (Nashville: Word Publishing, 1999).

7. Kingsiter, *Questions Muslims Ask.*

8. For further reading see:

> Dedat, Ahmad, and Anis Schoros. *Published Debate.* Islamic Society Library, 1992.
>
> Jeffrey, Grant R. *Jesus: The Great Debate.* Nashville: Word Publishers, 1999.
>
> Kingsiter, Del. *Questions Muslims Ask.* Center for Ministry to Muslims, 1991.
>
> Morey, Robert A. *Islamic Invasions.* Eugene, Ore.: Harvest House Publishing, 1992.
>
> Shorrosh, Anis A. *Islam Revealed.* Nashville: Thomas Nelson Publishers, 1988.

9. Peter G. Riddell and Peter Cotterell, *Islam in Conflict* (Leicester, England: IVP, 2003), 7-8.

10. Ibid., chapters 10–12, and page 193. Also a lecture by Riddell on the theme, "Muslim Views on the World" held at the London Institute for Contemporary Christianity and sponsored by the London Lectures Trust, October 23, 2003.

11. "U.S. Image Worsens in Europe Poll," news release credited to AFP (Agence Francaise de Presse), Washington, *The Korea Times* (March 18, 2004): 6.

Chapter 35: Literature and Media

1. Author's translation.

2. Telephone conversation in September 2003.

Chapter 36: Fellowship Formation

1. Omar Eby, *Fifty Years, Fifty Stories: The Mennonite Mission in Somalia, 1953-2003* (Scottdale, Pa.: Herald Press; Telford, Pa.: DreamSeeker Books, 2003), 37.

2. Omar Eby, *A Whisper in a Dry Land* (Scottdale, Pa.: Herald Press, 1968), 163-64.

3. Ibid.

4. Eby, *Fifty Years, Fifty Stories*, 37.

5. Ibid., 36.

6. At the opening of the secondary school, attended by then President Barre and other government officials, welcome banners expressed the anticipation of local and national leaders: "Scientific Socialism Turns Knowledge

into Practical Reality." As Omar Eby wrote in *Fifty Years, Fifty Stories*, 55, "Were the words 'a handwriting on the wall'? Would the slogan's acclaimed promise of a secular Eden be fulfilled? By the time Bertha Beachy again stood on the campus of Shebelli Secondary School twenty years later, the desolate, bombed-out classrooms [embodied] the bitter fruit of that harvest."

7. Ed and Jean Rissler quote, in Eby, *Fifty Years, Fifty Stories*, 56.

8. Eby, *Fifty Years, Fifty Stories*, 89.

9. Lederach's later reflections in Ibid., 105.

10. Ibid., 116.

11. Ibid, 119-24.

12. For further reading see:

> Eby, Omar. *Fifty Years, Fifty Stories: The Mennonite Mission in Somalia, 1953-2003*. Scottdale, Pa.: Herald Press; Telford, Pa.: DreamSeeker Books, 2003. Provides pithy vignettes from the half century of Mennonite involvement in Somalia. (See map, 137.)
>
> Shenk, Calvin E. *A Relevant Theology of Presence*. CIM: Mission Focus pamphlet, 1982.
>
> Shenk, David W. "Mennonite Presence and Church Development in Somalia 1952-1972." PhD dissertation, New York University, 1972.
>
> Checole, Alemu, et al. *A Global Mennonite History*, vol. 1 *Africa*. Arnold C. Snyder and John A. Lapp, general editors. Scottdale, Pa.: Herald Press, 2003. First in a series of books on the global history of Brethren in Christ and Mennonite Churches, sponsored by Mennonite World Conference. It should be noted that the section on Somalia is in need of significant correction.

13. Peter Falk, *Growth of the Church in Africa* (Kinshasa, Congo: Institute Superieur Theologique de Kinshasa, 1985), 71-72.

14. Paul E. Balisky, "Wolaitta Evangelists: A Study of Religious Innovation in Southern Ethiopia, 1937-75" (PhD dissertation, University of Aberdeen [Scotland], 1997), 85-88.

15. Makango Tesfaye, "The Impact of Evangelism, among the Muslim in Badawacho District" (research paper for BTh degree, Meserete Kristos College, Addis Ababa, 2003), 1-47.

16. Samuel Bateno, "Report" (1996): 1-2. (Available in the MKC Headquarters Office, Addis Ababa).

17. Tesfaye, "The Impact of Evangelism," 6, 11, 21-36.

18. Gordon Nickel, *Peaceable Witness Among Muslims* (Scottdale, Pa.: Herald Press, 1999), 36-66; and Mike Brislen, "A Model for a Multi-Culture Church," *Missiology* 24 (1996): 355-67.

Chapter 37: Contextualization

1. Phil Parshall, *New Paths in Muslim Evangelism* (Grand Rapids: Baker Book House, 1980), 53.

2. Eugene O'Neill, *Long Day's Journey into Night*, 1st ed. (New Haven: Yale University Press, 1955), 154.

3. Gordon Nickel, ed., "Mennonites Meeting Muslims" newsletter, May 1999.

4. Ed McManness, "Contextualizing Jesus Among Muslims" (presentation at An Anabaptist Consultation on Islam, Harrisonburg, Va., November 2003).

5. I discuss these themes in *No God But God: Paths to Muslim-Christian Discussion on God's Nature* (Maryknoll, N.Y.: Orbis Books, 2003), 19ff.

6. First Corinthians 9:22. Even when Paul had reason to be critical of others' cultures, he remained courteous (see examples in Ephesus, Acts 19:37; Antioch of Pisidia, Acts 13:16-41; and Athens, Acts 17:1-4).

7. Missiology and martyrology have long been two sides of the same coin. See 2 Timothy 4:6-7.

8. Seamus Heaney's poem "At the Well-Head" was originally published in the anthology, *Spirit-Level* (1996). I first read the poem in *Opened Ground: Selected Poems of Seamus Heaney, 1966-1996* (New York: Farrar, Straus and Giroux, 1998), 408.

9. Kosuke Koyama, *Water Buffalo Theology* (Maryknoll, N.Y.: Orbis Books, 1974).

10. Matthew 5:13-16.

11. J. Denny Weaver, *The Nonviolent Atonement* (Philadelphia: Westminster John Knox Press, 1997).

12. Two excellent resources on this subject are *A Violent Evangelism: The Politics and Religious Conquest of the Americas* (Louisville: Westminster John Knox Press, 1991), and George Tinker's, *Missionary Conquest: The Gospel and Native American Cultural Genocide* (Minneapolis: Fortress Press, 1993).

13. Although Abraham Joshua Heschel's theological conclusions seem at times to be contradictory, the conclusions stated here are based on reading *Who Is Man?* (Stanford, Calif.: Stanford University Press, 1965).

14. Jonah 4:4.

15. Matthew 9:9.

16. A recent book by David W. Shenk, *Journeys of the Muslim Nation and the Christian Church: Exploring the Mission of Two Communities* (Scottdale, Pa.: Herald Press, 2003), looks at some of the "big picture" theological questions that greatly impact the way that contemporary Muslim and Christian communities are relating to each other.

17. Acts 10.

18. Quoted from my book, *No God But God*, 17.

Chapter 39: Open Doors Through Walls

1. Abd al-Masih, *The Main Challenges for Committed Christian in Serving Muslim* (Austria, Villach: Light of Hope Publications, 1996).

2. Tokumboh Adeyemo, *Christ's Ambassadors in an Islamic Context* (Institute for Reformational Studies, 1986), 1-14.

3. Rebecca Manley Pippert, *Out of the Salt Shaker* (Leicester: IVP, 1978), 25.

4. John D. Robb, "Prayer as a Strategic Weapon in Frontier Mission," *International Journal of Frontier Mission* 98 (Jan. 1991).

Chapter 40: Questions That Muslims Address

1. N. A. Newmann, ed., *The Early Christian Dialogues: A Collection of Documents from the First Three Islamic Centuries (632-900 A.D.)* (Hatfield, Pa.: Interdisciplinary Biblical Research Institute, 1993).

2. A contributing factor to the tensions was the distribution of some Christian literature in the Mogadishu market by a couple of the first believers.

3. Lesslie Newbigin, *Honest Religion for Secular Man* (London: SCM, 1996).

4. Ali Shari'ati, *On the Sociology of Islam*, trans. from the Persian by Hamid Algar (Berkley: Mizan Press, 1979).

5. John Landis Ruth, *The Earth Is the Lord's* (Scottdale, Pa.: Herald Press, 2001), 275-87, 294-96, 321-22.

6. Tarif Khalidi, *The Muslim Jesus* (Cambridge: Harvard University Press, 2001), 9-22, 45.

7. Badru D. Kateregga and David W. Shenk, *A Muslim and A Christian in Dialogue* (Scottdale, Pa.: Herald Press, 1997), 206.

8. Miroslav Volf, *After Our Likeness, the Church as the Image of the Trinity* (Grand Rapids, Mich.: Eerdmans, 1988), 127-257.

9. Andrew Rippin, *Muslims: Their Religious Beliefs and Practices* (New York: Routledge, 2002), 210.

10. David Shenk, et al., *The People of God* (Nairobi: Evangel, 1976).

11. For further reading see:

> Cragg, Kenneth. *The Call of the Minaret*. Maryknoll, N.Y.: Orbis Books, 1985.
>
> Kateregga, Badru D., and David W. Shenk. *A Muslim and a Christian in Dialogue*. Scottdale, Pa.: Herald Press, 1997.
>
> McDowell, Bruce and Anees Zaka. *Muslims and Christians at the Table*. Phillipsburg: P & R Publishing, 1999.
>
> Nickel, Gordon D. *Peaceable Witness Among Muslims*. Scottdale, Pa.: Herald Press, 1999.
>
> Rippin, Andrew. *Muslims: Their Religious Beliefs and Practices*. New York: Routledge, 2002.
>
> Shenk, David W. *Journeys of the Muslim Nation and the Christian Church: Exploring the Mission of Two Communities*. Scottdale, Pa.: Herald Press, 2003.
>
> Van Gorder, A. Christian. *No God But God: A Path to Muslim-Christian Dialogue on God's Nature*. Maryknoll, N.Y.: Orbis Books, 2002.

Chapter 42: Counsel to the Anabaptist Community

1. Hava Lazarus-Yafeh, "Is there a Concept of Redemption in Islam?" in her *Some Religious Aspects of Islam* (Leiden: E. J. Brill, 1981), 48-57. Muzammil Husain Siddiqi, "The Doctrine of Redemption: A Critical Study," in *Islamic Perspectives: Studies in Honour of Mawlana Sayyid Abul A'la Mawdudi*, eds. Khurshid Ahmad and Zafar Ishaq Ansari, 91-102 (Leicester: The Islamic Foundation, 1979). W. Knietschke, "The Koran Doctrine of Redemption," *The Moslem World* 2:1 (1912): 60-65. See also Frederick M. Denny, "The Problem of Salvation in the Quran: Key Terms and Concepts," in *In Quest of an Islamic Humanism: Arabic and Islamic Studies in Memory of Mohamed al-Nowaihi*, ed. A. H. Green, 196-210 (Cairo: The American University of Cairo Press, 1984); and Badru D. Kateregga and David W. Shenk, *A Muslim and a Christian in Dialogue*, (Scottdale, Pa.: Herald Press, 1997), 141.

INDEX

Halmahera, 125

Hanes, Jim, 210

Hange, Roy, 117

Hange, Roy and Marin, 105

Hargeisa, 109

Harper, Dr. Howard, 156

Harregieh, 228

Harrisonburg, Virginia, 231

Hartono, Paulus, 301

Hasan, 56

Hasan, Enver, 357-59

Hassan, Prince, 67

Hazim Patriarch, 70

Heaney, Seamus, 421

Hebrew God, 130

Hebron, 178, 247, 251-54

Heckman, Bruce, 394

Heckman, Joyce and Bruce, 384

Hege, Nathan, 227

Heinrich, Alfred, 195

Henry VIII, 278n

Herat, 157

Heschel, Abraham Joshua, 423

Hess, Mahlon, 107

Hiebert, Clarence and Ferne, 157

Hiebert, J. N. C., 165

Hiroshima, 77

Hoekema, Alle, 102

Holland, 67, 104

Holy Spirit, 232, 296-97, 302, 315, 323-24n, 331, 337, 349, 368, 382, 412, 438, 440, 451-53

Honduras, 182

Hoover, Jon, 302

Horn of Africa, 260

Hostetler, Marion, 217

Hostetler, Mike and Virginia, 177-78

Hungary, 101

Huntington, Samuel P., 74, 94, 142, 261

Husein, 56

Hussein, Hajji, 409-10

Hussein, Saddam, 69

Hyderabad, India, 103, 164, 338

I

Ibn Abi Bakr, Muhammad, 138

Ibrahima, 210

Ibu, 209

Ignatius IV, Patriarch of Antioch, 105

India, 97, 100, 104, 114, 117, 165, 338, 346, 471

Indian-Pakistan border, 114

Indonesia, 73-74, 96-98, 102, 105-06, 112, 116, 118, 120, 122-27, 169-72, 174-75, 233, 298-99, 302. *See also* Muria, Indonesia

Iran, 106, 176. *See also* Qom, Iran

Iraq, 64, 69-70, 114, 120, 468

'Isa, 210, 307, 311-12

Isaac, 259, 306, 316, 385n

Isaiah, 132

Ishmael, 306, 385n, 456

Islamabad, 73

Israel, 97, 103, 130, 178, 182, 201, 276n. *See also* Israel-Palestine; Palestine

Israel-Palestine, 217, 247-48, 255, 262, 364

Italy, 267

Iye, Ali Moussa, 266

Contributors

Abd el Rab is from Egypt. For the last fourteen years he has lived in Canada where he is the founder of Arabic Ministries, which functions under the auspices of MBMS International. He is a graduate of Cairo Theological Seminary, has a law degree from Alexandria University (Egypt), and is a doctoral student in Old Testament at Florida University.

For many years **Yakuta Abdo** shared in the life and ministry of her husband, Kelifa Ali. Kelifa was one of six Meserete Kristos leaders who was imprisoned by the Marxist regime in Ethiopia (1982-86). Both Yakuta and Kelifa have roots within distinguished Ethiopian Muslim families. Yakuta's choice as a teenager to follow Christ was a decision that was much challenged by her family. She presently lives at Salunga, Pennsylvania.

Adana Abd el Rab works with her husband, Abd el Rab. She focuses on women's Arabic ministries.

Ali El-shariff Abdallah Emmanuel works with Family Life Network in Winnipeg, Manitoba.

Bertha Beachy has served for twenty-five years in Somali ministries with Eastern Mennonite Missions (EMM). This included eighteen years in Somalia, two years in Somali literacy in Kenya, and five years on a joint Mennonite Central Committee/EMM appointment as mission representative for Somali ministries based in Nairobi.

Timothy Bergdahl has served as a missionary in Pakistan for six years and is currently director of Long Term Ministries for Mennonite Brethren Missions and Service International. He is a graduate of Mennonite Brethren Biblical Seminary with an MDiv in world mission, and of Fuller Theological Seminary with an MA in cross-cultural studies. He is currently completing a PhD at Fuller on the intercession of Muhammad and the atonement of Jesus Christ.

Jonathan Bonk, executive director of the Overseas Ministries Study Center in New Haven, Connecticut (www.omsc.org), is editor of the *International Bulletin of Missionary Research*, and project director for the *Dictionary of African Christian Biography* (www.dacb.org).

Joe Bontrager is the U.S. regional director for Virginia Mennonite Board of Missions.

Jonathan Bornman serves among the Wolof in Senegal with the Africa Inter-Mennonite Mission and with Mennonite Mission Network. He and his wife, Carol, commenced their ministry with the Wolof in 1999.

Mike Brislen and his wife, Cindy, have served in Djibouti since 1988 on appointment with Eastern Mennonite Missions. At present Mike teaches English in a government high school.

Donna Entz began her service in Senegal in 1977, along with her husband, Loren. They represent three Mennonite agencies: Africa Inter-Mennonite Mission, Mennonite Mission Network, and Mennonite Church Canada Witness.

Loren Entz began his service in Senegal in 1977, along with his wife, Donna. They represent three Mennonite agencies: Africa Inter-Mennonite Mission, Mennonite Mission Network, and Mennonite Church Canada Witness.

Sara Fast is a graduate of Tabor College, and a current student at Mennonite Brethren Biblical Seminary, where she plans to graduate in spring 2005 with an MA in intercultural mission. After graduation she hopes to participate in a mission team in Asia that combines community development and church formation.

Herb Friesen and his wife, Ruth, began their twenty-eight years of service with Mennonite Brethren Missions and Service International (MBMSI) in Afghanistan in 1968. Herb's vocation has been starting eye hospitals and specialized training programs for Afghan doctors. Ruth has had a busy "gate ministry" with Afghan widows during their time in Pakistan. Since their retirement in 1996 they have served as MBMSI global partners as volunteers investing three to five months a year in Afghanistan and Pakistan.

A. Christian van Gorder is a global practitioner of dialogue with Muslims, and his recent book, *No God But God: A Path to Muslim-Christian Dialogue on God's Nature* (Orbis Books, 2003), is an exploration of de-Westernized contextual theological discourse with Muslims. He has taught missiology and world religions at Messiah College, and in 2005 will begin teaching Islamic studies at Baylor University.

Lydia Harder teaches at the Toronto School of Theology (TST), Conrad Grebel College, and is involved in the adult education program of her congregation and the larger conference (MCEC). She has been engaged in the Iranian Shi'a- Mennonite dialogues for the past five years through her work at the Toronto Mennonite Theological Centre at TST.

Ahmed Haile teaches courses related to peacemaking at Daystar University in Nairobi, Kenya. He has been actively engaged in the peace process within Somalia.

Roy Hange served for ten years in the Middle East doing development, ecumenical and interfaith encounter, and peace building under Mennonite Central Committee (MCC) in the countries of Egypt, Syria, and Iran. He established MCC's presence in Syria in 1991 and was co-country representative there with his wife, Maren, until 1997. In 1998 he served in Qom, Iran, where he and Maren participated in interfaith encounter and peace building. They were the first Christians to ever live in Qom. Roy currently co-pastors Charlottesville Mennonite Church in Virginia with Maren.

Susan Kennel Harrison is a pastor at Fairview Mennonite Home in Cambridge, Ontario, a recent graduate of Toronto School of Theology (TST), and Toronto coordinator of Mennonite Central Committee's exchange between Imam Khomeini Education and Research Institute in Qom, Iran, and the Toronto Mennonite Theological Centre at TST.

Bruce Heckman and his wife, Joyce, have served in various capacities in the Middle East, including assignment with Eastern Mennonite Missions. Currently Bruce is one of the directors of Immerge, a training program in the Lancaster, Pennsylvania, area that seeks to equip people for presence and service among Muslims.

Jane Hooley has served with Eastern Mennonite Missions (EMM) in Somalia and Sudan, and at present serves as administrative assistant for EMM's Asia and Middle East program.

Jon Hoover is a Mennonite minister who for several years has taught at Dar Comboni for Arabic Studies in Cairo, Egypt. He received his PhD in Islamic studies from the University of Birmingham in 2002. He has recently been appointed as assistant professor of Islamic studies at the Near East School of Theology in Beirut, Lebanon.

Loren Horst is president of Virginia Mennonite Board of Missions.

Marian Hostetler served in Algeria from 1961-70 on appointment with Mennonite Board of Missions, and later with Eastern Mennonite Missions in Djibouti for five years. Her interest in Islam and the North Africa region has inspired the writing of a primer on Islam and the history of Mennonite ministries in Algeria.

Mesach Krisetya has been a professor of pastoral theology for many years at the Universitas Kristen Satya Wacana, Salatiga, Indonesia. He has carried numerous responsibilities in the Indonesian GKMI synod and within Mennonite World Conference where he served as president (1997-2003).

John A. Lapp is executive secretary emeritus of Mennonite Central Committee, has served as dean, provost, and professor of history at Goshen College, and has taught at Eastern Mennonite University and Associated Mennonite Biblical Seminaries. He has authored numerous articles and several books and currently coordinates the Global Mennonite History Project of the Mennonite World Conference.

John F. Lapp and his wife, Sandra, served in the Middle East with Mennonite Board of Missions and Mennonite Central Committee (MCC). They taught from 1989 to 1991 in the Mar Elias High School in Ibillin, Israel, and later served as MCC Country Representatives for Palestine, living in Jerusalem from 1991-96. At present John is director for West Asia and Middle East with the Mennonite Mission Network.

Wayne and Jeannie Larson serve in media in the Middle East with the Mennonite Mission Network.

Chantal Logan was born in Paris and has an MA from the University of Paris, and a PhD from the University of Limoges, France. She and her husband, Mark, have served for many years with the Church of the Brethren missions in South America. For the last seven years they have served with Eastern Mennonite Missions (EMM) in Djibouti, and then with EMM and Mennonite Central Committee as co-directors of the Somali program.

Mark Logan served with his wife, Chantal, for many years with the Church of the Brethren missions in South America. For the last seven years they have served with Eastern Mennonite Missions (EMM) in Djibouti, and then with EMM and Mennonite Central Committee as co-directors of the Somali program.

Ronald J. R. Mathies is executive director of Mennonite Central Committee.

Ed McManness and his wife, Joan, began their journey with Muslims in South East Asia in 1988. They have served as Eastern Mennonite Missions appointees, as well as relating to the local Mennonite missions vision and outreach. At present Ed is one of the visionaries developing Immerge, a training program in the Lancaster, Pennsylvania, area that seeks to prepare persons for service in Muslim communities.

Bedru Hussein Muktar is vice-president of the Mesrete Kirstos College in Ethiopia. He is a former vice-president of the Mennonite World Conference, and has served as executive secretary of Meserete Kristos Church for eight years. He grew up as a Muslim and was converted to Christ in 1966. Since then he seeks to faithfully witness for Christ among Muslim people. He is a graduate of Eastern Mennonite Seminary.

Gordon D. Nickel lived in India as a youth where his parents served in mission. He teaches cross-cultural ministry at the ACTS Seminaries in Langley, British Columbia. He has a PhD in Qur'anic studies from the University of Calgary. He and his wife, Gwenyth, have served for ten years in Pakistan and India with Mennonite Brethren Missions and Service International (MBMSI).

Harold E. Reed and his wife, Barbara, served in Somalia for many years, as well as in Eastern Mennonite Missions administration in a variety of responsibilities. He has also served as pastor and bishop in the Lancaster Mennonite Conference.

A. James Reimer is a professor of religion and theology at Conrad Grebel University College, and Toronto School of Theology, and director of Toronto Mennonite Theological Centre.

Lindsey Robinson is conference minister and pastoral resource person for Lancaster Mennonite Conference. He is pastor at Locust Lane Mennonite Church in Harrisburg, Pa.

Jeanne Sahawneh and her husband, William, serve in Jordan in a variety of ministries.

William Sahawneh's roots are the Baptist Church in Jordan. Now a member of the Washington Community Fellowship, he and his wife, Jeanne, serve in a variety of ministries in Jordan.

Lamin Sanneh is a naturalized U.S. citizen who was born in Gambia, West Africa, and educated on four continents. He has studied classical Arabic and Islam and received his PhD in Islamic history at the University of London. He was a professor at Harvard University for eight years before moving to Yale University in 1989 as the D. Willis James Professor of Missions and World Christianity. He is editor-at-large of *The Christian Century,* and is the author of over a hundred articles on religious and historical subjects, and of several books.

Walter Sawatsky is professor of church history and mission at Associated Mennonite Biblical Seminaries. He has been involved in ministry and scholarship of the former Soviet Union and East Europe since 1973 under Mennonite Central Committee sponsorship. He is editor of *Mission Focus: Annual Review.*

Darren Schaupp and his wife, Cindi, have served among Muslims in Kenya with Eastern Mennonite Missions since 1997.

Mary Mae Schwartzentruber is the minister of missions for the Mennonite Conference of Eastern Canada, Kitchener, Ontario.

Patricia Shelly is professor of Bible and religion at Bethel College, North Newton, Kansas. From 1996-2000 she served in Jerusalem as the director of Mennonite Central Committee's program in the West Bank and Gaza. For the past twenty years she has led numerous study seminars in Israel/Palestine.

Calvin E. Shenk is professor emeritus of religion at Eastern Mennonite University. He and his wife, Marie, have served for fourteen years in Ethiopia with Eastern Mennonite Missions, and recently they have been engaged in teaching, dialogue, and writing in Jerusalem. This has been a joint appointment with Mennonite Central Committee, Eastern Mennonite Missions, and the Mennonite Mission Network.

Jewel Showalter is area representative for the Middle East/North Africa for Eastern Mennonite Missions' Global Ministries. For seven years (1982-89) she and her husband, Richard, served in ministries of presence and witness in the countries of Turkey and the Turkish Republic of North Cyprus.

Joe Showalter is president of Rosedale Mennonite Missions.

Richard Showalter serves as president of Eastern Mennonite Missions. He is a teacher, preacher, and writer with experience in church planting, pastoral leadership, and evangelism in the United States, Africa, and the Middle East.

Jay Smith is a PhD candidate at the Guthrie Center for Islamic Studies London and has a ThM in missions/Islamic studies from Fuller Theological Seminary. Since 1983 Jay and his wife, Judy, have been on appointment with Brethren in Christ World Missions in ministries among Muslims in Senegal, France, and now in London.

Bob Stauffer is director of missions for Eurasia for Rosedale Mennonite Missions.

Muhamud Siad Togane is a teacher of English literature in Montreal, an advocate for peace among the Somali people, a poet and an author of books on peacemaking within pathos, and an advocate for missions in the Mennonite Fellowship of Montreal where he is a member.

Dorothy Jean Weaver is a professor of New Testament at Eastern Mennonite Seminary. Since 1995 she has been a regular visitor and participant in ministries concerned for justice and reconciliation in the Middle East.

Barbara Witmer, with her husband Lamar, has served on Eastern Mennonite Missions assignment among the Somali people in Somalia and Kenya. At present she works as a volunteer in refugee advocacy and support in the Lancaster, Pennsylvania, area.

J. Dudley Woodberry is professor of Islamic studies at Fuller Theological Seminary and is considered one of the foremost Christian scholars on Islam. He holds a PhD from Harvard University, and an MA in Arab studies from the American University in Beirut, Lebanon. His missionary experience has been in Pakistan, Afghanistan, and Saudi Arabia. He is author of numerous articles and book chapters and has edited several books on Christian-Muslim relations.

Lawrence M. Yoder trained pastors from 1970-79 for the Javanese Mennonite Church, which developed among the largely Muslim population of north Central Java, Indonesia. For this assignment Yoder received special training in Islamic studies at Columbia University in New York, and then worked with Javanese historian Dr. Sigit Heru Soekotjo in preparing a history of that church. He has a PhD from Fuller Seminary School of World Mission and is presently professor of missiology at Eastern Mennonite Seminary.

Tom Yoder and his wife, Karen, served in Albania on appointment with Virginia Mennonite Board of Missions for seven years. Currently they serve as consultants for the Eastern Mennonite Missions/ Virginia Mennonite Board of Missions Albania program.

The Editors

James R. Krabill, with his wife, Jeanette, served with Mennonite Board of Missions (MBM) for twenty years (1976-1996). For much of this time, he was a Bible and church history teacher among African-initiated churches in Ivory Coast. He is the author of *The Hymnody of the Harrist Church Among the Dida of South-Central Ivory Coast, 1913-1949* (Frankfurt: Peter Lang, 1995), *The Short-Term Experience: Current Trends/Future Challenges*, *Does Your Church "Smell" Like Mission?*, and *Anabaptism and*  *Mission*, a bibliography co-edited with Chad Mullet Bauman featuring 3,250 titles of Anabaptist-Mennonite writings on mission-related themes. From 1995-2002, Krabill provided oversight to MBM's Mission Advocacy and Communication division, and since then, has served as Senior Executive for Global Ministries at Mennonite Mission Network.

David W. Shenk was born in Tanzania to pioneer Mennonite missionaries. He and his wife, Grace, served with Eastern Mennonite Missions (EMM) in Muslim ministries in East Africa (Somalia and Kenya) for sixteen years, prior to his nineteen years in missions' administration with EMM and several years with Lithuania Christian College where he served as academic dean and professor in theology. David has authored over a dozen books, including his latest, *Journeys of the Muslim*

Nation and the Christian Church: Exploring the Mission of Two Communities (Herald Press, 2003). At present he serves as global missions consultant with EMM.

Linford Stutzman with his wife, Janet, has been involved in church planting and leadership in Munich, Germany; Perth, Australia; and Harrisonburg, Virginia. He is the author of *With Jesus in the World: Mission in Affluent Societies* (Herald Press, 1992), co-editor with David W. Shenk of *Practicing Truth: Confident Witness in Our Pluralistic World* (Herald Press, 1999), and has authored numerous articles on mission and culture. Linford is currently associate professor of culture and mission at Eastern Mennonite University. He also directs the John Coffman Center at Eastern Mennonite Seminary. With his wife he has led semester-long study programs in the Middle East since 2001.